MOON

NASHVILLE TO NEW ORLEANS

Road T

MARGARET L

CONTENTS

Although every effort was made to make sure the information in this book was accurate when going to press, research was impacted by the COVID-19 pandemic. Some things may have changed during this crisis. Be sure to confirm specific details when making your travel plans.

NASHVILLE TO NEW ORLEANS ROAD TRIP
Southern Mississippi
New Orleans
NATCHEZ TRACE PARKWAY SOUTHERN TERMINUS
CYPRESS SWAMP LOOP TRAIL
MISSISSIPPI
LOUISIANA
ALABAMA
FLORIDA
Gulf of Mexico
Delta National Forest
Bienville National Forest
Homochitto National Forest
DeSoto National Forest
DeSoto National Forest
Talladega National Forest
Conecuh National Forest
Mississippi River
Tombigbee River
Bastrop
Winnsboro
Canton
Ridgeland
Vicksburg
Jackson
Rocky Springs
Port Gibson
Church Hill
Natchez
Philadelphia
Scooba
Meridian
Demopolis
Selma
Montgomery
Greenville
Troy
Laurel
State Line
Andalusia
McComb
Hattiesburg
Columbia
Lettsworth
Franklinton
Wiggins
Mobile
St. Francisville
Baton Rouge
Hammond
Abita Springs
Opelousas
Pensacola
Fort Walton Beach
Gulfport
Moss Point
Slidell
Lafayette
Gulf Shores
Panama City
Laplace
New Orleans
New Iberia
0
40 mi
0
40 km
© MOON.COM

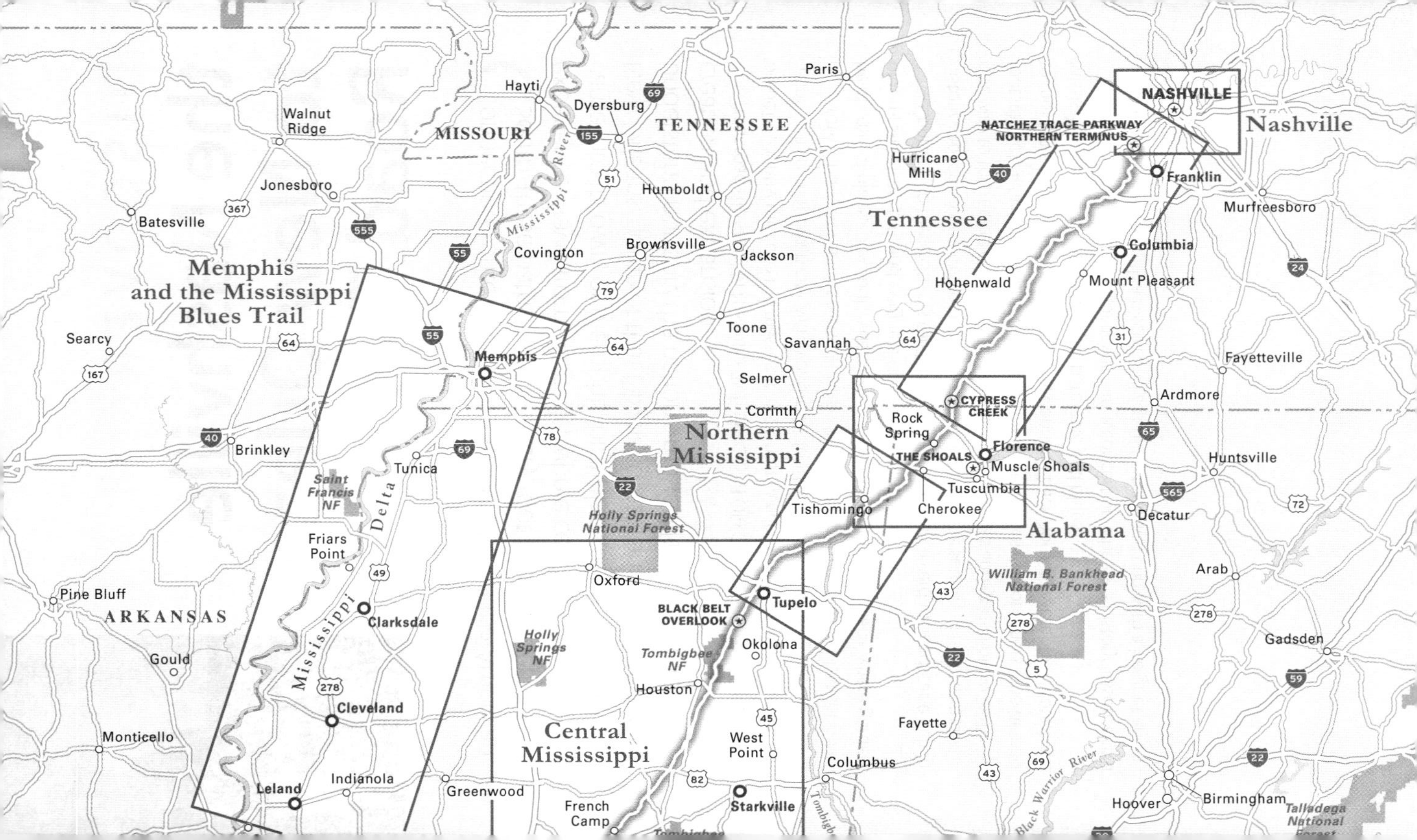
Memphis and the Mississippi Blues Trail
Northern Mississippi
Central Mississippi
Tennessee
Nashville
Alabama
NASHVILLE
NATCHEZ TRACE PARKWAY NORTHERN TERMINUS
CYPRESS CREEK
THE SHOALS
BLACK BELT OVERLOOK
MISSOURI
TENNESSEE
ARKANSAS
Mississippi River
Mississippi Delta
Black Warrior River
Saint Francis NF
Holly Springs National Forest
Holly Springs NF
Tombigbee NF
William B. Bankhead National Forest
Talladega National Forest
Paris
Hayti
Dyersburg
Walnut Ridge
Jonesboro
Batesville
Humboldt
Hurricane Mills
Franklin
Murfreesboro
Covington
Brownsville
Jackson
Columbia
Mount Pleasant
Hohenwald
Searcy
Toone
Savannah
Fayetteville
Memphis
Selmer
Corinth
Ardmore
Brinkley
Tunica
Rock Spring
Florence
Muscle Shoals
Tuscumbia
Huntsville
Tishomingo
Cherokee
Decatur
Friars Point
Oxford
Arab
Pine Bluff
Clarksdale
Tupelo
Okolona
Gadsden
Gould
Houston
Cleveland
Fayette
Monticello
West Point
Columbus
Leland
Indianola
Greenwood
French Camp
Starkville
Hoover
Birmingham

DISCOVER the Nashville to New Orleans Road Trip

Connecting some of the most iconic cities in the American South, these paths trace the very root of the American experience. Travel from Nashville, where country music came into its own, or Memphis, birthplace of the blues, to New Orleans, home of that Dixieland jazz, and you'll better understand not only the nation's musical legacy, but also its creation and expansion.

Your road trip starts in Nashville with the Grand Ole Opry, a radio show that brought country music to the masses. It also boasts a rich civil rights legacy, and a reputation as a cosmopolitan city with world-class food and entertainment.

You'll end in boisterous New Orleans, where jazz is perhaps the loudest sound in a heady mix of blues, rock, soul, zydeco, and Cajun music. It's also a place where gardens bloom, streetcars run, and beignets make everything sweeter.

Connecting these cities is the Natchez Trace Parkway, a verdant landscape rich in history and lore. Along this route your pace will slow as the sounds of raucous music give way to the melodies of birds and the rustling of leaves and grass. Follow in the footsteps of Native Americans, Civil War soldiers, and thousands of others who helped to mold this region into its current form. Continue back north to Memphis through the Mississippi Delta and lose yourself in barbecue and blues.

This journey is an outdoor adventure, a concert on wheels, a history lesson, and a culinary quest. Start it with a biscuit and a country tune and end with a beignet and a sax riff.

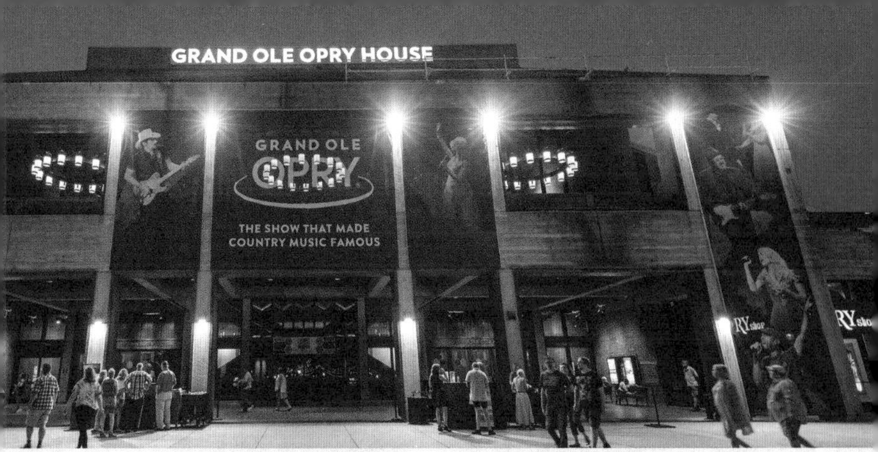

GRAND OLE OPRY HOUSE
GRAND OLE OPRY
THE SHOW THAT MADE COUNTRY MUSIC FAMOUS

10 TOP EXPERIENCES

1 **Listen to Live Music:** Country at the world-famous **Grand Ole Opry** (page 64) in Nashville? Blues at Memphis's **Juke Joints** (page 217)? Jazz at **Preservation Hall** (page 360) in New Orleans? Whatever sound you like, you can—and should—hear it on this trip.

2 **Let the Good Times Roll: Mardi Gras** (page 365) in New Orleans is something you shouldn't miss. But if you can't make it before Lent begins, you have a year-round opportunity at **Blaine Kern's Mardi Gras World** (page 348).

3 **Get Lit:** From **Eudora Welty** (page 297) to **Tennessee Williams** (page 240) and **William Faulkner** (page 263), literary legends have deep roots in the region.

4 **Eat like a Local:** Nashville's **hot chicken** (page 94), Memphis's **barbecue** (page 228), Mississippi Delta's **tamales** (page 251), and New Orleans' **Cajun** and **Creole cuisine** (page 391) are just some of the unforgettable foodie fun.

5 Honor the Civil Rights Movement: Learn about the fight for equality that continues to shape the South at the **Civil Rights Room at the Nashville Public Library** (page 45), the **Medgar Evers Home Museum National Monument** (page 298), the **Mississippi Civil Rights Museum** (page 295), and the **National Civil Rights Museum** (page 199). >>>

6 See Mississippi River Views: Enjoy the sky's color show over the water in **Memphis** (page 214)—or anywhere along the **Mississippi Delta.** >>>

I AM
A MAN
I AM
A MAN
LOANS

7 Raise a Glass: There's no shortage of options: wine along the **Natchez Trace** (page 123), craft beer in **Memphis** (page 232), and legendary cocktails at **Cathead Distillery** (page 301), to name a few. >>>

8 Learn Civil War History: Stories of the traumatic conflict that changed the Nation are told at **Fort Negley** (page 58), and **Vicksburg** (page 303) and **Shiloh** military parks (page 171). <<<

9 Get Artsy: Pick up a pre-made concert poster or make one at **Hatch Show Print** (page 79). Join a class taught by a Mississippi expert at the **Bill Waller Mississippi Craft Center** (page 293), or admire masterpieces in **New Orleans** (page 340). >>>

10 **Take a Hike:** You may just want to stretch your legs or enjoy the scenery, but you'll discover that even the trails are full of stories (page 24).

PLANNING YOUR TRIP

Where to Go

This drive along the Natchez Trace Parkway originates in Nashville, crosses through Tennessee, cuts across the northwest corner of Alabama, and then traverses much of Mississippi before ending in Natchez. From there, you're just a short drive from New Orleans.

Nashville

Nashville is the epicenter of **country music.** It's home to the **Grand Ole Opry,** the **Country Music Hall of Fame and Museum,** and hundreds of **recording studios.** It's the place where thousands of musicians and songwriters come to make it, and the city's nightlife is all the richer for it. **Fine arts** and a contemporary **culinary scene** appeal to sophisticates, while **museums, historical sites,** and the unusual **Tennessee State Capitol** recall the city's history.

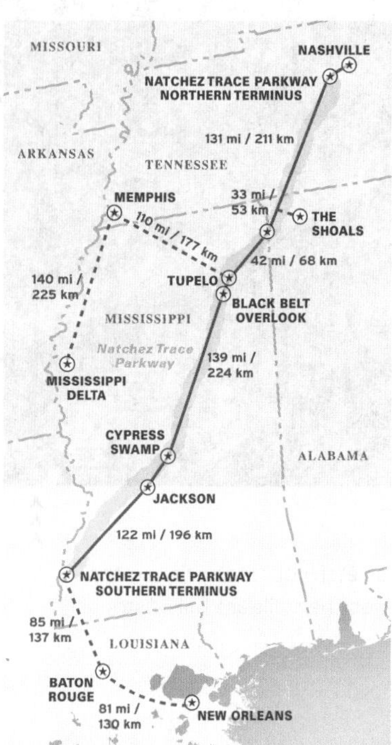

The Trace: Tennessee

This is where your drive starts: at the northern terminus of the **Natchez Trace Parkway.** This northernmost stretch features **rolling hills, secluded hikes,** and significant **historic sites,** including the somber and reverential **Meriwether Lewis Monument and Gravesite.** Close to the parkway are quaint suburbs and towns, including **Franklin** and **Leiper's Fork,** where you can visit **Civil War sites** and spot country music celebrities.

The Trace: Alabama

The **shortest section** of the Natchez Trace Parkway covers just the tiny northwest corner of Alabama but contains tons of history. Contemplate the somber **Wichahpi Commemorative Stone Wall,** an homage to the Trail of Tears. Close to the Trace, the **Shoals** region is home to **Muscle Shoals,** an important part of music history, and **Florence,** which is a charming epicenter of fashion and design.

The Trace: Northern Mississippi

This part of the state is known as "the hills" of Mississippi. And along this winding stretch of the parkway, you'll find **scenic views** and opportunities for **camping, hiking,** and **bicycling.** This section ends in **Tupelo,** birthplace of the King of Rock 'n' Roll, Elvis Presley. The **Natchez Trace Parkway Headquarters and Visitor Center** is the essential stopping point for information about the Natchez Trace.

Memphis and the Mississippi Blues Trail

This route starts in **Memphis,** Tennessee, and winds south for 170 miles into the Mississippi Delta. The **blues** were born

Top: the Natchez Trace Parkway; bottom: a jazz band performing in the French Quarter, New Orleans

in Memphis, and they still call Memphis home in **nightclubs** on **Beale Street** and around the city. But Memphis is more than music. It's an urban center with **fine dining, parks,** and **art museums.** Watch the resident ducks at **The Peabody Memphis** or fuel up with a plate of **barbecue.**

Drive through the Mississippi Delta to explore the **roots of American music** and listen to the blues in **juke joints.** Visit **small towns** that are home to big history, like **Clarksdale, Cleveland,** and **Greenwood.**

The Trace: Central Mississippi

Through **farmland** and past **Indian mounds,** the Natchez Trace Parkway is a leisurely, easy drive in this section of the Magnolia State. Exit the parkway for two of the state's academic and tourism treasures: **Oxford** and **Starkville.** Plan leisurely stops to stroll these quintessential college towns.

The Trace: Southern Mississippi

The southernmost stretch of the parkway is bookended by two of the state's most significant cities—the capital city of **Jackson** and historic **Natchez,** the **southern terminus** of the Trace. This is an opportunity to explore **civil rights sites, Civil War battlefields,** and **antebellum homes** and gardens.

New Orleans

New Orleans is unlike any other city, steeped as it is in many unique cultures. Its reputation of being a party place is accurate, but it's also home to **beautiful architecture, museums, gardens,** and, of course, tempting Cajun and Creole food. Louisiana capital **Baton Rouge** has some of NOLA's similar charms, but also its own traditions, institutions, and a mammoth campus.

When to Go

The Natchez Trace Parkway is compelling year-round. Visitors are steady throughout the year, with July and October slightly more popular times to travel the road. **Spring** is the most desirable time to visit. Colorful wildflowers will be in bloom, making overlooks and hikes stunning, but greenery won't yet block vistas, as happens in summer. In spring the days will be long enough to get miles and stops in on the Trace before sunset, but summer's crowds won't yet be nabbing campground spaces. Spring weather is temperate, not the oppressive heat of summer.

Summer is the peak travel season for Nashville and Memphis, when crowds and temperatures are at their highest. It's also when some of the biggest music festivals and events are going on. In New Orleans, summer is the least crowded time to visit; hurricane season is June-September.

Fall is also popular; the parkway is one of the best places in the South to see the leaves change. Stark white cotton bolls in bloom are a breathtaking contrast to the rich yellows and golds on the trees. Fall is a good time to explore Nashville, Memphis, and New Orleans, as the temperatures are cooler and the crowds have dispersed.

Winter is generally low season for this region—except in New Orleans, when people flock to the city for Mardi Gras and temperate weather. The Trace is rarely troubled by inclement weather, as the region sees little snow.

Preparing to Bike the Trace

If you're traveling the Trace by bicycle, as many do, you should plan ahead, as 444 miles is a significant ride. People of all fitness levels, ages, and abilities complete this ride, which ESPN rates as one of the 10 best bike routes in the country. The lack of dangerous road traffic combined with beautiful scenery and mild weather makes it particularly appealing to newbies and experienced pedalers alike.

cycling on the Natchez Trace Parkway

Before you begin, figure out approximately how many miles you plan to bike a day. If you plan to do the trip in a week, you'll need to average at least 75 miles per day, with limited detours. Make a **training plan** that gets you up to that mileage.

Wondering what to bring? Here's a start:

A bike. Obviously, you'll need to buy or rent a bicycle. The entirety of the parkway is paved, so a road or touring bike is your best bet (as opposed to a mountain bike).

Changes of clothes, particularly rain gear. Thunderstorms in the South can be soakers. So, while you want to pack light, you also want to have the clothes you need when Mother Nature shows you who's boss. Layering is key.

Clip-in shoes. If clip-ins and cleats are your thing, bring 'em. If not, that's fine, too, but in either case bring shoes (and hiking boots) to wear when not on your bike.

Locks. You'll want your gear to be safe when you hike, explore towns on side trips, and take breaks for food.

Maps. Some of the parkway has limited cell service. Have a paper (better yet, laminated) map in case your GPS fails you.

Snacks. You may not need gas on a bike, but your body needs fuel. Have protein bars or other snacks in your pack.

Padded shorts. It's 444 miles on a bike seat. Enough said.

Reflective gear and lights. It isn't recommended that you bike on the Trace at night. Remember, there are limited roadway lights. But you'll still want to make sure you can be seen when the sun is down. A helmet, first-aid kit, and safety gear are also essential.

A good attitude. You never know what will happen on a long trek. Some cyclists say the repetitive nature of the landscape bores them silly. Others find it meditative. Traffic, storms, construction, wild turkeys: Who knows what you will encounter? Keep an open mind and keep pedaling.

Companions. Many tour companies offer guided or supported bike rides on the Trace (meaning a van carries your meals and gear while you ride). These are great options for those who don't want to be on two wheels alone on the road. See the **Trace by Bicycle** section in *Essentials* (page 415) for more information on tour companies and links to websites with maps and recommendations.

If You're Looking For...

With 444 miles through three states, the Natchez Trace Parkway and its surrounding communities have something for everyone. Plan your trip based on your interests.

- **Music:** Almost every stop in this book has great music roots and music history. Head to **Nashville** for country, **The Shoals** for rock, **New Orleans** for jazz, and **Memphis, Jackson,** and **Clarksdale** for the blues.
- **Civil Rights History:** The fight for Civil Rights shaped—and is still shaping—the South. Learn more in **Memphis, Nashville,** and **Jackson**.
- **Native-American History:** Start in The Shoals learning about the Trail of Tears at **Wichahpi Commemorative Stone Wall**. Stop at **Chickasaw Village Site** near Tupelo and end at the **Grand Village of the Natchez Indians State Historic Site** in **Natchez.** Along the way the Trace offers context of Native-American life, including a number of significant burial mounds.
- **Hiking:** The north section of the Natchez Trace Parkway in Tennessee is prime territory for lacing up your boots. Put in some miles on the **Highland Rim Trail.**
- **Nightlife: Nashville, Memphis**, and **New Orleans** are the obvious choices, and **Clarksdale** has live music seven days a week and friendly locals who will hang out with you all night long.
- **Tasty Food:** Again, there is no shortage of great eats on this trip. Unexpected concentrations of gems can be found in **Oxford** and **Greenwood.**

Before You Go

Fly into **Nashville International Airport** and out of New Orleans's **Louis Armstrong New Orleans International Airport.** Memphis, Jackson, and Huntsville and Birmingham, Alabama, are other nearby cities that are good alternatives for those who want to do just a portion of the drive.

Pack light, particularly if you want to see the Natchez Trace by bicycle, motorcycle, or on horseback. Take **hiking boots** and **sunscreen** for exploring the Trace's many scenic pleasures, and tents and sleeping bags if you plan to camp.

If you're planning to stop over in the cities on this route, make **advance reservations.** Nashville sees demand spike during the summer music festival season. Football games in the Mississippi college towns of Oxford and Starkville make fall a tough time to find a hotel room. Everyone wants a New Orleans hotel during Mardi Gras (February or March) and Jazz Fest (April or May). Natchez is almost exclusively a B&B town, and these small inns are often booked in advance during the town's Spring and Fall Pilgrimage.

Most B&Bs along the Trace accommodate bicycle travelers. Call ahead to confirm there are safe spaces to store your gear.

Investigating Our Shared History

People who take road trips down the Natchez Trace Parkway and the Blues Highway tend to be people who like to learn about history. Every turn in the road is an opportunity to learn about those who came before—but much of that history is not pretty. This land has been the ground for cruelty against Native Americans who were forced from their ancestral homes. It was the battlefield for much of the bloodiest combat of the U.S. Civil War. Year after year, the atrocities of enslavement were perpetuated—and racism persists despite the continuing fight for Civil Rights.

Travel provides us with important opportunities to learn more about our neighbors and our nation. We encourage you to travel with an open mind, to allow yourself to feel uncomfortable when you encounter darkness in our shared history, and to continue to talk about what you see and learn along the way. Great care was taken to include sites that accurately and sensitively represent U.S. History. Sites that focus solely on nostalgia or misrepresent experiences of Native Americans and Black Americans have been omitted. Many sites are re-examining the ways in which they present this material and may update tours and museum exhibits as time goes on. Ultimately it's up to you to determine if particular sites are appropriate to visit.

Driving Tips

The Natchez Trace Parkway is a scenic 444-mile paved road managed by the National Park Service. The entire parkway is well marked with brown **mile markers** on the east side of the road. Crossroads are also marked, and there are signs at intersections letting you know how many miles to the next major city. It is very difficult to get lost on the Trace if you pay attention. Some of the stops have maps posted in their parking areas as well.

There are virtually no commercial stops on the route. That means you must exit the parkway at major crossroads to get gas. Some of the stops on the parkway have restrooms and vending machines, and there are three official campgrounds on the Trace, but for the most part, you'll need to exit for restaurants and accommodations as well.

Many people travel the Trace on **bicycle.** If you are in a car, you *must* allow at least three feet for cyclists when passing. You should pass in the opposite lane (when safe) when there are bicyclists present.

Cell phone reception can be spotty on much of the parkway, though generally reliable in the cities. Most hotels, even small B&Bs, have Wi-Fi, making it possible to connect on the road.

Drought and soil conditions can cause what the Park Service calls "severe cracking and movement of the parkway motor road surface" in Mississippi. In a car, you may not notice these conditions, but on motorcycle or bicycle you may encounter a high number of potholes.

It's rare for roads to be closed for inclement **weather.** Pay attention to alerts on this route for snow, tornadoes (during extreme temperature changes), dense fog, and flash floods; check with park rangers (662/680-4025) to get updated weather forecasts. They will also know about any unexpected road closures due to construction. That information is also posted on the parkway website (www.nps.gov/natr). Note that the Trace is a two-lane road with frequent pullouts. If a bridge or road is closed due to an accident, patience will be required. If a road is blocked due to an accident, you have to wait for it to clear or backtrack and find a detour.

HIT THE ROAD

The 12-Day Nashville to New Orleans Road Trip

With just under two weeks, you can wind your way from one epic music and food city to the next. The total drive is **620 miles;** 444 of these curve down the National Park Service's Natchez Trace Parkway. You'll hear everything from country to Creole; visit the birthplace of the King and places where civil rights stood proud.

The trip will take longer on two wheels or horseback, and the Natchez Trace is well-suited for such modes of transport. Check out the *Essentials* chapter (page 415) for more specifics on planning such a journey.

The parkway mileposts are numbered from south to north, so it's easy to **start your trip in New Orleans** and follow this guide in reverse to end your journey in Nashville. Either way, your trip is book-ended by good food and music. If you have more time, it is easy to add in the Mississippi Delta and Memphis and loop back to Nashville.

Days 1-2: Nashville

Spend your first two days in Nashville (see details and suggestions on page 35).

Day 3: Tennessee

NASHVILLE TO ALABAMA BORDER
(120 MI/194 KM)

Up and at 'em! Fuel up both yourself and your car with biscuits from **Loveless Cafe** and gasoline from a nearby station. Your first stop on the Natchez Trace Parkway is a prime photo spot: the **Double Arch Bridge.**

If you're up for exiting the scenic parkway, you have several good options for food, drink, and entertainment in **Franklin, Leiper's Fork,** and **Columbia,** which is where you'll find the **President James K. Polk Home & Museum.** Other highlights include the **Franklin Theatre.** While in Franklin, you can visit Carnton and learn some Civil War history.

Along the Trace itself you should stop at the **Meriwether Lewis Monument and Gravesite,** which is a somber memorial to a man who helped the country expand. This is also where to camp for the night before crossing into Alabama.

Day 4: Alabama

ALABAMA BORDER TO MISSISSIPPI BORDER
(30 MI/48 KM)

You'll be covering fewer miles on the Trace today but plenty of territory when it comes to Native American, music, and military history. Stop at the **Wichahpi Commemorative Stone Wall** and learn about the Trail of Tears.

Take a side trip to The Shoals region, where the namesake cities of Muscle Shoals, Florence, Sheffield, and Tuscumbia offer myriad opportunities. Muscle Shoals is home to important music sites like **Muscle Shoals Sound Studio** and **FAME Studios.** Shop for unique clothing items or souvenirs in Florence, then tuck in for the night.

Day 5: Northern Mississippi

MISSISSIPPI BORDER TO TUPELO
(45 MI/73 KM)

Don't forget to get gas before heading back to the Trace. Next you'll head south on the Trace, bound for Tupelo, stopping at **Bear Creek Mound** and **Pharr Mounds** on the way.

Once you arrive in Tupelo, sample the blueberry doughnuts at **Connie's Fried Chicken,** and then head to the **Elvis Presley Birthplace,** where you'll honor the King's legacy and learn how he got to be who he was. Catch live music at the **Blue Canoe,** then head back to your hotel so you can be rested and ready to go in the morning.

Top: the Double Arch Bridge along the Natchez Trace Parkway in Tennessee; **bottom:** FAME Studios in Muscle Shoals

Best Hikes

The Natchez Trace Parkway isn't just a great drive. It's also an access road to great walks, some short, some long. Here are a few of the best.

- **Garrison Creek (milepost 427.6):** As the northern terminus of the Highland Rim Trail, this is the place serious hikers go to escape the hubbub. Make it long and strenuous, or just do a quick section (page 121).
- **Wichahpi Commemorative Stone Wall (milepost 338):** Meditate and contemplate while walking along this mile-long unmortared wall, which honors those who walked the Trail of Tears (page 145).

Chisha Foka Multi-Use Trail

- **Rock Spring (milepost 330.2):** Take a 20-minute hike to a bubbling brook, sheltered from the sun under a canopy of trees (page 146).
- **Bailey's Woods Trail (Oxford):** Though doing this 20-minute wooded walk means taking a side trip to Oxford, Mississippi, it's worth it for the chance to visit William Faulkner's home, which connects to the trail (page 263).
- **Cypress Swamp Loop Trail (milepost 122):** Less than a half mile, this boardwalk stroll spans a serene swamp of water tupelos and bald cypress (page 283).
- **Chisha Foka Multi-Use Trail (milepost 95-105):** A paved path winds next to the parkway and is great for walkers, strollers, hikers, and bikers (page 291).

Day 6: Central Mississippi

TUPELO TO RIDGELAND (275 MI/443 KM WITH OXFORD)

Before you leave Tupelo, stop by the **Natchez Trace Parkway Headquarters and Visitor Center** on the Trace itself. This is the best place on the 444-mile route to meet with rangers, ask questions, watch a film, and buy some souvenirs.

Gas up the car for the 45-minute drive to Oxford, home of Ole Miss. Wander the **University of Mississippi** campus, where you can tour the **University Museum** and several of the campus's historic civil rights sights. Visit **Rowan Oak,** William Faulkner's home, then get lunch in **The Square,** the center of all things Oxford.

You have about an hour on the road to hook back up with the parkway (remember to fuel up). Then continue south. Two of five Native American ceremonial mounds are visible at the **Owl Creek Mounds Archaeological Site,** just off the parkway. Stop here to see sites that were likely temples and then head south to the six burial mounds at **Bynum Mounds.**

Take a quick hike at **Cypress Swamp,** then make for **Ridgeland,** another 150 miles down the Trace, to spend the night.

Days 7-8

RIDGELAND TO NATCHEZ (110 MI/177 KM)

Ridgeland is just east of Jackson, Mississippi's capital city. You have many

Top: Elvis Presley Birthplace in Tupelo; **bottom:** beignets at Café Du Monde in New Orleans

Best of Southern Cuisine

Honey-baked hams, biscuits, and pecan pies: A trip through the Deep South is tasty. Of course you can find hummus and kombucha, but when in the South. . . . Here's where to eat some regional specialties.

- **Loveless Cafe, Nashville:** They may not be the best biscuits in Nashville, but they are the most iconic, and they're at the northern terminus of the parkway (page 95).
- **Odette, Florence:** Locally grown and raised ingredients are incorporated in modern interpretations of classic dishes at this Alabama staple (page 158).
- **Connie's Fried Chicken, Tupelo:** This is the place to stop for fried chicken, biscuits, and blueberry doughnuts (page 184).
- **City Grocery, Oxford:** Oxford's food scene was transformed by this restaurant, which serves Coca-Cola ribs, barbecue oysters, and other Southern specialties in a renovated stable (page 265).
- **The Biscuit Shop, Starkville:** A good biscuit isn't hard to find in the South, but these are some of the best, with varieties you never imagined (page 276).
- **Carriage House Restaurant, Natchez:** Fried chicken and blue plate specials are served in Stanton Hall (page 313).
- **Jacques-Imo's Café, New Orleans:** Stop by this popular spot for innovative Creole and Cajun, huge portions, and sassy service (page 391).

blueberry doughnuts at Connie's Fried Chicken

museums from which to choose on your days in Jackson. The perfectly preserved **Eudora Welty House and Garden** feels like the author has just run out to lunch and she'll be back in a few. The civil rights collection at the **Margaret Walker Center** on the Jackson State campus, and the **Smith Robertson Museum** show different perspectives on the state's complicated civil rights history.

From Jackson you'll head back on the Trace for the last piece of your parkway drive. Appreciate the leisurely pace as you drive, stopping to read historical signs. Allocate enough time at **Mount Locust Historic House,** an 1800s building and grounds with cemeteries, walking trails, and more. Drive on to **Emerald Mound,** because while you may have seen a lot of Indian mounds on this trip, this is one on which you can climb. Like Mount Locust, **Elizabeth Female Academy** is one of the few remaining buildings (or portions thereof) on the parkway.

You've made it to the southern terminus! Natchez is known for its antebellum architecture. You can admire the historic architecture at **Garden Song B&B**. Sit by the fire or stroll the gardens and then head to **King's Tavern** for flatbread and beer for dinner. The restaurant, which may be haunted, is in the oldest building in the state.

Day 9

NATCHEZ TO BATON ROUGE

(100 MI/161 KM)

From Natchez, take US 61 south and continue to Baton Rouge, capital of Louisiana. Tour both **Louisiana's Old State Capitol** and the current **Louisiana State Capitol,** an art deco limestone stunner. Drive through **Spanish Town,** the city's oldest neighborhood, dating to 1805. Visit the **Old Louisiana Governor's Mansion,** which first resident Huey Long wanted to look like the White House.

Order savory and sweet pies at **Elsie's Plate & Pie** for dinner. Continue the history vibe by spending the night at the **Watermark** hotel, housed in an old bank.

Days 10-12

BATON ROUGE TO NEW ORLEANS

(110 MI/177 KM)

Yes, you could get from the state capitol to the Big Easy by taking I-10, but it is worth the extra miles (about 30 more) and the extra time to take the **Great River Road.** Admire the local architecture with lovely trees dripping with Spanish moss, plus a restaurant, museum, and even places to stay overnight. Continue on along the south edge of Lake Pontchartrain as you roll into **New Orleans** (see details and suggestions on page 324).

If You Have More Time Days 13-15: Memphis

NEW ORLEANS TO MEMPHIS

(400 MI/645 KM)

If you are not ready to stop exploring, add on to your trip by heading from New Orleans to Memphis through the Mississippi Delta. On your way north stop in Greenwood to eat at **Fan and Johnny's.** Visit the nearby **Robert Johnson Grave.** Stop and pay your respects to Emmett Till, whose murder at the site of **Bryant's Grocery & Meat Market** sparked the civil rights movement. Spend the night at **Travelers Hotel** in **Clarksdale** and listen to live music at **Red's Blues Club.** Swing by the **Gateway to the Blues Museum** in Tunica before you ease into Memphis (see details and suggestions on page 193).

Day 16

BACK TO NASHVILLE

(275 MI/443 KM)

Make it a loop by ending up where you started, by heading east from Memphis to Nashville. From Memphis, learn about Tina Turner and her childhood at the **West Tennessee Delta Heritage Center** before continuing on to Hurricane Mills to visit **Loretta Lynn's Ranch.** Connect back to the northern terminus of the Natchez Trace Parkway and then drive back to Nashville.

Music of the Trace

To travel along the Natchez Trace Parkway and through the Mississippi Delta is to be immersed in music that reflects the experiences of the people that have shaped this region. You don't even need to seek it out; you'll hear it in casinos and laundromats, on front porches and street corners, from Nashville country to New Orleans jazz.

Whether you prefer an intimate space or a place where you can kick up your heels and twirl, you'll find your musical fit on this road trip.

If you like songwriters and stories...

Find a listening room. This is an acoustic setup, often in the round, and the bread-and-butter of Nashville songwriters. Plan ahead and get tickets for **The Bluebird Café** or be spontaneous and head to **The Listening Room Café.**

If you want to dance...

Join Memphians at **Paula & Raiford's Disco,** which has been where locals have gone to shake their booty since 1976. In

With Less Time

Leiper's Fork

Not every period in life allows for a leisurely drive down the Natchez Trace Parkway, with 12 days to stop and explore. If your vacation days are in limited supply, here are options for shorter getaways. Each is less than 300 miles and can be done in four action-packed days:

Memphis to Nashville

Start in the Bluff City, listening to **Memphis's** music, understanding its role in the Civil Rights movement, and eating its food. When sated, start heading east. Stop in **Brownsville** to tour the **West Tennessee Delta Heritage Center** and see the Flagg Grove School, once where Tina Turner had her humble beginnings. Outsider art installation, **Mindfield,** is near by. Continue on **Hurricane Mills** to visit Loretta Lynn's Ranch. Next up are the trifecta of small Middle Tennessee towns—**Columbia, Leiper's Fork,** and **Franklin**—each with charming downtown areas, shopping, restaurants, and historic sights. Take a short drive on the **Natchez Trace Parkway,** where you can hike to overlooks and waterfalls and see the magnificent **Double Arch Bridge** and the northern terminus. End your trip in **Nashville,** where you can two-step your way through more music, history, and hot chicken.

Jackson to Natchez

One of the most popular sections of the **Natchez Trace Parkway** runs the 104.5 miles from **Ridgeland** to the southern terminus. Start in **Jackson**, and learn about the blues and Civil Rights and dining out I the big city (and state capitol) before checking out local artists at the **Bill Waller Mississippi Craft Center**. On the Trace you'll see rolling hills and lovely scenery, plus **Emerald Mound** and **Mount Locust Historic House**. Detour through **Vicksburg, Port Gibson, Lorman,** and **Rodney** where you'll learn about the Civil War, see the haunting **Windsor Ruins**, and eat delicious fried chicken while being serenaded. Finish your trip in **Natchez**, where more than four-hundred years' of history is on display in historic homes and museums.

Jackson, it's **The Iron Horse Grille** that gets people's feet tapping.

If a guitar rift is your jam...

Clarksdale has what you want, particularly at **Red's Blues Club** and **Ground Zero Blues Club.**

If you want live music in the middle of the day...

Head to honky-tonks like **Robert's Western World** and **Layla's** along Broadway in Nashville. In Clarksdale, check out weekend breakfast with a live show at **Bluesberry Cafe.**

If you want to hear the gospel sounds that led to Nashville's Music City moniker...

Make time to see the **Fisk Jubilee Singers** perform at Fisk University.

If you want to go behind the scenes...

Head to Alabama to visit the **Muscle Shoals Sound Studio** and **FAME Studios** to learn about how the Muscle Shoals Sound changed rock music.

If you like affordable shows and hanging with the college crowd...

Check out **Proud Larry's** in Oxford.

If you want river views...

Natchez's **Under-the-Hill Saloon** has been on the banks of the Mississippi since the 1800s and still offers a good time.

If you want to pay homage to the greats...

Go to Tupelo to visit the **Elvis Presley Birthplace**, or Indianola for the **B. B. King Museum and Delta Interpretive Center**—then stick around and catch a show at the museum's **Club Ebony**.

If you want a quick hit...

New Orleans's **Preservation Hall** hosts legendary shows that typically last less than an hour.

If you love a crowd and want to bar hop...

New Orleans's **Bourbon Street,** Memphis's **Beale Street,** and Nashville's **Broadway** are high-density thoroughfares for live music and people.

Nashville

Nashville

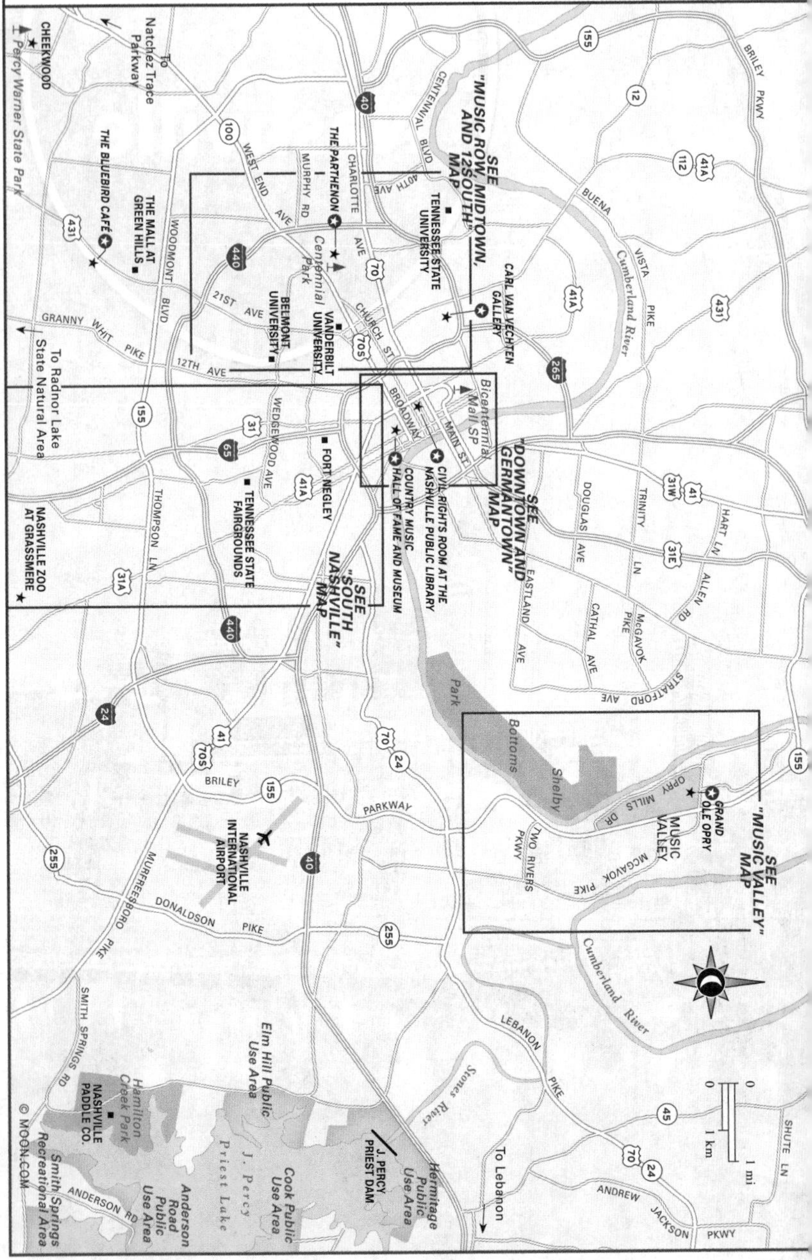

SEE "MUSIC ROW, MIDTOWN, AND 12SOUTH" MAP
SEE "DOWNTOWN AND GERMANTOWN" MAP
SEE "SOUTH NASHVILLE" MAP
SEE "MUSIC VALLEY" MAP
CHEEKWOOD
Percy Warner State Park
To Natchez Trace Parkway
THE BLUEBIRD CAFÉ
THE MALL AT GREEN HILLS
To Radnor Lake State Natural Area
NASHVILLE ZOO AT GRASSMERE
THE PARTHENON
Centennial Park
TENNESSEE STATE UNIVERSITY
CARL VAN VECHTEN GALLERY
VANDERBILT UNIVERSITY
BELMONT UNIVERSITY
Bicentennial Mall SP
CIVIL RIGHTS ROOM AT THE NASHVILLE PUBLIC LIBRARY
COUNTRY MUSIC HALL OF FAME AND MUSEUM
FORT NEGLEY
TENNESSEE STATE FAIRGROUNDS
Cumberland River
Shelby Bottoms Park
GRAND OLE OPRY
MUSIC VALLEY
NASHVILLE INTERNATIONAL AIRPORT
Elm Hill Public Use Area
J. Percy Priest Lake
J. PERCY PRIEST DAM
Hermitage Public Use Area
Cook Public Use Area
Anderson Road Public Use Area
Hamilton Creek Park
NASHVILLE PADDLE CO.
Smith Springs Recreational Area
Stones River
To Lebanon
CENTENNIAL BLVD
40TH AVE
CHARLOTTE AVE
MURPHY RD
WEST END AVE
WOODMONT BLVD
21ST AVE
GRANNY WHIT PIKE
12TH AVE
CHURCH ST
BROADWAY
MAIN ST
WEDGEWOOD AVE
THOMPSON LN
BRILEY PKWY
BUENA VISTA PIKE
DOUGLAS AVE
TRINITY LN
HART LN
ALLEN RD
EASTLAND AVE
CATHAL AVE
McGAVOK PIKE
STRATFORD AVE
OPRY MILLS DR
TWO RIVERS PKWY
McGAVOCK PIKE
BRILEY PARKWAY
MURFREESBORO PIKE
DONALDSON PIKE
LEBANON PIKE
SMITH SPRINGS RD
ANDERSON RD
ANDREW JACKSON PKWY
SHUTE LN
0 1 km
0 1 mi

Highlights

★ **Country Music Hall of Fame and Museum:** Learn about the genre's complex roots and then you'll be ready to explore the city's live music bounty (page 39).

★ **Civil Rights Room at the Nashville Public Library:** The public library houses the best exhibit about the historic Nashville sit-ins of 1960 and their role in the U.S. civil rights movement (page 45).

★ **Carl Van Vechten Gallery:** This museum on the Fisk University campus houses a remarkable collection of American art, a gift from Alfred Stieglitz (page 49).

★ **The Parthenon:** This life-size replica of the Greek Parthenon, complete with a statue of Athena, is a gathering place, a museum, and one of the reasons Nashville is called "the Athens of the South" (page 54).

★ **Grand Ole Opry:** Get an introduction to the depth and breadth of country music (page 64).

★ **The Bluebird Café:** The quintessential Nashville listening room hosts intimate music sessions with the people who really do write the songs (page 66).

There are songs in the air all around this city—in the honky-tonks lining lower Broadway, in the studios along Music Row, and in Music Valley, modern home of the Opry.

During the annual Country Music Association (CMA) Music Festival in June, the whole city is alive with the foot-tapping rhythm of country music. But locals like Jack White, Robert Plant, and the Kings of Leon have done their part to make Music City's sound more than just twang.

Nashville is also the city where performers and songwriters come to make it in the music business. Listening rooms and nightclubs all over the city are the beneficiaries of this abundance of hopeful talent, and their creativity and energy seep into almost everything in this city.

It is wrong to think that music, country or otherwise, is all there is to Nashville. After the Civil War and Reconstruction, Nashville became known as the Athens of the South because it was a center for education and the arts. Nashville offers visitors much more than a night at the Opry: Art buffs love the Frist Art Museum, Carl Van Vechten Gallery, and Cheekwood art museum, not to mention neighborhood and downtown gallery districts. The Nashville Symphony Orchestra plays in the elegant, acclaimed, and renovated Schermerhorn Symphony Center downtown.

Downtown is dominated by tall office towers and stately government buildings, including the state capitol. Meat-and-three restaurants serve irresistible Southern-style meals, East Nashville welcomes award-winning chefs, while eateries along Nolensville Pike reflect the ethnic diversity of the city. This is a city that strikes many notes but sings in perfect harmony.

Planning Your Time

In just **two days** you can see a few of the city's attractions and catch a show at the Grand Ole Opry before taking off down the Trace. Musical pilgrims, history enthusiasts, and outdoors enthusiasts should plan to spend more time—up to a week—in Music City.

Downtown is a good home base for many visitors. Hotels are within walking distance of many attractions, restaurants, and nightclubs. They are also the most expensive accommodations in the city. Visitors who are primarily interested in seeing a show at the Grand Ole Opry or shopping at Opry Mills can shack up in Music Valley, where there is a wide cross-section of affordable hotel rooms, as well as the luxury of the Opryland Resort.

If you're planning to fly to town and rent a car, bike, or motorcycle for the Natchez Trace Parkway exploration, you might as well pick up your rental upon arrival. While some neighborhoods, like downtown and 12South, are walkable, it's easier to explore the city with transportation, and you can opt for accommodations outside of the city center. There are affordable boutique hotels in midtown and East Nashville. The city's lone hostel is in midtown and is a good choice for budget travelers.

Getting There

Car

Driving is the most popular way to get to Nashville. The city is 250 miles from Atlanta, 330 miles from St. Louis, 400 miles from Charlotte, 550 miles from New Orleans, and 670 miles from Washington DC.

No fewer than three major interstate highways converge in Nashville. I-40 runs east-west, connecting Nashville with Knoxville and Memphis. I-65 runs north-south, connecting the city with Louisville, Kentucky, and Birmingham,

Two Days in Nashville

Day 1

Arrive in Nashville. Check in early to a swanky hotel, such as the historic **Hermitage Hotel** or the modern **21c Museum Hotel.** Leave your bags so you can make the most of the day unencumbered.

Set out on foot to the **Civil Rights Room at the Nashville Public Library,** where you'll learn about the city's role in the national movement.

From there head to the **Tennessee State Capitol** and then down the hill for lunch at one of the many restaurants at the **Nashville Farmers Market.** Next, take a walk through **Bicentennial Capitol Mall State Park,** which is between Germantown and downtown. Take the tour of the **Tennessee State Museum.** After hearing the carillon bells play "The Tennessee Waltz," check out **First Horizon Park,** home of baseball's Nashville Sounds, then head back downtown.

Spend the afternoon at the **Country Music Hall of Fame and Museum** and **RCA Studio B.** Grab a **Goo Goo Cluster** from the flagship store as you head back to the hotel to get ready for the evening.

Start the night off with drinks and dinner at **Pinewood.** Walk down the hill and spend the evening drinking and dancing at lower Broadway's **honky-tonks.** Or check out the show playing at the **Ryman Auditorium**—if you're in town between Thanksgiving and New Year's Eve, you'll be able to see the **Grand Ole Opry**—or the riverside **Ascend Amphitheater.**

Day 2

Get in the car and drive through the historic **Fisk University** campus. Stop at both the **Carl Van Vechten Gallery** and **Aaron Douglas Gallery** on campus.

Make your way to **Arnold's Country Kitchen** for a late breakfast. Standing in line with a crowd of locals and tourists will whet your appetite.

Sated with biscuits, head to bucolic **Centennial Park** and the majestic **Parthenon.** The replica is striking from the outside, but take the time to go inside and see the museum and the shining gold *Athena* sculpture. Grab a snack from one of the many food trucks that gather in Centennial Park.

Drive through midtown and check out **Vanderbilt University** and **Music Row,** where you might see celebs on their way to meetings with their record label executives.

Alabama. I-24 travels at a southeastern angle down to the city, connecting it with the cities of Clarkesville, Georgia, and St. Louis in the north, and Chattanooga and Atlanta in the south.

Air

Nashville International Airport (BNA, 1 Terminal Dr., 615/275-1675, www.flynashville.com) is eight miles east of the city center. To get downtown from the airport, head west on I-40; it's a short 15-minute drive. The flat one-way taxi fare from the airport to downtown or Music Valley is $25. The airport has been renovated Music City style. It has outposts of local restaurants and musicians playing live music (and selling CDs).

Airport Transportation

Many of the major hotels offer shuttles from the airport; there's a kiosk on the lower level of the terminal to help you find the right one. There is a designated ride-hailing area on the ground floor where you can find your Lyft or Uber driver.

Bus

Greyhound (800/231-2222, www.greyhound.com) serves Nashville, with

Best Restaurants

★ **Arnold's Country Kitchen:** It's worth standing in line for some of the best Southern food around, served cafeteria style (page 88).

★ **Capitol Grille:** This elegant restaurant has its own farm and herd of cattle—bringing farm-to-table to a new level (page 89).

★ **Butcher & Bee:** Low light and an open kitchen combine with an inventive small plates menu to give this restaurant its community feel (page 93).

★ **Prince's Hot Chicken Shack:** Nashville-style hot chicken is in hot demand across the country. Eat it at the place that invented it (page 94).

★ **Bastion:** With just 24 seats and an open kitchen, this restaurant offers an interactive evening with some of the best chefs in the city (page 94).

★ **Plaza Mariachi:** You'll feel like you've gone south of the border at this spirited Mexican marketplace featuring food, music, and dancing (page 94).

★ **Loveless Cafe:** With its iconic signage and famous biscuit recipe, this is a must for breakfast (page 95).

bus service to the city from Memphis, Jackson, Chattanooga, and Knoxville, Tennessee, as well as Paducah and Bowling Green, Kentucky. The **Greyhound station** (709 5th Ave. S, 615/255-3556) is well marked and well staffed, with ample parking, and is several blocks west of downtown. Expect to pay about $50 for a one-way ticket from Memphis to Nashville if you buy directly at the station, or about half that if you buy in advance online. **Megabus** (https://us.megabus.com) leaves from this same station to Louisville, Birmingham, Atlanta, Chattanooga, and other Southern cities.

Getting Around

Driving

The easiest way to get around Nashville is by car. Although visitors staying downtown will be able to find plenty to do and places to eat within walking distance, many of the best attractions are located outside of the city center.

A dozen different major rental agencies have a presence at the airport, including **Alamo** (615/340-6546, www.alamo.com), **Avis** (615/361-1212, www.avis.com), and **Hertz** (615/361-3131, www.hertz.com). Most agencies also have outposts near downtown.

Parking

There is metered parking on most downtown streets, but some have prohibited-parking signs effective during morning and afternoon rush hours. Always read the fine print carefully.

There is plenty of off-street parking in lots and garages. Expect to pay about $22 a day for garage parking. **Park It! Downtown** (www.parkitdowntown.com) is a great resource for finding downtown parking deals, plus information about the shuttle to Nissan Stadium during downtown events.

Public Transportation

Nashville's **Metropolitan Transit Authority** (MTA, www.nashvillemta.org) operates city buses. Pick up a map and schedule from either of the two downtown visitors centers or online.

Best Accommodations

★ **Downtown Sporting Club:** This isn't just a hotel, but a four-floor "'from-rise-to-rest" activity center (page 95).

★ **Union Station:** This hotel, a renovated train station, will capture your imagination (page 96).

★ **Hermitage Hotel:** More than a century old, this is the most historic hotel in town (page 96).

★ **Hutton Hotel:** Enjoy sleek luxury with a clean conscience at this ecofriendly hotel (page 98).

★ **The Russell:** This former church is now a boutique hotel with stunning stained glass windows (page 99).

★ **Gaylord Opryland Resort:** Other hotels in town, even the nicest ones, are just that: hotels. This is a full-on resort with a water park (page 100).

★ **Hotel Preston:** An airport hotel doesn't have to be generic; this one has tons of personality in addition to a convenient location (page 100).

Few tourists ride the buses because they can be difficult to understand if you're new to the city. One favorite is the **Music City Circuit,** a free bus that runs between downtown and the Gulch. These blue and green Circuit buses stop at 75 different spots on three routes. Another helpful route is the **Opry Mills Express,** which travels from downtown Nashville to Music Valley, home of the Grand Ole Opry, Opryland Hotel, and Opry Mills, the shopping mall. The Opry Mills Express departs the Bridgestone Arena 13 times a day on weekdays. Fare is $1.70 one-way ($0.85 for senior citizens). You can pick up a detailed route timetable from either of the two downtown visitors centers or online.

Commuter Rail

The **Music City Star Rail** (615/862-8833, www.rtarelaxandride.com) operates Monday to Friday, several times a day. Trains connect Donelson, Hermitage, Mount Juliet, and Lebanon to downtown Nashville (near Broadway and First Avenue). There is often additional service during special events, such as the Fourth of July celebration downtown.

One-way tickets can be purchased for $2-5.25 from vending machines at any of the stations. You can pre-purchase single-trip tickets, 10-trip packs, and monthly passes at a discount online. For a complete list of ticket outlets, contact the railway.

Taxis

Licensed taxicabs have an orange driver permit, usually displayed on the visor or dashboard. Several reliable cab companies are **Allied Cab Company** (615/333-3333, www.nashvillecab.com), **Checker Cab** (615/256-7000, www.nashville-taxicab.com), **American Music City Taxi** (615/865-4100, www.musiccitytaxi.com). Taxi rates are $3 to start plus $2 per mile.

Ride-hailing companies, including **Lyft** and **Uber,** are popular in Nashville. Download their apps to find a local to drive you to your destination. **Joyride Nashville** (615/285-9835, http://joyrideus.com/nashville) offers rides around downtown in a golf cart for a pay-what-you-wish model (drivers work on tips alone). Many of the drivers are happy to provide recommendations and tours as well as transportation.

Orientation

Even locals are perplexed by Nashville's city planning, with street names that repeat and change, and few straight roads. The interstates are a little easier to navigate than side streets. I-65 and I-24 create a tight inner beltway that encircles the heart of the city. I-440 is an outer beltway that circles the southern half of the city, while I-40 runs east to west. Briley Parkway, shown on some maps as TN-155, is a highway that circles the north and east perimeters of the city.

City residents use the interstates not just for long journeys, but also for short crosstown jaunts. Most businesses give directions according to the closest interstate exit.

Non-interstate thoroughfares emanate from Nashville like spokes of a wheel. Many are named for the communities that they eventually run into. Murfreesboro Pike runs southeast from the city; Hillsboro Pike (Route 431) starts out as 21st Avenue South and takes you to Hillsboro Village and Green Hills. Broadway becomes West End Avenue and takes you directly to Belle Meade and, eventually, the Loveless Cafe and the northern terminus of the Natchez Trace Parkway.

Nashville is built on a hill. Walking between Broadway and the state capitol is perfectly doable, but on a hot summer day, or with small children in tow, you may need to take breaks (or hop on one of the free Music City Circuit buses).

Downtown and Germantown

Downtown is Nashville's economic and tourism hub, not to mention the geographic center of the city. This is the heart of Music City's beat. **Lower Broad** is lined with **honky-tonks** with Western swing music playing almost any hour of the day. In addition to some of the city's biggest attractions, downtown is home to hotels, restaurants, and great views of the **Cumberland River.** Nearby, **The Gulch** is populated by high-rises filled with **restaurants, bars,** and **shops.**

Historic **Germantown** is chock-full of **chef-driven restaurants and bars** locals love to frequent. North of downtown, Capitol Hill is home to the **Tennessee State Capitol.**

Music Row, Midtown, and 12South

Midtown is where the work gets done: It's home to **Vanderbilt University** and Music Row, where record deals are signed. The 12South neighborhood is abuzz with activity: It boasts thoughtful **boutique shopping,** compelling **restaurants,** and an active nightlife, from **live music venues** to **comedy clubs.** The area lends itself to leisurely strolls down neighborhood streets. The **Belmont** and **Vanderbilt University** campuses bring youthful energy to the area. South of the city center are several distinct neighborhoods: **8th Avenue South,** close to downtown, is the antiques district. Along 12th Avenue below Wedgewood Avenue is **12South.** An influx of young professional property owners has given rise to restaurants, boutiques, and coffee shops.

East Nashville

East Nashville has a love-hate relationship with the "hip" moniker it has earned over the years. This always-changing neighborhood just east of downtown is home to stylish **vintage boutiques** and purveyors of handcrafted goods, not to mention many of the city's **tastiest restaurants** and **best watering holes.**

Music Valley

Close to the airport and the home of the **Grand Ole Opry** and **Opry Mills,** Music Valley is designed for tourists. Here you'll find **affordable hotels** and motels, kitschy attractions, **family-friendly restaurants,** and a few gems that even locals secretly love to frequent. It's a quick drive from the airport along Briley Parkway.

Belle Meade

Belle Meade, is actually a city with its own government. Named after an antebellum plantation, Belle Meade, the city, was historically home to Nashville's elite, and it possesses one of the most wealthy zip codes in America. The neighborhood is 7 miles southwest of downtown and 5 miles southwest of Centennial Park. The northern terminus of the Natchez Trace Parkway is 9 miles west of Belle Meade.

South Nashville

South Nashville doesn't have the cohesive neighborhood feel that some other parts of the city have. What the area may lack in clear borders, however, it makes up for in worthy destinations: the **Nashville Zoo at Grassmere** and the best **international cuisine** in Nashville.

Sights

Downtown and Germantown

This is the tourism and entertainment hub of Nashville. Walk along Lower Broad, as the blocks from 5th Avenue to the river are called, and you will pass dozens of different bars (honky-tonks), restaurants, and shops catering to visitors. The vibe of lower Broadway has become more like New Orleans' Bourbon Street in recent years, particularly on weekend nights. Parking is not permitted on this stretch of Broadway and diagonal crosswalks funnel revelers through the intersections. Expect crowds.

★ Country Music Hall of Fame and Museum

The distinctive design of the **Country Music Hall of Fame and Museum** (222 5th Ave. S., 615/416-2001, www.countrymusichalloffame.org, 9am-5pm daily, adults $25.95, seniors $23.95, children 6-12 $15.95, free for children 5 and under) is the first thing you will notice about this monument to country music. Vertical windows at the front and back of the building resemble piano keys, the sweeping arch on the right side of the building portrays a 1950s Cadillac fin, and from above, the building resembles a bass clef. The Hall of Fame was first established in 1967, and its first inductees were Jimmie Rodgers, Hank Williams, and Fred Rose. The original hall was located on Music Row, but in 2002 it moved to this signature building two blocks off Broadway in downtown Nashville.

Country music fans are drawn by the carload to the Hall of Fame, where they can pay homage to country's greatest stars, as well as to the lesser-known men and women who influenced the music. Those who aren't fans when they walk in generally leave with an appreciation of the genre's varied roots. The hall's slogan is "Honor Thy Music."

The museum is arranged chronologically, beginning with country's roots in the Scotch-Irish ballads sung by the southern mountains' first settlers, and ending with displays on some of the genre's hottest stars of today. In between, exhibits detail themes, including the rise of bluegrass, honky-tonk, and the world-famous Nashville Sound, which introduced country music to the world.

There are a half dozen private listening booths where you can hear studio-quality recordings of seminal performances, as well as a special display of a few of the genre's most famous instruments. Here you can see Bill Monroe's mandolin, Maybelle Carter's Gibson, and Johnny Cash's Martin D-355.

If you are interested in learning something about country music while you're here, splurge on the audio guide ($5), which adds depth to the exhibits.

The Hall of Fame itself is set in a rotunda. Brass plaques honor the 100 inductees, and around the room are the

Downtown

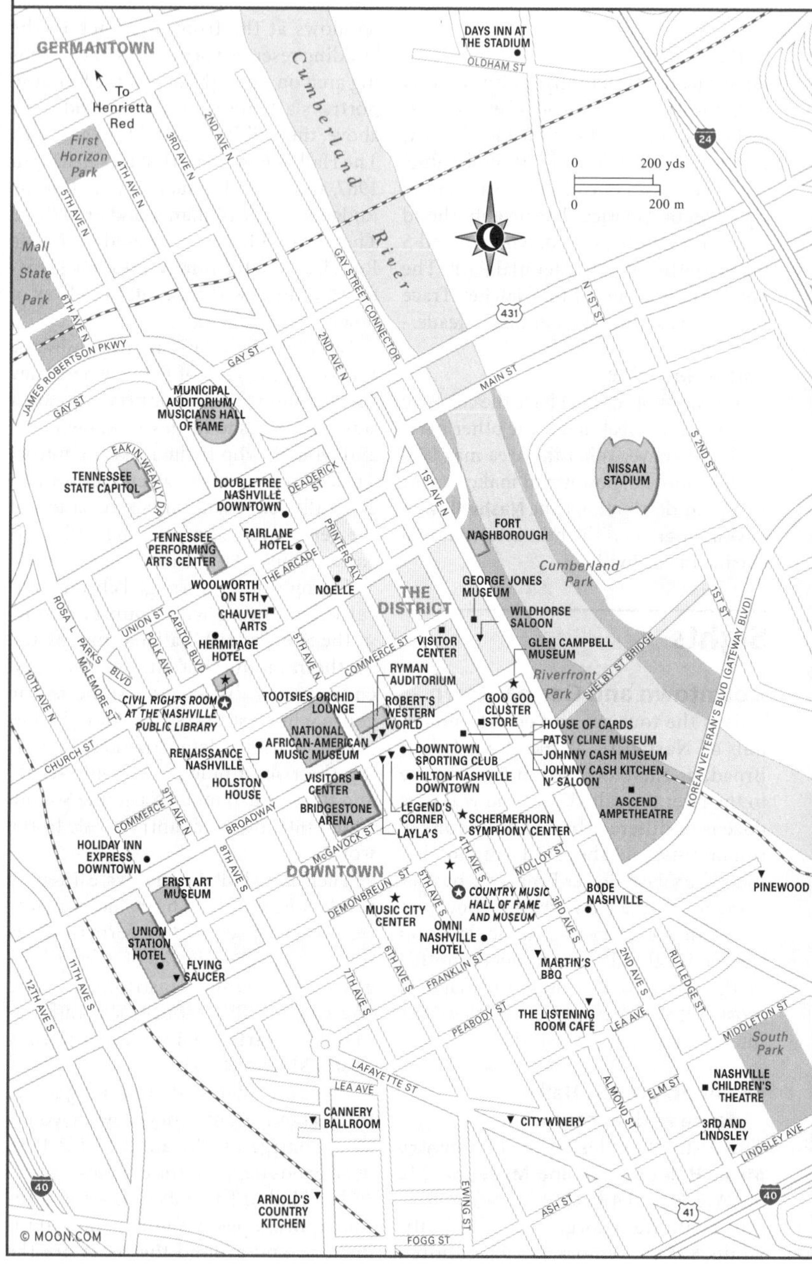
GERMANTOWN
To Henrietta Red
First Horizon Park
Mall State Park
Cumberland River
DAYS INN AT THE STADIUM
OLDHAM ST
0 200 yds
0 200 m
24
431
2ND AVE N
3RD AVE N
4TH AVE N
5TH AVE N
6TH AVE N
GAY STREET CONNECTOR
N 1ST ST
JAMES ROBERTSON PKWY
GAY ST
MAIN ST
MUNICIPAL AUDITORIUM/ MUSICIANS HALL OF FAME
EAKIN-WEAKLY DR
TENNESSEE STATE CAPITOL
DOUBLETREE NASHVILLE DOWNTOWN
DEADERICK ST
1ST AVE N
NISSAN STADIUM
S 2ND ST
FAIRLANE HOTEL
PRINTERS ALY
THE ARCADE
TENNESSEE PERFORMING ARTS CENTER
FORT NASHBOROUGH
Cumberland Park
WOOLWORTH ON 5TH
NOELLE
THE DISTRICT
GEORGE JONES MUSEUM
CHAUVET ARTS
WILDHORSE SALOON
UNION ST
CAPITOL BLVD
POLK AVE
ROSA L PARKS BLVD
HERMITAGE HOTEL
5TH AVE N
COMMERCE ST
VISITOR CENTER
GLEN CAMPBELL MUSEUM
SHELBY ST BRIDGE
1ST ST
KOREAN VETERAN'S BLVD (GATEWAY BLVD)
RYMAN AUDITORIUM
Riverfront Park
MCLEMORE ST
10TH AVE N
CIVIL RIGHTS ROOM AT THE NASHVILLE PUBLIC LIBRARY
TOOTSIES ORCHID LOUNGE
ROBERT'S WESTERN WORLD
GOO GOO CLUSTER STORE
HOUSE OF CARDS
PATSY CLINE MUSEUM
JOHNNY CASH MUSEUM
JOHNNY CASH KITCHEN N' SALOON
NATIONAL AFRICAN-AMERICAN MUSIC MUSEUM
CHURCH ST
RENAISSANCE NASHVILLE
DOWNTOWN SPORTING CLUB
HOLSTON HOUSE
VISITORS CENTER
HILTON NASHVILLE DOWNTOWN
ASCEND AMPETHEATRE
BRIDGESTONE ARENA
LEGEND'S CORNER
LAYLA'S
SCHERMERHORN SYMPHONY CENTER
COMMERCE ST
9TH AVE N
BROADWAY
McGAVOCK ST
HOLIDAY INN EXPRESS DOWNTOWN
8TH AVE S
DOWNTOWN
4TH AVE S
MOLLOY ST
FRIST ART MUSEUM
DEMONBREUN ST
5TH AVE S
COUNTRY MUSIC HALL OF FAME AND MUSEUM
3RD AVE S
BODE NASHVILLE
PINEWOOD
MUSIC CITY CENTER
OMNI NASHVILLE HOTEL
UNION STATION HOTEL
FLYING SAUCER
6TH AVE S
FRANKLIN ST
MARTIN'S BBQ
2ND AVE S
RUTLEDGE ST
11TH AVE S
12TH AVE S
7TH AVE S
PEABODY ST
THE LISTENING ROOM CAFE
LEA AVE
MIDDLETON ST
South Park
LAFAYETTE ST
LEA AVE
ALMOND ST
ELM ST
NASHVILLE CHILDREN'S THEATRE
CANNERY BALLROOM
CITY WINERY
3RD AND LINDSLEY
LINDSLEY AVE
40
ARNOLD'S COUNTRY KITCHEN
EWING ST
ASH ST
41
40
© MOON.COM
FOGG ST

words "Will the Circle Be Unbroken?" from the hymn made famous by the Carter Family.

The only way to visit Music Row's famous **RCA Studio B,** where Elvis once recorded, is to buy your ticket at the museum box office and hop on the Hall of Fame's guided tour bus. The tour takes about an hour, including the 10-minute drive to Music Row and back. The Studio B tour is an additional fee to your admission, but you can buy it as a package all at once. The Platinum Package (adults $40.95, children $30.95) includes the audio tour, museum admission, and Studio B.

The Taylor Swift Education Center is an interactive space where kids and parents can learn to play instruments and think creatively about songwriting and music making during scheduled programs. The museum has several gift shops, one of which is chock-full of much of the music you hear in the museum. The iconic Hatch Show Print store, art gallery, and printing facility is now in the Hall of Fame complex as well.

Ryman Auditorium

Thanks to an $8.5 million renovation in the 1990s, and another $14 million in 2015, the historic **Ryman Auditorium** (116 5th Ave. N., 615/889-3060, www.ryman.com, 9am-4pm daily, adults $24.95, children $16.95) remains one of the best places in the United States—let alone Nashville—to hear live music. Built in 1892 by Capt. Thomas Ryman, the Union Gospel Tabernacle, as the Ryman was then called, was designed as a venue for the charismatic preaching of Rev. Samuel P. Jones, to whom Ryman owed his own conversion to Christianity.

Managed by keen businesswoman Lula C. Naff during the first half of the 20th century, the Ryman began to showcase music and performances. In 1943, Naff let the Ryman host a popular barn dance called the Grand Ole Opry. The legacy of this partnership gave the Ryman its place in history as the so-called Mother Church of Country Music.

The Opry remained at the Ryman for the next 31 years. After the Opry left in 1974, the Ryman fell into disrepair and was virtually condemned when Gaylord Entertainment, the same company that owns the Opry, decided to invest in the grand old tabernacle. Today, it is a popular concert venue, booking rock, country, and classical acts, plus comedy and more. Performers still marvel at the fabulous acoustics of the hall and like to show them off, playing a number or two without a mic. The Opry returns here during the Christmas season, and in the summer there's a weekly bluegrass series.

Seeing a show at the Ryman is by far the best way to experience this historic venue, but if you can't do that, pay the admission fee to see a short video and explore the auditorium on your own, which includes museum-style exhibits about the musicians who have performed here through the ages. You can sit a few minutes on the old wooden pews and even climb on stage to be photographed in front of the classic Opry backdrop. A guided tour that takes you backstage (adults $30, children $25) isn't just for die-hard fans. It gives lots of insight into how stars behaved when they were behind these famous walls. The guides tend to throw in an extra tall tale or two. Plus, you get to walk on the storied stage yourself. More than one marriage proposal has taken place at this point on the tour.

Stop by Café Lula (www.cafelula.net, 10:30am-5pm daily, with extended hours during events) for snacks.

John Seigenthaler Pedestrian Bridge

Built in 1909, the Sparkman Street Bridge was slated for demolition in 1998 after inspectors called its condition "poor." But citing the success of the Walnut Street Bridge in revitalizing downtown Chattanooga, Tennessee, advocates succeeded in saving the bridge.

The now-named **John Seigenthaler Pedestrian Bridge** reopened in 2003 as a footbridge and bike bridge.

Today, the John Seigenthaler Pedestrian Bridge connects East Nashville neighborhoods with downtown. It was frequently featured on TV because of its great views of the city, and many folks get their iconic Music City photos taken there (including this author). It is named after the civil rights crusader and journalist. At the base of the east side of the bridge is **Cumberland Park** (592 S. 1st St., 615/862-8508, www.nashville.gov/parks, dawn-11pm daily) and the East Bank Landing's kayak, canoe, and paddleboard launches.

Johnny Cash Museum

The **Johnny Cash Museum** (119 3rd Ave. S., 615/256-1777, www.johnnycashmuseum.com, 9am-7pm daily, adults $19.95, seniors and military $18.95, children $15.95) looks like a small storefront with a tiny gift shop. But back behind the cash register is a wealth of information on all things Johnny Cash. The collection was amassed by one fan-turned-collector, and it features interactive listening booths, the jumpsuit the Man in Black wore when he flipped the bird in public, and other memorabilia from a varied and lauded career. Locals are crazy for the rebuilt stone wall that was taken from Cash's fire-destroyed suburban home. This is one of the city's most visited attractions.

Patsy Cline Museum

Housed above the Johnny Cash Museum, the **Patsy Cline Museum** (119 3rd Ave. S., 2nd floor, 615/454-4722, www.patsymuseum.com, 9am-7pm daily, adults $18.95, seniors, students, and military $17.95, children 6-15 $14.95, free for children 5 and under) chronicles the life of the legendary country artist. Visitors can view Cline's personal belongings and relevant artifacts, many of which were donated by her family, who are delighted to have so many people learn about the vocalist's short but significant life. Exhibits include a replica of the soda shop where she worked and her home, and videos about her career. Admission is separate from the Johnny Cash Museum.

Glen Campbell Museum

Learn all about the Rhinestone Cowboy at the **Glen Campbell Museum** (111 Broadway, Ste. 200, 615/258-5576, www.glencampbellmuseum.com, 9am-5pm daily, adults $19, seniors and military $18, youth ages 6-17 $15, free for children 5 and under). The museum features family photos, golf memorabilia, and other artifacts from the singer's storied career.

George Jones Museum

Known as "the Possum," George Jones was a country music great who passed away in 2013 at the age of 81. He struggled with alcohol abuse: He famously drove a John Deere tractor to the liquor store once because his brother-in-law hid his car keys, and was known for being a no-show for performances. His wife devoted her time to helping him get better. Now she's devoting her time to preserving his musical legacy. The **George Jones Museum** (128 2nd Ave. N., 615/818-0128, http://georgejones.com, 10am-8pm daily, adults $17, seniors $10, military $12, youth $7, free for children 5 and under) is filled with artifacts from his life and career, from stage costumes to awards to, yes, a replica of that John Deere tractor. Some exhibits include a hologram of Jones, to give the experience of seeing the legend. A rooftop bar looks out at the Cumberland River.

Tennessee Sports Hall of Fame

Sports fans will enjoy the **Tennessee Sports Hall of Fame** (Bridgestone Arena, 501 Broadway, 615/242-4750, www.tshf.net, 10am-5pm Tues.-Sat., adults $3, children $2). Located in a state-of-the-art 7,500-square-foot exhibit space inside Bridgestone Arena, the hall chronicles the history of sports in Tennessee from the 1800s to today's heroes.

Customs House

Located at 701 Broadway, the old Nashville **Customs House** is a historic landmark and architectural beauty. Construction on the Customs House began in 1875, and President Rutherford B. Hayes visited Nashville to lay the cornerstone in 1877. The building is an impressive example of the Victorian Gothic style. It was designed by Treasury architect William Appleton Potter and was completed in 1916. Although it is called a customs house, the building served as the center of federal government operations in the city: Federal government offices, courts, and treasury offices were housed in the building.

Frist Art Museum

Nashville's foremost visual art space is the **Frist Art Museum** (919 Broadway, 615/244-3340, http://fristartmuseum.org, 10am-5:30pm Mon.-Wed. and Sat., 10am-9pm Thurs.-Fri., 1pm-5:30pm Sun., adults $15, seniors and students $10, military $8). The Frist is located in a stately building that once housed the 1930s downtown post office (and there's still a working post office in the basement). High ceilings, art deco finishes, and unique hardwood tiles distinguish the museum. Look carefully in the hallways, and you can see the indentations in the walls from folks who leaned here while waiting for their turn in line at the post office.

The Frist puts on about 12 major visiting exhibitions annually. At any given time, you will see 3-4 different exhibits, many of which are regional or national premieres, plus nighttime concerts and events. There are typically plenty of ongoing educational activities paired with

Top to bottom: the Country Music Hall of Fame; Patsy Cline Museum; Glen Campbell Museum

the exhibitions. ArtQuest, a permanent part of the Frist, is an excellent hands-on arts activity room for children and their parents. The Frist's café serves better-than-expected salads and sandwiches, and has a nice patio for alfresco dining.

Downtown is dominated by large office buildings and federal, state, and city government structures. From Commerce Street northward to the state capitol, you will find historic churches, museums, and hordes of office workers.

Tennessee State Capitol

Set on the top of a hill and built with the formality and grace of classic Greek architecture, the **Tennessee State Capitol** building (600 Charlotte Ave., 615/741-0830, http://capitoltn.gov, tours 8am-4pm hourly Mon.-Fri., free) strikes a commanding pose overlooking downtown Nashville. Construction of the capitol began in 1845, two years after the state legislature finally agreed that Nashville would be the permanent capital city. Even with the unpaid labor of convicts and enslaved people, it took 14 years to finish the building.

The capitol is built of limestone, much of it from a quarry located near present-day Charlotte and 13th Avenues. In the 1950s, extensive renovations were carried out, and some of the original limestone was replaced. The interior marble came from Rogersville and Knoxville, and the gasoliers were ordered from Philadelphia. The capitol was designed by architect William Strickland, who considered it his crowning achievement and who is buried in a courtyard on the north end of the capitol.

Visitors are welcome at the capitol. Ask at the information desk for a printed guide that identifies each of the rooms and many of the portraits and sculptures both inside and outside the building. If the legislature is not in session, you can go inside both the House and Senate chambers, which look much as they did back in the 19th century. In the 2nd-floor lobby, you can see two bronze reliefs depicting the 19th and 14th amendments to the U.S. Constitution, both of which were ratified by the State of Tennessee in votes held at the capitol.

Guided tours of the capitol depart hourly 9am-3pm Monday-Friday. Ask at the information desk inside for more details.

Other important state buildings surround the capitol. The **Library and Archives** (403 7th Ave. N.) sits directly west of the capitol and next to the **Tennessee Supreme Court** (401 7th Ave. N.). The **Tennessee War Memorial** (301 6th Ave. N.) is a stone plaza on the south side of the capitol and a nice place to people-watch (and where, in 2000, Al Gore told supporters he would fight on in the presidential election against George W. Bush).

Tennessee State Museum

In 2018, the **Tennessee State Museum** (1000 Rosa L. Parks Blvd., 615/741-2692,

www.tnmuseum.org, 10am-5pm Tues.-Wed. and Fri.-Sat., 10am-8pm Thurs., 1pm-5pm Sun., free) moved from the basement of the building that houses the Tennessee Performing Arts Center to a new, custom-designed facility next to Bicentennial Capitol Mall State Park. With the move, the museum and its exhibits found new life. The walls are chockfull of interactive displays that show more of the breadth and depth of the Volunteer State. The children's area, designed by local artist Lucie Rice, is a bright, colorful space where you literally walk into maps of the state. There's an excellent overview of Tennessee history from Native Americans to the New South era of the 1880s. Exhibits detail the state's political development, explore the Revolutionary and Civil Wars, and profile famous Tennesseans including Andrew Jackson and Davy Crockett. They also cast a spotlight on the lifestyles and diversions of Tennesseans of various eras, from early frontierspeople to a free African American family before emancipation. Special artifacts include the top hat worn by Andrew Jackson at his presidential inauguration, a musket that belonged to Daniel Boone, and the jawbone of a mastodon that called Tennessee home some 10,000 years ago. The 137,000-square-foot building itself is big and open and afford great views of Bicentennial Mall, and easy access to the Nashville Farmers Market, which can be a good place for post-museum lunch.

★ Civil Rights Room at the Nashville Public Library

The **Nashville Public Library** (615 Church St., 615/862-5800, 9am-6pm Mon.-Fri., 9am-5pm Sat., 2pm-5pm Sun., free) houses a powerful exhibit (615/862-5782, www.library.nashville.org/civilrights/home.html) on the movement for civil rights that took place in Nashville in the 1950s and 1960s. Nashville was the first Southern city to desegregate public services, and it did so relatively peacefully,

Civil Rights Room at the Nashville Public Library

setting an example for activists throughout the South.

The story of the courageous men and women who made this change happen is told through photographs, videos, and displays in the **Civil Rights Room at the Nashville Public Library.** The library is a fitting location for the exhibit since the block below on Church Street was the epicenter of the Nashville sit-ins during 1960.

Inside the room, large-format photographs show school desegregation, sit-ins, and a silent march to the courthouse. A circular table at the center of the room is symbolic of the lunch counters where young students from Fisk, Meharry, American Baptist, and Tennessee A&I sat silently and peacefully at sit-ins. The table is engraved with the 10 rules of conduct set out for sit-in participants, including to be polite and courteous at all times, regardless of how you are treated. A timeline of the national and Nashville civil rights movements is presented above the table.

Inside a glass-enclosed viewing room you can choose from six documentary videos, including an hour-long 1960 NBC news documentary about the Nashville sit-ins. Many of the videos are 30 minutes or longer, so plan on spending several hours here if you are keenly interested in the topics.

The centerpiece of the Civil Rights Room is a glass inscription by Martin Luther King Jr., who visited the city in 1960 and said, during a speech at Fisk University: "I came to Nashville not to bring inspiration, but to gain inspiration from the great movement that has taken place in this community."

Nashville is planning a new and much-needed museum dedicated to its African American history and culture, which will be located at the corner of Jefferson and 8th Avenues, near the farmers market. Until this museum is built, the Nashville Public Library is the best place to learn about the city's racially segregated past and the movement that changed that.

The Civil Rights Room is on the 2nd floor of the library, adjacent to the room that houses its Nashville collection.

The Arcade

One of Nashville's most distinctive urban features is the covered arcade that runs between 4th and 5th Avenues and parallel to Union Street. The two-story arcade with a gabled glass roof was built in 1903 by developer Daniel Buntin, who was inspired by similar arcades he saw in Italy.

From the moment it opened, the **Arcade** (65 Arcade Alley, 615/248-6673, http://thenashvillearcade.com) was a bustling center for commerce. Famous for its peanut shop, the Arcade has also been the location of photo studios, jewelers, and a post office for many years. Today, restaurants (including Manny's House of Pizza) crowd the lower level, while art galleries, artists' studios, and professional offices line the 2nd floor. Don't miss the bustling activities here during the Art Crawl on the first Saturday of the month.

Downtown Presbyterian Church

William Strickland, the architect who designed the Tennessee State Capitol, also designed the **Downtown Presbyterian Church** (154 5th Ave. N., 615/254-7584, http://dpchurch.com; services 11am Sun., free), a place of worship now on the National Register of Historic Places. Built in 1848 to replace an earlier church destroyed by fire, the church is in the Egyptian revival style that was popular at the time. It is, however, one of only three surviving churches in the country to be built in this style.

Downtown Presbyterian, which added the word "Downtown" to its name in 1955, was used as a Union hospital during the Civil War, and it is where James K. Polk was inaugurated as Tennessee governor in 1839. Visitors are welcome to come for a self-guided tour at 2pm

The Nashville Sit-Ins

Greensboro, North Carolina, is often named as the site of the first sit-ins of the American civil rights movement. But, in truth, activists in Nashville carried out the first "test" sit-ins in late 1959. In these test cases, protesters left the facilities after being refused service and talking to management about the injustice of segregation. In between these test sit-ins and the moment when Nashville activists would launch a full-scale sit-in campaign, students in Greensboro took that famous first step.

The Nashville sit-ins began on February 13, 1960, when a group of Black students from local colleges and universities sat at a downtown lunch counter and refused to move until they were served. The protesting students endured verbal and physical abuse (white opposition, for example, extinguished cigarettes on the arms of the Black students), and were arrested.

Community members raised money for the students' bail, and Black residents of the city began an economic boycott of downtown stores that practiced segregation. On April 19, the home of Z. Alexander Looby, a Black lawyer who was representing the students, was bombed. Later the same day, students led a spontaneous, peaceful, and silent march through the streets of downtown Nashville to the courthouse. Diane Nash, a student leader, asked Nashville mayor Ben West if he thought it was morally right for a restaurant to refuse to serve someone based on the color of his or her skin. Mayor West said, "No."

The march was an important turning point for the city. The combined effect of the sit-ins, the boycott, and the march in 1960 caused Nashville to be the first major Southern city to experience widespread desegregation of its public facilities. The events also demonstrated to activists in other parts of the South that nonviolence was an effective tool of protest.

The story of the young people who led the Nashville sit-ins is told in the book *The Children* by David Halberstam. In 2001, Nashville resident Bill King was so moved by the story of the protests that he established an endowment to fundraise for a permanent civil rights collection at the Nashville Public Library. In 2003, the **Civil Rights Room at the Nashville Public Library** was opened. It houses books, oral histories, audiovisual records, microfilm, dissertations, and stunning photographs of the events of 1960. The words of one student organizer, John Lewis, who went on to become a congressman from Georgia, are displayed over the entryway: "If not us, then who; if not now, then when?"

Tues.-Thurs.; groups of five or more can call in advance.

Musicians Hall of Fame & Museum

Not to be confused with the Country Music Hall of Fame, the **Musicians Hall of Fame & Museum** (MHOF) (401 Gay St., 615/244-3263, www.musicianshalloffame.com, 10am-5pm Mon.-Sat., adults $25, seniors and military $22, youth $15) honors the people who pick and strum. Not necessarily the stars and not the songwriters, but the guitar players and drummers and others, regardless of genre or instrument, who make a song something to which we want to tap our toes. The MHOF was displaced when the city built the mammoth Music City Center. Located in Municipal Auditorium—once the city's leading concert venue—since 2013, the MHOF displays memorabilia and instruments from the unsung heroes of the industry. Inductees are nominated by current members of the American Federation of Musicians and others. An 8,500-square-foot Grammy Museum Gallery expansion is in the works.

21c Museum Nashville

One of the country's most cutting-edge contemporary art collections is inside a hotel. The **21c Museum Nashville**

(223 3rd Ave. N., 615/610-6400, www.21cmuseumhotels.com, 24 hours daily, free) opened in Nashville in 2017 with a mission to make contemporary art part of everyday life. Exhibits rotate annually and tend to be thought-provoking works.

National Museum of African American Music

The **National Museum of African American Music** (211 7th Ave. N., Ste. 420, 615/488-3310, http://nmaam.org, 9am-5pm daily, adults $24.95, seniors and students $18.75, free for children under 7) has been in the works for decades and honors groundbreaking African American music and artists across genres including gospel, jazz, the blues, and hip hop. It opened in 2020 in a new 5th and Broadway complex, across from Bridgestone Arena, and features interactive displays, listening rooms, and more. Exhibits also cover the civil rights movement and the Harlem Renaissance, putting the music in context of the larger issues of the times.

Bicentennial Capitol Mall State Park

Tennessee celebrated its 100th anniversary in 1896 with the construction of the beloved Centennial Park, so it must have seemed like a good idea to celebrate its 200th anniversary in much the same way. The **Bicentennial Capitol Mall State Park** occupies 19 acres on the north side of the capitol building. It offers excellent views of the capitol, which towers over the mall. The mall and the capitol are separated by a steep hill and more than 200 steps, which may look daunting but are worth the climb for the views and access to downtown.

The mall has dozens of features that celebrate Tennessee and Tennesseans, including a 200-foot granite map of Tennessee embedded in concrete; a River Wall with 31 fountains, each representing one of Tennessee's rivers; and a timeline with Tennessee events, inscriptions, and notable quotes from 1796 to 1996. A one-mile path that circles the mall's perimeter is popular with walkers and joggers, and a 2,000-seat amphitheater is used for special events. The park may be a civics lesson incarnate, but it is also a pleasant place to pass the time. Ninety-five carillon bells (for the state's 95 counties) play "The Tennessee Waltz" every hour on the hour.

To the west of the mall is the amazing **Nashville Farmers Market** (900 Rosa L. Parks Blvd., 615/880-2001, www.nashvillefarmersmarket.org, 8am-6pm Sun.-Thurs., 8am-8pm Fri.-Sat.), where you can buy fresh produce, flowers, gourmet breakfasts and lunches, and locally made crafts. Locals often picnic in the mall with goodies from the market. There's plenty of free parking here, but don't speed. Because this is a state park, tickets come from the state police, and they're pricier than metro Nashville tickets.

Fisk University

Founded in 1866 to educate newly freed African Americans, **Fisk University** (1000 17th Ave. N., 615/329-8500, www.fisk.edu) has a long and proud history as one of the foremost Black colleges in the United States. W. E. B. Du Bois attended Fisk, graduating in 1888, and Booker T. Washington married a Fisk alumna and sent his own children to Fisk. In more modern times, Knoxville native and poet Nikki Giovanni attended Fisk.

Fisk sits at the corner of Jefferson Street and Dr. D. B. Todd Jr. Boulevard, about 10 blocks west of downtown Nashville. The campus is a smattering of elegant red-brick buildings set on open green lawns, although a few more modern buildings, including the library, detract from the classical feel. One of the oldest Fisk buildings is **Jubilee Hall,** on the north end of the campus, which is said to be the first permanent building constructed for the education of African Americans in the country. It was built with money raised

Fisk's Stieglitz Collection

When photographer **Alfred Stieglitz** died in 1946, his wife, **Georgia O'Keeffe,** herself one of the most important artists of her generation, was left with the responsibility of giving away his massive art collection. Stieglitz had collected more than 1,000 works by artists who included O'Keeffe, Arthur Dove, Marsden Hartley, Charles Demuth, and John Marin. He also owned several African sculptures.

Stieglitz's instructions regarding this art collection were vague. In his will he asked O'Keeffe to select the recipients "under such arrangements as will assure to the public, under reasonable regulations, access thereto to promote the study of art."

O'Keeffe selected several obvious recipients for parts of the collection: the Library of Congress, the National Gallery of Art in Washington, the Metropolitan Museum of Art, the Art Institute of Chicago, and the Philadelphia Museum of Art. Nashville's **Fisk University** was a surprise, and Carl Van Vechten, a writer, photographer, and friend of Stieglitz and O'Keeffe, is credited with making the suggestion. Van Vechten was keenly interested in African American art and was close friends with Fisk president Charles Johnson.

The Stieglitz Collection at Fisk consists of 101 remarkable works of art, including 2 by O'Keeffe, 19 Stieglitz photographs, prints by Cézanne and Renoir, and 5 pieces of African tribal art.

Cash-strapped Fisk sought to sell parts of the collection to raise funds. An agreement between the university and Walmart heiress Alice Walton's Crystal Bridges Museum in Bentonville, Arkansas, means that the collection spends every two years in Bentonville and then returns to Fisk for two years. The $1 million from the partnership allowed Fisk to remodel and hire curatorial staff, and also to highlight the school's impressive collections of works by African American artists while the Stieglitz is in Bentonville.

by the Fisk Jubilee Singers, who popularized Black spirituals during a world tour 1871-1874. Another notable building is the **Fisk Little Theatre,** a white clapboard building that once served as a Union hospital during the Civil War.

The **Aaron Douglas Gallery** (Jackson St. and 17th Ave. N., 7:45am-10pm Mon.-Thurs., 7:45am-5pm Fri., 1pm-5pm Sat., 2pm-10pm Sun., free) houses Fisk's collection of African, African American, and folk art. It also hosts visiting exhibits and others by Fisk students and faculty. It is named after painter and illustrator Aaron Douglas, who also established Fisk's first formal art department. The gallery is located on the top floor of the Fisk library. **Cravath Hall** houses several Aaron Douglas murals that, while in need of restoration, are worth seeing. If a curator at the Van Vechten is available, you may be lucky enough to have them take you on a quick guided tour of the murals, as well as a small art gallery on the third floor of the library.

Fisk welcomes visitors, but there is no central information desk or printed guide. A map is posted just inside the library, and this is the best place to start your visit. Historical markers provide details of each of the main campus buildings. To see the famous painting of the Jubilee Singers, enter Jubilee Hall and bear right to the Appleton Room, where it hangs at the rear.

★ Carl Van Vechten Gallery

The **Carl Van Vechten Gallery** (Dr. D. B. Todd Jr. Blvd. and Jackson St., 615/329-8720, 10am-4pm Mon.-Fri., adults $10, seniors $6, college students $5, free for children) is named for the art collector who convinced artist Georgia O'Keeffe to donate to Fisk a large portion of the work and personal collection of her late husband, Alfred Stieglitz. The

The Jubilee Singers

In 1871, Fisk University needed money. Buildings at the school established in old Union army barracks in 1866 were decaying while more and more African Americans came to seek education.

So, in what might later be considered a very Nashville-style idea, the school choir withdrew all the money from the university's treasury and left on a world tour. The nine singers were Isaac Dickerson, Maggie Porter, Minnie Tate, Jennie Jackson, Benjamin Holmes, Thomas Rutling, Eliza Walker, Green Evans, and Ella Sheppard. Remembering a biblical reference to the Hebrew "year of the jubilee," Fisk treasurer and choir manager George White gave them their name, the Fisk Jubilee Singers.

The choir struggled at first, but before long audiences were singing their praises. They toured first the American South, then the North, and in 1873 sailed to England for a successful British tour. Their audiences included William Lloyd Garrison, Wendell Phillips, Ulysses S. Grant, William Gladstone, Mark Twain, Johann Strauss, and Queen Victoria. Songs like "Swing Low, Sweet Chariot" and "Nobody Knows the Trouble I've Seen" moved audiences to tears. The singers introduced the spiritual to mainstream white audiences and erased negative misconceptions about African Americans and African American education.

In 1874, the singers returned to Nashville. They had raised enough money to pay off Fisk's debts and build the university's first permanent structure, an imposing Victorian Gothic six-story building now called **Jubilee Hall.** It was the first permanent structure built solely for the education of African Americans in the United States.

Every October 6, the day in 1871 that the singers departed Fisk, the university recalls their struggle and their triumph with a free convocation featuring the modern-day Jubilee Singers. Jubilee Day, as it is called, also includes a pilgrimage to their gravesites to lay wreaths made from campus magnolia leaves.

collection includes works by Stieglitz and O'Keeffe, as well as acclaimed European and American artists, including Pablo Picasso, Paul Cézanne, Pierre-Auguste Renoir, Diego Rivera, Arthur Dove, Gino Severini, and Charles Demuth. For seven years a legal battle waged in courts as the college sought to sell parts of the collection to raise funds. Fortunately, a compromise was struck. Crystal Bridges Museum of American Art (http://stieglitzcollection.crystalbridges.org) in Bentonville, Arkansas, entered into a partnership with Fisk, allowing both institutions to display the collection; rotating every two years.

The collection is one worth seeing, and the new funds and partnership make that more possible, because the gallery now has a staff and regular hours. The school's works by African American artists are impressive as well, and make the gallery a worthwhile detour even when Stieglitz is not in residence. The gallery is closed when school is not in session; check the website for exact annual spring and fall break dates.

Meharry Medical College

Just across Dr. D. B. Todd Jr. Boulevard from Fisk is **Meharry Medical College** (1005 Dr. D. B. Todd Jr. Blvd., 615/327-6000, http://home.mmc.edu), the largest private, comprehensive, historically Black institution educating medical professionals. It was founded in 1876 as the Medical Department of the Central Tennessee College of Nashville, under the auspices of the Freeman's Aid Society of the Methodist Episcopal Church.

Meharry was at one time responsible for graduating more than half of all Black doctors and nurses in the United States. Today it has an enrollment of almost 800 students.

Marathon Village

This "new" neighborhood actually dates back to 1881. A former auto factory, **Marathon Village** (1305 Clinton St., www.marathonvillage.com) now houses sleek urban condos, restaurants, Nelson's Green Brier Distillery, Bang Candy Company, and shops, including Antique Archaeology Nashville, owned by Mike Wolfe of *American Pickers* TV fame. It's also becoming a destination for entertainment, thanks to live music venue Marathon Music Works, one of the best places to see non-country concerts, and Third Coast Comedy Club, the city's first comedy club, featuring stand-up, improv, and sketch acts. Of course, the architecture brings in history buffs who love the buildings' bones.

Hadley Park

Founded in 1912, **Hadley Park** (1037 28th Ave. N., 615/862-8451, dawn-dusk daily) is believed to be the oldest public park developed for African Americans in the South and, most likely, the United States. The park got its start when Fisk University president George Gates requested that the city buy land and create a park for its Black citizens. This was in the era of segregation, so other city parks were not open to Black people. The request was granted, and the park opened in July 1912. An old farmhouse was converted into a community center, and benches and a playground were installed. It is now home to a state-of-the-art gym and fitness center, computer labs, meeting rooms, and tennis courts.

Music Row, Midtown, and 12South

Home to the business end of the country music industry, Music Row can be found along 16th and 17th Avenues south of where they cross Broadway. While there are few bona fide attractions here, it is worth a jaunt to see the headquarters of both major and independent music labels all in one place (this might be your best chance for a celebrity sighting).

Music Row's most famous, or infamous, landmark is ***Musica,*** the sculpture at the Music Row traffic circle. The sculpture, by local artist Alan LeQuire, caused a stir when it was unveiled in 2003 for the larger-than-life anatomically correct men and women it depicts. Regardless of your views on art and obscenity, it is fair to say that *Musica* speaks more to Nashville's identity as the Athens of the South than as Music City USA.

RCA Studio B

As a rule, the music studios in Music Row are open for business, not tours. The lone exception is historic **RCA Studio B** (1611 Roy Acuff Pl., 615/416-2001, http://studiob.org, $30.95-40.95). The RCA studio was the second recording studio in Nashville and the place where artists including the Everly Brothers, Roy Orbison, Dolly Parton, Elvis Presley, and Hank Snow recorded hits. Also called the RCA Victor Studio, this nondescript studio operated from 1957 to 1977. Visitors on the one-hour tour, which departs from the Country Music Hall of Fame downtown, hear anecdotes about recording sessions at the studio and see rare footage of a 1960s Dottie West recording session.

Tours can only be purchased in conjunction with admission to the Country Music Hall of Fame. Tours depart hourly 10:30am-2:30pm daily.

The Upper Room Chapel and Museum

Three million Christians around the world know the Upper Room Daily Devotional Guide, a page-a-day pocket devotional available in 106 countries and 40 languages. Headquartered in Nashville, the Upper Room Ministry has established a bookstore, museum, and chapel to welcome visitors. **The Upper Room Chapel and Museum** (1908 Grand Ave., 800/972-0433, http://chapel.upperroom.org, 8am-4:30pm Mon.-Thurs.,

Midtown and West End

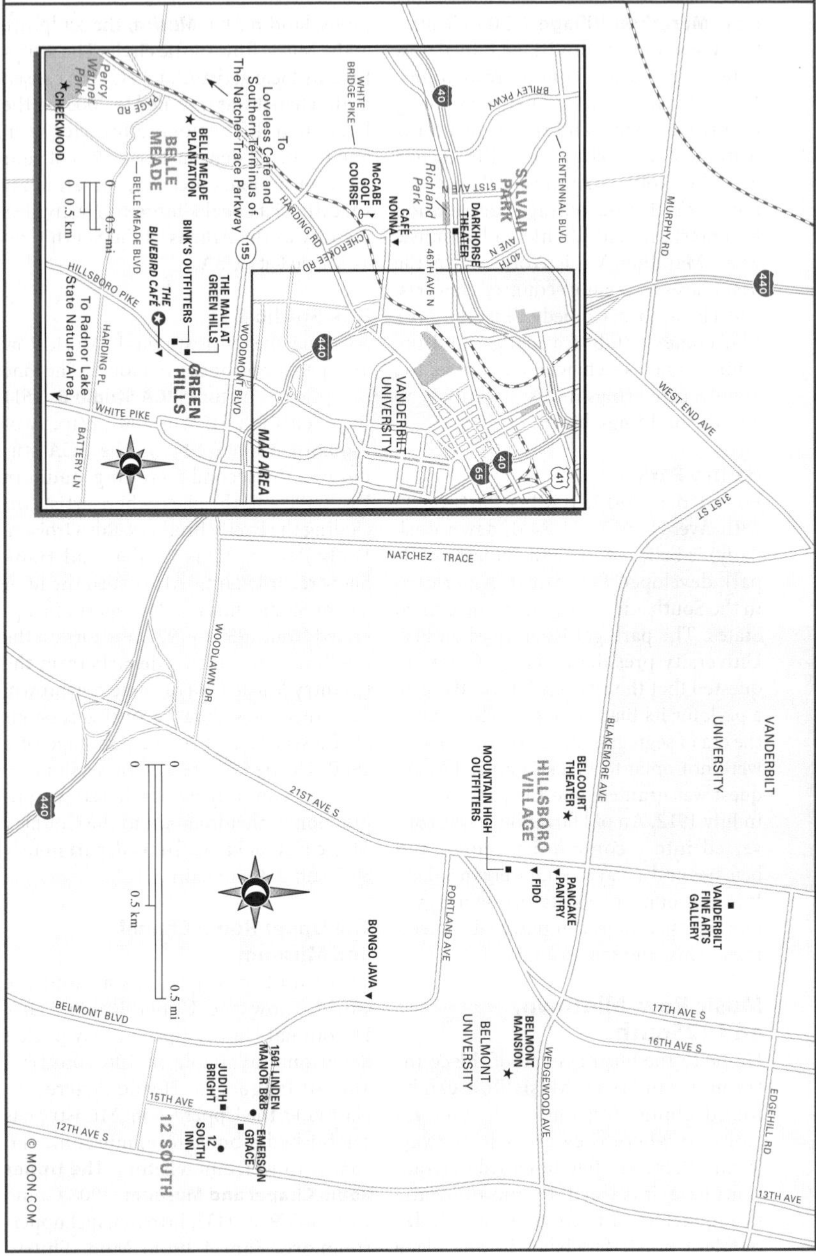

VANDERBILT UNIVERSITY
MURPHY RD
440
WEST END AVE
31ST ST
NATCHEZ TRACE
BLAKEMORE AVE
WOODLAWN DR
21ST AVE S
440
BELCOURT THEATER
HILLSBORO VILLAGE
MOUNTAIN HIGH OUTFITTERS
PANCAKE PANTRY
FIDO
VANDERBILT FINE ARTS GALLERY
PORTLAND AVE
BONGO JAVA
0 0.5 mi
0 0.5 km
17TH AVE S
16TH AVE S
BELMONT MANSION
BELMONT UNIVERSITY
WEDGEWOOD AVE
EDGEHILL RD
BELMONT BLVD
1501 LINDEN MANOR B&B
JUDITH BRIGHT
EMERSON GRACE
12 SOUTH INN
12 SOUTH
15TH AVE
12TH AVE S
13TH AVE

CENTENNIAL BLVD
BRILEY PKWY
40
SYLVAN PARK
51ST AVE N
40TH AVE N
DARKHORSE THEATER
Richland Park
46TH AVE N
CAFE NONNA
McCABE GOLF COURSE
WHITE BRIDGE PIKE
CHEROKEE RD
HARDING RD
To Loveless Cafe and Southern Terminus of The Natchez Trace Parkway
155
440
VANDERBILT UNIVERSITY
MAP AREA
40
65
41
PAGE RD
Percy Warner Park
CHEEKWOOD
BELLE MEADE PLANTATION
BELLE MEADE
BELLE MEADE BLVD
0 0.5 mi
0 0.5 km
BINK'S OUTFITTERS
THE MALL AT GREEN HILLS
GREEN HILLS
WOODMONT BLVD
THE BLUEBIRD CAFÉ
HILLSBORO PIKE
HARDING PL
To Radnor Lake State Natural Area
WHITE PIKE
BATTERY LN

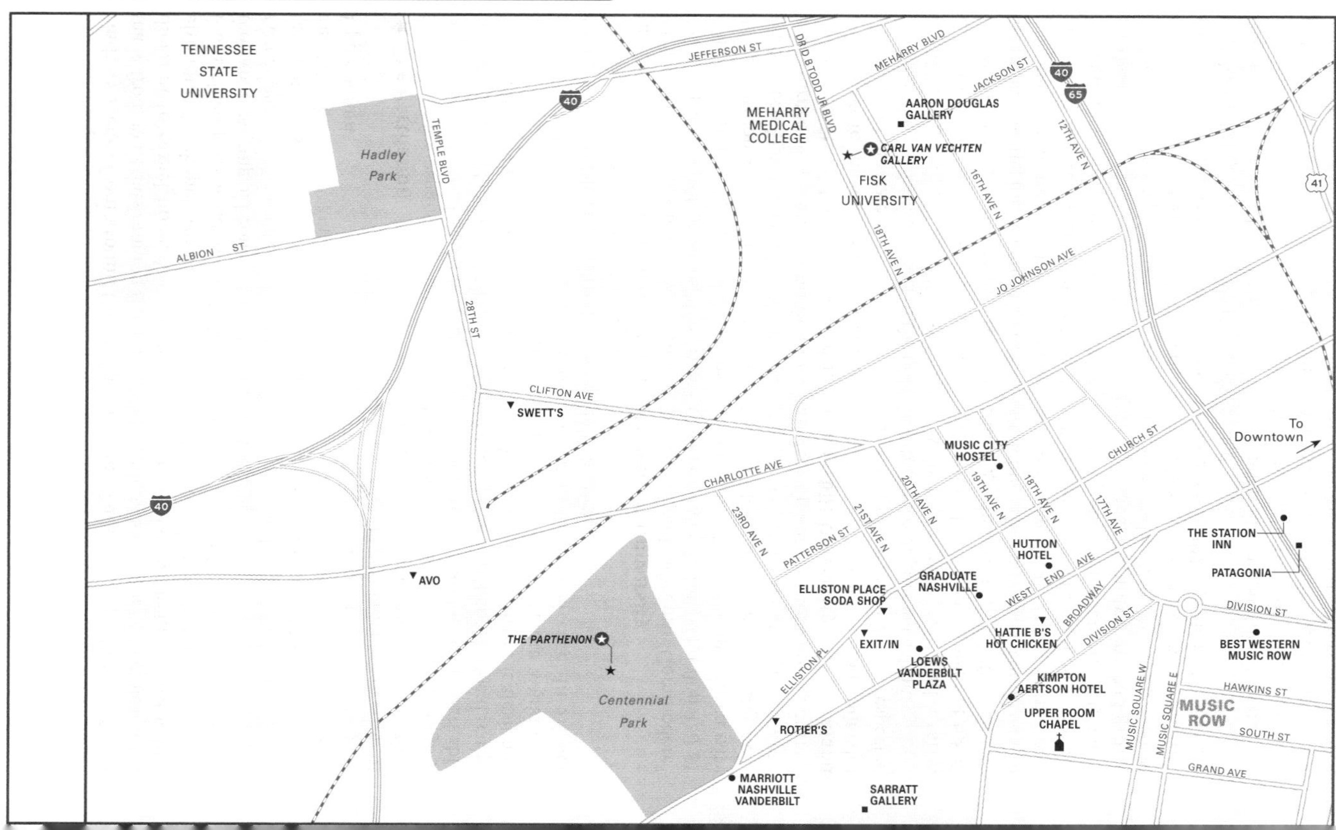
TENNESSEE STATE UNIVERSITY
Hadley Park
ALBION ST
TEMPLE BLVD
28TH ST
JEFFERSON ST
40
MEHARRY BLVD
DR D B TODD JR BLVD
JACKSON ST
MEHARRY MEDICAL COLLEGE
AARON DOUGLAS GALLERY
CARL VAN VECHTEN GALLERY
FISK UNIVERSITY
40
65
12TH AVE N
16TH AVE N
18TH AVE N
JO JOHNSON AVE
41
CLIFTON AVE
SWETT'S
To Downtown
MUSIC CITY HOSTEL
CHURCH ST
CHARLOTTE AVE
40
23RD AVE N
21ST AVE N
20TH AVE N
19TH AVE N
18TH AVE N
17TH AVE
PATTERSON ST
HUTTON HOTEL
THE STATION INN
PATAGONIA
AVO
GRADUATE NASHVILLE
ELLISTON PLACE SODA SHOP
WEST END AVE
BROADWAY
DIVISION ST
THE PARTHENON
EXIT/IN
LOEWS VANDERBILT PLAZA
HATTIE B'S HOT CHICKEN
DIVISION ST
BEST WESTERN MUSIC ROW
ELLISTON PL
KIMPTON AERTSON HOTEL
Centennial Park
UPPER ROOM CHAPEL
MUSIC SQUARE W
MUSIC SQUARE E
HAWKINS ST
MUSIC ROW
SOUTH ST
ROTIER'S
GRAND AVE
MARRIOTT NASHVILLE VANDERBILT
SARRATT GALLERY

free, $5 suggested donation) features a small museum of Christian-inspired art, including a wonderful collection of Nativity scenes from around the world made from materials ranging from needlepoint to camel bone. Visitors may also tour the chapel, with its 8- by 20-foot stained-glass window and 8- by 17-foot wood carving of Leonardo da Vinci's *Last Supper.* A 15-minute audio presentation discusses features of the carving and tells the history and mission of The Upper Room.

★ The Parthenon

In 1893, funds began to be raised for a mighty exposition that would celebrate the 1896 centennial of the state of Tennessee. Though the exposition would start a year later, in 1897, it would exceed all expectations. The old West Side Race Track was converted to a little city with exhibition halls dedicated to transportation, agriculture, machinery, minerals, forestry, and African Americans, among other themes. There were Chinese, Cuban, and Egyptian villages; a midway; and an auditorium. The exposition attracted 1.7 million people between May and October. While the event turned only a modest profit for its organizers, it no doubt contributed in other ways to the local economy and to the stature of the state.

When the exposition closed in the fall of 1897, all the exhibition halls were torn down except for a life-size replica of the Greek Parthenon, which had housed an art exhibit during the centennial. The exposition grounds were made into a public park, aptly named Centennial Park, and Nashvillians continued to admire their Parthenon.

The Parthenon replica had been built out of wood and plaster, and it was designed only to last through the centennial. Remarkably, it survived well beyond that. But by the 1920s, the Parthenon was crumbling. City officials, responding to public outcry to save the Parthenon, agreed to restore it.

Today, the **Parthenon** (Centennial Park, 2500 West End Ave., 615/862-8431, www.nashville.gov/parthenon, 9am-4:30pm Tues.-Sat., 12:30pm-4:30pm Sun., adults $6, seniors and children $4) remains one of Nashville's most iconic landmarks. It's most beautiful from the outside, particularly when lit dramatically at night.

As breathtaking as it is from the exterior, it's worth paying to go inside the Parthenon. The landmark has three gallery spaces; the largest is used to display works from its permanent collection of 63 pieces of American art. The other two galleries host interesting, changing exhibits. But upstairs is the remarkable 42-foot statue of Athena, by local sculptor Alan LeQuire. Athena is designed to replicate how the statue would have looked in ancient Greece, in all her golden glory.

Vanderbilt University

Named for philanthropist "Commodore" Cornelius Vanderbilt, who donated $1 million in 1873 to found a university that would "contribute to strengthening the ties which should exist between all sections of our common country," **Vanderbilt University** (211 Kirkland Hall, 615/322-7311, www.vanderbilt.edu) is now one of the region's most respected institutions of higher education.

A private research university, Vanderbilt has an enrollment of 6,800 undergraduates and 5,700 graduate students. The university comprises 10 schools, a medical center, public policy center, and The Freedom Forum First Amendment Center. Originally just 75 acres, the university had grown to 250 acres by 1960. When the George Peabody School for Teachers merged with Vanderbilt in 1979 another 53 acres were added.

Vanderbilt's campus life is vibrant, and there is a daily roll call of lectures, recitals, exhibits, and other special events for students, locals, and visitors alike. Check the website for an up-to-date listing of all campus events.

Prospective students and their parents can sign up for a campus tour. Vanderbilt also offers a self-guided tour of the campus's trees, which form the Vanderbilt Arboretum. Most trees on the tour are native to Nashville and Middle Tennessee. This is a nice activity for people who want to hone tree identification skills. Download the podcast, print a copy of the tour from the website, or contact the university for more information.

Vanderbilt University also has two excellent art galleries: the **Sarratt Gallery** (Sarratt Student Center, Vanderbilt Pl. near 24th Ave., 615/343-0491, http://vanderbilt.edu/sarrattgallery, 9am-9pm Mon.-Fri., 10am-10pm Sat.-Sun. Sept.-mid-May, 9am-4:30pm Mon.-Fri. mid-May-Aug., free), which has a more contemporary bent, and the **Vanderbilt University Fine Arts Gallery** (1220 21st Ave. S., 615/322-0605, 11am-4pm Mon.-Fri., 1pm-5pm Sat.-Sun. Sept.-early May, noon-4pm Tues.-Fri. 1pm-5pm Sat. early May-mid-June, free), which includes works that demonstrate the development of both Eastern and Western art, plus six different traveling exhibits annually. The Fine Arts Gallery is near the intersection of West End and 23rd Avenues. Both galleries are closed or limit their hours during university holidays and semester breaks, so it's a good idea to call ahead.

There is designated visitor parking in several lots on the Vanderbilt campus. Look on the eastern edge of the sports facilities parking lot off Natchez Trace, in the Wesley Place parking lot off Scarritt Place, or in the Terrace Place parking lot between 20th and 21st Avenues, north of Broadway. Pay attention to these signs, as the university parking monitors do ticket those who park in prohibited areas.

Top to bottom: Athena at The Parthenon; RCA Studio B; Vanderbilt University

Belmont University

The school for girls founded in the Belmont Mansion in 1890 evolved in 1913 to the Ward-Belmont School for Women and in 1951 to coed Belmont College. Since 1991, it has been **Belmont University** (1900 Belmont Blvd., 615/460-6000, www.belmont.edu), a higher-education institution with links to the Tennessee Baptist Convention. Today Belmont is a fast-growing university with highly respected music and music business programs. In 2011, the school opened the first new law school in the state in the last century. Belmont, which hosted one of the 2008 presidential debates, has a student enrollment of 6,400. Campus tours are available twice a day on weekdays.

Several Belmont facilities are of interest to the public, including the **Curb Event Center** (2002 Belmont Blvd., 615/460-8500), which hosts sporting events, concerts, and lectures.

Belmont Mansion

The elaborate "summer home" of Adelicia Acklen was constructed in 1853 and was named Belle Monte. **Belmont Mansion** (1900 Belmont Blvd., 615/460-5459, www.belmontmansion.com, 9:45am-3:30pm Mon.-Sat., 10:45am-3:30pm Sun., adults $15, seniors and military $14, students $10, youth ages 13-18 $7, children 6-12 $5), as it is known today, is a monument to the excesses of the Victorian age.

Adelicia was born to a wealthy Nashville family in 1817. When she was 22, Adelicia married Isaac Franklin, a wealthy bachelor 28 years her senior. When Franklin died seven years later, Adelicia inherited his substantial wealth. Adelicia remarried to Joseph Acklen, a young lawyer, and together they planned and built Belmont Mansion. The home was built in the Italian style, with touches of Egyptian revival style.

The home boasted 36 rooms and 16,000 square feet of space, including a grand gallery where the Acklens hosted elaborate balls and dinner parties. The property included a private art gallery, aviary, zoo, and conservatory, as well as a lake and acres of manicured gardens. After the Civil War, Adelicia traveled to Europe, where she purchased a number of paintings and sculptures that are now on display in her restored mansion.

Shortly before her death, Adelicia sold Belmont to two female educators, who ran a girls school from the property for 61 years. Later, it was purchased by the founders of Belmont College.

Visitors to the mansion are given a 45-minute guided tour of the property, which includes the downstairs sitting and entertaining rooms and three of the upstairs bedrooms. To get here, enter "1700 Acklen Avenue" in your GPS.

Music Valley

A collection of tourist attractions separated from the rest of Nashville by the Cumberland River, **Music Valley** is most known for being the new home of the Grand Ole Opry. The area was one of those hit hardest by the 2010 flood, leading to some significant improvements and upgrades, along with some closures. This strip of motels, restaurants, and country music "museums" is tourist-centric. It is more campy than authentic, although it does offer some fun, affordable ways to explore Music City's kitsch.

If you're game, however, head straight for **Cooter's Place** (2613 McGavock Pike, 615/872-8358, www.cootersplace.com, 9am-8pm Sun.-Thurs., 9am-9pm Fri.-Sat., free), a gift shop and museum dedicated to the *Dukes of Hazzard* television show. The museum features a mind-boggling array of toys, ornaments, and model cars manufactured in the 1970s and 1980s to profit off the Dukes' popularity. You can also see one of the bright-orange Dodge Chargers that became the Dukes' icon. In the gift shop, buy a pair of "official" Daisy Dukes or any number of General Lee souvenirs. Cooter's Place is operated by Ben Jones, who

Music Valley

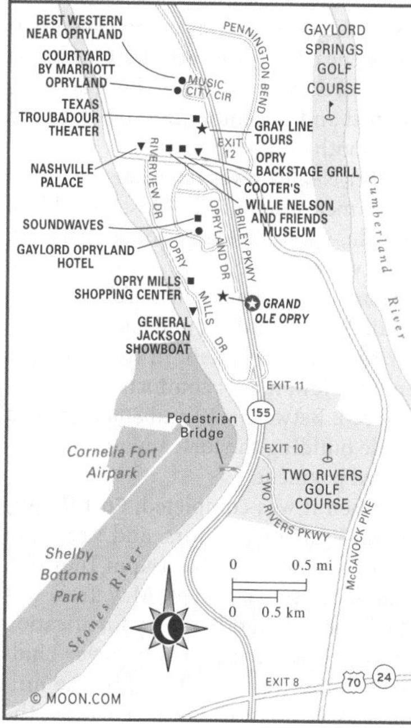

played Cooter, the affable sidekick mechanic, in the original television series. In recent years, Jones has been one of the forces behind DukeFest, a wildly popular annual celebration of fast cars and the General Lee held at the Nashville Motor Speedway. Jones has been determined to keep the signature Confederate flag as part of the art associated with the *Dukes of Hazzard*, despite the racist implications of the flag.

A few doors down from Cooter's Place, you will find **Willie Nelson and Friends Museum and General Store** (2613A McGavock Pike, 615/885-1515, http://willienelsongeneralstore.com, 8:30am-9pm daily, $10), which showcases a number of things that once belonged to Willie Nelson, including his golf bag, a replica of his tour bus, and the guitar he played during his first performance at the Grand Ole Opry. Many of the Willie Nelson items were purchased by museum operators Jeannie and Frank Oakley at an IRS auction.

Grand Ole Opry House

Since 1974, the Grand Ole Opry has been most often staged at the specially built **Grand Ole Opry House** (2802 Opryland Dr., 615/871-6779, www.opry.com) in Music Valley. This is the Opry's sixth regular home, and it was completely renovated after it was shuttered due to the 2010 flood. The Opry House may have been closed, but the Opry went on. The show still made the airwaves for every scheduled performance, playing at different venues around town while construction went on around the clock.

With the renovated Opry came an updated backstage tour. Daytime tour tickets go on sale two weeks in advance and are generally offered every 15 minutes; if you are buying tickets to a show, you can also purchase postconcert backstage tours. On this docent-led tour you'll get to see dressing rooms, learn lots of Opry history, and hear plenty of juicy stories about performers and their backstage behavior. One of the highlights of the guided tour is going on stage and having your photo taken under the lights. If you book a postshow tour, you'll see a performer or two. Tickets are $33 for adults, $27 for children; VIP tour $150 after a show; daytime tours are $33 adults, $28 children. The Opry performs at least two times a week, Friday and Saturday, with additional shows on Tuesday night most weeks.

Belle Meade

Cheekwood

Plan to spend a full morning or afternoon at **Cheekwood** (1200 Forrest Park Dr., 615/356-8000, http://cheekwood.org, 9am-5pm Tues.-Sun., adults $20, seniors $18, students and children $13-16, plus $5 parking per vehicle) so you can experience the full scope of this magnificent art museum and botanical garden. Galleries in the Cheekwood mansion house the museum's American and European collections, including an excellent contemporary art collection. Cheekwood has the largest public collection of works by Nashville artist William Edmondson, the sculptor and stoneworker. Cheekwood usually displays items from its permanent collection as well as traveling exhibitions from other museums. Many exhibits have special ties with Nashville.

But the Cheekwood is far more than just an art museum. The mansion overlooks hundreds of acres of gardens and woods, and it is easy to forget that you are near a major American city when you're at the Cheekwood. Walk the mile-long **Carell Woodland Sculpture Trail** past works by 15 internationally acclaimed artists, or stroll past the water garden to the Japanese garden. There are dogwood gardens, an herb garden, a delightful boxwood garden, and much more. Wear comfortable shoes and pack a bottle of water so you can enjoy the grounds in comfort.

The Cheekwood owes its existence to the success of the coffee brand Maxwell House. During the 1920s, Leslie Cheek and his wife, Mabel Wood, invested in the new coffee brand being developed by their cousin, Joel Cheek. Maxwell House proved to be a success and earned the Cheeks a fortune, which they used to buy 100 acres of land in West Nashville. The family hired New York residential and landscape architect Bryant Fleming to create a 30,000-square-foot mansion and neighboring gardens. Cheekwood was completed in 1933.

Leslie Cheek lived in the mansion just two years before he died, and Mabel lived there for another decade before deeding it to her daughter and son-in-law, who later offered it as a site for a museum and garden. Cheekwood opened to the public in 1960.

Fort Negley

Early in the Civil War, the Union army determined that taking and holding Nashville was a critical strategic link in their victory. So after Nashville fell in 1862, the Federals wasted no time fortifying the city against attacks. One of the city's forts was Fort Negley, built between August and December 1862 on St. Cloud Hill south of the city center.

Fort Negley owes its existence to the 2,768 men who built it. Most were Black people, some free and some enslaved, who were pressed into service by the Union army. These men felled trees, hauled earth, and cut and laid limestone for the fort. They slept in the open and enjoyed few, if any, comforts while they labored. Between 600 and 800 men died while building the fort, and only 310 received payment.

When it was completed, **Fort Negley** (noon-4pm Tues.-Thurs. and 9am-4pm Fri.-Sat. June-Aug., noon-4pm Tues.-Fri. and 9am-4pm Sat. Sept.-May, free) was the largest inland masonry fortification in North America. It was never challenged and was abandoned by the military after the war, but it remained the cornerstone of one of Nashville's oldest African American communities, now known as Cameron-Trimble. During the New Deal, the Works Progress Administration rebuilt large sections of the crumbling fort, and it became a public park.

Fort Negley has been designated a UNESCO Slave Route site for its efforts to document the contributions of both enslaved and freed Black people. The **visitors center** includes a museum on the fort's history and Nashville's role in the Civil War. A paved trail loops around the base of the fort, and raised boardwalks take you through the fortifications themselves; some of the boardwalks need repair, so heed signage. Historical markers tell the story of the fort's construction and detail its military features. Fort Negley is also one of the great places to take in views of Music City, and wildflowers bloom on the hillside.

African American Heritage

Part of what makes Nashville the city it is—from the Civil War to civil rights, baseball to Oprah—is its African American heritage. Music City is home to four historically Black colleges and universities and a number of African American historical and cultural sites. Here are some of the highlights:

- More than 2,700 men, most of them Black—some free, some enslaved—toiled to build **Fort Negley** (http://nashville.gov), what was then the largest inland masonry fortification and a strategic fort in the Civil War. As many as 800 people died while building the fort, and many more African American soldiers died during the Battle of Nashville. The Union army did not supply weapons to the Black soldiers or enslaved people; they were forced to protect themselves with whatever tools they had.
- Head to the **Civil Rights Room at the Nashville Public Library** (http://library.nashville.org) to learn about the men and women who participated in the historic sit-ins in Nashville and their role in the desegregation of public services nationwide.
- **First Horizon Park,** the new home of the Nashville Sounds, was built on the site of **Sulphur Dell,** which used to be baseball's home in the city. In the 1930s, it was the center of African American baseball in the South.
- The **Fisk Jubilee Singers** (www.fiskjubileesingers.org) were the first world-touring musical group and, thanks to Queen Victoria, the inspiration for the Music City moniker for Nashville. Today they continue to sing spirituals for audiences worldwide.
- Founded in 1912, **Tennessee State University** (www.tnstate.edu) is a historically Black university and boasts many illustrious African American graduates, among them Oprah Winfrey and Olympic champion Wilma Rudolph.
- The **National Museum of African American Music** (www.nmaam.org) opened in 2020 and is the first museum dedicated to recognizing and celebrating the musical accomplishments of African Americans. The space features five galleries covering more than 50 genres of music, including the blues, hip-hop, and R&B, along with historical context.

In the recent past, the park had fallen into disrepair, and its future looked uncertain. But the city has committed to its preservation and is building a park adjacent to the fort (on the site of the former baseball stadium).

City Cemetery

Right next to Fort Negley Park, off Chestnut Street, is the old **City Cemetery** (1001 4th Ave. S., www.thenashvillecitycemetery.org, dawn-dusk daily). Opened in 1822, City Cemetery was the final resting place of many of Nashville's most prominent early citizens, including founder James Robertson; William Driver, the U.S. Navy captain who named the flag "Old Glory"; Mabel Lewis Imes and Ella Sheppard, members of the original Fisk Jubilee Singers; and 14 Nashville mayors.

During the Civil War, the cemetery was contracted to bury more than 15,000 Union and Confederate dead, although they were later reinterred in different cemeteries.

Visitors are welcome 9am-5pm daily; if the gate is locked, call the phone number

The Battle of Nashville

During most of the Civil War, Nashville was occupied by Federal forces. After Fort Donelson, 90 miles northeast of Nashville, fell in mid-February 1862, Nashville was in Union hands. The Union turned Nashville into an important goods depot for the Northern cause and set strict rules for city residents during occupation.

As the war drew to a close in late 1864, Nashville was the site of what war historians now say was the last major battle of the Western Theater.

The Battle of Nashville came after a string of defeats for the Confederate army of Tennessee, commanded by John Bell Hood. After his bloody and humiliating losses at Spring Hill and Franklin a few miles south, Hood moved north and set up headquarters at Travellers Rest, the home of John Overton. His plan was to set up his troops in an arc around the southern side of the city. Union major general George H. Thomas did not plan to wait for Hood's attack, however. He devised to attack first and drive the Confederates away from Nashville.

A winter storm and frigid temperatures delayed the battle. For two weeks, from December 2 to 14, 1864, the two armies peered at one another across the no-man's-land between the two lines. Then, at dawn on December 15, 1864, the Union attack began. Union troops on foot and horse, including at least four U.S. Colored Infantry brigades made up of African American soldiers, attacked various Confederate posts around the city. By the close of the first day of fighting, Hood withdrew his troops two miles farther south from the city.

The dawn of the second day of battle augured more losses for the Confederates. Unable to hold their line against the Union assault, they fell back again. As darkness fell, Union major general Thomas wired Washington to announce his victory. Pursued by a Union cavalry commanded by Major General James Wilson, what remained of the Confederate army of Tennessee marched south, and on the day after Christmas they crossed the Tennessee River into Alabama. Four months later, the war was over.

The **Battle of Nashville Preservation Society, Inc.** (www.bonps.org) offers guided tours ($100-150) of the battlefield sites. Customers drive their own vehicle and the guide rides along; prices are per vehicle, not per person.

on the gate to be let in. Consult the information board in the Keeble Building for help with your self-guided tour. Guided tours and special events, such as living history tours, garden tours, and historical lectures, take place on the second Saturday of each month. The events are aimed at telling the history of Nashvillians who are buried at this historical cemetery.

Adventure Science Center

Children and their caretakers will enjoy the hands-on science education available at the **Adventure Science Center** (800 Fort Negley Blvd., 615/862-5160, www.adventuresci.com, 10am-5pm daily, adults $18, children $14). Interactive exhibits explore how the body works, the solar system, and other scientific areas. A multistory climbing tower in the building's center features a giant guitar and other instruments.

The center's **Sudekum Planetarium** (www.sudekumplanetarium.com, additional $8) is the largest planetarium in Tennessee. The 164-seat planetarium offers a variety of space-themed shows. There are also star-viewing parties, gravity-suspending rides, and other exhibits about space flight, the moon, the solar system, and other things found in space.

Tennessee Central Railway Museum

Railroad enthusiasts should make a detour to the **Tennessee Central Railway Museum** (220 Willow St., 615/244-9001, http://tcry.org, 9am-3pm Tues.-Sat., free). This institution is best known for its special railroad excursions, but it also collects railroad equipment and paraphernalia, which are on display at the museum. The museum is located in an otherwise industrial area between the interstate and the railroad tracks, one block north of Hermitage Avenue and east of Fairfield Avenue.

Nashville Zoo at Grassmere

See familiar and exotic animals at the **Nashville Zoo at Grassmere** (3777 Nolensville Pike, 615/833-1534, www.nashvillezoo.org, 9am-6pm daily mid-Mar.-mid-Oct., 9am-4pm daily mid-Oct.-mid-Mar., adults $16, seniors $14, children ages 3-12 $11, free for children under 2, parking $7). Many of the zoo's animals live in beautiful habitats like Lorikeet Landing, Gibbon Islands, and Bamboo Trail. The zoo's meerkat exhibit, featuring the famously quizzical and erect animals, is one of its most popular. The Wild Animal Carousel is an old-time carousel with 39 brightly painted wooden animals.

The zoo is located at Grassmere, the onetime home and farm of the Croft family. The historic Croft farmhouse has been preserved and is open for guided tours in October and December.

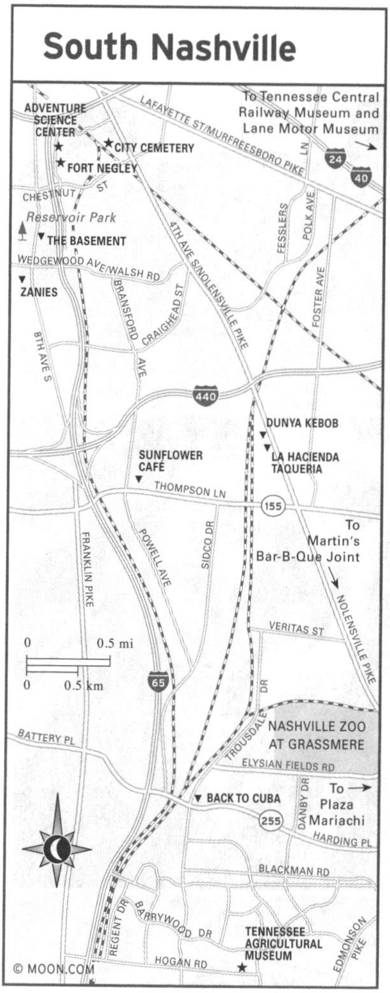

South Nashville

South Nashville

Lane Motor Museum

Kids and adults alike will relish the one-of-a-kind, off-the-beaten-track **Lane Motor Museum** (702 Murfreesboro Pike, 615/742-7445, www.lanemotormuseum.org, 10am-5pm Thurs.-Mon., adults $12, seniors $8, youth ages 6-17 $3, free for children 5 and under). Based in an old Sunbeam Bread bakery, the museum has the largest collection of European cars and motorcycles in the country. In fact, the collection is so large that the museum rotates exhibits. Here you'll find all manner of vehicles, from early hybrids and steam engines to a car so small it can be "reversed" merely by picking it up with a lever and putting it down facing the other direction. The amphibious cars are a delight. There's also a decent play area for kids who need a break.

Greater Nashville

Tours

NashTrash Tour

Nashville's most notorious tour guides are Sheri Lynn and Brenda Kay Jugg, sisters who ferry good-humored tourists

around town in a big pink school bus. The **NashTrash Tour** (615/226-7300, www.nashtrash.com, $35-40) is a raunchy, rollicking, rib-tickling tour of city attractions, some of which you won't even find in this guidebook. Be prepared to be the butt of some of the jokes yourself. Its "I Got Trashed" T-shirts have a double meaning. You'll snack on canned cheese, and there's a pit stop to buy beer. Not appropriate for children or adults who aren't comfortable laughing at themselves and others. As Sheri Lynn says, "If we haven't offended you, just give us some time." NashTrash Tours sell out early and often. If you think you want this perspective of the city, make your reservation now. Tours depart from the Nashville Farmers Market.

Gray Line Tours

Nashville's largest tour company, **Gray Line** (1307 Lebanon Pike, 615/883-5555 or 800/251-1864, http://graylinetn.com) offers more than 12 different sightseeing tours of the city. The three-hour Discover Nashville tour costs $49 per adult and includes entrance to the Ryman Auditorium and the Country Music Hall of Fame, and stops at other city landmarks.

The 3.5-hour Homes of the Stars tour takes you past the domiciles of country stars, including Jack White, Taylor Swift, Dolly Parton, and others for $59. There is also a hop-on, hop-off double-decker tour for $34 (children $15) and a 2.5-hour Nashville Walking Food tour ($52).

General Jackson Showboat

Gaylord Opryland's **General Jackson Showboat** (577 Opryland Dr., 615/889-1000, http://generaljackson.com, tickets $30-135) offers campy, big-budget-style musical shows on the stage of a giant riverboat as it lumbers down the Cumberland River. Show dates and

Top to bottom: Fort Negley; the Nashville Zoo at Grassmere; Lane Motor Museum

times vary by season, but typically there are midday lunch and evening dinner cruises. Because of the meal and the live entertainment, these cruises aren't necessarily the best way to see the river, as you're focused on the stage rather than the scenery.

River Queen Voyages

Choose between several different kayak tours down the Cumberland River with **River Queen Voyages** (615/933-9778, http://rqvoyages.com, hours vary May-Oct., $32-140). The three-mile guided tour starts in Shelby Bottoms Greenway, winding under railway bridges, and ending downtown with the skyline in sight. The four-mile, two-hour option takes you from Opryland to Shelby Bottoms.

Walk Eat Nashville

Former *Tennessean* editor Karen-Lee Ryan started her **Walk Eat Nashville** (locations disclosed upon reservation, 615/587-6138, www.walkeatnashville.com, tour times vary, $65) walking culinary tours as a way to show off her neighborhood of East Nashville. They were so popular, she soon expanded to midtown and downtown. The walking tours include food tastings at six restaurants and artisan food shops. Ryan and her informative guides narrate as you walk (and taste) and you get the benefit of her considerable knowledge of the city. You'll leave satisfied, but not full.

Tennessee Central Railway

The **Tennessee Central Railway Museum** (220 Willow St., 615/244-9001, www.tcry.org) offers an annual calendar of sightseeing and themed railway rides in central Tennessee, including kids' trips, Old West shoot-outs, and murder mysteries. Excursions include fall foliage tours, Christmas shopping expeditions, and trips to scenic small towns. All trips run on the Nashville and Eastern Railroad, which runs east, stopping in Lebanon, Watertown, Cookville, or Monterrey. Prices vary based on the trip but run $32-160 for adults.

These tours are not just train rides, but well-organized volunteer-led events. You might get "robbed" by a Wild West bandit (the cash goes to charity) or taken to a scenic winery. The volunteers know their railroad trivia, so feel free to ask questions. The cars vary depending on what is available, but one car doubles as a gift shop and another is a concession stand, although you are welcome to bring your own food on the train. Trips sell out early, so book your tickets well in advance.

Entertainment and Events

From live music to theater, Nashville offers visitors plenty of diversions. Even if you are not a fan of country music, you will find plenty to do in Music City.

Live Music Venues

No trip to Nashville is complete without listening to some live music. Music City overflows with musicians and opportunities to hear them. So whether you catch a show at the Opry, stake out a seat at The Bluebird Café, or enjoy a night at the symphony, be sure to make time for music during your visit.

Even before you arrive in the city, you can plan out your nights, thanks to the **Nashville Convention and Visitors Corp.** (www.visitmusiccity.com). Through a handy feature on the NCVC website you can check out upcoming concerts a month or more in advance. Many venues will let you buy tickets in advance over the phone or online. But don't panic if you can't plan ahead; because there are so many shows, there is always something that hasn't sold out.

While you're here, you must experience two of the city's most iconic venue types. The **honky-tonk** is a loud, dance-friendly spot for Western swing. **Listening rooms** are quiet spots where songwriters shine; most play acoustically—this is not the place to chat with your friends during a show.

Published on Wednesday, the ***Nashville Scene*** provides detailed entertainment listings and recommendations. The ***Nashville Tennessean,*** the city's daily paper, publishes its entertainment insert on Friday. **Now Playing Nashville** (www.nowplayingnashville.com) is a great resource for both entertainment listings and discounted tickets. Now Playing Nashville has a kiosk in the Nashville airport.

★ Grand Ole Opry

If there's any one thing you really must do while in Nashville, it's go to see the **Grand Ole Opry** (2804 Opryland Dr., 615/871-6779 or 800/733-6779, www.opry.com, $55-109). Really. Even if you think you don't like country music. For more than 90 years this weekly radio showcase of country music has drawn crowds to Nashville. Every show at the Opry is still broadcast live on WSM, a Nashville AM radio station. Shows are also streamed online, and some are televised on cable. But nothing beats the experience of being there.

The Opry runs Tuesday through Saturday nights, with two shows (7pm, 9:30pm) on Saturday. Shows start and end right on time.

Every Opry show is divided into 30-minute segments, each of which is hosted by a different member of the Opry. This elite country music fraternity includes dozens of stars that you've heard of and others you haven't. The host performs two songs—one at the beginning of his or her half-hour segment and one at the end. In between the host will introduce two or three other performers, each of whom will sing about two songs. In between segments, the announcers read radio commercials and stagehands change around the stage set.

It's a fast-paced show that keeps your toes tapping. Even when the biggest stars appear on the Opry stage, they rarely

Grand Ole Opry

sing more than a few numbers. Fans are welcomed, and even encouraged, to walk to the front of the seating area to take photographs during the performances.

The Opry usually releases the full lineup for each show about a week in advance. Some fans wait until then to buy their tickets so they're sure to catch a big-name artist. The best advice is to buy tickets to any show at all. Each show is carefully balanced to include bluegrass, classic country, popular country, and, sometimes, gospel or rock. It's a true showcase that music and Americana fans will enjoy.

Most Opry shows take place in the Grand Ole Opry House, a 4,400-seat auditorium. A circle of the original stage from the Ryman Auditorium was cut out and placed in the center of the Opry House stage, and it's here that artists perform. During the Christmas season the Opry returns to its Ryman roots (and the Radio City Rockettes take the Opry House stage).

Tickets for the Opry House's guided **backstage tour** (adults $23-30, children $23) go on sale two weeks in advance; times vary based on the time of year and day. The tours include a peek at the Green Room, Opry stars' mailboxes, and other behind-the-scenes treasures. If you book one of the evening tours, you're likely to see performers jamming in folding chairs after a show. Glitzy costumes, juicy stories, and a chance to walk on that stage are all part of the tour offerings. It's also possible to book combination packages that include the backstage tour, an Opry performance, and accommodations and meals at the Gaylord Opryland Resort.

Ascend Amphitheater

This open-air concert venue offers the chance to rock out by the river in Metro Riverfront Park. Between folding seats, box seats, and the lawn, it can hold 6,800 concert-goers, all of whom get a view of the skyline and great sightlines of the stage. **Ascend Amphitheater** (310 1st Ave. S., 615/999-9000, www.ascendamphitheater.com, hours and cost vary by event) is the place to see a big show, with big-name national acts on the schedule as well as the Nashville Symphony. Locals have been known to picnic nearby to listen to shows without being inside.

Ryman Auditorium

The most famous music venue in Nashville, the **Ryman Auditorium** (116 5th Ave. N., 615/889-3060, http://ryman.com, cover varies) continues to book some of the best acts in town, of just about every genre you can imagine. In 2015, a $14 million renovation gave the Ryman a café, better entrances and ticket areas, and a revamped backstage tour. The hall still boasts some of the best acoustics around, but the pew-style bench seats are just as uncomfortable as ever. Seeing the reverence performers have for this venue makes it hard to

The Origins of the Grand Ole Opry

Nashville's most famous broadcast can trace its roots to October 1925, when Nashville-based National Life and Accident Insurance Company opened a radio station in town. Its call letters (then and now), WSM, stood for "We Shield Millions," the company's motto.

WSM hired George D. "Judge" Hay, a radio announcer who had worked in Memphis and Chicago, to manage the station. Hay—who, while in Chicago, had announced one of the nation's first live country radio shows—planned to create a similar program in Nashville.

On November 25, 1925, Hay invited a 78-year-old fiddler, Uncle Jimmy Thompson, to perform live on Saturday night over the radio airwaves. The response was electric, and WSM continued to broadcast live old-time music every Saturday night. In May 1927, Hay was segueing from the previous program of classical opera to the barn dance, and he came up with the famous name: "For the past hour, we have been listening to music taken largely from Grand Opera. From now on, we will present the Grand Ole Opry," he said. The name stuck.

During the first few years, most Opry performers were unknowns. But as the show gained popularity, some acts were able to make it professionally, including Uncle Dave Macon, the Vagabonds, and the Delmore Brothers. By 1939, the Opry gained a slot on the NBC radio network, allowing it to reach a national audience.

notice anything else. Musicians love to show off the acoustics here, often playing a song or two without a mic.

Country Music Hall of Fame

The **Country Music Hall of Fame** (222 5th Ave. S., 615/416-2001, http://countrymusichalloffame.org) hosts concerts, readings, and musical discussions regularly in an auditorium located inside the hall. These daytime events are often aimed at highlighting one type of country music or another, but sometimes you'll find big names playing. Entry is free with your paid admission to the hall, so it is a good idea to plan your trip to the hall on a day when there's a concert scheduled (separate admission to concerts is not typically available). Check the website for a listing of upcoming events.

Marathon Music Works

The 14,500 square feet at **Marathon Music Works** (1402 Clinton St., 615/891-1781, www.marathonmusicworks.com, prices vary by event) are some of Nashville's most progressive when it comes to concert-going. Located in the historic Marathon Village, this venue has exposed brick, a swanky VIP loft area, multiple bars, and plenty of space for cutting the rug. Musical acts booked run the gamut from The Black Belles to the Yonder Mountain String Band.

★ The Bluebird Café

No other music venue is as quintessentially Nashville as **The Bluebird Café** (4104 Hillsboro Pike, 615/383-1461, http://bluebirdcafe.com, cover varies). It's intimate and homey. This listening room books some of the best up-and-coming country and acoustic acts in the business, as well as the songwriters who penned the lyrics you are used to hearing other people sing. There is no talking during the acts and virtually none of the usual bar pickup scene. In short, The Bluebird is a place where music comes first and everything else is a distant second.

Opened in 1982 by Amy Kurland, The Bluebird is located in a nondescript shopping mall a few miles south of Hillsboro Village. While it started out as a casual restaurant with live music, over the years it evolved into a destination for music

Let's Go Honky-Tonkin'

Layla's

It may be known locally as honkytonk, honky tonk, or honky-tonk, and it may be used as a noun (a bar that plays Western swing, where people dance), a verb (dancing to Western swing), or an adjective (a descriptor of the type of music), but one thing is for sure, in Nashville honky-tonk is what makes Music City sing.

These bars are across the city, but the main strip is found along lower Broadway in the heart of downtown. They play a specific strain of country and western swing music, with a live band. Small or large, these venues all have some empty space to cut the rug, because dancing is an essential part of Nashville honky-tonk.

The best places to go honky-tonking include: **Tootsie's Orchid Lounge, Nudie's Honky Tonk, Layla's, Legends Corner,** and **Robert's Western World.** Most of these establishments are open to all ages during the day but convert to 21 and over after 6pm. They typically don't have a cover charge, although when the cowboy hat is passed for the band, don't forget to drop a few dollars in.

lovers who appreciate its no-nonsense take on live music, and who hope that they just might stumble onto the next big thing. The Bluebird is famous as an early venue for then-unknown Garth Brooks, but its stage has also hosted the likes of Emmylou Harris, Kathy Mattea, Gillian Welch, Trisha Yearwood, and Steve Earle.

The Bluebird is open every night of the week, and most evenings the entertainment starts at 6pm. Cover is usually under $15. There are just 20 tables and a few additional seats at the bar, so, depending on the show, you have to be on your toes to get a spot. Reservations are only taken online and are in high demand. Generally, reservations open about three weeks before the date. Some shows are first-come, first-seated only.

Once you've successfully nabbed a seat at The Bluebird, sit back and enjoy some fine live music (but really, no talking—you will be shushed).

Texas Troubadour Theatre

Known as the Texas Troubadour, Ernest Tubb started a tradition when he set up a live radio show at the back of his Broadway record shop. The **Ernest Tubb's Midnite Jamboree** was broadcast after the Opry shut down across the street, and it lived up to its name. The Jamboree continues, now broadcast from the **Texas Troubadour Theatre**

(Music Valley Village, 2416 Music Valley Dr., 614/255-7503, http://etrecordshop.com, no cover). Located across the street from the Gaylord Opryland Resort, the Jamboree gets started early in the evening, while the Opry is still on, but things really get swinging after midnight.

The Texas Troubadour Theatre is also home to the **Cowboy Church** (2416 Music Valley Dr., nashvillecowboychurch.com). Every Sunday at 10am, locals and tourists dressed in anything from shorts to Stetsons gather here for a lively praise-and-worship country gospel church service led by Dr. Harry Yates and Dr. Joanne Cash Yates. The church was founded in 1990 with just six souls; today it attracts hundreds to its weekly services. Country and gospel music legends make cameo performances now and again, but the real star is Jesus.

Concert Series

Thursday nights in August and September transform downtown's Public Square Park for **Live on the Green** (www.liveonthegreen.com, free). The outdoor concert series tends to attract indie rock acts, and the crowd is young, hip, and socially aware. Food and arts and crafts vendors line the sidewalks under tents.

Also taking place on Thursday nights in the summer, **Bluegrass Nights at the Ryman** (116 5th Ave. N., 615/889-3060, http://ryman.com, 7:30pm Thurs. late June-late July, $29.50) is a concert series that features some of the best pickers in the country. Starting in June and ending in July, this Ryman Auditorium series is always popular.

Held in early summer and early fall, **Musicians Corner** (2500 West End Ave., http://musicianscornernashville.com, 5pm-9pm Fri-Sat. May-June, 5pm-9pm Thurs. Sept., free) is a concert series at an eponymous location inside Centennial Park. There's some permanent seating in the form of stone benches, but most people bring blankets and camp chairs and hang for the day. Food trucks and kids' activities are on-site, but the focus is the music.

Nightlife

Clubs

Most bars and clubs (except for honky-tonks) charge a cover when there is a performer, while songwriter nights and open mics are usually free.

Country

Nashville's most colorful country music establishments are the honky-tonks that line Broadway. These all-day, all-night bars and music clubs cater to visitors, who take advantage of the high energy, cheap beer, and talented musicians found here. Whether you're looking for a place to drown your sorrows or kick off a night on the town, Broadway's honky-tonks are a good place to go. They are always open and typically free, although you are encouraged to contribute when the hat is passed for the band.

Tootsie's Orchid Lounge (422 Broadway, 615/299-1585, www.tootsies.net, 10am-3am daily, no cover) is painted purple and exudes classic country every day of the week beginning as early as 10am. Three doors down from Tootsie's is **Robert's Western World** (416 Broadway, 615/244-9552, www.robertswesternworld.com, 11am-3am Mon.-Sat., noon-3am Sun., no cover), voted the city's best honky-tonk. Originally a store selling boots, cowboy hats, and other country music regalia, Robert's morphed into a bar and nightclub with a good gift shop. Another choice is **The Stage on Broadway** (412 Broadway, 615/726-0504, www.thestageonbroadway.com, 11am-3am daily, no cover), with a large dance floor and music every night. A cozy, dark dance hall, **Layla's** (418 Broadway, 615/726-2799, www.laylasnashville.com, noon-midnight Sun.-Mon., noon-1am Tues., noon-2am Wed.-Sat., no cover) offers that honky-tonk trifecta: cheap beer, a hot dog cart, and no cover. Head to the back entrance (which opens onto the alley next to the Ryman) or the upper floor for more space. After 6pm, entry is for the 21-plus crowd only. Memorabilia of Nashville's past adorns the walls at **Legends Corner** (428 Broadway, www.legendscorner.com, 10am-3am daily, no cover), a popular and authentic club for live music and rollicking crowds.

Nudie's Honky Tonk (409 Broadway, www.nudieshonkytonk.com, 11am-3am Mon.-Thurs., 10am-3am Fri.-Sun., no cover) might be one of the newer honky-tonks on Lower Broad, but it has a serious connection to the past. Owned by the same folks who opened the Johnny Cash Museum, this bar celebrates all things Nudie Cohn. Nudie was the tailor who made suits for Johnny Cash and Elvis, among others. The bar is also a museum, with many of Nudie's famous works behind glass and one of his ostentatious cars, a $400,000 Cadillac El Dorado, hanging from the wall.

Mega country star Alan Jackson bought one of Lower Broad's long-time honky-tonks, The Wheel, and opened **AJ's Good Time Bar** (421 Broadway, 615/678-4808, www.ajsgoodtimebar.com, 1pm-2:30am Mon.-Wed., 11am-2:30am Thurs.-Sun.). The honky-tonk, named after one of Jackson's popular songs, features a focus on country music.

The **Wildhorse Saloon** (120 2nd Ave. N., 615/902-8200, http://wildhorsesaloon.com, 11am-midnight Mon.-Thurs., 11am-3am Fri.-Sun., cover varies) is a boot-scootin', beer-drinkin' place to see and be seen that's occupied almost exclusively by tourists. The huge dance floor is often packed with cowboys and cowgirls line dancing to the greatest country hits. Free dance lessons are offered every day (times vary by season). The Wildhorse books big-name acts many nights of the week, including country music, roots rock, and classic rock stars. From 10pm on, the Wildhorse is a 21-and-over club. The

Top to bottom: Tootsie's Orchid Lounge; Nudie's Honky Tonk; The Listening Room Café

Tennessee Waltzing

In Nashville you hardly need to find a dance club to boogie. There is (quite literally) music in the streets; people will start moving whenever the mood strikes. The carillon bells play "The Tennessee Waltz" every hour on the hour at Bicentennial Mall, and it can be hard to resist the urge to start waltzing right there in public, whether you have a partner or not.

But if you want more structured dance environs, no worries. There are dance floors, lessons, and places to cut the rug all over town. Downtown's **Wildhorse Saloon** (120 2nd Ave. N., 615/902-8200, www.wildhorsesaloon.com) offers dance lessons every single day of the week. This stop isn't considered particularly authentic by locals, but the lessons are free, the music is loud, and there's usually a good crowd.

Monday nights transform East Nashville's **The 5 Spot** (1006 Forrest Ave., 615/650-9333, www.the5spot.club) into a throwback party with swing dancing and Motown tunes. Despite taking place on a school night, it is regularly packed and lasts into the wee hours.

Nashville Palace (2611 McGavock Pike, 615/889-1540, www.nashville-palace.com) near Opryland is a good bet for line dancing without the downtown hubbub. **Plaza Mariachi** (3955 Nolensville Pike, 615/373-9292, www.plazamariachi.com) offers free salsa dancing classes many nights of the week.

Wildhorse is owned by Gaylord, the same folks who own the Ryman, Opryland, and the Opry, and often offers deals for hotel guests. There is a shuttle back to the Opryland Hotel for folks staying there.

It doesn't look like much (or anything) from the outside, but inside this cinder-block box is the city's most popular venue for bluegrass and roots music. **The Station Inn** (402 12th Ave. S., 615/255-3307, www.stationinn.com, 7pm-midnight daily, cover $10-20) is perhaps the country's best bluegrass club, and it showcases fine artists every night of the week. The homey, casual club opens nightly two hours before the music begins, typically at 7pm or 9pm. This is a 21-and-over club, unless you come with a parent or guardian. There is no cover for the Sunday-night bluegrass jam, at which almost everyone who is anyone picks up an instrument and plays. On Tuesday nights the beloved **Doyle & Debbie Show** (615/999-9244, www.doyleanddebbie.com; $20) takes the stage and offers its send-up of the music scene through live musical satire. Tickets must be purchased in advance. This cheeky show often sells out.

The Nashville Palace (2611 McGavock Pike, 615/889-1540, www.nashville-palace.com, 11am-midnight Sun.-Mon., 11am-2am Tues.-Sat., cover varies) is an old-school restaurant, nightclub, and dance space across from the Gaylord Opryland Resort. If your image of Nashville is line dancing and whatever you've seen in movies, this place is more likely to meet your mental image than anywhere on Lower Broad. Live music is on tap daily with start times for scheduled acts ranging from 5pm to 10pm. The patio makes for a good middle ground—if you want to hear music but not be right in the center of it all.

If you're looking to see up-and-coming singer-songwriters and, you know, actually be able to listen to what they're saying and singing, **The Listening Room Café** (618 4th Ave. S., 615/259-3600, www.listeningroomcafe.com, 11am-3pm and 4pm-11pm Mon.-Fri., 10am-3pm and 4pm-11pm Sat., cover $5-12 with a $7 food-drink minimum pp per show when seated) fits the bill. It books local bands and the occasional national act and has a full menu and bar, including a popular brunch. Large tables make this venue popular with groups who want to go out together. Unlike at other listening rooms, there are no rules against conversation, but the idea is to be attentive to the songwriters.

Jazz and Blues

If you need to get that country twang out of your head, a good dose of the Memphis blues will do it. **B. B. King's Blues Club** (152 2nd Ave. N., 615/256-2727, http://bbkings.com/nashville, 11am-11pm Mon.-Thurs., 11am-1am Fri.-Sat., 11am-10pm Sun., cover $3-10) is a good place to start for a night of the blues. The club is a satellite of King's original Beale Street club in Memphis, and it books blues acts every night.

In Printer's Alley, the **Bourbon Street Blues and Boogie Bar** (220 Printer's Alley, 615/242-5837, www.bourbonstreetbluesandboogiebar.com, 11am-3am daily, cover varies) is a hole-in-the-wall nightclub that specializes in New Orleans-style jazz and blues.

Eclectic

Clubs listed here may book a rock band one night and folk the next. Always check the free weekly *Nashville Scene* for the latest entertainment listings.

The **Exit/In** (2208 Elliston Pl., 615/321-3340, www.exitin.com, ticket prices vary) has been a favorite rock music venue for years, although it also books alternative country, blues, and reggae. Located on Elliston Place, the club is convenient to Vanderbilt and downtown.

The Basement (1604 8th Ave. S., 615/254-8006, http://thebasementnashville.com, cover varies) calls itself a cellar full of noise, but it's a good kind of noise. Indie rock is the most common art form here, but it books other types of acts, too. The Basement's "New Faces Nite" on Tuesday is a popular place to hear singer-songwriters. Admission is 21 and over, unless accompanied by a parent or guardian. The brick walls and subterranean feel give The Basement its cool atmosphere. Park behind the club and on side streets. The team behind The Basement has also expanded into East Nashville with **The Basement East** (917 Woodland 8th Ave. S., 615/645-9174, http://thebasementnashville.com, cover varies). This venue quickly became one of the city's leading places to hear new and non-country music, and it's open seven days a week.

Located in an old warehouse that has been home to a flour mill, jam factory, and country music concert hall, **Cannery Ballroom** (1 Cannery Row, 615/251-3020, www.mercylounge.com, cover varies) and its sisters, **Mercy Lounge** and **The High Watt,** are cool venues for live music. Cannery Ballroom is a large, somewhat cavernous space with lots of nice cherry-red touches, hardwood floors, and a shiny red bar. It can hold up to 1,000 people. Mercy Lounge upstairs is a bit more intimate, with a capacity of up to 500 people. The High Watt, also upstairs, holds similarly small shows. Mercy hosts 8 Off 8th on Monday nights, a no-cover open mic where eight different bands each perform three songs. All three venues book rock, country, soul, and other acts.

A neighborhood bar and grill, **3rd and Lindsley** (818 3rd Ave. S., 615/259-9891, www.3rdandlindsley.com, cover varies) showcases rock, alternative, progressive, Americana, soul, and R&B music. Over the years it has developed a reputation for booking good blues acts. It serves a full lunch and dinner menu, the bar is well stocked, and the club offers a great atmosphere and sound quality. Most Monday nights host The Time Jumpers, a Western swing band including Vince Gill and many other talented musicians.

Yes, **The City Winery** (609 Lafayette St., 615/324-1010, www.citywinery.com/nashville, 5pm-10pm Mon.-Thurs., 5pm-11pm Fri., 10:30am-2pm and 5pm-11pm Sat., 10:30am-2pm and 5pm-10pm Sun., ticket prices vary) live music venue/restaurant/wine bar is a chain (it has locations in Chicago, New York, Atlanta, and

Boston). But it's the brainchild of Michael Dorf, who created the iconic Knitting Factory club earlier in his career, which means that the musical lineup is impressive. Tickets typically include seating, so you can eat and drink and not crane your neck to see the act; dining begins two hours prior to showtime. This isn't a place where people generally get up and dance.

Modeled after Los Angeles's Magic Castle, **House of Cards** (119 3rd Ave. S., 615/730-8326, www.hocnashville.com, 5pm-midnight Mon.-Sat., 10:30am-3pm and 6pm-midnight Sun., no cover) is an adults-only magical evening in the making. For the price of dinner ($34-62), you'll also get a magic show in its separate theater, as well as see many smaller tableside acts from card tricks to mentalist performances. You are not allowed to take photos in the venue (lest you document the floating table or ghost playing the piano), so it makes for a good opportunity to be present and enjoy. Don't miss the amazing collection of antique playing cards hanging on the walls. House of Cards is "hidden" underneath the Johnny Cash Museum. It might sound hokey, but it's a fun night out. Reservations are recommended, and there's a basic dress code: jackets required for men and no flip-flops or tank tops.

Bars

Many bars in Nashville are also clubs, but there are some that are more traditional bars without live music.

Downtown

A few blocks from downtown, away from the honky-tonks and near the Frist Art Museum, you'll find one of the city's best beer bars. Behind the Union Station Hotel on the west side of downtown, the **Flying Saucer** (111 10th Ave. S., 615/259-3039, www.beerknurd.com, 11am-midnight Sun.-Thurs., 11am-2am Fri.-Sat., no cover) has one of the best selections of beer in town. There are more than 200 beers from which to choose—and 83 of them are on tap. If you are going to be in town for a while, join the "UFO Club." After you taste 200 beers, you receive a "ring" that adorns the walls and ceilings. Monday is pint night, when you can get $4 pints of just about any of the beers on the wall.

Music row, Midtown, and 12South

Elliston Place is home to college hangouts (thanks to its location just blocks from Vanderbilt), several live music clubs, and a few neighborhood bars.

There's no sign on the exterior, but that hasn't kept people across the country from discovering **Patterson House** (1711 Division St., http://thepattersonnashville.com, 5pm-1am Sun.-Wed., 5pm-3am Thurs.-Sat., no cover). Cocktails are mixed with care, and there's no standing room. You must have a seat in order to be served, both of which contribute to a civilized cocktail hour.

Built in the steam room of an old laundry, **Old Glory** (1200 Villa Pl., #103, 615/679-0509, 5pm-1am Sun.-Thurs., 5pm-2am Fri., noon-2am Sat.) is one of the most striking bars in the city. It can be tricky to find the entrance (in the alley-like corridor of Edgehill Village, behind Taco Mamacita), but when you get there, you'll see it was worth the exploration. Order a carefully crafted seasonal cocktail plus a few smart appetizers, such as *harissa* carrots with leeks and goat cheese ($9).

Gay and Lesbian Nightlife

You don't have to be gay to enjoy **Tribe** (1517-A Church St., 615/329-2912, http://tribenashville.com, 3pm-1am Mon.-Thurs., 3pm-3am Fri., 11am-3am Sat., 11am-1am Sun., no cover), but it helps to be beautiful, or at least well dressed. The dance floor at this Midtown hangout is one of the best in the city. Martinis and other specialty drinks are the poison of choice at this standard-setting club, which stays open until the wee hours.

Celebrity Bars

What's next after you become a big country music artist? Open your own bar and music venue on Broadway, of course. Here's a quick overview of which bars might result in a megastar sighting:

- Alan Jackson bought former honky-tonk The Wheel and turned it into **AJ's Good Time Bar** (421 Broadway, 615/678-4808, www.ajsgoodtimebar.com).
- Country megastar and Nashville local Dierks Bentley opened **Whiskey Row** (400 Broadway, 629/203-7822 http://dierkswhiskeyrow.com).
- *The Voice* judge and country music hottie Blake Shelton teamed up with Ryman Hospitality to open **Ole Red** (300 Broadway, 615/780-0900 www.olered.com), and there's a location in East Tennessee, too.
- The initials at **FGL House** (120 3rd Ave. S., 615/961-5460, http://fglhouse.com) stand for Florida Georgia Line, the band that owns this multi-level bar.
- Famous duo Big & Rich are behind **Redneck Riviera** (208-210 Broadway, http://redneckrivieranashville.com), which opened in late 2017.
- Singer Gavin DeGraw and his brother are behind **Nashville Underground** (105 Broadway, 615/964-3000, www.nashunderground.com).
- There's no cover at **Jason Aldean's Kitchen + Rooftop Bar** (307 Broadway, http://jasonaldeansnashville.com), but if you're headed here just for the view, note that the rooftop has different hours than the rest of the bar.
- Behind a historic building facade, Luke Bryan's **Luke's 32 Bridge** (301 Broadway, www.lukes32bridge.com) has three floors with music, an outdoor patio, and a sushi menu.

Right next door to Tribe is **Play** (1519 Church St., 615/322-9627, http://playdancebar.com, 9pm-3am Wed.-Thurs. and Sun., 8pm-3am Fri.-Sat., cover varies), the city's highest-energy gay club, with drag shows and performances by adult-film stars.

Women outnumber men at the **Lipstick Lounge** (1400 Woodland St., 615/226-6343, www.thelipsticklounge.com, 5pm-1am Tues.-Fri., 10am-3am Sat., 10am-1am Sun., cover varies), a cool yet homey club in East Nashville. Live music, pool, and great food attract a crowd nearly every night.

Comedy

If it's stand-up comedy you want, head to **Zanies** (2025 8th Ave. S., 615/269-0221, http://nashville.zanies.com, ticket prices vary), where you can hear stand-up comics every weekend and some weeknights. Doors open 30-90 minutes prior to show time. Opened in 2016, **Third Coast Comedy Club** (1310 Clinton St., 615/745-1009, www.thirdcoastcomedy.club, showtimes and prices vary) is a classic, dedicated comedy club with improv, sketches, and more.

There are many other spots to amuse you, including **The Doyle & Debbie Show** at **The Station Inn** (402 12th Ave. S., 615/999-9244, http://www.doyleanddebbie.com) and the **NashTrash Tour** (615/226-7300, www.nashtrash.com, $35-40).

The Arts

Before Nashville was Music City, it was the Athens of the South, a city renowned for its cultural, academic, and artistic life. Universities, museums, and public arts facilities created an environment for artistic expression unparalleled by any other Southern city. It has an opera company of its own, not to mention an award-winning symphony (and symphony center), an innovative arts scene, and ample opportunities to sample contemporary and classic music, film, and theater.

Theater

Opened in 2013, **OZ Arts** (6172 Cockrill Bend Circ., 615/350-7200, www.ozartsnashville.org) is a 500-seat arts space in an off-the-beaten-track location, producing the city's most groundbreaking theater and dance. Many of the artists it brings to town are world-renowned disrupters. You won't see revivals of plays from your youth here.

The **Nashville Repertory Theatre** (505 Deaderick St., 615/782-4040, www.nashvillerep.org) is Tennessee's largest professional theater company. It stages five big-name shows plus the Ingram New Works project annually. The Rep performs in the Tennessee Performing Arts Center, located in the James K. Polk Cultural Center in downtown Nashville. This is the same building that houses the Tennessee State Museum, plus some Nashville Opera performances and the Nashville Ballet. Some of its productions have included *The Crucible, I Hate Hamlet,* and *Doubt*. The season runs October-May.

Artists' Cooperative Theatre (no phone, http://act1online.com), a.k.a. **ACT 1,** is an organization dedicated to bringing theatrical gems, both classic and modern, to Nashville audiences. Founded in 1989, ACT 1 has presented productions of more than 90 of the world's greatest plays. Each year the theater puts on four or five productions. ACT 1 performs at the Darkhorse Theater (4610 Charlotte Ave.).

New theatrical works are given the spotlight by the **Actors Bridge Ensemble** (Darkhorse Chapel, 4610 Charlotte Ave., 615/498-4077, http://actorsbridge.org), a theater company for new and seasoned actors. It brings provocative and new plays to Nashville, often performing at the Belmont Black Box Theater in midtown.

Circle Players (www.circleplayers.net) is the oldest nonprofit, all-volunteer arts association in Nashville. As it's a community theater, all actors, stagehands, directors, and other helpers are volunteers. The company stages four or five performances every year at theater locations around the city. Performances include classic theater, plus stage adaptations of popular cinema and literature.

Children's Theater

Nashville Children's Theatre (25 Middleton St., 615/252-4675, www.nashvillechildrenstheatre.org) is the oldest children's theater company in the United States. During the school year, the company puts on plays for children from preschool to elementary-school age in its colorful theater. In the summer there are drama classes for youngsters, plus lots of activities that include Mom and Dad.

Don't miss the **Marionette Shows at the Nashville Public Library** (615 Church St., 615/862-5800). Using marionettes from the collection of former library puppeteer Tom Tichenor, plus others, the library's children's room staff put on excellent one-of-a-kind family entertainment. They also offer the Puppet Truck, run by Wishing Chair Productions, the library's puppet troupe.

Music

The **Nashville Symphony Orchestra** (1 Symphony Pl., 615/687-6400, www.nashvillesymphony.org) is housed in the remarkable Schermerhorn Symphony Center next to the Country Music Hall of Fame, one of the downtown buildings that was renovated as a result of 2010 flood damage. Nominated for four Grammy Awards and selling more recordings than any other American orchestra, the symphony is a source of pride for Music City. Costa Rican conductor Giancarlo Guerrero is the symphony's seventh music director.

The symphony puts on more than 200 performances each year, including classical, pops, and children's concerts. Its season spans September-May. Buying tickets online is a breeze, especially since you can easily choose where you want to sit. There is discounted parking for symphonygoers in the Pinnacle at Symphony Place, across the street from the Schermerhorn.

During the summer, the symphony plays its **Centennial Park Concert Series** at several locations around town. Head to the Centennial Park band shell on Saturday nights to hear free big-band, ballroom, and classical concerts with other parkgoers. It is a classic Nashville experience.

The **Blair School of Music** (2400 Blakemore Ave., 615/322-7651) presents student, faculty, and visiting artist recitals frequently during the school year. Vanderbilt University's music school, Blair addresses music through academic, pedagogical, and performing activities.

Opera

Middle Tennessee's only opera company, the **Nashville Opera Association** (www.nashvilleopera.org, 615/832-5242) puts on an average of four main-stage performances per season (Oct.-Apr.) and does a six-week tour to area schools. They perform at the Tennessee Performing Arts Center (505 Deaderick St.) and the Noah Liff Opera Center (3622 Redmon St.).

Ballet

Founded in 1981 as a civic dance company, the **Nashville Ballet** (505 Deaderick St., www.nashvilleballet.com) became a professional dance company in 1986. Entertaining more than 40,000 patrons each year, the ballet performs both classical and contemporary pieces at the Tennessee Performing Arts Center (505 Deaderick St.) or Martin Center for Nashville Ballet (3630 Redmon St.).

Festivals and Events

January to March

There's only one day all year that the **Hermitage,** the home of Andrew Jackson (4580 Rachel's Ln., 615/889-2941, www.thehermitage.com, 9am-5pm daily) is free to the public, and that's to celebrate the former president's victory at the Battle of New Orleans. The free day is typically on a weekend closest to January 8.

More than 150 dealers set up in the Music City Center for the upscale **Antiques and Garden Show of Nashville** (201 Fifth Ave. S., 615/352-1282, http://antiquesandgardenshow.com, $20-25) in February. One of the largest such shows that combines indoor furniture and outdoor garden antiques, the event includes workshops, demonstrations, and vintage finds to meet most budgets and tastes. Proceeds from the show benefit Cheekwood.

Many Nashville music events celebrate the performers. But the **Tin Pan South Songwriters Festival** (http://tinpansouth.com) honors the people who come up with the lyrics for all those great tunes. Typically held the last week of March, Tin Pan South, organized by the Nashville Songwriters Association International, schedules performances at venues across the city.

April to May

The **Country Music Television Music Awards** (www.cmt.com) was country music's first fan-voted awards show. Founded in 2002, the show lets fans participate in both the first and final rounds of voting. The show is broadcast live on television from Nashville, usually from the Bridgestone Arena.

The Hermitage

Andrew Jackson's plantation and home, 16 miles east of Nashville, is the area's most well-known historical tourist attraction. **The Hermitage** (4580 Rachel's Ln., 615/889-2941,http://thehermitage.com, 9am-5pm daily, adults $22, seniors $19, students 13-18 $17, children 9-12 $12, free for active military and children 5 and under) is where Jackson retired following his two terms as president of the United States, and it is where he and his beloved wife, Rachel, are buried.

Jackson bought the property in 1809; he and Rachel initially lived in a rustic log cabin, which has since been restored. Jackson ran a successful cotton plantation on the property. In 1819, he and Rachel started construction of what is now the mansion. They moved in two years later.

At the end of Jackson's second term in office in 1837, he retired to the Hermitage and lived here happily until his death in 1845. Following President Jackson's death, the Hermitage remained in family hands until 1853, when it was sold to the state of Tennessee to pay off the family's debts. It was restored and opened as a museum in 1889. Many of the furnishings are original, and even the wallpaper in several rooms dates back to the years when Jackson called it home.

Jackson's legacy is tarnished by his racist policies that caused significant harm to African Americans and Native Americans. The Hermitage has a number of educational opportunities, including the In Their Footsteps Tour: The Lives of the Hermitage Enslaved, which details the horrors of life as an enslaved person. To learn more, take an add-on wagon tour, offered April-October ($10).

Unfortunately, The Hermitage does not do as detailed a job talking about the Trail of Tears, the forceable removal of more than 60,000 Native Americans from their ancestral homes, which Jackson oversaw beginning in 1831. (For more on the Trail of Tears, see page 420).

Understanding Jackson's history, his presidency, his policies, the Trail of Tears, and the Battle of New Orleans is useful background information for the road trip detailed in this book, including the Natchez Trace Parkway and the city of New Orleans. For that reason, some travelers may want visit, although many may not.

Film lovers throughout the country look forward to the **Nashville Film Festival** (http://nashvillefilmfestival.org), held every April at Regal Hollywood Stadium 27 and RPX Nashville. The film festival was founded in 1969 as the Sinking Creek Film Celebration. These days, upwards of 20,000 people attend the weeklong event, which includes film screenings, industry panels, and lots of parties.

The **Rock 'n' Roll Nashville Marathon** (www.runrocknroll.com) takes place every April. More than 15,000 professional and amateur runners take part, and tens of thousands more come out for the live music and cheer squads that line the racecourse. The postrace concert usually boasts nationally known country music artists.

Held in Centennial Park, the May **Tennessee Crafts Fair** (http://tennesseecrafts.org) showcases the work of more than 180 fine craftspeople. Some 45,000 people come to the three-day event every year, which also includes craft demonstrations, a food fair, and entertainment. The fair repeats in September.

For something a little different, plan to attend the **Iroquois Steeplechase** (www.iroquoissteeplechase.org) at Percy Warner Park. Taking place on the second Saturday of May, the race is the nation's oldest continuously run weight-for-age steeplechase in the country. Fans in sundresses or suspenders and hats enjoy watching some of the top horses in the country navigate the race course. You can pay for general admission to sit on the hillside overlooking the stadium. Pack a blanket, food, and drinks (and mud boots if it has rained recently), and you'll have an excellent day. Various tailgating tickets are available and are priced according to how good the view is from the parking spot.

June to August

What was once called Fan Fair and is now hosted by the Country Music Association and called the **CMA Music Festival** (www.cmaworld.com) is a four-day mega-music show in downtown Nashville. The stage at Riverfront Park along the Cumberland River is occupied by day with some of the top names in country music. At night the hordes move to Nissan Stadium to hear a different show every night. Four-day passes, which cost $200-400 per person, also give you access to the exhibit hall, where you can get autographs and meet up-and-coming country music artists, although there are plenty of free shows going on at the same time. This is one of Nashville's biggest events of the year, and you are wise to buy your tickets and book your hotel early. Get a room downtown so you don't need a car.

Early June sees Nashville's gay, lesbian, bisexual, and transgender community show its colors at the **Nashville Pride Festival** (www.nashvillepride.org), a two-day event at Public Square Park.

Independence Day (www.visitmusiccity.com/july4th) is celebrated in a big way with fireworks and a riverfront concert that's broadcast live on television. The event is free and attracts upwards of 100,000 people every year.

The **Music City Brewer's Festival** (www.musiccitybrewersfest.com) is a one-day event at the Music City Walk of Fame downtown. Come to taste local brews, learn about making your own beer, and enjoy good food and live music. Tickets are required, and the event usually sells out.

The temperature is almost always hot at the **Music City Hot Chicken Festival,** but so is the chicken. This east side event (http://hot-chicken.com/festival) is a feast of Nashville's signature spicy pan-fried dish (always served on white bread with a pickle).

The **Tomato Art Festival** (www.tomatoartfest.com) is a tongue-in-cheek celebration of tomatoes and the hip, artsy vibe of East Nashville. Events include a parade of tomatoes, the "Most Beautiful Tomato Pageant," biggest and smallest tomato contests, tomato toss, and Bloody Mary taste-off. The festival usually takes place on the second Saturday of August.

September to October

A multi-venue conference/music showcase, the **Americana Music Festival** (www.americanamusic.org), a.k.a. AmericanaFest, has become one of the city's most popular events. Professionals (musicians, songwriters, producers, and more) come for the connections and the workshops during the day. Locals join them at night for concerts—more than 215 at 14 different venues—that show off the genre. There's an awards show and an end-of-week big budget concert at Ascend Amphitheatre.

Jubilee Day at Fisk University (www.fisk.edu) is held on October 6, the anniversary of the day the Fisk Jubilee Singers set out in 1871 to raise funds for their school. The day includes a convocation and free concert, free admission at the Carl Van Vechten Gallery, and a pilgrimage to the singers' tombstones. This is one of the most powerful events in the city, and shouldn't be missed if you are in town on October 6.

November to December

The **Franklin American Mortgage Music City Bowl** (www.musiccitybowl.com) pits a Southeastern Conference team against a Big Ten rival. This nationally televised football game is held at Nissan Stadium and typically includes a night-before free concert downtown.

Bachelorette City

Nashville Pedal Tavern

You'd be forgiven for thinking that Las Vegas is the go-to city for people looking for a party before they get hitched. While that may be true for bachelor parties, when it comes to bachelorette parties, everything is coming up Music City. In recent years Nashville has become the bachelorette party destination, thanks to its centralized district of restaurants, bars, and live music. Here's how to celebrate the bride-to-be in Music City:

Where to get ready: Bach Weekend (www.bachweekend.com) can help you plan the perfect party weekend. East Nashville's **Darling Salon and Blowout Bar** (1049 W. Eastland Ave., 615/200-7745, www.darlingsalon.com) will do blowouts for your crew to keep you looking sleek in high humidity. **Cured Nail Salon** (813 Gallatin Ave., 615/953-6284, www.curednails.com) is the sleekest-looking nail salon you've visited. **Eastside Nails** in the Shoppes on Fatherland (1006 Fatherland St., 615/988-0449) is the place for themed nail art.

What to do: An offbeat tour with a drink or two on the side is a popular way to get your party started. **Music City Party Tub** (pickup point at The Turnip Truck in The Gulch, 321 12th Ave S., 615/669-0722, www.musiccitypartytub.com) and **Nashville Pedal Tavern** (1504 Demonbreun St., 615/390-5038, www.nashvillepedaltavern.com) are two fun options. **Acme Feed and Seed Nashville** (101 Broadway, 615/915-0888, www.acmefeedandseed.com) offers free mechanic bull rides for bachelorettes, if you're feeling brave (and have good balance).

Where to stay: Pick a place that gives you and your friends the ability to hang out together in a communal space. A few hotels designed for such festivities (with perks like bunk beds and in-room cocktails) include: **Downtown Sporting Club** (411 Broadway, 615/271-4395, www.downtownsportingclub.com); **Vandyke Bed and Beverage** (105 S. 11th S., 615/730-5023, www.vandykenashville.com); and **Bode Nashville** (401 2nd Ave. St., 844/431-2633, www.bode.co). **The Dive Motel & Swim Club** (1414 Dickerson Pike, www.thedivemotel.com) has a disco ball in every room.

Where to get a souvenir: Nashvillian **Judith Bright** (2307 12th Ave. S., 615/269-5600, judithbright.com) makes custom jewelry. Everyone can buy the same ring or bracelet but swap out colored gemstones for a personalized touch. You can watch the pieces being made in the small 12South studio, and the surrounding neighborhood has a number of murals that make a good backdrop for a selfie or group photo.

New Year's Eve near downtown Nashville at Bicentennial Mall, called **Music City Midnight** (www.visitmusiccity.com/newyearseve) includes—what else?—a music note drop. This is one of the biggest celebrations in the country, with big crowds and lots of free outdoor fun. It has been part of the national program *Dick Clark's New Year's Rockin' Eve*. Mega acts like Kings of Leon and Keith Urban play free concerts.

Shopping

You'll find many good reasons to shop in Nashville. Who can pass up Western wear in Music City? Fine boutiques cater to the well-heeled in tony West End. Downtown you'll find unique art and gifts. East Nashville is a mecca for those who crave handmade goods. Many of the museums have excellent gift shops.

Nashville's largest flea market takes place on the fourth Saturday of every month at the Tennessee State Fairgrounds. The **Tennessee State Fairgrounds Flea Market** (615/862-5016, www.thefairgrounds.com) is a bargain lover's dream, with thousands of sellers peddling clothes, crafts, and all sorts of vintage and used housewares, often at lower prices than you'd find in bigger cities. The fairgrounds are on 4th Avenue, south of downtown. Admission is free, but parking is $5.

Downtown and Germantown

The Texas Troubadour, Ernest Tubb, founded his famous record store on Broadway in 1947. The **Ernest Tubb Record Shop** (417 Broadway, 615/255-7503, http://etrecordshop.com, 10am-10pm Sun.-Thurs., 10am-midnight Fri.-Sat.) remains a good source of classic and modern country music recordings, as well as DVDs, books, clothing, and souvenirs. At the back of the shop you can see the stage where Ernest Tubb's Midnite Jamboree was recorded and aired after the Grand Ole Opry on Saturday nights. The Jamboree still airs, but it's recorded at the Texas Troubadour Theatre in Music Valley. JesseLee Jones, the owner of Robert's Western World, bought the record shop in 2020 in an effort to keep it open and preserved.

After Ernest Tubb, the most famous place to shop in Nashville is **Hatch Show Print** (224 5th Ave. S., 615/577-7710, http://hatchshowprint.com, 9:30am-6pm daily). Hatch has been making colorful posters for more than a century, and its iconic letterpress style is now one of the trendiest looks in modern design. It continues to design and print handouts, posters, and T-shirts for local and national customers. Gaze at the cavernous warehouse operation and buy small or large samples of the shop's work, including reproductions of classic country music concert posters. This is a great place to find a special souvenir of your trip to Nashville or just see another part of Music City's history. Hatch posters are up all over town, including in the airport.

If you need clothes to fit the Nashville part, **Boot Country** (304 Broadway, 615/259-1691, 10am-10:30pm Mon.-Thurs., 10am-11pm Fri.-Sat., 11am-7:30pm Sun.) specializes in all styles and sizes of cowboy boots and often offers a free pair of boots when you buy two pairs. It's popular with both tourists and locals for its deals. **Manuel Exclusive Clothier** (2804 Columbine Pl. , 615/321-5444, 9am-6pm Mon.-Fri.) is the Western wear designer to the stars. This is a clothing shop where cowboy shirts start at $750 and jackets at more than $2,000. This is where to go when you want a custom outfit for your big stage debut.

As the neighborhood of Germantown has gentrified, boutiques have popped up left and right. **Abednego** (1210 4th Ave. N., 615/712-6028, www.abednegoboutique.com, 11am-6pm Tues.-Sat., 11am-4pm Sun.) carries local- and other American-made clothes and accessories. Owned by a local musician, Abednego

Where to Stock Up for a Road Trip

If you're about to embark on the 444-mile trip down the Natchez Trace, you need to stock up. These are the best places in the area to find quality camping and hiking gear, waterproof supplies, water bottles, and everything else you need for hiking and other outdoor activities. The salespeople at these spots can offer tips about traveling on the Trace.

- **Friedman's Army/Navy Surplus & Outdoors** (2101 21st Ave. S., 615/297-3343, www.friedmansarmynavyoutdoorstore.com, 9am-6pm Mon.-Sat.)
- **Cumberland Transit** (2807 West End Ave., 615/321-4069, http://cumberland transit.com, 10am-6pm Mon.-Sat., noon-5pm Sun.)
- **Bass Pro Shops at Opry Mills** (323 Opry Mills Dr., 615/514-5200, http://basspro.com, 10am-9pm Mon.-Sat., 10am-7pm Sun.)
- **Patagonia** (601 Overton St., 615/747-2535, www.patagonia.com, 10am-7pm Mon.-Fri., 11am-7pm Sat., 11am-5pm Sun.)
- **Binks Outfitters** (4015 Hillsboro Pike, 615/298-1700, www.binksoutfitters.com)
- **Mountain High Outfitters** (1608 21st Ave. S., 615/730-6627, http://mountain highoutfitters.com)

stocks goods for men and women in a minimalist loft-like environment.

New York transplants Ivy and Josh brought their interior design eyes to the South. The duo opened a Germantown atelier called **Wilder** (1212 4th Ave. N., 615/679-0008, www.wilderlife.com, 10am-5pm Wed.-Mon.) to show off their transformational wares. Come browse the furnishing, textiles, lighting, mirrors, and more, all with a modern sensibility and many not found elsewhere in the area.

While downtown, check out the many art galleries. One of the most accessible and eclectic, **Chauvet Arts** (215 5th Ave. of the Arts, 615/254-2040, www.chauvetarts.com, 11am-5pm Tues.-Sat.) offers outsider art, the works of local artists, and other contemporary works ranging from the avant-garde to the everyday. Perhaps the most cosmopolitan of all Nashville's galleries, **The Rymer Gallery** (233 5th Ave. of the Arts, 615/752-6030, www.therymergallery.com, 11am-5pm Tues.-Sat.) installs thought-provoking exhibits with works from artists of national renown. The Rymer is also home to Nashville's **Herb Williams** (www.herbwilliamsart.com), a gifted artist who creates sculpture from crayons. Williams's work has been on display in the White House and other prestigious addresses.

The upper level of **The Arcade** (http://thenashvillearcade.com), between 4th and 5th Avenues, houses several artist studios that open as galleries during downtown's monthly **Art Crawl,** which takes place the first Saturday of each month.

Music Row, Midtown, and 12South

For new and used CDs, DVDs, and vinyl, go to **Grimey's New and Preloved Music** (1060 East Trinity Ln., 615/226-3811, www.grimeys.com, 10am-8pm Mon.-Sat., noon-6pm Sun.). Here you'll find a wide selection of country, as well as rock, folk, blues, R&B, and other genres. The staff is knowledgeable and friendly.

A boot is not just a boot—at least

not in Nashville, where boots are a status symbol as much as footwear. And in a town that loves boots, people really love **Lucchese Boot Co.** (503 12th Ave. S., 615/242-1161, www.lucchese.com, 10am-7pm Mon.-Sat., noon-6pm Sun.). Pronounced "LU-kay-see," this brand has been around since 1883, but only since 2012 has it had its own retail shop in The Gulch.

If you want to *make* your own music, head to **Gruhn Guitars** (2120 8th Ave. S., 615/256-2033, http://guitars.com, 10am-6pm Mon.-Sat.), a guitar shop with one of the best reputations in the music world. Founded by guitar expert George Gruhn, the shop is considered by some to be the best vintage guitar shop in the world. Shiny guitars, banjos, mandolins, and fiddles look like candy hung up on the walls of the Broadway storefront, which serves both up-and-coming and established Nashville musicians.

Third Man Records (623 7th Ave. S., 615/891-4393, http://thirdmanrecords.com, 10am-6pm daily) is a record label, recording studio, and record store all in one fairly small building. The idea behind the label is simple: All the music in the building has Jack White's stamp on it in some way. It's not a bad thing. Blue Series records are recorded by bands traveling through town, recording one or two songs, and are available on seven-inch vinyl. Green Series are nonmusical recordings, such as spoken word, poetry, or instructional discussions.

At **Hey Rooster General Store** (1711 21st Ave. S., www.heyrooster.com, 10am-6pm Mon.-Sat., 10am-4pm Sun.), proprietor Courtney Webb stocks lovely handmade gifts from art to jewelry, plus prepared foods and ingredients, as well as a few books.

Walk in the doors of this small, unassuming house, and you'll find a jewelry shop that has attracted the attention of stylists, filmmakers, and celebrities. **Judith Bright** (2307 12th Ave. S., 615/269-5600, http://judithbright.com, 10am-6pm Mon.-Sat., noon-6pm Sun.) trains a team of women to make reasonably priced jewelry, including earrings, necklaces, and bracelets with gemstones. Most of the work is done off sight, but in a small studio in the house you can watch them switch out stones and size a piece just for you.

Kimberly Lewis helped retail brands like BCBGMAXAZRIA expand before she decided to open her own 12South shop, **Emerson Grace** (2304 12th Ave. S., 615/454.6407, www.emersongracenashville.com, 10am-6pm Mon.-Sat., 11am-5pm Sun.). Her considerable experience allowed her to create a shop with a focus on women's clothing that is stylish and well-edited, offering brands not otherwise found in Nashville.

Bargain-hunting fashionistas cannot skip **UAL** (2918 West End Ave., 615/340-9999, http://shopual.com, 9am-8pm Mon.-Fri., 10am-8pm Sat.-Sun.). Designer samples of clothes, handbags, shoes, and jewelry are shoved onto crowded racks in this shop near the Vanderbilt campus. UAL stocks both men's and women's clothing, but the women's selection is significantly larger. There are also locations in Hillsboro Village (1814 21st Ave. S., 615/540-0211) and 12South (2900 12th Ave. S. 615/891-3052), as well as in New Orleans.

Owned by famous singer-songwriter Holly Williams (granddaughter of Hank), **White's Mercantile** (2908 12th Ave. S., 615/750-5379, http://whites-mercantile.com, 10am-6pm Mon.-Sat., noon-5pm Sun.) is a modern general store stocked with high-end gifts, home decor, artsy trinkets, and kitchenware. Williams says she seeks inspiration for the shop when she's out on the road. There's another outpost in New Orleans.

Celebrities like Gwyneth Paltrow love 12South's **Imogene + Willie** (2601 12th Ave. S., 615/292-5005, http://imogene-andwillie.com, 10am-6pm Mon.-Thurs., 10am-7pm Fri.-Sat., noon-5pm Sun.). The shop carries clothes for men and women, but its specialty is custom-fit blue jeans at a price tag of $200 and up.

Nashville native Reese Witherspoon launched the flagship location of her shop/lifestyle brand **Draper James** (2608 12th Ave. S., 615/997-3601, www.draperjames.com, 10am-6pm Mon.-Wed., 10am-7pm Thurs.-Sat., 11am-5pm Sun.) in her hometown. Find pillows, cocktail napkins, and more—with a Southern twist.

Ceri Hoover (2905 12th Ave. S., #105, 615/200-0991, http://cerihoover.com, 11am-6pm Tues.-Fri., 10am-6pm Sat., 11am-5pm Sun.) designs luscious high-end leather handbags, shoes, and wallets. These accessories are head-turners, and on the arms of most of the city's most fashionable people.

East Nashville

There are two collections of small boutiques in East Nashville, great for browsing for local goods. The bigger is the **Shoppes on Fatherland** (1006 Fatherland St., 615/227-8646, http://fatherlanddistrict.com), which has art galleries, clothing shops, and even a place for fly-fishing gear. Here you'll find **Project 615** (www.project615.org, 11am-6pm Mon.-Thurs., 10am-6pm Fri.-Sat., noon-5pm Sun.), which puts local landmarks like the Trace's Double Arch Bridge on T-shirts, and **Gift Horse** (http://gifthorsenashville.com, 11am-6pm Tues.-Sat., 10am-6pm Sat., noon-4pm Sun.), which stocks plenty of cards and art prints from local makers. The other collection of stores, **1108 Shops at Woodland** (1108 Woodland St., hours vary by store), which includes several vintage clothing boutiques.

Owner Joelle Herr, who, earlier in her career, worked for Avalon Travel, built **The Bookshop** (1035 W. Eastland Ave., #105, 615/485-5420, www.herbookshop.com, 10am-7pm Mon.-Fri., 10am-6pm Sat., 10am-5pm Sun.), a tiny but mighty bookstore based on her good instincts and professional experience. Herr selects everything that graces these pretty,

The Bookshop

well-designed shelves, including a mix of fiction, non-fiction, local interest, and children's books. The Bookshop connects through an inner hallway to next-door-neighbor **Kettner Coffee Supply** (1035 W. Eastland Ave., 7am-3pm daily). Kettner is a coffee shop with a few delicious menu items (including soft-serve ice cream) and space to host The Bookshop's Lit Club, silent book club, and other events.

It's a family affair at **Harlan Ruby Gift Shop** (805 Woodland St., #301, 615/955-0565, www.harlanruby.com, 10am-6pm Mon.-Fri., 9am-3pm Sat.-Sun.), an umbrella for several creative businesses run by a mother and her daughters. You'll be delighted by the surprises in this modern party supply and gift shop, stocking locally made artwork, housewares, and hipster greeting cards, plus a "balloon bar" with unusual options like unicorns, cacti, margarita glasses, and oh-so-trendy rose gold letters and numbers. The youngest daughter (who is school-age) runs Hankabee Button Co., which is a part of the shop.

In another city, **Fanny's House of Music** (1101 Holly St., 615/750-5746, http://fannyshouseofmusic.com; 10am-6:30pm daily) might be considered unusual. It's a woman-owned, guitar-centered music store with a vintage clothing shop mixed in. But in Nashville, it's par for the course. The staff can help you find a guitar that's comfortable for you to play, regardless of gender or size. There are new, used, and vintage guitars and gear, and the guitar techs do a superb job of getting the road dings out of your axe. There are almost always folks sitting around jamming while you shop.

Music Valley

The discount mall **Opry Mills** (433 Opry Mills Dr., 615/514-1000, http://simon.com, hours vary by store) is the city's most maligned favorite destination. Locals love to hate it—because it replaced the old Opryland amusement park on this same site and because it is so popular (it's one of the area's leading tourist attractions); lines for the parking lot back up along Briley Parkway. If you live near other national-brand outlet malls, you don't need to come here. But if good deals on name-brand merchandise appeal to you, or you are looking to kill time before a show at the Opry, Opry Mills is the mall for you. Brands include Old Navy, Disney, LEGO, Coach, Kate Spade, Ann Taylor, H&M, and Torrid. The mammoth Bass Pro Shops is a great place to get gear before heading out on the Trace. The famous wax museum **Madame Tussauds** (515 Opry Mills Dr., www.madametussauds.com/nashville, 10am-9pm Mon.-Sat., 11am-7pm Sun., $19-55) has an outpost in Opry Mills. As expected, it is chock-full of country music stars' likenesses and kitsch.

South Nashville

A famous owner (novelist Ann Patchett) meant that the opening of **Parnassus**

Books (3900 Hillsboro Pike, 615/953-2243, www.parnassusbooks.net, 10am-8pm Mon.-Sat., noon-5pm Sun.) made national headlines. Located in a strip mall across from the Mall at Green Hills, Parnassus specializes in a well-edited selection, personal service, and literary events for both kids and adults.

Near the old 100 Oaks Mall in South Nashville you'll find Nashville's largest and most popular antiques mall. **Gaslamp Antiques & Decorating Mall** (100 Powell Ave., 615/297-2224, www.gaslampantiques.com, 10am-6pm Mon.-Sat., noon-6pm Sun.) is squeezed behind a Staples and next to a Home Depot. It has more than 150 vendors and a great selection of all types of antiques.

Sports and Recreation

Parks

Centennial Park

Nashville's best city park, **Centennial Park** (2500 West End Ave., 615/862-8400, dawn-11pm daily) is best known as home of the Parthenon. The edifice is the center of activity at this 132-acre gem, but Centennial Park is also just a pleasant place to relax. A small lake provides a habitat for ducks and other water creatures, and there are walking and running trails, a dog park, bicycle rental stations, children's play areas, and more. Something is almost always going on here, particularly in the summer, with frequent live music and Shakespeare in the Park performances (Aug.-Sept.).

Radnor Lake State Natural Area

Just seven miles southwest of downtown Nashville, **Radnor Lake State Natural Area** (1160 Otter Creek Rd., 615/373-3467, 6am-dusk daily) provides an escape for visitors and residents of the city. Eighty-five-acre Radnor Lake was created in 1914 by the Louisville and Nashville Railroad Company, which impounded Otter Creek to do so. The lake was to provide water for the railroad's steam engines. By the 1940s, the railroad's use of the lake ended, and 20 years later the area was threatened by development. Local residents, including the Tennessee Ornithological Society, successfully rallied against development, and Radnor Lake State Natural Area was established in 1973.

There are six miles of hiking trails around the lake, and Otter Creek Road, which is closed to vehicular traffic, is open to bicycles and walkers. A nature museum at the visitors center describes some of the 240 species of birds and hundreds of species of plants and animals that live at Radnor. The visitors center is open 9:30am-6pm daily (closed 1pm-2pm; restrooms open at 7am).

Edwin and Percy Warner Parks

The largest city parks in Tennessee, **Edwin and Percy Warner Parks** (7311 TN-100, 615/370-8051, www.nashville.gov, dawn-11pm daily) are a 2,600-acre oasis of forest, fields, and quiet pathways located just nine miles southwest from downtown Nashville. Nashvillians come here to walk, jog, ride bikes and horses, and much more. The parks have scenic drives, picnic facilities, playgrounds, cross-country running trails, an equestrian center, bridle trails, a model-airplane field, and athletic fields. Percy Warner Park is also home to the Harpeth Hills Golf Course, and Edwin Warner Park has a nature center that provides year-round environmental education. The nature center also hands out maps and other information about the park.

Warner Parks hosts the annual Iroquois Steeplechase in May. A 10-mile bridle path is open to horseback riding year-round. Visit the park's **Equestrian Center** (2500 Old Hickory Blvd.) for more information.

J. Percy Priest Lake

J. Percy Priest Lake (miles 6-7 of the Stones River, www.percypriestlake.org)

was created in the mid-1960s when the U.S. Army Corps of Engineers (USACE) dammed Stones River east of Nashville. The lake is a favorite destination for fishing, boating, swimming, paddling, and picnicking.

J. Percy Priest Lake sprawls over 14,200 acres. Access is provided through more than a dozen different parks and access areas on all sides of the lake. Many of these areas bear the names of communities that were inundated when the lake was created.

The lake's main **visitors center,** operated by the USACE, is at the site of the dam that created the lake. The visitors center is on Bell Road at exit 219, off I-40 heading east from downtown Nashville. There you will find a lake overlook and one of four marinas on the lake.

The USACE operates three day-use **swim areas** (6am-7pm daily Apr.-Oct.) that have sand beaches, bathrooms, and other amenities for a day in the water. These swim areas are located at Anderson Road, Cook Campground, and Seven Points Campground. There is a $5 vehicle fee at Anderson and Cook.

Greenways

Nashville has a remarkable network of connected green spaces, thanks to its **greenways** (www.nashville.gov/greenways). The master plan is for this system to eventually connect the entire city. Today there are more than 190 miles of paved pathways and 80 miles of primitive trails used by bicyclists, runners, dog walkers, and more. The greenways run through the city's prettiest natural areas and, in places, along the Cumberland River. Some greenways include nature centers and other educational facilities. For the most part, the routes are clean and safe. Good maps are available for download from **Greenways for Nashville** (www.greenwaysfornashville.org).

Biking

Nashville has a fast-growing bike culture, and it's easy to pedal your way across the city to see its highlights. It's easy to connect to more than 90 miles of greenways and 130 miles of bike lanes and shared-use bike routes.

Nashville's only dedicated mountain bike trail is at **Hamilton Creek Park** (www.nashville.gov) on J. Percy Priest Lake, on the east side of the Nashville airport. This 10-mile bike trail consists of an eastern trail, better for beginning bikers, and a western trail, for advanced bikers. The two trails meet at a tunnel that crosses Bell Road.

The **Harpeth Bike Club** (www.harpethbikeclub.com) is Nashville's largest bike club. It organizes weekend and weekday group rides April-October, plus races and social events where you can meet other bike enthusiasts.

Bike Shops

There are several good bike shops in Nashville. If you need bike gear, repairs, or advice before you head out on the Trace, check out **Cumberland Transit** (2807 West End Ave., 615/321-4069, http://cumberlandtransit.com, 10am-6pm Mon.-Sat., noon-5pm Sun.) or **Trace Bikes** (8080B TN-100, 615/646-2485, http://tracebikes.com, 10am-6pm Mon.-Fri., 10am-5pm Sat., noon-6pm Sun.), next to the Loveless Cafe near the Natchez Trace Parkway. East Nashville's **Shelby Avenue Bicycle Co.** (1629 Shelby Ave., 615/925-3274, http://shelbybicycle.com, 11am-6pm Wed.-Fri., 10am-4pm Sat., noon-4pm Sun.) rents bikes, sells bikes, and does bike repairs. The focus at **Halcyon Bike Shop** (2802 12th Ave. S., 615/730-9344, http://halcyonbike.com, 10am-6pm Tues.-Sat., noon-5pm Sun.) is restored and recycled bicycles. It has a great repair shop, fun accessories, and a passionate staff.

Water Sports

Nashville's easy access to multiple rivers and lakes makes it a natural gateway for kayaking, canoeing, and stand-up paddleboarding. **Nashville Paddle Co.** (2901 Bell Rd., 615/682-1787, www.nashvillepaddle.com, hours vary daily May-Sept., $25-45) offers lessons and rentals for stand-up paddleboarding, which is well suited for Middle Tennessee's flat water. (Full disclosure: The author of this book is one of the owners of Nashville Paddle Co.)

While primarily designed as an add-on for guests of the Gaylord Opryland Resort, the mammoth **SoundWaves** (2800 Opryland Dr., 615/458-6802, www.soundwavesgo.com, 10am-9pm daily, $40-55 pp) is an indoor/outdoor water park that's open to the resort's guests as well as the public, and jam-packed with fun and sun. It includes a 315,000-gallon wave pool with adults-only pools, kids' pools, a massive LED movie screen, several giant water slides, a lazy river, a surfing simulator, food trucks, and more. No detail has been overlooked: You can eat, drink, and lounge, or play in the water all day. Since much of the park is indoors, it allows for frolicking even when the weather isn't fine. Party rooms can accommodate groups of 10, 16, or 30 for events such as birthday parties, bachelorette parties, and family reunions and are available in four-hour blocks, with all-day access to the park and complimentary parking.

Spectator Sports

Football

You cannot miss 68,000-seat **Nissan Stadium,** home of the NFL's **Tennessee Titans** (1 Titans Way, 615/565-4000, www.titansonline.com). The stadium towers on the east bank of the Cumberland River, directly opposite downtown. The Titans moved to this stadium (then called LP Field) in 1999 and initially sold out almost every home game. But a spotty win-loss record in recent years has made

Nissan Stadium is the home of the NFL's Tennessee Titans.

tickets easier to come by. If you want to see a game on short notice, your best bet is the online NFL ticket exchange, where season ticket holders can sell their seats to games they don't want to attend. The stadium also hosts many other events, including CMA Music Festival concerts.

Baseball

What an appropriate name for a minor-league baseball team. The **Nashville Sounds** (19 Junior Gilliam Way, 615/690-4487, www.nashvillesounds.com, tickets $10-40) are an affiliate of the Oakland Athletics, and they play about 30 home games a year June-October. In 2015 the team moved to the spectacular **First Horizon Park** between downtown and Germantown. The new stadium has a guitar-shaped scoreboard, plus a mini-golf course (yes, inside the stadium), better-than-average-stadium food and drink from **The Band Box** (http://thebandboxnashville.com), and great sightlines. There's an alcohol-free section, too.

Ice Hockey

Nashville proved itself to be a hockey town when its beloved National Hockey League franchise, the **Nashville Predators** (501 Broadway, 615/770-7800, www.nhl.com/predators), went to the Stanley Cup playoffs in 2017. It was a sweet victory for fans who fought to keep the team in the city in the face of lackluster support from the community with a "Save the Predators" campaign. The Predators play in the 20,000-seat Bridgestone Arena, located on Broadway in the heart of downtown. Home games include live country music performances and other activities for the fans. The regular season begins in October and ends in early April. Single-game tickets start at $24-35 and can cost as much as $400.

Sports fans will enjoy the **Tennessee Sports Hall of Fame** (Bridgestone Arena, 501 Broadway, 615/242-4750, www.tshf.net, 10am-5pm Tues.-Sat., adults $3, children $2), which is in the exhibit space of the arena.

College Sports

In addition to Nashville's smorgasbord of professional and semiprofessional sports teams, the city's colleges provide lots of good spectator sports. Vanderbilt plays football, men's and women's basketball, and baseball in the Southeastern Conference. Tennessee State University and Belmont University play Division 1-A basketball, and Lipscomb University is a member of the Atlantic Sun Division. Vanderbilt football games are an unusual sporting event, as students traditionally dress in coats and ties or dresses and high heels.

Food

You can eat in a different restaurant each day in Nashville and never get bored. Southern cooking stars at meat-and-three diners, signature hot chicken, and barbecue joints, fine-dining restaurants cater to the well-heeled, and international eateries reflect the city's diversity.

More than a few high-profile chefs—including *Chopped*'s Maneet Chauhan, Ford Fry, and world-famous Jonathan Waxman—have opened local kitchens.

Downtown and Germantown

The Arcade

One of two downtown food destinations, the **Arcade** is an old outdoor shopping mall that lies between 4th and 5th Avenues. The ground floor of the Arcade is full of small, casual restaurants that cater to the downtown lunchtime crowd with quick, cheap eats. Upstairs are a few art galleries and artists' studios. Most restaurants at the Arcade have limited seating inside, or you can sit outside and watch the world go by.

There are also several sandwich shops and **Manny's House of Pizza** (15 Arcade, 615/242-7144, http://mannyshouseofpizza.com, 11am-4pm Mon.-Fri., $3-6), which many consider the city's best slice.

Southern

Run, don't walk, to ★ **Arnold's Country Kitchen** (605 8th Ave. S., 615/256-4455, www.arnoldscountrykitchen.com, 10:30am-2:45pm Mon.-Fri., $7-10) for some of the best Southern cooking in town. Set in a red cinder-block building on the southern edge of downtown, Arnold's is a food-lover's dream. Start out by grabbing a tray at this cafeteria-style spot and select from chocolate pie, juicy sliced tomatoes, turnip greens, squash casserole, macaroni and cheese—and that's just the "vegetables." Choose a vegetable plate, or a meat-and-three for just about a buck more. Common meat dishes include ham, baked chicken, fried fish, and beef tips. All meals come with yeast rolls or corn bread. The full lunch, plus a drink, will run you less than $10. There's almost always a line out the door.

There's no shortage of fried chicken south of the Mason-Dixon. Even so, people often throng to one of the three locations of **Puckett's Grocery & Restaurant** (500 Church St., 615/770-2772, http://puckettsgro.com, 7am-10pm Sun.-Thurs., 7am-11pm Fri.-Sat.) for what folks say is among the area's best fried chicken. The downtown outpost of this regional mainstay has classic Southern food (don't skimp on the fried green beans) in a casual, often crowded environment. There's live music many nights and a full bar, but the real appeal is stick-to-your-ribs comfort food in a restaurant that will get you in and out in time to see a show at the Ryman.

In 2018, the **Woolworth on Fifth** (221 5th Ave., 615/891-1361, http://woolworthonfifth.com, 11am-9pm Mon.-Thurs., 11am-10pm Fri., 9:30am-10pm Sat., 9:30am-9pm Sun., $7-32) opened as a Southern restaurant, cookbook library, event space, and keeper of history, with many fixtures from the original drugstore and a re-created lunch counter where the 1960s civil rights sit-ins took place. Some critics are concerned that the venture appropriates this painful history for monetary gain, while other see it as a way to raise awareness of the history that took place here. The multimedia "Big Idea" discussion and music series that takes place downstairs is particularly thoughtful.

John Carter Cash remembers his famous parents taking him to Swett's for fried chicken as a child. So, it makes sense than when the owners of **Johnny Cash's Kitchen & Saloon** (121 3rd Ave., 615/209-9504, www.cashkitchenandsaloon.com, 11am-10pm Mon.-Wed., 11am-3am Thurs., 9am-3am Fri.-Sat., 9am-10pm Sun., $8-14) were looking for someone to serve meat-and-threes to the

Not Just for Vegetarians

Nashville, with its hot chicken and its meat-and-threes, isn't known as a vegetarian paradise. But as its food scene in general has become more varied, so have the vegetarian options. Here's a look at some of the more interesting options for those looking for a plant-based meal (or two). Don't worry, omnivores, everyone will find something to eat at these spots:

- **AVO** (3 City Ave., #200, 615/329-2377, www.eatavo.com): The entire menu at this quirky local favorite is plant-based, raw, and gluten-free. The AVOcado margarita (made with avocado, aged tequila, cilantro, and lime) is the talk of the town.
- **Graze** (1888 Eastland Ave., 615/686-1060, www.grazenashville.com): This "plant-based bistro and bar" is at home in hip East Nashville, serving dinner as well as weekend brunch. Here, the cheese is made from cashews, the hot "chicken" sandwich is made with meat-free tempeh, and the banh mi is filled with seitan. There are also a handful of juices and smoothies for those looking for sustenance in liquid form.
- **Wild Cow** (1100 Fatherland St., 615/262-2717, http://thewildcow.com): Despite the perhaps misleading name, this East Nashville joint is all about vegetarian and vegan fare made with organic and locally sourced ingredients when possible. Choose from salads, tacos, and bowls filled with grains or greens.
- **Sunflower Cafe** (2834 Azalea Pl., 615/457-2568, www.sunflowercafenashville.com): This Berry Hill house is home to a vegetarian cafeteria-style restaurant with a changing selection of entrées and sides served in meat-and-three style, albeit without the meat. Many of the offerings are vegan and gluten-free as well.

masses downtown, they'd turn to the Swett family. Come here for reasonably priced, cafeteria-style Southern dishes, including cakes, pies, and baked potato casserole. There are live music stages—playing Johnny Cash music—on both floors. Upstairs is a bar with a fireplace and stained glass windows; downstairs is the restaurant. Both are designed to look like Johnny and June's home. After 8pm, the venue is open for the 21-and-over crowd only.

Barbecue

In walking distance to downtown's honkytonks and with a great backyard beer garden, **Martin's Bar-B-Que Joint** (410 4th Ave. S., 615/288-0880, 11am-10pm Sun.-Thurs., 11am-midnight Fri.-Sat., $8-35) is one of the city's favorite barbecue houses. It serves pulled pork, barbecue spareribs, smoked wings, and beef brisket, plus all the side dishes you could want: coleslaw, green beans, potato salad, and the best corn cakes this side of town. Martin's has several other locations around town.

Contemporary

Rub elbows with legislators, lobbyists, and other members of the jet set at the ★ **Capitol Grille** (231 6th Ave. N., 615/345-7116, www.capitolgrillenashville.com, 6:30am-11am, 11:30am-2pm, and 5pm-10pm daily, $10-65). Located on the ground floor of the elegant Hermitage Hotel and a stone's throw from the Tennessee State Capitol, this is the sort of restaurant where marriages are proposed and deals are done. The menu is fine dining at its best: choice cuts of meat prepared with exacting care and local ingredients (grown at the nearby Farm at Glen Leven). The provenance of each dinner entrée (elk, pork, sea bass) is noted on the menu. Adjacent to the Capitol Grille is the old-school **Oak Bar,** a wood-paneled and intimate spot for pre- or post-dinner drinks.

Built in the old Trolley Barns that look out over downtown, **Pinewood** (33 Peabody St., 615/751-8111 www.pinewoodsocial.com, 7am-1am Mon.-Fri., 9am-1am Sat.-Sun., pool open 11am-11pm daily summer, $7-25) has something for everyone—literally. This breakfast, lunch, brunch, dinner, and late-night restaurant is designed to appeal, no matter whether you need a cup of coffee while you check your e-mail or if you want to bowl with friends at one of the six lanes here. There's even a small pool open in summer. The cocktails are delicious, as is the fried broccoli.

From the team behind Pinewood and Bastion, along with Nashville native and chef Julia Sullivan, **Henrietta Red** (1200 4th Ave. N., 615/490-8042, www.henriettared.com, 5:30pm-10pm Tues.-Fri., 10am-2pm and 5:30pm-10pm Sat.-Sun., bar until 11pm Tues.-Thurs., midnight Fri.-Sat., $12-26) is a seafood-friendly barroom, with an emphasis on seasonal contemporary cooking. The room is sleek and well-designed, and buzzing with activity, making for a space that's loud but not overbearing. The marble-topped oyster bar is popular with locals from the surrounding Germantown neighborhood. Henrietta Red is one of the more coveted dining spots in town; reservations are recommended.

International

Maneet Chauhan is known for appearing on *Iron Chef America, The Next Iron Chef,* and *Chopped.* She opened **Chauhan Ale & Masala House** (123 12th Ave. N., 615/242-8426, http://chauhannashville.com, 11am-2:30pm and 5pm-10pm Sun.-Thurs., 11am-2:30pm and 5pm-11pm Fri., 5pm-11pm Sat., $12-34). The eatery brought Indian street food and a fusion of dishes and tastes to a city that wasn't known for its Indian cuisine. The vibe is fun and friendly, the cocktails go down easy, and there is even an interpretation of a Nashville hot chicken dish. She also owns several other restaurants, including **Chaatable** (345 40th Ave. N.), which focuses on Indian street food.

Diners and Coffee Shops

Next door to the Johnny Cash Museum, **Sun Diner** (105 3rd Ave. S., 615/742-9099, http://sundinernashville.com, 24 hours daily, $15-20) is downtown's 24-hour diner, with a menu that pays homage to Sun Records. This is where to get a doughnut breakfast sandwich. Due to its prime location, prices are higher than at traditional diners.

Desserts

Nashville's legendary candy company **Goo Goo Cluster** (116 3rd Ave. S., 615/490-6685, http://googoo.com, 10am-7pm daily) has been selling sweets for more than a century. In this flagship red, white, and blue location, you'll find the company's full array of sweets, plus some varieties made only in this open kitchen. Watch the chef create something you'll love. Goo Goo-branded hats, T-shirts, Hatch Show Print posters, and other goodies are also for sale. Don't miss the historical exhibit about the brand.

Farmers Markets

The **Nashville Farmers Market** (900 Rosa L. Parks Blvd., 615/880-2001, www.nashvillefarmersmarket.org, daily, hours vary by merchant) has undergone a resurgence in recent years and, as a result, is one of the best places to grab an interesting meal in the city. The outdoor components of the market include a farm shed with fresh produce year-round. This is a growers' market, so produce is farmed locally. When you're hungry, head to the interior for the Market House food court, with choices ranging from Southern specialties to Caribbean cuisine. **Jamaicaway** (615/255-5920, 10:30am-6pm Sun.-Fri., $9) serves oxtail, steamed fish, and

Jamaican patties. Other options include Mexican food, wood-fired pizza, local beers, barbecue, and Greek dishes, as well as enough baked goods to give you a toothache. The monthly **night market** brings specialty food and drink, plus live music, dancing, and a magical ambience.

Music Row, Midtown, and 12South

Southern

One of Nashville's most beloved meat-and-threes is **Swett's** (2725 Clifton Ave., 615/329-4418, http://swettsrestaurant.com, 11am-8pm daily, $8-12), family owned and operated since 1954. People come from all over the city to eat at this Nashville institution, which combines soul food, Southern cooking, and barbecue with great results. The food is homemade and authentic, down to the mashed potatoes, vinegary greens, and yeast rolls. Start by grabbing dessert—the pies are excellent—and then move on to the good stuff at this cafeteria-style spot: Country-fried steak, pork chops, meatloaf, fried catfish, and ham are a few of the usual suspects. A standard plate comes with one meat, two sides, and a yeast roll or corn bread, but you can add more sides if you like. Draw your own iced tea—sweet or unsweet—and then find a seat if you can.

For some people, Nashville-style hot chicken, that spicy, local delicacy, is only authentic if it is served pan-fried in a shack without air-conditioning or adequate seating. If that's your criteria, then this is not the spot for you. But for many people **Hattie B's Hot Chicken** (112 19th Ave. S., 615/678-4794, http://hattieb.com, 11am-10pm Mon.-Thurs., 11am-midnight Fri.-Sat., 11am-4pm Sun. $12-22) is the answer to their hot chicken prayers. The recipes are delicious, with options for everyone ranging from mild to Shut the Cluck Up, with all the amenities of a traditional restaurant, including beer and some vegetarian-friendly side dishes. There are also locations in West Nashville (5209 Charlotte Ave., 615/712-7137) and Melrose (2222 8th Ave. S., 615/970-3010).

Contemporary

To describe **The Catbird Seat** (1711 Division St., 615/810-8200, http://thecatbirdseatrestaurant.com, 5:30pm-9pm Wed.-Sat., $135) as a restaurant is a bit of a misnomer. It is a culinary performance that happens to include dinner. There are just 32 seats in this U-shaped space. Once you get a coveted reservation (available online only), you'll be treated to a seasonal meal made before your eyes. Reservations are accepted up to 30 days in advance. The multicourse tasting menu is $135 per person without drinks. The nonalcoholic pairings are as inventive as the wines.

International

For the best Italian food in Nashville, head west to the neighborhood of Sylvan Park, where you'll find **Caffe Nonna** (4427 Murphy Rd., 615/463-0133, www.caffenonna.com, 5pm-9pm Mon.-Thurs., 5pm-10pm Fri.-Sat., $12-24). Inspired by Chef Daniel Maggipinto's own *nonna* (grandmother), the café serves rustic Italian fare. Appetizers include salads and bruschetta, and entrées include the divine Lasagne Nonna, made with butternut squash, ricotta cheese, spinach, and sage. The service at Caffe Nonna is friendly and attentive, and the atmosphere is cozy, but the space is small. Call ahead for a table.

Located just west of the Kroger grocery store, **K&S World Market** (5861 Charlotte Pike, 615/353-8681, 8:30am-8pm daily), the second in a chain whose original location is on Nolensville Pike, will keep any foodie happy for hours with its obscure and unusual food items. In the same shopping center you'll find Nashvillians' favorite Vietnamese restaurants, **Kien Giang** (5825 Charlotte Pike, 615/353-1250, 11am-9pm Tues.-Sun., $6-12) and **Miss Saigon** (5849 Charlotte Pike,

615/354-1351, http://misssaigontn.com, 10am-9pm Wed.-Mon., $7-12).

Diners and Coffee Shops

There's a lot of hype surrounding Nashville's favorite breakfast restaurant, the **Pancake Pantry** (1796 21st Ave. S., 615/383-9333, www.thepancakepantry.com, 6am-3pm Mon.-Fri., 6am-4pm Sat.-Sun., $6-14). Founded in 1961, the Pantry serves some of the most popular pancakes in the city. Owners say that the secret is in the ingredients, which are fresh and homemade. Many of the flours come from Tennessee, and the syrup is made right at the restaurant. The menu offers no fewer than 21 varieties, and that doesn't include the waffles. On weekend mornings and many weekdays, the line for a seat at the Pantry goes out the door.

In today's retro-happy world, it isn't too hard to find an old-fashioned soda shop. But how many of them are the real thing? **Elliston Place Soda Shop** (2111 Elliston Pl., 615/327-1090, www.ellistonplacesodashop.com, 7am-8pm Mon.-Thurs., 7am-10pm Fri.-Sat., $5-11), near Centennial Park and Vanderbilt, is one of those rare holdovers from the past, and it's proud of it. The black-and-white tile floors, lunch counter, and Purity Milk advertisements may have been here for decades, but the food is consistently fresh and good. Choose between a sandwich or a plate lunch, but be sure to save room for a classic milkshake or slice of hot pie with ice cream on top.

Nashville's original coffee shop, **Bongo Java** (2007 Belmont Blvd., 615/385-5282, www.bongojava.com, 7am-8pm daily, $3-9) is just as popular as ever. Located near Belmont University, Bongo is regularly full of students chatting, texting, and surfing the Internet, thanks to free wireless Internet. Set in an old house with a huge front porch, Bongo feels

Top to bottom: Fido; Hattie B's Hot Chicken; Plaza Mariachi homey and welcoming, and a bit more on the hippie side than other Nashville coffee shops. Expect the latest in coffee drinks, premium salads, and sandwiches. Breakfast, including Bongo French toast, is served all day.

Bongo Java's big brother, **Fido** (1812 21st Ave. S., 615/777-3436, www.bongojava.com/fido-cafe, 7am-11pm daily, $5-13) is more than a coffee shop. It is a place to get work done, watch deals being made, and see and be seen. Take a seat along the front plate-glass windows to watch the pretty people as they stroll by. In addition to coffee, sandwiches, and salads, baked goods are on the menu.

Said to have the best burger in Nashville, **Rotier's** (2413 Elliston Pl., 615/327-9892, www.rotiersrestaurant.com, 11am-3:30 pm Mon.-Sat., $7-16) is also a respected meat-and-three diner. Choose from classic sandwiches or comfort-food dinners. The Saturday breakfast will fuel you all day long. Ask about the milkshake, a city favorite that appears nowhere on the menu. Don't miss the hash brown casserole.

East Nashville

Contemporary

★ **Butcher & Bee** (902 Main St., 615/226-3322, http://butcherandbee.com, 11am-2pm and 5pm-10pm Mon.-Thurs., 11am-2pm and 5pm-11pm Fri., 10am-2pm and 5pm-11pm Sat., 10am-2pm and 5pm-10pm Sun., $14-20) serves Israeli-influenced tapas—the whipped feta is joy in a bowl—in an ambience that is hip but not intimidating. At the end of the night your check will be delivered inside of a book.

On a small side street, **The Treehouse** (1011 Clearview Ave., 615/454-4201, http://treehousenashville.com, 5pm-11pm Mon.-Wed., 5pm-1am Thurs.-Sat., $12-29) was named after the actual treehouse on the property when it was owned by fiddle player Buddy Spicher. Locals love to dine outside, where it does feel like you are eating in a treehouse, albeit one with good service and solid, seasonal dishes and great cocktails.

With a full wood-fired hearth (and stacks of wood to burn out front), **Pelican & Pig** (1010 Gallatin Ave., 615/730-6887, www.pelicanandpig.com, 5pm-10pm Tues.-Sun., $14-35), fires up seasonal American specialties, accompanied by fresh-baked sourdough (finished in that same hearth). Vegetable dishes are savory and flavorful enough to stand alone as main dishes. Don't skip dessert. The talented chef couple also owns **Slow Hand Coffee + Bakeshop** (1012 Gallatin Ave., 7am-4:30pm Mon.-Sat., 7am-3pm Sun.) next door and know their way around a baked good.

International

Mas Tacos Por Favor (732 McFerrin Ave., 615/543-6271, 11am-9pm Mon.-Fri., 10am-9pm Sat. $10-14) began as a beloved food truck, but this brick-and-mortar restaurant with full bar has surpassed it in popularity. The menu—featuring its tasty tacos, soups, and other Mexican delights—is bigger than seems possible given the tiny kitchen, and specials change throughout the week. Order at the window; there's almost always a line, but it moves quickly. The patio provides great East Nashville people-watching.

Diners and Coffee Shops

To call **Barista Parlor** (519B Gallatin Ave., 615/712-9766, www.baristaparlor.com, 7am-6pm daily, $8-16) a coffee shop is an understatement. It's more an art gallery where the coffee is the work of art. Housed in a renovated auto shop, this is a big, well-designed space with signage made by local artists, uniforms crafted by local designers, interesting furniture, and attentive servers. They take coffee seriously and are happy to answer your questions about their pour-over style and different blends. Be patient as your caffeine fix is prepared.

When Julia Jaksic moved from New York to Nashville, she wanted to open what she thought the city was missing: an all-day café. Turns out, the city was missing it, and now you may need to wait for a table. **Café Roze** (1115 Porter Rd., 615/645-9100, www.caferoze.com, 8am-10pm daily, $12-22) serves thoughtfully created food made fresh to order, with menu items like a vegetable bowl, a creative salad, and an egg dish. It also has a full bar and an Instagrammable interior. The café is popular with the population of makers and musicians who work offbeat hours.

The Bongo East coffee shop transforms in the afternoons and evenings into **Game Point Café** (107 S. 11th St., http://gamepointcafe.com, 615/777-3278, noon-10pm Sun.-Thurs., noon-11pm Fri.-Sat., $5-10 food, $10 pp minimum suggested for game playing), a fun community center. Choose from one of more than 300 board games in the restaurant's library, each categorized by type of game, number of required players, and ease of play. A game concierge helps you select the right game for your group, learn the rules, and settle disputes. The space attracts a wide variety of guests, locals and tourists alike, from families with kids to bachelorette parties.

South Nashville

Southern

Nashville's most sublime food experience is not to be found in a fine restaurant or even at a standard meat-and-three cafeteria. The food that you'll still be dreaming about when you get home is found at ★ **Prince's Hot Chicken Shack** (5814 Nolensville Pike, 615/801-9388, http://princeshotchicken.com, 11am-10pm Mon.-Thurs., 11am-midnight Fri., 11:30am-midnight Sat., $6-26). There is lots of hot chicken in Nashville, but Prince's invented it. It comes in three varieties: mild, hot, and extra hot. Most will find the mild variety plenty spicy, so beware. Your food is made to order, and Prince's is very popular, so the wait often exceeds 30 minutes. Take heart, though—Prince's chicken is worth the wait.

Contemporary

★ **Bastion** (434 Houston St., 615/490-8434, www.bastionnashville.com, 5:30pm-9:30pm Wed.-Sat., bar 5pm-2am Tues.-Sat., à la carte menu $9-19) is one of the best restaurants in town, helmed by James Beard award-nominated chef Josh Habiger. Bastion has just 24 seats—the idea being that you can have an up-close-and-personal experience with the staff as they work. Bastion offers an à la carte menu that they recommend combining into a five-course meal. Reservations, which include an advance ticket/deposit, are essential. The restaurant can't accommodate groups of more than six people.

International

Nolensville Pike is a mecca for international food. Mexican marketplace ★ **Plaza Mariachi** (3955 Nolensville Pike, 615/373-9292, www.plazamariachi.com, 11am-9pm Tues.-Wed., 11am-1am Thurs.-Fri., 11am-2am Sat., 11am-9pm Sun.) features a number of restaurants mixed in with grocery stores, clothes shops, and other services. Dining highlights include Argentinean steak house Tres Gauchos, sweets shop Ninas Nieves De Garrafa, and walk-up ceviche bar El Ceviche Loco. During the day there's often live music, and at night you can take free salsa lessons. The atmosphere can feel a little like being on a cruise ship—lots of flashing lights and faux scenic backdrops—but the food is fun, affordable, and festive. Also on Nolensville Pike is **Dunya Kabob** (2521 Nolensville Pike, 615/242-6664, 11am-9pm daily, $5-11). Nashville has a large Kurdish immigrant population, and this is the place to try the cuisine. It serves specialties of chicken, lamb, beef and seafood kabobs as well as gyro sandwiches.

Not far from Nolensville, you'll find another international favorite in a shopping center. **Back to Cuba** (4683

Trousdale Dr., 615/837-6711, 11am-9pm Tues.-Sat., $8-12) serves traditional Cuban favorites: Grilled sandwiches of pork, ham, cheese, and pickle are a popular choice at lunchtime. For dinner, try the roast pork or grilled shrimp, and don't skip the lacy fried plantains and spicy black beans.

Greater Nashville

Southern

The ★ **Loveless Cafe** (8400 TN-100, 615/646-9700, www.lovelesscafe.com, 7am-9pm daily, $7-17) is an institution, and some may argue it's a state of mind. The Loveless got its start in 1951, when Lon and Annie Loveless started to serve good country cooking. Over the years the restaurant changed hands, but Annie's biscuit recipe remained the same, and it was the biscuits that kept Nashvillians coming back for more. The biscuits are fluffy and buttery, the ham salty, and the eggs, bacon, and sausage will hit the spot. The supper and lunch menu includes Southern standards like fried catfish and chicken, pit-cooked pork barbecue, pork chops, and meat loaf, as well as a few salads. Loveless is about 20 miles from downtown Nashville; plan on a 30-minute drive along TN-100. It's the last place you'll pass before getting on the Natchez Trace Parkway.

Accommodations

Nashville houses some 35,000 hotel rooms, with another 11,000 in the works. That's because a lot of people want to come to Music City. Accommodations range from historic downtown hotels to standard motels, many of which have Music City touches, from recorded wake-up calls from country stars to guitar-shaped swimming pools.

Downtown and The Gulch have the most appealing and convenient hotels. More budget-friendly options are found in midtown and Music Valley.

Downtown and Germantown

$150-200

Located across Broadway from the Frist Art Museum, **Holiday Inn Express Nashville-Downtown** (920 Broadway, 615/244-0150, www.ihg.com, $145-270) offers a comfortable compromise between value and location. It has an on-site fitness room, free wireless Internet, a business center, and a guest laundry. Guest rooms have desks, coffeemakers, and two telephones. Suites (from $157) have refrigerators and microwave ovens. All guests enjoy free continental breakfast. On-site parking is available for $30 a day. The Holiday Inn is about five blocks from lower Broadway.

Downtown has lots of new hotels that were born out of old, renovated buildings. But **The Fairlane** (401 Union St., 615/988-8511, www.fairlanehotel.com, $159-497) is different for its retro 1970s feel. The old bank building features mid-century furnishings and one-of-a-kind furniture. Beds have cup holders in the headboards and service is impeccable. There's an on-site coffee shop and two restaurants, one of which has an outdoor patio. The gym—called "Jim"—features Peloton bikes.

Over $200

Strategic Hospitality, the local company that runs some of the city's best restaurants (Pinewood, page 89, and The Catbird Seat, page 91, to name two), opened ★ **Downtown Sporting Club** (411 Broadway, 615/271-4395, www.downtownsportingclub.com, $225-270), a hybrid hotel concept, in 2019. Hotel rooms are on the third floor of the Broadway building, with axe throwing, a rooftop bar, a coffee shop, and more entertainment above and below. It may seem crazy to try to sleep in the center of all the Broadway action, but thanks to floor-to-ceiling windows using special sound-proofing glass panes, white noise machines, and ear plugs, it is possible. Forgot something? A vending machine is stocked with toiletries, snacks, phone chargers, and hair ties—sold at drugstore prices.

Nashville's creative class has come together to create the 220-room **Noelle** (200 4th Ave. N., 615/649-5000, http://noelle-nashville.com, $249-649). The luxury hotel is situated in the former Noel Place building, which dates to 1930. Artwork adorning the rooms and public spaces is care of Bryce McCloud of Isle of Printing, and he also runs a print shop/art gallery on the hotel's ground floor. There's a rooftop deck for hotel guests. **Makeready Libations & Liberation, The Trade Room** lobby bar, and **Hidden Bar** are open to the public. Also check out **Drug Store Coffee,** operated by Andy Mumma of Barista Parlor, and fashionable **Keep Shop,** run by a local creative consultant.

Holston House (118 7th Ave., N., 615/392-1234, http://holstonhousenashville.hyatt.com, $169-569) is an art deco beauty with a boutique hotel feel. Decor includes some Nashville touches without falling into country music kitsch, and the breakfast and lunch counter is a throwback to a different time. But as part of the Hyatt chain, it also has major hotel amenities. The absurdly generous number of electrical outlets in the lobby means you can work as long as you need without your laptop losing juice, and the rooftop pool is perfect for when you need a break.

One of Nashville's most notable downtown hotels is ★ **Union Station** (1001 Broadway, 615/726-1001, www.unionstationhotelnashville.com, $191-280), a 125-room hotel located in what was once the city's main train station. High ceilings, lofty interior balconies, magnificent iron work and molding, and an impressive marble-floored great hall that greets guests make this one of Nashville's great old buildings, which was renovated in 2016. Union Station is a refined hotel, with amenities like free turndown service, a fun fitness center, Wi-Fi, and room service. Because the hotel is in an old train station, rooms vary depending on what their former use was. Some have cathedral ceilings, stylish furnishings, and a subtle art deco touch; others are updated and modern, but small.

The all-suite **Hilton Nashville Downtown** (121 4th Ave. S., 615/620-1000, www.hilton.com, $174-404) is next door to the Country Music Hall of Fame, Broadway's honky-tonks, and the home of the Nashville Symphony. All of the hotel's 330 suites have two distinct rooms—a living room with sofa, cable television, microwave oven, refrigerator, and coffeemaker, and a bedroom with one or two beds. The rooms are appointed with modern, stylish furniture and amenities. An indoor pool, workout room, valet parking, and two restaurants round out the hotel's amenities.

The last of a dying breed of hotels, the ★ **Hermitage Hotel** (231 6th Ave., 615/244-3121, www.thehermitagehotel.com, $300-800) has been the first choice for travelers to downtown Nashville for more than 100 years. The 123-room hotel was commissioned by prominent Nashville citizens and opened for business in 1910, quickly becoming the favorite gathering place for the city's elite. Prominent figures including Al Capone, Gene Autry, seven U.S. presidents, and modern country stars have stayed at the Hermitage. Guests enjoy top-of-the-line amenities, including 24-hour room service, pet walking, and valet parking. Rooms are furnished in an opulent style befitting a luxury urban hotel and have refreshment centers, marble baths, and high-speed wireless Internet access. Many rooms have lovely views of the capitol building and city. Check for last-minute specials on its website, when rates will dip to $200. You can choose to have $2 from your room rate contributed to the Land Trust for Tennessee.

The Omni Nashville Hotel (250 5th Ave. S., 615/782-5300, www.omnihotels.com, $225-545) is adjacent to the 1.2 million-square-foot Music City Convention Center. It has more than

80,000 square feet of meeting and event space, more than 800 guest rooms, and easy access to the convention center, the Hall of Fame, restaurants, and other attractions south of Broadway. Don't miss the cool displays of musicians' costumes in the hallway that connects Hatch Show Print to the hotel.

The **21c Museum Hotel** (221 2nd Ave. N., 615/610-6400, www.21cmuseumhotels.com, $199-600) has 124 rooms as well as a contemporary art museum inside. The public is welcome to tour the museum for free, while guests enjoy rooms ranging from a single king bed to suites with terraces. Perks include free Wi-Fi, free bottled water, a docking station for your phone, bathrobes, and original art in every room. The hotel also features **Gray and Dudley,** a lovely a bar and restaurant with the same caliber of art.

For those who prefer more private accommodations, **The 404 Hotel** (404 12th Ave. S., 615/242-7404, http://the404hotel.com, $199-319) is a good option. It has just five rooms and an on-site manager who provides "invisible service," making The 404 a luxury hotel for people who don't want to stay in a hotel. Rooms have sumptuous linens, work by local artists, fruit and pastries, and free Wi-Fi. It's walking distance to all of The Gulch's charms but is not a place for kids under 15 or pets. Adjacent to the hotel, in an old shipping container, is **404 Kitchen,** an award-winning 56-seat restaurant.

The **Thompson** (401 11th Ave. S., 615/262-6000, www.thompsonhotels.com, $232-441) offers Nashville a lot of things that seem at odds with one another: It is in the heart of The Gulch, but still quiet enough to sleep. It's in a modern high rise, but feels like a small, boutique hotel. Enjoy pet-friendly rooms with hardwood floors, midcentury modern-style furnishings, honor bars with local spirits, Bluetooth speakers, and rain showers. Several on-site eating and drinking options are worth visiting, including **Marsh House,** which has impeccable service and a lovely Southern menu, and the hopping **L.A. Jackson** rooftop bar, plus a coffee shop on the 1st floor.

Music Row, Midtown, and 12South

Under $100

The **Music City Hostel** (1809 Patterson St., 615/497-1208, www.musiccityhostel.com, $33-135) is among doctors' offices and commercial buildings in between downtown Nashville and Elliston Place. The low-slung '70s-style building looks like nothing much on the outside, but inside it is cheerful, welcoming, and a comfortable home base for budget travelers. Music City Hostel offers the usual dorm-style bunk-bed accommodations, as well as a handful of private apartments. You can also book a private bedroom with private bath plus shared kitchen and common room. Common areas include a large kitchen, dining room, reading room, cable TV room, computer with Internet access, and coin laundry. The entire facility is smoke-free. Parking is free, and the hostel is within walking distance of restaurants, a bus stop, a car rental agency, a post office, and hospitals. It is a hike to get downtown on foot from here.

$150-200

A bed-and-breakfast choice in this part of the city is **1501 Linden Manor B&B** (1501 Linden Ave., 615/298-2701, www.nashville-bed-breakfast.com, $195-295). This cheerful yellow-brick home on a corner lot has three guest rooms, each with stylish furniture and hardwood floors; one room has a private whirlpool, and another has a fireplace.

Over $200

The **Graduate Nashville** (101 20th Ave., 615/551-2700, www.graduatehotels.com/nashville, $199-295) has a motto: "We are all students." But this isn't a divey college hangout. With fun art, lots of lounging space, and a bar with an animatronic backup band for your karaoke needs, this is the place to stay if you want to feel connected to the campus community.

For luxurious accommodations near Vanderbilt, consider **Loews Vanderbilt Plaza** (2100 West End Ave., 615/320-1700, www.loweshotels.com, $256-532), a 340-room hotel on West End Avenue close to Centennial Park and Hillsboro Village. Loews boasts 24-hour room service; luxurious sheets, towels, and robes; natural soaps; and spacious bathrooms. Guests enjoy in-room tea kettles and top-of-the-line coffee, evening turndown service, and free high-speed Internet access. Many rooms have views of the Nashville skyline. Premium rooms provide guests with access to the concierge lounge, continental breakfast, evening hors d'oeuvres, and a cash bar. All guests can enjoy a fine fitness room, spa, art gallery, and gift shop.

You can't get closer to Vanderbilt University than the **Marriott Nashville Vanderbilt** (2555 West End Ave., 615/321-1300, www.marriott.com, $179-279). Set on the northern end of the university campus, the Marriott has 301 guest rooms, six suites, and meeting space. It is across West End Avenue from Centennial Park, home of the Parthenon, and a few steps from Vanderbilt's football stadium. It has an indoor pool, full-service restaurant, concierge lounge, ATM, and business center.

★ **Hutton Hotel** (1808 West End Ave., 615/340-9333, www.huttonhotel.com, $229-400) is Nashville's eco-friendly darling. It emphasizes sustainability in details such as its bamboo flooring and use of biodegradable cleaning products. The swanky hotel is near the Vanderbilt campus and offers an easy commute to Music Row and downtown, but regular visitors stay here less for the great location and more for the ambience. The lobby and guest rooms are stocked

latch hook portrait of Minnie Pearl by Margaret Timbrell at the Graduate Nashville

with well-edited art collections, and the bathrooms include sleek granite showers. The pet-friendly property also has all the expected amenities, such as flat-screen TVs and Wi-Fi access. An added bonus is the likelihood of a celebrity sighting.

Rising next to the Vanderbilt campus is the 180-room **Kimpton Aertson Hotel** (2021 Broadway, 615/340-6376, www.aertsonhotel.com, $217-595). Perks include free bike rentals, an 8th-floor pool deck with cabanas, and a 17th-floor indoor/outdoor event space. Enjoy free coffee and tea in the morning in the lobby, referred to as the "living room." **Henley,** the swanky 1st-floor restaurant, is a favorite of locals (be sure to check out the cocktail list) and adjacent **Caviar & Bananas** is an excellent place to grab better-than-average takeout for a picnic. Kimpton hotels are well-known for their pet-friendliness; there's no extra charge for pet beds, mats, or water bowls in your room.

East Nashville

$100-150

You'll can that ★ **The Russell** (819 Russell St., 615/861-9535, www.russell-nashville.com, $121-175) used to be a church from its restored stained glass windows and headboards repurposed from pews. The boutique hotel has 23 rooms, and its lobby—which includes reading areas stocked with titles from The Bookshop (page 82) and a podcasting studio—is a stunner. The Russell donates a portion of each room rate to organizations supporting the city's unhoused population, such as Shower Up, a truck that provides people living on the streets opportunities for a hot shower. Note there's no elevator for humans to the 2nd floor (although there is one for luggage).

$150-200

The Big Bungalow (618 Fatherland St., 615/256-8375, www.thebigbungalow.com, $145-275), a Craftsman-style early-1900s town house, offers three guest rooms, each with its own private bath and television. Guests have shared access to a computer (no wireless Internet), microwave, and refrigerator. Common areas are comfortable and stylish, with tasteful decor and hardwood floors. This is a pet-free, nonsmoking facility; children over 10 are welcome. The bed-and-breakfast is about seven blocks from the John Seigenthaler Pedestrian Bridge, which takes you to the heart of downtown.

Vandyke Bed and Beverage (105 S. 11th S., 615/730-5023, www.vandyke-nashville.com, $249) is a liquor-themed hotel with a large open-air bar. Each of the luxury hotel's eight rooms is named after a different beverage—champagne, whiskey, wine, beer, tequila, gin, vodka, and rum—and come with decor and glassware appropriate to that drink. Some rooms have bunk beds for bachelorette parties or family groups. Two rooms on the ground floor are wheelchair-accessible; higher levels and the rooftop bar are not. While the hotel serves food and drinks in the bar, this isn't a full-service establishment. You'll be carrying your own bags and, before check-in, directed to an app to open your room door.

Music Valley

Under $100

The all-suite **Best Western Suites Near Opryland** (201 Music City Cir., 615/902-9940, www.bestwestern.com, from $112) is a comfortable compromise between the luxury of the Opryland Hotel and the affordability of a motel. Each of the hotel's 100 suites has a couch, desk, high-speed Internet access, coffee- and tea maker, microwave, ironing board, and refrigerator. Rooms with whirlpool tubs are available for about $80 more per night. Guests enjoy an on-site fitness room, 24-hour business center, outdoor pool, free continental breakfast, and weekday newspaper. The Best Western is located along a strip of motels and restaurants about one mile from the Grand Ole Opry and other Opryland attractions.

$150-200

Guests at the **Courtyard by Marriott Opryland** (125 Music City Cir., 615/882-9133, www.marriott.com, $146-194) enjoy refurbished rooms with soft beds, wireless Internet, coffeemakers, ironing boards, and refrigerators. The on-site restaurant serves breakfast, and business rooms come with a desk, dataport, voicemail, and speakerphone.

Over $200

Said to be the largest hotel without a casino in the United States, the ★ **Gaylord Opryland Resort** (2800 Opryland Dr., 615/889-1000, www.marriott.com, $199-450) is more than just a hotel. The 2,881-room luxury resort and convention center is built around a nine-acre indoor garden. Glass atriums let in sunlight, and miles of footpaths invite you to explore the climate-controlled gardens. Highlights include a 40-foot waterfall and flatboats that float along a river.

Set among the gardens are dozens of restaurants and cafés, ranging from casual buffets to elegant steakhouses. Hundreds of room balconies overlook the gardens, providing some guests with views of the well-kept greenery, even in winter. If you stay, choose between a traditional view looking outside the hotel and an atrium view.

The property has a full-service salon, spa, and fitness center; multiple swimming pools (indoor and outdoor); on-site child care and "kids' resort"; and a car rental agency. You can walk to Opry Mills mall and the Grand Ole Opry from the hotel or take the free shuttle. Guest rooms are luxurious and feature coffee- and tea makers; two telephones; wireless Internet access; pay-per-view movies, games, and music; daily national newspapers; and other usual amenities. Service is impeccable. Press the "consider it done" button on the phone in your room, and any of your needs will be met. Guests can buy onetime or daily passes on the downtown shuttle for about $20 a day, and the airport shuttle costs $30 round-trip. Self-parking is $24 a day; valet is $32 per day.

The hotel offers resort-style packages that add on other Gaylord-owned attractions and properties. These often include tickets to the Grand Ole Opry, a ride on the General Jackson Showboat, trips into Nashville to visit the Ryman Auditorium or the Wildhorse Saloon, and extras like spa visits, golf games, and access to the hotel's SoundWaves water park. Many of these packages are a good deal for travelers who want to pay one price for their whole vacation. Christmastime always brings interesting kid-friendly packages.

Airport

$150-200

★ **Hotel Preston** (733 Briley Pkwy., 615/361-5900, www.hotelpreston.com, $93-296) is a boutique hotel near the airport. Youthful energy, modern decor, and up-to-date rooms set this property apart from the crowd. The "You-Want-It-You-Got-It" button in each room beckons the 24-hour room service, and whimsical extras, including a lava lamp, pet fish, and an art kit, are available by request when you check in. Two restaurants, including the Pink Slip bar and nightclub, which features a sculpture by local artist Herb Williams, is known to both locals and hotel guests as a place with friendly barkeeps and good energy.

Information and Services

Visitors Centers

Nashville's main **visitors center** (615/259-4747, www.visitmusiccity.com/visitors, 8am-5:30pm Mon.-Sat., 10am-5pm Sun.) is at the corner of 5th Avenue and Broadway, inside the Bridgestone Arena. Here you can pick up brochures, get a free map, and find answers to just about any question. It is open late when there is an event at Bridgestone.

There is another visitors center a few blocks uptown (150 4th Ave. N., 615/259-4730, 8am-5pm Mon.-Thurs., 8am-4pm Fri.).

Emergency Services

Dial 911 for police, fire, or ambulance in an emergency. For help with a traffic accident, call the **Tennessee Highway Patrol** (800/736-0212).

Because health care is such a big industry in Nashville, there are a lot of hospitals. The **Monroe Carell Jr. Children's Hospital at Vanderbilt** (2200 Children's Way, 615/936-1000, www.childrenshospitalvanderbilt.org) is among the best in the country. **Saint Thomas Midtown Hospital** (2000 Church St., 615/284-5555, www.sthealth.com) and **Saint Thomas West** (4220 Harding Pl., 615/222-2111, www.sthealth.com) are other major players.

Rite Aid, CVS, Walgreens, and the major grocery store chains have drugstores all over Nashville. Try the **CVS** at 426 21st Avenue South (615/321-2590, www.cvs.com) if you need 24-hour service. Many drugstores have urgent care clinics inside.

The Trace:
Tennessee

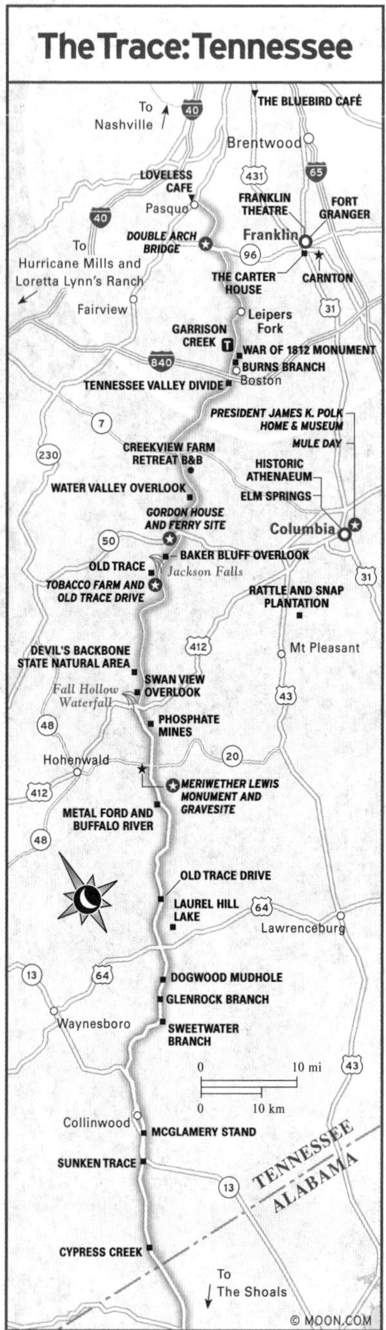

The hills roll and the road winds. The sun rises over wildflower meadows and peeks through lush green tree canopies. You've just left Nashville, but it already seems worlds away.

The Tennessee section of the parkway isn't the best known—Mississippi holds that honor. But it reliably immerses you into the scenic wonderland that is the Trace. As soon as you hop on at the northern terminus, just 17 miles southwest of downtown Music City, you're transported into a lush forest. No matter the time of year, you'll witness nature's bounty, be it colorful leaf changing in the fall (September and October) or riotous flower blooms in the spring (April and May). This may be the only stretch of the Trace where you can experience truly cold temperatures in the winter. You may even get relief from the southern summer heat and humidity under the shade of these trees.

The idea of a road trip like one down the Natchez Trace is that the journey is the destination. Unlike a drive *to* a national park, in this case, the drive *is* the national park. On your leisurely 131-mile drive you'll pass through green, green grasses, historic landmarks and Native American monuments, campgrounds, waterfalls, hiking trails, and the best bridge on the entire Trace. One of the Trace's most solemn monuments, the gravesite of Meriwether Lewis, is found on this stretch, as well as numerous opportunities for hikes and picnics.

Quick detours and side trips off of the Natchez Trace in Tennessee offer access to Civil War and presidential history, good food, and great live music (we're close to Music City, U.S.A., after all).

Highlights

★ **Double Arch Bridge:** This arched bridge is an iconic feat of engineering and the ultimate selfie stop (page 108).

★ **Mule Day:** Celebrate the work animals that were essential to farmers and the area's growth at this four-day festival (page 126).

★ **Meriwether Lewis Monument and Gravesite:** The famous explorer's gravesite is both somber and scenic (page 134).

★ **President James K. Polk Home & Museum:** James Polk's ancestral home gives insight into the 11th president (page 124).

★ **Tobacco Farm and Old Trace Drive:** Learn about the crop that once covered these hills and take a drive on the Old Trace (page 132).

Best Restaurants

★ **Merridee's Breadbasket:** Its founder may have grown up in Minnesota, but this restaurant has become synonymous with Southern cooking (page 117).

★ **Red Pony Restaurant:** Innovative Southern food is served in a cosmopolitan setting (page 118).

★ **Puckett's Grocery & Restaurant:** Legendary Southern eats, great live music, and perfect people-watching pack 'em into Puckett's (page 120).

★ **Muletown Roasted Coffee:** Head here for a cup of locally roasted goodness (page 127).

You're likely to meet strangers who will become friends, many with good yarns to tell and recommendations for great roadside barbecue.

Route Overview

This section of the Trace, southwest of Nashville through to the Alabama border, covers **131 miles.** There are more than 25 interesting overlooks, historical markers, and sites to see on this stretch of the Trace alone. This stretch could easily take **two days,** without leaving the Trace itself, and it's a great excuse to **camp overnight** at the Meriwether Lewis Monument and Gravesite Campground.

Side trips into Franklin, Leiper's Fork (a favorite home of Nashville celebrities), and Columbia could add another two days to your itinerary. If you want to camp, hike more, and enjoy the great outdoors, you won't be bored if you add another day or two to your trip.

Driving Considerations

This northern section of the Natchez Trace could be waylaid by snow and ice in the winter. Even light snowfall here is rare enough that roads aren't often salted or plowed. Drive with caution if you happen to be on the Trace during or after a snowfall.

Fuel and Services

This section of the Trace is the least remote, running near suburban **Franklin** and **Leiper's Fork** as well as **Columbia,** all towns with a plethora of amenities, including places to sleep, eat, gas up, and play. The proximity to these towns also means that you're likely to be near a cell tower for some of your drive, although cell service should never be taken for granted anywhere on the Trace.

Many people like to have their last meal before hitting the road at the famous **Loveless Cafe** in Nashville, which is less than a mile from the terminus of the Natchez Trace. Grab some of their famous biscuits, take a photo of the iconic sign, and then get gas at the adjacent Shell station on TN-100 and McCrory Lane. Attached to the station is the delicious **Bar-B-Cutie** restaurant, if that's more your taste.

Just north of McGlamery Stand (milepost 352.9) is the town of **Collinwood,** a good place to stop and get gas. Once you're there, drive two blocks west to the **Wayne County Welcome Center** (219 E. Broadway, 931/724-4337, 9am-5pm daily) for parkway maps and information about attractions in the area.

Getting to the Starting Point

Start at the very beginning. Or, as the Trace mile markers say, at the very end: **Milepost 444** is just 17 miles southwest of downtown Nashville. Get here by turning south onto the Trace from TN-100. The entry onto the Trace is well-marked with National Park signage. The first sight, the

Best Accommodations

★ **Creekview Farm Retreat B&B:** Spend the night on a working farm (page 123).

★ **The Inn at Bigby Creek:** This former home of a Columbia mayor makes for swanky lodging on 1.5 pretty acres (page 128).

★ **Meriwether Lewis Monument and Gravesite Campground:** It may sound creepy to set up your tent near a gravesite, but this solemn spot is full of history and great vistas (page 135).

★ **Fall Hollow B&B and Campground:** This is a perfect spot for groups that can't decide between camping and glamping (page 137).

Double Arch Bridge, is at milepost 438, just six miles from the starting point.

Car, Motorcycle, or Bicycle

If you're not bringing your own car, motorcycle, or bicycle for this epic road trip, you can rent one in Nashville, a major city with many options. Nashville International Airport (BNA) is on the opposite side of town from the Natchez Trace, about a 28-mile drive. If you are flying into town to start your road trip, the airport is as good a place as any to pick up a rental car. Most of the major car rental companies, including **Avis** (300 N. 1st St., 615/743-4740, www.avis.com), **Enterprise** (1700 8th Ave. S., 615/254-6181, or 1 Terminal Dr., 833/898-21498, http://enterprise.com), and **Budget** (1803 Church St., 615/366-0806, http://budget.com), have desks at the airport, and rates are often competitive. There are also car rental offices downtown and at many of the major hotels.

The siren song of the open road is loud on the Natchez Trace, and many choose to answer it from a motorcycle. If you don't have your own, rent from **EagleRider Nashville** (401 Fesslers Ln., 615/850-7993, http://eaglerider.com, 9am-5:30pm Mon.-Sat.), which, despite its name, is in Murfreesboro, about 50 miles from the northern Trace terminus. **Sloan's Motorcycle and ATV Supercenter** (2233 NW Broad St., Murfreesboro, 615/225-6057, 9am-6pm Mon.-Fri., 8:30am-4pm Sat.) and **Moonshine Harley-Davidson** (7128 S. Springs Dr., Franklin, 615/274-4158, www.moonshineharley.com, 10am-7pm Mon.-Fri., 9am-6pm Sat., 11am-5pm Sun.) are other options.

If you prefer your two wheels nonmotorized, stop at **Trace Bikes** on TN-100 (8080-B TN-100, 615/646-2485, http://tracebikes.com, 10am-6pm Mon.-Fri., 10am-5pm Sat., noon-4pm Sun.) for rentals and helpful gear for touring this road on bike power. Trace Bikes is not open on Sunday.

Air

As Nashville has grown and become more of a tourist destination, **Nashville International Airport** (BNA, http://flynashville.com) has grown, too. In 2019, it saw more than 18.3 million travelers through its gates and announced significant expansion plans. The airport is easy to navigate and is the best bet for flying into Music City. BNA offers email updates that tell travelers when to expect congestion, so they can plan accordingly.

The airport is filled with local art and restaurants, live music, and comfortable waiting areas for those picking up passengers. There's even a health clinic for routine medical care. Most of the major airlines serve BNA, including Delta,

Fuel Up

The noncommercial aspect of the Natchez Trace can also be its downfall. No billboards! No businesses! No bright lights! No gas stations.

Don't let an empty tank stop your road trip. Here's a quick list of places to exit the parkway in Tennessee so that you can refuel at the closest gas station. (Some stops may take you to small towns, others will be just a single service station.) The National Park Service also posts a list of nearby supply stations at most Trace rest areas, although the list is not updated regularly.

- **Milepost 444:** Exit at TN-100, just east of the northern terminus.
- **Milepost 438:** Exit at TN-96; drive seven miles west.
- **Milepost 429:** Exit at TN-46; drive one mile east toward Leiper's Fork.
- **Milepost 391.1:** Exit at US 412; drive seven miles west.
- **Milepost 385.9:** Exit at TN-20; drive six miles west to Hohenwald, which has many options.
- **Milepost 369.9:** Exit at US 64; drive less than 0.75 mile west.
- **Milepost 354.9:** Exit at TN-13; drive less than 0.5 mile east to Collinwood.

United, Southwest, Frontier, American, JetBlue, Alaska, and AirCanada.

Exchange currency at **SunTrust Bank** near A/B concourse or at the **Business Service Center** (Wright Travel, 615/275-2660) near C/D concourse.

Many of the major hotels offer shuttles from the airport; there's a kiosk on the lower level of the terminal to help you find the right one. BNA was the first airport in the United States to include "transportation network companies" such as Lyft and Uber in their plans. There is a designated ride sharing area on the ground floor where hotel shuttles wait.

Train and Bus

Amtrak does not have service to Nashville. **Greyhound** (709 5th Ave. S., 615/255-3556, www.greyhound.com) fully serves Music City, with daily routes that crisscross the state in nearly every direction. In 2012 the city opened a LEED-certified depot, about 20 miles from the terminus of the Natchez Trace. The environmentally friendly building has parking for passenger pickup, a restaurant, a vending area, and ample space for buses. Service goes to major cities in most directions, including Atlanta, Chattanooga, Memphis, and Louisville.

Budget-friendly **Megabus** (http://us.megabus.com) also leaves from the same station. Megabus boasts free Wi-Fi on board and, perhaps because of that, attracts a younger clientele.

★ Double Arch Bridge (MP 438)

Just six miles into the drive on the Natchez Trace, you come to milepost 438. Nothing like starting off a trip with one of the highlights. This bridge is a feat of engineering and design.

At its most utilitarian, the bridge allows the two-lane Natchez Trace to span TN-96, which takes you off the Trace and into charming Franklin. But this bridge is much more than merely practical and, as

A Day on the Trace: Tennessee

For a great day on Tennessee's Trace, fuel up in suburban Franklin at **Puckett's Grocery and Restaurant.** Stroll these quaint downtown streets, window shopping and taking in the restored **Franklin Theatre**.

Now it's time to fuel up the car and enter the parkway at TN-96, right at the base of the breathtaking **Double Arch Bridge.** Not only is this a feat of engineering, but its scale and beauty help frame the scenery you are about to see on your drive.

Lace up the hiking boots for a walk along the **Highland Rim Trail** section of the Natchez Trace National Scenic Trail. This 24-mile path has many entrance points, so you can modify the hike for as short or long a distance as you like. **Burns Branch** is a good place for a quick less-than-two-mile walk to stretch your legs and take in the flora and fauna, but still leave time for more exploring down the parkway. Next head to the **Gordon House and Ferry Site,** one of only two remaining structures on the Trace. Think about what this rest area would have meant to early settlers and take an easy walk to the ferry site on the Duck River and back to the parking lot.

History continues on your side trip to Columbia, where you can get gas, eat, and tour the **President James K. Polk Home & Museum,** residence of the 11th president of the United States. See the work of local artists and each lunch at **CAB Cafe.** If you'd rather grab picnic supplies for dining on the Trace, stop at **Bypass Deli** before the 20-minute drive back to the parkway. Continue to admire the road's vistas and historical monuments before pulling into the parking lot at **Fall Hollow Waterfall** (milepost 391.9). Walk to the bottom (take a hiking pole) to gaze at nature and reflect on everything you've seen.

It's a quick six-mile drive to **Meriwether Lewis Monument and Gravesite,** the last stop of the day. Find a site at the campground for the night and then enjoy the trails and the monument. For a complete list of every stop along the Trace, download the detailed National Park Service maps (www.nps.gov/natr).

Get up early the next day to finish this section of the route (about 50 miles) before crossing into Alabama.

a result, is one of the most-photographed stops on the Trace. Built in 1994, it was the first bridge in the country built from segments of concrete (in the end there were 122 arch segments). The arches aren't symmetrical, and instead flow with the rolling hills of the countryside.

There are two places to stop and take it all in. The first is the northern pull-off just before the bridge on the right side of the road, called **Birdsong Hollow** (milepost 438), about 155 feet above the valley. You can park in this small lot and walk just a few steps to see the bridge from above, and even walk along the bridge itself, but you can't stop your car on the bridge. In the thick of summer, some of the view may be obstructed by foliage. There are no amenities other than parking and epic views.

Tragically, the Double Arch Bridge is one of several bridges on the parkway that have become spots where people have attempted and committed suicide. There are several initiatives underway, with celebrity support from country singer Wynonna Judd and former senator (and medical doctor) Bill Frist, to create barriers to make jumping from the 155-foot-tall bridge more difficult. There is signage to address this along the bridge; don't hesitate to call 911 if you see someone who needs help. If you need help, call the **National Suicide Prevention Lifeline** (800/273-8255).

The best view of the bridge itself is from the second pull-off. From the parkway, cross the bridge and follow the sign for the exit to TN-96. Turn left off the Trace. The road swoops back toward the bridge and takes you to a **pull-off** with several parking spaces and a view that takes in the scope of the bridge. Afterward, return to the parkway from the way you came.

TN-96 to Franklin

For much of its life, Franklin was just another small town in Tennessee. The bloody Battle of Franklin that took place in the fields surrounding the town on November 30, 1864, was probably the single most important event to take place there. Like other towns in the region, it took many years for Franklin to fully recover from the impact of the Civil War.

Starting in the 1960s, Franklin underwent a metamorphosis. Construction of I-65 near the town spurred economic development. Today, Franklin is a well-heeled bedroom community for Nashville professionals and music industry bigwigs. The city, whose population runs around 81,000, is the seventh largest in Tennessee and one of the wealthiest in the state. What sets Franklin apart from other towns in the state is the effort it has made to preserve and protect the historic downtown. Its location, only 20 miles from Nashville and just a quick, straight drive along TN-96 from the Double Arch Bridge, is also a major plus.

Franklin's attractions are all within a few miles of the city center.

The city of Franklin is currently making efforts to better depict the ugly side of its military history. The Fuller Story Project (https://visitfranklin.com/fuller-story-project) is part of an effort to erect five markers around downtown that tell the story of enslaved Black Americans, reconstruction, the riot of 1867, and more. A bronze statue of a U.S. Colored Troop is being built outside the courthouse. These efforts have been opposed by the Daughters of the Confederacy (www.franklintn.gov/our-city/the-fuller-story).

Leaving the Trace

The drive to Franklin from the Double Arch Bridge is about 10 miles and takes about 15 minutes. Cross the bridge, then turn left at the first intersection. After 0.5 mile on this frontage road, make a right onto TN-96 East. Continue for just under 10 miles to reach Franklin.

This is a good place to stop for gas. There's a BP station at the southwest corner of TN-96 and Downs Boulevard. Thanks to the landscaping, it can be hard to see from the road, but it's there.

Getting Around

Traffic can be heavy in and around Franklin. Because it's a bedroom community for commuters working in Nashville, the morning and afternoon rush hours are to be avoided.

Franklin offers a **trolley bus service** (http://tmagroup.org/franklin-transit, 6:30am-6pm Mon.-Fri., 8:30am-6pm Sat., adults $1, children $0.50) in town and to outlying areas. The trolleys run three different routes. Kids small enough to sit in your lap ride free. You can pick up a full schedule and route map from the visitors center or download it from the website for the TMA Group (http://tmagroup.org).

Sights

Franklin Theatre

A neon-lit gem in historic downtown Franklin is the **Franklin Theatre** (419 Main St., 615/538-2076, www.franklin-theatre.com, box office noon-5pm Sun.-Mon., 11am-6pm Tues.-Sat.), a 1937 movie theater that had seen better days when it finally closed in 2007. In 2011, it reopened after an $8 million restoration, funded primarily by donations from locals through the efforts of the Heritage Foundation. The renovation is spot on, bringing the theater, including its striking outdoor marquee, back to its former glory. Lush carpeting, detailed wallpaper, comfortable seats—everything

Franklin

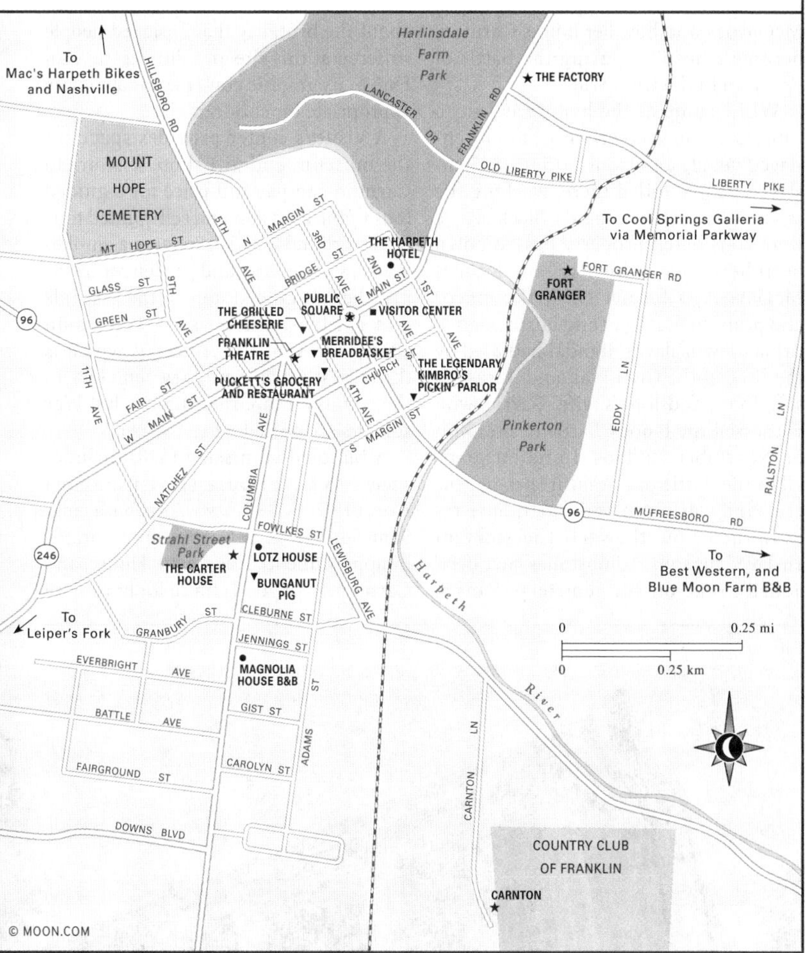

about the theater evokes moviegoing in a different era.

But the Franklin Theatre isn't stuck in the past. Many modern amenities make it a great place to have a night out, such as a concession stand that serves beer, wine, and spirits, with a menu that delineates Jack Daniel's from bourbon and whiskey. The Franklin Theatre hosts live concerts as well as films, ranging from black-and-white classics to recent releases. Because so many celebrities live in and near Franklin, the concert lineup tends to be all-star.

Carnton

When Robert Hicks's novel *The Widow of the South* became a best seller in 2005, the staff at the former plantation known as **Carnton** (1345 Carnton Ln., 615/794-0903, http://boft.org, 9am-5pm Mon.-Sat., noon-5pm Sun., adults $18, children

6-15 $8, free for children under 5) noticed an uptick in the number of visitors. The novel is a fictionalized account of Carrie McGavock and how her home, Carnton, became a hospital during the Battle of Franklin in the Civil War.

While some of the history is lost to time, Carnton was certainly built by enslaved people and from 1815 to 1865 enslaved people toiled there, working the sawmill and in the orchards. Black people were considered property passed down by inheritance, which is how Randal McGavock, a former Nashville mayor and prominent lawyer and businessman, came to own slaves. Randal had died by the time of the Civil War, and it was his son, John, and John's wife, Carrie, who witnessed the bloody Battle of Franklin on November 30, 1864. In recent years, all of the Battle of Franklin sites in general, and Carton in particular, have reexamined how they tell the story of enslaved persons. Tombstones have been added to the on-site cemetery to mark the graves of the enslaved who are buried there. The Slavery and Enslaved Tour at Carnton & Carter House goes into detail about the brutality that enslaved people suffered at this site and during the war. Due to its graphic content, it may not be appropriate for children.

A visitors center provides space for the museum and gift shop. Visitors to Carnton can pay full price for a guided tour of the mansion and self-guided tour of the grounds, which include a smokehouse, slave house, and garden, or $5 for just the self-guided tour of the grounds and gardens. There is no admission charged to visit the cemetery, which is the largest private military cemetery in the country. More than 1,500 Civil War soldiers are buried here.

A bundled admission ($30) includes access to **Lotz House** (1111 Columbia Ave., 615/790-7190, www.lotzhouse.com, 9am-5pm Mon.-Sat., 1pm-4pm Sun. or by appointment), The Carter House, and Carnton. It's a good choice for hard-core

Carnton

history buffs but perhaps too much Civil War lore for one day for the average visitor.

Fort Granger

An unsung attraction, **Fort Granger** (113 Fort Granger Dr., 615/794-2103, www.franklin.gov, dawn-dusk daily, free) is a lovely and interesting place to spend an hour or so. Built between 1862 and 1863 by Union forces, the earthen fort occupies 14.5 acres on a bluff overlooking the Harpeth River just south of downtown Franklin. The fort, built by Capt. W. E. Merrill during the Federal occupation of Franklin, was the largest fortification in the area. It saw action twice in 1863 and also in 1864 during the Battle of Franklin.

Many features of the fort remain intact for visitors. You can walk around portions of the breastworks. The interior of the fort is now a grassy field, perfect for a summer picnic or game of catch. An overlook at one end of the fort provides an unmatched view of the surrounding countryside.

You can reach Fort Granger two ways. One is along a short but steep trail departing Pinkerton Park on Murfreesboro Road, east of town. Or you can drive straight to the fort by heading out of town on East Main Street. Turn right onto Liberty Pike, right onto Eddy Lane, and, finally, right again onto Fort Granger Drive.

The Carter House

Some of the fiercest fighting in the Battle of Franklin took place around the farm and house belonging to the Carter family on the outskirts of town. The family took refuge in the basement while Union and Confederate soldiers fought hand to hand right above them. Today, **The Carter House** (1140 Columbia Ave., 615/791-1861, www.boft.org, 9am-5pm Mon.-Sat., 11am-5pm Sun., adults $18, children $8) is the best place to come for a detailed examination of the battle and the profound human toll that it exacted on both sides.

You will see hundreds of bullet holes, which help to illustrate the ferocity of the fight. Guides describe some of the worst moments of the battle and bring to life a few of the people who fought it. The house also holds a museum of Civil War uniforms and memorabilia, including photographs and short biographies of many of the men who were killed in Franklin. A video about the battle shows scenes from a reenactment.

If you can't get enough Civil War history, consider one of the packages that offer discounts on joint admission to nearby Lotz House (www.lotzhouse.com), The Carter House, and Carnton.

Tours

Pick a topic (Civil War history, ghosts, food, crime, etc.) and **Franklin on Foot** (114 E. Main St., 615/400-3808, www.franklinonfoot.com, adults $15-49) will lead you on a walking tour that meets your needs. Most tours occur daily,

The Americana Music Triangle

The Americana Music Triangle (http://americanamusictriangle.com) is a collection of three themed driving routes linking Nashville, Memphis, and New Orleans, forming a triangle. Like the Mississippi Blues Trail, it aims to show the evolution of and connections between nine different genres of music that developed in this area—including gospel, R&B, jazz, country, and bluegrass—starting with the Paleo-Indians, who came to the Mississippi Delta in 40,000 BC. Many of the stops and sights on the trail, including those in Franklin and Leiper's Fork, are detailed in these pages, but the website also lists upcoming music events and is worth checking out.

but book ahead to be sure. Want something faster? Try **Franklin Segway Tours** (615/905-6263, iridefranklin.com, $69); tours leave from Handy Hardware (731 Columbia Ave.). The 90-minute experience includes 30 minutes of training and a 60-minute guided Segway tour.

Entertainment and Events

Live Music

Founded by a songwriter, **The Legendary Kimbro's Pickin' Parlor** (214 S. Margin St., 615/567-3877, www.legendarykimbros.com, 4pm-3am daily) is a hoppin' place to hear live music. With several stages, it can host a mellow listening-room-style performance or a louder, more raucous pickin' party. Guitars hang on the wall in case you want to grab one and join in. Some nights there will be a cover; whether there is or not, don't forget to tip the band. Because so many musicians and songwriters live in Franklin and Leiper's Fork, it is not unusual to see big names perform here.

Festivals and Events

Spring

One of the city's biggest festivals of the year is the **Main Street Festival** (615/591-8500, http://williamsonheritage.org, Apr.) during the last full weekend of April. Local arts and crafts are the major draw of this showcase, which also includes food, music, theater, and children's activities. The event is hosted by the Heritage Foundation of Franklin & Williamson County.

The town's Rotary Club organizes the annual Franklin Rodeo (www.franklinrodeo.com, May), a weeklong event in May that includes a Rodeo Parade, Miss Tennessee Rodeo pageant, and a Professional Rodeo Cowboys Association (PRCA)-sanctioned rodeo with steer wrestling and bronco and bull riding. It takes place at the Williamson County Ag Expo Park (4215 Long Ln. #100, 615/595-1227), and proceeds go to local service projects.

Summer

During the first full weekend of June you can join the **Heritage Foundation on a Town and Country Tour of Homes** (http://williamsonheritage.org, June). Tours go to private and historic homes that are closed to the public during the rest of the year.

Franklin celebrates Independence Day with Franklin on the Fourth (http://visitfranklin.com, July 4), a patriotic family concert on the public square. The fireworks finale takes place near Mack Hatcher/Hillsboro Road.

During the last weekend in July the city celebrates Bluegrass Along the Harpeth (615/390-3588, www.bluegrassalongtheharpeth.com, July, free), a music festival featuring bluegrass, old-time string bands, and buck dancing.

The Williamson County Fair (www.williamsoncountyfair.org, Aug.) starts on the first Friday in August and features agricultural exhibits, a midway, live entertainment, and competitions.

It takes place at the Williamson County Ag Expo Park (4215 Long Ln. #100, 615/595-1227).

Fall

Re-enactors descend on Franklin for **Blue and Gray Days** (www.boft.org, Nov.), two days of living history, including a Civil War soldiers' camp. The events are staged at The Carter House (1140 Columbia Ave., 615/791-1861) and Carnton (1345 Eastern Flank Circle, 615/794-0903).

In just a few years the **Pilgrimage Music & Cultural Festival** (http://pilgrimagefestival.com, Sept.) has become a major player on the concert festival circuit, which is really saying something in the land of Bonnaroo. The fest, which takes place in September at The Park at Harlinsdale Farm (239 Franklin Rd., 615/794-2103), attracts acts including Grace Potter, the Foo Fighters, Hall & Oates, and Kacey Musgraves. Megastar and Tennessee native Justin Timberlake is one of the partners in the festival.

Winter

During the second full weekend of December, the city of Franklin is transformed into a bustling Victorian town at **Dickens of a Christmas** (http://williamsonheritage.org, Dec.). There are costumed characters like Oliver Twist, carolers, artisans, strolling minstrels, and unique foods.

Shopping

Shopping is Franklin's greatest attraction (at least for those not interested in Civil War history). Trendy downtown shops, the unique environment of **The Factory**, and proximity to a major mall make this a destination for shoppers. It is also one of Tennessee's most popular antiques shopping destinations.

Antiques

Franklin declares itself the New Antiques Capital of Tennessee. Indeed, antiquing is one of the most popular pursuits of Franklin's visitors. The best place to start antiquing is the **Franklin Antique Mall** (251 2nd Ave. S., 615/790-8593, www.franklinantiquemall.com), located in the town's old icehouse. The mall is a maze of rooms, each with different goods on offer. Possibilities include books, dishware, quilts, furniture, knickknacks, and housewares.

Just outside the Franklin Antique Mall are at least five other antiques shops to roam through, including J. J. Ashley's (125 S. Margin St., 615/791-0011), which specializes in French and English country accessories, as well as European furniture. Scarlett Scales Antiques (246 2nd Ave., 615/791-4097, http://scarlettscales.com), located in a 1900s shotgun house, has American country furnishings, accessories, and architectural elements arriving daily.

Downtown

Retail is alive and well in Franklin's downtown. West Main Street is the epicenter of the shopping district, although you will find stores scattered around other parts of downtown as well. Home decor, classy antiques, trendy clothes, and specialty items like candles, tea, and gardening supplies are just a few of the things you'll find in downtown Franklin.

Most shops are open by 10am, and many stay open until the evening to catch late-afternoon visitors. You can easily navigate the downtown shopping district on foot.

Bink's Outfitters (421 Main St., 615/599-8777, www.binksoutfitters.com, 10am-9pm Mon.-Sat., 11am-7pm Sun.) is the perfect place to stock up on outdoor clothing and equipment before biking or hiking the Trace.

Check out **Jondie** (412 Main St., 615/807-2386, www.jondie.com, 10am-6pm Mon.-Wed., 10am-7pm Thurs., 10am-8pm Fri.-Sat., 11am-6pm Sun.) for women's clothing and accessories, then pop into **Avec Moi** (418 Main St.,

615/791-9121, www.avecmoifranklin.com, 10am-5:30pm Mon.-Thurs., 10am-9pm Fri., 10am-6pm Sat., noon-4pm Sun.) for both vintage and new jewelry.

The city's best bookstore is Landmark Booksellers (114 E. Main St., 615/791-6400, www.landmarkbooksellers.com, 10am-5pm daily), found about a block east of the town square. It has a wide selection of used and new books, including many regional and rare titles. It is friendly and welcoming, with fresh coffee for sale in the mornings.

For the best in paper, gift wrap, and stationery, go to **Rock Paper Scissors** (317 Main St., 615/791-0150, www.rockpaperscissor.com, 10am-6pm Mon.-Fri., 10am-5pm Sat.). Head to **Tin Cottage** (123 S. Margin St., 615/472-1183, www.tincottage.com, 10am-6pm Mon.-Thurs., 10am-8pm Fri.-Sat., noon-5pm Sun.) for local prepared foods and kitchen goodies, housewarming gifts, and the thank-you gift for the person holding down the fort at home while you travel.

The Factory

Franklin's most distinctive retail center is **The Factory** (230 Franklin Rd., 615/791-1777, www.factoryatfranklin.com). A 250,000-square-foot complex of 11 old industrial buildings, The Factory once housed stove factories and a textile mill. In the mid-1990s, Calvin Lehew bought the dilapidated eyesore and began the lengthy process of restoring the buildings and converting them to a space for galleries, retail shops, restaurants, and other businesses.

Today, The Factory is a vibrant commercial center for the city of Franklin. It houses a refreshing array of local independent retailers, including galleries, salons, candy shops, and a pet boutique. Across the street The Little Cottage (324 Liberty Pike, 615/794-1405, www.thelittlecottagechildrensshop.com, 9:30am-5pm Mon.-Fri., 10am-5pm Sat.) sells children's fashions.

Sports and Recreation

To add a little height (and adrenaline) to your Franklin area recreation, head to **SOAR Adventure Tower** (3794 Carothers Pkwy., 615/721-5103, www.soaradventure.com, 10am-9pm Tues.-Thurs., 10am-10pm Fri.-Sat., 10am-8pm Sun. June-July, adults $45, children 8-17 $40, children 3-7 $35), where you can climb obstacles in the sky. Or opt for the easy float of **Middle Tennessee Hot Air Adventures** (615/584-6236, www.tnballoon.com, shared flight $200/passenger, private two-passenger flight $750).

If you're looking for a bike ride before heading out on the Trace, try **Mac's Harpeth Bikes** (1110 Hillsboro Rd., 615/472-1002, www.macsharpethbikes.com, 10am-6pm Mon.-Wed., 10am-7pm Thurs., 10am-5pm Sat.).

Parks

Franklin's **Parks Department** (615/794-2103, www.franklin.gov) is in charge of the city's network of parks, encompassing more than 700 acres of land.

Pinkerton Park (405 Murfreesboro Rd.), just southeast of town off Murfreesboro Road, is a pleasant city park. Walking trails, playgrounds, and picnic tables draw dozens of town residents, who come to exercise or simply relax. A short hiking trail takes you to Fort Granger, overlooking the city. You can also take the Sue Douglas Berry Memorial pedestrian bridge over the Harpeth River and walk the six blocks to the town square.

Jim Warren Park (705 Boyd Mill Ave.) is a large public park with baseball and softball fields, tennis courts, covered picnic areas, and 2.5 miles of walking trails. Take a stroll around a Civil War monument and 61-acre historic battle site at **Winstead Hill Park** (4023 Columbia Ave.). The park also has a short walking trail and restrooms. **Aspen Grove Park** (3200 Aspen Grove Dr.) offers 14 acres of fun, including a half-mile walking trail, a creek (Spencer Creek), playground, and picnic pavilion with grills.

The Park at Harlinsdale Farm

One of the most famous Tennessee Walking Horse breeding farms is now a public park. **The Park at Harlinsdale Farm** (239 Franklin Rd.) was a famed Franklin landmark for many years, thanks to a very famous horse. Midnight Sun, a stallion, was a world champion Walking Horse in 1945 and 1946, and all subsequent champions can trace their ancestry to him.

In 2004, Franklin bought the 200-acre farm for $8 million, and three years later the first 60 acres opened as a public park. It is a pleasant place to walk or picnic, with a dog park, a pond for catch-and-release fishing, and a 5K turf track.

Food

The best choice for baked goods, coffee, and light fare, including soups, salads, and sandwiches, is ★ **Merridee's Breadbasket** (110 4th Ave., 615/790-3755, www.merridees.com, 7am-5pm Mon.-Wed., 7am-9pm Thurs.-Sat., $3-11). Merridee grew up in Minnesota and learned baking from her mother, a Swede. When Merridee married Tom McCray and moved to Middle Tennessee in 1973, she kept up the baking traditions she had learned as a child. In 1984, she opened Merridee's Breadbasket in Franklin. Merridee McCray died in 1994, but her restaurant remains one of Franklin's most popular. Merridee's also bakes fresh bread daily; take home a loaf of the always-popular Viking bread.

Puckett's Grocery & Restaurant (120 4th Ave. S., 625/794-5527, http://puckettsgro.com, 7am-9pm Sun.-Thurs., 7am-10pm Fri.-Sat. $7-15), the Leiper's Fork institution, has a second location in Franklin (plus outposts in Nashville and Columbia). The Franklin shop offers

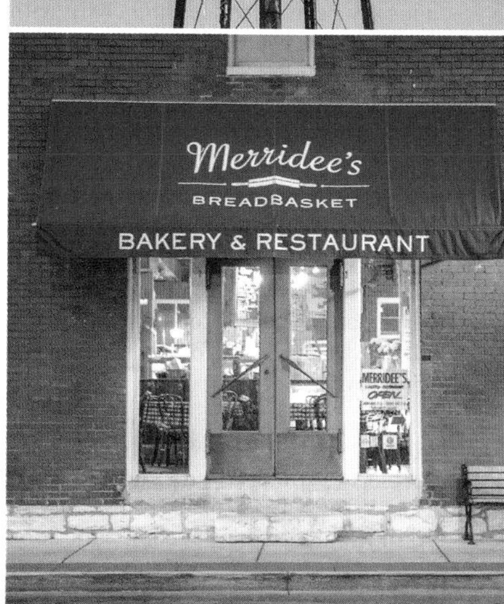

Top to bottom: Franklin Theatre; The Factory; Merridee's Breadbasket

traditional breakfasts with eggs, bacon, country ham, and biscuits, and plate lunches during the day. In the evening, order a handmade burger, a Southern dinner of fried catfish, or a traditional steak, chicken, or fish entrée. For vegetarians, there's a veggie burger or a vegetable plate, as well as salads. Do not skip the fried green beans. There's almost always a crowd, regardless of whether or not there's live music on tap.

★ **Red Pony Restaurant** (408 Main St., 615/595-7669, http://redponyrestaurant.com, 4pm-10pm Mon.-Thurs., 4pm-11pm Fri.-Sat., $26-55) is a Franklin favorite. The chefs call the menu "sophisticated Southern," which translates to lots of bacon, okra, grits, and game meats served in innovative ways. Red Pony is a perfect place to celebrate a birthday or anniversary.

Nashville ooey-gooey sensation, the **Grilled Cheeserie** (334 Main St. 615/905-0467, 11am-8pm daily, $8-16), has an outpost in Franklin. Order one of their creative grilled cheese sandwiches are build your own combo.

Need a cup of joe before you hit the road? **Frothy Monkey** (125 5th Ave. S., 615/600-4756, www.frothymonkey.com, 6am-9pm Mon.-Thurs., 6am-10pm Fri., 7am-10pm Sat., 8am-9pm Sun., $6-17) is a locally beloved coffee shop chain with solid sandwiches and salads. Need other kinds of drinks? Try **Juice Bar Franklin** (232 5th Ave. N., 615/656-1144, www.ilovejuicebar.com, 7am-6:30pm Mon.-Fri., 8am-6:30pm Sat., 11am-5pm Sun., $6-10) for the healthy stuff and **Mantra Artisan Ales** (216 Noah Dr. #140, 615/628-8776, www.mantrabrewing.com, 3pm-9pm Mon.-Thurs., 3pm-10pm Fri., noon-10pm Sat., noon-6pm Sun.) for adult beverages. Mantra is only a taproom and does not serve food.

Franklin Farmers Market

The **Franklin Farmers Market** (230 Franklin Rd., 615/592-1337, www.franklinfarmersmarket.com, 8am-noon Sat.) takes place at the rear of The Factory. This is one of the finest small-town farmers markets in the state, featuring a wide variety of fruit and vegetable growers and cheese, milk, and meat sellers, as well as craftspeople and live music.

Accommodations

Franklin has two types of accommodations: cozy bed-and-breakfast inns and chain motels. The bed-and-breakfasts are located in downtown Franklin and the surrounding countryside. This is also a good area to search for alternative accommodations, like those offered on **Airbnb** (http://airbnb.com).

A hotel room shortage in Nashville has meant higher prices in all the surrounding areas. A few good bets for affordable rooms include the **Comfort Inn Franklin** (4202 Franklin Commons Ct., 615/591-6660, http://comfortinn.reservations.com, $95-135), which offers free Wi-Fi and complimentary breakfast, and allows pets.

The **Magnolia House Bed and Breakfast** (1317 Columbia Ave., 615/794-8178, www.bbonline.com/tn/magnolia, $175-215) is less than a mile from downtown Franklin, near The Carter House. A large magnolia tree shades the early-20th-century Craftsman home. There are four guest rooms, each with a private bath. Common areas include a polished sitting room, cozy den, and sunroom that looks out on the quiet residential neighborhood.

A hip, urban option is **Aloft/Cool Springs** (7109 S. Springs Dr., 615/435-8700, www.aloftnashvillecoolsprings.com, $129-184). The hotel boasts a saltwater pool, a better-than-average hotel bar, and a good location for business or recreation in Franklin.

The 119-room **Harpeth Hotel** (130 2nd Ave., 615/206-7510, http://harpethhotel.com, $184-286) is Franklin's luxury hotel, with high-end amenities; a full-service restaurant, **1799 Kitchen & Cocktails;** and a coffee shop on-site. It is part of Hilton's Curio Collection.

Back to the Trace

Take TN-96 west for just under 10 miles. Turn left when you see the brown Natchez Trace Parkway sign just before the Double Arch Bridge. Follow this frontage road for about 0.5 mile, then turn left to get back on the Trace, headed south.

Leiper's Fork (MP 428)

Part bucolic small town, part rarified enclave, Leiper's Fork is a pleasant place to spend a few hours—or a lifetime. The town runs for several miles along Leiper's Fork, a tributary of the West Harpeth River. Beautiful old farmhouses line Old Hillsboro Road, which serves as the main thoroughfare through town.

One of the earliest settlers of the area was the Benton family, including Thomas Hart Benton, who would go on to become a U.S. senator from Missouri. For many years, Leiper's Fork was called Hillsboro after Hillsborough, North Carolina, where many of its early settlers came from. There is another Hillsboro in Coffee County, Tennessee, however, so when this Hillsboro petitioned for a post office in 1818, the U.S. Postal Service insisted that it change its name. Leiper's Fork was born.

Acclaimed furniture maker Dick Poyner was from the Leiper's Fork area. Poyner, formerly enslaved, was famous for his sturdy ladder-back wooden chairs, one of which is on display at the Tennessee State Museum in Nashville.

Leiper's Fork's die-hard locals who are seriously proud of their town. Art galleries and antiques shops line the short main drag. A few bed-and-breakfasts in the area make it a viable place to rest before the next leg of your trip.

Many music powerhouses, from producers to performers, live here, including Justin Timberlake, who owns two businesses. But, please, if you see a celebrity, don't make a fuss. They choose to live in Leiper's Fork to be away from the crowds. When you do see them around town, expect them to be in boots and jeans, just like everyone else.

Leiper's Fork is less than two miles off the Trace. Take the exit at milepost 428 for TN-46, which will veer right onto an unnamed frontage road for 0.1 mile. At the intersection with TN-46, turn right and follow the highway. Turn left at the stop sign, then continue for about a mile on the highway to reach the Leiper's Fork Historic District.

Entertainment and Events

Friday night is songwriter night at **Puckett's Grocery & Restaurant** (4142 Old Hillsboro Rd., 615/794-1308, www.puckettsofleipersfork.com). For $30 you can enjoy dressed-up dinner—fresh seafood, poultry, and steak are usually among the options—at 7pm and an in-the-round performance from Nashville singer-songwriters starting at 8:30pm. Or pay $12 for the concert only. Reservations are essential for either, so call ahead. Check the website to find out who is performing.

Jailhouse Industrys operates the **Leiper's Fork Lawnchair Theatre** (http://leipersforklawnchairtheater.com, 615/477-6799) behind Leiper's Creek Gallery (4144 Old Hillsboro Rd.) from May to September. Bring your lawn chair or blanket and enjoy classic movies and kids' favorites on Friday and Saturday nights, plus concerts.

Shopping

This is the town to browse for one-of-a-kind gems. Leiper's Fork retailers are generally open 10am-5pm Wednesday-Saturday and 1pm-5pm Sunday.

The Leiper's Creek Gallery (4144 Old Hillsboro Rd., 615/599-5102, www.leiperscreekgallery.com) is the finest gallery in town. It shows a wide selection of paintings by local and regional artists and hosts arts events year-round.

The 3,000-square-foot **Serenite**

Maison (4149 Old Hillsboro Rd., 615/599-2071, www.serenitemaison.com) houses a well-edited inventory thanks to the smart design sense of Alexandra Cirimelli. A California transplant, Cirimelli has appeared on an episode of *American Pickers* and is known for finding her well-heeled clients (including Holly Williams and several actors from *Nashville*) the perfect farm table or pie safe for their kitchen. Don't overlook the pickin' corner, where locals stop in to play the antique guitars, banjos, and mandolins that hang on the walls.

High-end, Western-style clothing from jeans to boots is on the shelves at **Moo Country** (4208 Old Hillsboro Rd., 615/614-3796, www.moocountry.com, 11am-5pm Tues.-Thurs., 10am-5pm Fri.-Sat., noon-5pm Sun.).

Food

★ **Puckett's Grocery & Restaurant** (4142 Old Hillsboro Rd., 615/794-1308, www.puckettsofleipersfork.com, 7am-9pm Wed.-Sun., $6-25) is the heartbeat of Leiper's Fork. An old-time grocery with a small dining room attached, Puckett's serves breakfast, lunch, and dinner to the town faithful and visitors alike. The original country store opened in 1953. In 1998, Andy Marshall bought the store and expanded the restaurant offerings. Solid country breakfasts are the order of the day in the mornings, followed by plate lunches. Dinner specials include catfish nights, family nights, and a Saturday-night seafood buffet. Friday night—for which reservations are essential—the grocery turns upscale with a supper club and live music. Puckett's hours vary by season, so it's best to call ahead, particularly for dinner.

The Davis General (5600 Leipers Creek Rd., 615/830-8503, 8am-3pm Wed.-Sat.) is more than a gas station, with an excellent deli offering sandwiches, cinnamon rolls, and great picnic foods.

Serenite Maison

Accommodations

Innkeepers Eric and Samantha have three different places to stay under the name **Pot N' Kettle Cottages** (615/864-3392, www.potnkettlecottages.com, $160-485). The cottages, all on the same street, are within walking distance of downtown Leiper's Fork and sleep 5-9 people. Amenities include bicycles to cruise around town and Wi-Fi. Discounts are available for groups that book more than one cottage at a time.

Garrison Creek (MP 427.6)

The history is as rich as the forest at this creek and trailhead. In the 18th century the woods gave way to a garrison (hence the name) to protect troops from Native American attacks. The long-gone fort was used again in the parkway's history, most recently as a base during road construction.

Today a paved lot at the site of the former fort includes plenty of parking spots, restrooms, and picnic tables nestled under the shady trees, and room for horse trailers (in the back of the lot). It makes a good place to stretch your legs and eat lunch.

Walk just a few minutes from the parking lot to see small Garrison Creek, which winds its way through the forest. Unlike other waterways along the Trace, this creek is too shallow for swimming. But it makes for pretty scenery and a place for dogs or horses to take a drink.

As the northern terminus of the Highland Rim Trail section of the Natchez Trace National Scenic Trail, **Garrison Creek Trailhead** is popular with day hikers, backpackers, and equestrians. You will need to cross the creek if you decide to hike here. There's not a bridge, but several logs and fallen trees make crossing possible.

This is also the starting point for November's 46-mile **Natchez Trace Trail Run** (www.hardwinadventures.com), an out-and-back double marathon trail run.

This is the last restroom stop until Gordon House and Ferry Site (milepost 407.7).

Burns Branch (MP 425.4)

This picnic area and parking lot on the left side of the road offers a nice, shady respite. It is well-marked with official signage and the lot is paved.

The tree canopies here are perfect for offering shade in the heat of summer and for admiring color in the fall. There are picnic tables and a small creek for a contemplative rest stop. There are trash receptacles but no other amenities.

From Burns Branch it's possible to hike a section of the **Highland Rim Trail,** part of the greater Natchez Trace National Scenic Trail, going either north

Hiking the Highland Rim Trail

Today the Natchez Trace Parkway is an easily traveled roadway for drivers, bikers, cyclists, and equestrians. Two centuries ago, it was a more arduous trip. The **Natchez Trace National Scenic Trail** (www.nps.gov/natt) offers the chance to experience the undeveloped landscape of the area as travelers did so many years ago.

The Natchez Trace National Scenic Trail is composed of five different trails totaling more than 60 miles. Tighten your hiking boot laces: The Leiper's Fork District of the Natchez Trace National Scenic Trail runs for 24 miles, starting near milepost 427 and ending at milepost 408, where TN-50 crosses the parkway. This trail, part of the **Highland Rim Trail,** is one of several preserved sections of the Old Trace.

The most popular access point for the Highland Rim Trail is from **Garrison Creek** (milepost 427), the northernmost entrance. Heavy rains may make conditions muddy. Be sure that you aren't accidentally trespassing on private property: Stay on the marked trail at all times.

Garrison Creek to Burns Branch

Garrison Creek is one of the most popular places to hit the Highland Rim Trail section of the Natchez Trace National Scenic Trail, not only because it's the most scenic, but because it's so easy to access—it's also the northern terminus of the trail. The first part of the trail is an open meadow, with no shade to speak of, but it soon winds its way next to Garrison Creek.

Start here to complete the full 24-mile southbound trek—or do any number of shorter hikes. It's just 2.3 miles from Garrison Creek to Burns Branch and 3.7 miles to the Tennessee Valley Divide. Most of this section is well shaded by trees, except for the access points next to the parking lots.

From Garrison Creek you can hike or ride south, where you can take in several sights and, if you are on foot, check out several small side trails, most of which are small dirt paths of the Old Trace and not accessible to horses. While here, stop quickly at the small stone **War of 1812 Memorial** (milepost 426.3), near a spot that was cleared for use as a postal road in the early 1800s.

Burns Branch to the Tennessee Valley Divide

Continue 2.3 miles to Burns Branch, where you'll work out your thighs and calves on rolling hills (rather than steep inclines). The dense forest provides shade from the hot summer sun, although serious trail runners prefer this path in winter, when some of the lush green overgrowth is gone and they can make their way without foliage or branches in the way. When you get to Burns Branch, you'll find a parking lot on the left side of the road and several picnic tables along this branch of the creek. Enjoy lunch in the shade and rest, or continue on toward the Tennessee Valley Divide, which offers similar scenery on a longer hike. Most walkers and hikers just do the section to Burns Branch, so if you continue on, you'll have few companions on your hike. Some locals do use this space for trail running, so pay attention and move aside if someone wants to pass you.

toward Garrison Creek or south as far as the Gordon House and Ferry Site. Good signage makes it clear which way to go, should you decide to hike. This rest stop offers hitching posts and has room for trailers in the parking lot, for those looking to traverse the trail on horseback.

The Natchez Trace Wine Trail

The Natchez Trace Parkway isn't Napa Valley by any stretch of the imagination. But just off the Tennessee section of the Trace, there are four places to stop and explore nearby wineries.

Housed in a log cabin, **Grinder's Switch Winery** (2119 Hwy. 50 W. Loop, Centerville, 931/729-3690, http://gswinery.com, noon-5pm daily) has sweet and dry reds and whites. The bucolic green landscape is the appeal here, but there is an urban tasting room in Nashville's Marathon Village as well. Grinder's Switch is 20 miles west of the Trace where it intersects with TN-50.

Sweet wines, free tastings, and live music are the draw of **Keg Springs Winery** (361 Keg Springs Rd., Hampshire, 931/285-0589, http://kegsprings.com, 11am-6pm Wed.-Sun.). Keg Springs is just a short distance east of the parkway along Keg Springs Road, but you must travel south past Devil's Backbone State Natural Area and exit at US 412 East, then work your way north along Ridgetop Road and Catheys Creek Road to reach the winery.

Novelty fruit wines, dry reds, and a pastoral setting are the calling cards of **Amber Falls Winery & Cellars** (794 Ridgetop Rd., Hampshire, 931/285-0088, http://amberfallswinery.com, 10am-6pm Mon.-Fri., 10am-8pm Sat., 12:30pm-6pm Sun.). Amber Falls is near Keg Springs. Exit the Trace at US 412 East. After about two miles, turn north onto Ridgetop Road to reach the winery.

Old World techniques, with an emphasis on sustainable growing, is the philosophy at **Natchez Hills Vineyard** (109 Overhead Bridge Rd., Hampshire, 931/285-2500, http://natchezhills.com, noon-5pm Wed.-Sun.). Natchez Hills is just off US 412. From the Trace, turn onto US 412 East and continue for about six miles. When US 412 turns north, continue straight onto Overhead Bridge Road to reach the winery.

Tennessee Valley Divide (MP 423.9)

This well-marked rest stop, which is on the left side of the road, may at first look like another of the parkway's magnificent scenic views. And it is, offering an open meadow and a wide, open expanse for taking in the big sky and the fresh air. But this spot also has both geographical and historical significance.

Rivers and streams on the south side of the divide flow to the Duck and Tennessee Rivers, while those to the north head to the Cumberland River (a 600-plus-mile river that wends its way through downtown Nashville). Historically, this divide was significant because it was the boundary between the Chickasaw Nation (to the south) and the United States (to the north). In the mid-1800s the Chickasaw people, along with other Native American tribes, were forced from their homes along what was to become known as the Trail of Tears. Today the Chickasaw Nation is largely in Oklahoma.

From this spot it's possible to hike a section of the **Highland Rim Trail,** part of the greater Natchez Trace National Scenic Trail, going either north toward Garrison Creek or south as far as the Gordon House and Ferry Site. This spot is a hiker-only access point.

Creekview Farm Retreat B&B (MP 416)

The three-bedroom ★ **Creekview Farm Retreat B&B** (5177 Leipers Creek Rd., Santa Fe, 931/446-7993, $120-170) is on a working farm, just three miles from the parkway itself. But don't worry. You can admire the livestock from a screened-in porch; no one is going to make you do farm chores. In colder months, the fireplace is the perfect place to curl up and reflect on your travels and your trip. Guests are welcome to use the B&B's kitchen (breakfast is provided, of course). Children are welcome, but those traveling with pets will need to stay elsewhere.

To get here, exit the parkway at TN-7 (milepost 416) and head east for less than one mile to Leipers Creek Road. Turn south (right) and drive for less two miles to reach the B&B.

TN-7 to Columbia

Columbia is the seat of Maury County. Founded in 1809 and named for Christopher Columbus, Columbia was the commercial hub for Middle Tennessee's rich plantations. In 1850 it became the third-largest city in Tennessee, behind Nashville and Memphis. A decade later Maury County was the wealthiest county in the whole state. The city's prominence did not survive, however. The economic trauma of the Civil War was largely to blame.

No city in all of Tennessee, if not the country, is more closely associated with mules than Columbia. During the 19th and early 20th centuries, Columbia's mule market opened on the first Monday of April, and people flocked here to buy and sell mules. Other towns, including Lynchburg and Paris, were known for large "First Monday" sales, but Columbia's was the largest. As a nod to its roots, the city is home to the Muletown Music Festival, with big-name acts, each October.

Today, Columbia has a charming, revitalized downtown, particularly around the picturesque courthouse square, and thriving maker and artist community.

Leaving the Trace

Exit the parkway at TN-7 (milepost 416) and head east for 17 miles. TN-7 (also known as Water Valley Road) winds its way into downtown Columbia. Stay on it until you hit North Garden Street (Business 412), then turn right. Continue five blocks until you are in the center of the charming downtown district. The total drive time for this 20-mile drive should be less than 30 minutes.

★ President James K. Polk Home & Museum

The 11th president of the United States, James Knox Polk, was born in North Carolina but moved to Middle Tennessee with his family when he was 11 years old. Before moving to town, Polk's family lived for several years on a farm north of Columbia, from where Polk's father ran successful plantations, speculated in land, and was involved in local politics.

The home where Polk lived as a teenager and young man in Columbia is the only house remaining, besides the White House, where Polk ever lived. It is now known as the President James K. Polk Home & Museum (301-305 W. 7th St., 931/388-2354, www.jameskpolk.com,

9am-5pm Mon.-Sat., 1pm-5pm Sun. Apr.-Oct., 9am-4pm Mon.-Sat., 1pm-5pm Sun. Nov.-Mar., adults $12, seniors $10, youths 6-18 $8, free for children under 6) and is dedicated to Polk's life and presidency. Free parking is available along High Street or in the lot across 7th Street.

The home has furnishings that belonged to President Polk and his wife, Sarah, while they lived at the White House. Other pieces come from Polk Place, the home that the couple planned and built in Nashville following the end of Polk's presidency in 1849. Sadly, Polk died of cholera just five months after leaving office and so had little opportunity to enjoy the home; Sarah Polk lived for another 42 years following her husband's death, and she spent them all at Polk Place.

The Polk home in Columbia was comfortable, but not luxurious, for its time. It was while living here that Polk began his career as a Tennessee lawyer and eventually won his first seat in the U.S. House of Representatives. He would go on to serve 14 years in the House, four of them as Speaker. He was governor of Tennessee from 1839 to 1841 and defeated Henry Clay, a Whig, to become president in 1845. Polk's presidency was defined by his drive to expand the Union westward, and it was during his term in office that the United States added California, Texas, and Oregon to the territory of the United States.

Historic Athenaeum

Once part of a famous finishing school for girls, the **Historic Athenaeum** (808 Athenaeum St., 931/381-4822, http://historicathenaeum.com, tours 10am-4pm Thurs.-Sat., by appointment Mon.-Wed., Feb.-Dec., $5), formerly called the Athenaeum Rectory, is also an unusual architectural gem. Designed and built by Maury County master builder Nathan Vaught, the rectory was the home of Rev. Franklin Gillette Smith and his family. Smith came to Columbia from Vermont

President James K. Polk Home & Museum

in 1837 to run the Columbia Female Institute, an Episcopal girls' finishing school.

In 1851, Smith decided to open his own school for girls. He built the Columbia Athenaeum School next to the rectory, which remained his family home. Its name refers to Athena, the goddess of wisdom, and has come to mean "seat of learning."

For 52 years the Athenaeum educated young women in art, music, history, science, and business. The Athenaeum remained open until 1904; after the deaths of Reverend Smith and his wife, it was operated by their son. From 1904 to 1914, the Athenaeum served as the community's high school, and in 1915 the school was torn down and the Columbia High School built in its place. The Athenaeum Rectory was preserved, however, and visitors can tour the Moorish-Gothic structure that housed the parlor and reception area for the school.

The building is operated by the Association for the Preservation of Tennessee Antiquities (www.theapta.org) and is open only for tours and special events. For a week every summer it offers the 1861 Athenaeum Girls' School, when 14- to 18-year-old girls dress up in period clothing and study topics like etiquette, penmanship, and archery.

★ Mule Day

Columbia's **Mule Day** (931/381-9557, www.muleday.com, Apr.) takes place over four days in mid-April and is perhaps the thing for which Columbia is best known. The festival's roots are in the First Monday mule market that took place in Columbia during the period when work animals were indispensable to Tennessee farmers. In many cases, mules were a farmer's most valuable asset—a good pair of mules could make a poor farmer rich.

Mules were more expensive than horses or oxen because they were more highly prized. They were said to be stronger, smarter, and more surefooted than other work animals. Their temperament can be stubborn, but some mules are easy and willing to work. For this reason, mule breeders were important, influential, and, often, quite wealthy.

Today's Mule Day is more festival than mule market, although the event still includes mule sales, mule and donkey seminars, and mule shows and competitions. The highlight is Saturday morning's Mule Day Parade, when thousands of people crowd to see school bands, mules, and colorful troops parade down the road. There is also live music, storytelling, dancing, gospel singing, and the crowning of the Mule Day Queen. Activities take place at various locations in Columbia, but the heart of Mule Day is the Maury County Park on Lion Parkway.

Shopping

Boutiques are Columbia's bread and butter. **Needle and Grain** (510 N. Garden St., 931/548-6686, http://needleandgrain.com, 10am-5pm Mon.-Fri., 10am-4pm Sat.) is a mercantile that stocks home decor, fabrics, gifts, and supplies for DIY craft projects. Don't be surprised to find community craft-making on Mule Day.

Since 1955, **Ted's Sporting Goods** (806 S. Main St., 931/388-6387, www.tedssportinggoods.com, 8am-5:30pm Mon.-Fri., 8am-4pm Sat.) has been the place to stock up on whatever you need for an outdoor adventure on the Natchez Trace.

Duck River Books (12 Public Sq., 931/548-2665, http://duckriverbooks.com, 10am-6pm Mon.-Sat.) is an independent bookstore with lots of staff recommendations if you need assistance finding that perfect tome.

The visual arts scene in Columbia is robust. Housed in an 1870s home is **Gallery 205** (205 W. 6th St., 931/548-2291, 1pm-5pm Wed.-Sat.), a mecca of contemporary art. **W7thCo Gallery** (107 W. 7th St., 931/446-1900, http://w7thco.com,

10am-6pm Wed.-Sat. noon-4pm Sun.) is focused entirely on historical photographs of Columbia, printed from a salvaged collection from the Orman Studio, which was a Columbia photo studio for 80 years. The **Columbia Arts Building** (307 W. 11th St., 931/384-8347, www.columbiaartsbuilding.com, hours vary by business) is home to studios, galleries, and a café.

If you need assistance as you cycle the parkway, stop at **Spinning Spoke** (11 Public Sq., 931/548-8313, www.spinningspoke.com/trek-columbia, 10am-6pm Mon.-Fri., 9am-6pm Sat.).

Sports and Recreation

One of the reasons travelers take a detour from the Trace in this area is to take advantage of the area's blueways. The **River Rat's Canoe Rental** (4361 US 431, 931/381-2278, http://riverratcanoe.com, 9am-6pm Mon.-Fri., 8am-6pm Sat.-Sun. Apr.-Oct., $25-55) offers self-guided Class I trips via canoe or kayak, either five miles (starting at Milltown Dam coming back to River Rat's, about 3-4 hours) or nine miles (starting at River Rat's to Carpenter's Bridge, about 5-6 hours). Rentals include life jackets, paddles, and a ride to the river. Have your own gear? Ask about shuttle service only.

What does an equestrian need? Hiking, biking, birding, fishing, swimming, and campgrounds designed for campers traveling with horses. That's **Chickasaw State Park** (20 Cabin Ln., Henderson, 731/989-5141, http://tnstateparks.com, 8am-10pm daily, free). There are rowboats and pedal boats for rent on Lake Placid, and horses are also available for rent to ride on the hour-long trail. Areas of interest also include the Brewer's Cabin (built in 1876), Sagamore Lodge (Arts and Crafts style building built in the 1930s), and the Aviary (which houses an owl and a red-tailed hawk). Want to stay longer? Check out one of the 13 cabins ($80-145), which sleep up to six people.

Food

Located on the courthouse square, **Square Market and Café** (36 Public Sq., 931/840-3636, www.squaremarketcafe.com, 9am-4pm Mon.-Thurs., 9am-9pm Fri., 10:30am-9pm Sat., $8-11) serves breakfast and lunch throughout the week and dinner on Friday and Saturday nights. The weekday menu features salads, sandwiches, and soups. The signature Polk's Roasted Pear Salad of greens, blue cheese, walnuts, and roasted-pear vinaigrette is a favorite for lunch. There is live music, too.

Get more than a cup of coffee at ★ **Muletown Roasted Coffee** (23 Public Sq., 931/901-0220, www.muletowncoffee.com, 6am-8pm Mon.-Sat.), where you can hang out and learn all the Columbia goings-on. This hip coffee shop roasts its own beans and sells bags of coffee (including single origin options) for $12-20, along with espresso drinks, drip coffee, and pastries.

Hattie Jane's (16 Public Sq., 931/490-0229, http://hattiejanescreamery.com, noon-6pm Thurs.-Sun., $4-8) is a small-batch ice cream scoop shop and coffee house. Come here for a treat while strolling around the courthouse square.

If you're headed to New Orleans, you might as well get excited with some NOLA-inspired cuisine at **River Terrace** (1000 Riverside Dr., 931/223-5135, www.riverterracerestaurant.com, 4pm-8:30pm Mon.-Sat., $8-34). Start the meal off with some specialty martinis. Chef Randy Landry is a New Orleans native, so he knows his way around the kitchen.

The **Bypass Deli** (1323 S. James Campbell Blvd., 931/381-9634, 8am-10pm Mon.-Sat., $4-8) serves affordable basics, such as burgers, sandwiches, po'boys, and salads. This is a great takeout option to accompany the Trace's pretty picnic spots.

Inside the Columbia Arts Building, **CAB Cafe** (306 W. 11th St., 931/505-2533, www.columbiaartsbuilding.com, 4pm-9pm Thurs., 4pm-10pm Fri., 10am-10pm

Sat., 10am-7pm Sun.) serves avocado toast, cheese fries, and other treats in a welcoming environment surrounding by works of local artists.

The Dotted Lime (1907 Shady Brook St., 931/548-8445, www.thedottedlime.com, 7am-5pm Tues.-Fri., 7am-3pm Sat. $10-18) is a family-owned, entirely (yes, 100 percent) gluten-free restaurant. The menu changes often, with options like a breakfast burger, pizzas, and chicken and waffles.

Accommodations

Columbia has many decent chain hotel options. A host of motels are found around exit 46 on I-65, about 10 miles east of Columbia. Locally owned, the **Richland Inn** (2405 Pulaski Hwy., 931/381-4500, www.richlandinncolumbia.com, $85-125) is a 107-room inn with singles, doubles, and suites. There is a continental breakfast and a family restaurant next door.

Built in 1960, ★ **The Inn at Bigby Creek** (1306 Trotwood Ave., 931/982-6226, www.innatbigbycreek.com, $150) might be more modern than the word "inn" usually conjures up. But this house, the former home of a Columbia mayor, is a perfect getaway. There are three guest rooms, with amenities like free Wi-Fi, private bathrooms, high-end sheets, and a full breakfast. Stroll through the 1.5 acres before continuing your travels.

Back to the Trace

It should take you no more than 30 minutes to rejoin the parkway at milepost 416 from downtown Columbia. Take North Garden Street (Business 412) north, then turn left onto North James Campbell Boulevard. Continue on this road, which turns into TN-7 in about 0.5 mile, for a total of about 17 miles. Pass under the parkway, then turn right and follow the road to rejoin the parkway.

Water Valley Overlook (MP 411.8)

If you haven't used the wide-angle lens or panoramic setting on your camera phone yet, this scenic overlook on the left side of the road is the place to give it a try. The parking lot is small, but you'll be looking at the expanse of rolling hills and Middle Tennessee foliage. Picnic tables provide a perfect place to rest and overlook the top of a ridge, with an impressive 180-degree view of the Water Valley. Unlike some other vantage points along the parkway, this view is rarely obscured by brush or other growth. This is one of the wide-open places on the parkway where you can imagine seeing what early settlers saw when they first came to the area. Today you may see some farms and houses in the distance but no other significant development, traffic, or billboards.

The overlook is well-marked with the signature parkway signage.

Gordon House and Ferry Site (MP 407.7)

As a modern-day stop along the parkway, the **Gordon House and Ferry Site,** the 200-year-old home of John Gordon and Dolly Cross Gordon, just south of TN-50, may not look imposing. But centuries ago, this two-story brick building near the Duck River was essential. It was a trading post, a place to cross the river, a refuge after a long journey, and it signaled that Nashville was close by.

One of the Captain of the Spies (the name for the leaders of Andrew Jackson's scouting units), John Gordon fought from the Battle of Talladega in 1813 through the Battle of Horseshoe Bend in 1814, and he was partially responsible for some of the country's worst legacies: forcing Native Americans from their homeland.

While he was at war, he supervised long distance the building of this Federal-style house, designed to be elegant but also safe in a frontier environment. The Gordon House and Ferry Site is not open to visitors (due to unsafe conditions), but exploring the grounds and the exterior is a worthy stop along the parkway, as this is one of only two buildings remaining from the Old Trace era. It is listed on the National Register of Historic Places, and was restored to 1818 style after it was acquired by the NPS in the 1970s.

Follow the short paved trail from the parking area, past the house, and imagine yourself as one of the early travelers along the Old Trace. From there, turn right. You'll find a bridge to cross the small Fattybread Branch creek (something those who walked these footsteps centuries ago would not have found) to the old ferry site on the banks of the wider, faster-moving Duck River. This ferry ran for nearly 100 years (long after the trading post was no longer necessary), making travel easier and helping trade in the area thrive until a bridge was built. This is a gently sloped walk, with equal parts shade and sun, and shows off the variety of the Water Valley landscape.

The site has restrooms and picnic tables and, as the closest place to the southern terminus of the **Highland Rim Trail,** is a good place to stock up on water. Walk 0.3 mile north to the TN-50 parking lot, where you'll find hitching posts for horses, ample parking, and signage to take you the few hundred feet to the trailhead.

Baker Bluff Overlook (MP 405.1)

Pull into the Baker Bluff Overlook, on the left side of the road, to take in a view of the area farmland and the Duck River

Top to bottom: Gordon House and Ferry Site; Baker Bluff Overlook; Jackson Falls

from above. Informative signage explains the conservation methods that local farmers use today to help preserve these pristine surroundings. This is one of only a few vantage points on the Tennessee section of the parkway where you are looking at farmland from above and don't have views obscured by trees, no matter the time of year.

This spot is popular with photographers wanting to get the perfect shot. The overlook view is to the east, so your best bet is to try to stop in the afternoon or before sunset so that the sun is at your back. This is a scenic and educational stop, as well as pit stop, as it has a restroom and several picnic tables. From here you can hike a steep descent to Jackson Falls.

Baker Bluff Trail

Distance: 0.75 mile one-way
Duration: 40-60 minutes
Difficulty: Moderate

After taking in the sights from the overlook, follow the signed Baker Bluff Trail down to Jackson Falls (which is also the next stop on the parkway). The first section of this trail from Baker Bluff is an ascent, a steep 0.1 mile uphill, before heading downhill toward the falls. This trail is short, less than a mile, but very steep. Depending on weather conditions and how sure-footed you are, it may take you 20-30 minutes each way. If you have a hiking pole with you, this is a good place to use it.

Like many hikes along the Trace, this one is wooded, which is great for shade but means you may have to maneuver around branches on your way. While this trail takes you to Jackson Falls, and you may hear the water from here, there is not a vantage point of the water until you get to milepost 404.7, so many people choose to do the hike from the parking lot at Jackson Falls.

Jackson Falls (MP 404.7)

As is the case with many landmarks in Tennessee, these falls were named for President Andrew Jackson. No one knows if he actually ever took in their beauty, but regardless, you shouldn't miss them. Fortunately, this scenic stop is designed to accommodate everyone.

Following the signs for Jackson Falls, pull into the parking lot by turning right off the Trace. You'll loop underneath it to end up on the left side of the parkway. You'll see both the standard arrowhead-shaped parkway sign and a brown directional one pointing the way.

There are benches (plus restrooms) at the top of the falls, where you can take in some of the view without walking. But if you're up to it, walk at least halfway down the path, which is paved for the beginning. From here you can stop at a bench and look at the water crashing over the limestone rock. Or, continue farther (about 900 feet downhill, in total), to the base of the falls. This is a popular hike for Nashvillians looking to get out of the city.

This is the last restroom stop until Meriwether Lewis Monument and Gravesite (milepost 385.9).

Jackson Falls Trail

Distance: 900 feet one-way
Duration: 30 minutes
Difficulty: Moderate

The trail down to a clear pool and a view of Jackson Falls is paved in concrete, which makes this steep 900-foot-long hike considerably easier to navigate. The trail is short, but steep, and could take 15 minutes to walk each way. When you get to the bottom, there's some serious payoff for your exertion: a clear pool and dramatic waterfalls cascading down a limestone outcropping. The water is clear and

Hurricane Mills: Loretta Lynn's Ranch

Loretta Lynn's Ranch

What Graceland is to Elvis, Hurricane Mills is to country music star Loretta Lynn: a must-stop for fans and a fun diversion for everyone else. Lynn recalls going for a Sunday drive in the countryside west of Nashville in the early 1960s. That was when she and her late husband, Oliver Lynn, first saw the 1817 plantation home where they would eventually raise their family. "I looked up on this big ole hill and said, 'I want that house right there,'" she is reported to have said.

The mansion that Lynn bought is now just one of a handful of attractions based around her celebrity at the Western-themed **Loretta Lynn's Ranch** (8000 Hwy. 13 S., 931/296-7700, www.lorettalynnranch.net, guided tour $25 for adults, free for children 10 and under). It's located in Hurricane Mills, a town that time would have forgotten were it not for her—and now she owns the whole shebang: Even the U.S. Postal Service rents the Hurricane Mills Post Office from Miss Loretta! Lynn and her family still live part of the year in Hurricane Mills (though no longer in the mansion), so a sighting is possible if unlikely.

Loretta Lynn's Ranch feels a little bit like an amusement park without rides. There's a small Western town's worth of offbeat attractions and re-created buildings, plus walking trails, swimming pools, restaurants, and gift shops, plus a year-round campground (campsites $20, RV sites $35-40, cabins $100-200, additional $50 fee for pets). Even Lynn's old tour bus is parked nearby for photo ops. There are also canoe and kayak rentals, horseback riding options, yoga festivals, chuckwagon races, and occasional concerts by Lynn and other musicians.

The museum tours (Coal Miner's Daughter Museum, Doll and Fan Museum, Loretta's Frontier Homestead, Grist Mill Museum, Native American Artifacts Museum) are open April 1-November 1 and are generally closed during the winter. Call ahead to confirm.

Getting There

From Jackson Falls, exit the parkway at TN-50. Drive northwest for 35 miles; you'll pass over the Duck River several times. Turn right (north) on TN-13 and drive 7 more miles to reach the entrance to Hurricane Mills. From the gate you'll drive 4-5 more miles in the complex to get to the different attractions and campgrounds.

runs year-round. Even when other small creeks dry up in Tennessee's hot summers, this water keeps flowing—at least at a trickle. The small Jackson Branch used to flow directly into the Duck River, but floods, erosion, and other factors ate away at the bluffs, creating these falls.

At the bottom of the falls is a bench, as well as some flat rocks perfect for perching on to dip your toes in the pool. This is more a wading spot than a swimming hole—the pond isn't particularly big or deep.

Old Trace (MP 403.7)

All along the official Natchez Trace Parkway are places where the Old Trace, the original road that was most active from the 1790s to the early 1800s, intersects. At each of these spots, you can get out and stretch your legs for a quick out-and-back hike.

To see this section, pull into the parking lot on the right side of the road at the Old Trace sign. Here, follow signage for an easy 2,000-foot walk, which shouldn't take more than 10-15 minutes, along a ridge with a view of the Duck River. As you wend your way through the forest and look out at the farmland, think about how different this once was for soldiers and explorers than it is for modern travelers on the parkway.

As you drive south to the next landmark, there's a tiny **cemetery,** but it isn't marked and doesn't have a parking lot. Less than 0.5 mile from milepost 403.7, look for a bridge and pull over just before it. On the left side is the Cathey Family cemetery. The graves are very close to the end of the bridge, perhaps 30 steps away, although due to foliage, you may not see them as you drive by. Only a few of the tombstones are legible. Be respectful of the dead and their families if you choose to stop and take a look, and pay attention to traffic as you are pulling off and on the road.

Old Trace Walk

Distance: 2,000 feet one-way
Duration: 15 minutes
Difficulty: Easy

At milepost 403.7 is a 2,000-foot section of the Old Trace. This ridgeway walk gives you a glimpse of what passage along the route was like before there was a paved parkway. This small hike should take no more than 15 minutes at a leisurely pace. It offers shade from the hot summer sun, as much of the trail goes through the dense forest of the area. At certain vantage points you'll have views of the Duck River Valley below. This is an out-and-back path, not a loop, so when it dead-ends, turn around to return to the parking lot.

★ Tobacco Farm and Old Trace Drive (MP 401.4)

At this mile marker, pull off the parkway on the left and to see an old tobacco farm and to drive a dirt portion of the Old Trace.

First, you'll see a tobacco farm from the early 1900s, complete with old wooden barn and tobacco both growing in the ground and hanging to dry inside the barn.

Park in the lot and follow the signage for a very easy, flat walk through a field. This replica of the kind of tobacco farm that would have existed here before the Park Service took over shows you how the land on and around the Trace has sustained its residents and neighbors for generations. This stop is a great one for those traveling with kids, as the signage explains exactly what they are witnessing.

If that's enough for you, you can simply exit the parking lot and continue south on the parkway. Or, you can drive on a one-way dirt road that is a section of the Old Trace for about two miles. This dirt road isn't suitable for RVs or other oversized vehicles, but it's easy (if dusty) for standard cars or motorcycles.

This very narrow loop road winds through the forest and brings you back to the parking lot where you started. Most preserved sections of the Old Trace are for hiking or horseback riding only. This is one of only a few portions of the Old Trace that allow cars. Along the short drive, you'll get several vantage points of the surrounding valley and its wildflowers, trees, and wildlife. Look for wild turkeys roaming here.

Devil's Backbone State Natural Area (MP 394)

Technically, this park is adjacent to the Trace, not on it. Stop here to take a pretty, moderate-effort hike through the woods, without a lot of other people around. Devil's Backbone was named a Class 1 Scenic Recreation Area in 1997. It has a diversity of flora and fauna that can be seen during the hike.

Enter the parking lot at milepost 394 (on the right side of the road). There are no amenities for non-hikers here.

Devil's Backbone Hike

Distance: 3.2-mile loop
Duration: 1.5 hours
Difficulty: Moderate

This 3.2-mile hiking trail starts at the parking lot and gives hikers an experience out in the Highland Rim (not to be confused with the Highland Rim Trail), the ridge of a geographic basin. This hike winds beside a creek and loops back to the starting point. Despite the short distance, there are about 200 feet of elevation change, making for some steep areas, but it should be easy enough for the average hiker. A babbling brook crosses the trail and breaks up the forest scenery, primarily comprising oak, hickory, and tuliptree.

Folks often liken this hike to the one at Meriwether Lewis Monument and Gravesite (milepost 385.9), given the terrain, the difficulty, and the foliage. But Devil's Backbone is typically much less crowded than the Meriwether Lewis hike—great for those who want to commune with nature in solitude.

Because this area isn't used often, the trail can be overgrown. Few blazes mark the way, so pay attention in order to stay on the trail.

Swan View Overlook (MP 392.5)

Pull in to this small, well-marked parking lot up the hill on the right side of the road and grab the camera. There aren't any restrooms or other amenities, but you want to stop for a good view of the water tower in nearby Hohenwald, to the west. Hohenwald is the highest elevation town between New Orleans and Chicago, and a quick photo shouldn't be missed, particularly during leaf-changing season. Unlike much of the Trace, which is dense with forest and leaves, here the views of the rolling hills, Swan Creek, and farmland are uninterrupted.

Fall Hollow Waterfall (MP 391.9)

After pulling into the parking lot at this stop, you only need to step about 10 feet away from your car to hear and see Fall Hollow. But venture beyond the parking lot to an easy, paved pathway. The path leads to a wooden bridge and platform about halfway down the falls with a simple bench where you can sit and take in the sights and sounds of the waterfall. In the late summer butterflies flitter around like a scene from a Disney movie. This is easily one of the prettiest places on the Tennessee section of the Trace and a great spot for a picnic. (Picnic tables are at the top, but it's better to stay here if you can nab a spot on the bench.)

For a bit longer and steeper hike, continue past the bench onto the unimproved dirt path to the bottom of the falls. You will see more dramatic water cascades at this spot. This is a good spot to use a trekking pole. The path to the bottom is undeveloped and steep, and may take an additional 10 minutes to walk.

Phosphate Mine

(MP 390.7)

Take a short (0.2-mile round-trip) walk on sunken ground to get a glimpse of what remains of an 1800s phosphate mining town called Gordonsburg. In fact, the land here was so rich in limestone phosphate that nearby Mount Pleasant was once known as the Phosphate Capital of the World. See the old mine shaft and foliage that has grown over the limestone. While the sunken path seems similar to Old Trace sections, it is, in fact, an abandoned railroad route, used to take the phosphate from mine to market. This is an out-and-back walk and is largely shaded. The pullout is on the right side of the road; there are no other amenities at this stop.

★ Meriwether Lewis Monument and Gravesite (MP 385.9)

Meriwether Lewis, the U.S. army captain and private secretary to President Thomas Jefferson, is best known as the leader, along with William Clark, of the Lewis and Clark Expedition to the Pacific Ocean from 1804 to 1806. The **Meriwether Lewis Monument and Gravesite** (www.nps.gov/natr) sits along the Natchez Trace Parkway about seven miles east of Hohenwald. This is where Lewis died, under mysterious circumstances, while traveling the Trace bound for Washington DC in 1809.

According to accounts, Lewis, who was appointed governor of the Louisiana Territory following his successful expedition, was upset by accusations of financial mismanagement. He was traveling to Washington to clear his name, and on the night of October 11, 1809, he stayed at Grinder's Stand, a homestead whose owners boarded travelers along the Trace. In the morning, Lewis was found shot to death in his bed. His death was called a suicide, although a few months later a friend came to investigate the circumstances and pronounced that Lewis was murdered. Lewis was just 35 years old when he died.

While the circumstances of Lewis's death remain a mystery, his legacy lives on. Plan to spend time here exploring his story as well as the great outdoors. Several monuments to Lewis have been erected at and around his gravesite, with ample signage. Chief among them is the monument over the grave. This solemn stone column was erected by the state of Tennessee in 1848 to commemorate Lewis's life. If the top seems broken or unfinished, don't be surprised: The design represents a life cut short.

If you are at the site on a weekend, stop in the small log cabin (noon-4:15pm Fri.-Sat., free) near the site where the original Grinders' Stand stood. No one knows

for sure what the inn where Lewis spent his last night looked like, but this replica mimics the style of the day. Inside are interpretive displays about his life.

The complex also offers flat, wheelchair-accessible pathways through central Tennessee landscape. These walkways allow you to commune with nature, despite the crowds. All of the paths are on a well-marked loop, taking you past the Grinder's Stand site and the monument, across a section of the Old Trace and Little Swan Creek, and back to the parking lot. The interior driving road leads to smaller loops for picnic areas, restrooms, and the campground.

This site also houses a pioneer cemetery near the gravesite. In 1927 the National Park Service placed commemorative markers at each gravesite to represent the lives of early residents of the area, more than 100 in all. The site also has a small visitors center and museum (800/305-7417) with detailed educational displays about the Corps of Discovery. The museum tends to be open Friday-Sundays April-September, but call to confirm if this is an essential part of your planning.

The site is on the west side of the parkway. Exit to the right before TN-20 near milepost 386.

Accommodations

The ★ **Meriwether Lewis Monument and Gravesite Campground** (800/305-7417, free) has 32 campsites. There are no fees and reservations are not accepted; this is a first-come, first-served situation. Stays are limited to 14 consecutive days. There's a cross-section of wooded, secluded spots, and some with wide-open views of the landscape. All of the spots are fairly close to one another, but thanks to the foliage that grows so quickly in this climate, you won't feel like the folks in the site next to you can see into your tent.

the Meriwether Lewis Monument and Gravesite

Meriwether Lewis: The Man Behind the Legend

Being half of perhaps the most famous explorer team in U.S. history, Meriwether Lewis (1774-1809) is tied inexorably to his partner William Clark. But Lewis, who died along the Natchez Trace and whose gravesite with its memorial is on the parkway (milepost 385.9), is a legend in his own right.

Born in Virginia in 1774, Lewis grew up about 10 miles from Monticello, the home of Thomas Jefferson, who would be a mentor and friend to Lewis.

Lewis served in the Frontier Army, rising through the ranks. By 1801 President Jefferson appointed Lewis to be his personal secretary. In 1803, Congress had approved an expedition of the territory acquired in the Louisiana Purchase. Lewis's military training, his interest in plant life, his intellect, and his diplomatic and leadership skills made him a natural choice to lead this epic undertaking. William Clark, under whom Lewis had served in the army, was named co-commander of the expedition that would change the American West.

The team started in St. Louis, Missouri, in May 1804. With the help of Sacagawea, a Shoshone woman, the team traveled by boat, on foot, and on horseback. By November 1805 they had reached the Pacific coast, successfully completing the first transcontinental expedition. But the 8,000-mile trip was difficult physically and mentally. Lewis, Clark, and the rest of their group—now referred to as the Corps of Discovery—coped with everything from harsh weather conditions to hunger on the trek. At one point Lewis was accidentally shot in the thigh during a hunting trip. At another point he slipped and fell more than 20 feet in a cave, saving himself by using a knife to stop his fall.

On their return, the team was treated like celebrities and heroes. Lewis was named governor of the Louisiana Territory and set to work to publish the journals of their voyage, documenting the plants and animals they encountered, as well as the people and the geography.

Lewis died at age 35 of gunshot wounds along the Natchez Trace. Lewis likely suffered from depression, and the transition back to everyday life after the expedition was difficult. The journals, with their observations deemed crucial to the development of the American West, were being published at a slower pace than expected. Lewis was in debt, and may have suffered from malaria, a disease that, untreated, could cause hallucinations. He also suffered from alcoholism and had attempted suicide in the past.

Despite his untimely death, there's no question that America would not be the country it is without Lewis's service, his intellectual pursuits, and his vision.

TN-20 to Hohenwald

The unassuming county seat of Lewis County, Hohenwald developed in the 1890s when a railroad was built through the rural county. Starting in 1895, immigrants from Switzerland moved to the area as part of a settlement scheme advanced by a Swiss American developer, J. G. Probst. The immigrants laid out and built New Switzerland immediately adjacent to the older town of Hohenwald. The two communities are now united.

Tucked into the rural landscape of central Tennessee near the small town of Hohenwald, more than 20 African and Asian elephants retired from circuses and zoos have found refuge at The Elephant Sanctuary, a 2,700-acre park that's not open to the public. At the **Elephant Discovery Center** (27 E. Main St., 931/796-6500, www.elephants.com, 9am-4pm Tues.-Sat. or by appointment), you can watch videos of the elephants in the sanctuary, look at photo exhibits, and browse the gift shop, where proceeds from purchases benefit the sanctuary.

Leaving the Trace

Downtown Hohenwald is an easy 10-minute, six-mile drive northwest on TN-20 from the Meriwether Lewis Monument and Gravesite.

Natural Bridge

One of the area's most remarkable natural attractions, a **double-span natural bridge** (Tennessee Fitness Spa and Retreat, 299 Natural Bridge Rd., 800/235-8365 or 931/722-5589, www.tennesseefitnessspa.com, by appointment Sun. Mar.-Nov., free) is hidden away at a privately owned and operated spa. A tributary of the Buffalo River has etched away at the bedrock for thousands of years, eventually creating a natural bridge formation that is marvelous to look at.

The bridge invites exploration. You can walk along the side of the trickling stream and climb up to view the bridge from above. The sight of layer upon layer of rock, which has been carved out over many thousands of years, is remarkable. A few hundred yards from the natural bridge is a small cave, also open to visitors. Lights have been placed inside to make it easy to explore.

Natural Bridge is along State Route 99, between Hohenwald and Waynesboro. Tennessee Fitness Spa, the property owner, allows the public to visit Natural Bridge and the cave on Sundays only, 9am-5pm. Check in at the office first.

Entertainment and Events

Amber Falls Winery & Cellars (794 Ridgetop Rd., 931/285-0088, http://amberfallswinery.com, 10am-6pm Mon.-Fri., 10am-8pm Sat., 12:30pm-6pm Sun.) has a tasting room and a live music series called Music on the Ridge.

The emphasis at **Keg Springs Winery** (361 Keg Spring Rd., 931/285-0589, www.kegspringswinery.net, 11am-6pm Wed.-Sun.) is fruit wines, including blackberry, peach, cherry, and strawberry.

There's a beautiful porch at **Natchez Hills Vineyard** (109 Overhead Bridge Rd., 931/285-2500, www.natchezhills.com, noon-5pm Wed.-Sun.). Enjoy an umbrella-shaded table while you sip your wine.

Food

Stop for lunch (sandwiches and more) or to pick up homemade Amish baked goods and snacks at **Yoders Homestead Market** (3555 Summertown Hwy., 931/796-1646, 9am-5pm Mon.-Sat.). There's a table where you can sit outside and admire the well-kept garden, as well as one inside. A small general store section includes games and books for kids and homeopathic health supplies. Bring cash or checks; credit cards are not accepted.

Accommodations

Sometimes you're traveling with folks who want different things. Some people want to pitch a tent, while others want a real mattress. At ★ **Fall Hollow B&B and Campground** (1329 Columbia Hwy., 931/796-1480, http://fallhollow.com, primitive campsites $10-20, RV sites $35-40, cabins $69, B&B rooms $80-100), both options are possible. The B&B has two motel-style rooms, plus two rooms in the main house; rates include breakfast. The campground has 21 RV hookup sites, plus tent camping and a bathhouse with heated showers.

Back to the Trace

From central Mount Pleasant, it's a quick drive back to the Trace. Hop on TN-20 heading east and drive for about six miles. Turn left onto Meriwether Lewis Park Road, then right onto Campground Road. Another right turn gets you back on the Trace headed south.

Metal Ford and Buffalo River (MP 381.8)

Named for the smooth stone bottom of the Buffalo River that flows here, Metal Ford is a good place to rest. Pull into the parking lot on the right side of the parkway. The river bank is just steps away from the lot, as are a few picnic tables. There are no other amenities here.

Follow the easy, signed 0.15-mile loop trail through the woods and along the river bank. This is a nearly flat walk that should take about 10 minutes. In the early 1800s a steel mill stood at this site. There are few remnants from the facility, but signage both in the parking lot and along the trail helps you imagine how the area might have looked when it was active.

This was one place where settlers used to cross the Buffalo River. It can be fast moving, but is relatively shallow and about 25 feet wide in summer (though width and depth will vary based on rain levels). Because its banks are accessible, this spot is a popular swimming hole in hot summer months. Wear water shoes and beware slippery rocks.

Old Trace Drive (MP 375.8)

This pullout on the left side of the road leads you onto a section of the original Old Trace. Unlike some of the Old Trace sections that are only open to foot traffic, this 2.5-mile loop is open to vehicles, making it a great option for those who want to see the Old Trace but aren't interested in hiking.

Drive slowly (keep it to 20 mph or less) and watch for three distinct overlooks of the surrounding countryside. Because this is a narrow, one-way road and it's difficult for cars to pass each other, it isn't recommended that you stop or park on the drive. This old road is only suitable for cars, motorcycles, and bicycles. It isn't an option for those traveling by RV.

Laurel Hill Lake (MP 370)

If you have a rod and reel with you, you'll want to detour three miles east to **Laurel Hill Lake;** exit the parkway onto US 64/TN-15, near milepost 370, then turn left at Peter Cave Road and follow Brush Creek Road to the lake entrance. This state-managed lake is one of several in Tennessee specifically designed for anglers. You'll need a state fishing license ($6.50 per day Tennessee residents, $40.50 for three days for non-residents), which you can buy at the **Laurel Hill Tackle and Deli** (39 Peter Cave Rd., 931/762-7200, 6am-7:40pm daily, closed Wed. Labor Day-Memorial Day and when the fishing is too tempting for the folks here to resist). From there, you can rent a kayak, launch your own boat, or sit on shore to cast your reel. You'll need to sign in to launch at the lake, regardless of whether or not someone is in the shop. Recreational boating is not permitted.

Accommodations

Nearby **Laurel Hill Trail & Camp** (27 Smith Rd., Lawrenceburg, 931/722-4442, http://laurelhilltn.com, $10-25) offers a campground with 38 trailer hookups (water and electric) and restrooms. There are barns to keep horses in, as well as horse trails, making it a great place to stop if you're an equestrian Trace traveler.

Glenrock Branch (MP 364.5)

Nestled below a parking lot on the left side of the road is a natural amphitheater, a sweet area consisting of a small creek and a limestone bluff. Unlike at many other stops along the parkway, you can't see its wonders from the road. Park in the small lot, where you'll also find picnic tables and restrooms. At the top of the rocky area, look down and you can see the amphitheater and the short loop trail. The trail down to the amphitheater is steep but short (fewer than 50 steps), and the payoff is one of the prettiest picnic areas on the parkway.

Some of the signage on the parkway calls this "Lower Glenrock." There's also an easy 0.6-mile out-and-back trail to Upper Glenrock, another picnic area.

Sweetwater Branch (MP 363)

This creek was so named because the water was fresh (or "sweet") to the Trace pioneers who stopped to drink here. This pullout on the right side of the road offers only a few parking spots and trailhead access.

Sweetwater Branch Walk

Distance: 0.5-mile loop
Duration: 20 minutes
Difficulty: Moderate

Consider taking a quick stroll along Sweetwater Branch. It's a quiet, pretty area along the creek banks. This is the last hiking trail before you cross the Alabama-Tennessee state line. The walk includes some stairs and hilly terrain, so it isn't appropriate for wheelchairs.

TN-13 to Collinwood

Tiny Collinwood (population 982) is yards away from milepost 355. You won't spend an enormous amount of time here, but it is a worthwhile detour for information, restrooms, or a place to stay. Particularly if you are seeing the Trace on two wheels, this is a good place to rest between Nashville and Tupelo.

The **Wayne County Welcome Center** (219 E. Broadway St., 931/724-4337, www.waynecountychamber.org, 9am-5pm daily) is a notably well-stocked source of information. Stop here for maps, weather and road conditions, and friendly advice.

Food and Accommodations

A cute white frame house is home to **The Dragonfly** (100 2nd Ave. N., 931/724-6400, 8am-5pm Mon., 7am-5pm Tues.-Fri., 9am-5pm Sat., $6-18), a coffee shop with a great sweet tooth.

If you are pedaling your way down the parkway and need a place to sleep, consider **Miss Monetta's Country Cottages** (400 W. Tennessee St., 931/724-9309, www.missmonettas.com). It offers two non-smoking cottages, each with three bedrooms, satellite TV, and places to safely store bicycles overnight. Cottages sleep up to 5 or 6 people. Base rates are $90 for 1-2 people in the original cottage and $60 for 1 person in the newer cottage, with surcharges of $10 for each additional person.

Back to the Trace

Exit the parkway at TN-13 near milepost 355, and drive 0.2 mile west to the Wayne County Welcome Center. Retrace your steps to return to the parkway.

McGlamery Stand (MP 352.9)

This stop on the right side of the road is the site of an old frontier trading post (also called a "stand") for Trace travelers, reportedly established in 1849 by Jon McGlamery. The closest village was named McGlamery Stand in his honor. The stand didn't make it through the Civil War, but today you can still see an old fire tower among the trees and admire the foliage from cute rocking chairs near the parking area. There aren't any other amenities at this site.

Sunken Trace (MP 350.5)

The name says it all. This section of the Old Trace was often too waterlogged and sunken to allow wagons and horses to traverse it. Here, three preserved pathways come together to the right side of the parking lot, evidence of how Trace travelers would alter their route depending on which area was most easily crossed. The pull-off for this stop is on the left side of the road.

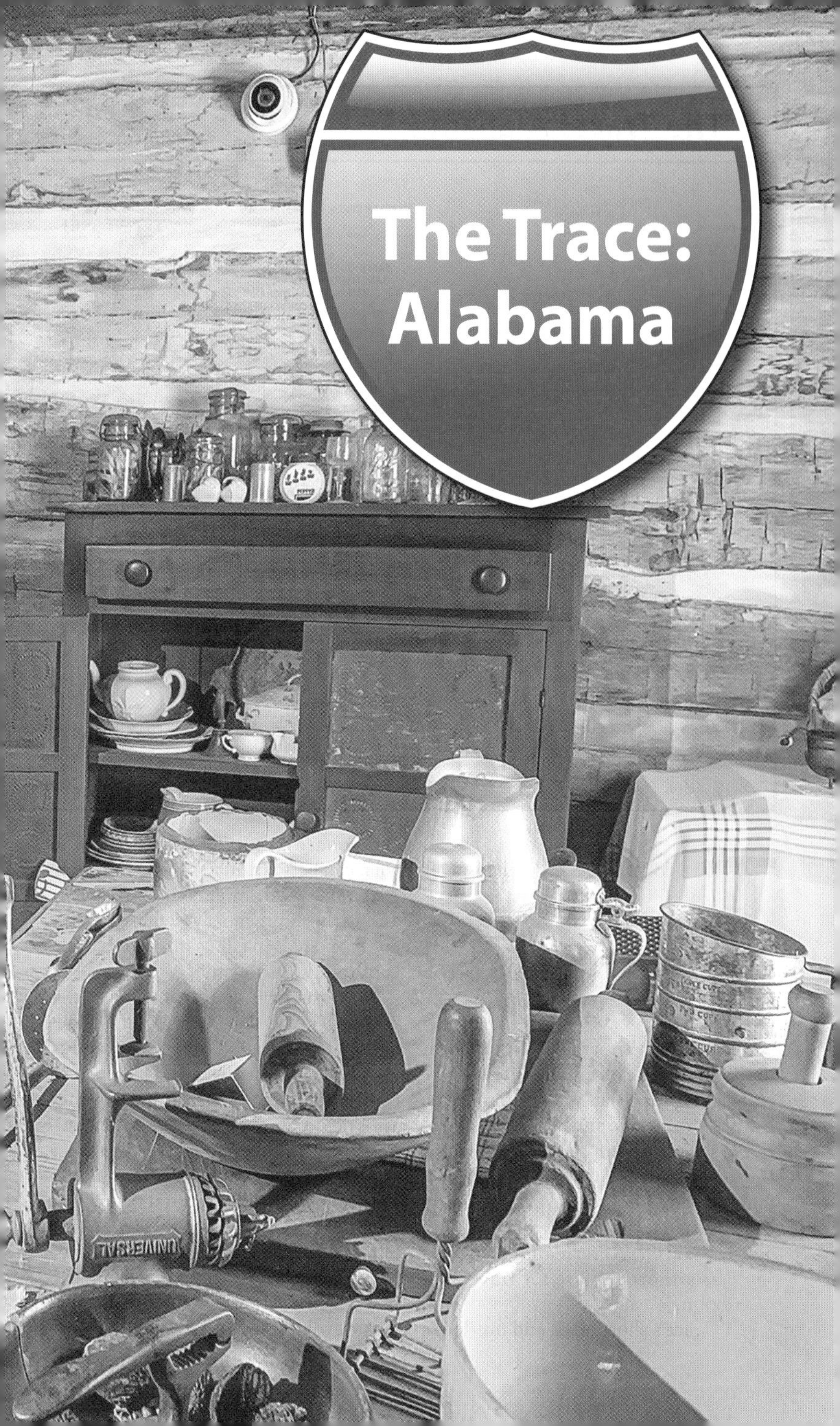
The Trace:
Alabama

The Trace: Alabama

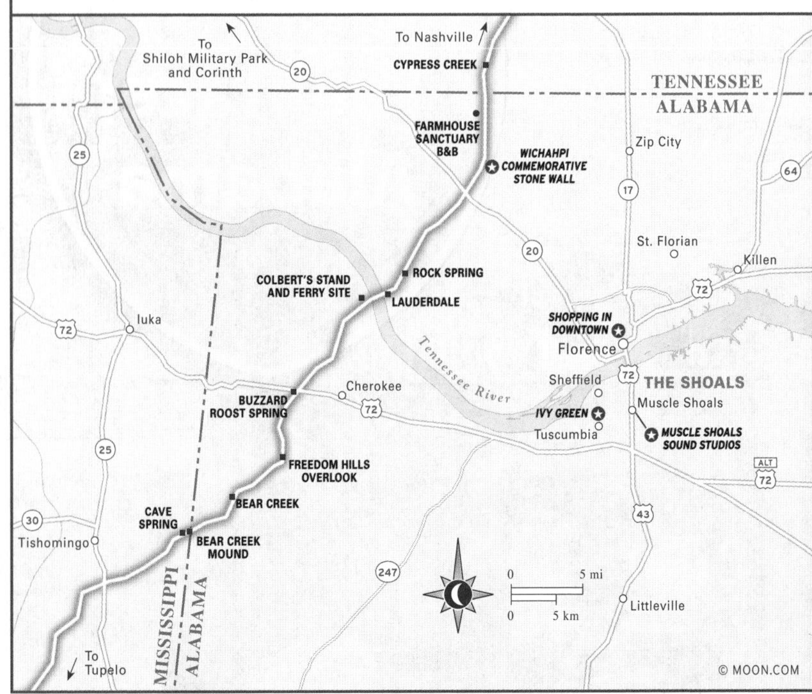

The Trace runs through just a small corner of Alabama, only 33 miles of the parkway's total 444.

Among them are a moving monument to the Trail of Tears and the sites of several former inns that sheltered soldiers, Native Americans, and other travelers.

This section of the Trace, while short, was essential for General Andrew Jackson's soldiers to travel south during the Battle of New Orleans. Long before, Native Americans used this route as a thoroughfare for traversing the region.

The Trace's short hikes and overlooks and wooded oases offer a shady respite to what can be hot summer temperatures in Alabama. Wildflowers bloom in spring and early summer, leaves change to oranges and reds in fall. Winter is crisp and cool, but generally mild.

The essential side trip on US 72 takes you to The Shoals region, sometimes called the Quad Cities: Tuscumbia, Muscle Shoals, Sheffield, and Florence. In addition to their Civil War history, they are known for their creative communities—particularly Florence, which has a strong designer and maker community—outdoor recreation, and importance to American musical history. The Muscle Shoals documentary renewed worldwide interest in the sound that continues to play an important role in the nation's music evolution.

Highlights

★ **Wichahpi Commemorative Stone Wall:** This wall, built one stone at a time, is one man's moving tribute to the tragic Trail of Tears (page 145).

★ **Ivy Green:** Reacquaint yourself with Helen Keller's inspirational story of perseverance at her birthplace (page 150).

★ **Muscle Shoals Sound Studio:** Visit one of the most influential music studios in the country, a restored gem where many legendary performers have recorded (page 153).

★ **Shopping in Downtown Florence:** Explore the funky and eclectic boutiques in this creative town (page 155).

Best Restaurants

★ **Rattlesnake Saloon:** This underground Western-themed restaurant is an experience (page 149).

★ **Odette:** This restaurant highlights farm-to-table cuisine with an update on Southern classics—plus delicious craft cocktails (page 158).

★ **Trowbridge's Ice Cream and Sandwich Bar:** This beloved old-fashioned soda fountain serves all your favorite childhood desserts (page 159).

★ **Yumm Thai Sushi and Beyond:** Find sushi along with noodles, rice dishes, and other Asian-inspired flavors (page 159).

Route Overview

There are just eight stops on this **33-mile** section of the Trace, but they are some of the Trace's most powerful and most scenic, including a somber reminder of U.S. history. It's worth setting aside at least **one day and one night** to explore the area.

Just 14 miles southeast of the Trace, The Shoals offer an entertaining side trip and the region's best music, creative maker cultures, and, of course, great food. Plan to spend at least one night in the area, using your campground or hotel as your home base to explore. All four cities have their charms, but Florence has the highest concentration of restaurants and hotels, as well as a robust college campus. Depending on how much time you want to spend at museums, shopping, and at restaurants, you easily could stretch this to two or three nights. Muscle Shoals's sights are essential stops on the Americana Music Triangle routes.

You'll likely have cell service for the entirety of your short drive in Alabama. If you are in need of bike, motorcycle, or car repair, this is one of the best areas to look for what you need before you head south into more remote areas.

Getting to the Starting Point

Car, Motorcycle, or Bicycle

As you drive or ride southbound on the Trace, you slip from Tennessee into Alabama as you ease past the state-line sign.

From **Memphis,** it's a 2.5-hour, 150-mile drive east along US 72 to milepost 320 on the Trace. To reach the Wichahpi Commemorative Stone Wall, the first stop of this section, you'll need to head north on the Trace for about 18 miles.

If you're coming from **Huntsville,** it's possible to join the Trace as well as enjoy The Shoals by taking I-565 and US 72 ALT west. This 80-mile route takes you through the Quad Cities and then north to the Wichahpi Commemorative Stone Wall, the first stop on the Alabama section of the route. This drive takes about 1.5 hours. From Huntsville, take I-565 west for about seven miles, after which the interstate ends and becomes US 72 ALT. In another few miles, AL-20 joins with US 72 ALT and you'll cross the Tennessee River into Decatur, a small city with beautiful views of Wheeler Lake. Continue west for another 40 miles until you reach the US 43/US 72 East junction. Turn right onto US 72 East, following signs for Florence/Muscle Shoals. In less than a mile you'll be in the heart of Muscle Shoals. (See *US 72 to The Shoals,* on page 148, for ideas on how to spend some time in this area.) To get to the Trace from Florence, the city north of the river, hop on AL-20 West for about 14 miles. Follow signs for Natchez Trace Parkway by exiting on the right, then

Best Accommodations

★ **Muscle Shoals Music House:** Sleep where stars like Bob Dylan once did in this scenic B&B (page 160).

★ **Residence Inn Marriott:** This is a surprisingly well-appointed chain hotel with spot-on service (page 161).

★ **Stricklin Hotel:** A renovated 1946 building is now a modern boutique hotel in the heart of downtown Florence (page 161).

★ **Farmhouse Sanctuary B&B:** It's just steps (or pedal strokes) from the Trace (page 161).

turning right at the stop sign to go north on the parkway. In 1.5 miles, turn right at the intersection with County Road 8 to reach the Wichahpi Commemorative Stone Wall.

Air

This isn't the easiest section of the Trace to access by air, but if that's your preference, the **Memphis International Airport** (MEM, 2491 Winchester Rd., 901/922-8000, www.flymemphis.com) is a good choice. MEM is served by Delta, Southwest, United, and other major airlines, with a number of nonstop routes. The three-concourse airport offers free Wi-Fi and many local dining options. It is a 2.5-hour, 150-mile drive from the airport to Florence.

The **Huntsville International Airport** (HSV, www.flyhuntsville.com) is closer to this portion of the Trace—just over 62 miles, an hour's drive, from Florence—but it is a smaller airport, with mostly regional destinations served. American, Delta, and United serve this northeastern Alabama city.

Train and Bus

Memphis Central Station (545 S. Main St., www.amtrak.com) is a stop on **Amtrak**'s 900-mile City of New Orleans route, which runs from New Orleans to Chicago, and has three stops in Alabama, although none of them are particularly convenient to The Shoals: Anniston (180 miles), Birmingham (117 miles), and Tuscaloosa (122 miles).

Greyhound (www.greyhound.com) serves Florence, stopping at the Quik Mart (348 Cox Creek Pkwy.). Fares are cheap—starting at $16 from Memphis, but the ride takes more than 16 hours. Greyhound offers free Wi-Fi on board.

★ Wichahpi Commemorative Stone Wall (MP 338)

The first stop while heading south on the Trace after crossing the Alabama-Tennessee state line (milepost 341.8) is the somber, yet inspiring, **Wichahpi Commemorative Stone Wall** (256/764-3617, 8am-4pm daily, free), referred to by locals as "Tom's Wall."

The late Tom Hendrix spent more than 30 years building what has become the largest unmortared wall in the country. The mile-long wall is a monument to Hendrix's great-great grandmother, Te-lah-nay, and her journey on the Trail of Tears. Each stone, hand-placed by Hendrix (or visitors) beginning in 1988, symbolizes a single step Te-lah-nay took. Today the wall includes stones from more than 120 different countries.

Fuel Up

Here's a quick list of places to exit the parkway in Alabama so that you can refuel at the closest gas station. (Some stops may take you to small towns, others will be just a single service station.)

The National Park Service also posts a list of nearby supply stations at most Trace rest areas, although the list is not updated regularly.

- **Milepost 338:** Exit at Lauderdale County Road 8; drive four miles east, then turn right (southeast) on AL-157 to the Pure station/Cloverdale Quick Mart.
- **Milepost 336:** Exit at AL-20; drive less than three miles east to the Haddock Quick Stop station in Florence.
- **Milepost 320:** Exit at US 72; drive less than two miles east to Cherokee. The BP station on the south side of Lee Highway/US 72 is the most convenient. There's also an Exxon station to the west of the Trace on US 72—again, about two miles away.

Once here, you can walk in solitude along the maze-like wall, reflecting on its significance and the way in which the United States has treated Native Americans. The land is largely flat and easy to traverse, with many places to stop and rest along the way. Some parts of the path may be difficult for wheelchairs to maneuver. Much of the wall winds its way under oak tree canopies, providing welcome shade in the hot Alabama summer. Some people believe certain stones have specific properties, such as one that is said to cure infertility.

The entrance to this magnificent site is not technically on the Trace itself, but in recent years the National Park Service and Trace enthusiasts have embraced it and are helping to spread the word. If you are traveling with a large group (10 people or more), call to reserve a time for a tour.

Set aside at least 30 minutes to walk along the wall; double that if you want to sit and listen to stories told by Hendrix's family. Visitors are welcome to bring their own rocks to add to the wall. Please note that Hendrix's family considers this a sacred space; treat it respectfully.

Take the first left turn (east) after milepost 338 onto County Road 8 (CR-8). The entrance to the monument is well-marked 150 yards down on the right. Because it isn't an official Trace stop, this is one of the few places on the Trace where you won't see clear signage (though the signage for County Road 8 is clear), so watch the milepost markers. There's typically plenty of parking across the street by the cotton field on County Road 319. To get back on the Trace after you visit the wall, simply turn around on CR-8, drive 150 yards, and turn left to continue heading south on the parkway.

Rock Spring (MP 330.2)

The first true Alabama Trace stop is a pretty oasis and easy hike. On the left side of the road, follow a short road to a loop parking lot. The parking lot is not visible from the parkway, so look for signage on the right.

From here you can access a simple half-mile **loop trail** to a bubbling spring. Allot about 20 minutes to walk in this shaded oasis. The terrain is easy, with some picturesque square stepping stones that enable you to cross Colbert Creek (this portion isn't wheelchair accessible). Birders and wildlife-watchers love this area because the spring provides a home to beavers, ruby-throated hummingbirds,

A Day on the Trace: Alabama

Any day is a great day to be in this tiny corner of Alabama. It starts off with much of what makes the Trace so special: local history, Native American spirituality, and scenic views at **Wichahpi Commemorative Stone Wall** (a.k.a. Tom's Wall). Start here by strolling the mile-long wall built by the late Tom Hendrix to honor his ancestors. Head back on the Trace for a few minutes to take in more views along a 20-minute hike at **Rock Spring.**

After that, it will be time to fuel up, which you can do by driving the 20-plus miles to The Shoals. On the way, stop at the **Key Underwood Coon Dog Cemetery** and honor the memorials people have left for their faithful companions. From there, grab lunch at one of downtown Florence's delicious eateries, such as **Odette,** topping off your meal with an ice cream sundae from **Trowbridge's Ice Cream and Sandwich Bar.** Browse the city's creative shopping community with stops at **Billy Reid** and **Alabama Chanin.**

Even if you don't have time to tour either spot, drive by **Muscle Shoals Sound Studio (3614 Jackson Highway)** and **FAME Studios** in Muscle Shoals, important sights in music history. Pull into the **Stricklin Hotel,** then explore downtown Florence on foot, perhaps with a cocktail at **On the Rocks** and dinner at **Ricatoni's Italian Grill.** Catch live music at the **FloBama Music Hall** before turning in for the night.

The next morning, feast at Big Bad Breakfast before returning to the Trace via US 72 (just under 30 miles) to finish this section of the route (about 12 miles) before crossing into Mississippi. For a complete list of every stop along the Trace, download the four detailed National Park Service maps (www.nps.gov/natr).

salamanders, and other wildlife. This is a good place to take in wildflowers as well, particularly in the late summer and early fall, when delicate jewelweed is in bloom.

Other than a few parking spots, picnic tables, and the trail, there are no other amenities at this stop. Don't confuse this stop with **Rocky Springs,** at milepost 54.8, which is one of the Trace's three campgrounds.

Lauderdale (MP 328.7)

This picnic area on the shore of the Tennessee River is the best spot for views of the John Coffee Memorial Bridge. The bridge, which is the longest on the parkway, was built in 1964. It's named for John Coffee, who fought with Andrew Jackson in the Battle of New Orleans. Coffee was married to an aunt of Rachel Donelson, Jackson's wife. From this vantage point it's easy to imagine how difficult it was for settlers to traverse the river in the 1700s without the aid of such a bridge.

This is the only road immediately to the north of the bridge, so it's very easy to spot. Entrance to the loop parking lot is on the left side of the road.

Colbert's Stand and Ferry Site (MP 327.3)

In its heyday, Colbert's Stand was an essential stop on the Old Trace. George Colbert and his brother Levi operated a ferry that took Trace travelers across the Tennessee River from 1800 to 1819. George also ran an inn on this site. Lore suggests that Colbert once charged Andrew Jackson $75,000 to ferry his Tennessee militiamen across the river, a princely sum in those days.

After crossing the Tennessee River, pull off the Trace into a well-marked park on the right side of the road. There are restrooms at the Colbert's Ferry site,

The Remembrance Wall One Man Built

One of the country's most compelling landmarks was started as a quiet family monument. Tom Hendrix had heard the stories about his great-great-grandmother, Te-lah-nay, a member of the Yuchi tribe, who was forced from her home, like many Native Americans during the Indian Removal Act of 1830. After her exile to Oklahoma, Te-lah-nay spent five years walking back home to Florence, Alabama, longing for the Tennessee River that she believed sung to her.

Motivated by an elder of the Yuchi tribe who said to him: "All things shall pass. Only the stones will remain," Hendrix started to build a wall to honor Te-lah-nay's journey home, with just his own hands (and, eventually, more than three trucks, 22 wheelbarrows, and some 3,500 pairs of gloves). No stonemasons or other professionals pitched in.

For years this site, a monument of irregular height and thickness, was simply called "Tom's Wall" (and most locals still refer to it as such). But lore goes that one day, a spiritual person named Charlie Two Moons walked the length of the wall and said to Hendrix: "The wall does not belong to you, Brother Tom. It belongs to all people. You are just the keeper. I will tell you that it is *wichahpi,* which means 'like the stars.' When they come, some will ask, 'Why does it bend, and why is it higher and wider in some places than in others?' Tell them it is like your great-great-grandmother's journey, and their journey through life: It is never straight."

Now it is officially called the **Wichahpi Commemorative Stone Wall,** after Charlie Two Moons's vision, and is registered in the Library of Congress. Hendrix wrote a self-published book, *If the Legends Fade* (www.ifthelegendsfade.com), about Te-lah-nay and other Native American women, filled with legends of the Tennessee River and other stories. Hendrix passed away in 2017 at age 83. His son now maintains the site, with hopes of preserving it, and their family history, for generations.

the only stop with such amenities in the Alabama section of the Trace (the next restrooms are at Tishomingo State Park at milepost 304.5).

From the parking lot, walk 50 yards up the path to see where the inn once stood. Here you'll find exhibits—a joint effort of the Chickasaw Nation and the Natchez Trace Parkway Association—about the rich Native American history at this site.

US 72 to The Shoals

Tuscumbia, Muscle Shoals, Sheffield, and **Florence** are four cities sometimes called the Quad Cities, in a region referred to as The Shoals. These neighboring towns have long been rich in music history, creative communities, and natural beauty. U.S. history comes alive here, too, with many Native American and Civil War sites. World-class golf courses and water sports on the Tennessee River attract lovers of the outdoors.

Until recently, The Shoals had been something of an insider secret, thanks to its location, tucked away in northwest Alabama. In 2013, the documentary *Muscle Shoals* was released, and the secret was out. Now folks are flocking here to see the place where Black and white musicians have long worked together in harmony.

Leaving the Trace

The cities can be reached a number of ways from the parkway, but the easiest and most direct is to take US 72 (near milepost 320) and head east about 20 miles. To get to downtown Tuscumbia, take US 72 for 19 miles, then turn left (north); the road continues as US 72. Sixth Street marks Tuscumbia's downtown area.

US 72 continues north for several

blocks into Muscle Shoals. As the highway travels north, you'll pass Sheffield on the west. Take either 2nd Street or Hatch Boulevard to get into downtown Sheffield. To reach Florence, stay on the highway as it crosses the river. Park near Pine and Court Streets to explore downtown Florence.

Stopping at the Rattlesnake Saloon

It's just a quick detour off US 72 on the way to The Shoals to the famous ★ **Rattlesnake Saloon** (1292 Mt. Mills Rd., 256/370-7220, www.rattlesnakesaloon.net, 11am-10pm Thurs.-Sat., 11am-3pm Sun. Apr.-Sept., 11am-10pm Thurs.-Sat. Feb.-Mar. and Oct.-Nov., $4-12). It's worth the extra miles—when else will you be able to eat in a Western-themed restaurant that also happens to be nestled under a rock? This quirky restaurant features burgers, nachos, nightly live music, and is the type of place where everyone is wearing cowboy boots. It's popular, so be prepared to wait. If you're coming in spring or fall, bring a jacket. Natural rock outcroppings form a three-sided cave. So, even when you are seating in the cave, you are exposed to the elements and it can get cold. There is limited seating indoors, in a structure built into the side of the rock. You'll lose the cave ambience if you sit indoors, but you get more of the Old West saloon vibe. Alcohol is only served until 5pm.

The walk from the parking lot to the restaurant takes about 10 minutes down a steep driveway with a number of stairs. If you're not up for the trek, there's a shuttle that will transport you. Wait under the "taxi" structure in the parking lot.

Rattlesnake Saloon also offers some untraditional accommodations. You can spend the night in a silo for $72 (for two people) or opt for a campsite ($10-27) or cabin ($150). There's a sense of camaraderie here; if you're looking to hang out with other travelers, this is the place.

Get to the restaurant from the Trace by taking US 72 east for about eight miles. Turn right (south) onto Mount Mills Road and continue for about seven miles. To continue on to The Shoals after you've eaten, continue south down Mount Mills Road for one mile, then turn left onto Bald Knob Road. After about a mile, turn left (north) onto AL-247. In about seven miles, turn right (east) to pick up US 72.

Sights

Tuscumbia

The **Alabama Music Hall of Fame** (617 US 72 W., 256/381-4417, www.alamhof.org, 9am-5pm Tues.-Sat., adults $10, seniors and students $8, children under 12 $6, free for children 5 and under) honors the state's musicians as well as its musical legacy, particularly in the genres of pop, rock, country, gospel, blues, and R&B. The lobby features bronze stars on the floor—its Walk of Fame—and a chandelier that projects a light show set to music. Exhibits include plaster casts of Lionel Richie and Sonny James, a wax figure of Hank Williams, costumes worn by members of St. Paul & the Broken Bones, and instruments and memorabilia from the many (and often surprising) pop culture and music icons who have a connection to the state of Alabama. A recording studio lets you record your own video or single from a catalog of songs, many of which have a connection to the area.

The coonhound is a quintessential part of the Southern landscape. In 1937 a man named Key Underwood buried his faithful companion, Troop, at the site that would later become the **Key Underwood Coon Dog Cemetery** (Coondog Cemetery Rd., 256/412-5970, http://coondogcemetery.com, dawn-dusk daily). Today it's a one-of-a-kind site, where only coon dogs can be buried, and where tombstones demonstrate loving devotion to pals named Smoky, Ralston, and, of course, Troop. More than 185 coonhounds are now buried here. Each Labor Day, the Friends of the Coondog Cemetery host a celebration, with music, dancing, and a liar's contest. The cemetery is off US 72,

seven miles southwest of Tuscumbia. Turn right on Coondog Cemetery Road and follow signs.

Built in 1972, the **Tennessee Valley Museum of Art** (511 N. Water St., 256/383-0533, www.tvaa.net, 9am-5pm Mon.-Fri. 1pm-3pm Sun., adults $5, students and children $3, free Sun.) is the art museum of this corner of Alabama. The permanent exhibit houses the Martin Petroglyph and a set of boulders with Native American carvings from 600-1,000 years ago. Traveling exhibits feature photography, painting, and other fine art.

A historical white-brick building built in 1881, the **Colbert County Courthouse** (201 N. Main St., 256/386-8500, 8am-4:30pm Mon.-Fri., free) still houses county government offices. It was damaged by a fire in 1908, and the clock tower you see today was added during the renovations.

★ Ivy Green

Built in 1820 by Helen Keller's grandparents, **Ivy Green** (300 N. Commons St., West Tuscumbia, 256/383-4066, www.helenkellerbirthplace.org, 8:30am-4pm Mon.-Sat., adults $6, seniors $5, students $3) is the birthplace and historic home of the brilliant woman who would become a leader for education and rights for the blind and deaf. Tours are available for the home, which is listed on the National Register of Historic Places, as well as the grounds. The clapboard house has been left mostly how it was in Keller's time.

One of the highlights of the 640-acre property is the well pump where "Miracle Worker" Anne Sullivan taught the young Keller to spell out "water" with hand symbols, connecting those symbols to a concrete meaning. By the end of that day, Keller, who had been largely unable to communicate, knew 30 words. Six

Top to bottom: Rattlesnake Saloon; Ivy Green; Muscle Shoals Sound Studio

months later she knew the alphabet and 625 words.

While the building itself is interesting, it is the stories told here of Sullivan and Keller's friendship and hard work that are compelling for kids and adults alike. *The Miracle Worker* is performed here each summer as part of the annual Helen Keller Festival.

Ivy Green is in West Tuscumbia, two miles north of US 72.

Muscle Shoals

Muscle Shoals is one of the fastest-growing cities in Alabama and, of its Quad Cities brethren, the best known—thanks, in part, to the 2013 documentary that bears its name. Today most visitors come to the area to learn about its musical heritage and to make music themselves.

To reach downtown Muscle Shoals from the parkway, take US 72 for 25 miles (stay on US 72 as it turns north), then turn right on Avalon Avenue. It is less than three miles from Tuscumbia to Muscle Shoals.

A major regional landmark built in the 1920s, the **Wilson Lock and Dam** (704 S. Wilson Dam Rd., 256/764-5223, www.tva.gov) made it possible for The Shoals to become a major transportation hub for the area. One of 10 locks on the 650-mile Tennessee River, it's the highest single lift lock east of the Rocky Mountains and provides both electricity and flood protection to the region. With a normal lift between 93 and 100 feet, Wilson Lock and Dam is a feat of engineering. When construction began in 1918, this dam, named for Woodrow Wilson, was the largest hydroelectric installation. Call ahead because the dam may be closed for cleaning or security reasons. The dam is 1.3 miles south of US 72, on the banks of the Tennessee River.

FAME Studios

What do Etta James, the Osmonds, Aretha Franklin, Cher, Alicia Keys, Otis Redding, and Jamey Johnson have in common? They're all part of the long list of performers who have recorded at **FAME Studios** (603 Avalon Ave., 256/381-0801, http://famestudios.com, tours at 9am and 4pm Mon.-Fri., tours on the hour 10am-2pm Sat., $10). This legendary recording studio was founded in 1961 by Rick Hall. During its heyday in the 1960s, it was one of the few places in the country where Black and white musicians could record together without incident, in part because its remote location kept it off the radar of those outside the music industry. But many musicians would travel to work here (and still do), and it was here that the famous Muscle Shoals sound was born.

Hall was famously difficult to work with and, in 1969, his four sessions musicians (including bass player David Hood, father to the Drive-By Truckers' Patterson Hood and the only one who is still a working musician) tired of his treatment. They opened a competing studio, Muscle Shoals Sound Studio, which welcomed even bigger acts—like the Rolling Stones.

Hall's wife, Linda, offers guided tours of this still-working studio. You'll hear many stories about Hall and the musicians who've recorded here, although less context is provided than on the Muscle Shoals Sound Studio tour. The walls are heavy with music memorabilia. Avalon Avenue is one block east of US 72.

W. C. Handy Birthplace, Museum, and Library

The name William Christopher Handy may not be immediately familiar. But when you immerse yourself in his life at the **W. C. Handy Birthplace, Museum, and Library** (620 W. College St., 256/760-6434, www.wchandymuseum.org, 10am-4pm Tues.-Sat., adults $12, children $6), you'll realize you were familiar with his music.

The modest cabin that was W. C. Handy's birthplace in 1873 is now the site of this museum, which houses

The Muscle Shoals Sound

FAME Studios in Muscle Shoals

People in Muscle Shoals like to say that music is in the water here. The area was the birthplace of W. C. Handy, known as "The Father of the Blues." Sun Studio and Sun Records owner Sam Phillips, also known as "The Father of Rock and Roll," was born in Florence.

But perhaps it's Rick Hall who deserves the most credit for creating the Muscle Shoals sound, which is funk-meets-soul-meets-rock. Hall created an all-white house band, Muscle Shoals Rhythm Section, and helped them record at his FAME Studios in 1967. In 1969, the group moved on to form their own Muscle Shoals Sound Studio in nearby Sheffield. From there they got big, and became known as The Swampers, a moniker that stuck only after Lynyrd Skynyrd name-checked them in "Sweet Home Alabama": "Now Muscle Shoals has got the Swampers; And they've been known to pick a song or two." Eventually The Swampers and Hall had a falling out over pay. The four musicians knew their worth and left FAME and went to the Muscle Shoals Sound Studio in 1969, further cementing the area's soulful sound as an iconic part of American music.

Due to its then-remote location, the studios were places in the 1960s where Black and white artists felt they could make music together and record together without push-back or negativity.

considerable memorabilia from the man who created St. Louis Blues, Beale Street Blues, and Memphis Blues. Handy is considered the "Father of the Blues." The African American composer had a significant impact not just on blues, but on the music that eventually would become rock 'n' roll.

Tour guides are knowledgeable and impart a lot of information about Handy's roll in modern music. There are several good videos that offer additional context. Artifacts include Handy's piano and lots of sheet music. The museum also helps organize the W. C. Handy Music Festival each July and a birthday party for Handy each November. College Street is six blocks north of US 72.

Sheffield

Tiny Sheffield, Alabama, is the oft-forgotten member of the Quad Cities, sometimes overshadowed by Muscle Shoals' music and Florence's creative scene. But Sheffield is crucial in a tour of the area, given its role in U.S. history and music. In 1815 General Andrew Jackson brought his troops here to cross the Tennessee River on the way to the Battle of New Orleans. Several sites important to the Muscle Shoals sound, such as the legendary Muscle Shoals Sound Studio, are technically in Sheffield city limits.

Sheffield is slightly northwest of the other Shoals cities. To get there from the parkway, follow US 72 east for 20 miles (into Tuscumbia), then turn right on Hook Street, which will become Montgomery Avenue. Follow this for 10 miles.

★ Muscle Shoals Sound Studio

Perhaps once the best-known music studio in Muscle Shoals and also known by its address, **3614 Jackson Highway** (256/978-5151, http://muscleshoalssoundstudio.org, 10am-4pm Mon.-Sat., adults $15, military and seniors $13, students $10, free for children 10 and under) is listed on the National Register of Historic Places. It may look familiar: It's appeared on the cover of a Cher album named after the famous address. Between 1969 and 1978, this was the place musicians including Bob Seger, Paul Simon, and the Rolling Stones came to record. After it closed, though, it fell into disrepair and was nothing more than a place to take a photo. After the *Muscle Shoals* documentary, Dr. Dre and Jimmy Iovine from Beats Electronics decided to make a sizeable philanthropic gift toward its restoration. Muscle Shoals Sound Studio reopened in 2017, fully restored to its 1969 glory down to its retro plaid couches. Musicians such as The Black Keys have come to record here since.

In addition to nabbing the requisite selfie in front of the famous sign, you should take a **tour of the studios** (tours hourly on the half-hour 10:30am-3:30pm Mon.-Sat.). In addition to viewing memorabilia, you'll hear stories about the music history made here—for instance about the rift between Rick Hall and The Swampers that led to them leaving FAME Studios to create this one. Tours are offered on a first-come, first-served basis (no reservations accepted).

Florence

From early Native American explorers and Civil War soldiers to 19th-century musicians and contemporary artists, Florence has been attracting people for generations. Much of the quaint downtown district is on the National Register of Historic Places; most of the buildings were constructed between 1880 and 1920. Allow time to stroll here, and for shopping, listening to music, eating, and drinking.

Florence is 29 miles east of the parkway on US 72. Park near Pine and Court Streets to explore downtown.

In 1974 former University of North Alabama (UNA) president Robert M. Guillot brought a 35-pound lion cub to the campus. Named Leo, the lion spent the next 14 years helping lead the school to victory. The original Leo died in 1988, but the tradition didn't, and a long succession of lions came to campus. Today Leo III and Una (a female lion companion) live next to a waterfall in the 12,764-square foot **George Carroll Lion Habitat** (1 Harrison Plaza, 800/825-5862, www.una.edu/lioncam, free), the only live lion mascot on a U.S. campus. Note that there is not an official address for the habitat, but the main address for UNA brings you to the main parking lot and fountain at the front of campus, which are adjacent to the habitat.

One of the Quad Cities' oldest buildings, **Pope's Tavern and Museum** (203 Hermitage Dr., 256/760-6439, 10am-4pm Tues.-Sat., adults $5, students $2) has been a stagecoach stop, a tavern, an inn, a hospital, and an army command center (for both the North and South). Today it is an affordable, engaging museum chock-full of artifacts, particularly those from the Civil War era. Don't miss the vertically strung piano, one of only four ever made.

Frank Lloyd Wright Rosenbaum House

Architecture critic Peter Blake once called four of Frank Lloyd Wright's buildings among America's most beautiful. One of them was **Rosenbaum House** (601 Riverview Dr., 256/718-5050, http://wrightinalabama.com, 10am-4pm Tues.-Sat., 1pm-4pm Sun., $10 adults, $5 students and seniors), the only Frank Lloyd Wright building in the state of Alabama.

Rosenbaum House is an example of Wright's utilitarian Usonian-style architecture, and perhaps one of its best examples. The L-shaped red brick house was designed to be affordable and functional and was built for Mildred and Stanley Rosenbaum and their family. It is one of the few Wright homes with an addition designed by Wright himself (the Rosenbaums had four boys who needed a little more room to roam than the original design afforded). Mildred donated the house to the city of Florence in 1999, and some of her weavings are on display inside. The house has a strong connection to the outdoors, where the large lot blends with the house through the tall glass windows. Tours last 45 minutes. Admission sales are in the gift shop across the street from the house.

Florence Indian Mound Museum

While the state of Mississippi is home to the largest number of Native-American mound sites in the South, the **Florence Indian Mound Museum** (1028 S. Court St., 256/760-6427, 10am-4pm Tues.-Sat., 1pm-4pm Sun., adults $5, children $2) is a worthy stop in Alabama. The small museum is well-designed for exploration, with interactive displays, artifacts in kid-height pullout drawers, and several videos. It sits at the base of a 43-foot-high ceremonial mound, the summit of which offers 360-degree views and is accessed by a 68-step staircase.

Kennedy-Douglas Center for the Arts

The city of Florence oversees the three adjacent houses that comprise the **Kennedy-Douglass Center for the Arts** (217 E. Tuscaloosa St., 256/760-6379, www.kdartcenter.org, 9am-4pm Mon.-Fri., free). Exhibitions change regularly (more than once a month) and are always offered at no charge. A robust schedule of lectures, workshops, and other programming rounds out the offerings. The small giftshop is chockful of quality art supplies and crafts for kids.

Festivals and Events

Food and wine flow during the **Florence Wine Fest** (118 E. Mobile St., www.florencewinefest.com, May, $65-200) at Mobile Plaza. Proceeds benefit local charities, and wine to take home is available at a discount.

The Kennedy-Douglass Center for the Arts in Florence presents **Arts Alive** (217 E. Tuscaloosa St., www.alabamaartsalive.com, 9am-5pm Sat., 10am-5pm Sun., May), an annual juried arts show in Wilson Park.

The week-long **Helen Keller Festival** (www.helenkellerfestival.com, June) brings antique car shows, live music, amusement rides, and more to Tuscumbia's Spring Park (1 Spring Park Rd.). This festival is timed to coincide with the annual production of *The Miracle Worker*, produced at Ivy Green, Keller's birthplace.

The 10-day **W. C. Handy Music Festival** (www.wchandymusicfestival.com, July) celebrates the Father of the Blues. Since 1982 this festival has been played around Tuscumbia—in churches, bars, and parks.

Florence favorite designer hosts a summer party, **Billy Reid Shindig** (www.billyreid.com/shindig11, Aug., $150-2,900), with music, food, and fashion. It's a community event that draws lots of celebrities.

The **Trail of Tears Commemorative Motorcycle Ride** (http://al-tn-trailoftears.

net, Sept.) revs its engines from Bridgeport to Waterloo, Alabama, along the Trail of Tears on the third Saturday of September each year.

★ Shopping

Florence has long fostered a culture of creativity, with a particular strength in fashion. As a result, the shopping scene is especially eclectic. Designers Billy Reid and Natalie Chanin, who both have outposts in Florence, have attracted others to this corner of the state. Expect to find lots of one-of-a-kind items in the many boutiques.

Downtown Florence

Court Street is Florence's main drag, and it's where some of the top shops dress their windows. Stroll this historic area, especially between Tennessee and Tombigee Streets, to window shop or stock up on gifts, home decor, and women's clothing and jewelry.

Perhaps most responsible for the new Southern preppie movement is **Billy Reid** (114 N. Court St., 256/767-4692, www.billyreid.com, 10am-6pm Mon.-Thurs., 10am-7pm Fri.-Sat.). This designer has stores in New York, New Orleans, Atlanta, Austin, Charleston, Dallas, Houston, Nashville, Chicago, and Washington DC. But the multi-story headquarters is in an old Florence bookstore, selling designs for both women and men. The brand combines Southern aesthetics with New York fashion and helped put Florence on the map. Even if you're not in the market for pricey threads, stopping in the well-designed store is worthwhile. You can also book a room designed by Reid at the nearby Gunrunner Hotel.

Printers & Stationers Inc. (113 Court St., 256/764-8061, http://printersandstationers.com, 8am-5pm Mon.-Fri., 11am-4pm Sat.) was founded in 1933 and stocks stationery and invitations, as

Top to bottom: Florence Indian Mound Museum; Arts Alive; Alabama Chanin

you'd expect, plus fun gifts and accessories. Tucked inside the Stricklin Hotel, **Reclaimed Spirit by Stacey** (315 N Court St., 256/633-7788, www.reclaimedspiritbystacey.com, 9am-2:30pm Sun.-Fri., 9am-5pm Sat.) sells locally made and designed jewelry, gifts, and souvenirs. **Studio 23** (333 E College St., 256/247-2601, http://shopstudio23.com, 10am-5pm Tues.-Sat.) is home to a collection of artists' studios. Browse their booths to find jewelry, woodwork, paintings, sculptures, and textiles.

Check out **Alabama Outdoors** (119 N. Court St., 256/764-1809, http://alabamaoutdoors.com, 10am-7pm Mon.-Sat., noon-5pm Sun.) to buy clothing suitable for the state's great weather and open spaces. This statewide chain offers clothing and gear for outdoor adventuring of all sorts, from climbing to skiing to hiking.

North Florence

Locals consider Wood and Royal Avenues to be North Florence, even though the area is just a quick walk (about a mile) north of historic downtown. Situated above the University of North Alabama campus, the area is dotted with antiques shops and has more of a residential vibe than downtown.

Alabama Chanin (462 Lane Dr., 256/760-1090, http://alabamachanin.com, 10am-5pm Mon.-Fri.), the company started by Florence native Natalie Chanin, is another brand that has defined the town. Alabama Chanin sells clothing and other goods made from organic cotton grown and sewn in the United States (and, in many cases, in the state). For those who are so motivated, the company also offers workshops to learn the signature design technique.

Marigail Mathis (1631 Darby Dr., 256/555-5555, http://marigails.myshopify.com, 10am-5pm Mon.-Sat.) sells contemporary women's clothing, including brands such as Eileen Fisher, BB Dakota, and Lilla P NYC. A wood-sided house is home to **Frolic** (1326 N. Pine St., 256/710-1937, 11am-5pm Tues.-Wed., 10am-5pm Thurs.-Fri., 10am-4pm Sat.), where fashion-forward yet affordable women's clothing rules the racks. Most items are in the $25-50 range.

Tuscumbia

Downtown Tuscumbia has a few boutiques worth browsing including **Audie Mescal Clothing** (101 N. Main St., 256/314-6684, www.audiemescal.com, 10am-5:30pm Mon.-Sat.), which specializes in women's clothing, with brands including Johnny Was and Traffic People. **Cold Water Books** (101 W. 6th St., 256/381-2525, 7am-8pm Sun.-Thurs., 7am-9pm Fri., 9am-9pm Sat., 1pm-5pm Sun.) is an independent bookshop and café housed in a historic building from the 1800s.

Sports and Recreation

A namesake spring runs through **Spring Park** (1 Spring Park Rd., Tuscumbia,

256/386-5670, 9am-9pm daily), which boasts a playground, picnic pavilions, and a stage that is well-used for live music and other shows year-round. Don't miss the water show and lighted waterfall. You can even trout fish here (in season and with a license, of course).

The **Cypress Lakes Golf & Tennis Club** (1311 E. 6th St., Muscle Shoals, 256/381-1232, www.cypresslakesgolfandtennis.com, 7am-7pm Tues.-Sun., greens fees $15-42) is open to the public. Of the 18 holes, 15 have a water challenge. There are five sets of tees, so the course accommodates golfers of all skill levels. Tennis courts and a swimming pool are also open in warm weather.

Alabama's **Robert Trent Jones Golf Trail** (www.rtjgolf.com) is not just a golf course (or a collection of golf courses): It is the largest golf course construction project ever attempted. Today the trail includes 26 golf courses at 11 different sites across Alabama, including two 18-hole courses in Muscle Shoals: **Fighting Joe** and **Schoolmaster** (990 SunBelt Pkwy., Muscle Shoals, 256/446-5111, greens fees $65 and up).

In Sheffield, the preserved wood-and-metal **Old Railroad Bridge** (2100 Ashe Blvd., Sheffield, http://oldrailroadbridge.com, dawn-dusk daily, free), built in 1840, was once the main way to cross the Tennessee River. This bridge no longer fully spans the river. Walk 0.75 mile out to get great views of the river or connect to nearby walking trails for a longer (yet still easy) hike.

Pretty **Wilson Park** (E. Tombigee St. and Wood Ave., Florence) is in the center of Florence's downtown, across the street from the stately Florence-Lauderdale public library. You can get to the fountain in the center of the park by following one of four pathways, one from each corner of the park. The fountain is a great backdrop for photos. The park houses a **sculpture of W. C. Handy,** Father of the Blues. Numerous events, including the juried Arts Alive show, Music in the Park,

Robert Trent Jones Golf Trail

Haunted Ghost Tour, and the Alabama Renaissance Faire, take place here.

If seeing so many equestrians along the Trace has you wanting to ride horseback, head to **Seven Springs Lodge** (1292 Mt. Mills Rd., Tuscumbia, 256/370-7218, www.rattlesnakesaloon.net/lodge, $10 per day). The lodge offers 20,000 acres of woodland for horseback riding, as well as camping ($10-27), fishing, and stables for those with their own horses. Guided horseback rides are offered the second week of each month.

Just five miles off of US 72, **Hawk Pride Mountain Offroad** (3834 Hawk Pride Mountain Rd., Tuscumbia, 256/349-4150, www.hawkpridemountainoffroad.com, drivers $15-35, passengers $10-20, free for children under 10) is a 1,000-acre park with ATV trails, rock crawling trails, and other outdoor activities. Want to stay and play? Camping, cabins, and RV sites are available, too.

Beardo Outdoors (256/577-5138, 8am-3pm daily, rental rates begin at $35) leads guided paddling trips down Cypress Creek, the Tennessee River, and other waterways. Reservations are required 72 hours in advance. Kayaks and paddleboards are available.

Food

Tuscumbia

A soda fountain housed in an 1833 building, **The Palace Ice Cream and Sandwich Shop** (100 S. Main St., 256/386-8210, 11am-5pm Mon.-Sat., $8-12) is one of those time-travel kind of stops. A bicycle hangs from the ceiling, the waitresses call you "sweetie," and the milkshakes are delicious. The Palace offers a full lunch menu, with burgers, sandwiches, and more, but most people just come for the ice cream.

Old-school Southern cooking sticks to your ribs at local favorite **City Restaurant** (108 W. 5th St., 256/383-9809, 7am-3pm Mon.-Fri., $7-12). The menu changes daily but is chock-full of classics, such as meatloaf, fried chicken, and pot pie. The downtown location means you'll see lots of local government officials here during lunch.

Muscle Shoals

A regional chain, **Champy's Chicken** (120 2nd St., 256/389-9985, http://champyschicken.com, 10:30am-10pm Sun.-Thurs., 10:30am-midnight Fri.-Sat., $7-20) serves fried chicken, beans, coleslaw and other traditional sides, and plenty of beer. Live music makes it a popular hangout as well as a place to eat. The decor is eclectic.

Florence

People love to eat in Florence as much as they like to shop. Start your culinary tour at ★ **Odette** (120 N. Court St., 256/349-5219, www.odettealabama.com, 11am-11pm Tues.-Thurs., 11am-1am Fri.-Sat., 11am-3pm Sun., $7-30), where you'll find a menu featuring farm-to-table cuisine with lots of Southern influences and ingredients. Pair your meal with a drink from the craft cocktail menu.

Casual but tasty, **306 Barbecue** (322 N. Court St., 256/766-5665, http://306bbq.com/florence, 11am-10pm Sun.-Thurs., 11am-11pm Fri.-Sat., $5-19) has a big menu of all things barbecue, including chicken, pork, and beef, in salads, sandwiches, and on plates. The bar offers a fun hangout atmosphere. There's also a location in Muscle Shoals (400 Avalon Ave., 256/850-3100).

Get started in the morning with brown sugar bacon and grits at John Currence's **Big Bad Breakfast** (315 N. Court St., 256/415-8545, http://bigbadbreakfast.com, 7:30am-2pm daily, $8-14), which is connected to the Stricklin Hotel. Smaller portions and lots of caffeine are on the menu at **Rivertown Coffee Company** (117 N. Seminary St., 256/765-7128, http://rivertowncoffee.co, 7am-10pm Mon.-Thurs., 7am-11pm Fri., 9am-11pm Sat., $6-10), which also servers a robust lunch and dinner crowd.

Perhaps Florence's best-loved eatery,

★ **Trowbridge's Ice Cream and Sandwich Bar** (316 N. Court St., 256/764-1503, 9am-5:30pm Mon.-Sat., $2-5) is an old-fashioned ice cream parlor and sandwich shop, just like Grandma used to love. Grab a stool at the fountain and enjoy pimento cheese sandwiches, ham salad, chicken salad, and more, or go straight for dessert. The options are all your childhood favorites: malts, milkshakes, ice cream sodas, and sundaes.

★ **Yumm Thai Sushi and Beyond** (117 N. Court St., 256/349-2074, http://yummthaisushiandbeyond.com, 11am-2pm and 5pm-9pm Mon.-Thurs., 11am-2pm and 5pm-10pm Fri.-Sat., $10-27) delivers what its name promises: sushi and contemporary maki, as well as curries and rice and noodle dishes. Vegetarian options are available. When the weather is nice, choose the cute sidewalk seating out front and take in the downtown energy.

Brick walls and a wood-burning oven combine for a cozy experience at **Ricatoni's Italian Grill** (107 N. Court St., 256/718-1002, www.ricatonis.com, 11am-10pm daily, $11-30). This two-story downtown eatery serves Italian classics such as pizza, pasta, and chicken marsala.

Nightlife

FloBama Music Hall (311 N. Court St., 256/764-2225, http://flobamadowntown.com, 11am-10pm Mon., 11am-1:30am Tues.-Thurs., 11am-2am Fri.-Sat.) is both a full-service restaurant ($7-10) and a live music venue with a stage and projection screens. Enjoy Southern barbecue, including ribs, whole smoked chickens, their signature hickory-smoked wings, and sandwiches.

A stop on the North Alabama Craft Beer Trail (www.northalabama.org/trails/craft-beer), **Singin' River Brewery** (526 E. College St., 256/349-2294, www.singinriverbrewing.com, 4pm-9pm Tues.-Fri., 2pm-9pm Sat., 1pm-6pm Sun.) is The Shoals' casual hangout for locally brewed beer.

Craft cocktails, funky hot dog combinations, nachos, flatbreads, and late-night hours make **Wildwood Tavern** (180 Mobile St., 256/349-2139, www.keepflorencefunky.com, 11am-2am Mon.-Sat., 4pm-2am Sun.) a go-to for locals and visitors alike. The drink menu includes spiked lemonades, craft cocktails with boutique ingredients such as shrubs, and funky drinks made with Fruity Pebbles-infused simple syrup.

In the basement of the Stricklin Hotel, the **Boiler Room** (313 N. Court St., 256/693-0074, http://stricklinboilerroom.com, 5pm-midnight Mon.-Thurs., 5pm-2am Fri.-Sat., 2pm-10pm Sun.) has arcade games, foosball, Skee-Ball, and a bowling alley.

On the Rocks (110 N. Court St., 256/760-2212, http://florenceontherocks.com, 4pm-2am daily) is a friendly neighborhood pub with live music. The crew supports a lot of local causes, so the neighborhood shows up. Expect traditional bar food and burgers ($7-13).

Accommodations

Tuscumbia

There are a number of dependable chain hotels in the area, as well as options like the **Key West Inn** (1800 US 72, 256/383-0700, www.staycobblestone.com, $74-117). You may not feel like you're in Florida, but with in-room refrigerators and microwaves, free Wi-Fi, a hot tub, and a free continental breakfast, you will feel perfectly comfortable. The hotel has just 43 rooms, so the staff has time to attend to your requests. The US 72 location makes it a quick drive to and from the parkway.

Every campsite at **Heritage Acres RV Park** (1770 Neil Morris Rd., 256/383-7368, www.heritageacresrvpark.com, $33-42) has water, sewer, and electrical hookups, plus 48 TV channels. This is a great place to do laundry and check email if you are traveling by RV. The park is open year-round and offers free Wi-Fi.

Colbert County Rose Trail Campground (9395 Riverton Rose Rd., 256/360-2764, $13-18) is in nearby Cherokee (not to be confused with Cherokee County, which is farther away) on Pickwick Lake. This is a scenic place to park the RV, with access to electricity, water, sewage, bathhouse, and boat ramps. During the late night in the winter, water access may be shut off to keep water lines from freezing, but it is turned back on in the morning.

Muscle Shoals

A serviceable hotel with free Wi-Fi and a basic breakfast, the **Days Inn** (2701 Woodward Ave., 256/248-9755, www.wyndhamhotels.com, $63-83) is right off of US 72 and close to Wilson Dam.

Park your RV and camp at **Colbert County Alloys Park and Campground** (180 Alloys Park Lake, 256/577-9619, www.colbertcounty.org, $20) on Wilson Lake. Electricity, water, sewage, bathhouse, and boat ramps are open year-round.

Sheffield

You don't have to be famous (or talented) to stay at ★ **Muscle Shoals Music House** (117 Lakewood Dr., 256/436-9990, $109-116). This two-room B&B on the banks of the Tennessee River claims to be where Bob Dylan and others stayed when they came to record at Muscle Shoals Sound Studio. Room rate includes breakfast. Free Wi-Fi is offered. A two-night stay is required.

Florence

With its views of the Tennessee River, the **Marriott Shoals Hotel & Spa** (10 Hightower Pl., 256/246-3600, www.marriott.com, $124-179) is a favorite getaway for travelers. The 360-degree views from the top of the hotel are unparalleled. Rooms include free mini-fridges

Top to bottom: Singin' River Brewery; Gunrunner Hotel; Stricklin Hotel

and are pet friendly (additional $75 fee). The hotel has both indoor and outdoor pools, a fitness center, a spa, and two onsite restaurants.

The ★ **Residence Inn Marriott** (1000 Sweetwater Ave., 256/764-9966, www.marriott.com, $89-139) is a surprising find. The all-suites hotel features rooms with kitchens, a nice pool with outdoor seating, and an outdoor barbecue area. The hotel has green hotel certification, nice sculptures in the hallways, and decent views. The free breakfast has plenty of gluten-free and non-pork options.

Each of the 10 rooms in the funky **Gunrunner Hotel** (310 E. Tennessee St., 855/269-4724 or 256/349-5464, http://gunrunnerhotel.com, $180-300) has a different theme—such as one inspired by Frank Lloyd Wright and another designed by local fashionista Billy Reid. The lobby is an interesting industrial-chic second-story communal space decorated with guitars signed by some of the hotel's famous guests. There's an adjacent spa and coffee shop.

Housed in a carefully updated and restored historic building, the ★ **Stricklin Hotel** (317 N. Court St., 256/248-9982, www.thestricklin.com, $140-190) is a charming boutique hotel with downtown Florence right outside. The hotel is home to the **Big Bad Breakfast** restaurant, **Boiler Room** bar, and charming **Reclaimed Spirit by Stacey** shop. Because the Stricklin is near several downtown bars and close to the University of North Alabama campus, it can be loud at night.

If you want the great outdoors, combined with great fishing, look into **Joe Wheeler State Park** (4403 McLean Dr., 256/247-1184, www.alapark.com, $77-222 rooms and cabins). This 2,550-acre park on Wheeler Lake includes a lodge with restaurant and convention center, an 18-hole golf course and clubhouse, and a marina. A 2019 tornado closed the campsites indefinitely; check the website for updates.

Along the Trace

★ **Farmhouse Sanctuary B&B** (8775 County Road 5, 256)/349-2652, $119-169) is a working farm with five bed and breakfast rooms right off the Trace near Wichahpi Commemorative Stone Wall. Each room has its own bathroom. The proximity to the Parkway makes it a good pick for folks seeing the Trace on bicycle, and there's secure bike parking at your disposal while you're enjoying the meadow views, outdoor fireplace, and having a comfortable night's sleep. Don't leave without tasting some homemade honey (the innkeepers are beekeepers, too) and sourdough bread.

Information and Services

Visitor Information

The 7,500-square-foot **Florence/Lauderdale Visitor's Center** (200 Jim Spain Dr., 256/740-4141 or 888/356-8687, 9am-5pm Mon.-Fri., 10am-4pm Sat.) has a design inspired by Frank Lloyd Wright and a wealth of information on all the sights and sounds of The Shoals. Take a break on benches made from local wood and take your time perusing all the information inside on the region, much of which is stored on interactive iPad displays. There's a Frank Lloyd Wright model and a well-stocked gift shop with a lot of locally made goods as well as copies of the *Muscle Shoals* documentary. The staff is particularly friendly and helpful. The center is on the edge of McFarland Park.

Medical and Emergency Services

Shoals Hospital (201 W. Avalon Ave., Muscle Shoals, 256/386-1600, www.shoalshospital.com) has a full emergency room. **Helen Keller Hospital** (1300 S. Montgomery Ave., Sheffield, 256/386-4196, www.helenkeller.com) is a full-service hospital with an emergency room.

The **Muscle Shoals Police Department** (1000 Avalon Ave., Muscle Shoals, 256/383-6746, www.mspolice.org) is centrally located. The **Sheffield Police**

Alabama Fishing

fishing in Alabama

Northwest Alabama is an angler's paradise. Once you get a fishing license, check out these nearby places to cast your rod and reel:

- **Joe Wheeler State Park** (4401 McLean Dr., Rogersville, 256/247-6971, $3 parking fee) is a favorite of bass fishers, but it's also a good place to find catfish, crappie, bream, and stripe. The park is about an hour's drive east of the Natchez Trace. Take US 72 east for 38 miles to AL-101/Wheeler Dam. Drive north for 12 miles, where you'll reconnect with US 72. Turn right, drive east for four miles, and then turn right on McLean Drive.
- **Wilson Lake** (www.wilsonlake.info) is a reservoir on the Tennessee River, which is home to smallmouth and spotted bass, plus sunfish, catfish, and more. Wilson Lake is 22 miles east of the parkway on US 72.
- **Pickwick Lake** (www.tennesseelakeinfo.com) is chock-full of crappie, bass, and catfish. It is northwest of the parkway near Waterloo. Exit near milepost 333 at County Road 14 and continue east for 10 miles to the lake entrance.

Department (600 N. Montgomery Ave., Sheffield, 256/383-1771) is downtown.

Repair Services

For those traveling the Trace by hog, **Natchez Trace Harley-Davidson** (595 US-72 Alt., Tuscumbia, 256/383-5814, 9am-6pm Mon.-Sat., noon-5pm Sun.) is the place to stop for parts, gear, and more.

The **Spinning Spoke Cycle Hub** (221N S. Seminary St., Florence, 256/349-5302, www.spinningspoke.com, 10am-6pm Mon.-Fri., 9am-5pm Sat.) is a Trek bike dealer in the heart of downtown Florence, and will service all manner of cycles. Expedited service may be available if you need to get back on the Trace ASAP.

Back to the Trace

Retrace your steps on US 72, heading west for about 20 miles from Tuscumbia to get back to the parkway. You'll rejoin the Trace near milepost 320, where you can continue your drive south.

Buzzard Roost Spring (MP 320.3)

Once called Buzzard Sleep, Buzzard Roost was a shelter for travelers run by Levi Colbert, a Chickasaw chief and brother of George Colbert. Together the two brothers ran Colbert's Ferry, which took early settlers across the Tennessee River. Like his brother's stand, Levi's was well regarded as a place where weary travelers could rest and eat. The spring here was a water source for the Colbert house.

The site of Levi's stand and that of his brother seem very close to one another, just seven miles apart on the parkway. But in the days of the Old Trace, it may have taken as long as two hours to reach one stand from the other on horseback.

The physical building no longer exists. Informational signs, including some with buttons playing recorded messages, give you a sense of what life was like for travelers who stopped here. The short trail to the spring itself includes many rock steps. While the walk isn't particularly strenuous or long, it does have elevation changes and is not wheelchair accessible. It's worth the walk down, as the water in the spring is impossibly clear and the stairs shaded, making the area a refuge on a hot Alabama day. Some visitors claim to have witnessed ghosts or paranormal activity at this stop, as well as at Colbert's Ferry.

Buzzard Roost isn't visible from the road, but clear signage makes its entrance, on the right side of the parkway, hard to miss. There are no other amenities at this stop.

Freedom Hills Overlook (MP 317)

This quick stop features the **highest point** on the Trace in the state of Alabama. If you stop in spring, summer, or fall, when leaves are still on the trees, it's unlikely that you'll be able to see the type of view expected at an overlook. In winter, you may have more of a chance, but much of the overlook is gone, as trees have blocked the view over the years. It remains a pretty oasis, particularly for fall foliage. To get the full experience, take the 0.25-mile paved path up and back. A few benches at the top allow you to recover from the initial steep ascent.

Access to this overlook is well-marked on the right side of the parkway and the parking area is visible from the road. There are no other amenities.

The Trace:
Northern
Mississippi

The Trace: Northern Mississippi

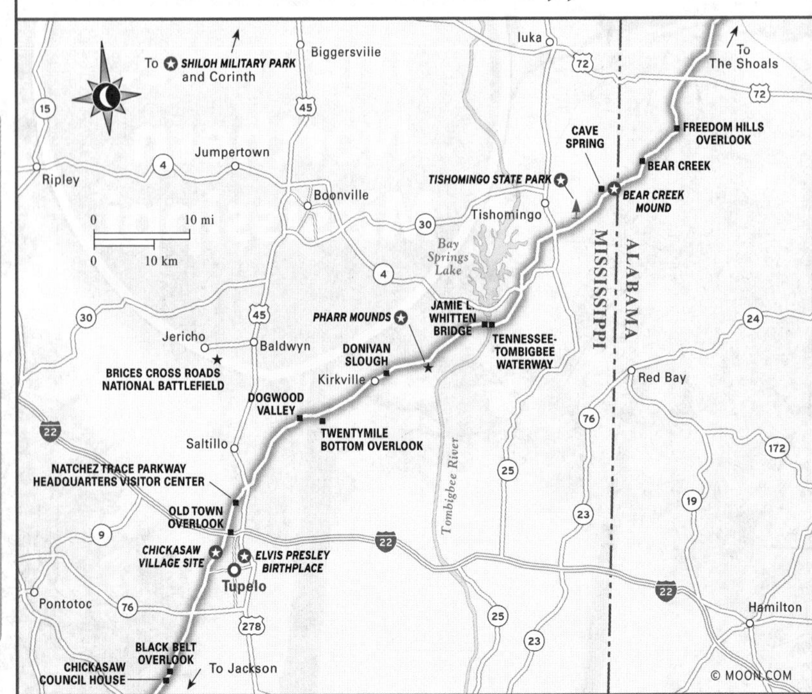

You don't have to have a particularly active imagination to picture the significance this section of land had on the country.

Beyond the forty-three miles of the paved Natchez Trace Parkway, there are also opportunities to walk in the deep grooves of the sunken Old Trace, the original trail worn by thousands of footsteps of Native Americans, settlers, and travelers.

The entirety of this stretch of the road trip, from milepost 304.5 south to 261.8, takes place in Mississippi: Seek shelter under shady dogwoods and oaks during the hot summer sun or choose to explore the other three seasons of the year, when the forecast will be more temperate.

The main stop in this corner of Mississippi is just a short drive off the parkway. Tupelo is known for its contribution to the American music scene—it's the birthplace of Elvis Presley. Nearby Corinth is ripe with history and small-town charm.

Route Overview

The northern Mississippi section of the Natchez Trace Parkway starts at the Alabama-Mississippi border and continues south just past the city of Tupelo. It's **43 miles,** just about 10 percent of the entire length of the Trace. But this section, nestled in the hills of the Magnolia State, is chock-full of sights to see, including three significant archaeological sites,

Highlights

★ **Shiloh National Military Park:** Rolling hills and scenic views are a bucolic balance to the bloody battlefield history (page 171).

★ **Bear Creek Mound:** This site was likely once a temple or chief's house circa AD 1100-1300 (page 174).

★ **Pharr Mounds:** With eight Native American burial mounds, this stop is among the most significant in the state (page 176).

★ **Chickasaw Village Site:** Imagine how life was for Native Americans on the Trace at this expansive former village (page 179).

★ **Elvis Presley Birthplace:** It's a powerful stop, not just for fans of the King of Rock 'n' Roll, but for anyone who appreciates music history (page 180).

Best Restaurants

★ **Abe's Grill:** Classic breakfasts, lunches, and baked goods, plus local diner chit-chat have made Abe's a Highway 72 institution (page 174).

★ **Connie's Fried Chicken:** Come for the chicken and biscuits; stay for the blueberry doughnuts (page 184).

★ **Forklift:** Modern and friendly, this neighborhood joint isn't serving your mama's Southern food (page 185).

★ **Blue Canoe:** Enjoy local beer, local bands, and local dishes made from local ingredients. Bring a Sharpie to sign the walls (page 185).

scenic hikes, several powerful war monuments, the headquarters for the parkway operations, and a trip to Tupelo, the city that gave us the King of Rock 'n' Roll.

One day is sufficient to see this portion of the Trace. Spend at least one night in Tupelo, the charming city just five miles off the Trace. Plan to use Tupelo as your command center to explore the region's music (including many things Elvis), delicious food, and one-of-a-kind shopping. If you're a true U.S. history buff, you add a day to your schedule to spend adequate time at the historic battlefields. They are packed with information and you don't want to feel rushed.

Driving Considerations

On this part of the parkway, you may encounter that urban affliction: traffic. The parkway's proximity to Tupelo means it does usher more cars through, particularly during rush hour. The section near Pharr Mounds, one of the most popular sights on the Trace (milepost 286.7) also sees some traffic delays on weekend days.

Fuel and Services

This section of the Trace is short—43 miles—and close to a major city, so the risk of running out of gas is low. Take advantage of a side trip to **Tupelo** to stock up on essentials for yourself and the car, bicycle, or motorcycle. You'll likely have cell service for most of your drive in northern Mississippi, with the best reception as you get closer to Tupelo.

The **Natchez Trace Parkway Headquarters and Visitor Center** (milepost 266; 2680 Natchez Trace Pkwy., Tupelo, 800/305-7417 or 662/680-4027, www.nps.gov, 8am-4:30pm daily) is on this stretch and is the place to stop for any and all parkway-related services. Allot enough time here to talk to rangers about the Trace.

Tune your radio to 1610AM for recorded information about some of the sights and stops along the way.

For bicycle help in Tupelo, there are several options very close to the parkway. Check in with **Trails and Treads** (549B Coley Rd., 662/690-6620, 10am-6pm Mon.-Fri., 9am-6pm Sat.), about 3.5 miles from the Trace. **Bicycle Pacelines** (2120 W. Jackson St., 662/844-8660, www.bicyclepacelines.net, 11am-6pm Mon.-Fri., 10am-4pm Sat.) is just 100 yards from milepost 260.8. **Core Cycle and Outdoors** (1697 N. Coley Rd., 662/260-5266, corecycleandoutdoor.com, 9:30am-6pm Mon.-Sat.) is another good resource.

Getting to the Starting Point

Car, Motorcycle, or Bicycle

As you drive or ride southbound on the Trace, you'll ease over the border from Alabama into Mississippi, north of Tishomingo State Park and the town of Tishomingo. Save for a small brown sign

Best Accommodations

★ **Bear Creek Saloon Guesthouse:** Close to the parkway, this is a great option for those bicycling the Trace (page 175).

★ **Tishomingo State Park:** Camp here with gear or reserve a historic Civilian Conservation Corps cabin (page 175).

★ **Piney Grove Campground:** Whether you have an RV or a tent, this is the place to stay on the Tenn-Tom Waterway (page 176).

★ **Moon Lake Farm B&B:** Enjoy the great outdoors with views and horseback rides, followed by a cozy night's sleep inside (page 186).

marking the state line, you won't notice a difference in the parkway.

From **Memphis,** it's about 130 miles (just over two hours) to reach Tishomingo State Park, the first major stop on this section of the route. Take US 72 east for about 115 miles. This route goes through Corinth, Mississippi, a town rich in Civil War history. You can stop in the charming downtown for lunch or continue to the Trace. Exit US 72 at MS-25 (following signs for Iuka/Fulton), and continue south on MS-25 for about 13 miles. Follow signs for Tishomingo State Park and turn left onto County Road 90 to get to the park.

To get to the beginning of this section of the drive from **Huntsville,** Alabama, it's a 60-mile drive west along US 72. You'll join the Trace where US 72 intersects with the Trace, at milepost 320. Take the Trace for about 13 miles south to reach the Mississippi border.

Stopping in Corinth

If you're starting from Memphis, you'll drive through the town of Corinth, Mississippi. This charming town of 15,000 is one of the state's historic treasures. Once the crossroads of the Mobile and Ohio and Memphis and Charleston Railroads, Corinth was a major transport hub during the Civil War. Union and Confederate troops battled for control of Corinth, with the Union Army emerging the victor in October 1862.

Air

This isn't the easiest section of the Trace to access by air, but if that's your preference, the **Memphis International Airport** (MEM, www.flymemphis.com) is a good choice. MEM is served by Delta, Southwest, United, and other major airlines, with a number of nonstop routes. The three-concourse airport offers free Wi-Fi and many local dining options. The Memphis airport is 148 miles/2.5 hours from downtown Florence.

The **Huntsville International Airport** (HSV, www.flyhuntsville.com) is closer to this portion of the Trace, but it is a smaller airport, with mostly regional destinations served and higher prices. American, Delta, and United serve this northeast Alabama city. Huntsville is 62 miles/70 minutes from downtown Florence.

Contour Airlines flies between Nashville and **Tupelo Regional Airport** (www.flytupelo.com) five times a day for as little as $29.

Train and Bus

Train travel to the Trace is a tough proposition; riding the rails isn't the most efficient way to get around this area. **Amtrak** operates out of Memphis's **Central Station** (545 S. Main St., www.amtrak.com), a stop on the 900-mile City of New Orleans route, which runs from New Orleans to Chicago. Central Station is conveniently located downtown, where

Fuel Up

Thanks to the proximity to Tupelo on this section of the route, you're unlikely to be far from a gas station. Here's a quick list of places to exit the parkway in northern Mississippi so that you can refuel at the closest gas station. (Some stops may take you to small towns, others will be just a single service station.)

The National Park Service also posts a list of nearby supply stations at most parkway rest areas, although the list is not updated regularly.

- **Milepost 302.8:** Exit at MS-25 and drive three miles north to reach two gas stations, one with a convenience store.
- **Milepost 282.2:** Exit at MS-371 (signs for Baldwyn). Go west (left) in 0.2 mile to follow MS-371, then turn right in 0.3 mile to get onto MS-370. Drive west on MS-370 for 12 miles to US 45 in Baldwyn. A Texaco, a Shell, a Chevron, and several other gas stations are on the highway north and south of 370.
- **Milepost 266:** Exit at MS-145 and drive 1.5 miles south to Tupelo.
- **Milepost 263:** Exit at McCullough Boulevard and drive 0.3 mile west. Alternatively, drive 0.6 mile east to Tupelo.

most major rental car companies have offices.

Greyhound (www.greyhound.com) serves Tupelo (2611 S Eason Blvd.) from Nashville, Memphis, and Jackson.

Budget-friendly **Megabus** (http://us.megabus.com) serves Memphis from Atlanta, Birmingham, Chicago, Dallas, Little Rock, and St. Louis, from a station (3033 Airways Blvd.) near the Memphis airport. Megabus boasts free Wi-Fi on board.

Corinth

Historic Corinth (www.corinth.net) is one of Mississippi's richest treasures, and in recent years the city has embraced its past as a significant Civil War site. Corinth isn't right off the Natchez Trace, but US 72 runs through it, making it a natural stop if you are headed to the parkway from Memphis or Huntsville. It is a 40-minute drive from Corinth (from US 72 and then on MS-25) to get to the parkway.

Once the spot where the Mobile & Ohio and Memphis & Charleston Railroads met, Corinth was named for the city in Greece that was also a crossroads for major transport lines. Being a hub made Corinth crucial to the Civil War; capturing the city gave troops unfettered access to the rail lines. Union and Confederate troops battled here, until the Union army won control in 1862.

If you don't have much time in town, you can get a taste with **60 Sights in 60 Minutes** (http://60sights60minutes.com). This self-guided walking tour takes you through Corinth's tree-lined downtown streets, which are dotted with historic sites, stores, and restaurants; painted footprints help you easily navigate town. Download the PDF from the website or grab a brochure at the **Corinth Area Convention and Visitors Bureau** (215 N. Fillmore St.).

Sights

Corinth Civil War Interpretive Center

The 15,000-square-foot **Corinth Civil War Interpretive Center** (501 W. Linden St., 731/689-5696, www.nps.gov/shil,

A Day on the Trace: Northern Mississippi

Rise and shine bright and early! This is going to be a jam-packed day and you don't want to miss a thing. Today's destination is Tupelo, which is about 43 miles along the Trace from the Alabama-Mississippi border. On the way there, stop at the archaeological wonders at **Bear Creek Mound** and **Pharr Mounds.** Take a hike at the **Chickasaw Village Site,** which is just outside of Tupelo proper. For a complete list of every stop along the Trace, download the four detailed National Park Service maps (www.nps.gov/natr).

Your first stop in Tupelo must be **Connie's Fried Chicken** for one of their famous blueberry cake doughnuts. Make your way to the **Elvis Presley Birthplace,** where you'll learn about the King of Rock 'n' Roll and his connections to the area.

Next it's time for some late afternoon shopping downtown, including a stop at **Tupelo Hardware Company,** where Elvis got his first guitar. Feast on modern Southern food at **Forklift,** then get back in the car and head over to **Blue Canoe** for local beer and live music before you call it a night. Spend the night just 15 minutes from downtown Tupleo at the bucolic **Moon Lake Farm B&B.**

8am-5pm daily, free), a separate unit of the Shiloh National Military Park, is a significant draw to Corinth. If you're here for Civil War history, this is where to start. The museum showcases a number of artifacts and informational films that help put the battles fought here into context, as well as affecting public art displays. As you walk up the steps to the entrance, notice the bronze replicas of soldiers' gear set in the sidewalk. These reproductions show the scale of the gear soldiers had to carry and compare those objects with your own. Visit The Stream of American History Fountain and Liberty Pool. This modern art creation uses the placement of different objections to show the timeline of the struggles toward reunification.

Park rangers are on hand to answer questions. The building and exhibits are ADA compliant, but the museum is a steep walk uphill from the parking lot; you are permitted to drop off guests at the door and then return to park. It's a 20-minute drive from the interpretive center north to the Shiloh Battlefield Visitor Center.

Corinth Contraband Camp

As Union troops occupied the city of Corinth in 1862, enslaved people from surrounding areas escaped and sought safety behind the military lines. After the Preliminary Emancipation Proclamation, the **Corinth Contraband Camp** (1055 Pittsburg Landing Rd., 731/689-5696, www.nps.gov/shil, sunrise-sunset daily, free) was created, a community where eventually 6,000 escapees lived. It became a cooperative farm, turning a profit and providing a first step to freedom for the formerly enslaved. They lived and worked here until December 1863 when the camp was relocated to Memphis. Today, the site is a moving tribute to this part of the Civil War story and preserved by the National Park Service and city of Corinth. Take a half-mile walk through the park and admire bronze sculptures and signage about the experience. Download the app and the sculptures will come to life and tell their stories.

This is an unmanned stop, without park rangers on-site or restrooms. It has an ample parking lot and is wheelchair-accessible.

★ Shiloh National Military Park

True military history buffs will want to make their way to **Shiloh National Military Park** (1055 Pittsburg Landing Rd., Shiloh, 731/689-5696, www.nps.gov/shil, sunrise-sunset daily, free). Run by the National Park Service, this 4,000-acre park in Shiloh, Tennessee, preserves the Shiloh and Corinth battlefields, two of the bloodiest sites from the Civil War.

At the time, the April 1862 Battle of Shiloh was the largest ever fought in the country. In just two days, more than 3,400 soldiers on both Union and Confederate sides were killed and 2,000 captured. Ultimately, the Union troops, led by Generals W. H. L. Wallace and Benjamin Prentiss, won the battle, outfoxing the surprise attack from the Confederate army under command of General P. G. T. Beauregard. The nation was shocked by the brutality on both sides. It was this battle that brought home what was happening to many.

Start with the exhibits at the **Shiloh Battlefield Visitor Center,** which includes a 32-minute orientation film. Then grab a free map (or download one online) and use it to tour battlefield sites in order. Color-coded signage shows the troop positions of each of the armies on each day of the battle. The majority of the park is accessible from a driving route. Also here are some hiking trails as well as the Shiloh National Cemetery—don't miss the views of the Tennessee River from the bluff at the cemetery—and Shiloh Indian Mounds. It is easy to spend the better part of a day here.

To get to Shiloh from the Trace, exit the Trace at AL-20 (milepost 336). Drive northwest across the Tennessee state line, where the road turns into TN-69, for a total of 31 miles. Turn left on TN-128 for 2.8 miles. Turn left again on TN-22 for 9 miles to Pittsburg Landing Road. From downtown Corinth it is a half-hour drive to the military park. Take Fulton Drive 4 miles until it hits MS-2. Turn right (east) and continue 15/6 miles to the park entrance. You will cross over the Tennessee state line.

Verandah-Curlee House

The 1857 **Verandah-Curlee House** (705 Jackson St., 662/287-9501, http://verandahcurleehouse.com, 9am-2pm Mon., 9:30am-4pm Thurs.-Sat., 1pm-4pm Sun., adults $8, youth and seniors $5, free for children under 12) served as headquarters for both Confederate and Union generals during the war.

Corinth Coca-Cola Museum

The brainchild of Kenneth Williams, president of Corinth Coca-Cola Bottling Group and a local philanthropist, the **Corinth Coca-Cola Museum** (601 Washington St., 662/415-7998, www.corinthcoke.com/coke-museum, free) is a treasure-trove of all things related to the iconic soft drink. Anytime the bottling plant is open—which is most nonholidays year-round—the museum is open, so you can take a self-guided walk through Coke memorabilia that includes old delivery trucks, promotional giveaways, and a soda fountain.

Lake Hill Motors Motorcycle Museum

You'll think you're in the wrong place when you arrive at the **Lake Hill Motors Motorcycle Museum** (2003 US 72, 662/287-4451, www.lakehillmotors.com, 8am-5pm Mon.-Fri., 8am-3pm Sat., free)—it's located inside Lake Hill Motors, an ATV and Marine showroom—but go on in and tell the friendly sales staff you're here to see the motorcycles. Your jaw will drop at the century's worth of motorcycles on display. Some have informational signage or a funny mannequin behind the wheel.

Dream Riderz Classic Cars & Collectibles

More than 80 classic cars are on display at **Dream Riderz Classic Cars & Collectibles** (913 US 45, 662/331-1980, http://dreamriderz.com, 11am-7pm Wed.-Thurs., 11am-9pm Fri.-Sat., adults $10, military $7, children 12 and under $5), a pristine museum about a 10-minute drive south of downtown Corinth. The collection consists of gems that belong to the museum's owner as well as private collectors who occasionally pop by to take their wheels out for a spin, plus some cars that were rescued from the now-shuttered Tupelo Automobile Museum. The total collection numbers more than 200, so the cars on display rotate. Tour guides are knowledgeable.

Shopping

Wick Street is downtown Corinth's main shopping strip, chock-full of independent boutiques. Wandering along the storefronts and meeting locals is a lovely way to pass an afternoon. Must-stops include **Love & A Dog** (625 Wick St., 662/872-3288, www.shoploveandadog.com, 10am-5:30pm Mon.-Fri., 10am-3pm Sat.), which stocks women's and kids' clothing, plus lots of stuff for Fido. **Shirley Dawg's** (629 Wick St., 662/284-0111, http://shirleydawgs.com, 10am-5pm Mon.-Fri., 10am-3pm Sat.) has a pup at the cash register, but the merchandise is for humans and primarily includes clothing and outdoor gear. **Taylor Wick & Co.** (622 Wick St., 662/649-8986, www.shoptaylorwick.com, 10am-5pm Tues.-Fri., 10am-3pm Sat.) stocks candles, lotions, and other gift items. **Rowan House** (604 Wick St., 662/396-2299, www.shoprowanhouse.com, 10am-4:30pm Mon.-Thurs., 10am-5pm Fri., 10am-3pm Sat.) features locally made art and gift items.

Food

Borroum's Drug Store (604 E. Waldron St., 662/286-3361, 9am-5pm Mon.-Fri., 9am-3pm Sat., $2-9) is the oldest continuously operating drugstore in Mississippi but, more importantly, a classic soda fountain and lunch counter. This is the place to listen to locals tell tall tales as you eat your lunch. Order a slugburger, a Corinth Depression-era dish that consists of ground meat and potato flour that

Top to bottom: Shiloh National Military Park; Shirley Dawg's; Abe's Grill

stretches the protein further. Equally essential to local culture is ★ **Abe's Grill** (803 US 72 W., 662/286-6124, 5am-3pm Mon.-Fri., $2-7), a classic, no-frills, counter-service diner that has been serving some of the South's best biscuits as well as a chocolate chip cookie that has been named the state's best. Try the chocolate gravy.

Nestled in one of Corinth's renovated historic buildings, **Pizza Grocery** (800 Cruise St., 662/287-3200, www.pizzagrocery.com, 11am-2pm and 5pm-8pm Mon.-Thurs., 11am-2pm and 5pm-9pm Fri.-Sat., $9-23), serves classic Italian dishes including pizza, as well as beer. If the weather is good, nab a table on the patio.

Since 1972 **Russell's Beef House** (104 US 72, 662/287-5150, 4:30pm-9pm Sun.-Thurs., 4:30pm-10pm Fri.-Sat., $6-20) has been the place to go for a steak and salad bar. It's a no-frills spot—and it doesn't have a liquor license—but the meats can't be beat. Chef Russell Smith also owns **Smith. Restaurant** (603 N. Fillmore St.) downtown.

It's the Mississippi Delta that's most known for tamales (page 251), but if you need a fix while in Corinth there's **Dillworth's Tamales** (702 Wick St., 662/223-3296, 10am-7pm Mon.-Sat., 2pm-6pm Sun., $1.50-48), which has a drive-up window. Afterward, you can pop by **Lauren's Cake Shop** (103 Taylor St., 662/415-7961, 11am-5pm Wed.-Fri., 11am-2pm Sat., $2-6) for a cupcake dessert.

Accommodations

With its convenient location off US 72, plus a pool, gym, and free breakfast, the **Hampton Inn** (2107 US 72 W., 662/286-5949, www.hilton.com, $112-154) is a dependable option for an overnight stay.

★ Bear Creek Mound (MP 308.8)

Immediately after crossing the state line into Mississippi you'll see the entrance to Bear Creek Mound and Village Site on the right side of the road. From there you'll be able to see a square, flat-topped mound that has existed since around AD 1100-1300, part of what is referred to as the Mississippian period in geology.

It may look like just a grassy knoll now, but the mound, likely built in stages, was intended for either ceremonial use or as a residence for an elite member of a tribe, like a chief. Archaeological excavations by the National Park Service suggest that the mound was the site of a temple or a chief's home, which would have been made of mud plaster and wooden posts. This is different from a burial mound, which you'll see at Pharr Mounds (milepost 286.7).

Over the years, Bear Creek's mound height had been reduced by plowing. After the 1965 excavation by the NPS, it was restored to its estimated original dimensions: approximately 8 feet high and 85 feet wide.

This mound was likely within a village, possibly dating back as far as 8000 BC. Nearby Bear Creek made for an environment rich in wildlife, and thus a fertile area for hunting and gathering.

Native American sites are protected by the Antiquities Law of Mississippi and the federal Archaeological Resources Protection Act. Treat these areas with respect for the many generations who came before.

There are no amenities here, but it is an essential stop, a place to understand and appreciate the long history of the Trace.

Cave Spring (MP 308.4)

Cave Spring is an oasis along the parkway. This rock cavern was carved by underground water slowly eroding the surrounding limestone. The cave itself is not safe to enter; instead, you can take an easy walk on a paved loop path next to the cave entrance.

As you walk along the outside of the cave, you'll see the limestone and other sediments that have piled up over time, creating a layer cake of rock that's more than one story high. The namesake spring may resemble a small pond, so it can be hard to imagine how this water was responsible for carving away at stone. In the summer, this is a shaded, cool place, and in the autumn, migrating butterflies are in abundance.

It takes just a few minutes to walk the path and see the cave. There are stairs on each end, so the lower portion is not wheelchair accessible. However, you can take in the cave spring area from an observation point above.

The water is not safe to drink and there are no other amenities. To get to Cave Spring from the parkway, take the well-marked loop road on the right, which leads to the parking lot.

Accommodations

Less than three miles from Cave Spring and just 0.75 mile off the parkway is ★ **Bear Creek Saloon Guesthouse** (1338 MS-30, Tishomingo, 334/332-3474, www.bearcreekinnsms.com, $80). This unhosted guesthouse was once a family retreat and now sleeps 1-3 people (with a queen bed and twin bed). It also has a kitchen and laundry facilities. Because of its proximity to the Trace, it's perfect for those traveling by bicycle. Children are welcome, but pets are not allowed. The owners have provided a fire pit as well as information on food delivery.

Tishomingo State Park (MP 304)

Named for Chief Tishomingo, once leader of the Chickasaw Nation, **Tishomingo State Park** (105 County Road 90, 662/438-6914, www.mdwfp.com, $4 for up to six people) is more than 1,500 acres, a great place to recreate near the Trace. Limestone outcroppings provide the backdrop for lots of outdoor recreation options, including canoeing on 45-acre Bear Lake, fishing on well-stocked Bear and Haynes Lakes, swimming (ages 13 and older $6, children 3-12 $4), picnicking, disc golf, volleyball, rock climbing, and hiking on the park's 13 miles of trails. One of the most popular paths is the **Bear Creek Outcropping Trail,** which starts at a 200-foot swinging bridge and continues for 3.5 miles. Rock climbing is allowed in the park, but you must bring your own gear and obtain a permit when you pay the park entrance fee. Three-day Mississippi fishing licenses (601/432-2400, http://mdwfp.com/license/fishing) are $15 for nonresidents and $3 for those who live in the state.

To get to the park, turn right to exit the Trace at milepost 304. Drive for 0.5 mile, then turn right onto County Road 90; the park's gatehouse, where you pay the entrance fee, is just several hundred feet along this road.

Accommodations

The park offers ★ **campsites** for tents and RVs (61 sites, $15-28) and historic Civilian Conservation Corps **cabins** ($60-85), many of which are ringed by wildflowers and ferns in the spring. The cabins have fireplaces and screened porches. There is also an accessible cottage (linens not included). To make a reservation, call (662/438-6914) or book online (http://mississippistateparks.reserveamerica.com).

Eight miles south of the park in the tiny railroad town of Belmont is the **Belmont Hotel** (121 Main St., 662/454-7948). This 10-room hotel looks straight out of a movie set. Sit on the porch or in the renovated red lobby and talk to the innkeepers about the lore surrounding this 1924 building. A stay here is the only reason to come to Belmont.

Tennessee-Tombigbee Waterway (MP 293.2)

This 234-mile-long canal linking the Tennessee River with the Tombigbee River opened in 1985, but the Tenn-Tom Waterway had been discussed for centuries leading up to its construction. In fact, Louis XIV once considered such a proposal. Congress mulled it over as early as 1810. Finally, in 1946 the U.S. Army Corps of Engineers approved a plan for a canal to connect the two bodies of the water and in 1971 building began.

Admire the feats of engineering that went into the canal at this stop on the Trace, where you'll cross the waterway via the **Jamie L. Whitten Bridge,** which is named after the Mississippi congressman who helped make the canal a reality.

This stop on the right side of the road has a loop parking area with access to picnic areas and pretty, albeit not secluded, views of the waterway and bridge. It's particularly lovely at sunset, when the sky's colors hit the water.

Accommodations

Just before milepost 293.2, you can exit the Trace at John Rankin Highway to explore the Tennessee-Tombigbee landscape. There are eight different **campgrounds** managed by the Army Corps on the Tenn-Tom Waterway, five of which are in Mississippi. ★ **Piney Grove Campground** (662/728-1134, starting at $22), the closest to the parkway, has 141 RV sites, with a swimming beach, laundry, electricity, and other amenities. To get there, exit John Rankin Highway (County Road 3501) and take it north to County Road 3550, about 13 miles. Entrance to the campground will be on the left. Retrace your steps to return to the parkway.

★ Pharr Mounds (MP 286.7)

One of the best-known and most significant stops on the Natchez Trace is **Pharr Mounds,** a complex of eight burial mounds that comprise the largest archaeological site in northern Mississippi, and one of the largest in the region.

Built between AD 1 and 200, in what's referred to as the Middle Woodland period, these mounds range in height from 2 to 18 feet, in an area of about 90 acres (about 100 football fields). In 1966, the National Park Service excavated four of the mounds and found fire pits, human remains, and ceremonial artifacts. Some of these artifacts included copper objects,

decorated ceramics, lead ore like galena and mica, and a greenstone pipe. Copper, galena, mica, and greenstone aren't originally from Mississippi, so they must have been brought from long distances. This indicates that the local people participated in a trade network.

From the parking lot you can see three of the mounds—giant camelback shapes covered in grass. It's easy to spot the largest mounds, but the smaller ones may be all but invisible. The Park Service allows some of the area surrounding the mounds to be harvested for hay, so depending on the time of year, you may see some hay bales. The juxtaposition of the bales against the larger, green mounds can make for a striking visual. While observing, stay on the pathways, which are about 400 yards from the mounds. Remember to treat the area with the respect it deserves.

There are restrooms but no other amenities. These are the last restrooms until **the Natchez Trace Parkway Headquarters and Visitor Center** (page 178). The parking area for Pharr Mounds is on the left side of the parkway. The mounds are visible from the road.

Donivan Slough

(MP 283.3)

A slough is a swamp that might appear stagnant but, in fact, has moving water. And that's what you'll find at this small, pretty stop on the right side of the parkway. A wooded boardwalk trail circles the swamp. The slough is home to bald cypress, tulip poplar, sycamore, and water oak trees that thrive in this moist environment. You'll see cypress "knees" (the roots of the cypress trees popping up through the water), and in the spring, wildflowers dot the land.

There's a picnic table near the parking lot, which is a good spot for a rest. There are no other amenities. The parking lot is directly off the parkway.

Pharr Mounds

Donivan Slough Trail

Distance: 0.4-mile loop
Duration: 15 minutes
Difficulty: Easy

The trail is an easy 15-minute (less than 0.5 mile) loop on a boardwalk, accessible from the parking lot. It's shaded from the hot summer sun and a few degrees cooler, too. During the heat of the summer, if there has been drought, the water levels may be very low, but the foliage is worth taking in, regardless. After hard rains, water levels will be high, but thanks to the boardwalk you'll stay dry. Signage is posted along the trail, with brief information about the various flora.

Accessing the path requires descending about 15 steps (with a handrail) to access the trail; there is no wheelchair ramp. If you are walking near sunset in the summer, you may want to use bug spray or wear long sleeves.

Twentymile Bottom Overlook (MP 278.4)

At this overlook along the parkway you can take in the scope and depth of the landscape of the Old Trace from above. Drive up the hill on the right side of the parkway. From the hill, you can look out at the now-developed farmland and imagine what a hard route the area below (the "bottom") was for Native Americans, early settlers, soldiers, and others. This is also one the few spots where you can get a scenic view of the paved parkway itself from above, making it a great photo op.

This parking lot is an out-and-back, not a loop, so those in large RVs or with horse trailers may want to avoid this stop. (It is clearly marked with a "no circular drive" sign.) Neither the overlook nor the parking area is visible from the road.

Dogwood Valley (MP 275.2)

This easy 15-minute walk along a portion of the Old Trace on the right side of the parkway, is located, unsurprisingly, in a valley of dogwood trees. Dogwoods are a beloved tree in the south, and are known for their white or pink four-petal flowers. Some of the dogwoods in this valley are more than 100 years old and no longer flower. There's lots of signage along the way to teach you about this favorite tree. The walk is in the sunken part of the Old Trace and is not suitable for those in wheelchairs.

Natchez Trace Parkway Headquarters and Visitor Center (MP 266)

The one stop everyone traveling a section of the Trace should make is at the **Natchez Trace Parkway Headquarters and Visitor Center** (2680 Natchez Trace Pkwy., Tupelo, 800/305-7417 or 662/680-4027, www.nps.gov, 8am-4:30pm daily). This is the hub for all things Trace-related. Park rangers run a well-stocked gift shop and small museum, which includes a short orientation video narrated by country star Amy Grant. Any questions you have—from the history of the Trace to where to eat lunch—can be answered by the knowledgeable staff. This is also the place to send postcards, buy souvenirs for friends and family at home, or to get your National Parks Passport stamped. The gift shop has very basic concessions (just soda and candy)—there aren't meal options. Plenty of free maps are available, not just for the Tupelo area, but for the entirety of the parkway.

Ranger-led tours and other activities take place here, including the popular Read with a Ranger program (monthly, free). You'll find ample parking for cars, trailers, and RVs, and plenty of picnic tables, restrooms, and other amenities. There are several short nature walks off of (and visible from) the parking lot, perfect for walking the dog or stretching your legs. You can jump on a longer hiking trail (part of the Natchez Trace Scenic National Trail) that connects you to Old Town Overlook (2.5 miles each way) and the Chickasaw Village Site (4 miles each way). These are relatively moderate hikes with elevation changes and are not wheelchair-accessible.

Old Town Overlook (MP 263.9)

Old Town Overlook is named for a Chickasaw village whose name has been lost to history. At this spot, early Trace pioneers had a lovely view of that village, which they dubbed "Old Town." Today you can pull over on the right side of the road and see a thriving pond with turtles and other wildlife at this scenic spot. Rest and take in the views of both nature and the parkway itself. Unlike some other overlooks on the parkway, this one is in a meadow, so there isn't a lot of overgrowth blocking the vista.

It's possible to hike 2 miles south from here to the Chickasaw Village Site or 2.5 miles north to the Natchez Trace Parkway Headquarters and Visitor Center. This stretch is part of the Natchez Trace Scenic National Trail. Look for signage to direct you along the trails. These are easy, out-and-back hikes.

The driveway to the overlook is on the right when you enter the pullout; the pond is to the left.

★ Chickasaw Village Site (MP 261.8)

If you want to imagine what life along the Trace was like for the Native Americans who lived and traveled here, be sure to devote plenty of time to the **Chickasaw Village Site.**

Archaeologists believe that the Chickasaw people had a fort and several summer dwellings here in the 1700s, in what's now a wildflower-strewn meadow. A modern covered shelter has artist renderings of how the fort would have looked. Occasionally there are ranger-led activities at this site. Check the National Park Service website (www.nps.gov) or at the Natchez Trace Parkway Headquarters and Visitor Center for details.

There are several options for hikes. The first is an easy, sun-dappled 15-minute loop walk with signage pointing out the various plants that the Chickasaw used in their daily life for food and medicine. The 0.3-mile loop is slightly hilly but relatively easy. Stay to the right and you'll end up back behind the information shelter where you started. Perhaps because this trail is so close to Tupelo, it's very well maintained, with regular volunteer help, and you won't encounter as much overgrowth as on some other Trace trails.

If you are up for a longer hike, you can take the trail to the right of the shelter (in the left corner if you are in the parking lot) two miles to Old Town Overlook or four miles to the **Parkway Visitors Center.**

This is one of the larger stops along the Trace and plans are in the works for an extensive expansion of the Chickasaw heritage interpretation found here. The long driveway on the right has a gate, which is closed after dusk. Neither the parking area nor the site itself is visible from the road. There are no picnic tables or other amenities.

Tupelo

Tupelo is a place where you can have lots of unexpected fun. It's population is just 38,000, but local businesses employ many more; the town's working population is closer to 100,000—so it has the energy of a city.

Nestled in a region called the Hills of Mississippi, Tupelo is home to rich American music history—famous locals have included Elvis Presley himself—and there's a modern live music scene. More than 25 colorful guitar sculptures are planted around town to remind you this is a place that likes to play music. There are also plenty of museums to explore art and Civil War history, and more than enough places to eat and drink before you rejoin the Natchez Trace Parkway.

Tupelo was the first city to gain electricity under President Franklin Roosevelt's Tennessee Valley Authority initiatives. Don't miss the lighted neon TVA arrow sign on your way to downtown at the intersection of Main and Gloster. This landmark has been part of city history since 1945.

Several exits from the parkway lead to the city of Tupelo. The most direct way is to exit the parkway at US 45. Take US 45 for five miles, exiting at Front Street. Once you reach the intersection of Front Street and Main Street, you'll be in downtown Tupelo.

Sights

Brices Cross Roads National Battlefield

The mammoth **Brices Cross Roads National Battlefield** (US 45 and MS-370, Baldwyn, 662/365-3969, www.nps.gov/brcr, 9am-5pm Tues.-Sat., free) marks an important moment in American history. In June 1864 the scrappy Confederate army, led by Major General Nathan Bedford Forrest, defeated the larger Union army. Some counts suggest that as many as five times more Union troops died here than Confederate soldiers. This battle, also referred to as the Battle of Guntown or Tishomingo Creek, allowed the soldiers to secure supply lines between Nashville and Chattanooga, Tennessee.

History buffs should plan to spend at least 90 minutes at this collection of sites about 20 miles north of Tupelo.

The best-known site is a one-acre section of the battlefield, which includes an imposing concrete monument topped by an eagle. The **monument,** at the corner of the park near MS-370, honors those who lost their lives in the battle. It's surrounded by cannons and foliage. Pay your respects at the 96 Confederate graves at **Bethany A. R. P. Church Cemetery,** visit the church that became a field hospital after the battle, and walk along interpretive trails. These sites are close together, so it's an easy walk to see it all.

Nearby, in the town of Baldwyn, is the **Final Stands Interpretive Center** (607 Grisham St., Baldwyn, 662/365-3969, www.finalstands.com, 9am-5pm Tues.-Sat., adults $5, children under 12 $2). This center has a 4,000-square-foot building with artifacts, museum-style exhibits, a bookstore, and two short films, for those who want to immerse themselves in the battle.

To get to Brices Cross Roads from Tupelo, take US 45 north for nearly 10 miles, exiting at MS-348. Go west for less than a mile, then turn right (north) onto County Road 833. Go five miles and continue straight when CR 833 becomes MS-370. The entrance will be on your right.

★ Elvis Presley Birthplace

If there is one thing for which Tupelo is known, it is the **Elvis Presley Birthplace** (306 Elvis Presley Dr., 662/841-1215, http://elvispresleybirthplace.com, 9am-5:30pm Mon.-Sat. and 1pm-5pm Sun. May 1-Sept. 30, 9am-5pm Mon.-Sat. and 1pm-5pm Sun. Oct. 1-Apr. 30, adults $19, seniors $15, children $9), which includes

Tupelo

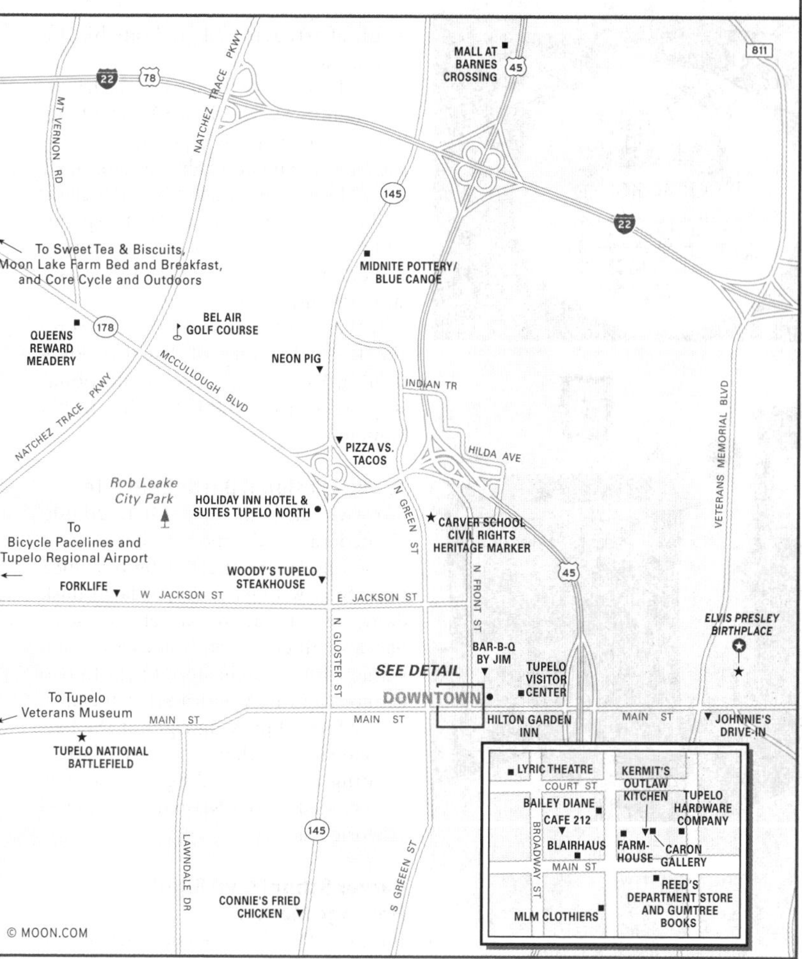

the house Elvis was born in, a museum, his childhood chapel, a gift shop, and much more.

Elvis Aaron Presley was born on January 8, 1935, in this two-room house that's been restored to its original condition. The family didn't live in the house long—hard financial times befell them. Elvis's talent was evident at a young age. When he was 11, his mother bought him a guitar at Tupelo Hardware Company. His pastor taught him to play, and the gospel music he learned in Tupelo influenced his entire career.

You can stop by the birthplace and see the exterior of the small home, as well as the chapel and one of the family's cars, without taking the **Grand Tour** (adults $19, seniors $15, children $9). But it's worth the cost to hear about how the blues and gospel influenced Elvis and how he created his signature sound,

leading him to be the best-selling solo artist in history. With the tour, you'll also be able to go inside the museum, which is full of artifacts that celebrate his life and music.

It's also possible to take just the **house tour** (adults $9, children $3). The Elvis Presley Birthplace is a physically compact site, and it's accessible for fans of all ages. The grounds are lovely and include walking trails, gardens, a reflective pond, and a dynamic sculpture called *Becoming* depicting Elvis as a child and then as a larger-than-life star.

If the visit leaves you wanting more, check out the city of Tupelo's **Elvis Driving Tour**, which has 13 additional stops relating to the King's life in his hometown.

Tupelo National Battlefield Site

For two days in July 1864, 20,000 Confederate and Union soldiers fought at the **Tupelo National Battlefield** (2083 Main St., www.nps.gov/tupe, dawn-dusk daily, free). Today the battlefield resembles a small city park. It houses a small statue with an eagle atop it next to two cannons and an American flag. It can be tricky to find parking right at the battlefield site, but there is plenty of street parking on surrounding blocks. The site is listed on the National Register of Historic Places.

Carver School Civil Rights Heritage Marker

Built in 1939, Carver Elementary School was an important part of the Tupelo civil rights movement, as a school for Black students as well as a meeting place for the Black community. The **Carver School Civil Rights Heritage Marker** (910 N. Green St.), standing in front of what is still an elementary school today, acknowledges this history.

Top to bottom: Chickasaw Village; Elvis Presley Birthplace; Tupelo Veterans Museum

Oren Dunn City Museum

Housed in a converted dairy barn inside Ballard Park, the **Oren Dunn City Museum** (689 Rutherford Rd., 662/841-6438, www.tupeloms.gov, 9am-5pm Mon.-Fri., free) tells the story of Tupelo, Mississippi Hill Country, and Chickasaw cultural history. This is a great place to take the kids for an hour or two, thanks to its playgrounds, picnic areas, and a lakeside walking trail. The museum hosts the annual Dudie Burger Festival and the Dogtrot Rockabilly Festival.

Tupelo Veterans Museum

The **Tupelo Veterans Museum** (689 Rutherford Rd., 662/844-1515, 9am-4pm Tues.-Fri., 10am-3pm Sat., free) houses an impressive collection of military artifacts, but its beautiful and solemn grounds near Ballard Park are what make this a must-stop. Inside check out Civil War memorabilia and a document signed by Abraham Lincoln, plus uniforms and equipment from the Korean, Vietnam, and Gulf Wars. Outside see planes, flags, and memorials in a beautiful setting. **The Vietnam Veterans Replica Wall** is designed to look like the memorial in Washington DC and is inscribed with the 58,267 names of those who did not return.

Entertainment and Events

An art deco-style building near downtown, the historic **Lyric Theatre** (201 N. Broadway St., 662/844-1935, www.tct.ms) is home to many of Tupelo's performing arts productions by the Tupelo Community Theatre. TCT also operates **TCT Off Broadway** (213 E. Franklin St.), an 80-seat cabaret space. Ticket prices and show times vary by performance. The Lyric is said to be haunted by a ghost named Antoine; it was used as a makeshift hospital after the 1936 tornado.

Folks in Mississippi love a festival. The Dudie Burger, named for the Dudie Diner, was a Tupelo mainstay, a burger made with meat, flour, and water (it is similar to Corinth's slugburger). The diner is now part of the Oren Dunn City Museum, which brings the burger back for one day a year at the **Dudie Burger Festival** (662/841-6438) each May. May also brings people to downtown Tupelo for the two-day **GumTree Festival** (http://gumtreefestival.com), which includes a juried visual arts exhibition and singer/songwriter contest.

The **Tupelo Elvis Festival** (http://tupeloelvisfestival.com) honors hometown King Elvis Presley with live music for four days in early June.

Elvis' musical legacy still rings through Tupelo. Many restaurants and bars, including the **Blue Canoe** and **Forklift,** offer live music on a regular schedule.

Shopping

Shopping in downtown Tupelo is a browser's dream, with lots of small boutiques with one-of-a-kind wares. Come here for jewelry, housewares, and gourmet eats.

You'll find jewelry, repurposed antiques, and art at **FarmHouse** (530 W. Main St., 662/269-2934, www.farmhousetupelo.com, 10am-5:30pm Mon.-Sat., 1pm-5pm Sun.).

Even if you are not a shopper, you must stop at the historic **Tupelo Hardware Company** (114 W. Main St., 662/842-4637, www.tupelohardware.com, 7am-5:30pm Mon.-Fri., 7am-noon Sat.). Open since 1926, this is a traditional hardware store, but it is where Elvis Presley's mother, Gladys, bought him his first guitar. He wanted a .22 caliber rifle for his birthday, but she didn't want him to have a gun, so she bought the guitar instead and history was born. The store has a plaque out front and is one of the stops on the Elvis Driving Tour.

Caron Gallery (128 W. Main St., 662/205-0351, http://thecarongallery.com, 10am-5pm Mon.-Fri., 10am-4pm Sat.) represents more than 50 artists from the state of Mississippi. Interior design firm **Blair Haus** (208 W. Main

St., 662/269-2513, www.blairhaus.com, 10am-5pm Mon.-Fri., 11am-4pm Sat.) has a small storefront space that sells furniture, linens, and artwork.

The emphasis at **Bailey Diane** (1695 N. Coley Rd., 662/432-4139, http://baileydiane.com, 10am-5pm Mon. and Sat., 10am-6pm Tues.-Fri.) is on women's clothing, most at affordable price points under $50. **MLM Clothiers** (108 S. Spring St., 662/842-4165, www.mlmclothiers.com, 9am-6pm Mon.-Fri., 10am-5pm Sat.) claims to be the oldest men's clothing store in Mississippi.

First opened in 1905 as a dry goods general store, **Reed's Department Store** (131 Main St., 662/842-6453, www.reedsms.com, 9:30am-5:30pm Mon.-Sat.) is now a favorite Southern department store with clothing for men, women, and children. There's a second Reeds location in the **Mall at Barnes Crossing** (1001 Barnes Crossing Rd., 662/842-6453, 10am-9pm Mon.-Sat., 1pm-6pm Sun.), as well as in Starkville. Connected to Reed's is **Gum Tree Books** (111 S. Spring St., 662/842-6453, www.reedsms.com/bookstore, 9:30am-5:30pm Mon.-Sat.), a small but well-stocked bookstore with an emphasis on Southern writers and a popular children's story hour.

Not downtown, but worth the drive (and next to the Blue Canoe) is **Midnite Pottery** (2004 N. Gloster St., 662/842-8058, 10am-5pm Mon.-Fri., 10am-3pm Sat.), a pottery studio with a creative local take on ceramics. Come for dishes, platters, and candles, some of which can be personalized. The pottery studio is connected to the retail shop, so if you time it right you might see some of the pieces being made.

Food

★ **Connie's Fried Chicken** (821 S. Gloster St., 662/842-7260, 6am-8pm Mon.-Fri., 6am-2pm Sat., 7am-2pm Sun., $8) is often

Top to bottom: Blue Canoe; Midnite Pottery; Queens Reward Meadery referred to as the "Café Du Monde of Tupelo," a reference to New Orleans's famous beignet spot. Connie's is a chicken shack, sure, but one that also sells delicious blueberry doughnuts, a Tupelo favorite. The doughnuts are light and sweet, and are also featured as an ingredient in other local desserts. The fried chicken is tasty, too, and the biscuits are flaky, but the reason to come to Connie's is the doughnuts. Go ahead and get a dozen to go.

When in Tupelo, you must eat somewhere Elvis ate. And that somewhere should be **Johnnie's Drive-In** (908 E. Main St., 662/842-6748, 8am-9pm Mon.-Sat.). The King loved the dough burgers—hamburgers with flour added to stretch the meat further in lean times. Fried green beans, fried chicken, eggs, and biscuits round out the no-frills menu. If it isn't crowded, you may be able to sit in Elvis's favorite booth, but car service is also available if you don't want to go inside.

If you're looking for a modern take on Southern food—using time-honored techniques and fresh ingredients—★ **Forklift** (1103 W. Jackson Ave., 662/510-7001, www.forkliftrestaurant.com, 4pm-9pm Tues.-Thurs., 4pm-10pm Fri., 11am-2pm and 4pm-10pm Sat., 11am-2pm Sun.) is a good find. The menu includes blackened catfish and barbecue shrimp. This is a neighborhood favorite, with a regular live music schedule and a popular Sunday brunch.

Woody's Tupelo Steakhouse (619 N. Gloster St., 662/840-0460, www.woodyssteak.com, 4:30pm-8:30pm Mon., 4:30pm-9pm Tues.-Thurs., 4:30pm-9:30pm Fri.-Sat., $10-40) isn't your run-of-the-mill northern steakhouse, thanks to its wild game menu options, like quail and alligator. Locals like the burgers, po'boys, and catfish, and the karaoke lounge on Thursday nights.

Locals are passionate about ★ **Blue Canoe** (2006 N. Gloster St., 662/269-2642, www.bluecanoebar.com, 3pm-midnight Mon.-Thurs., 3pm-1am Fri., 2pm-1am Sat., $7-14), a bar and restaurant with live music and a better-than-bar-food menu. There are two things you shouldn't skip: the fries with "crack dip" (an addictive sausage and cheese sauce) and the bread pudding, made with blueberry doughnuts from Connie's Fried Chicken. This is a great place to try local beers on tap or watch a football game. The fine folks behind Blue Canoe also own **Pizza vs. Tacos** (1010 N. Gloster St., 662/432-4918, 4pm-9pm Tues.-Thurs., 4pm-10pm Fri.-Sat., 11am-8pm Sun., $3.75-18), which serves exactly what its name suggests. Kids eat free during the week. Try the dill pickle pizza.

The farm-to-table menu at **Kermit's Outlaw Kitchen** (124 Main St., 662/620-6622, www.kermitsoutlawkitchen.com, 11am-2pm Mon.-Wed., 11am-2pm and 5pm-10pm Thurs.-Sat., $13-40) changes weekly, but it always features fresh, local, and delicious ingredients. Don't miss the Vegetable Art Project, a vegetarian entrée made with local seasonal veggies. Owned by the same folks, **Neon Pig Café** (1203 N. Gloster St., 662/269-2533, http://eatneonpig.com, 11am-9pm Mon.-Sat., 11am-4pm Sun., $6-35) is a two-room homage to all things pork. Order tacos, sandwiches, or burgers for take out or to eat in, or avail yourself of the butcher shop. This is a popular spot; lines can be long at night.

A casual coffee shop, **Cafe 212** (212 Main St., 662/844-6323, www.cafe212tupelo.com, 7:30am-2pm Mon.-Fri., $5-7) serves coffee all day and lunch 11am-2pm. In addition to salads, grilled sandwiches, and cold sandwiches, there's a Blue Suede Grill inspired by Elvis: a grilled sandwich with bananas, peanut butter, and honey.

When in the South you don't want to miss the opportunity for a good pimento cheese sandwich. Order one at **Sweet Tea & Biscuits Café** (2025 McCullough Blvd.,

662/322-7322, www.sweetteaandb.com, 11am-2pm Tues.-Sat., $8-9.50). The BLT made with fried green tomatoes is another South-inspired favorite.

If you can't resist the siren call of barbecue, **Bar-B-Q by Jim** (203 Commerce St., 662/840-8800, www.bbqbyjimsmokehouse.com, 10:30am-6pm Mon.-Wed., 10:30am-7:30pm Thurs.-Sat., $5-18) is a mainstay. The smoked chicken salad is modern twist on a classic.

A charming escape just two blocks from the Natchez Trace Parkway, **Queens Reward Meadery** (1719 McCullough Blvd., 662/823-6323, http://queensreward.com, 10am-8pm Tues.-Wed., 10am-10pm Thurs.-Sat.) is Mississippi's first meadery. Sip some of the wine-like beverages, which are made from local honey. Queens Reward doesn't serve food, but food trucks often hang out in the parking lot. There's lovely outdoor space—dogs welcome—and nice tables for board games inside.

Accommodations

Tupelo has many chain hotels, totaling more than 1,900 rooms, many of which are affordable and well-located. There are also several options from **Airbnb** (www.airbnb).

The ★ **Moon Lake Farm B&B** (3130 Endville Rd., 662/420-1423, www.moonlakefarm.com, $129-149) has three guest rooms, all with their own entrances and decks offering great views of the property. You can fish on-site and go horseback riding.

Hampton Inn & Suites Tupelo/Barnes Crossing (1116 Carter Cove, 662/821-0317, www.hilton.com, $92-147) is close to the mall. Choose from standard rooms or suites with kitchens. Take advantage of the outdoor pool, free hot breakfast, free Wi-Fi, and fitness center. Also nearby is the **Holiday Inn Express & Suites Tupelo** (1612 McClure Cove, 662/620-8184, www.ihg.com, $79-143), with a free breakfast buffet and indoor pool.

King City Cycles

Several hotels dot Gloster Street. The **Hilton Garden Inn** (363 Main St., 662/718-5500, hilton.com, $99-169) is Tupelo's best bet for a centrally located hotel. It has all the standard amenities, plus a pool, and is within walking distance to downtown's charms.

Information and Services

You can't miss the **Natchez Trace Parkway Headquarters and Visitor Center** (2680 Natchez Trace Pkwy., 800/305-7417, 8am-4:30pm daily) as you drive by. The headquarters has an interpretive center, a gift shop with some snacks, bathrooms, ample parking, picnic areas, and access to hiking trails. This is a great place to get questions answered from knowledgeable rangers. For information about the city's attractions, stop by the **Tupelo Visitors Center** (399 Main St., 662/841-6521, www.tupelo.net, 8am-5pm Mon.-Fri., free), which has interactive displays about Elvis, including listening stations, and a small gift shop. While here, grab a map to the 14-stop **Elvis Driving Tour** and find the places that were influential to the King. The center is a stop on the **Mississippi Blues Trail** and has a marker out front.

If you want to rent a bike around town for a few hours, check out **King City Cycles** (rentals from $3 for 30 min.). You must download the Koloni app (http://koloni.me) to start your rental.

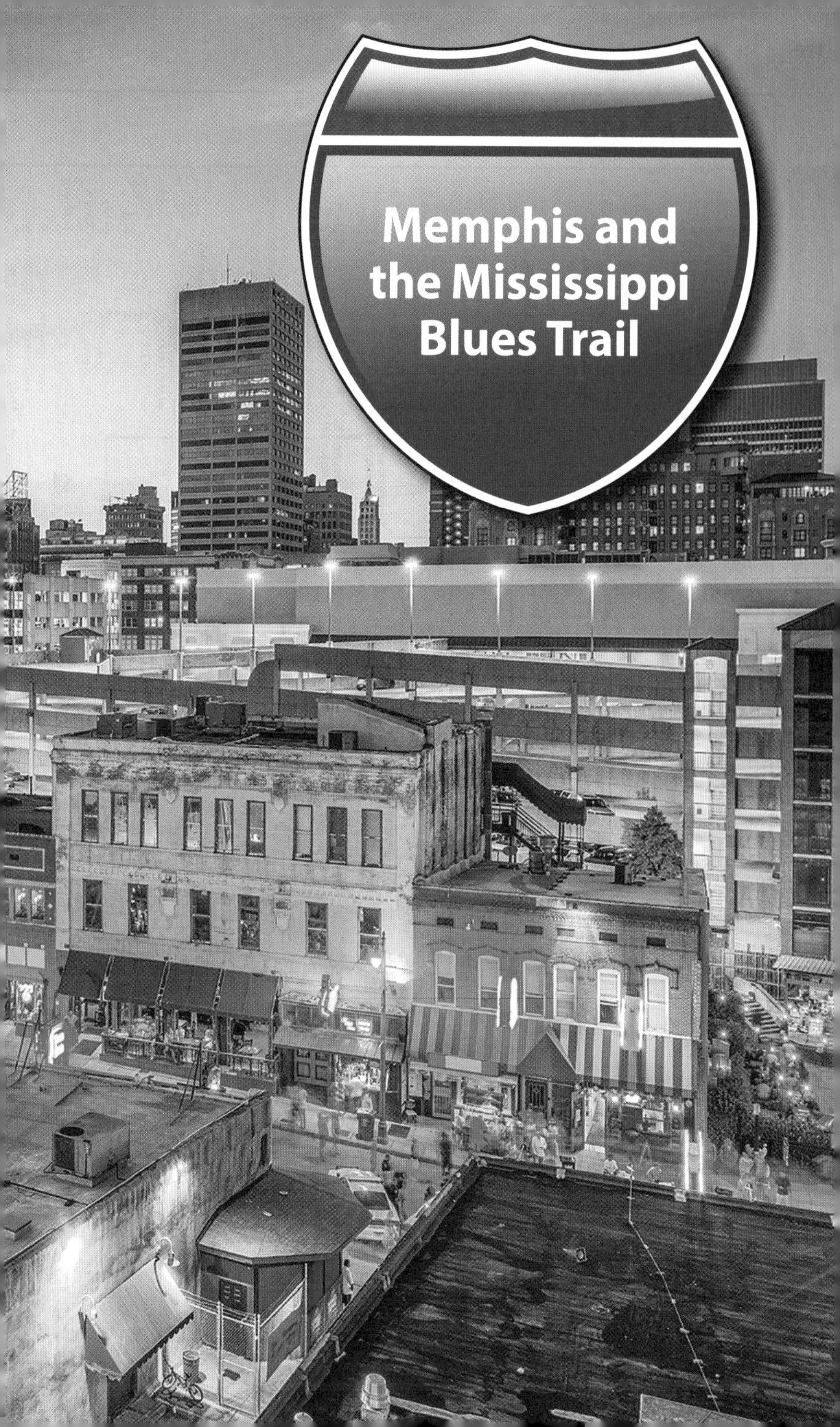
Memphis and
the Mississippi
Blues Trail

Memphis

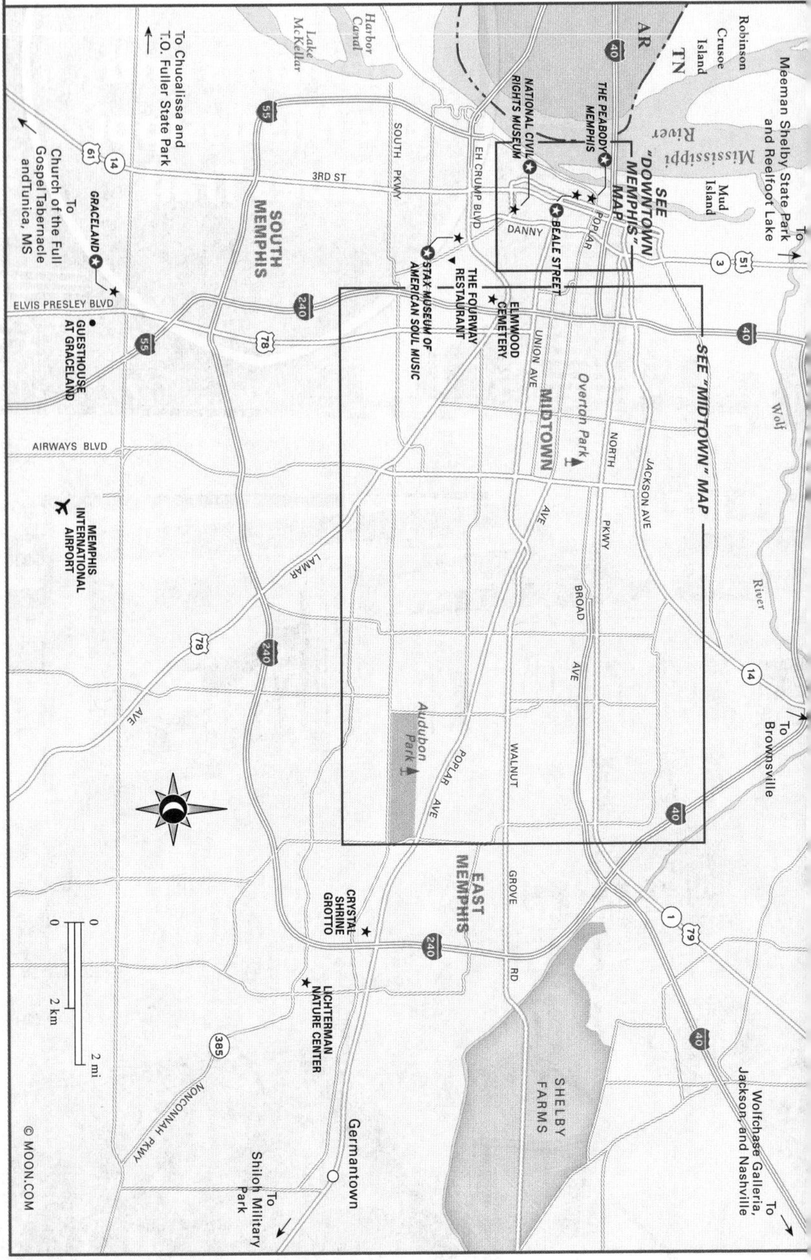

To Meeman Shelby State Park and Reelfoot Lake
Wolf River
To Brownsville
To Wolfchase Galleria, Jackson, and Nashville
Robinson Crusoe Island
Mississippi River
Mud Island
TN
AR
SEE "DOWNTOWN MEMPHIS" MAP
SEE "MIDTOWN" MAP
JACKSON AVE
NORTH PKWY
BROAD AVE
THE PEABODY MEMPHIS
POPLAR
Overton Park
BEALE STREET
MIDTOWN
UNION AVE
NATIONAL CIVIL RIGHTS MUSEUM
DANNY
ELMWOOD CEMETERY
WALNUT GROVE RD
SHELBY FARMS
EH CRUMP BLVD
THE FOURWAY RESTAURANT
EAST MEMPHIS
POPLAR AVE
STAX MUSEUM OF AMERICAN SOUL MUSIC
Audubon Park
SOUTH PKWY
Harbor Canal
CRYSTAL SHRINE GROTTO
Germantown
LICHTERMAN NATURE CENTER
Lake McKellar
3RD ST
LAMAR AVE
SOUTH MEMPHIS
To Shiloh Military Park
NONCONNAH PKWY
To Chucalissa and T.O. Fuller State Park
GRACELAND
ELVIS PRESLEY BLVD
GUESTHOUSE AT GRACELAND
AIRWAYS BLVD
MEMPHIS INTERNATIONAL AIRPORT
To Church of the Full Gospel Tabernacle andTunica, MS
0 2 mi
0 2 km
40 51 3 14 79 1 240 55 78 385 61

Highlights

★ **Beale Street:** The street that gave birth to the Memphis blues celebrates its legacy every single night of the week (page 196).

★ **National Civil Rights Museum:** For years the Lorraine Motel represented merely the tragic assassination of Martin Luther King Jr. Today, it tells the story of the African American struggle for civil rights (page 199).

★ **The Peabody Memphis:** Even the ducks in the fountain get the red-carpet treatment at this landmark hotel. The lobby is a must-visit (page 201).

★ **Stax Museum of American Soul Music:** Irresistible soul music is what made Stax famous in the 1960s. Exhibits bring to life the work of Otis Redding, the Staple Singers, Isaac Hayes, and more (page 207).

★ **Dockery Farms:** Both the Delta's cotton-farming history and its blues-music significance are explored at this preserved cotton gin (page 244).

★ **Grammy Museum Mississippi:** The role of the Delta and the blues in American music is beautifully laid out to see and hear in this museum (page 245).

★ **B. B. King Museum and Delta Interpretive Center:** This institution demonstrates not just King's superior talent in guitar playing, but his connection to the Delta region that raised him (page 247).

Memphis has a legacy as rich and complicated as its history. It's a city of the South, a cultural, culinary, and musical melting pot that has been shaped by the Mississippi River that runs alongside it and, of course, by Elvis. But Memphis has also been formed by its history of racist violence and protests; Martin Luther King Jr. was assassinated here more than 50 years ago, changing the city forever.

Still, this is a city that lives in the present. Today, it continues to celebrate food, music, and the visual arts. To really love Memphis, study its past and embrace its future. Do so with an open mind and enough time to explore. And of course, slow down for some signature barbecue.

From Memphis, you can drive south to explore a section of the Mississippi Delta along the Mississippi Blues Trail, through towns including Clarksdale, Indianola, and Greenwood, where you'll find markers, museums, houses, and other sights important to understanding the evolution of American music.

Planning Your Time

You can knock out Memphis's main attractions in a weekend. If you have more time to soak up the city's special mojo—the music, food, and laid-back attitude—by all means do; you won't regret it. But Memphis makes for a great starting spot for sections of the Mississippi Delta, including stops along the Mississippi Blues Trail, and connecting to the Natchez Trace Parkway. It's a great place in which to fly into if you want to explore the college-town charms of Oxford, Mississippi, or see the maker and music culture of Muscle Shoals, Alabama, and then continue south of the parkway.

The city center is home to the best bars, restaurants, sports venues, live-music clubs, and, of course, Beale Street. Downtown is also the liveliest, and one of the safest, parts of Memphis after the sun sets. While a lot of Memphis's attractions are downtown, others are located in the eastern and southern stretches of the city. A free shuttle is available to Graceland and Sun Studio from downtown, but for other attractions like the Stax Museum of American Soul Music and the Memphis Brooks Museum of Art, you will need a car or taxi. Take note that two of the city's best barbecue joints (a Memphis must), as well as its hopping live music venues are not within walking distance of downtown.

Safety

A word about safety: In some circles, Memphis has a reputation as being "dangerous" and, certainly, official statistics confirm that it has its share of crime, like anywhere else (less than Baltimore and Detroit in 2018 but slightly more than Chicago, for example). Police and community groups have made some strides in changing this, and this shouldn't deter you from visiting this gem of a city.

However, it can't hurt to remind yourself of general best practices for personal safety. Memphians say, "stow it, don't show it"; don't leave valuables in your parked car and don't carry valuables on your person that you don't need. Be aware of your surroundings when you're out and about (don't walk around with headphones or your head buried in your phone, and if you're drinking, stay mindful). At night, stick to well-populated areas. Certain areas, including around the airport and Graceland, are not ideal for strolling around at night. Most restaurants, bars, live music venues, and hotels have security teams; ask someone to escort you to your car or wait with you for your ride-share or taxi if you feel uncomfortable.

Two Days in Memphis

Day 1

Arrive in Memphis and check into a downtown hotel, such as **The Peabody Memphis** or **Memphis Central Station Hotel.** Head straight to **Graceland** to immerse yourself in the world of the King. Eat lunch at **Coletta's** and feast on Elvis's favorite pizza. Then visit **Sun Studio,** where Elvis recorded his first hit. When you return downtown, eat dinner at **Dyer's Burgers** on **Beale Street** in memory of the King, then stroll down along Beale Street in the evening. Barhop and listen to the blues, or just take it all in from the street, where you'll be surrounded by many new friends.

Day 2

Take the **Beale Street walking tour** in the morning, stopping at the **W. C. Handy Home and Museum.** Take your picture with the Elvis statue and go treasure hunting at **A. Schwab.** Eat lunch in at **Puck Food Hall,** then go to the **National Civil Rights Museum,** followed by a trip to the **Stax Museum of American Soul Music** and **Blues Hall of Fame Museum** in the afternoon. Head to dinner at **The Liquor Store** and then to **Minglewood Hall** for a night of live music.

Getting There

Car

Memphis is located at the intersection of two major interstate highways: I-40, which runs east-west across the United States, and I-55, which runs north-south from St. Louis to New Orleans.

From **Tupelo,** it's a 110-mile, two-hour drive along I-22 to Memphis.

To get to Memphis directly from **Nashville,** it's a 211-mile, 3-hour drive along I-40.

From **New Orleans** it is a six-hour drive for 400 miles along I-55, but it is more fun if you stop in the towns of the famous Highway 61/Blues Highway. From **Clarksdale** (and other locations in the Mississippi Delta) it is a 75-mile drive on this route.

Air

Memphis International Airport (MEM, 901/922-8000, www.flybymemphis.com) is 13 miles south of downtown Memphis. The airport's main international travel insurance and business services center (901/922-8090) is in ticket lobby B and is open daily. Here you can exchange foreign currency, buy travel insurance, send faxes, make photocopies, and buy money orders and travelers checks. A smaller kiosk near the international arrivals and departures area at gate B-36 is open daily and offers foreign currency exchange and travel insurance. There is free Wi-Fi throughout the airport.

To get to midtown Memphis, take I-240 north. To reach downtown, take I-55 north and exit on Riverside Drive. The drive takes 20-30 minutes.

Airport Shuttle

TennCo Express (901/527-2992, www.tenncoexpress.com) provides a shuttle service from the airport to many downtown hotels. Tickets are $20 one-way and $30 round-trip. Look for the shuttle parked in the third lane near column number 14 outside the airport terminal. Shuttles depart every half hour 7:30am-9:30pm. For a hotel pickup, call at least a day in advance.

Train

Amtrak (800/872-7245, www.amtrak.com) runs the City of New Orleans train daily between Chicago and New Orleans, stopping in Memphis on the way. The southbound train arrives daily at Memphis's **Central Station** (545 S. Main St.,www.amtrak.com) at 6:27am, leaving about half an hour later. The northbound

Best Restaurants

★ **Central BBQ:** This spot pleases both those who like their barbecue dry rubbed and those who prefer sauce (page 228).

★ **The Beauty Shop:** The setting may be kitschy, but the kitchen serves seriously good food (page 229).

★ **The Liquor Store:** Enjoy the Cuban vibe, the food, the drink, and the midtown community in this restaurant housed in what used to be, yes, a liquor store (page 229).

★ **Delta Meat Market:** Cole Ellis's modern take on Southern classics elevates Cleveland dining (page 246).

★ **Fan and Johnny's:** Welcoming and innovative, this eatery might be the Delta's best-kept secret (page 249).

★ **Steven's Bar-B-Q:** Eat a Delta tamale in the region's heart (page 250).

train arrives at 10pm every day. It is an 11-hour ride overnight between Memphis and Chicago, and about 8 hours between Memphis and New Orleans. Ticket and baggage service is available at Central Station 5:45am-11pm daily.

Bus

Greyhound (3033 Airways Blvd., 800/231-2222, www.greyhound.com) runs daily bus service to Memphis from around the country. Direct service is available to Memphis from a number of surrounding cities, including Jackson and Nashville, Tennessee; Tupelo and Jackson, Mississippi; Little Rock and Jonesboro, Arkansas; and St. Louis, Missouri. The Greyhound station (3033 Airways Blvd., 901/395-8770) is open 24 hours a day.

Budget-friendly **Megabus** (http://us.megabus.com) also serves Memphis from six cities (Atlanta, Birmingham, Chicago, Dallas, Little Rock, and St. Louis) from the same location. Megabus boasts free Wi-Fi on board.

Getting Around

Car

Driving is the most popular and efficient to get around Memphis. Downtown parking is plentiful if you are prepared to pay; an all-day pass in one of the many downtown parking garages costs about $12. Traffic congestion peaks at rush hours and is worst in the eastern parts of the city and along the interstates.

Public Transportation

Buses

The **Memphis Area Transit Authority** (901/274-6282, www.matatransit.com) operates dozens of buses that travel through the greater Memphis area. For information on routes, call or stop by the North End Terminal on North Main Street for help planning your trip. The bus system is not used frequently by tourists. A daily pass is available for $3.50; weekly passes are $16.

Trolleys

Public trolleys (www.matatransit.com) run for about two miles along Main Street from the Pinch District in the north to Central Station in the south, and circle up on a parallel route along Riverfront Drive. Another trolley line runs about two miles east on Madison Avenue, connecting the city's medical center with downtown. The Main Street line runs

Best Accommodations

★ **Hotel Indigo Memphis Downtown:** Retro and modern, this is one of downtown's sleekest sleeps (page 234).

★ **The Peabody Memphis:** This historic hotel is also the city's most famous, at least in part due to its resident ducks (page 234).

★ **Travelers Hotel:** The center of Clarksdale is a fun place to be, and this hotel also makes it feel like home (page 243).

★ **Cotton House Hotel:** This upscale hotel is located amid restaurants, shops, and museums, right in the center of the city's action (page 246).

★ **The Alluvian:** Make a reservation at the spa and have a Greenwood getaway at this swanky hotel (page 250).

every 10-15 minutes at most times, the Madison Avenue line runs every 15 minutes, and the Riverfront line runs every 20 minutes.

Fares are $1 per ride. You can buy an all-day pass (known as a fast pass) for $3.50 or a three-day pass for $9. All passes must be purchased at the North End Terminal at the northern end of the Main Street route. Trolleys accept both cash and transit passes on board. Daily fast passes are usable on both trolleys and fixed-route buses and can be purchased at the North End Terminal (444 N Main St.) as well.

Sun Studio Free Shuttle Bus

Sun Studio runs a free **shuttle** (www.sunstudio.com/shuttle-schedule) between Sun Studio, the Memphis Rock 'n' Soul Museum at Beale Street, and Graceland. The first run stops at the Graceland Heartbreak Hotel at 9:55am, Graceland at 10am, Sun Studio at 10:15am, and the Memphis Rock 'n' Soul Museum at 10:30am. Runs continue throughout the day on an hourly schedule. The last run picks up at Heartbreak Hotel at 5:55pm, Graceland Plaza at 6pm, and Sun Studio at 6:15pm.

The shuttle is a 12-passenger black van painted with the Sun Studio logo. The ride is free, but consider tipping your driver. The published schedule is a loose approximation, so it's a good idea to get to the pickup point early in case the van is running ahead.

Motorcycle and Bicycle

If you are considering seeing the Natchez Trace Parkway on two wheels, Memphis is a good place to find them. **Bumpus Harley Davidson** (2160 Whitten Rd., 901/401-9279, http://bumpushdmemphis.com, 9am-6pm Mon.-Fri., 9am-4pm Sat., 11am-3pm Sun.) rents seven different Harley models and has storage for your car and extra belongings while you are on the road.

For bicycles, or parts and repairs for your existing bikes, try **Peddler Bike Shop** (3548 Walker Ave., 901/327-4833, http://peddlerbikeshop.com, 9am-6pm Mon.-Fri., 9am-5pm Sat., 1pm-5pm Sun.), which has three other locations in the greater Memphis area. The shop also offers bike rentals. **Bike Plus** (9445 Poplar Ave., 901/755-7233, http://bikesplus.net, 10am-6pm Mon.-Fri., 10am-5pm Sat.) is a full-service shop with two locations, each with repairs and rentals.

Taxis

Memphis has a number of taxi companies, and you will usually find available cabs along Beale Street and waiting at the airport. Otherwise, you will need to call for a taxi. Some of the largest companies are **Yellow Cab** (901/577-7777, www.yellowcabofmemphis.com), **City Wide Cab** (901/722-8294, www.citywidetaxi.net),and **Metro Cab** (901/322-2222, http://ridememphis.com). Expect to pay $25-35 for a trip from the airport to downtown; most fares around town are under $10. Taxis accept credit cards.

App-based ride-sharing services like **Uber** and **Lyft** ($15-20 from the airport to downtown) operate in Memphis and have agreements with the local government to allow them to make stops at the airport and other destinations.

Sights

Downtown

Downtown refers to the area south of Union Avenue in the city center. It is the heart of Memphis's tourist district. Also contained within the downtown district is the area known as the **South Main Arts District,** a strip of several blocks along and near Main Street that is home to small boutiques, art galleries, restaurants, condos, and historical architecture. South Main is about a 15-minute walk or a 5-minute trolley ride from Beale Street.

★ Beale Street

If you want to delve into the history and character of Memphis music, your starting point should be **Beale Street,** home of the blues.

Beale Street has two distinct personalities. During the day it's a laid-back place for families or adults to stroll, buy souvenirs, and eat. You can also stop at one of several museums and attractions located on the street. At night, Beale Street is a strip of nightclubs and restaurants, a great place to people-watch, and one of the best places in the state to catch live blues seven nights a week.

Within **Elvis Presley Plaza** is a statue of Memphis's most famous native son, Elvis Presley, depicted during his early career.

W. C. Handy Home and Museum

The story of Beale Street cannot be told without mentioning William Christopher Handy, whose Memphis home sits at the corner of Beale Street and 4th Avenue. The building was originally located at 659 Jeanette Street, but it was moved to Beale Street in 1985. Now the **W. C. Handy Home and Museum** (352 Beale St., 901/527-3427, www.wchandymemphis.org, 10am-5pm Tues.-Sat. summer, 11am-4pm Tues.-Sat. winter, adults $6, children $4) is dedicated to telling the story of Handy's life. It was Handy who famously wrote, in his "Beale Street Blues": "If Beale Street could talk, married men would have to take their beds and walk, except one or two who never drink booze, and the blind man on the corner singing 'Beale Street Blues.' I'd rather be there than anyplace I know."

The Handy museum houses photographs of Handy's family, one of his band uniforms, and memorabilia of the recording company that he founded. You can also hear samples of Handy's music. For more on Handy, visit the modest cabin where he was born, that is now **W. C. Handy Birthplace, Museum, and Library** in Florence.

Orpheum Theatre

Near the corner of Beale and Main Streets is the **Orpheum Theatre** (203 S. Main St., 901/525-3000, www.orpheum-memphis.com). This site has been used for entertainment since 1890, when the Grand Opera House opened there with a production of *Les Huguenots.* Later, the opera house presented vaudeville shows and theater. Fire destroyed it in 1923, but in 1928 it reopened as the Orpheum, a movie theater and performing arts venue for the likes of Duke Ellington, Cab Calloway, Bob Hope, and Mae West. The Orpheum remains one of the city's premier venues for the performing arts, with

Downtown Memphis

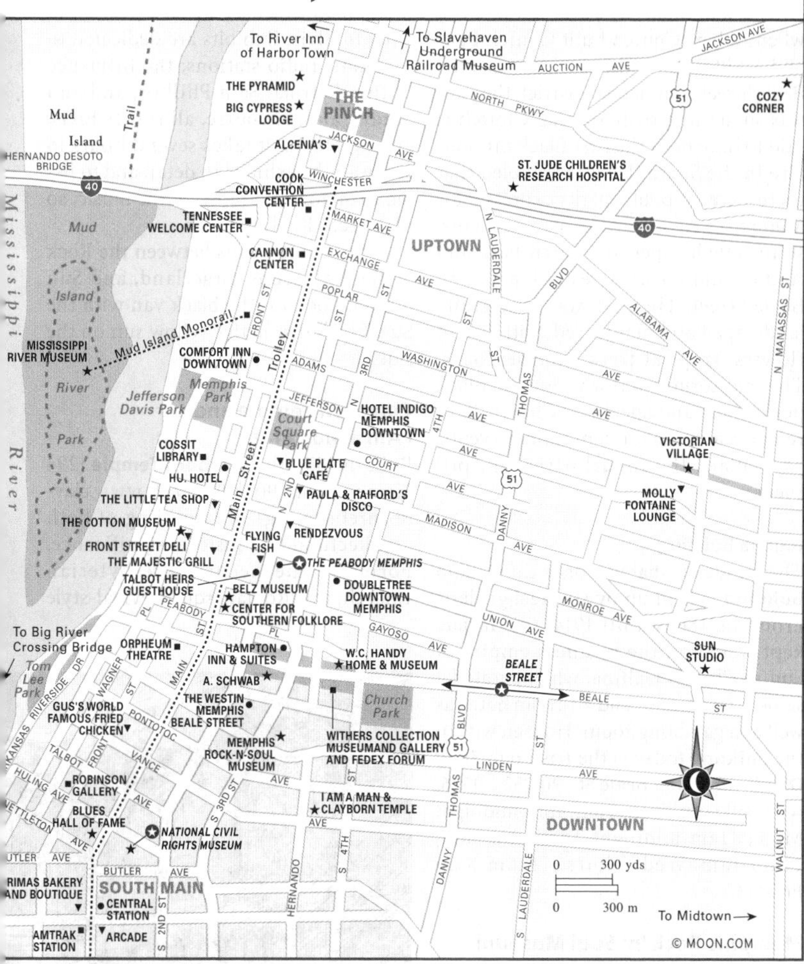

Broadway productions, mainstream musical artists, and movies.

First Baptist Beale Street Church

The **First Baptist Beale Street Church** (379 Beale St.) was built between 1868 and 1885 and is home to one of the oldest African American congregations in Memphis. In the 1860s, the congregation started to meet under brush arbors at the present location, and the first temporary structure was erected in 1865. The cornerstone was laid for the present building in 1871. The First Baptist Beale Street Church was an important force in Memphis's African American history. It was here that Black Memphians published their first newspapers, the *Memphis Watchman* and the *Memphis Free Speech and Headlight.*

Church Park

Today, **Church Park** (4th St. and MLK Ave.) is a humble city park. But in 1899, when Robert Church built Church Park and Auditorium at the eastern end of the Beale Street commercial district, the park was something truly special. Church is said to have been the first Black millionaire in the South. He was troubled that there were no public parks expressly for Memphis's African American residents, so in 1899 he opened Church Park and Auditorium on six acres of land along Beale Street. The park was beautifully landscaped and manicured, with bright flowers, tropical trees, and peacocks. The auditorium was a venue for Black performers and speakers. Church Park remains a venue for community events, particularly the annual Africa in April event.

Gallina Building

The facade of what was once the **Gallina Building** is held up by six steel girders. From the 1860s until 1914, this facade kept watch on the business empire of Squire Charles Gallina, who operated a saloon, restaurant, and 20-room hotel, as well as a gambling room. Housed within the building today is the Irish pub **Silky O'Sullivan's** (183 Beale St., 901/522-9596, www.silkyosullivans.com, 4pm-midnight Mon., 11am-midnight Tues. and Sun., 11am-1am Wed.-Thurs., 11am-3am Fri.-Sat.).

Memphis Rock 'n' Soul Museum

Music fans should plan to spend several hours at the **Memphis Rock 'n' Soul Museum** (191 Beale St., 901/205-2533, www.memphisrocknsoul.org, 9:30am-7pm daily, adults $13, children 5-17 $10, free for children 4 and under), located right next to FedEx Forum, off Beale Street. An affiliate of the Smithsonian Institution, this museum tells the story of Memphis music from the Delta blues to *Shaft*. Start with a short video documentary, and then follow the exhibits with your personal audio guide, which includes recordings of dozens of Memphis-influenced artists, from B. B. King to Elvis. Exhibits are dedicated to Memphis radio stations; the influence of the Victrola, Sam Phillips, and Sun Studio; and, of course, all things Elvis, among others. It takes several hours to study all the exhibits in detail and to listen to all (or even most) of the music, so plan accordingly.

A free shuttle runs between the Rock 'n' Soul Museum, Graceland, and Sun Studio. Look for the black van with the Sun label's distinctive yellow sun on the side.

Clayborn Temple and I Am a Man Plaza

Built in 1887, the **Clayborn Temple** (294 Hernando St., 901/907-0532, www.claybornreborn.org) is a building of both architectural and historic significance. Formerly the Second Presbyterian Church, this Romanesque Revival-style

building, with its commanding presence and stained glass windows, was sold to the African Methodist Episcopal Church (AME) in 1949 and renamed Clayborn Temple. Efforts to restore the historic building are underway; once the church renovation is complete, you'll be able to hear the church choir singing on Sunday mornings.

In 1968, it became a key gathering place and a safe haven during the U.S. civil rights movement. Here, more than 1,000 sanitation workers organized a strike to protest unsafe working conditions. It wasn't unusual for Dr. Martin Luther King Jr. to stop here when in town—and it was at this temple that Dr. King gave his "I've Been to the Mountaintop" speech, the day before his assassination. The iconic "I Am a Man" signs that were part of the movement were also distributed here. In 2018—the 50th anniversary of King's death—the **I Am a Man Plaza** was dedicated next to Clayborn Temple. The plaza is a place of powerful remembrance, bearing the name of all the striking sanitation workers who sacrificed for their cause.

Clayborn Temple and the I Am a Man Plaza are stops on the U.S. Civil Rights Trail and the Memphis Heritage Trail. Nearby street parking is usually available.

★ National Civil Rights Museum

If you do nothing else while you are in Memphis, or, frankly, the state of Tennessee, visit the **National Civil Rights Museum** (450 Mulberry St., 901/521-9699, www.civilrightsmuseum.org, 9am-5pm Wed.-Mon., later summer hours, adults $16, students and seniors $14, children 5-17 $13, free for children 4 and under). Built on the Lorraine Motel site, where Dr. Martin Luther King Jr. was assassinated on April 4, 1968, the museum makes a thorough examination of the American civil rights movement, from slavery to the present day. Exhibits display original letters, audio recordings, photos, and newspaper clippings from

the National Civil Rights Museum

events including the Montgomery bus boycott, *Brown v. Board of Education,* Freedom Summer, and the march from Selma to Montgomery. Original and re-created artifacts, such as the bus where Rosa Parks made her stand in 1955 and the cell where Dr. King wrote his famous *Letter from a Birmingham Jail,* help to illustrate the story of civil rights.

When Dr. King visited Memphis in March and then again in April 1968, the Lorraine Motel was one of a handful of downtown hotels that welcomed African Americans. The room (and balcony and parking lot) where he spent his final hours has been carefully re-created, and a narration by those who were with King tells the shocking story of his death. Across Mulberry Street, in the building that was once the boardinghouse from where James Earl Ray is believed to have fired his sniper shot, exhibits probe various theories about the assassination, as well as the worldwide legacy of the civil rights movement.

This is a large museum, and it is overflowing with information, so visitors who want to give the displays their due attention should plan on spending 3-4 hours here. A good way to visit is to tour the Lorraine Motel exhibits first, take a break for lunch, and then go across the street for the second half of the museum when you are refreshed.

Spending half a day here is a powerful experience, and one that raises many thoughts about civil rights. Expect interesting conversations with your travel companions after coming here. The gift shop offers books and videos for more information on the topic.

Admission is free on Monday after 3pm to Tennessee residents. In June, July, and August the museum stays open until 6pm.

Blues Hall of Fame Museum

The **Blues Hall of Fame Museum** (421 Main St., 901/527-2583, www.blues.org, 10am-5pm Mon.-Sat., 1pm-5pm Sun., adults $10, students and military $8, free for children under 12 with an adult) has existed as an entity—a project of the Blues Foundation—since 1980. But the physical building that you can tour and experience didn't open until 2015. The $2.9 million building is across the street from the National Civil Rights Museum at the Lorraine Hotel. It celebrates the music for which Memphis is famous and honors the musicians who make it.

Belz Museum of Asian and Judaic Art

The **Belz Museum of Asian and Judaic Art** (119 S. Main St., 901/523-2787, www.belzmuseum.org, 10am-5:30pm Tues.-Fri., noon-5pm Sat.-Sun., adults $6, seniors $5, students $4, free for children under 5), formerly Peabody Place Museum, houses one of the largest collections of artwork from the Q'ing dynasty. Forged from the private collection of Memphis developers Jack and Marilyn Belz, owners of the Peabody and the now shuttered Peabody Place mall, the museum features some 1,000 objects, including an array of jade, tapestries, paintings, furniture, carvings, and other artifacts. The museum is also home to the largest U.S. collection of work by Israeli artist Daniel Kafri.

Uptown

Locations north of Union in the city center are considered part of uptown. Originally settled by German immigrants, the **Pinch District** is now a hub of restaurants and nightlife. It is also the gateway to residential neighborhoods farther north. You can walk to the Pinch, but the best way to get there is to ride the Main Street Trolley. Also part of the uptown area is **Harbor Town,** a planned riverside community with green spaces, views of the Mississippi, shops, and a hotel.

Cotton Museum

The **Cotton Museum** at the Memphis Cotton Exchange (65 Union Ave.,

901/531-7826, www.memphiscotton-museum.org, 10am-5pm Mon.-Sat., noon-5pm Sun., adults $10, seniors and students $9, military $8, children 6-12 $8, free for children under 6) is in the broad rectangular room that once was the nerve center of the Mid-South's cotton trade. The Cotton Exchange was established in 1873, and it was here that buyers and sellers of the South's most important cash crop met, and where fortunes were made and lost. Located just steps away from the Mississippi River, the Exchange was the trading floor of Cotton Row, the area of town that was defined by the cotton industry.

The Cotton Museum is home to exhibits about cotton's history, its uses, and the culture that its cultivation gave rise to in Memphis and the Mississippi Delta. There are several videos you can watch, as well as a live Internet feed of today's cotton exchange—now conducted entirely electronically. The nicest thing about the museum, however, is seeing the chalkboard where the prices of cotton around the world were written by hand. There is also a replica of the Western Union office, where buyers and sellers sent telegrams using an intricate system of abbreviations known only to the cotton trade. The museum expanded in 2010, adding more hands-on exhibits and an educational wing.

★ The Peabody Memphis

The Peabody Memphis (149 Union Ave., 901/529-4000, www.peabodymemphis.com) is the city's most famous hotel. Founded in 1869, the Peabody was one of the first grand hotels of the South, a place as well known for its elegant balls and big-band concerts as for the colorful characters who sipped cocktails at its famous lounge. Named in memory of the philanthropist George Peabody, the original hotel was at the corner of Main

Top to bottom: Orpheum Theatre; Blues Hall of Fame Museum; a Peabody duck

and Monroe. It closed in 1923, and a new Peabody opened two years later in its present location on Union Avenue. It remained the place to see and be seen for generations of Memphians and Delta residents. It was historian and journalist David Cohn who famously wrote in 1935 that "the Mississippi Delta begins in the lobby of the Peabody Hotel in Memphis."

Even if you don't stay here, you must stop by the elegant hotel lobby to see the twice-daily march of the **Peabody ducks** (a trip to Memphis is incomplete without this experience). The ducks live on the roof of the hotel and make the journey—by elevator—to the lobby fountain every morning at 11am. At 5pm they march out of the fountain, back onto the elevator, and up to their accommodations on the roof.

The hotel employs a duck master who takes care of the ducks and supervises their daily trip downstairs. Watching the ducks is free, frenzied, and undeniably fun. It is also one of the most popular activities among visitors to Memphis, so be sure to get there plenty early (at least a half hour) and secure a good vantage point along the red carpet (or on the balcony upstairs) to watch the ducks march.

Mud Island

In Memphis, it is sometimes possible to forget that you are just steps away from the great Mississippi River. A trip to **Mud Island** will cure this confusion. A narrow band of land in the river, Mud Island is home to the **Mud Island River Park and Mississippi River Museum** (125 N. Front St., 901/312-9190, www.mudisland.com, 10am-5pm Thurs.-Sun. Apr.-Oct., adults $10, children $8), which has exhibits about early uses of the river, steam- and paddleboats, floods, and much more. Last admission is one hour prior to closing. Admission to the park is free. You can walk across the monorail bridge for free; it offers a great photo/selfie opportunity.

The park's seasonal **Mississippi River Museum** begins with a refresher course on European exploration of this region—de Soto, La Salle, and Marquette and Joliet—followed by information about early settlement. The highlight is being able to explore a replica of an 1870s steamboat. In the Riverfolk Gallery there are wax depictions of Mark Twain, riverboat gambler George Devol, and steamship entertainers. The museum also remembers the numerous river disasters that have taken place along the Mississippi. Admission to the museum includes the **River Walk** at the Mud Island River Park, a five-block scale model of the entire Mississippi River, from Minnesota to the Gulf of Mexico. Walk alongside the model to see representations of cities along the river's path and read placards about the river's history.

Slavehaven Underground Railroad Museum

The legend of the Burkle Estate, a modest white clapboard house on North 2nd Street, has given rise to the **Slavehaven Underground Railroad Museum** (826 N. 2nd St., 901/527-3427, www.slavehavenmemphis.com, 10am-5pm Mon.-Sat. summer, 10am-4pm Mon.-Sat. winter, adults $12, seniors $11, youth $11). The museum tells the story of slavery and the legendary Underground Railroad, which helped thousands of enslaved people escape to freedom in the North (and, after the 1850 Fugitive Slave Act, to Canada). Jacob Burkle, a German immigrant and owner of the Memphis stockyard, is said to have built the Burkle Estate around 1850. Escapees would have hidden in a root cellar beneath the house before making the 1,500-foot trip to the banks of the Mississippi, where they journeyed farther north.

Skeptics say that there is no evidence of this story and even point to documents that show Burkle may not have purchased the property until 1871, well after the end of slavery. Advocates for the Underground Railroad story say that it

Tina Turner, Nutbush, and Sleepy John

West Tennessee Delta Heritage Center

Half welcome center, half museum complex, the **West Tennessee Delta Heritage Center** (121 Sunny Hill Cove, Brownsville, 731/779-9000, www.westtnheritage.com, 9am-5pm Mon.-Sat., 1pm-5pm Sun., free for self-guided tours or $7.50 for guided tours) is a good place to learn about the culture and history of Tennessee's Delta region. It comprises various museums, including the **West Tennessee Music Museum,** the **Hatchie River Museum,** and the **West Tennessee Cotton Museum,** which respectively examine the musical heritage of the region, the ecology of the nearby Hatchie River, and cotton, the region's most important crop.

But the star of the museum complex is the **Flagg Grove School,** which used to be a one-room schoolhouse. Anna Mae Bullock, better known as Tina Turner, grew up in nearby Nutbush (hence the title for her hit, "Nutbush City Limits") and attended the school in her childhood. It now houses some of her costumes, platinum and gold records, fan mail, an old yearbook, and other artifacts in sleek, modern exhibits that contrast with the old wood floors, chalkboards, and wooden desks. On November 26, Turner's birthday, the center serves cake and has other festivities.

The **"Sleepy" John Estes Home** is also here. The faded clapboard house was relocated to the center so visitors could see where the blues legend was living when he died in 1977. Estes was born in Ripley, Tennessee, in 1904 but lived most of his life in Brownsville. A blues guitarist and vocalist, Estes had a distinctive "crying" vocal style that made him sound like an old man, even on his early recordings. He made his recording debut in Memphis in 1929, and recorded regularly until the United States joined World War II in 1941. Estes spent the end of his life blind and living in poverty.

The heritage center also has displays about each of the counties in the region, with visitor information on each. There is also a gift shop stocked with some locally made goods, like scented candles that smell like kudzu and cotton. It's located at exit 56, just off I-40, less than an hour's drive east of Memphis (en route to Nashville).

Mindfield

While in Brownsville, head over to **Mindfield,** a collection of steel sculptures created by local artist Billy Tripp. At first glance it looks like an electrical transformer station, but this acre of creations is a remarkable work of outsider art. Begun in 1989, the sculptures, which are largely made from reclaimed steel and other material, continue to grow and change and will do so until Tripp's death, at which point the site will be the place of his interment. Today it stands seven stories tall in places and includes the artist's messages of optimism and open-mindedness. There's an opportunity to leave comments about your impressions of the works. Find *Mindfield* off US 70, one block away from the town square on the south side of West Main Street/TN-54, next to the Sunrise Inn motel.

was the nature of the railroad to be secret, so there is nothing unusual about a lack of concrete evidence.

Visitors today need not be too concerned with the details of the debate; the Slavehaven museum does a good job of highlighting the brutality of the slave trade and slavery and the ingenuity and bravery it took for the enslaved to escape. Perhaps the most interesting display is of the quilts that demonstrate the way that enslaved people used quilting patterns to send messages to one another. Other exhibits show advertisements for Memphis slave auctions and images from the early 20th century that depict damaging racial stereotypes.

The museum is operated by Heritage Tours of Memphis, and staff is available to conduct guided tours of the property.

The Pyramid

The Memphis **Pyramid** is the most physically dominating feature of the northern city skyline. Memphis's affiliation with all things Egypt began with its name and continued in 1897, when a large-scale replica of a pyramid was built to represent Memphis at the Tennessee Centennial Exhibition in Nashville. Pyramids were popular symbols on Memphis paraphernalia for many years.

The first serious proposal for a life-size pyramid to be built in Memphis was written in the 1970s, but the idea did not take off until the 1980s, when the city and county governments agreed to fund it. Denver developer Sidney Shlenker promoted the plan and promised restaurants, tourist attractions, and lots of revenue for the city. The 321-foot pyramid was built and opened in 1991, minus the money-making engines that Shlenker promised.

For years the $63 million "Great American Pyramid" sat empty. In 2015 **Bass Pro Shops at the Pyramid** (1 Bass Pro Dr., 901/291-8200, www.basspro.com/pyramid, 8am-10pm Mon.-Sat., 8am-7pm Sun.) opened what it modestly calls "one of the most dynamic, immersive retail stores in the world." This outdoor gear store includes a cypress swamp, 10 aquariums holding 600,000 gallons of water, a **Big Cypress Lodge** 105-room hotel (800/223-3333, www.big-cypress.com) with treehouse cabins, a spa, Ducks Unlimited National Waterfowling Heritage Center, Uncle Buck's Fishbowl and Grill nautical-themed restaurant, a giant 28-story freestanding elevator, and more. Obviously, this isn't an average store. There are regular **fish feedings** (10am and 3pm daily).

Midtown

East of downtown is midtown, a district of revitalized neighborhoods and the city's best park and art museum. The city's original suburb, midtown now seems positively urban compared to the sprawling 'burbs that creep farther eastward every year. Poplar Avenue is midtown's main artery, and a good point of reference when exploring by car.

Located in midtown is **Cooper-Young,** a residential and commercial neighborhood that lies around the intersection of Cooper Street and Young Avenue, as well as the **Broad Avenue Arts District. Crosstown,** named for the Crosstown Concourse mecca of restaurants, shops, and galleries that are housed in an old Sears warehouse, is also in midtown; this area is also referred to as the Medical District.

Sun Studio

It is well worth your time to drop by the famous **Sun Studio** (706 Union Ave., 901/521-0664, www.sunstudio.com, 10am-6:15pm daily, adults $14, free for children 5-11, under 5 not admitted), where Elvis Presley recorded his first hit, "That's All Right," and where dozens of blues, rock, and country musicians recorded during the 1950s. Founded by radioman and audio engineer Sam Phillips and his wife, Becky, the studio recorded weddings, funerals, events, and, of course, music. Phillips was interested in the blues, and his first recordings were of yet-unknown artists such as Rufus Thomas and Howlin' Wolf. In 1953, Elvis Presley came into the studio on his lunch break to record a $3 record of himself singing "My Happiness" for his mother. Phillips was not impressed with the performance, and it was not for another year—and thanks to the prodding of Phillips's assistant, Marion Keisker—that Phillips called Presley in to record some more. When Phillips heard Elvis's version of the blues tune "That's All Right," he knew he had a hit. And he did.

But the story of Elvis's discovery is just one of many that took place in the modest homemade Sun Studio, and this attraction is not just for Elvis fans. The one-hour tour of the studio leaves every hour on the half hour, and while you are

Midtown

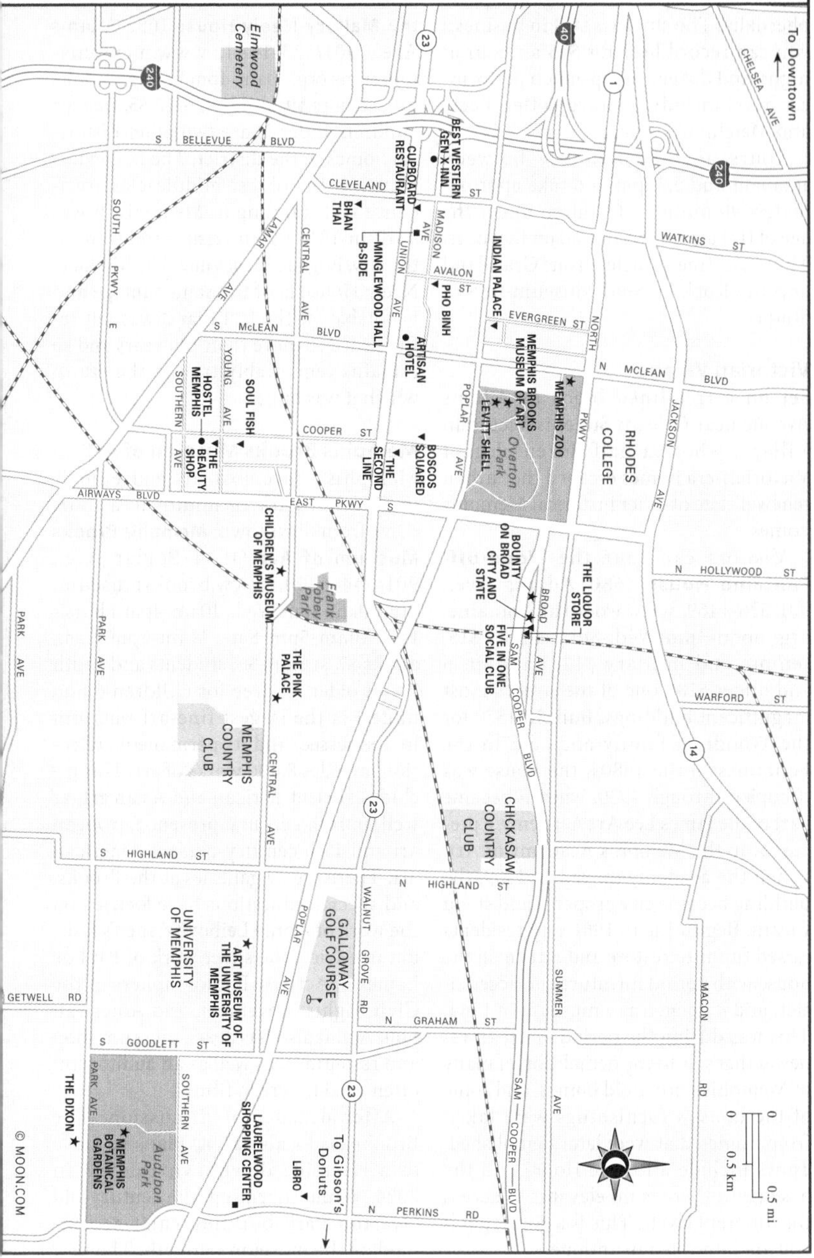

To Downtown
Elmwood Cemetery
240
23
40
1
S BELLEVUE BLVD
BEST WESTERN GEN-X INN
CUPBOARD RESTAURANT
CLEVELAND ST
BHAN THAI
MADISON AVE
UNION AVE
MINGLEWOOD HALL
B-SIDE
AVALON ST
PHO BINH
INDIAN PALACE
WATKINS ST
CHELSEA AVE
SOUTH PKWY E
LAMAR AVE
CENTRAL AVE
EVERGREEN ST
NORTH PKWY
S McLEAN BLVD
ARTISAN HOTEL
MEMPHIS BROOKS MUSEUM OF ART
MEMPHIS ZOO
LEVITT SHELL
N McLEAN BLVD
RHODES COLLEGE
JACKSON AVE
YOUNG AVE
SOUTHERN AVE
HOSTEL MEMPHIS
SOUL FISH
POPLAR AVE
Overton Park
COOPER ST
BOSCOS SQUARED
THE SECOND LINE
THE BEAUTY SHOP
AIRWAYS BLVD
EAST PKWY S
CHILDREN'S MUSEUM OF MEMPHIS
BOUNTY ON BROAD
CITY AND STATE
THE LIQUOR STORE
BROAD AVE
N HOLLYWOOD ST
Frank Tobey Park
FIVE IN ONE SOCIAL CLUB
PARK AVE
THE PINK PALACE
SAM COOPER BLVD
WARFORD ST
14
MEMPHIS COUNTRY CLUB
CHICKASAW COUNTRY CLUB
S HIGHLAND ST
N HIGHLAND ST
UNIVERSITY OF MEMPHIS
ART MUSEUM OF THE UNIVERSITY OF MEMPHIS
GALLOWAY GOLF COURSE
WALNUT GROVE RD
SUMMER AVE
MACON RD
GETWELL RD
N GRAHAM ST
S GOODLETT ST
THE DIXON
MEMPHIS BOTANICAL GARDENS
Audubon Park
LAURELWOOD SHOPPING CENTER
To Gibson's Donuts
LIBRO
N PERKINS RD
0 0.5 mi
0 0.5 km

waiting you can order a real fountain drink from the snack bar or browse the shop's collection of recordings and paraphernalia. The studio is still in business; you can record here for $75 an hour at night, and dozens of top-notch performers have, including Grace Potter, Beck, and Matchbox Twenty.

Tours are given hourly between 10:30am and 5:30pm and take approximately 90 minutes. Children under the age of five are not permitted on the tours. There are free shuttles from Graceland and the Rock 'n' Soul Museum to Sun Studio.

Victorian Village

Set on a tree-lined block of Adams Avenue near Orleans Street is Victorian Village, where a half dozen elegant Victorian-era homes escaped the "urban renewal" fate of other historical Memphis homes.

Visitors can tour the **Woodruff-Fontaine House** (680 Adams Ave., 901/526-1469, www.woodruff-fontaine.org, noon-4pm Wed.-Sun., adults $15, seniors and military $12, children 6 and under $10), one of the street's most magnificent buildings. Built in 1870 for the Woodruff family and sold to the Fontaines in the 1880s, the house was occupied through 1930, when it became part of the James Lee Art Academy, a precursor to the Memphis Academy of Art. When the academy moved in 1959, the building became city property and stood vacant. Beginning in 1961, city residents raised funds to restore and refurnish the house with period furniture and accessories, and it opened as a museum in 1964. This was during the period of urban renewal that saw to the demolition of many of Memphis's other old homes, and some of the house's furnishings were taken from homes that were later demolished. Tours include all three floors and the basement; there is no elevator to access the different levels. This is a good stop if you are interested in antiques.

The **Magevney House** (198 Adams Ave., 901/526-1484, free admission first Saturday of each month 1pm-4pm) and the **Mallory-Neely House** (652 Adams Ave., 901/523-1484, www.memphis-museums.org, 10am-4pm Fri.-Sat., adults $10, seniors $9, children 3-12 $5, free for children under 3) are two other historical homes in the district. The Magevney House is the oldest middle-class residence still standing in Memphis. It was built in 1836 by an Irish immigrant to the city, Eugene Magevney. The Mallory-Neely House is of the same vintage and is notable for the fact that it was not refurnished in more than 100 years and so remains remarkably true to the era in which it was built.

Memphis Brooks Museum of Art

Memphis's foremost art museum is in Overton Park in midtown, a short drive from downtown. **Memphis Brooks Museum of Art** (1934 Poplar Ave., 901/544-6200, www.brooksmuseum.org, 10am-8pm Wed., 10am-4pm Thurs.-Fri., 10am-5pm Sat., 11am-5pm Sun., adults $7, seniors $6, students and youth 7 and older $3, free for children 6 and under) is the largest fine-art museum in Tennessee, and its permanent collection includes 8,000 works of art. This includes ancient African and Asian art, as well as 14th century-present European art and 18th century-present American art. There are 29 galleries at the Brooks, and special exhibitions have focused on the work of Annie Leibovitz, men's fashion in Africa, the silver work of Paul de Lamerie, Activist Photographers of the Civil Rights Movement, and American Folk Art. It also has also a museum shop and restaurant, as well as an auditorium often used to screen films.

After decades of discussion, The Brooks (as locals call it) plans to move to a riverside downtown campus in 2024. While charming, the century-old Overton Park building can't accommodate the museum's growth. The new museum building—with a price tag of more than $110 million—will be connected to the Riverfront Greenway.

Memphis Zoo

The **Memphis Zoo** (2000 Prentiss Pl., 901/333-6500, www.memphiszoo.org, 9am-6pm daily Mar.-Oct., 9am-5pm daily Nov.-Feb., adults $18, seniors $17, children $13) is the proud steward of two giant pandas, Le Le and Ya Ya; large cats; penguins; lions; tropical birds; and 500 other animal species. More hippos have been born here than at any other zoo. The butterfly exhibit, open May-October, is a popular feature, and camel rides are available in the spring. The zoo is on the grounds of Overton Park. Parking is an additional $5 and a point of some contention in the city. (Parking on the grass during zoo events upsets those who use the magnificent Overton Park for other purposes. Be mindful when you visit until a solution is developed.) Tennessee residents with ID can get in for free on Tuesdays after 2pm, except in March.

South Memphis

During the day, visitors beat a path to south Memphis to see attractions like **Graceland** and the **Stax Museum of American Soul Music.** However, this is one of the most economically depressed areas of the city. Visitors should avoid this neighborhood at night, unless accompanied by a local who knows the way around.

★ Stax Museum of American Soul Music

Perhaps there is no place in Memphis that better tells the story of the city's legendary soul music than the **Stax Museum of American Soul Music** (926 E. McLemore Ave., 901/942-7685, http://staxmuseum.com, 10am-5pm Tues.-Sun., adults $13, seniors, students, and military $12,

Top to bottom: Sun Studio; Memphis Zoo; Stax Museum of American Soul Music

children 9-12 $10, free for children 8 and under). The museum tour starts with a short toe-tapping video that sets the scene for the musical magic that took place here during the 1960s.

Exhibits include the sanctuary of an old clapboard Delta church, which illustrates the connection between soul and gospel music. You can also see Booker T. Jones's original organ, Otis Redding's favorite suede jacket, and Isaac Hayes's 1972 peacock-blue gold-trimmed Cadillac Eldorado, Superfly.

The museum also winds you through the studio's control room and into the studio itself, slanted floors and all. If you want to try your hand at singing, there is a karaoke machine, as well as a dance floor in case you can't help but move to the music. The Stax Museum is a must-see for music enthusiasts but also an educational journey for those who don't know the story behind some of America's most famous songs. It sits next door to the Stax Music Academy, a present-day music school that reaches out to neighborhood youth.

Graceland

Drive south from downtown on Elvis Presley Boulevard to reach the King's most famous home, **Graceland** (3717 Elvis Presley Blvd., 901/332-3322 or 800/238-2000, www.graceland.com, 9am-5pm Mon.-Sat. and 9am-4pm Sun. Mar.-Oct., 9am-4pm daily Nov.-Feb., adults $69, seniors and students $62.70, children 5-10 $38, free for children 4 and under). The Graceland mansion is a National Historic Site that attracts more than 650,000 visitors annually. A 2017 expansion to the estate added a 200,000-square-foot entertainment complex called **Elvis Presley's Memphis,** which is separate from the mansion. It includes **Elvis: The Entertainer Career Museum, Presley Motors Automobile Museum,** and other exhibits, as well as **Graceland Soundstage,** a live music venue.

Graceland Elvis Grave

Visitors can choose from a variety of tour packages. The Elvis Entourage VIP and Elvis Experience Tour offer audio-guided tours of the mansion. The rest of the museums on the grounds are self-guided. If you can shell out $180 pp for the Ultimate VIP tour, you'll have a guided mansion tour, instead of the audio tour. There's also an option for seeing only Elvis Presley's Memphis + Planes Tour (adults $41.50, seniors $37.35, children 5-10 $21, free for children 4 and under) and skipping the mansion. The tour of the mansion itself takes about an hour and is essential to the Graceland experience. Don't consider skipping it unless you have seen it before or are really pressed for time.

A multimedia digital tour narrated by actor and Elvis fan John Stamos guides you through the ground floor of the mansion (the upstairs remains closed to the public) and several outbuildings that now house exhibits about Elvis's life and career. High points include watching the press conference Elvis gave after leaving the army, witnessing firsthand his audacious taste in decor, and visiting the Meditation Garden, where Elvis, his parents, and his grandmother are buried. There is also a plaque in memory of Elvis's lost twin, Jesse Garon. The tour plays many of Elvis's songs, family stories remembered by Elvis's daughter Lisa Marie Presley, and several clips of Elvis speaking. Among Graceland's exhibits are ***Elvis: That's the Way It Is,*** a documentary chronicling the legend's first Las Vegas performance, and ***I Shot Elvis,*** which features photos from the early years of his career and encourages museum guests to take a photo with a larger-than-life image of the King.

The exhibits gloss over the many challenges Elvis faced in his life—his addiction to prescription drugs, his failed marriage, and his unsettling affinity for younger women and firearms among them. But they showcase Elvis's generosity, his dedication to family, and his fun-loving character. The portrait that emerges is sympathetic and human for a man who is so often portrayed as larger than life.

The Graceland automobile museum features 33 vehicles, including his pink Cadillac, motorcycles, and a red MG from *Blue Hawaii,* as well as some of his favorite motorized toys, including a go-kart and dune buggy. His private planes include the *Lisa Marie,* which Elvis customized with gold-plated seat belts, suede chairs, and gold-flecked sinks. Other special Graceland exhibits include ***The Country Road to Rock: The Marty Stuart Collection, Elvis' Tupelo,*** and ***Icons: The Influence of Elvis Presley.***

On-site dining options includes barbecue at **Vernon's Smokehouse,** traditional American fare at **Gladys' Diner,** treats at **Minnie Mae's Sweets,** and grab-and-go items at **Rock 'n' Go,** which are fine options if you're peckish while touring, but there's certainly better food to be found elsewhere in Memphis.

The expansion also added **The Guest House at Graceland,** a 450-room hotel, but staying overnight here and immersing oneself in all things Elvis may not be for anyone but hard-core fans.

For more information on Elvis' humble beginnings, a trip to the Elvis Presley Birthplace in Tupelo is informative and satisfying. **Graceland Excursions** launched in 2018 and offers day trips departing from The Guest House at Graceland to historic music-centric regions relevant to the King, including to Tupelo (adults $99, children 5-12 $79) and the Mississippi Delta (adults $119, children $89).

Ticket counters, shops, museums, airplanes, restaurants, and parking lots are on the west side of Elvis Presley Boulevard, and here you board a shuttle to the Graceland mansion. The Graceland complex is surrounded by fast-food joints and a few souvenir shops lining the boulevard, but there's not a lot else in this part of town to attract tourists.

Elmwood Cemetery

Elmwood Cemetery (824 S. Dudley St., 901/774-3212, www.elmwoodcemetery.org, 8am-4:30pm daily), an 80-acre cemetery southwest of the city center, is the resting place of 70,000 Memphians—ordinary citizens and some of the city's most prominent leaders. It was founded in 1852 by 50 gentlemen who wanted the cemetery to be a park for the living as well as a resting place for the dead. They invested in tree planting and winding carriage paths so that the cemetery today is a pleasant, peaceful place to spend a few hours.

The cemetery is the resting place of Memphians like Annie Cook, a well-known madam who died during the yellow fever epidemic of 1878; Marion Scudder Griffen, a pioneering female lawyer and suffragette; and musician Sister Thea Bowman. Thousands of anonymous victims of the yellow fever epidemic were buried here, as were soldiers of the Civil War. Prominent citizens, including Robert Church Sr., Edward Hull Crump, and Shelby Foote, are also buried at Elmwood.

Visitors to the cemetery may simply drive or walk through on their own. But it is best to rent the one-hour audio guide ($10), which takes you on a driving tour and highlights 60 stops in the cemetery. Thanks to a well-written and well-presented narration, the tour comes closer than any other single Memphis attraction to bringing Memphis's diverse history and people to life.

The cemetery offers occasional lectures and docent-guided tours for $15 on select Saturday mornings. Call ahead or check the website to find out if any are scheduled during your visit. To find Elmwood, drive east along E. H. Crump Boulevard, turning south (right) onto Dudley, which dead-ends at the single-lane bridge that marks the entrance to the cemetery.

Docent-led walking tours of the 1,500 trees in the Carlisle S. Page Arboretum are also available for $15 per person.

Church of the Full Gospel Tabernacle

A native of Arkansas and longtime resident of Michigan, Al Green first made his name as one of history's greatest soul singers, with hits like "Let's Stay Together," "Take Me to the River," and "Love and Happiness." Following a religious conversion in 1979, he dedicated his considerable talents to God and founded the **Church of the Full Gospel Tabernacle** (787 Hale Rd.) in Memphis, where his Sunday sermons dripped with soulful gospel.

For almost 11 years, the Reverend Al Green left secular music, dedicating himself to God's music. He began his return to secular music in 1988, and in 1995 Green released the first of three new secular albums on Blue Note Records.

According to his official biography, *Take Me to the River,* Reverend Green faced some criticism when he returned to the secular scene. "I've got people in the church saying, 'That's a secular song,' and I'm saying, 'Yeah, but you've got Monday, Tuesday, Wednesday, Thursday, Friday, and Saturday to be anything other than spiritual. You've got to live those days, too!'" Reverend Green writes. In the book he says he has not neglected his duty to God: "The music is the message; the message is the music. So that's my little ministry that the Big Man upstairs gave to me—a little ministry called love and happiness."

Despite his rebirth as a secular soul performer, Al Green, now a bishop, still makes time for his church. He preaches regularly, but not every Sunday, and continues to sing the praises of God. The Sunday service at his Memphis church begins at 11:30am. Visitors are welcome, and you can come—within reason—as you are. Please show respect, though, by being quiet when it's called for and throwing a few bucks in the offering plate when it comes around. And don't forget that the church is a place of worship and not a tourist attraction. If you're not in town on Sunday, you can catch the weekly choir rehearsal on Thursday at 7pm. Don't bother to call ahead to find out if Reverend Green is preaching before you come out; the staff won't confirm or deny his schedule.

Metal Museum

As the only museum in the country devoted to the art and craft of metalwork, the **Metal Museum** (374 Metal Museum Dr., 901/774-6380, www.metalmuseum.org, 10am-5pm Tues.-Sat., noon-5pm Sun., adults $6, seniors and military $5, students and children $4) is an unusual delight. Formerly the National Ornamental Metal Museum, this complex is dedicated to preserving and displaying this craft. The permanent collection numbers more than 3,000 objects and ranges from contemporary sculpture to works up to 500 years old. The museum also hosts special exhibits several times a year that showcase various aspects of metalwork. There is also a working studio where you can observe the pros or take metalworking classes yourself. Demonstrations may be available on weekend afternoons; call the museum in advance to confirm.

The museum, located on a bluff overlooking the Mississippi River on the grounds of a former Marine hospital that dates to 1798, are an attraction in themselves. This is reputed to be the site where Spanish explorer Hernando de Soto and his men camped when they passed through the area in 1542.

Sections of the museum and grounds may be difficult to navigate in a wheelchair, although staff is available to help; call ahead as needed.

Directly across Metal Museum Drive is **Chickasaw Heritage Park,** sometimes referred to as De Soto Park, which has two Native American ceremonial mounds. Unlike burial mounds, which are sacred sites, you are allowed to walk to the top of these and will find great views of the Mississippi River and the museum grounds. There's also a marker indicating that this is the place where Hernando de Soto may have first seen the Mississippi.

C. H. Nash Museum at Chucalissa

Platform and ridge mounds along the Mississippi River are the main attraction at **Chucalissa Archaeological Site** (1987 Indian Village Dr., 901/785-3160, www.memphis.edu/chucalissa, 9am-5pm Tues.-Sat., 1pm-5pm Sun., adults $6, seniors and children 4-11 $4). The mounds were once part of a Choctaw Indian community that existed AD 1000-1550. The village was empty when Europeans arrived, and the word *chucalissa* means "abandoned house."

The largest mound would have been where the chief and his family lived. The present-day museum, operated by the University of Memphis, consists of an exhibit about the area's Native American population and a self-guided tour around the mounds and courtyard area, where games and meetings would have been held. There is also a 0.5-mile nature trail along the bluff overlooking the river.

East Memphis

East Memphis is where you will find large shopping malls with restaurants and movie theaters, major hospitals, the University of Memphis, and a few traffic jams. There are also a few attractions out here, including The Dixon Gallery and Gardens and Memphis Botanic Garden.

Crystal Shrine Grotto at Memorial Park Cemetery

Inside the mammoth Memorial Park Cemetery is one of Memphis's most offbeat attractions: the **Crystal Shrine Grotto** (5668 Poplar Ave., 901/302-9980, www.memorialparkfuneralandcemetery.com, 6am-8pm daily, free). Listed on the National Register of Historic Places, this faux stone cavern is described as the world's only human-made crystal cave. Walk over the bridge and through a faux tree to find yourself standing inside what seems like a geode, surrounded by biblical scenes documenting the life of Christ. The space is both kitschy and serene; while it may not feel sacred to some, even those who don't appreciate the religious iconography may appreciate the design, the craftsmanship, and the oddity of this mini park inside of a cemetery.

Made with five tons of crystals, the cave was started in 1935 by late artist Dionicio Rodríguez and finished by other artists in the early 1980s. Rodríguez was known for faux bois, specifically the sculpting of wood patterns from concrete, which can be seen in the grotto's exterior. The grotto area has a koi pond with pathways and stairs for climbing and exploring. The too-blue dyed water of the pond, tinted concrete, and colored lights amid the crystals is a lot to absorb.

Enter the cemetery from the Poplar Avenue side for the most direct route; head north from here to the grotto. (The Poplar Avenue gate closes at 10pm, while the Yates Road gate closes at 8pm.) There are some signs inside the cemetery, maps, and free fish food for the koi in the cemetery office. Do be respectful of mourners here, but don't feel uncomfortable about visiting the cemetery for fun. The folks at Memorial Park are proud of their tourist attraction, and it isn't unusual for Memphians to consider a trip here akin to a day at the park (the cave is naturally cool inside, which is an attraction during a hot Memphis summer). Also of note is that R&B singer Isaac Hayes (1942-2008) is buried near the grotto.

The Dixon Gallery and Gardens

The Dixon Gallery and Gardens (4339 Park Ave., 901/761-5250, www.dixon.org, 10am-5pm Tues.-Sat., 1pm-5pm Sun., adults $7, seniors and college students $5, children 7-17 $3, free for children 6 and under), an art museum housed inside a stately Georgian-style home, has an impressive permanent collection of more than 2,000 paintings, many of them French impressionist and post-impressionist style, including works by Monet, Renoir, Degas, and Cézanne. It also mounts a half dozen special exhibits each year; previous ones have showcased the art of Lester Julian Merriweather, Rodin, and Brian Russell.

The Dixon is an easy place to spend several hours, immersed first in art and then in walking the paths that explore the house's 17 acres of beautifully tended gardens. There is a cutting garden, woodland garden, and formal gardens, among others.

Admission to the Dixon is free 10am-noon Saturday and pay what you wish on Tuesday. It's also open late (8pm) the third Thursday of each month.

Memphis Botanic Garden

The 100-acre **Memphis Botanic Garden** (750 Cherry Rd., 901/636-4100, www.memphisbotanicgarden.com, 9am-6pm daily summer, 9am-4:30pm daily winter, adults $10, seniors $8, children 2-12 $5, free for children under 2) is home to more than 140 different species of trees and more than two dozen specialty gardens, including a Sculpture Garden, Azalea Trail, and Iris Garden. Trails meander through the gardens, but for the greatest fun buy a handful of fish food and feed the fish and ducks that inhabit the pond at the Japanese Garden. The garden puts on a number of events, including blockbuster concerts, workshops, plant sales, wine tastings, and programs for children. **Fratelli's Café at the Garden** (901/766-9900, 11am-2pm Mon.-Sat.) is a good option for lunch on-site.

Pink Palace

A good destination for families, the **Pink Palace** (3050 Central Ave., 901/636-2362, www.memphismuseums.org, 9am-5pm Mon.-Thurs., 9am-5pm and 6pm-9pm Fri., 9am-5pm Sat., noon-5pm Sun.) is a group of attractions rolled into one. The **Pink Palace Museum** (adults $15, seniors $14, children 3-12 $10, free for children under 2, free after 1pm Tues.) is a museum about Memphis, with exhibits about the natural history of the Mid-South region and the city's development. The museum is housed within the Pink Palace Mansion, the Memphis home of Piggly Wiggly founder Clarence Saunders. In 2018, following renovations, the mansion and its three exhibits—a replica of the first Piggly Wiggly supermarket, the Country Store, and the Clyde Parke Miniature Circus—reopened. While you're checking out the newly improved exhibits, don't miss the Pink Palace's refurbished grand staircase.

The Pink Palace is also home to the **Sharpe Planetarium,** which includes a 3-D movie theater and a theater-in-the-round called the AutoZone Dome, with daily screenings. Special package tickets are available for all the Pink Palace attractions.

Art Museum of the University of Memphis

The **Art Museum of the University of Memphis** (142 CFA Building, 901/678-2224, www.memphis.edu/amum, 9am-5pm Mon.-Sat., free) houses excellent but small exhibits of ancient Egyptian and African art and artifacts, along with a noteworthy print gallery. There are frequent special exhibitions. The museum is closed during university holidays and in between temporary exhibits. Parking is free after 4pm Friday and on weekends; otherwise it's $3 per hour or $15 per day in the parking garage.

Children's Museum of Memphis

You will know the **Children's Museum of Memphis** (2525 Central Ave., 901/458-2678, www.cmom.com, 9am-5pm daily, $15 admission, parking $4) by the large alphabet blocks outside spelling its acronym, CMOM. Bring children here for constructive and educational play: They can sit in a flight simulator and real airplane cockpit, climb through the arteries of a model heart, climb a skyscraper, and more. The museum has 26 permanent exhibits and several traveling exhibits. Beat the Memphis summer heat at the museum's **H2Oh! Splash Park** (Memorial Day-Labor Day 10am-5pm daily, $20 combination ticket includes museum entry), which has 40 water sprayers in which children can frolic.

The Children's Museum of Memphis is also home to the magnificent **Grand Carousel** ($3 per ride). Built in 1909 and moved to Memphis in 1923, it was a standby of Memphis childhoods for decades, until the closure of its home, the Libertyland amusement park. Savvy community members saved it and restored it and, in 2017, the carousel reopened at the museum, surrounded by a new pavilion. The restoration includes Elvis's favorite horse, as well as modifications to make the carousel wheelchair-accessible. The carousel runs on the quarter hour, with the last ride making its spin at 4:45pm daily.

Adults who are not accompanied by children are not permitted in the museum; however, they may visit the Grand Carousel, which is often rented for corporate events, weddings, and other private events. Even if you're not much of a merry-go-round fan, the craftsmanship and artistry are admirable.

Lichterman Nature Center

Lichterman Nature Center (5992 Quince Rd., 901/636-2211, www.memphismuseums.org/lichterman-overview, 10am-3pm Tues.-Thurs., 10am-4pm Fri.-Sat., adults $9, seniors $8, children ages 3-12 $5, free for children 2 and under, free to all Tues. 1pm-close) is dedicated to generating interest and enthusiasm for the Mid-South's nature. The park encompasses some 65 acres, and visitors will enjoy seeing native trees and flowers, including dogwood, lotus, and pine. It has a museum about the local environment, picnic facilities, and pleasant trails. Environmental education is the center's mission, and this certified arboretum is a popular destination for families and school groups.

Tours

History Tours

Heritage Tours of Memphis (901/527-3427, www.heritagetoursinmemphis.com, prices vary by tour) is the city's only tour company dedicated to presenting Memphis's African American history. Operated by Memphians Elaine Turner and Joan Nelson, Heritage Tours offers Black heritage, musical heritage, civil rights, and Beale Street walking tours. The company can also arrange out-of-town tours to area attractions, such as the **Alex Haley Museum and Interpretive Center** in Henning, Tennessee (adults $40, students 4-17 $30). Most local tours last about three hours.

The Black heritage tour starts at the W. C. Handy Home and Museum and includes a stop at the Slavehaven Underground Railroad Museum plus narration that tells the story of Black Memphians such as Ida B. Wells, Robert Church, and Tom Lee, and the events leading up to the assassination of Dr. Martin Luther King Jr. You will drive past the Mason Temple Church of God in Christ at 930 Mason Street, where Dr. King gave his famous "mountaintop" speech the night before his death.

River Tours

The **Memphis Queen Riverboat Tours** (901/527-2628, www.memphisriverboats.net, adults $20, seniors, college students, military, ages 13-17 $17, ages 3-12 $10, ages 2-3 $5, free for children 2 and under) leave daily at 2:30pm (boarding at 1:30pm) from the Port of Memphis, at the foot of Monroe Avenue on the riverfront. The afternoon tour lasts 90 minutes and takes you a few miles south of the city before turning around. Commentary tells some of the most famous tales of the river, but the biggest attraction of the tour is simply being on Old Man River. The **views** of the Memphis skyline from the water are impressive. Concessions are available on board. From May through August, an additional 5pm tour (boards 4:30pm) is offered Saturday and Sunday. The riverboats also offer dinner cruises at 7:30pm with live music for about $45 per person. See website to check dates and times.

Music Tours

Music-themed tours are the specialty at **Backbeat Tours** (126 Beale St. 901/527-9415, www.backbeattours.com, $20 and up, tickets must be reserved in advance). You will travel on a reconditioned 1959 transit bus and be serenaded by live musicians. Tours include the Memphis Mojo Tour (adults $30, students $28, children 7-12 $15, free for children 6 and under), which takes you to Memphis music landmarks like Sun

Studio and the Stax Museum, and the Hound Dog tour, which follows in Elvis Presley's Memphis footsteps. Backbeat can also take you to Graceland and offers two walking tours of Memphis—a Memphis Ghost Tour (adults $20, children 7-12 $13, free for children 6 and under), which explores the bloody and creepy side of history—and a Memphis historical walking tour (adults $25, children 7-12 $15, free for children 6 and under). Tickets must be reserved in advance.

Entertainment and Events

Memphis's vibrant, diverse personality is reflected in its entertainment scene. Blues, rap, R&B, and gospel are just some of the types of music you can hear on any given weekend. Alternative and indie rock find a receptive audience in Memphis, as do opera, Broadway productions, and the symphony. There's always a good excuse to go out.

Live Music

Memphis may be the birthplace of the blues, but there's a lot more to the music scene than that. It's true that you can catch live blues at a Beale Street nightclub or in a city juke joint. But you can also find hard-edge rock, jazz, and acoustic music most nights of the week. The best resource for up-to-date entertainment listings is the free weekly ***Memphis Flyer*** (www.memphisflyer.com), which comes out on Wednesday morning and includes a detailed listing of club dates and concerts.

Keep in mind that big-name artists often perform at casinos in Tunica, just over the state line in Mississippi. Many of these shows are advertised in Memphis media outlets, or check out the upcoming events on the **Tunica Convention and Visitors Bureau** website, www.tunicatravel.com.

Blues

One of the first things you should do when you get to Memphis is to find out if the **Center for Southern Folklore** (119 S. Main St., 901/525-3655, www.southernfolklore.com, 11am-6pm Mon.-Fri., 2pm-11pm Sat., 2pm-8pm Sun.) has concerts or activities planned during your stay. The center has been documenting and preserving traditional Memphis and Delta blues music since the 1970s. The free self-guided tour of all things traditional-Southern leads you through Heritage Hall. This is also the location of concerts, lectures, and screenings of documentaries; the center offers group tours and educational programs, and hosts the annual Memphis Music and Heritage Festival over Labor Day weekend. It often has live blues on Friday afternoon and offers a variety of special shows. This is one of the best places to hear authentic blues. The folklore store sells folk art, books, CDs, and traditional Southern food, and often hosts live music on Friday and Saturday nights. A sign stating "Be Nice or Leave" sets the tone as soon as you step into this colorful and eclectic shop, one of the best gift shops in the city. The center is a nonprofit organization and well worth supporting. You'll find live music in the Folklore Store most Friday and Saturday nights starting around 8pm.

Beale Street is the starting place for checking out Memphis's blues music scene. While some people lament that Beale has become a sad tourist shell of its former self, it can still be a worthwhile place to spend your evening. Indeed, no other part of Memphis has as much music and entertainment encompassing such a small area. On a typical night, Beale Street is packed with a diverse crowd strolling from one bar to the next. Beer seems to run a close second to music as the street's prime attraction, with many bars selling directly onto the street through concession windows. The "Big Ass Beer" cups used by many establishments say it all.

Nearly all Beale Street bars have live music, but one of the most popular is **B. B. King's Blues Club** (143 Beale St., 901/524-5464, www.bbkings.com/memphis, 11am-midnight Mon.-Thurs., 11am-2am Fri.-Sat., 9am-midnight Sun., cover $3-5 weekends). Local acts and some nationally known performers take the stage. B. B. King's draws a mostly tourist crowd, and it is a chain, but with the blues on full throttle, you probably won't care too much.

Also on Beale Street, **Blues City Café** (138 Beale St., 901/526-3637, www.bluescitycafe.com, 11am-3am Sun.-Thurs., 11am-5am Fri.-Sat., cover $3-5) books blues, plus a variety of other acts including doo-wop, zydeco, R&B, funk, and "high-impact rockabilly." The café-restaurant is one of the most popular on Beale Street, and its nightclub, **Rum Boogie Café** (182 Beale St., 901/528-0150, http://rumboogie.com, 11am-1am Sun.-Thurs., 11am-2am Fri.-Sat., cover varies), has an award-winning house band, Vince Johnson and the Boogie Blues Band, that performs most evenings.

Jazz

If you want a break from the blues, **King's Palace Café** (162 Beale St., 901/521-1851, http://kingspalacecafe.com, 11am-10pm Sun.-Thurs., 11am-1am Fri.-Sat.) specializes in jazz. Lots of wood paneling and red paint make the bar and Cajun restaurant warm and welcoming. This is an unpretentious place to have a meal or listen to live music. There is a $1 per person entertainment charge when you sit at a table.

Rock

Alfred's On Beale (197 Beale St., 901/525-3711, www.alfredsonbeale.com, 11am-3am Sun.-Thurs., 11am-5am Fri.-Sat., cover varies) has rock acts five nights a week. On Sunday evening, the 17-piece Memphis Jazz Orchestra takes the stage. The dance floor at Alfred's is one of the best on Beale Street.

Off Beale Street, the **Hi-Tone Cafe** (412 N. Cleveland St., 901/490-0335, 5pm-3am daily, www.hitonememphis.com, cover and ticket prices vary) is probably the best place to see live music in town. The Hi-Tone books all kinds of acts, from high-energy rockers to soulful acoustic acts. They are really committed to bringing good live music to Memphis. The cover charge for local shows is a few bucks, but tickets for bigger-name acts can run $20 and more. The bar serves respectable burgers and finger foods, excellent martinis, and lots of beer.

Nightlife

Who knew your designated driver would be a kangaroo? It's a reality with **Ride the Roo** (www.ridetheroo.com, 5pm-2am Fri.-Sat., $2 per ride, $5 for all-night pass), a sleek black mini-bus with a martini-wielding kangaroo on top, which makes 12 stops along nightlife-heavy areas in Overton Square and Cooper Young.

Downtown

You can head to Beale Street for a night out, regardless of whether or not you sing the blues.

Off Beale Street, **The Peabody Memphis** (149 Union Ave., 901/529-4000, www.peabodymemphis.com, 10am-midnight Sun.-Thurs., 10am-2am Fri.-Sat.) may be the best place to enjoy a relaxing drink. The lobby bar offers good service, comfortable seats, and a rarified atmosphere.

In the South Main district, **Earnestine and Hazel's** (531 S. Main St., 901/523-9754, http://earnestineandhazelsjukejoint.com, 5pm-3am Wed.-Sun.) is one of Memphis's most celebrated pit stops for cold drinks and a night out. Once a brothel, Ernestine and Hazel's now has one of the best jukeboxes in town. Take a seat upstairs in one of the old brothel rooms and watch South Main Street below. Rumor is the joint is haunted, but folks come here for the jukebox, not the spirits. Earnestine and Hazel's has a

Juke Joints

There are only two reasons to go to a juke joint full of blues: because you feel good or because you feel bad. A juke joint (or sometimes, "jook"), is a place where the music is great, the decor isn't much to look at, and the crowd is lively. In fact, the word "juke" may have come from the Gullah word meaning rowdy.

Memphis's Beale Street is a reliable source of music seven nights a week. But if you want to sneak away from the tourist crowd and catch some homegrown talent, head to a juke joint. Both in Memphis and in the Delta you can find places with great music and cheap drinks.

Opening and closing times are loose concepts at a juke joint. Live music is typical on Friday and Saturday nights and sometimes during the week. Generally music starts late (11pm) and finishes early (3am). Don't be surprised if the person you've engaged in conversation sitting next to you gets called to the stage sometime during the evening to play.

In general, there are only a few rules for getting along in a juke joint: Don't videotape without advance permission and tip the musicians handsomely.

Note that clubs tend to come and go. Often they don't have telephones. Or websites. Or signage. Asking a local is a great way to find a juke joint that'll be jumping. For more information, read Roger Stolle's book, *Mississippi Juke Joint Confidential* and schedule a trip to Clarksdale in April for the **Juke Joint Festival** (www.jukejointfestival.com) Stolle helped create.

- **Wild Bill's** (1580 Vollintine Ave., Memphis, 901/409-0081): The patriarch himself passed away in the summer of 2007, but what he established carries on. This legendary club is the quintessential juke joint: small and intimate, with an open kitchen serving chicken wings, and ice-cold beer served in 40-ounce bottles. It's home to the Wild Bill Band.

- **Mr. Handy's Blues Hall** (174 Beale St., Memphis, 901/528-0150): New Orleans has Preservation Hall. Memphis has Mr. Handy's Blues Hall. Everyone bad-raps Beale Street, but this tiny spot, connected to Rum Boogie Café, is the real deal. You'll feel like you are at the end of a country road in Mississippi.

- **Big S Grill** (1179 Dunnavant St., Memphis, 901/775-9127): Since the 1960s this unassuming white house has been a place where the music plays, the beer flows, and the barbecue cooks slowly.

- **Red's Blues Club** (390 Sunflower Ave., Clarksdale, 662/627-3166): This stop on the Blues Trail is open when Red wants to be open (and he'll be on-site, but may be watching basketball on the TV; don't bother him), with live blues care of some of the best musicians in Clarksdale.

- **Ground Zero Blues Club** (387 Delta Ave., Clarksdale, 662/621-9009, www.groundzerobluesclub.com) is bigger than a traditional juke joint, but it is designed to operate on the same principles, with live music from locals, the ability for those in the audience to join them on stage, lots of dancing, and laid-back décor.

- **Po' Monkey's** (99 Po' Monkey Rd., Merigold): This was *the* world-famous rural juke joint until Willie "Po' Monkey" Seaberry passed away in 2016. It no longer operates, but is a stop on the Blues Trail between Clarksdale and Cleveland and is worth a pause if you are interested in all things juke joint.

- **Blue Front Café** (107 E Railroad Ave., Bentonia, 662/528-1900): This is the oldest juke joint (that's still hopping) in the state, just outside of Yazoo City, and a stop on the Blues Trail.

similar vibe to a juke joint, but without the live music.

If beer's your thing, check out the growler station at **Joe's Wine & Liquor** (1681 Poplar Ave., 901/725-4252, http://joeswinesandliquor.com, 8am-11pm Mon.-Sat., 10am-5pm Sun.). Behind the iconic signage you'll find 30 beer taps.

If you like a velvet rope, a disco ball, and shaking booties, **Paula & Raiford's Disco** (14 S. Second St., 901/521-2494, 10pm-4am Fri.-Sat., $10-20 cover, cash only) is for you. Locals still call it Raiford's: Robert "Hollywood" Raiford opened his disco nearby in 1976 and ran it until 2007. In 2009 his daughter reopened the Memphis institution, adding her name, at the current location. Hollywood passed away in 2017, but Paula is keeping it going—with many family members at the door. Paula doesn't let anyone get away with anything: There are no drugs, no weapons, and no one gets in for free (seriously, staff shirts spell it out). Expect great people-watching and better music. The price of the cover increases after midnight.

Midtown

Murphy's (1589 Madison Ave., 901/726-4193, www.murphysmemphis.com, 11am-3am Mon.-Sat., noon-3am Sun.) is a neighborhood bar with a nice patio.

Perfect for a business date or after-work pit stop, **The Grove Grill** (4550 Poplar Ave., 901/818-9951, www.thegrovegrill.com, 11am-2:30pm and 3pm-9pm Mon.-Thurs., 11am-2:30pm and 3pm-10pm Fri.-Sat., 11am-2:30pm Sun.) is popular with office workers.

Two of Memphis's best sports bars are found in the eastern reaches of the city. **Brookhaven Pub & Grill** (695 W. Brookhaven Cir., 901/680-8118, www.brookhavenpubandgrill.com, 11am-2am daily) has big-screen plasma televisions, great beer on tap, and lots of fans. Tuesday night is Team Trivia night.

There's more to do than just watch the game at **Rec Room** (3000 Broad Ave., 901/209-1137, http://recroommemphis.com, 5pm-11pm Mon.-Thurs., 4pm-2am Fri., noon-2am Sat., noon-11pm Sun.). In addition to oversized screens for sports-watching, you can also get your game on with vintage video games, board games, and tabletop games such as foosball and Ping-Pong. Though Rec Room doesn't have a menu of its own, food trucks regularly pull up to the patio to tend to customers' cravings. Kids are welcome before 6pm if escorted by an adult; after 6pm, it's 21 and up. There's no cover for adults, a $5 wristband charge for those under 18, and video game/TV rooms cost $10-25 per hour to rent, depending on the day of the week.

The first heyday of **Lafayette's Music Room** (2119 Madison Ave., 901/207-5097, www.lafayettes.com, 11am-10pm Mon., 11am-10:30pm Tues.-Wed., 11am-midnight Thurs., 11am-2am Fri.-Sat., 11am-midnight Sun., ticket prices vary) was brief, but memorable, in the 1970s. It was shuttered for nearly four decades, during which time those who'd been there told tales of seeing performers like Kiss and Billy Joel there. Since reopening in 2014, Lafayette's has hosted live music seven days a week, including jazz, rock, and, of course, lots of blues. Its Overton Square location welcomes a steady stream of locals and tourists. Customer ages range a little older than at some other midtown venues and the lineup includes more recognizable names than some of the smaller venues in the neighborhood.

Minglewood was a town near Memphis, then a sawmill and a box factory, and a place workers went to have a good time. A song "Minglewood Blues" was written by Noah Lewis in 1928 and was so beloved in the blues tradition that even the Grateful Dead name-checked it. **Minglewood Hall** (1555 Madison Ave., 901/312-6058, www.minglewoodhall.com, box office 11am-3pm Mon.-Fri. and 4pm show days, door times and prices vary by show) is a live music venue that honors the history of the blues.

Yes, people still play the blues here, but all sorts of other genres as well, with a number of national names on the bill. Depending on the lineup, Minglewood Hall has more locals and fewer tourists in the audience than on Beale Street.

In the same complex as Minglewood is **B-SIDE** (1555 Madison Ave., 901/347-6813, 3pm-3am Mon.-Fri., 6pm-3am Sat.-Sun., cover $7-10), a relative newcomer to the Memphis live music scene. It features local bands for affordable cover prices. With a capacity of about 100 people, this is a nice, small venue to hear local music. The bar offers generous pours and a decent local craft beer selection.

LGBTQ Nightlife

Memphis is generally an inclusive place. Several of the city's most popular gay- and lesbian bars are in midtown.

Dru's Bar (1474 Madison Ave., 901/275-8082, http://drusbar.com, 1pm-midnight Sun.-Wed., 1pm-3am Thurs.-Sat.) is a welcoming bar that has weekly Drag Time and Beer Bust. The beer is cold and the liquor is BYO.

Club Spectrum Memphis (600 Marshall Ave., 901/292-2292, 9pm-4am Fri.-Sat.) is a gay-, lesbian-, and everyone-welcome dance club. This is a weekend-only spot to get your groove on.

The Pumping Station (1382 Poplar Ave., 901/272-7600, http://thepumpingstationmemphis.com, 4pm-3am Mon.-Fri., 3pm-3am Sat.-Sun.) is one of the city's favorite gay bars, with a full bar, craft beers on tap, and an outdoor beer garden (called The Backdoor Lounge, which is the only place you can smoke). It is housed in a building that once allowed a Jewish couple, evicted from another location, to open a liquor store, and is proud of its inclusive historical roots.

Located in a Victorian house decorated in a hodgepodge of styles, **Mollie Fontaine Lounge** (679 Adams Ave., 901/524-1886, www.molliefontainelounge.com, 5pm-3am Wed.-Sat., $8-11) welcomes a hodgepodge of guests. While not specifically an LGBTQ bar, its accept-everyone vibe has made it a defacto one. Order upscale cocktails, relax with live jazz music, and eat tasty Mediterranean- and Middle Eastern-inspired tapas. The food is upmarket and delicious, but people come here for the bar and the crowd.

The Arts

Memphis has a growing arts scene. **ArtsMemphis** (901/578-2787, www.artsmemphis.org) provides funding for more than 20 local arts groups and is a reliable source of information about upcoming events.

Major arts venues include the **Cannon Center for the Performing Arts** (255 N. Main St., 901/576-1200, www.thecannoncenter.com, box office noon-5pm Mon.-Fri. and two hours before showtime) and the **Orpheum Theatre** (203 S. Main St., 901/525-3000, www.orpheum-memphis.com, box office 9am-5pm Mon.-Fri.). They regularly book major artists and Broadway performances.

Galleries

With more than 1.8 million photographic images, the **Withers Collection Museum and Gallery** (333 Beale St., 901/523-2344, www.thewitherscollection.com, noon-10pm Tues.-Thurs., noon-11pm Fri.-Sat., 2pm-9pm Sun., adults $10, students and seniors $7) is one of the world's leading archives for images of the U.S. civil rights movement. Memphis native Ernest Withers (1922-2007) was a freelance photojournalist who documented the fight for equality. You can look at the historical images in changing themed exhibitions and also purchase prints for sale at this site on the Memphis Heritage Trail.

Historical photographs of Memphis and the Mississippi Delta are on display at **Robinson Gallery** (400 S. Front St., 901/576-0708, robinsongallery.com 11am-5pm Mon.-Fri.), primarily the work of former *Vogue* photographer Jack Robinson Jr. Photos capture the fashion and celebrities of the 1960s and 1970s, among other things. Robinson lived and worked in New York at the apex of his career, but he was a native of Meridian, Mississippi, and brought his understanding of the region to his art.

Theater

For theater, check out **Playhouse on the Square** (66 S. Cooper St., 901/726-4656, http://playhouseonthesquare.org, box office 10am-5pm Tues.-Sat., 1pm-5pm Sun.). This dynamic Memphis institution serves as home to several of the city's acting companies and puts on 15-20 different performances every year. It also offers theater classes, school performances, and pay-what-you-can shows.

Theatre Memphis (630 Perkins Ext., 901/682-8323, www.theatrememphis.org, box office 10am-5pm Tues.-Fri., 6pm curtain on performance weekdays, noon curtain Sat.-Sun.) is a community theater company that has been in existence since the 1920s. It stages about 12 shows annually at its theater in midtown.

Music

The **Memphis Symphony Orchestra** (610 Goodman Rd., 901/537-2525, www.memphissymphony.org, box office 9am-5pm Mon.-Fri.) performs a varied calendar of works year-round in its home at the Cannon Center for the Performing Arts (255 N. Main St.). The symphony was founded in 1952 and today has more than 850 musicians, staff, and volunteers.

Opera

Opera Memphis (Clark Opera Memphis Center, 6745 Wolf River Blvd., 901/202-4533, www.operamemphis.org) performs traditional opera at venues around town, including the historic Playhouse on the Square (66 S. Cooper St.) and the Germantown Performing Arts Centre (1801 Exeter Rd., Germantown). For the 30 days of September the company performs "pop-up" operas at different locations around the city.

Dance

Ballet Memphis (901/737-7322, www.balletmemphis.org) performs classical dance at the Playhouse on the Square (66 S. Cooper St.), the Orpheum (203 S. Main St.), and other venues throughout the city. The **New Ballet Ensemble** (901/726-9225, www.newballet.org) puts on performances around the city with "dancers in do-rags as well as tights," in the words of the *Commercial Appeal.*

Festivals and Events

Spring

Memphians celebrate their African heritage over a long weekend in mid-April. **Africa in April** (901/947-2133, www.africainapril.org) honors a specific country in Africa each year. Activities include cooking, storytelling, music, and a parade. The festival takes place at Church Park on the east end of Beale Street.

In early May, the Memphis-based Blues Foundation hosts the annual **Blues Music Awards** (www.blues.org), the Grammys of the blues world. Per the foundation, a nominee announcement, as well as ticket information for the event, is released each year in mid-December on their website.

Memphis in May (www.memphisinmay.org), the city's largest annual event, is really three major festivals rolled into one. The **Beale Street Music Festival,** which takes place at Tom Lee Park on the river, kicks things off with a celebration of Memphis music. Expect a lot of wow-worthy performers, plus many more up-and-coming talents. The festival has grown over the years, and it is now a three-day event with four stages of music going simultaneously. In addition to music, the festival offers excellent people-watching, lots of barbecue, cold beer, and festivity. You can buy daily tickets or a three-day pass for the whole weekend.

In mid-May, attention turns to the **World Championship Barbecue Cooking Contest,** a celebration of pork, pigs, and

Levitt Shell

Levitt Shell

Looking for a midtown local? **Levitt Shell at Overton Park** (1928 Poplar Ave., 901/272-2722, www.levittshell.org) is a good bet. Locals gravitate here because Levitt Shell hosts more than 50 free concerts a year. Past lineups have included The Soul Rebels, Cherry Poppin' Daddies, Steep Canyon Rangers, and Lera Lynn. Want to do Levitt like a local? Bring your own lawn chairs or blanket and chill out on the lawn. Concessions are sold and you can also bring your own food and drinks, including booze for those of age. There are also a few ticketed concerts every year, which are not free and to which outside food and drink are not permitted.

The space has history: It was built by the city in 1936 as part of the Works Progress Administration (WPA), designed by architect Max Furbringer. There were dozens of WPA band shells built, and Levitt is one of the few that remain in use. But more important to Memphians: On July 30, 1954, Elvis Presley had his first paid gig on this stage, opening for Slim Whitman.

Like many historic buildings, Levitt Shell (originally called Overton Park Shell and Shell Theater) sat vacant for many years. A neighborhood grassroots organization brought it back, raising funds for its renovation. The new Levitt Shell concert series launched in 2011.

Parking is generally free, and concerts are held rain or shine, but check ahead if you are concerned about more inclement weather. MATA bus routes 50 Poplar and 53 Summer make stops near Overton Park, while 50 Poplar stops closer to the shell.

barbecue that takes place in Tom Lee Park. In addition to the barbecue judging, it offers entertainment, hog-calling contests, and other piggy antics. If you're not part of a competing team, you can buy barbecue from vendors who set up in the park.

A sunset symphony caps off the month-long festivities. Book your hotel rooms early for **Memphis in May,** since many hotels, particularly those in downtown, sell out.

Summer

Carnival Memphis (901/458-2500, http://carnivalmemphis.org) is a Mardi Gras-style celebration, not a fairgrounds-esque event. It features a parade, fireworks, a ball, and more. This celebration raises funds for local children's charities.

Like carnivals elsewhere in the South, Carnival Memphis consists of several events, including the Crown & Sceptre Ball, Princess Ball, and a luncheon for businesses. Public ticket prices are released annually on the website.

The annual candlelight vigil at Graceland on August 15, the anniversary of Elvis's death, has grown into a whole week of Elvis-centric activities throughout Memphis. More than 30,000 people visit Graceland during **Elvis Week** (www.graceland.com/elvis-week), and during the vigil his most adoring fans walk solemnly up the Graceland drive to pay their respects at his grave. Special concerts, tribute shows, and movies are shown during the week as the city celebrates its most famous son even more than usual.

Fall

Since 2004 **Gonerfest** (www.goner-records.com/gonerfest) has been the showcase for artists on the Goner Records label. Held in September, the fest features shows at venues downtown as well as opening and closing shows at Goner's gazebo. Tickets are sold at the door for single concerts, but if you are hardcore there's also a "Golden Ticket" that will get you into each and every show for $75.

End-of-summer fairs are a tradition for Southern and rural communities all over the United States. The 10-day **Mid-South Fair** (662/280-9120, http://midsouthfair.org) in September is a bonanza of attractions: livestock shows, rodeos, agricultural judging, concerts, beauty pageants, exhibitions, carnival rides, funnel cakes, and cotton candy. The fair is held in northern Mississippi, about 30 miles south of Memphis.

In mid-September, the Cooper-Young neighborhood throws its annual jamboree at the **Cooper-Young Festival** (http://cooperyoungfestival.com). This street carnival includes an arts and crafts fair, live music, and food.

The annual **Southern Heritage Classic** (http://southernheritageclassic.com) is one of the South's big football games. But the matchup of two historically Black rival colleges, Jackson State University and Tennessee State University, is more than just a game—it is a serious citywide festival.

Winter

The colder weather welcomes a number of sporting events, including the **St. Jude Marathon and Half Marathon** (800/565-5112, www.stjudemarathon.org) in December, which is a qualifying race for the Boston Marathon. The **AutoZone Liberty Bowl** (901/795-7700, www.libertybowl.org) typically welcomes two of the National Collegiate Athletic Association's (NCAA) best football teams to town on New Year's Eve.

Taking place over the weekend closest to Elvis Presley's January 8 birthday, the **Elvis Birthday Celebration** (www.graceland.com) draws Elvis fans with special performances, dance parties, and a ceremony at Graceland proclaiming Elvis Presley Day.

Shopping

Downtown

A half dozen shops along Beale Street sell gifts and souvenirs of the city. **A. Schwab** (163 Beale St., 901/523-9782, http://a-schwab.com, noon-5pm Mon.-Wed., noon-7pm Thurs., 10am-9pm Fri.-Sat., noon-6pm Sun.) has served Memphis residents for more than 140 years, although it focuses now on odd, out-of-date, and hard-to-find items rather than traditional general-store necessities. Stop in for a souvenir or to visit the A. Schwab "museum," a collection of old-fashioned household tools and implements. The shop may stay open later in the summer depending on crowds.

Another good place for gift shopping is the **Center for Southern Folklore** (119 S. Main St., 901/525-3655, www.

southernfolklore.com, 11am-6pm Mon.-Fri., 2pm-11pm Sat., 2pm-8pm Sun.), which has books, art, and music focusing on the region.

Memphis Music (149 Beale St., 901/526-5047, http://memphismusicstore.com, 10am-midnight Mon.-Sat., noon-10pm Sun.) has a great selection of CDs and DVDs.

Head to the South Main Arts District to visit art galleries like **Robinson Gallery/Archives** (400 S. Front St., 901/576-0708, http://robinsongallery.com, 11am-5pm Mon.-Fri.), a photography gallery that houses the work of *Vogue* photographer Jack Robinson Jr.

Midtown

Shangri-La Records (1916 Madison Ave., 901/274-1916, www.shangri.com, noon-7pm Mon.-Fri., 11am-6pm Sat., 1pm-5pm Sun.), one of the city's best record stores, specializes in Memphis music. **Goner Records** (2152 Young Ave., 901/722-0095, www.goner-records.com, noon-7pm Mon.-Sat., 1pm-5pm Sun.) is both a record store and a record label.

The area between Cooper and East Parkway has the city's greatest concentration of antiques stores. **Flashback** (2304 Central Ave., 901/272-2304, www.flashbackmemphis.com, 10:30am-5:30pm Mon.-Sat., 1pm-5pm Sun.) sells both vintage furniture and clothes, including a whole lot of Levi's jeans.

Sports and Recreation

With a professional basketball team, excellent downtown baseball club, and lots of city parks, Memphis is a great city in which to watch sports and get active yourself.

Parks

Downtown

Named for the legendary blues composer W. C. Handy, **Handy Park** (200 Beale St.), located between 3rd Street and Rufus Thomas Boulevard, seems a tad out of place among Beale's nightclubs and restaurants. A statue of the park's namesake guards its gates. The park hosts occasional outdoor concerts and festivals.

The mile-long **Big River Crossing** (www.bigrivercrossing.com, 6am-10pm daily, free) boasts that it is the country's longest active pedestrian bridge, attracting cyclists, runners, walkers, and others. It spans the Mississippi River, linking downtown Memphis with Arkansas, and connects to a 10-mile corridor that is part of the **Big River Trail System** (www.bigrivertrail.com). This is one of the best options for getting outside and catching river views in the area. The bridge is illuminated with LED lights that dance every hour on the hour. To get to the base of the bridge from Memphis, head to Channel 3 Drive and Virginia Avenue West. There is street parking and some lot parking in nearby Martyrs Park. Note heavy rains can temporarily flood some of the trails on the Arkansas side.

Uptown

Tom Lee Park (spanning Riverside Dr.), a long, 30-acre, narrow grassy park that overlooks the Mississippi, is a popular venue for summertime festivals and events, including the Memphis in May festival's **World Championship Barbecue Cooking Contest.** It is also used year-round for walking and jogging and by people who simply want to look out at the giant river. The park is named for Tom Lee, an African American man who saved the lives of 32 people when the steamboat they were on sank in the river in 1925.

Located on the northern side of downtown Memphis, **Court Square** (62 N. Main St.), three blocks from the waterfront along Court Avenue, is a pleasant city park surrounded by historic buildings. Court Square is one of four parks included when the city was first planned in 1819. There are benches and trees, and it is a wireless Internet hot spot.

Midtown

Located in midtown Memphis, **Overton Park** (1914 Poplar Ave., www.overton-park.org) is one of the best all-around parks the city has to offer. This 342-acre park has a nine-hole golf course, nature trails through the woods, bike trails, an outdoor amphitheater called the Levitt Shell, and lots of green, open spaces. The park shares space with the Memphis Zoo and the Memphis Brooks Museum of Art, making the area a popular destination for city residents and visitors. Patience may be required when looking for a parking spot during an event at Overton.

South Memphis

Southwest of the city center, about a 15-minute drive from the airport, is **T. O. Fuller State Park** (1500 Mitchell Rd., 901/543-7581, http://tnstateparks.com, 8am-sunset fall-winter, 8am-7pm spring-summer). The visitors center is open 8:15am-4:15pm Mon.-Fri. Amenities at the 1,138-acre park include sheltered picnic areas, tennis courts, a golf course, a swimming pool ($5 per person ages 4 and up), basketball courts, a softball field, six miles of hiking trails, and camping facilities. T. O. Fuller State Park was the first state park east of the Mississippi River open to African Americans, and the second in the nation. An interpretive center features exhibits about the park's history, wildlife, and energy efficiency. A staff member must accompany visitors into the interpretive center.

East Memphis

Located near the University of Memphis and Oak Court Mall, **Audubon Park** (4161 Park Ave.) has a golf course, tennis courts, walking trails, and other sports facilities. The Memphis Botanic Garden is located here.

Memphians celebrate the fact that their largest city park, **Shelby Farms** (6903 Great View Dr. N., 901/222-7275, www.shelbyfarmspark.org), is five times the size of New York's Central Park. But

Overton Park

most of its 4,500 acres is pleasantly undeveloped. More than 500,000 people come here annually to go zip-lining, mountain biking, horseback riding, inline skating, walking, or running along the many trails. You can also fish, raft, canoe, or sail on the park's six lakes. The park has a wheelchair-accessible trail, areas for picnicking, and a shooting range. Other features include a visitors center, retreat center, event pavilion, boat kiosk, and wetland walk. Shelby Farms is on the eastern side of the city, just outside the I-40/I-240 loop that circles Memphis. It is easily accessible from exits 12 and 14 off I-40, and exit 13 off I-240. Or follow Walnut Grove Road from midtown.

Biking

Most cyclists in the city bike as a form of recreation, rather than transportation. The City of Memphis has established six **bike routes** that circle the city and various neighborhoods. These routes are marked and have designated parking and restroom facilities at the start. They are not bike paths—you share the road with cars—and normal safety measures are necessary.

The **Memphis Hightailers Bicycle Club** (www.memphishightailers.com) organizes frequent rides for various levels, with distances ranging 20-100 miles. Regularly scheduled Urban Bicycle Food Ministry rides are listed for people to help distribute food while riding 10-12 miles.

Several parks near Memphis are bike friendly. **Meeman-Shelby Forest State Park** (910 Riddick Rd., 901/876-5215, http://tnstateparks.com, 7am-10pm daily), north of the city, has five miles of paved bike paths, and cyclists use the main park roads for more extensive riding.

It is also noteworthy that the **Mississippi River Trail** (www.nps.org), a bicycle route that runs 3,000 miles from the headwaters of the Mississippi River in Minnesota to the Gulf of Mexico, runs through Memphis and on to Mississippi. For maps and details, go to www.lmrcc.org/outdoor-recreation/bicycling.

Spectator Sports

Basketball

The NBA's **Memphis Grizzlies** play at the massive FedEx Forum, one of the largest arenas in the NBA. Ticket prices range from under $20 to several hundred dollars. For ticket information, contact the **FedEx Forum box office** (191 Beale St., 901/205-2640, www.fedexforum.com, 10am-5:30pm Mon.-Fri.) or purchase through Ticketmaster. The NBA season runs October-April.

You can also watch the **University of Memphis Tigers** basketball team play November-April at FedEx Forum. Tickets are available from the FedEx Forum box office, or contact University of Memphis Athletics (www.gotigersgo.com) for more information.

Baseball

From April to October, the **Memphis Redbirds** (901/721-6000, www.memphisredbirds.com, $9-75) play AAA ball at the striking **AutoZone Park** in downtown Memphis. The stadium is bounded by Union Avenue, Madison Avenue, and 3rd Street, and is convenient to dozens of downtown hotels and restaurants. The Redbirds are an affiliate of the St. Louis Cardinals. Cheap tickets ($9) buy you a seat on the grassy berm, or you can pay a little more for seats in the stadium or boxes.

Food

Eating may be the best thing about visiting Memphis. The city's culinary specialties start—but don't end—with **barbecue.** Plate-lunch diners around the city offer delectable corn bread, fried chicken, greens, fried green tomatoes, peach cobbler, and dozens of other Southern specialties on a daily basis. And to make it even better, such down-home restaurants are easy on your wallet. For those seeking a departure from home-style fare, Memphis has dozens of fine restaurants, some old established eateries and other newcomers that are as trendy as those in any major American city.

Not sure where to start? Try a **Tastin' 'Round Town** food tour (901/310-9789, http://tastinroundtown.com). Choose from barbecue for $65 or Taste of Memphis for $50. These walking tours are multi-restaurant experiences that let you sample some of the city's best. Some tour times require a minimum of two tickets to purchase.

Memphis also has a decent **food truck scene.** Find one of the 24 trucks out and about (www.memphisfoodtruckers.org).

The closest gourmet grocery is in Harbor Town, the residential community on Mud Island, where **Cordelia's Market** (737 Harbor Bend Rd., 901/526-4772, http://cordeliasmarket.com, 7am-9pm daily) sells fresh produce, bakery goods, and staples. A deli in the back serves soups, salads, sandwiches, and a wide variety of prepared foods.

The **Memphis Farmers Market** (866/348-2226, www.memphisfarmersmarket.com, Sat. 8am-1pm Apr.-Oct., rain or shine, free) takes place in the pavilion opposite Central Station in the South Main part of town.

Downtown

Barbecue

Barbecue is serious business in Memphis. On the northern fringe of downtown Memphis is one of the city's most famous and well-loved barbecue joints: **Cozy Corner** (735 N. Parkway, 901/527-9158, www.cozycornerbbq.com, 11am-8pm Tues.-Sat., $7-20). Cozy Corner is tucked into a storefront in an otherwise abandoned strip mall; you'll smell it before you see it. Step inside to order barbecue pork, sausage, or bologna sandwiches. Or get a two-bone, four-bone, or six-bone rib dinner plate, which comes with your choice of baked beans, coleslaw, or barbecue spaghetti, plus slices of Wonder bread to sop up the juices.

Coletta's (1063 S. Parkway E., 901/948-7652, http://colettas.net, 11am-10pm Mon.-Thurs., 11am-11pm Fri., noon-11pm Sat., 1pm-9pm Sun., $4-15) is one of Memphis's time-loved restaurants, known for its famous barbecue pizza and for being Elvis's favorite pizza place.

Although aficionados will remind you that the ribs served at **Rendezvous** (52 S. 2nd St., 901/523-2746, http://hogsfly.com, 4:30pm-10:30pm Tues.-Thurs., 11am-11pm Fri., 11:30am-11pm Sat., $9-22) are not technically barbecue, they are one of the biggest barbecue stories in town. Covered in a dry rub of spices and broiled until the meat falls off the bones, these ribs will knock your socks off. The door to Rendezvous is tucked in an alley off Monroe Avenue. The smoky interior, decorated with antiques and yellowing business cards, is low-key, noisy, and lots of fun.

Southern

Tucked inside an unassuming storefront across from the valet entrance to the Peabody is **Flying Fish** (105 S. 2nd St., 901/522-8228, www.flyingfishinthe.net, 11am-9pm Sun.-Thurs., 11am-10pm Sat., $8-22), your first stop for authentic fried catfish in Memphis. If catfish isn't your thing, try the grilled or boiled shrimp, fish tacos, frog legs, or oysters. The baskets of fried seafood come with fries and hush puppies, and the grilled plates come with veggies, rice, and beans.

It would be a mistake to visit Memphis and not stop at **Gus's World Famous Fried Chicken** (310 Front St., 901/527-4877, http://gusfriedchicken.com, 11am-9pm Sun.-Thurs., 11am-10pm Fri.-Sat., $6-12) for some of their delicious fried bird. The downtown location is a franchise of the original Gus's, which is a half-hour drive northeast out of town along US 70, in Mason. It is no exaggeration to say that Gus's cooks up some of the best fried chicken out there: It is spicy, juicy, and hot. It's served casually wrapped in brown paper.

The **Arcade** (540 S. Main St., 901/526-5757, http://arcaderestaurant.com, 7am-3pm Sun.-Wed., 7am-10pm Thurs.-Sat., $5-11) is said to be Memphis's oldest restaurant. Founded in 1919 and still operated by the same family (with lots of the same decor), this restaurant feels like a throwback to an earlier time. The menu is diverse, with pizzas, sandwiches, and plate-lunch specials during the week, and breakfast served anytime.

Contemporary

The Majestic Grille (145 S. Main St., 901/522-8555, http://majesticgrille.com, 11am-10pm Mon.-Thurs., 11am-11pm Fri., 11am-2:30pm and 4pm-11pm Sat., 10am-2pm and 4pm-9pm Sun., $8-48) serves a remarkably affordable yet upscale menu at brunch, lunch, and dinner. It is in what was once the Majestic Theater, and the restaurant's white tablecloths and apron-clad waiters lend an aura of refinement. Don't pass on dessert, served in individual shot glasses, such as chocolate mousse, key lime pie, and carrot cake, among others.

If you're staying downtown, **Eighty3 food & drink** (83 Madison Ave., 901/333-1224, http://eighty3memphis.com, 6:30am-10:30am, 11:30am-2pm, and 5pm-10pm Mon.-Thurs., 11:30am-2pm and 5pm-11pm Fri., 6:30am-2pm and 5pm-11pm Sat., 6:30am-2pm and 5pm-10pm Sun., $15-38) is a reliable find-everything stop. You can feast on steaks and chops, with a "natural/organic/sustainable" slant. Or you can head here for bar snacks while watching your favorite sports team, streetside seating for people-watching, or even grab-and-go breakfasts perfect for taking to explore the city. Check out the happy hour (5pm-7pm Mon.-Thurs.).

It is hard to pigeonhole **Automatic Slim's Tonga Club** (83 S. 2nd St., 901/525-7948, http://automaticslimsmemphis.com, 11am-11pm Mon.-Thurs., 11am-1am Fri., 9am-1am Sat., 9am-11pm Sun., $10-27), except to say that this Memphis institution consistently offers fresh, spirited, and original fare. Named after a character from an old blues tune, Automatic Slim's uses strong flavors to create its eclectic menu; Caribbean and Southwestern influences are the most apparent. A meal here isn't complete without a famous Tonga Martini or one of the delectable desserts: Pecan tart and chocolate cake are good choices. Automatic Slim's is a welcome departure from barbecue and Southern food. Its atmosphere is relaxed, and there's often a crowd at the bar, especially on weekends, when there's live music.

Cafés and Diners

For the best burgers on Beale Street, go to **Dyer's Burgers** (205 Beale St., 901/527-3937, www.dyersonbeale.com, 11am-'til close Sun.-Thurs., 11am-'til close Fri.-Sat., $5-18). The legend says the secret is that Dyer's has been using the same grease (strained daily) since it opened in 1912. Only in Tennessee could century-old grease be a selling point. True or not, the burgers here are especially juicy. Dyer's also serves wings, hot dogs, milkshakes, and a full array of fried sides.

For coffee, pastries, and fruit smoothies, **Bluff City Coffee** (505 S. Main St., 901/405-4399, www.bluffcitycoffee.com, 6:30am-6pm Mon.-Sat., 8am-6pm Sun., $2-7.50) is your best bet in this part of the city. Located in the South Main district of galleries and condos, the shop is decorated with large prints of vintage Memphis photographs, and it is also a wireless Internet hot spot.

At **Primas Bakery and Boutique** (523 South Main St., 901/352-4193, www.primasbakeryandboutique.com, 6am-6pm Tues.-Fri., 11am-6pm Sat., 10am-3pm Sun., $2-36), two cousins offer a small selection of baked goods and sweets (hence the name: "primas" means "cousins" in Spanish). The charming shop in the South Main Arts District also sells Latin American-made gifts, clothing, and accessories.

Uptown

Southern

The Little Tea Shop (69 Monroe Ave., 901/525-6000, 11am-2pm Mon.-Fri., $5-10) serves traditional plate lunches through the week. Choose from daily specials like fried catfish, chicken potpie, and meat loaf with your choice of vegetable and side dishes by ticking off boxes on the menu. Every meal (except sandwiches) comes with fresh, hot corn bread that might as well be the star of the show. This is stick-to-your-ribs Southern cooking at its best, so come hungry. If you have room, try the peach cobbler or pecan ball for dessert. The staff's welcoming, yet efficient, style makes this perfect for a quick lunch.

The **Blue Plate Café** (113 Court Sq. S., 901/523-2050, 8am-2pm daily, $4-10) serves hearty breakfasts, plate lunches, and traditional home-style cooking. Its newsprint menu imparts wisdom ("Rule of Life No. 1: Wake up. Show up. Pay attention.") and declares that every day should begin with a great breakfast. It's not hard to comply at the Blue Plate. Eggs come with homemade biscuits and gravy, plus your choice of grits, hash browns, or pancakes. For lunch, try a meat-and-three or vegetable plate, slow-cooked white-bean soup, or a grilled peanut butter and banana sandwich. There is another location in an old house in midtown (5469 Poplar Ave., 901/761-9696, 6am-2pm Mon.-Sat., 7am-2pm Sun.).

Alcenia's (317 N. Main St., 901/523-0200, www.alcenias.com, 11am-5pm Tues.-Fri., 9am-3pm Sat., $9-13), located in the Pinch District, is among Memphis's best Southern-style restaurants. Known for its plate lunches, fried chicken, and pastries, Alcenia's has a style unlike any other Memphis eatery, witnessed in its offbeat decor of '60s-style beads, folk art, and wedding lace. Proprietor B. J. Chester-Tamayo is all love, and she pours her devotion into some of the city's best soul food. Try the spicy cabbage and deep-fried chicken, or the salmon croquette, and save room for Alcenia's famous bread pudding for dessert. Chicken and waffles is the Saturday morning specialty.

Midtown

Barbecue

★ **Central BBQ** (2249 Central Ave., 901/272-9377, http://cbqmemphis.com, 11am-9pm daily, $5-27) appeals to both those who love dry rub and those who want their sauces. Can't decide between the pulled pork, the brisket, and other local favorites? Easy solution: Get the combo platter. Central has several locations around town; they are, of course, centrally located, friendly, and clean.

Southern

Just follow the crowds to the **Cupboard Restaurant** (1400 Union Ave., 901/276-8015, http://thecupboardrestaurant.

com, 7am-8pm daily, $8-13), one of Memphians' favorite stops for plate lunches. The Cupboard moved from its downtown location to an old Shoney's about a mile outside of town to accommodate the throngs who stop here for authentic home-style cooking. The Cupboard gets only the freshest vegetables for its dishes. The meat specials change daily but include things like fried chicken, chicken and dumplings, hamburger steak with onions, and beef tips with noodles. The corn bread "coins" are exceptionally buttery. For dessert, try the lemon icebox pie.

The Women's Exchange Tea Room (88 Racine St., 901/327-5681, www.womans-exchange.com, 11:30am-1:45pm Mon.-Fri., 11am-1pm Sat., $8-15) feels like a throwback to an earlier era. Located one block east of the Poplar Street viaduct, the Women's Exchange has been serving lunch since 1936, and the menu has not changed much over the years. The special changes daily and always includes a choice of two entrées or a four-vegetable plate. Classics like chicken salad, salmon loaf, beef tenderloin, and seafood gumbo are favorites, and all lunches come with a drink and dessert. The dining room looks out onto a green garden, and the atmosphere is homey—not stuffy. The Exchange also sells gifts, housewares, and other knickknacks.

Contemporary

Memphis restaurateur Karen Blockman Carrier's **Mollie Fontaine Lounge** (679 Adams Ave., 901/524-1886, http://molliefontainelounge.com, 5pm-13am Wed.-Sat., $8-11) is an old-fashioned club where guests order upscale cocktails, relax with live music, and eat tasty Mediterranean- and Middle Eastern-inspired tapas. The restaurant has an upmarket but cozy atmosphere, with equal measures of funky and fine. The live piano jazz is the perfect backdrop for the restaurant's artistic small plates.

Libro (387 Perkins Ext., 901/800-2656, www.novelmemphis.com, 9am-8pm Mon.-Sat., 11am-2pm Sun., $14-18) is more than a bookstore café. Located inside Novel, this eatery has pastas, salads, entrées, a great wine list, and cocktails that elevate it to Italian restaurant status.

One of Memphis's most distinctive restaurant settings is an old beauty shop in the Cooper-Young neighborhood. ★ **The Beauty Shop** (966 S. Cooper St., 901/272-7111, http://thebeautyshoprestaurant.com, 11am-2pm and 5pm-10pm Mon.-Thurs., 11am-2pm and 5pm-11pm Fri.-Sat., 10am-3pm Sun., $23-27) takes advantage of the vintage beauty parlor decor to create a great talking point for patrons and food writers alike. The domed hair dryers remain, and the restaurant has put the shampooing sinks to work as beer coolers. At lunch, the Beauty Shop offers a casual menu of sandwiches and salads. For dinner, the imaginative cuisine of Memphis restaurateur Karen Blockman Carrier, who also owns Mollie Fontaine Lounge and Automatic Slim's Tonga Club, takes over.

If you enjoy your beer as much as or more than your meal, then head straight for **Boscos Squared** (2120 Madison Ave., 901/432-2222, www.boscosbeer.com, 11am-midnight Mon.-Thurs., 11am-3am Fri.-Sat., 10:30am-midnight Sun., $13-26). Boscos is a brewpub with fresh seafood, steak, and pizza. Its beer menu is among the best in the city, and many of the brews are made on the premises.

Bounty on Broad (2519 Broad Ave., 901/410-8131, http://bountyonbroad.com, 5pm-9:30pm Mon.-Thurs., 5pm-10pm Fri., 11am-2pm and 5pm-10pm Sat., 11am-2pm. Sun., $17-42) serves family-style dishes with a farm-to-table slant. Cash is not accepted, just credit cards.

The exterior of ★ **The Liquor Store** (2655 Broad Ave., 901/405-5477, www.thebroadliquorstore.com, 8am-2pm Mon., 8am-9pm Tues.-Sat., 8am-4pm Sun., $4-15) matches its name, but inside is one of the city's best restaurants and bars. The menu is loaded with flavorful

Cuban food and drinks, not to mention house-made Pop-Tarts and tres leches cake. The decor is Instagram friendly, with analog clocks, turning cake displays, and bright, tropical colors and motifs.

International

The **India Palace** (1720 Poplar Ave., 901/278-1199, www.indiapalacememphis.com, 11am-2:30pm and 5pm-9:30pm Mon.-Fri., 11am-3pm and 5pm-10pm Sat.-Sun., $11-17) is a regular winner in readers' choice polls for Indian food in Memphis. The lunchtime buffet is filling and economical, and the dinner menu features vegetarian, chicken, and seafood dishes. The dinner platters are generous and tasty.

Pho Binh (1615 Madison Ave., 901/276-0006, 11am-9pm Mon.-Sat., $4-9) is one of the most popular Vietnamese restaurants in town. You can't beat the value of the lunch buffet, but you can order from the dizzying array of Chinese and Vietnamese dishes, including spring rolls, vermicelli noodle bowls, rice, and meat dishes. There are lots of vegetarian options.

The atmosphere at **Bhan Thai** (1324 Peabody Ave., 901/272-1538, www.bhanthairestaurant.com, 5pm-9:30pm Sun.-Mon., 11am-2:30pm and 5pm-9:30pm Tues.-Fri., 5pm-10:30pm Sat., $14-25) in midtown is almost as appealing as its excellent Thai food. Set in an elegant 1912 home, Bhan Thai makes the most of the house's space, and seating is spread throughout several colorful rooms and on the back patio. Choose from dishes like red snapper, masaman curry, and roasted duck curry. The Bhan Thai salad is popular, with creamy peanut dressing and crisp vegetables.

It's the regulars who are happy at the **Happy Mexican Restaurant and Cantina** (385 S. 2nd St., 901/529-9991, www.happymexican.com, 11am-10pm

Top to bottom: The Arcade; The Beauty Shop; Gibson's Donuts

Mon.-Thurs., 11am-11pm Fri.-Sun., $7-15). Serving generous portions of homemade Mexican food for lunch and dinner, Happy Mexican is destined to become a downtown favorite. The service is efficient and friendly, and the decor is cheerful but not over the top. It's just a few blocks south of the National Civil Rights Museum. There are two other locations in the greater Memphis area.

Puck Food Hall (409 S. Main St., www.puckfoodhall.com, 8am-10pm Tues-Sat, 10am-4pm Sun., but hours may vary by vendor) is home to a number of food vendors, from pasta to ice cream to seasonal Mexican. Grab a craft cocktail from Bar 409 before heading out to the galleries in the area.

Raw Girls Memphis (http://raw-girls-memphis.myshopify.com) runs two food trucks that dole out cold-pressed juices, snacks, soups, salads, and sandwiches. The eats are as clean as it gets—free of gluten, dairy, and refined sugar, a boon for those navigating food allergies or sensitivities—featuring organic, locally grown produce to boot. Look for the trucks parked in midtown (242 S. Cooper St., 8am-6:30pm Tues.-Sat., noon-6pm Sun., $7-9) and East Memphis (5502 Poplar Ave., 8am-6:30pm Tues.-Sat., noon-6pm Sun.).

Cafés and Diners

Few restaurants have a larger or more loyal following in midtown than **Young Avenue Deli** (2119 Young Ave., 901/278-0034, www.youngavenuedeli.com, 11am-3am daily, $4-8), which serves a dozen different specialty sandwiches, plus salads and sides. The food is certainly good, but it's the atmosphere at this homey yet hip institution that really pulls in the crowds. There is live music most weekends, and the bar serves a kaleidoscope of domestic and imported beer, including lots of hard-to-find microbrews. The deli serves lunch and dinner daily.

Coffee shop and general store **City & State** (2625 Broad Ave., 901/249-2406, http://cityandstate.us, 7am-6pm Mon.-Fri., 8am-6pm Sat., 8am-2pm Sun.) peddles tea, coffee, pastries, and sandwiches alongside locally made goods for retail sale, right in the heart of the Broad Avenue Arts District. They take credit cards only.

Restaurant Iris chef Kelly English also runs a more casual restaurant, **The Second Line** (2144 Monroe Ave., 901/590-2829, www.secondlinememphis.com, 4pm-10pm Mon.-Thurs., 11am-'til close Fri.-Sun., $15-26), right next door. The kitchen rolls out New Orleans-inspired classics such as fried oyster po'boys and barbecue shrimp alongside global wild cards, like roasted beet and feta shawarma or roasted pork enchiladas.

South Memphis

Barbecue

Jim Neely's Interstate Bar-B-Que (2265 S. 3rd St., 901/775-2304, http://interstatebarbecue.com, 11am-10pm Mon.-Wed., 11am-11pm Thurs., 11am-midnight Fri.-Sat., 11am-7pm Sun., $5-23) was once ranked the second-best barbecue in the nation, but the proprietors have not let it go to their heads; this is still a down-to-earth, no-frills eatery. Large appetites can order a whole slab of pork or beef ribs, but most people will be satisfied with a chopped pork sandwich, which comes topped with coleslaw and smothered with barbecue sauce. For an adventure, try the barbecue spaghetti or barbecue bologna sandwich. If you're in a hurry, Interstate has a drive-up window, too, and if you are really smitten, you can order pork, sauce, and seasoning in bulk to be frozen and shipped to your home.

Southern

Gay Hawk Restaurant (685 S. Danny Thomas Blvd., 901/947-1464, 11:30am-3pm Mon.-Fri., 11:30am-5pm Sun., $6-10) serves country-style food that sticks to your ribs and warms your soul. Chef Lewis Bobo declares that his specialty

Brews in Bluff City

Memphians love their beer. There's never been a shortage of places to pop a cold one. Now the number of places that make beer in the city is increasing. Check out a few of these local microbreweries.

- The **Memphis Made Brewing Co.** (768 S. Cooper St., 901/207-5343, http://memphismadebrewing.com, 4pm-10pm Thurs.-Fri., 1pm-10pm Sat., 1pm-7pm Sun.) has some serious beer cred. Head brewer/co-founder Drew Barton was former head brewer at French Broad Brewery in North Carolina. Co-founder Andy Ashby also helped launch the Cooper-Young Beerfest. The brewery puts out three year-round brews plus a handful of seasonals. Try them in the taproom. There's no food on the menu, but local food trucks often stop by.
- Take a tour of **High Cotton Brewing Co.** (598 Monroe Ave., 901/543-4444, http://highcottonbrewing.com, 4pm-9pm Thurs.-Fri., noon-10pm Sat., noon-8pm Sun.) on Saturday at 3pm. The cost is $12 and includes a pint glass and samples. Or come by for a drink and live music throughout the week.
- Tours and brews that have been given nods from national magazines like *Men's Journal* are available at **Wiseacre Brewing Co.** (2783 Broad Ave., http://wiseacrebrew.com, 4pm-8pm Mon.-Thurs., 1pm-10pm Fri.-Sat.). The brewery was founded by brothers Kellan and Davin Bartosch, after the name their grandmother used to call them.
- **Crosstown Brewing Taproom** (1264 Concourse Ave., no phone, www.crosstownbeer.com, 4pm-8pm Mon.-Tues., 4pm-10pm Wed.-Thurs., noon-10pm Fri.-Sat., noon-8pm Sun.) offers quirky themed beers that reflect the identity of the Crosstown community. A rotating selection of food trucks and local restaurants that deliver supplement the taproom beers.

is "home-cooked food," and it really is as simple as that. The best thing about Gay Hawk is the luncheon buffet, which lets newcomers to Southern cooking survey the choices and try a little bit of everything. The Sunday lunch buffet practically sags with specialties like fried chicken, grilled fish, macaroni and cheese, greens, and much, much more. Save room for peach cobbler.

Since 1946 **The Four Way** (988 Mississippi Blvd., 901/507-1519, http://fourwaymemphis.com, 11am-7pm Tues.-Sat., 10am-5pm Sun. $6-11) has been an important part of Memphis life. Even when the city was segregated, this was a place where Black and white people were welcomed to dine together. Martin Luther King Jr. ate here when he was in town, and it was also a favorite of Elvis Presley. Today diners still love the soul food favorites: country-fried steak, turkey and dressing, pickled beets, and mac and cheese. Sundays are popular for to-go dinner orders as well as in-house dining, so lines can be long.

East Memphis

Contemporary

To many minds, Memphis dining gets no better than **Erling Jensen, The Restaurant** (1044 S. Yates Rd., 901/763-3700, www.ejensen.com, 5pm-10pm daily, $33-51). Danish-born Erling Jensen is the mastermind of this fine-dining restaurant that has consistently earned marks as Memphians' favorite restaurant. Understated decor and friendly service are the backdrop to Jensen's dishes, which are works of art. The menu changes with the seasons and is based upon availability. Meals at Jensen's restaurant should begin with an appetizer, salad, or soup—or all three.

Memphis's premier steak house is **Folk's Folly** (551 S. Mendenhall Rd., 901/762-8200, www.folksfolly.com, 5:30pm-10pm Mon.-Sat., 5:30pm-9pm Sun., $30-70), just east of Audubon Park. Diners flock here for prime aged steaks and seafood favorites. Seafood includes lobster, crab legs, and wild salmon. The atmosphere is classic steak house: The lighting is low, and there's a piano bar on the property.

Treats

Is there anything better than a doughnut shop that never closes? **Gibson's Donuts** (760 Mt. Moriah Rd., 901/682-8200, 24 hours daily, $2-8) has been a Memphis staple since 1967. Try the Crumb, which is just is as it sounds: a doughnut made from rolling it in the crumbs of other doughnuts. The pineapple fritter is so popular it often sells out. Prices are reduced after 11 pm.

Accommodations

There are thousands of cookie-cutter hotel rooms in Memphis, but travelers would be wise to look past major chains. If you can afford it, choose to stay in downtown Memphis. With the city at your doorstep, you'll have a better experience both day and night. Downtown is also where you'll find the most distinctive accommodations, including fine luxury hotels and charming inns.

Budget travelers have their pick of major chain hotels; the farther from the city center, the cheaper the room. Beware of very good deals, however, since you may find yourself in sketchy neighborhoods. There is a campground with tent and RV sites within a 15-minute drive of downtown at T. O. Fuller State Park.

Downtown

$150-200

The **Talbot Heirs Guesthouse** (99 S. 2nd St., 901/527-9772, www.talbotheirs.com, $130-275), in the heart of downtown, offers a winning balance of comfort and sophistication. Each of the inn's eight rooms has its own unique decor—from cheerful red walls to black-and-white chic. All rooms are thoughtfully outfitted with a full kitchen and modern bathroom, television, radio and CD player, sitting area, desk, and high-speed Internet. Little extras, like the refrigerator stocked for breakfast, go a long way, as does the cheerful yet efficient welcome provided by proprietors Tom and Sandy Franck. Book early since the Talbot Heirs is often full, especially during peak summer months.

Over $200

In 2007, Memphis welcomed the **Westin Memphis Beale Street** (170 George W. Lee Ave., 901/334-5900, www.westinmemphisbealestreet.com, $185-499), across the street from FedEx Forum and one block from Beale Street. The hotel's 203 guest rooms are plush and modern, each with a work desk, high-speed Internet, MP3-player docking station, and super-comfortable beds. The location can be noisy when Beale Street is in full swing. Expect to pay $30 a day for parking ($30 for valet).

The **Hampton Inn & Suites** (175 Peabody Pl., 901/260-4000, www.bealestreetsuites.hamptoninn.com, $165-333) is less than a block from Beale Street. The Hampton Inn has 144 standard rooms with high-speed Internet and standard hotel accommodations. The 30 suites ($239-333) have kitchenettes and separate living quarters. The entire hotel is nonsmoking. Add $18 per day for parking.

Uptown

$150-200

Memphis Central Station Hotel (545 S. Main St., 800/872-7245, http://

centralstationmemphis.com, $137-244) has transformed an old train station into a 124-room hotel in the heart of the South Main Arts District. Amenities include a listening room, bar, and restaurant, and, of course, lots of train memorabilia. There's a daily playlist of music pulled together specifically for hotel guests that you can play on speakers in your room.

If the ★ **Hotel Indigo Memphis Downtown** (22 N. B. B. King Blvd., 901/527-2215, www.ihg.com, $160-315, parking $20 per night) has a retro feel, it is because this swanky hotel was once the first Holiday Inn in Memphis. Lots of the vintage midcentury charm is intact, but has been upgraded with Frette linens and a pool in the center of the action.

Over $200

★ **The Peabody Memphis** (149 Union Ave., 901/529-4000, www.peabodymemphis.com, $300-500) is the city's signature hotel. Founded in 1869, the Peabody was the grand hotel of the South, and the hotel has preserved some of its traditional Southern charm. Tuxedoed bellhops greet you at the door, and all guests receive a complimentary shoeshine. Rooms are nicely appointed with free wireless Internet and in-room safes, as well as all the amenities typical of an upper-tier hotel. Several fine restaurants are on the ground floor, including the lobby bar, which is the gathering place for the twice-daily red carpet march of the famous Peabody ducks.

A 28-room boutique hotel on Mud Island, the **River Inn of Harbor Town** (50 Harbor Town Sq., 901/260-3333, www.riverinnmemphis.com, $300-680) offers great river views and a unique location that is just minutes from downtown. Set in the mixed residential and commercial New Urban community of Harbor Town, the River Inn provides guests with super amenities, like a fitness center, reading rooms on each floor, free parking, several restaurants, a rooftop bar, and a 1.5-mile walking trail. Even the most modest rooms have luxurious extras like a fireplace, chocolate truffle and wine turndown service, and gourmet breakfast. The River Inn offers the best of both worlds—a relaxing and quiet getaway that is still convenient to the center of Memphis.

With a name and look that aims to pay homage to the hues of Memphis and one of its best-known citizens, **Hu. Hotel** (79 Madison Ave., 866/446-3674, http://huhotelmemphis.com, $195-235, valet parking $28 per night) offers a modern aesthetic in an old Beaux Arts bank building. Formerly the Madison Hotel, Hu. Hotel now handles check-in at the coffee shop (the barista will hand you your key) and features sleek, minimalist guest rooms and a rooftop bar with great views of the mighty Mississippi, Big River Crossing, and AutoZone Park. It honors Hu Brinkley, the grandson of one of the founders of Memphis, and an icon in his own right, having served in the state legislature and as vice mayor.

It is hard to describe the **Big Cypress Lodge** (1 Bass Pro Dr., 800/223-333 or 901/620-4600, http://big-cypress.com, $385-800) without making it sound a little crazy. First of all, this 103-room hotel is inside a giant pyramid that houses a Bass Pro Shop retail store. Opulent rooms are designed to look like treehouses and duck-hunting cabins. Rooms overlook the cypress swamp filled with alligators and fish and the retail shopping of the Bass Pro Shop. But for all its quirkiness, this hotel, which opened in 2015, is a luxury resort, with all the associated amenities, including a spa and a bowling alley. Expect to pay a $20 resort fee plus $15 per day for parking.

Midtown

Midtown hotels are cheaper than those in downtown. By car or trolley line, they are convenient to city-center attractions as well as those in midtown itself.

Under $100

For affordable accommodations in Cooper-Young, check in to **Hostel Memphis** (1000 S. Cooper St., 901/273-8341, http://hostelmemphis.com, $25-55). Options include single-sex and co-ed dorm rooms for $25 per night or private rooms for $55 (all bathrooms are shared). The hostel offers Wi-Fi, continental breakfast, bike storage, and access to common areas.

$100-150

The **Best Western Gen X Inn** (1177 Madison Ave., 901/692-9136, www.bestwestern.com, $98-200) straddles downtown and midtown Memphis. It's about two miles from the city center along the Madison Avenue trolley line, so Gen Xers can get downtown on the trolley in about 15 minutes, with a little luck. The hotel, which has free parking and breakfast, is also accessible to the city's expansive medical center and the attractions around Overton Park. These rooms are standard hotel style, enhanced with bright colors, flat-panel plasma TVs, and a general aura of youthfulness. The whole hotel is nonsmoking, and guests enjoy a good continental breakfast and a special partnership with the downtown YMCA for gym use. This is a good choice for travelers who want to be near downtown but are on a budget, particularly those with a car. No pets are permitted.

Over $200

The five rooms available in **The James Lee House** (690 Adams Ave., http://jamesleehouse.com, 901/359-6750, $245-450) may be in one of the most opulent homes you've had the pleasure to stay in. The building may have been built in the 19th century, but the inn's amenities, such as wireless Internet and private gated parking, are 21st century.

Top to bottom: The Peabody Memphis; River Inn of Harbor Town; Hu.Hotel

South Memphis

There are two reasons to stay in south Memphis: the airport and Graceland. But even if you are keenly interested in either of these places, you should think twice about staying in this part of town. You will need a car, as some of these neighborhoods are seedy and south Memphis is not within walking distance of anything of interest. Book early for **Elvis Week** in August.

Under $100

The **Days Inn at Graceland** (3839 Elvis Presley Blvd., 901/410-3967, www.wyndhamhotels.com, $75-95) is one of the most well-worn properties in the venerable Days Inn chain. The hotel has amped up the Elvis kitsch; you can tune into free nonstop Elvis movies or swim in a guitar-shaped pool. There is a free continental breakfast.

The **Magnuson Grand Memphis Hotel** (1471 E. Brooks Rd., 901/207-7924, www.magnusonhotels.com, $38-125) is a tidy, safe oasis in an otherwise unappealing part of town. Before its remodel, being close to Graceland and the airport were the only draws of this budget hotel. It remains affordable, but now it has the added perk of being clean, with updated rooms and bathrooms, plus a restaurant and bar. Amenities include a decent outdoor pool, a small fitness room, and an upgraded lobby.

$150-200

Opened in 2016, **The Guest House at Graceland** (3600 Elvis Presley Blvd., 901/443-3000, http://guesthousegraceland.com, from $199) is a 430-room Elvis themed resort, not a mere hotel. The property has 20 themed suites, the designs of which were supervised by Priscilla Presley herself, and which evoke the feel of Graceland itself. In addition, the luxury hotel has two full-service restaurants (Delta's Kitchen, EP's Bar & Grill) and a grab-and-go café (Shake Rattle & Go) plus an outdoor pool and a 464-seat theater for performances and films. The decor is sleek and contemporary, but you still get plenty of Elvis kitsch. Pets weighing less than 35 pounds are welcome with an additional $35 daily fee. The appeal of the Guest House is its proximity to Graceland. If that's not of interest, there's not many reasons to stay here.

Camping

You can pitch your tent or park your RV just a 15-minute drive from downtown Memphis at **T. O. Fuller State Park** (1500 Mitchell Rd., 901/543-7581, http://reserve.tnstateparks.com, $25). The park has 45 tent and RV sites, each with a picnic table, fire ring, grill, lantern hanger, and electrical and water hookups.

On the north side of Memphis, **Meeman-Shelby Forest State Park** (910 Riddick Rd., Millington, 901/876-5215, http://reserve.tnstateparks.com, $25-125) is a half-hour drive from downtown. Stay in one of six lakeside cabins, which you can reserve up to one year in advance; book at least one month in advance to avoid being shut out. The two-bedroom cabins can sleep up to six people. Rates are $100-125 per night, depending on the season and day of the week. There are also 49 tent/RV sites ($25-27) with electrical and water hookups, picnic tables, grills, and fire rings. The bathhouse has hot showers.

Information and Services

Visitors Centers

The city's visitors center is the **Tennessee Welcome Center** (119 Riverside Dr., 901/543-6757, www.tnvacation.com/welcome-centers, 7am-9pm daily), located on the Tennessee side of the I-40 bridge. The center has lots of brochures and free maps and staff who can answer your questions. The center assists more than 350,000 travelers annually.

Emergency Services

Dial 911 in an emergency for fire,

ambulance, or police. The downtown police department is the **North Main Station** (444 N. Main St., 901/636-4099). Police patrol downtown by car, on bike, and on foot.

Hospitals

Memphis is chockablock with hospitals. Midtown Memphis is also referred to as Medical Center for the number of hospitals and medical facilities there. Here you will find the **Regional One Health** (877 Jefferson Ave., 901/545-7100, www.regionalonehealth.org), a 325-bed teaching hospital affiliated with the University of Tennessee; and the **Methodist University Hospital** (1265 Union Ave., 901/516-7000, www.methodisthealth.org), the 617-bed flagship hospital for Methodist Healthcare.

In east Memphis, **Baptist Memorial Hospital** (6019 Walnut Grove Rd., 901/226-5000, www.baptistonline.org/memphis) is the cornerstone of the huge Baptist Memorial Health Care System, with 771 beds.

St. Jude Children's Research Hospital (332 N. Lauderdale St., 901/595-4414, www.stjude.org) is one if the country's best-known institutions. It was founded by entertainer Danny Thomas in fulfillment of his promise to God to give back to those in need.

Mississippi Blues Trail

There are nearly 200 sites included as part of the **Mississippi Blues Trail** (http://msbluestrail.org). Visiting all of them is a considerable undertaking, but diehard blues fans will want to make a pilgrimage. The must-see stops covered in this guide delve into the history and influence of blues greats like Muddy Waters and B. B King. However, there are many more, some mere markers or plaques about artists from the town or what happened on that spot—even blues fans might want to skip some. Download the app for details on them all. If you're only casually acquainted with the blues, it's possible that you think this side trip isn't for you. But embarking on this trip may convert you!

If country music is more your style, there's also a smaller **Mississippi Country Music Trail** (www.mscountrymusictrail.org). It's not robust enough for exploration on its own, and Nashville is the heart of country music, but there is some overlap of sights on the Blues Trail.

This section covers **170 miles** of the Blues Trail in the Mississippi Delta, heading as far south as Leland/Greenville. Driving from Memphis through to Leland will take just over three hours, not including time for sightseeing and meals, so you'll want to devote at least two days to driving this route. Consider an overnight stay in Clarksdale or Cleveland and Greenwood before you turn back to Memphis. It's also possible to drive east along US 82 after visiting Indianola to cut back over to the Trace. This 100-mile, 1.5-hour drive will get you back onto the parkway at about milepost 204.

On this drive you'll visit Tunica, Clarksdale, Indianola, Greenwood, and Leland/Greenville. Make sure your car has good speakers and your phone is charged up, because you'll be in the mood to listen to a lot of music. Don't miss an opportunity to watch a world-class **Mississippi Delta sunset.**

Tunica

Getting There

Tunica is 30 miles southwest of downtown Memphis. It's a 40-minute drive down US 61 to get there. The **Tunica Airport** (209 S. Airport Blvd., 662/357-7320, http://tunicaairport.com) is small but may have deals that rival bigger airports.

Gateway to the Blues Museum

To some, Tunica is best known as a gateway to casinos, just over the state line from Memphis. But the **Gateway to the Blues Museum** (13625 US 61 N.,

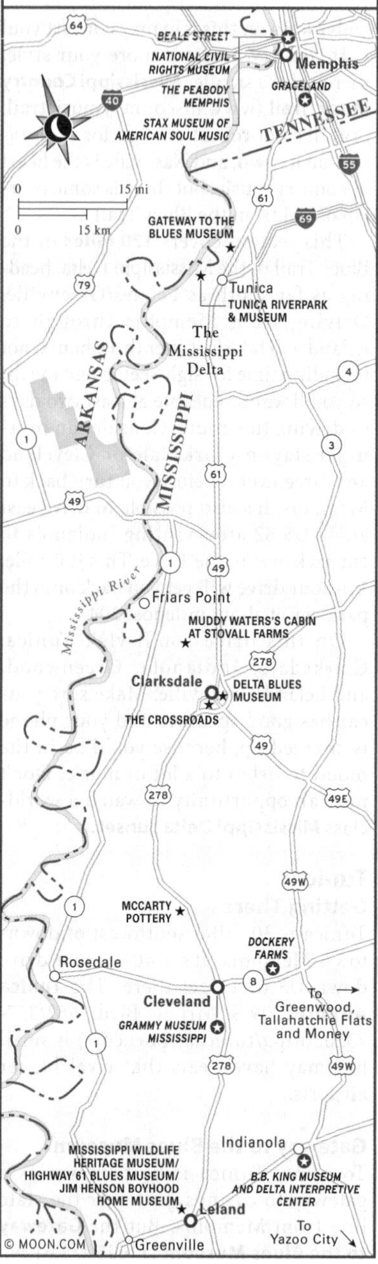

888/488-6422, www.tunicatravel.com, 8:30am-5pm Mon.-Fri., 10am-5pm Sat., 1pm-5pm Sun., adults $10, children 12 and under $5) shows Tunica is more than a place for slot machines. This must-stop 3,500-square-foot museum has six different galleries, where you can learn about the history of the blues and how the geography contributed to the genre. There's even an exhibition where you can record your own blues song (which will be emailed to you).

Housed in an old railroad station, the museum is connected to the **Tunica Visitors Center,** where you can get free information about the area. Even if you don't plan to stay overnight in Tunica, this is an essential stop if you want to get your bearings before immersing yourself in the Delta blues.

Tunica RiverPark & Museum

The **Tunica RiverPark & Museum** (1 Riverpark Dr., 866/517-4837, http://tunicariverpark.com, 9am-5pm Tues.-Sat., adults $10, seniors $9, children 12 and under $5) is a mammoth modern structure, with several floors of educational exhibits about the river and the Mississippi Delta. This is a great stop for families, as there are lots of interactive options, plus room to run around. Don't miss the river observation deck on the roof. The park has boat launches, if you are looking to get on the river.

Food

Tunica's Las Vegas-style casino resorts include many restaurants and bars per. If you're going to gamble, see a show, or go to the spa, these are decent add-ons. But if you're looking for something lower-key and more authentic to the Delta, try these instead.

Since 1969 **The Hollywood Cafe** (1585 Old Commerce Rd., Robinson, 662/363-1225, www.thehollywoodcafe.com, 10am-9pm Mon.-Thurs., 10am-10pm Fri.-Sat., $7-37) has been serving Southern classics such as fried catfish and

What is the Delta? Where is the Delta?

No, it is not the mouth of the Mississippi River. Yes, that is what "delta" often means. But the Mississippi Delta refers to the triangular piece of land between the Mississippi and Yazoo Rivers. These alluvial plains, created by the rivers, often flood, making them great for growing rice, cotton, and other crops.

So that's the technical definition. And you can see it on a map; the Delta runs about 200 miles long and 70 miles wide. But it takes up a much larger space in our collective imaginations. The oft-quoted author David Cohn wrote, "The Mississippi Delta begins in the lobby of the Peabody Hotel in Memphis and ends on Catfish Row in Vicksburg," and this is both a more accurate and poetic description of what and where the Delta is. It is a place where the land shapes the community. Where the farms stretch for miles and the cruise ships come in to dock. The blues play from porches where people still sit in rocking chairs.

Many people visit the Delta by taking a Mississippi River cruise, stopping in Greenville, Cleveland, and Clarksdale.

The pace in the Delta is slower, and not just because of the humidity and the heat mid-summer. This is a somewhere to pause, to eat a tamale, to sing the blues, and take in a river sunset.

pecan pie. It also claims to be the place where fried pickles first became famous. Come on a Saturday night and listen to the Grand Ole Opry over the radio while you dine. The restaurant has a full bar, which isn't true of lots of roadside eateries of this ilk.

You cannot miss the **Blue and White Restaurant** (1355 US 61, 662/363-1371, 5am-10pm daily, $6-22) as you drive down US 61—and you shouldn't miss it. Since 1924 this diner has a been a local draw. It is particularly popular with the pre-fishing and post-church crowds. Don't skip the doughnuts.

Accommodations

There are several casino hotels from which to choose in Tunica. **Horseshoe Casino** (1021 Casino Center Dr., 800/303-7463, www.caesars.com, $33-161) has all the basics—casino, restaurants, bars, shops, spas, shoe-shine stations, plus river views and the friendliest staff you'll ever meet. Even the valet parking is free.

Clarksdale

At the intersection of Old US 49 and Old US 61, Clarksdale is often referred to as The Crossroads. Legend goes that bluesman Robert Johnson sold his soul to the devil at this crossroads in exchange for his musical talent. Today the intersection (Desoto Ave. and N. State St./MS-161) is marked by a crossroads sign with giant guitars. This Mississippi Delta town was also important to civil rights history. In 1958 Martin Luther King Jr. visited the town for the first major meeting of what would become the Southern Christian Leadership Conference (SCLC).

While many places in the Mississippi Delta are known for their Mississippi Blues Trails stops, Clarksdale is perhaps the best stop if you want to actually hear the blues. There's live music seven nights a week (and many days, too). There are a whopping 11 Blues Trail markers in Clarksdale.

Getting There

Clarksdale is about a 35-minute drive from Tunica. Take US 61 36 miles south to get to the heart of Clarksdale.

On your way into Clarksdale from Friars Point, you can take a short detour and drive by the former site of **Muddy Waters's Cabin at Stovall Farms** (4146 Oakhurst Stovall Rd., 662/624-2153), where the legend was born. The sign is

If You Have More Time

If you can make your drive between Tunica and Clarksdale more leisurely, head to tiny Friars Point, where music is in the water. Country legend Conway Twitty (born Harold Lloyd Jenkins) was born here, and Robert Nighthawk, considered one of the foremost blues guitarists, lived here off and on for years, even working the town into song lyrics. Nighthawk's Blues Trail marker is right outside historic Hirsberg Drug Store, where many legendary musicians, including Robert Johnson, have played. Friars Point is also home to the **North Delta Museum** (784 2nd St., 662/902-7642, 9am-noon Mon.-Sat., adults $4, children under 7 $2), a small local heritage museum with lots of blues-related artifacts. Museum hours can be irregular; call in advance to confirm.

Friars Point is about a 45-minute drive south of Tunica along US 61. After about 25 miles on US 61, turn right onto Friars Point Road. Continue for about 8 miles, turn right onto Sheriff Ridge Avenue, then turn left onto Washington Street after two blocks. Make a right onto 2nd Street to get to North Delta Museum.

just past the entrance to the farm. From Friars Point, take Friars Point Road south for about three miles to MS-1 South. After about two miles, turn left onto Old River Road, which will soon turn into Oakhurst Stovall Road. Follow this for two miles to reach the cabin. Continue on Oakhurst Stovall Road for four miles to reach Clarksdale. In addition to being an important site in music history, this is a scenic place to take in the wonder of the Delta sky.

Delta Blues Museum

Created in 1979, the **Delta Blues Museum** (1 Blues Alley Ln., 662/627-6820, www.deltabluesmuseum.org, 9am-5pm Mon.-Sat. Mar.-Oct., 10am-5pm Mon.-Sat. Nov.-Feb., adults $10, children 6-12 $8, free for children under 6) is the state's oldest music museum. Housed in an old train depot, originally built in 1918 for the Yazoo and Mississippi railroad lines, it has both permanent and changing exhibitions. Muddy Waters's cabin has been relocated here from its original site a few miles northwest.

Tennessee Williams Rectory Museum

American playwright Tennessee Williams lived in Clarksdale when his grandfather, Reverend Walter E. Dakin, served as rector of St. George's Episcopal Church. Their home, next to the still-active, still-lovely church, is now the restored **Tennessee Williams Rectory Museum** (106 Sharkey Ave., 646/465-1578, http://tennesseewilliamsrectory-museum.com, open by appointment). The museum is chock-full of carefully researched information about the writer, his life, and his work. While an appointment is needed to tour the museum (24 hours advance notice minimum), it is well worth planning ahead to visit. The folks behind this museum also present the Mississippi Delta Tennessee Williams Festival each October.

Entertainment and Events

Nightlife

Clarksdale is charming, vibrant and chock-full of history. But the reason to come here is so that you can listen to live blues seven days a week, either at juke joints or at low-key places that emulate that vibe. Don't let the "nightlife" category fool you; you'll also find live music at breakfast and lunch. Bring cash to tip the band: This is their livelihood, and they play whether there is one person in the audience or 100.

Across from the Delta Blues Museum is the **Ground Zero Blues Club** (387 Delta Ave., 662/621-9009, www.groundzero-bluesclub.com, 11am-2pm Tues., 11am-11pm Wed.-Thurs., 11am-midnight

Fri.-Sat.), a restaurant and bar with live music. It is partly owned by actor and Mississippi Delta advocate Morgan Freeman, and is perhaps the best-known spot in the Delta. It is a large, tourist-friendly place done up in juke-joint style. The menu includes barbecue, catfish, and Delta tamales, but the draw is the music. Bring a Sharpie; visitors sign their name to any object in sight. You can even book one of the rooms upstairs and stay overnight.

An authentic juke joint with an erratic schedule and a hard-to-find entrance—it's the door to your right as you approach the building—**Red's Blues Club** (390 Sunflower Ave., 662/627-3166, 8pm-close Wed.-Sun., cover $7-10 cover, cash only) offers live blues by some of the best local musicians in a no-frills bar. Loose hours are given, but Red decides when he wants to open and close. There is a Blues Trail marker outside the entrance to Red's, discussing Big Jack Johnson, who played here regularly.

Bluesberry Cafe (235 Yazoo Ave., 662/627-7008, 6:30pm-midnight Mon., 7:30am-1pm Sat.-Sun., cash only) is known for its live blues breakfast, which also has a full menu of omelets and baked goods.

Other downtown live music options include **The New Roxy** (363 Issaquena Ave., 662/313-6220, www.newroxy.com) and **Hambone Art & Music** (111 E. 2nd St., 662/403-8810, http://stanstreet.com, 11am-5pm Tues.-Sat.).

Festivals and Events

If you really want to get your feet tapping, consider coming to Clarksdale for the **Juke Joint Festival** (www.jukejointfestival.com, Apr.) or the **Sunflower River Blues & Gospel Festival** (www.sunflowerfest.org, Aug.). Hotel rooms are at a premium during these times, so plan ahead.

Top to bottom: Muddy Waters's Cabin at Stovall Farms; Delta Blues Museum; Tennessee Williams Rectory Museum

The **Mississippi Delta Tennessee Williams Festival** (http://deltawilliamsfestival.com, Oct.) is a magnet for writers, readers, and dramatists.

Shopping

Downtown Clarksdale is dotted with cute boutiques and lots of opportunities for retail therapy. Your first stop in town should be the **Cathead Delta Blues & Folk Art** (252 Delta Ave., 662/624-5992, 10am-5pm Mon.-Sat., 11am-3pm Sun.). It's jam-packed with books, posters, shirts, records, and art. But more importantly, owner and author Roger Stolle is a fount of knowledge about Clarksdale, and has written a number of books about the area and its history, including *Mississippi Juke Joint Confidential*. Don't miss the opportunity to talk to him. Fashion designer **Brooke Atwood** (247 Delta Ave., 662/832-9789, www.brookeatwood.com, 11am-5:30pm Tues.-Sat.) brings big-city style to her Delta studio. **Collective Seed & Supply Company** (145 Delta Ave., 662/624-2381, www.collective-seed.com, 9am-5pm Tues.-Sat.) is a modern general store with plants, books, gifts, chocolates, and gourmet snacks.

Sports and Recreation

The fine folks at **Quapaw Canoe Co.** (291 Sunflower Ave., 662/627-4070, www.island63.com/clarksdale.cfm, $175-400) will take you out on adventures on the Mississippi River, with options from one day to three weeks. Check out the shop, which has custom art of the Mississippi River, books, and paddling gear.

Food

If listening to the blues is the first order of business in Clarksdale, going out to eat is the second. Plus many eateries also occasionally host live music.

Housed in an old commissary, **Hooker Grocery** (316 John Lee Hooker Ln., 662/624-7038, www.hookergrocer.com, 4pm-'til Wed.-Fri., 11am-9pm Sat.-Sun., $12-32) uses fine-dining techniques on Southern comfort food classics. The atmosphere is friendly and welcoming.

You could eat three squares a day and never get bored at **Yazoo Pass** (207 Yazoo Ave., 662/627-8686, www.yazoopass.com, 7am-9pm Mon.-Sat., $7-14). They serve sandwiches, salads, gumbos, tacos, and more! This is a good place for healthy alternatives to may of the fried delicacies of the South—but don't skip the baked goods for dessert.

Rest Haven (419 S. State St., 662/624-8601, 6am-3pm Mon.-Tues., 6am-8:30pm Wed.-Sat., $1.50-19) is a classic diner that also serves traditional Lebanese dishes.

Get your day started with affordable, classic eggs and bacon at **Our Grandma's House of Pancakes** (115 3rd St., 662/592-5290, 7am-2pm Mon.-Sat., 7am-3pm Sun., $1-8).

Meraki Coffee Roasters (282 Sunflower Ave., 662/351-2233, http://merakiroasting.com, 7am-1pm Mon., 7am-6pm Tues.-Sat., 1:30pm-6pm Sun., $2-13.50) hires young people so they can learn essential work skills on the job at this roasting company and coffee shop.

Accommodations

Recent years have seen an explosion of creative boutique hotels near the center of town, making it easy to find a place to stay so you can hang out and listen to music.

Rooms aren't fancy at the basic **Riverside Hotel** (615 Sunflower Ave., 662/624-9163, www.riversideclarksdale.com, $70-110), but you can sleep where both Duke Ellington and Ike Turner lived, and find a Blues Trail marker.

The Auberge Clarksdale Hostel (164 Delta Ave., 662/351-2220, http://aubergehostels.com, $26-111) feels more like a bed & breakfast than a run-of-the-mill hostel. It has a welcoming communal space with guitars you can use to practice the blues. Each sleeping area has its own charging station and private storage area. There are some rooms with private baths, though the communal baths are

The Blues Highway

For blues fans, there's no more important road than Highway 61. US 61 is often called the Blues Highway, and some say it rivals Route 66 as the most famous road in American music history. The highway also gave folks the ability to get out and move on when times got tough, as they often did.

Tons of songs reference the route and dozens of blues artists have recorded songs about Highway 61; Bob Dylan even named an album after it in 1965. But the first song about it was Roosevelt Sykes's "Highway 61 Blues," recorded back in 1932.

As is the case with Natchez Trace Parkway and the Old Trace, there's an original Old Highway 61 and a newer one that is part of the U.S. highway system. The old route (west of the new road) was winding and, in the state of Mississippi, largely unpaved. It was one long road from New Orleans to Grand Portage, Minnesota, near the Canadian border.

At first it may seem like this route ain't much to look at; true, like many highways, it goes through patches of desolation and clusters of commercial developments. But when it winds its way through the fields and the farms and open expanses for catching sunrises and sunsets, it can be a jaw-dropper. It is also the fastest way to see many of the sights along the Blues Trail and get a feel for the towns of the Mississippi Delta.

well-appointed and have dividers for privacy. Furnishings are modern and the owners live on-site.

The idea behind the sleek and modern ★ **Travelers Hotel** (212 3rd Ave., 662/483-0693, www.stayattravelers.com, $120-135) is that creative folks who want to come to Clarksdale to work on a project or play music can apply to work here or at the **Collective Seed & Supply Company,** owned by the same cooperative, in exchange for room and board (offsite). The result is a friendly and engaging staff and communal atmosphere; there are no TVs in the rooms, which encourages you to come down to the lobby, hang out, and talk to people. There's a small bar and fireplace.

For those staying a spell, the **Lofts at the Five and Dime** (211 Yazoo Ave., 888/510-9604, http://fiveanddimelofts.com, $125) offers apartment-style accommodations with full kitchens, TVs, and all the comforts of home.

Chateau Debris (111 Leflore Ave., 732/740-6155, http://chateaudebris.com) is a quirky, two-floor bed-and-breakfast with funky decor. It's a great option for small groups traveling together.

People who want to be in the center of all the action like **Ground Zero Blues Club Apartments** (387 Delta Ave., 662/645-9366, http://www.deltacottoncompany.com/services, $150-200), located right above the legendary blues club. Don't forget to pack ear plugs.

Former sharecropper shacks have been turned into one of Clarksdale's most iconic properties. The **Shack Up Inn** (001 Commissary Cir. Rd., 662/624-8329, www.shackupinn.com, $80-100) features more than 20 of these tiny cabins and rooms in a former cotton gin, plus a lobby, gift shop, and outdoor areas for sipping a cocktail and talking to (new or old) friends. Not everyone will be comfortable with the repurposing of spaces that housed brutal working conditions, but the Shack Up Inn has become a gathering place and a place to take part in music workshops, as well as hear music performed by locals. No bus tours are permitted and all guests must be older than 25. It is four miles north from the Shack Up Inn to downtown Clarksdale.

Information

Visit Clarksdale (www.visitclarksdale.com, 662/627-6149, 9am-5pm Mon.-Fri., 9am-noon Sat.) is a great resource for tours and sights in the area, as well as maps and other resources. Check out the free downloadable audio walking tour (www.visitclarksdale.com/tour).

Cleveland

Thanks to Delta State University and the quaint, thriving downtown, Cleveland has sweet shops and plenty of restaurants and bars, a lovely luxury hotel, plus a handful of reliable chains. Cotton Row and Sharpe Avenue run on each side of the grassy median in downtown Cleveland, and each blocked is dotted with boutiques, bars, and restaurants.

Getting There

Cleveland is about 40 minutes south of Clarksdale. To get there, take US 278 West/US 61 South for about 33 miles to get into town.

McCarty Pottery

On your way into Cleveland from Clarksdale you want to make a few stops en route. Since 1954 **McCarty Pottery** (101 St. Mary St., Merigold, 662/748-2293, www.mccartyspottery.com, 10am-4pm Tues.-Sat.) has been Mississippi's locally grown, best-known ceramics stop. Jamie and Stephen Smith, the godsons of Lee and Pup McCarty, have continued the tradition of making their own glazes and creating beautiful and practical pottery. Their pieces are sold throughout the Delta, but a side trip to see the studio (and the gardens) is worthwhile. **Peter's Pottery** (301 Fortune Ave., Mound Bayou, 662/741-2283, 10am-4pm Mon.-Tues. and Thurs.-Fri., 10am-3:30pm Sat.) makes ceramics from Mississippi mud in Mound Bayou, a Delta town founded by enslaved people.

★ Dockery Farms

Just outside of Cleveland is **Dockery Farms** (229 MS-8, 662/719-1048, www.dockeryfarms.org, dawn-dusk daily, $10 donation encouraged), a restored cotton farm and gin from 1895. Many

Dockery Farms

later-famous African American musicians, including Charley Patton, worked on this plantation and, some believe, birthed the blues here. At its peak, Dockery Farms was a self-sufficient town: It had schools, a post office, a blacksmith shop, stores, and a cemetery. Self-guided tours are available any time during daylight (there's a box in which you can drop your donation), and a number of videos on play help make sense of the site. If you have time, schedule a $10 tour through Bill Lester (wclester48@gmail.com). Check the Dockery Farms website for special events, such as educational programming and concerts. This is an essential stop on the Blues Trail as well as a lovely place to take in the Delta scenery.

★ Grammy Museum Mississippi

Opened in 2016, the **Grammy Museum Mississippi** (800 W. Sunflower Rd., 662/441-0100, www.grammymuseumms.org, 10am-5:30pm Tues.-Sat., 1pm-5:30pm Sun., adults $14, seniors $12, students and youth $8, free for children 4 and under) is the institution's first outside Los Angeles. This says a lot about how seriously the music establishment takes preserving the blues and educating people about the role the Mississippi Delta had in American music. In September 2016 it became the 192nd marker on the Mississippi Blues Trail.

This is a spectacular 28,000-square-foot facility. The building itself is designed to honor the architecture of the region, with a large front porch where people can hang out and listen to music, and building materials reflective of the types of materials used in the area, albeit on a much grander scale. The museum was purposefully located next to the campus of Delta State University, so that it can be an educational force was well as a tourism draw.

The Grammy Museum has more than 12 different interactive exhibits, many designed for you to share with your fellow tourists. Plan to stay for several hours to listen to all the music, including in a 140-seat theater that often has concerts. The museum does an excellent job of linking the blues to other genres. There are exhibits where you can try to make your own music and poignant displays of artifacts from musicians from the region. It has a decent gift shop as well.f

The Grammy Museum, by a function of its backers, is more professional than most of the other small, labor of love museums that dot US 61. To be sure, there's a homegrown quality in those other venues that is lost here. But the professionalism doesn't give way to slickness; the character of the Delta and its music has been preserved. The museum has the feel of an important American institution, albeit in an out-of-the-way place. It is one of four Blues Trail stops in Cleveland proper.

Delta State University

The lovely Delta State University campus has a number of worthwhile attractions for visitors. Essential to anyone wanting to learn more about the Mississippi Delta is the **Delta Center for Culture and Learning** (1003 W. Sunflower Rd., Ewing Hall, Ste. 130, 662/846-4311, http://deltacenterdsu.com). It's stocked with maps, books, and brochures about the region. Check the website for a schedule of upcoming educational programming. Casts of the faces of 50 blues musicians by artist Sharon McConnell hang in the Ewing Hall lobby where the center is located; it's worth checking out while in the building.

Tucked away on the third floor of the Charles W. Capps, Jr. Archives & Museum building is the surprising **Mississippi Delta Chinese Heritage Museum** (101 Fifth Ave., 662/846-4780, 8am-5pm Mon.-Thurs., 8am-4pm Fri., free). The moving museum has a number of displays about the Chinese American experience in the Delta.

Also on campus is **The Bologna Performing Arts Center** (1003 W. Sunflower Rd., 662/846-4625, http://bolognapac.com), Cleveland's main theater. It's worth checking out its lovely outdoor sculpture garden.

Martin and Sue King Railroad Heritage

Right on Cotton Row is the **Martin and Sue King Railroad Heritage** (115 S. Bayou Ave., 662/843-3377, http://clevelandtrainmuseum.com, 9am-noon and 1pm-4pm Mon.-Fri., 1pm-4pm Sat., free, donations encouraged), a friendly museum that tells the tale of the railroad that made the city of Cleveland what it is. The majority of the museum is taken up by a giant model railroad with secret windows, noisemakers, and a conductor who helps you explore it all.

Shopping

H Squared Boutique (126 N. Sharpe Ave., 662/843-4504, www.hsquaredladieswear.com, 10am-6pm Mon.-Fri., 10am-5pm Sat.) stocks fun women's clothing and accessories, and has a vintage convertible in the window that will make you want to go for a drive.

Mod + Proper (166 N. Sharpe Ave., 662/400-3111, http://shopmodandproper.com, 10am-5:30pm Mon.-Fri., 10am-5pm Sat.) stocks local gifts, jewelry, and accessories.

Cotton Row Book Store (333 Cotton Row, 662/843-7083, 10am-5pm Mon.-Fri., 10am-3pm Sat.) is a small shop with plenty of kids' books and current fiction.

Food

Pull in to **Airport Grocery** (3606 US 61, 662/843-4817, www.airportgrocerycleveland.com, 11am-10pm Mon.-Sat., 5-9pm Sun., $6-19). You'll find a friendly staff serving po'boys, tamales, and chili dogs in a casual but hipster environment. Don't miss the signature dessert: the Moon Man, a deep-fried moon pie. This is a casual, kid-friendly spot for lunch. Next door, **Mosquito Burrito** (118 E. Sunflower Rd., 662/441-1581, http://eatmosquitoburrito.com, 11am-9pm Mon.-Sat., $7-9) makes burritos and tacos with your choice of ingredients.

Delta native Cole Ellis traveled the world and cooked in kitchens in Charleston and Nashville before returning to his hometown to open ★ **Delta Meat Market** (215 Cotton Row, 662/444-6328, www.deltameatmarket.com, 7am-9pm daily, $7-49). Originally a butcher shop, restaurant, bar, and boutique grocer, it moved across the street in 2019 to the Cotton House Hotel. There, Ellis's food shines three meals a day, with creative twists on Southern classics using locally grown ingredients as well as imported specialties. While the restaurant serves hotel guests, it is also a draw for locals, and still has an in-house butcher shop.

Accommodations

Cleveland is a charming university town and a great place to explore the Delta, but in 2019 it got even better. That's when ★ **Cotton House Hotel** (215 Cotton Row,

662/843-7733, http://www.cottonhouse-cleveland.com, $124-191) opened. The hotel celebrates the region's heritage in attentive details such as U.S.-grown cotton sheets and towels and record players with blues music in the rooms. Cole Ellis's **Delta Meat Market** and rooftop **Bar Fontaine** satisfy any culinary cravings, and the location can't be beat. Just step right outside to be in the heart of the city's action.

Information and Services

Visit Cleveland (101 South Bayou, 662/843-2712, 8am-5pm Mon.-Fri) is right across the street from the Martin and Sue King Railroad Heritage museum, in an old train depot. It is stocked with lots of maps and good information on the Delta.

Bolivar Medical Center (901 MS-8 E., 662/846-0061, www.bolivarmedical.com) is centrally located near downtown Cleveland.

Indianola

Getting There

Indianola is about 30 miles south of Cleveland. Take US 278/US 61 south for nearly 10 miles, then turn left onto MS-448 and follow it for 15 miles.

★ B. B. King Museum and Delta Interpretive Center

The impressive **B. B. King Museum and Delta Interpretive Center** (400 2nd St., 662/887-9539, http://bbkingmuseum.org, noon-5pm Sun.-Mon., 10am-5pm Tues.-Sat. Apr.-Oct., noon-5pm Sun., 10am-5pm Tues.-Sat. Nov.-Mar., adults $15, seniors $12, students and children 5-7 $10, free for children 5 and under) chronicles the legend's rise to fame. In addition to showing his importance as a musician, it also lets his personality shine through (and if you don't know why he named his guitars Lucille, you'll find out). The galleries, located in an old cotton gin, cover the music of the Delta in the 1920s, Memphis in the 1950s, and beyond. There are high-tech recordings and videos and lots of artifacts. The museum opened in 2008; when King died in 2015 he was buried here and a garden with native plants was created in his honor. King was born in tiny Itta Bena, about 25 miles east of Indianola, and he was proud of his local roots. An expansion in 2020 included a new resting place for King and more educational space. The gift shop includes a lot of books and other educational materials about the blues.

Once an important African American nightclub, **Club Ebony** (404 Hanna Ave., 662/887-9539, 5pm-10pm Thurs., 5pm-1am Fri.-Sat.) hosted King and many others on its stage. It opened in 1948 and went through several owners over the years. When the most recent owners decided to retire in 2008, King bought the place to preserve it. It is one of three Indianola markers on the Mississippi Blues Trail and is now owned by the B B King Museum. It still gets hopping at night.

Food

There are two good options for down-home eats while in Indianola: **The Blue Biscuit** (501-503 2nd St., 662/645-0258, 11am-2pm Mon., 11am-2pm and 4pm-11pm Fri., 11am-2pm and 5pm-12:30am Sat., 5pm-10pm Sun., $7.50-14.50) and **Betty's Place** (301 Main St., 662/887-2627, http://bettyzplace.weebly.com, 10am-6pm Tues.-Thurs., 10am-7pm Fri.-Sat., $2.50-9.50).

Greenwood

The former agricultural capital of Greenwood is steeped in civil rights and blues history. Thanks to the Viking Cooking School, a great spa, and a downtown with good shopping and restaurants, it has a become a destination for girlfriend getaways. An easy walk to the banks of the Yalobusha River, Greenwood is also one of the best places to catch one of the famous **Mississippi Delta sunsets.**

Getting There

Greenwood is about 44 miles, 50 minutes, southeast of Cleveland. To get there, take MS-8 east to US 49 east to reach downtown.

Sights

Bryant's Grocery & Meat Market

One of the most troubling and traumatic stops on the U.S. Civil Rights Trail is **Bryant's Grocery & Meat Market** (Money Rd.). In 1955, 14-year-old Emmett Till came from Chicago to visit family in Mississippi for the summer. The white female shopkeeper at the dime store that was once here accused Till, an African American, of flirting with her. Her husband and his half-brother tracked the child down and brutally murdered him. When his body was returned to Chicago his mother made the decision to have an open casket funeral to display his mutilated body, a move that is largely credited for sparking the civil rights movement.

Tills's murderers were acquitted by an all-white jury, although later they admitted to the crime. The shopkeeper, Carolyn Bryant, also admitted later that she fabricated the details.

The actual grocery has fallen into disrepair, but there is signage here and a renovated gas station next door that gives you the feel of what the grocery may have looked like during the period.

This stop and Till's story are upsetting. It is an essential stop, but those traveling with children may want spend time beforehand considering how best to approach this part of our history with them.

There's no exact address here; the market is on the west side of the street, six miles north of Tallahatchie Flats and 10.5 miles north of downtown.

Robert Johnson Grave

Without Robert Johnson the Delta blues would not exist as we know them. Considered one of the best guitarists of all time, Johnson wrote 29 songs that influenced rock 'n' roll for the next generation. Legend suggests that he made a deal with the devil—selling his soul in order to master the blues—at the intersection of Old US 49 and Old US 61 in Clarksdale. Johnson died young—at the age of 27—poisoned at a juke joint by the husband of a woman with whom he was having an affair. There are three different places he is said to be buried, but the **Robert Johnson Grave** (63530 Money Rd.) at Little Zion Missionary Church is believed to be the actual site.

The cemetery at the church is well-marked, and there's Blues Trail signage, a box for making a donation to maintain the site, and plenty of parking. It is four miles north of downtown. This is one of eight Blues Trail markers in Greenwood.

Museum of the Mississippi Delta

Housed in a former factory, the **Museum of the Mississippi Delta** (1608 US 82, 662/453-0925, www.museumofthemississippidelta.com, 9am-5pm Mon.-Sat., adults $10, seniors $8, college students $6, youth 17 and under $5) offers an in-depth look at all things Delta. Exhibitions cover Native American history, agriculture, architecture, the Civil War, and visual arts. There's a swamp diorama and several dress-up opportunities for kids.

Back in the Day Museum

To understand more about Robert Johnson, the African American neighborhood of Baptist Town in which the museum is located, and the civil rights era, consider visiting the **Back in the Day Museum** (208 Young St., 662/392-5370, tours by appointment only, $10, more for neighborhood tours, negotiate your price upfront for the larger tours). Local resident Sylvester Hoover manages the museum, which is tiny and poorly lit—and chock-full of memorabilia. Whether you choose the quick museum visit narrated by Hoover or one of his more comprehensive neighborhood tours, you're sure to hear some tall tales about the area.

Bobbie Gentry Marker

Along the Tallahatchie River, there's a Mississippi Country Music Trail marker to Bobbie Gentry, who sang "Ode to Billie Jo," which mentioned the Tallahatchie Bridge. Gentry grew up in Greenwood.

Shopping

Downtown Greenwood is imminently strollable and great even just for window-shopping. Highlights include **Smith & Co.** (211 Fulton St., 662/453-4411, 10am-5:30pm Mon.-Sat.), which sells men's and women's clothing and gear for outdoor adventures. **Turnrow Books** (304 Howard St., 662/453-5995, www.turnrowbooks.com, 9am-5:30pm Mon.-Fri., 9am-5pm Sat.) is one of the South's best bookstores. Upstairs is a small café and an art gallery space. **The Mississippi Gift Company** (300 Howard St., 662/455-6961 or 800/467-7763, www.themississippigiftcompany.com, 9am-5:30pm Mon.-Sat.) is the place for souvenirs and anything made in Mississippi, whether it be chocolate or pottery. **The Viking Cooking School** (325 C Howard St., 662/451-6750, 10am-5:30pm Tues.-Sat.) is a big draw for its classes. The large shop has any and everything you could want for your kitchen.

Food

Mississippi chef Taylor Bowen-Ricketts named her modest, surprising eatery after her maternal grandparents. ★ **Fan and Johnny's** (117 Main St., 662/374-5060, 11am-2pm Mon.-Tues., 11am-2pm and 6pm-9pm Wed.-Fri., $10-25) has a creative menu, with seasonal dishes and takes on Southern eats, such as a pimento cheese queso. There are occasional pop-ups and extended hours, so it is worth checking hours when you get to town.

Tucked into an assuming strip mall, **Honest Abe Donuts** (201 W. Park Ave.,

Top to bottom: B. B. King Museum and Delta Interpretive Center; Betty's Place; Bryant's Grocery & Meat Market

662/455-2575, 6am-8pm Mon.-Sat., 6am-5pm Sun., $3-24) is one of the best places in town to grab those famous Delta tamales to-go.

Walk into ★ **Steven's Bar-B-Q** (208 Fulton St., 662/453-0313, 5am-8pm Mon.-Sat., $1.50-19) and you'll feel like you have walked into Mayberry (in fact, *The Andy Griffith Show* may be playing on the TV). In addition to barbecue, Steven's also serves tamales great for eating while walking around taking in downtown's sights—or on-site, where you can enjoy the small-town feel with the friendly locals, eager to share their town with strangers.

Since 1933 **The Crystal Grille** (423 Carrollton Ave., 662/453-6530, www.crystalgrillms.com, $6-13) has been Greenwood's go-to diner, with classic Italian and American dishes on the menu. But most people come here for the pie.

In a strip mall off the main road, behind another Mexican restaurant and inside a market, **San Miguel Arcangel** (522 W. Park Ave. B, 662/451-7766, 11am-3pm Thurs., 11am-8pm Fri., 10am-3pm Sat.-Sun.) is worth seeking out. The menu is full of fresh street tacos and other classics.

Accommodations

One of the swankiest hotels in the Delta, ★ **The Alluvian** (318 Howard St., 662/453-2114, www.thealluvian.com, $218-360) offers a respite from everyday chaos. Check in and relax in the sumptuous beds, reserve a treatment at the spa (across the street), and dine downstairs at **Giardina's,** which has a number of private booths for a date night. Full breakfast is included on the rooftop patio and top-floor library.

On the banks of the Tallahatchie River, on the famous Money Road, **Tallahatchie Flats** (58458 County Rd. 518, 662/453-1854 or 662/458-1948, http://tallahatchieflats.com, $85-125) rents six different sharecropper-style homes arranged in a motel-style. There's a tavern for private events only.

Information and Services

Visit Greenwood (225 Howard St., 662/453-9197, www.visitgreenwood.com) has itineraries and maps for any interest, whether it is seeing all the sights where *The Help* was filmed, architecture, or stops on the Civil Rights Trail or the Blues Trail.

Leland/Greenville

The adjacent Delta towns of Leland and Greenville are home to several quirky stops.

US 61 runs right into downtown Leland. Several of the city's sights are designed to highlight Leland's past: part hard-drinking music hub and part genteel Southern getaway. The **Leland Blues Project Murals** (www.highway61blues.com) showcase some of its history. There are five Blues Trail markers in Leland.

Just eight miles west on US 82 at the Mississippi River is Greenville, the area's commercial hub, with museums, restaurants, and hotels.

Getting There

Leland is 15 miles west of Indianola on US 82, a 20-minute drive. Greenville is another eight miles west, an additional 10-minute drive.

Highway 61 Blues Museum

The old Montgomery Hotel in the heart of downtown is home to the **Highway 61 Blues Museum** (307 N. Broad St., Leland, 662/686-7646, www.highway61blues.com, 10am-5pm Mon.-Sat., $7). This is a labor of love, jam-packed with blues artifacts and info compiled by local enthusiasts. This particular museum has more visual art, including paintings and photography by Delta artists, than most music museums. If you call ahead, they'll do their best to have some musicians show up to play while you peruse, an experience no blues fan should miss. As is

Tamale Trail

Tamales are as intrinsic a part of the Delta as the Mississippi River is. As far back as 1928 Reverend Moses Mason sang about them; and in 1936, blues legend Robert Johnson sang about tamales in "They're Red Hot." How did what many think of as a Latin American dish come to be so prevalent in the Delta? Some believe that the Native American mound-builders who lived in this area 2,000 years ago made them, with their food culture centered around corn. The more common story goes that migrant laborers from Mexico, after the end of the U.S.-Mexican War in 1848, came to work in the cotton fields and introduced tamales to local Black field hands, who got hooked on them and adapted them, using ingredients with which they already cooked—meat and corn meal—to create the Delta tamale.

Today, you can find a variety of tamales in the area, but most don't stray too far from the signature recipe: pork, beef, or turkey, encased in corn meal (which makes them a little gritty), and then wrapped in a corn husk and tied with string. In general they are spicier and smaller than a tamale you'd find in Latin America.

There's no better way to explore the Delta than taste-testing tamales. They're usually sold in paper bags of 3, 6, or 12. Find your favorite; here are some options, from north to south:

- **Dillworth's Tamales** (702 Wick St., Corinth, 662/223-3296, 10am-6pm Mon.-Sat., 1pm-5pm Sun.)
- **Airport Grocery** (3606 US 61, Cleveland, 662/843-4817, www.airportgrocerycleveland.com, 11am-10pm Mon.-Sat., 5-9pm Sun.)
- **Abe's Bar-B-Q** (616 N. State St., Clarksdale, 662/624-9947, www.abesbbq.com, 10am-8:30pm Mon.-Sat., 11am-2pm Sun.)
- **Ground Zero Blues Club** (387 Delta Ave., Clarksdale, 662/621-9009, www.groundzerobluesclub.com, 11am-2pm Tues., 11am-11pm Wed.-Thurs., 11am-midnight Fri.-Sat.)
- **Honest Abe Donuts** (201 W. Park Ave., Greenwood, 662/455-2575, 6am-8pm Mon.-Sat., 6am-5p Sun.)
- **Steven's Bar-B-Q** (208 Fulton St., Greenwood, 662/453-0313, 6am-8pm Mon.-Fri., 11am-3pm Sat.)
- **Hot Tamale Heaven** (1427 MS-1 S., Greenville, 662/702-511611am-9pm Mon.-Thurs., 11am-10pm Fri.-Sat., 11am-6pm Sun.)
- **Doe's Eat Place** (502 Nelson St., Greenville, 662/334-3315, www.doeseatplace.com, 5-9pm Mon.-Sun.)
- **Solly's Hot Tamales** (1921 Washington St., Vicksburg, 601/636-2020, 10:30am-7pm Tues.-Sat.)
- **The Tamale Place** (2190 S. Frontage Rd., Vicksburg, 601/634-8900, 10am-8pm Mon. and Wed.-Sat.)

For more information on the tamale trail, including oral histories with tamale-makers, check out www.southernfoodways.org/oral-history/hot-tamale-trail and plan to come to Greenville in October for the annual **Delta Hot Tamale Festival** (662/378-3121).

If You Have More Time

If you want to extend your Blues Trail experience and can spend a little extra time in the Delta, it's worth adding a stay in Yazoo City, which is 65 miles south of Leland and en route if you are heading to either Vicksburg or Ridgeland and Jackson.

Main Street is Yazoo City's primary thoroughfare, and you'll know you're in the right place when you see brightly covered building after brightly colored building. The linchpin of this design is the **Main Street Hotel** (203 S. Main St., 662/751-8886, www.mainsthotel.com, $95-165), a collection of apartment-style hotel rooms with full kitchens, laundry, and balconies overlooking Main Street.

Wander around and check out the restaurants and boutiques on Main Street. **Downtown Marketplace** (231 S. Main St., 662/746-5031, 9am-5:30pm Mon.-Sat.) is a collection of vendors selling antiques, vintage items, and handmade goods. Don't let the name fool you: **Webb Pharmacy** (216 S. Main St., 662/746-3253, 8am-6pm Mon.-Fri., 8am-1pm Sat.) is a great place to stock up on Yazoo Toffee, Mississippi Cheese Straws, and other local treats. **Tom's on Main** (219 S Main St, 662/716-0505, 11am-2pm Mon.-Thurs., 11am-2pm and 6pm-9pm Fri., 11am-2pm Sat., $4.25-9) is a popular breakfast and lunch spot. **P-Reaux's Cajun Mudbugs & Shrimp** (124 Water St., 662/746-4460 or 662/571-3292, 11am-2pm and 5pm-8:30pm Tues.-Thurs., 11am-10pm Sat., $6-25) is the place for local seafood.

In nearby **Bentonia,** 16 miles south of Yazoo City via US 49, **Blue Front Café** (107 E. Railroad Ave., 662/528-1900) is home to the oldest juke joint in Mississippi, one of the more reliable places to have a live blues experience. Hours vary, but it tends to be open Friday and Saturday nights.

There are five Blues Trail markers in the area. For more suggestions, check out **Visit Yazoo** (http://visityazoo.org).

the case at many homespun museums, you should allow plenty of time to have conversations with the passionate staff.

Jim Henson Boyhood Home Museum

When in Leland you must swing by the **Jim Henson Boyhood Home Museum** (415 SE Deer Creek Dr., Leland, 662/686-7383, www.birthplaceofthefrog.org, 10am-5pm Mon.-Sat. late May-early Sept., 10am-4pm Mon.-Sat. early Sept.-late May, free, donations encouraged). Henson was born in the Delta, and his family donated many artifacts to this odd roadside museum chock-full of Muppets and memorabilia, such as a large Kermit the Frog sitting on a lily pad, straight out of *The Muppet Movie*. The gift shop is well-stocked, but tiny.

Mississippi Wildlife Heritage Museum

Opened in 2017, the **Mississippi Wildlife Heritage Museum** (304 N. Broad St., Leland, 662/686-7085, www.mswildlifeheritagemuseum.com, 10am-5pm Mon.-Fri., adults $10, seniors $7, free for children 16 and under) displays artifacts relating to the region's agricultural past inside a renovated hardware store downtown.

Winterville Indian Mounds & Museum

Native American mounds are among the treasures in this part of the country. **The Winterville Indian Mounds & Museum** (2415 MS-1 N., Winterville, 662/334-4684, 9am-5pm Tues.-Sat., free) has 12, hand-made mounds, including one that is 55-feet tall. A museum with archaeological artifacts, such as pottery and animal bones, provides a glimpse into the rich history of the Native American tribes that lived and thrived in the area. and The museum is six miles north of downtown Greenville.

Greenville History Museum

You'll be shocked by how much material is jam-packed into this two-story museum on local history. One could spend several hours looking through the chronological displays and organized binders of information and photos at the **Greenville History Museum** (409 Washington Ave., Greenville, 662/335-5802, 9am-5pm Mon.-Fri., adults $5, children under 15 $3). The museum is a one-man show, and sometimes he locks the front door on slow days. Go ahead and ring the bell, or call and he'll let you in.

1927 Flood Museum

You need to call ahead to book an appointment to visit the **1927 Flood Museum** (118 S. Hinds, Greenville, 662/347-2782, by appointment, $5), but if you are interested in how the Delta landscape changed based on this event, it is worth the advance planning. The small museum is housed in the oldest structure in downtown Greenville. Both the Tunica RiverPark & Museum and the Museum of Mississippi History in Jackson have more information on the flood.

Food

With an ice cream parlor, general store, and deli, **Downtown Butcher and Mercantile** (509 Washington Ave., Greenville, 662/702-5185, www.downtownbutcher.com, 9am-5:30pm Mon.-Fri., 9am-5pm Sat., $6-13) can help you with a quick meal or road trip supplies.

Giant delicious hash browns and a homemade secret sauce are some of the reasons that people flock to **Jim's Cafe** (314 Washington Ave., Greenville, 662/332-5951, 7am-2pm Mon.-Sat., $8-12). It has been serving breakfast and lunch to locals for generations.

Yes, **Doe's Eat Place** (502 Nelson St., Greenville, 662/334-3315, www.doeseatplace.com, 5pm-9pm daily, $9-78) has a full menu of steaks and more. But the reason people come from far and wide is for the tamales. Doe's is located on Nelson Street, once a bustling center of African American life in the Delta. It has one of three Blues Trail markers in Greenville.

Accommodations

Note that the water in the Leland/Greenville area comes from an aquifer that winds through cypress swamps. This can make the water coming out of the taps brown in color. It is safe to drink, but most hotels will provide bottled water if you prefer.

Right above Downtown Butcher and Mercantile, **Lofts at 517** (517 Washington Ave., Greenville, 662/702-5202, www.loftsat517.com, $185-295) offers apartment-style accommodations in an old renovated Sears store. When it rains, you can hear the drops hitting the metal roof. Note that there are no wheelchair-accessible rooms.

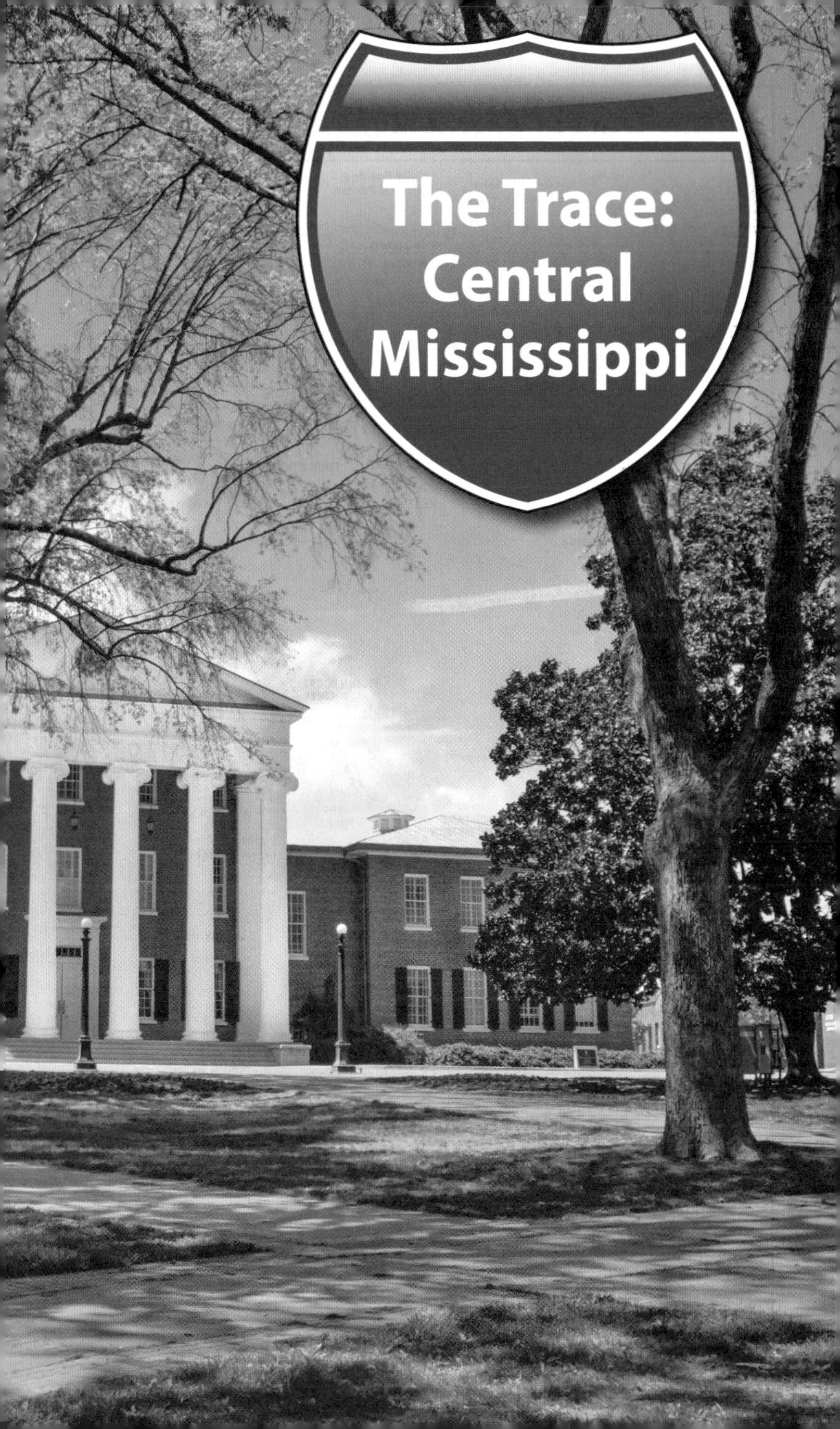
The Trace:
Central
Mississippi

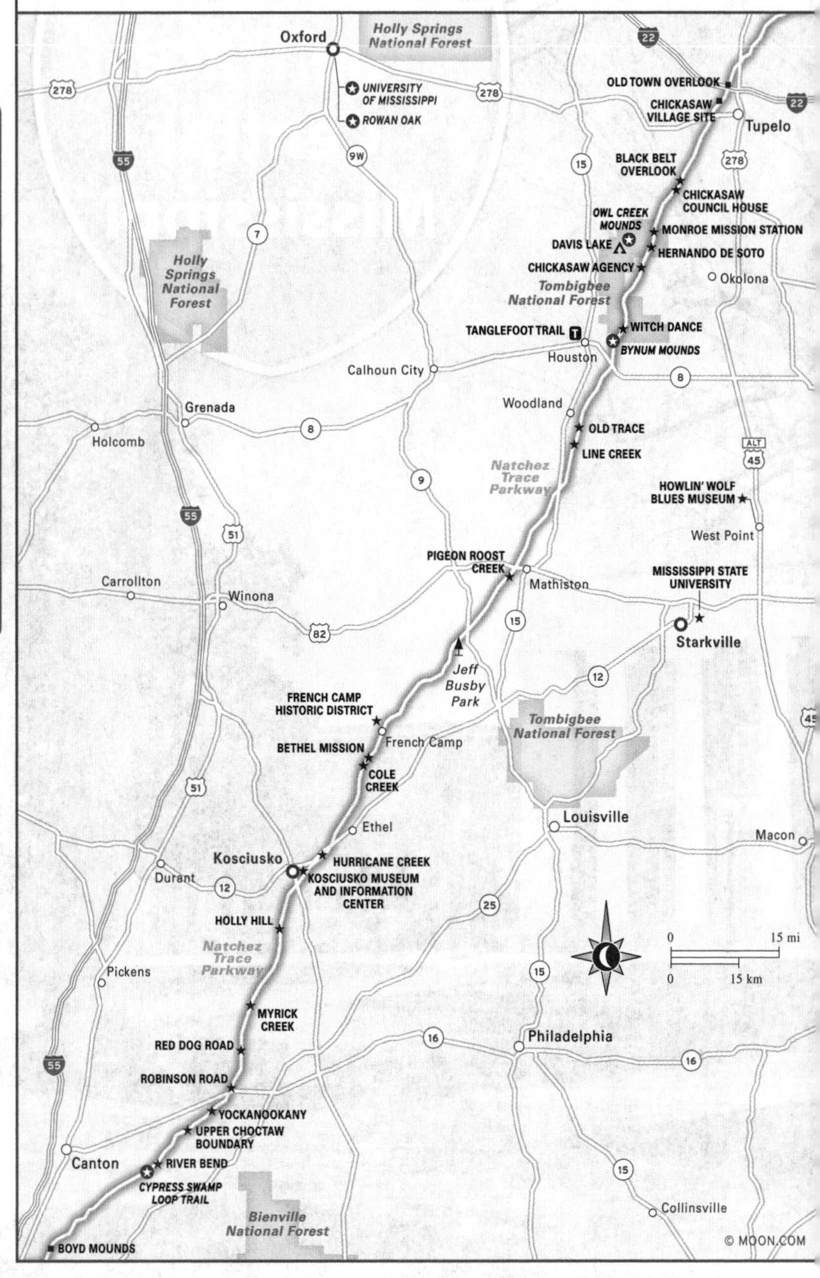
The Trace: Central Mississippi
Oxford
Holly Springs National Forest
UNIVERSITY OF MISSISSIPPI
ROWAN OAK
OLD TOWN OVERLOOK
CHICKASAW VILLAGE SITE
Tupelo
BLACK BELT OVERLOOK
CHICKASAW COUNCIL HOUSE
OWL CREEK MOUNDS
MONROE MISSION STATION
DAVIS LAKE
HERNANDO DE SOTO
CHICKASAW AGENCY
Okolona
Tombigbee National Forest
TANGLEFOOT TRAIL
WITCH DANCE
BYNUM MOUNDS
Houston
Calhoun City
Grenada
Holcomb
Woodland
OLD TRACE
LINE CREEK
Natchez Trace Parkway
HOWLIN' WOLF BLUES MUSEUM
West Point
PIGEON ROOST CREEK
Mathiston
MISSISSIPPI STATE UNIVERSITY
Starkville
Carrollton
Winona
Jeff Busby Park
FRENCH CAMP HISTORIC DISTRICT
French Camp
BETHEL MISSION
COLE CREEK
Louisville
Macon
Ethel
Kosciusko
HURRICANE CREEK
KOSCIUSKO MUSEUM AND INFORMATION CENTER
Durant
HOLLY HILL
Pickens
MYRICK CREEK
RED DOG ROAD
Philadelphia
ROBINSON ROAD
YOCKANOOKANY
UPPER CHOCTAW BOUNDARY
Canton
RIVER BEND
CYPRESS SWAMP LOOP TRAIL
Bienville National Forest
Collinsville
BOYD MOUNDS
0 15 mi
0 15 km
© MOON.COM

Highlights

★ **University of Mississippi:** Explore the history and charms of Ole Miss (page 261).

★ **Rowan Oak:** Visit the family home that served as William Faulkner's creative inspiration (page 263).

★ **Owl Creek Mounds:** These unusually shaped Native American mounds are a sight to see (page 268).

★ **Bynum Mounds:** Some of the Trace's most significant archaeological sites are beneath these six burial mounds (page 270).

★ **Cypress Swamp Loop Trail:** This easy boardwalk trail meanders through water tupelos and bald cypress, offering four seasons of beauty (page 283).

Best Restaurants

★ **Oxford Canteen:** The state's best grilled cheese sandwich (and more) is served in an old gas station-turned-restaurant (page 265).

★ **City Grocery:** John Currence's restaurant put Oxford (and Southern) dining on the map (page 265).

★ **Bottletree Bakery:** At this popular diner-turned-bakery, order a delicious pastry for breakfast to start your morning right (page 265).

★ **The Biscuit Shop:** Indulge in delicious biscuits of unusual varieties—but hurry, they sell out fast (page 276).

The parkway winds its way through the northern section of Tombigbee National Forest, so all you can see for miles is green.

Central Mississippi is also one of the places to clearly see the marks of former users of the Trace. Before Native Americans were forcibly removed from their land via the Trail of Tears, this region was the epicenter of the Chickasaw and Choctaw Nations; the former sites of their villages and lives are marked along this section. At times in its history the Trace has been called both the "Chickasaw Trail" and the "Path to Choctaw Nation." Several burial mounds further explore what life was like when the Chickasaw lived here.

There are opportunities to get out and experience these wilds, including one of the three campgrounds on the parkway, and fishing and water recreation options on Davis Lake.

Route Overview

This section of the drive covers the Natchez Trace Parkway from mileposts 261 to 122, with a number of opportunities to get off the parkway and explore.

Starting at Black Belt Overlook and ending at Cypress Swamp, the Central Mississippi section of the Trace covers a **139-mile** stretch of parkway, all within the state of Mississippi. This is a doable section for **one day,** allotting plenty of time for nature walks and hikes and to explore Owl Creek Mounds and French Camp at a leisurely pace.

Side trips are possible to Mississippi's best-known college towns, both of which have their own charms. The drive to **Oxford** is 45 miles (40 minutes) each way, although it would be hard to take advantage of all Oxford has to offer without spending at least one night; two is better. The side trip to **Starkville** is about 20 miles (30 minutes) each way and could be done as a day trip, albeit a busy one.

Driving Considerations

This section of the parkway is well-maintained, and there are ample pullouts to allow for safe sightseeing. The speed limit is 50 mph. Dense fog is occasionally an issue on fall and winter mornings.

Fuel and Services

This section of the drive, both on the Trace and on the side trips to **Oxford** and **Starkville,** is composed of rural roads connecting metropolitan areas. While you are in the cities and smaller towns, you'll have access to gas, restaurants, bike repair, and other basic services. When you're on the scenic rural stretches, you may not have cell service.

Best Accommodations

★ **The Z Bed & Breakfast:** This welcoming inn is a home-away-from-home in Oxford (page 266).

★ **Davis Lake Campground:** Commune with nature under the stars here (page 269).

★ **The Courtyard by Marriott at the Mill at MSU:** Connected to a historic cotton mill and a new convention center, this hotel combines old and new Starkville (page 276).

★ **Jeff Busby Campground:** It's one of just three places you can camp overnight on the parkway itself (page 277).

★ **French Camp B&B:** Learn about the Trace of yore at this hideaway (page 278).

Tune your radio to 1610AM for recorded information about some of the specific sights and stops along the way.

Getting to the Starting Point

Car, Motorcycle, or Bicycle

As you leave Tupelo, you'll slide back onto the parkway and ride southbound on the Trace. This portion of the route starts about 10 miles outside of Tupelo.

From **Memphis,** it's about 120 miles (two hours) to reach Black Belt Overlook, the first major stop on this section of the route, via the most direct route, I-22. However, it's also possible to visit **Oxford** on your way to the parkway by taking I-55 south from Memphis, then US 278/MS-6 east. This 140-mile route will take about 2.5 hours, not including any time you choose to spend in Oxford.

To get to the beginning of this section of the drive from **Birmingham,** Alabama, it's a 150-mile, two-hour drive west along I-22. This route will take you directly into Tupelo. From there, head south on the Trace.

Budget Car Rental (2763 W. Jackson St., 662/840-3710, 8am-8pm Mon.-Fri., 8am-1pm Sat., noon-8pm Sun.) is near the Tupelo Regional Airport. **Enterprise Car Rental** (551 Daybrite Dr., 662/842-2237, 7:30am-6pm Mon.-Fri., 8am-1pm Sat.) is south of downtown Tupelo.

Air

This isn't the easiest section of the Trace to access by air, but if that's your preference, the **Memphis International Airport** (MEM, www.flymemphis.com) is a good choice. MEM is served by Delta, Southwest, United, and other major airlines, with a number of nonstop routes. The three-concourse airport offers free Wi-Fi and many local dining options.

Birmingham-Shuttlesworth International Airport (BHM, 5900 Messer Airport Hwy., www.flybirmingham.com) is served by Delta, Southwest, United, and American Airlines. The easy-to-navigate airport has free Wi-Fi.

Contour Airlines (http://contourairlines.com) offers small craft service to **Tupelo Regional Airport** (2763 W. Jackson St., 662/841-6570, www.flytupelo.com) from Nashville five times a day for as little as $29.

Train

Train travel to the Trace is a tough proposition; riding the rails isn't the most efficient way to get around this area. **Amtrak** operates out of **Memphis Central Station** (545 S. Main St., www.amtrak.com), a stop on the 900-mile City of New Orleans route, which runs from New Orleans to Chicago. Central Station is conveniently located downtown, where

Fuel Up

Nothing puts a damper on a road trip like noticing you are nearly out of gas when you are miles from a filling station. Here's a quick list of places to exit the parkway between Tupelo and Kosciusko so that you can refuel at the closest gas station. (Some stops may take you to small towns, others will be just a single service station.)

The National Park Service also posts a list of nearby supply stations at most Trace rest areas, although the list is not updated regularly.

- **Milepost 260:** Exit at MS-6/Main Street, the last exit before you leave Tupelo. Drive east one mile to a Marathon or Texaco station or west one mile to a Shell.
- **Milepost: 255.7:** Exit at Palmetto Road and drive 0.7 mile east to Palmetto Quick Stop in Verona.
- **Milepost 239:** Exit at MS-32 and drive east nine miles to a cluster of five or six gas stations. This route often has heavy truck traffic.
- **Milepost 219.6:** Exit at MS-46 and drive one mile west to Mantee.
- **Milepost 204.2:** Exit at US 82. Drive east one mile to the Shell station in Mathiston or two miles west to Fox Run Quick Stop.
- **Milepost 195.3:** Exit at MS-9 and drive six miles south to Europa.
- **Milepost 159.8:** Exit at MS-19, near the Kosciusko Information Center. Drive one block north to Parkway Pure.
- **Milepost 135.5:** Exit at MS-16 and drive 1.5 miles west toward Canton to Michael's 16 station.

most major rental car companies have offices.

Birmingham also has Amtrak service from New Orleans and Atlanta, operating out of a small station (19th St. N., www.amtrak.com).

Bus

Greyhound serves the Bluff City via the **Memphis Bus Station** (3033 Airways Blvd., www.greyhound.com). The station is adjacent to the Memphis International Airport and close to major car rental companies. The Greyhound routes to Memphis are through Birmingham, Dallas, Jackson, Nashville, and St. Louis.

The Greyhound bus from Memphis, Atlanta, and Birmingham stops in **Tupelo** at a supermarket (1074 N. Eason Blvd., 662/842-4557, 10am-5pm daily).

Budget-friendly **Megabus** (3033 Airways Blvd., http://us.megabus.com) serves both Memphis and Birmingham and boasts free Wi-Fi on board.

US 278 to Oxford

The city of Oxford is unlike anywhere else in the state of Mississippi. Founded in May 1837, it was built on land that had once belonged to the Chickasaw Nation. It was named after Oxford, England, aspiring to be a university town. By 1841 the Mississippi legislature indeed voted to make Oxford the home of the University of Mississippi, the state's first, and the city's fate as an intellectual hub was sealed. Today, Ole Miss, as it is called, is a major public university.

A Day on the Trace: Central Mississippi

If you've only got one day in this region, start early so you'll be hungry by the time you arrive in Oxford. After the 40-minute drive to Oxford from the Trace, drive up to **Big Bad Breakfast** to caffeinate and feast on a large Southern breakfast, then head over to **Rowan Oak** for a tour of William Faulkner's home.

Leave the car parked and wander through Wood Trail to the **University of Mississippi** campus. Take in a few important sights, such as the **Lyceum,** where civil rights history was made. Walk back to the car and head to **The Square** for a quick lunch from **Oxford Canteen.** Then you'll have time to browse the many shops there. Don't miss **Square Books,** which is a lively space. Swing by **Bottletree Bakery** for some pastries for the car ride, and then drive the 40 minutes back to the parkway. You will have driven about 110 miles total in the first part of your day.

Check out some important parkway sights along the way, including **Owl Creek Mounds** and **Bynum Mounds.**

Stretch your legs at **Cypress Swamp** and then continue into southern Mississippi (see page 287) and head to Ridgeland, near milepost 100, to spend the night. If that 150 miles on the Trace is too much driving after Oxford, pick a B&B in **Kosciusko** (near milepost 160) to crash in for the night. For a complete list of every stop along the Trace, download the detailed National Park Service maps (www.nps.gov/natr).

Life hasn't always been easy in Oxford. In 1864 the city was nearly destroyed when Union troops set fire to the town. It was rebuilt, and in 1962 conflict came again, when James Meredith entered the University of Mississippi as its first African American student, amid protests of more than 2,000 people.

Like many college towns, today Oxford is known for its rich intellectual and cultural life, having been home to authors ranging from William Faulkner to John Grisham, plus a tradition of art and music.

Few sights are far from one another in this small town. Unless you are visiting during the height of summer heat and humidity, Oxford is a walkable town.

Leaving the Trace

As you are driving south on the Trace, after leaving Tupelo exit the parkway at MS-6/Main Street/US 278 near **milepost 260**. Drive west for 45 miles (40 minutes); about 9 miles in, the road will jog to the right and then the left. Turn right (north) onto South Lamar Boulevard. You'll reach downtown Oxford in about 1.5 miles.

Sights

★ University of Mississippi (Ole Miss)

First things first: No one calls the **University of Mississippi** (123 University Circle, 662/915-7211, http://olemiss.edu) by its proper name. It's "Ole Miss." Founded in 1848, the school today has more than 24,000 students. The city itself has a population of nearly 24,000, so it is easy to see how the school dominates this area.

Wandering through campus reveals a picture-perfect backdrop. The **Lyceum** building is the center of the Ole Miss campus. The bullet holes above the doorway are a sign of the violence that broke out in 1962 when James Meredith tried to integrate the then-white-only school. Behind the building is a civil rights monument with Meredith's figure.

Ventress Hall, built in 1889, was the first major building erected on campus after the Civil War. It is said that author William Faulkner helped paint and renovate this building as a young man. **The Grove** is the open space where tailgating becomes a pastime before football games.

The **University Museum** (University Ave. and 5th St., 662/915-7073, http://museum.olemiss.edu, 10am-6pm Tues.-Sat., free) has an impressive collection and exhibition space. While the museum is free, there is an additional fee for special exhibits (adults $5, seniors $4, children $3). Guided tours are available by request. Past exhibitions have included Greek and Roman antiquities and the work of photographer William Eggleston. Drive through campus or walk via the lovely Bailey's Woods Trail from Rowan Oak. The museum operates Rowan Oak and the Walton-Young Historic House, which is closed for renovations.

The **J. D. Williams Library** (1 Library Loop, 662/915-5855, hours vary by month) has an impressive archive, including William Faulkner collections, Civil War and civil rights materials, and comprehensive blues music materials. It's an excellent place to pass a few hours.

On weekdays, you'll need a visitor parking pass ($3 daily) to park on campus. Order one ahead of time online (662/915-7235, http://olemiss.edu/parking/visitors.html) or purchase one onsite at the Lyceum Circle welcome booth. There are a few metered spots on campus that don't require a permit (exact change only).

Oh, and if you hear anyone say, "Hotty Toddy," just say "Hotty Toddy" right back. It's the Ole Miss greeting, school cheer, and football game chant.

The Square

Nothing else fully encapsulates Oxford's charms as does **The Square** (Jackson Ave. and Courthouse Sq., http://visitoxfordms.com), its historic town square and center of the city. Three different bookstores (technically outposts of the same store) bring author readings, live music, and discussions to the area. Live music venues, bars, and restaurants attract faculty and students from Ole Miss, as well as other locals and tourists. There are plenty of shops, too, of the higher-end

the L. Q. C. Lamar House Museum

and university-focused sort. You could easily spend a weekend within walking distance of The Square.

L. Q. C. Lamar House Museum

A National Historic Landmark, the **L. Q. C. Lamar House Museum** (616 N. 14th St., 662/513-6071, www.lqclamarhouse.com, 1pm-4pm Fri.-Sun., free) is dedicated to preserving the legacy of Lucius Quintus Cincinnatus Lamar II. Lamar was a senator and U.S. Secretary of the Interior (under President Grover Cleveland) and was included in President John F. Kennedy's Pulitzer Prize-winning book, *Profiles in Courage,* for his work trying to reunite the North and the South after the Civil War.

Housed in Lamar's former home, the museum is a labor of love. It is chock-full of information—more than the average history buff can read. The building itself has been restored, and docents can explain some of the decisions that were made in the restoration process.

★ Rowan Oak (William Faulkner House)

Even those who don't think of themselves as fans of the great Southern writer William Faulkner (1897-1962) will be charmed by **Rowan Oak** (916 Old Taylor Rd., 662/234-3284, www.rowanoak.com, grounds dawn-dusk daily, house 10am-4pm Tues.-Sat., 1pm-4pm Sun. Aug.-May, 10am-6pm Mon.-Sat., 1pm-6pm Sun. June-July; grounds free, house $5), his former family home. The Greek Revival-style house, sitting on 29 acres, offers insight about the Nobel and Pulitzer Prize winner, as well as his creative process. Rowan Oak feels like Faulkner is just out for a walk, with his outline for *A Fable* scrawled on the walls to help him focus and numbers scribbled next to the phone in the 1844 building. Faulkner restored much of the home himself.

These grounds are said to be the inspiration for Yoknapatawpha County, the fictional setting for all but three of Faulkner's works. The grounds connect to the University of Mississippi campus through the **Bailey's Woods Trail** (www.museum.olemiss.edu/baileys-woods-trail). It takes about 20 minutes to walk the length of this National Recreational Trail, which comes out at the University Museum. The trail is about two-thirds of a mile long and is well-maintained. Four footbridges span steep areas in the woods.

If you want more than a self-guided look around, call ahead to schedule a tour. Note that the entrance to the home is easy to miss when rounding the bend on Old Taylor Road. From town, drive slowly after passing 10th Street, then turn right.

North of University Avenue and up a few blocks is **Saint Peter's Cemetery** (Jefferson Ave. and N. 16th St.), where you can see William Faulkner's tombstone. The large monument is close to the sidewalk and is often covered with whiskey bottles that fans leave for their favorite author.

Cedar Oak

Many structures were lost to fire by the Union troops during the Civil War. **Cedar Oak** (601 Murray St., no phone, www.cedaroaks.org, 11am-4pm Fri., 1pm-4pm Sun., free) survived, not because the armies spared it, but because Molly Turner Orr, the sister of William Turner, the man who built the house, organized a group of people to fight the fire. In the mid-1900s Cedar Oak was moved 2.2 miles away from its original location.

Tours of the Greek Revival structures are scheduled only on Fridays, although you may be able to make an appointment for another day by calling in advance.

Burns-Belfry Museum

Burns Methodist Episcopal Church was a church organized by freed African Americans. This beautiful 1910 brick building is now home to the **Burns-Belfry Museum** (710 Jackson Ave. E., 662/281-9963, www.burns-belfry.com, noon-3pm Wed.-Fri., 1pm-4pm Sun., free), a multicultural center that invites discussions of civil rights, slavery, and more. The museum exhibits are professional and thought-provoking. While the museum is free, donations are accepted to fund expansion and educational programs.

Entertainment and Events

Performing Arts

Originally built in the 1800s as a livery stable for William Faulkner's family, **The Lyric** (1006 Van Buren Ave., 662/234-5333, www.thelyricoxford.com, box office noon-5pm Wed.-Fri.) is the place to see concerts, film festivals, and other live events in Oxford.

People come to **Proud Larry's** (211 S. Lamar Blvd., 662/236-0050, www.proudlarrys.com, 11am-midnight Mon.-Wed. and Sat., 11am-1am Thurs.-Fri., 11am-2pm Sun.) for the impressive lineup of live music acts. It also doubles as a restaurant.

The **Thacker Mountain Radio Hour** (http://thackermountain.com, 6pm Thurs., fall and spring, free) is a lively, smart live radio show with author readings and music, broadcast from **Off Square Books** (129 Courthouse Sq.). Arrive early if you want a good seat. The show is rebroadcast every Saturday at 7pm on Mississippi Public Radio. It's produced only in the fall and spring.

Festivals and Events

Held over a week in late July at Ole Miss, the **Faulkner and Oknapatawpha Conference** (www.outreach.olemiss.edu/events/faulkner) discusses the work of Oxford's favorite son. A celebration of all things related to the written word, the **Oxford Conference for the Book** (http://oxfordconferenceforthebook.com) is held for three days in March each year at Ole Miss.

The **Double Decker Festival** (Historic Courthouse Sq., 662/232-2477, http://doubledeckerfestival.com) started as a modest event on a double-decker bus imported from England. Now it's a two-day fest of music, arts, and food each April.

The **Southern Foodways Alliance** (662/915-3368, www.southernfoodways.org) hosts a number of workshops and conferences all year, but the fall symposium is the sell-out. Chefs, food professionals, and people who just like to eat come to learn about Southern cooking through multimedia presentations.

Shopping

Oxford's historic courthouse square, a.k.a. **The Square** (Jackson Ave. and Courthouse Sq.), is the hub of downtown and the place to start shopping.

Square Books (160 Courthouse Sq., 662/236-2262, www.squarebooks.com, 9am-9pm Mon.-Sat., 9am-6pm Sun.) actually has three locations on The Square. Aside from the main outpost, there's **Square Books Jr.** (111 Courthouse Sq., 662/236-2207, 9am-7pm Mon.-Sat., 11am-5pm Sun.), just for kids, and **Off Square Books** (129 Courthouse Sq., 662/236-2828, 9am-8pm Mon.-Sat., noon-5pm Sun.), the company's "lifestyle and leisure" location. Off Square is also home of the Thursday night **Thacker Mountain Radio Hour** (http://thackermountain.com).

Amy Head Cosmetics (301 S. Lamar Blvd., 662/513-0711, www.amyheadcosmetics.com, 10am-5:30pm Mon.-Fri., 10am-5pm Sat.) sells a boutique makeup line.

Belles and Beaus (1005 Van Buren Ave., 662/236-6880, www.bellesandbeausoxford.com, 9:30am-6pm Mon.-Sat.) is the place for kids' clothing. Both **Lulu's Shoes and Accessories** (265 N. Lamar Ste. V, 662/234-4111, www.shopluox.com, 10am-6pm Mon.-Sat., 11am-3pm Sun.) and **My Favorite Shoes** (138 Courthouse Sq., 662/234-0059, 10am-5:30pm Mon.-Thurs., 10am-6pm Fri.-Sat.) are go-tos for women's clothing, jewelry, shoes, and accessories.

Looking for something one of a kind? **Mississippi Madness** (141 Courthouse Sq., 662/234-5280, 10am-5:30pm Mon.-Sat.) has gifts and home decor from Mississippi artists. The motto of **Neilson's** (119 Courthouse Sq., 662/234-1161, http://neilsonsdepartmentstore.com, 9am-5:30pm Mon.-Sat.) is "Where trends meet tradition." This Southern department store was established in 1839, so they know about tradition.

In the heart of downtown, **The End of All Music Record Store** (103A Courthouse Sq., 662/281-1909, http://theendofallmusic.com, noon-6pm Mon., 10am-6pm Tues.-Sat., noon-5pm Sun.) stocks country, rock, jazz, and anything else you want.

Food

The Square

Housed in an old gas station, ★ **Oxford Canteen** (766 N. Lamar Blvd., 662/638-3393, www.oxfordcanteen.com, 8am-8pm Tues.-Sat., 10am-2pm Sun., $5-11) is the all-day favorite for locals wanting Vietnamese coffee, brisket grilled cheese, and other elevated classics from Chef Corbin Evans.

Chef John Currence is the man responsible, in large part, for Oxford's culinary renaissance. ★ **City Grocery** (152 Courthouse Sq., 662/232-0808, http://citygroceryonline.com, 11:30am-2:30pm and 6pm-10pm Mon.-Thurs., 11:30am-2:30pm and 6pm-10:30pm Fri.-Sat., 11am-2:30pm Sun., $10-45) was his first Oxford restaurant, one that combines fine dining with traditional Southern ingredients in an old livery stable. There's a casual bar menu upstairs and a more traditional fine dining experience downstairs. City Grocery is so much a part of the city fabric that some locals have standing reservations and their "own" table. Another John Currence restaurant, **Bouré** (110 Courthouse Sq., 662/234-1968, http://citygroceryonline.com, 11am-10pm Mon.-Thurs., 11am-10:30pm Fri.-Sat., $11-40) serves Creole-inspired dishes from the second floor of The Square.

Expect a wait at ★ **Bottletree Bakery** (923 Van Buren Ave., 662/236-5000, 7am-2:30pm Tues.-Fri., 8am-2pm and 3pm-9pm Sat., 8am-2pm Sun., $6-8), a funky diner-turned-bakery with freshly made pastries and sandwiches.

Football legend Eli Manning reportedly counts **Ajax Diner** (118 Courthouse Sq., 662/232-8880, www.ajaxdiner.net, 11:30am-10pm Mon.-Sat., $7-30) as a favorite. Both the lunch and dinner menus highlight soul food, such as turnip green dip, po'boys, and fried catfish.

A sleek, modern pizza parlor, **Saint Leo** (1101 Jackson Ave. E., 662/380-5141, www.eatsaintleo.com, 11am-midnight Mon. and Wed.-Sat., 11am-9pm Sun., $13-36) is a sophisticated favorite of locals looking for alternatives to Southern food. They make some of their cheeses (ricotta and mozzarella) and cure some of their meats (pork belly) in-house.

Stop for sweets at **Oxford Creamery** (309 N. Lamar Blvd., 662/638-3245, http://theoxfordcreamery.com, 11am-9pm Sun.-Wed., 11am-11pm Thurs.-Sat., $3-10), a "farm to cone" ice cream shop.

North Lamar

The food served at chef John Currence's morning spot, **Big Bad Breakfast** (719 N. Lamar Blvd., 662/236-2666, http://citygroceryonline.com, 7am-1:30pm Mon.-Fri., 8am-3pm Sat.-Sun., $7-14) features ingredients such as house-cured Tabasco and brown sugar bacon. Also from John Currence's City Grocery group, **Snackbar** (721 N. Lamar Blvd., 662/236-6363, http://citygroceryonline.com, 5:30pm-10pm Mon.-Thurs., 5:30pm-10:30pm Fri.-Sat., $10-32) is a trendy eatery with a raw bar, charcuterie, and small plates.

Tired of grits and fried chicken? **Jinsei Sushi** (713 Lamar Blvd., 662/234-0109, www.jinseioxford.com, 5pm-10pm daily, $5-17) is a sleek sushi bar with traditional sashimi and *nigiri*, plus contemporary maki and hot dishes, including a wagyu steak that you sear yourself on a hot rock.

Accommodations

If you want a hotel room the weekend of a big football game or other event at Ole Miss, book as far ahead as possible.

Inn at Ole Miss Hotel & Conference Center (120 Alumni Dr., 662/234-2331, www.theinnatolemiss.com, $109-135) has 146 rooms, with standards in the original Alumni House building and deluxe rooms in an addition. Deluxe rooms are a little bigger and have sleeper sofas. The hotel offers all the standard amenities, such free Wi-Fi and a fitness center (with an outdoor pool), plus a shuttle to downtown Oxford. Rates include breakfast.

A quirky boutique hotel located on The Square, **Graduate Oxford** (400 N. Lamar Blvd., 662/234-3031, http://graduateoxford.com, $96-359) is a favorite of locals as well as visitors, thanks to the rooftop bar The Coop and the lobby lounge decorated with vintage books. Pets are welcome in this funky hotel.

There are several decent chain hotels in Oxford. **Courtyard by Marriott** (305 Jackson Ave. E., 662/638-6014, www.marriott.com, $94-394) has the standard amenities, plus a Green Roof Lounge that serves dinner and cocktails. **The Hampton Inn Oxford/Convention Center** (103 Ed Perry Blvd., 662/234-5565, www.hilton.com, $76-199) is a nonsmoking hotel with a fitness center, pool, and free Wi-Fi. **Holiday Inn Express & Suites Oxford** (112 Heritage Dr., 662/236-2500, www.ihg.com, $75-168) touts a business center, free breakfast bar, fitness center, and free Wi-Fi.

Walking distance to downtown, ★ **The Z Bed & Breakfast** (1405 Pierce Ave., 281/804-8022, http://thez-oxford.com, $120-150) is a quirky, homey B&B with three rooms, each tastefully and uniquely decorated. Prices include full homemade breakfast plus wine and cookies nightly. There are two bikes available for your use, plus the backyard has a fire pit and grill. The owners have two other properties in town, The Z Shanty and The White House, which are appropriate for larger parties and family reunions.

Blue Creek Cabin (535 MS-30, East Oxford, 662/238-2897, www.bluecreekcabin.com, $138 s/d, $69 for each additional guest) is a good option for those not traveling with young kids (no children under the age of 10 are allowed) who want something a little different. This is a two-bedroom 1800s log cabin with shared bathroom and kitchenette.

A Victorian-style home converted into a B&B, with a horse pasture to boot, **Oak Hill Stables** (670 County Rd. 101, 662/234-8488, www.oakhillstables.net, $100-200) isn't your average hotel. There are also guest rooms available in a converted barn.

Ravine (53 County Rd. 321, 662/234-4555, www.oxfordravine.com/inn, $135-300) is also a log cabin-style B&B with rooms with kitchenettes. Amenities include Wi-Fi, breakfast, and a pool. There's a 70-seat restaurant on the premises.

The Barn Loft at Willowdale Farm (28 County Rd. 225, 662/801-8600, http://thefarmatwillowdale.com, $78-156) is good if you want more than just a bedroom. Rent out the loft, the upper level of a barn that's been fashioned into a living space with a porch, living room, kitchen, washer and dryer, two bedrooms, a sleeper sofa, and a bathroom.

Information and Services

Your first stop in town should be the charming **Visit Oxford Visitor's Center** (1013 Jackson Ave. E., 662/232-2477 or 800/758-9177, http://visitoxfordms.com, 8am-5pm Mon.-Fri., 11am-3pm Sat.,). The office is filled with maps, information, and Southern hospitality.

Get bicycles serviced and find parts at **Oxford Bicycle Company** (407 Jackson Ave. E., 662/236-6507, 10am-6pm Mon.-Fri., 10am-4pm Sat.).

Baptist Memorial Hospital (1100 Belk Blvd., 662/636-1000, www.baptistonline.org) is a full-service hospital.

Back to the Trace

To return to the parkway from downtown Oxford, take Lamar Boulevard south to US 278. Turn left and continue for 38 miles east. Exit to the right to continue on US 278 (following signs for US 278/MS-6/Main Street). Drive the last nine miles to the parkway, where you'll pass under the Trace, then turn right to rejoin the Trace near **milepost 260.** Turn left (follow signs for Jackson) to continue south.

If you don't mind skipping a few miles of the parkway, you can shave off about five minutes of driving time without missing any sights. About 38 miles east of Oxford, at the US 278/MS-76 junction, continue on MS-76 instead of exiting. Continue for almost eight miles. You'll pass underneath the parkway, exit to the right (south), then turn left to rejoin the parkway near **milepost 257,** heading south.

Top to bottom: Square Books; Oxford Canteen; The Z Bed & Breakfast

The Louisiana Purchase

For 10,000 years the Natchez Trace has been a route inland from the Mississippi River. Native Americans, hearty pioneers, even wildlife, would use it as access to food and water.

President Thomas Jefferson negotiated treaties with both the Chickasaw and Choctaw Nations for use of this land, hoping to connect the frontier to the settled eastern sections of the United States. When the Louisiana Purchase, which covered 828,000 square miles, was signed in 1803, there was even more motivation to have reliable access to the new land.

In 1806, motivated by their $11 million investment, Congress authorized construction to build roads on what had been the centuries-old Natchez Trace. For most of its history, travel on the Trace went northward. Settlers with their goods would travel by boat south on the Mississippi River and then return north via the Trace by foot or on horseback, which is why the milepost markers begin in Natchez and end in Nashville. Construction began in 1934. In 1938, the route was designated the Natchez Trace National Parkway.

Black Belt Overlook (MP 251.9)

This scenic overlook on the right side of the road offers a wide open view of the pastoral landscape of central Mississippi. In another era, this land was under the sea, as archaeologists can tell from the shells and other marine organisms deposited to form the limestone. Over time, that limestone morphed into fertile soil of various colors. The area got its name from the rich black soil. Much of the region's "Black Belt" was once used for growing cotton.

Make a quick stop to take a few photos. The area has a U-shaped pull-in that can be seen from the road. There aren't any amenities.

Chickasaw Council House (MP 251.1)

This stop might not look like much as you turn left into the small pullout. In the 1820s, however, it was an important site: the capital of the Chickasaw Nation. In the council house that once stood here, tribal elders met to sign treaties and set laws and policies. Each summer more than 2,000 Chickasaw people came to receive an annual payment for lands they had sold to the federal government. The Pontotoc Creek Treaty of 1832, which ceded the last of the Chickasaw land east of the Mississippi River to the U.S. government, was signed here.

There are no physical remains of the council house at this site.

★ Owl Creek Mounds (MP 243.1)

Near milepost 243.1 is a worthwhile detour off of the parkway, in the Tombigbee National Forest. The **Owl Creek Mounds Archaeological Site** (dawn-dusk daily, free) consists of two Native American ceremonial mounds built AD 1100-1200. It's possible to see two mounds, one of which has a somewhat unusual crescent shape. However, archaeologists believe that there once were five mounds in this area. The taller mound likely housed a temple or chief's home. Research suggests that these mounds were used for a short time—less than a century.

There are paved pathways around the mounds, so you can explore from all sides. Clear, easy-to-read signage makes this an educational stop. Because they are not on the parkway, these mounds are not part of the National Park system, but instead are protected by the U.S. Forest Service. These were sacred spaces and should be treated with respect.

To get here, exit the Trace to the right just past the Hernando de Soto site, following signs for Owl Creek Mounds Archaeological Site and Davis Lake. Turn right on Davis Road and drive for three miles, past the Chickasaw OHV Trail. The mounds will be on your right. To return to the parkway, retrace your steps for three miles, turn left to rejoin the Trace, then turn right to continue south on the parkway.

Davis Lake Recreation Area

Instead of returning to the parkway from Owl Creek, another option is to continue on Davis Road for one mile (a total of four west of the parkway) to reach **Davis Lake Recreation Area** (877/444-6777), a 200-acre lake that's inside the **Tombigbee National Forest** (601/285-3264). This is a place to swim, fish, and hike, with a few miles of easy walking trails. Three-day Mississippi fishing licenses (601/432-2400, http://mdwfp.com/license/fishing) are $15 for nonresidents and $3 for state residents.

The **Chickasaw OHV Trail** (662/285-3264, Apr.-Oct., $10 per ATV), which you'll pass on your way from the Trace, offers 12 miles of motorized trails for all-terrain vehicles. Eighteen miles of horseback riding trails and lots of birdwatching round out the fun. Leashed pets are allowed in the area and campgrounds but not on the beach.

★ **Davis Lake Campground** (662/285-3264, www.recreation.gov, starting at $20/night) has more than 20 campsites, 14 of which are on the lake itself. Some of the campsites have electricity, and there are showers and other amenities. Davis Lake is one of two campgrounds in Tombigbee National Forest. The other, Choctaw Lake, is south of Starkville and farther from the parkway.

Follow Davis Road to reach the park entrance and ranger station. To return to the parkway, drive east on David Road for four miles. Turn left to exit Davis Road, then right to continue south on the Trace.

Chickasaw Agency

(MP 241.4)

Between 1802 and 1825, when this section of the Trace was the heart of Chickasaw Nation, the federal government sent representatives to the Chickasaws (one of whom was James Robertson, the founder of Nashville). The agency functioned similarly to a modern-day embassy. The agents' presence helped broker peaceful relations between the Chickasaws and white settlers. Their responsibilities also included removing trespassers and recovering stolen horses. During the winter, they were largely alone in the wilderness. During the summer thousands of Kaintucks, those hardy boatmen traveling north, would stop at the agency for sleep or nourishment.

Today this is just a historical marker on the Trace. The pullout is on the right side of the road, with a U-shaped parking area. The marker is visible from the road and there are no other amenities.

Witch Dance (MP 233.2)

This stop's alluring name comes from lore that says that witches once gathered here to dance and the grass withered beneath their feet wherever they touched the ground. There is a hidden spot here where grass stubbornly refuses to grow. (Hint: Look for it behind the sign and under the trees.)

This stop is popular with those traveling the Trace with horses or on bicycle. It's a staging area for the Witch Dance Horse Trail in Tombigbee National Forest, with hitching posts and camping only for those traveling with horses or on bicycle. Signage marks the designated camping areas. The horseback riding trails are 9 and 15 miles long.

Amenities include restrooms, water fountains (most outdoor water is turned off in winter, but indoor faucets still flow), and several picnic areas. The next restroom stop headed south is not until the Jeff Busby Campground (milepost 193.1).

There are two ways to access Witch Dance. On the right side of the road before you get to the driveway there is a small pull-in parking area with a few steps up to the building with the restrooms. You can see this from the road. If all you need is a bathroom break, this works well. If you have a trailer, want to picnic, and would like to see where the witches once danced, pass the building and turn right into the marked driveway. It winds around and puts you on the opposite side of the bathrooms (this is also the accessible side for those in wheelchairs). There's plenty of parking and access to the trails.

★ Bynum Mounds (MP 232.4)

This is one of the most significant sites on the parkway. Bynum Mounds' six burial

Bynum Mound

mounds were built between 100 BC and AD 100 (known as the Middle Woodland period). Just two of the mounds, the two largest, have been restored to their original appearance and are available for public viewing. Detailed signage and displays give you an in-depth archaeological experience.

The southernmost of the two restored mounds, called Mound A, contained the remains of a woman, with copper spools at each wrist, placed between two burned oak logs at the mound's base. In addition, cremated remains of two other adults and a child were found.

The largest mound, Mound B, covered a log-lined crematory pit. Here the Park Service found greenstone axe heads, copper spools, and other objects that didn't come from Mississippi. These finds demonstrate the long-distance trade networks used by the people living at the time.

These are sacred spaces and should be treated with respect. Stay on the well-marked paved pathways to circle the mounds and read the signage. Stop at the simple shelter off of the parking lot that has illustrated signage about what life would have been like on the Trace in the Middle Woodland period.

The Bynum Mounds site is not visible from the parkway, giving this stop an intimate feeling, even though it is quite large. Exit the parkway on the left side of the road and follow the driveway to the parking lot. There are no amenities.

MS-8 to Houston

For cyclists who need a place to spend the night, **Bridges-Hall Manor B&B** (435 N. Jackson St., Houston, 662/456-4071, $98-105) is less than five miles west from Bynum Mounds in the small town of Houston, Mississippi. The home has five rooms, each with a private bath, and safe spots to park your wheels. You'll enjoy a full Southern breakfast in the morning to send you on your way. Houston has gas stations and a Walmart if you need supplies.

To get to Bridges-Hall from the parkway, drive (or ride) one mile south from Bynum Mounds. Head west on MS-8 (you'll exit on the left to loop around). Ride four miles west to Jackson Street, and turn right (north).

Line Creek (MP 213.1)

A sole picnic table on the shaded banks of a small creek is what remains at what was once a significant spot on the Trace. This small creek was recognized by the Chickasaw and Choctaw people as the boundary between the two nations. It remained until the tribes were forced west on the Trail of Tears. Over the years Line Creek's meandering path has changed slightly, but this marker is very close to the original spot. Nearby was a stand, run by Noah Wall and his Choctaw wife, that offered food and shelter for travelers.

The U-shaped pullout and parking area is on the west side of the parkway. There are no other amenities.

US 82 to Starkville

A restored, vibrant downtown and the campus of Mississippi State University make sweet Starkville worth visiting. It's also known for its rabid fans of State's football team, the Bulldogs. If you're planning to visit in the fall, check football schedules in advance, book hotel rooms early, and don't forget the cowbell.

Native Americans lived in this area and worked the land for hundreds—even thousands—of years. Artifacts suggest people lived here more than 2,000 years ago. White settlers moved in after the Trail of Tears forced the Choctaw and Chickasaw people west in the 1830s. Once known as Boardtown, because of the clapboards made in a mill here, in 1835 the name of the town was changed to Starkville.

Leaving the Trace

From Line Creek, drive south on the Trace to **milepost 204.5.** Exit on the left, following signs for US 82/Mathiston. From the exit road, turn right and take US 82 east for 12 miles. Turn right to get on MS-182 and drive southeast for nine miles. Turn right on Jackson Street to reach Starkville's downtown, near the Hotel Chester. This drive should take less than 30 minutes.

Sights

Mississippi State University

Mississippi State University (75 B.S. Hood Dr., 662/325-2323, www.msstate.edu), referred to simply as "State," is the reason most people come to Starkville. The school, once Mississippi A&M, has more than 21,600 students—in a town with a population of 25,300. All over town you'll see signs proclaiming "Hail State," and most signage will be in the school color of maroon.

There are several free student-led campus tours (662/325-5198, www.visit.msstate.edu/publictours), including a children's tour, an art tour, a historical tour, and more. Tours are offered year-round; call at least two weeks in advance to reserve your spot. If you are with a big group, book at least two weeks in advance. For guided art tours, call 662/325-2970.

In addition to **Davis Wade Stadium,** where the Bulldogs play, there's lots to see. The Welcome Center lobby is home to the Cullis & Gladys Wade Clock Museum, which boasts more than 400 American-made clocks dating back to the 1700s.

The life of the 18th president is well documented at **Ulysses S. Grant Presidential Library** (449 Hardy Rd., 662/325-4552, www.usgrantlibrary.org, 7:30am-5pm Mon.-Fri., 10am-2pm Sat., free). The library contains more than 15,000 linear feet of correspondence, clothing, cannons, and other Civil War memorabilia.

The school hosts many concerts and theater performances as well as academic lectures by State and visiting faculty, as well as the student-run **Magnolia Film Festival** each February. Everything comes to a halt for football here, so check game schedules before visiting.

West Point: Home to Howlin' Wolf

While many of the Mississippi Blues Trail highlights are in the Delta, there's one worth a detour for true-blue blues fans.

His given name was Chester Arthur Burnett, but everyone knows him as Howlin' Wolf. Considered one of the pioneers in electrifying the Delta blues, he was born near West Point, which is where **Howlin' Wolf Blues Museum** (307 E. Westbrook St., 662/295-8361, call for a tour, donations accepted) is located. It might seem off-putting to visit a museum open by appointment only, but museum curator Jeremy Klutts can be there within 10 minutes during normal business hours. Klutts hopes the museum will soon expand to a larger facility, but for now he is an engaging guide who will take you through the history of Howlin' Wolf. The museum is about one block from a West Point Blues Trail marker (East Street and East Broad Street), which commemorates Howlin' Wolf with a statue.

The **Black Prairie Blues Festival** (www.wpnet.org), formerly the Howlin' Wolf Memorial Blues Festival, is held annually in September. The rest of the year, if you want to hear good blues, head over to **Anthony's Good Food Market** (121 W. Main St., 662/494-0316, www.anthonysgoodfoodmarket.com, 5pm-9:30pm Tues.-Thurs., 5pm-10pm Fri.-Sat., $8-50). Up the street from Anthony's, there's a mural and an adjacent blue wall where visitors are encouraged to leave notes for the Wolf; it's a lovely, low-tech, interactive tribute that prevents graffiti elsewhere.

To get to West Point, exit the parkway at MS-8. It will turn into US 45 ALT; follow that for 30 miles to get to downtown West Point. Heading out of town, follow US 45 ALT heading south for 20 miles to get to Starkville. The drive will take about an hour.

Overstreet School

Constructed in 1897, **Overstreet School** (307 S. Jackson St.) was the first elementary school in Starkville and became the cornerstone for what is now the charming residential Overstreet Historic District. The building was renovated in 1949 and is a beautiful example of art moderne, a type of architecture that focuses on clean horizontal lines. The building's striking Indian motif honors the original residents of the area.

Architecture fans should take some time to explore the 180 homes in this area, just south of downtown. The Overstreet Historic District was added to the National Register of Historic Places in 1992 and includes examples of Craftsman, Victorian, art deco, and art moderne buildings.

Starkville City Jail

Johnny Cash was held overnight in 1965 in the **Starkville City Jail** (111 Dr. D. L. Conner Dr., 662/323-2421, www.sheriff.oktibbeha.ms.us/division/jail). It was this event that inspired Cash's song "Starkville City Jail." The building isn't much to look at, but its history makes it worth a drive-by (while listening to the song, of course).

The Cotton District

The Cotton District (104½ Maxwell St., www.cottondistrictms.com) is considered one of the first New Urbanism developments in the world. The movement supports walkable mixed-use neighborhoods, with restaurants, bars, and places to live. Starkville's Cotton District was founded by developer Dan Camp in the 1960s, revitalizing a community that was in disrepair after the local cotton mill closed. Buildings inspired by Greek Revival, Classical, and Victorian architecture offer people an opportunity to live, work, and study in a walkable community. The **Cotton District Arts Festival** (www.cdafestival.com) is held here each April.

Oktibbeha County Heritage Museum

The historical Gulf Mobile and Ohio Railroad depot has been brought back to life as the **Oktibbeha County Heritage Museum** (206 Fellowship St., 662/323-0211, http://oktibbehaheritagemuseum.com, 1pm-4pm Tues.-Thurs. and by appointment, free), a surprisingly comprehensive museum to Starkville's history. You'll find artifacts about the region's growth, an old medical office, music, taxidermy, and displays about locals who have made it big, such as Portland Trailblazers basketball player Travis Outlaw. The museum is run by volunteers, so don't panic if it opens a few minutes late. It's also possible to call and schedule a private tour. Don't miss the outdoor garden, which emphasizes water conservation.

Entertainment

Starkville Community Theatre performs at **Playhouse on Main** (108 E. Main St., 662/323-6855, www.sct-online.org, tickets $10-15) in the heart of downtown. There are typically four productions annually with a nine-show run for each.

The Greater Starkville Development Partnership's office is the home to the **GSDP Art Gallery** (200 E. Main St., 662/323-3322, http://starkville.org, 8am-5pm Mon.-Fri.). This isn't a full art gallery, but it is centrally located downtown and is worth browsing while you're strolling. Local artists are well represented.

Shopping

Downtown Starkville is chock-full of shops with handmade goods and jewelry, clothing, and art appealing to a college student crowd (and their parents).

Start at the **Idea Shop at MSU** (114 E. Main St., 662/325-3521, http://shop.ideashopmsu.com, 1pm-9pm Wed.-Fri., 8am-5pm Sat.-Sun.), a maker space for

Top to bottom: Mississippi State University; Idea Shop at MSU; Oktibbeha County Heritage Museum

More Cowbell!

When shopping in Starkville you'll see—in every store, bar, and even gas station—cowbells. Cowbells have been rung at State football games since at least 1940, when the football team had an undefeated season. People debate which styles are best and which best help cheer the Bulldogs to victory, but a popular choice is a long-handled, bicycle-grip bell made of thin and tightly welded shells. Many cowbells are handed down in families, from one alumnus to the next. Monogrammed versions are given as gifts to new students and to women being courted by potential suitors.

Cowbells are a much-loved football game tradition at Mississippi State University.

Technically, the bells were outlawed by the Southeastern Conference (SEC), the football governing body, in 1974, but State fans kept sneaking them in and ringing them, making a game at Davis Wade Stadium one of the loudest you'll ever witness. In 2010 the SEC reversed the ruling, acknowledging that the cowbell was an integral part of the school's tradition. However, students and alumni alike must "ring responsibly."

If you plan on experiencing Starkville like a local, there are just two phrases you need to know: "Hail State" and "More cowbell!"

students and locals, with a small boutique in front. Artists sell the wares they make in the studio space, so you're guaranteed to find items—from jewelry to textiles—that you won't find elsewhere.

Curio (116 E. Main Street, 662/323-0929, www.curiobrands.com, 10am-6pm Mon.-Sat.) sells candles and fragrant skin care products.

Libby Story (308 University Dr., 662/323-1426, http://libbystory.com, 10am-6pm Mon.-Fri., 10am-5pm Sat.) is a hip, funky women's clothing shop in an old auto parts store (there's also a location in Ridgeland). **Swanky B** (209 E. Main St., 662/546-0897, www.swankyb.com, 10am-6pm Mon.-Fri., 10am-4pm Sat.) has women's clothing with a young, trendy vibe. **L.A. Green Boutique** (117 E. Main St., 662/324-6280, http://shoplagreen.com, 10am-6pm Mon.-Sat.) has women's and men's shoes, clothing, some home decor, and works by local artists.

The Book Mart (120 E. Main St., 662/323-2844, 9am-5:30pm) is a lovely bookstore with an adjacent café and a decent selection of Hail State gear.

Since 1905, **Reed's** (302 University Dr., 662/323-2684, http://reedsms.com, 9:30am-6pm Mon.-Sat.) has catered to Mississippi shoppers looking for outdoor gear and clothing. This location, unlike the one in Tupelo, sells plenty of cowbells.

Farmers and artisans sell their goodies at the **Starkville Community Market** (200 E. Main St., 662/323-3322, http://visit.starkville.org, 4pm-6pm Tues., 7:30am-10:30am Sat. May-Aug.), which is also a great local hangout.

Food

You won't go hungry in Starkville, a town that's proud of its agricultural roots and Southern culture.

Two Brothers Smoked Meats (103-C Rue du Grand Fromage, 662/617-8095, 11am-10pm Tues.-Sat., 11am-2pm Sun., $7-13) makes burgers, tacos, and sandwiches with all manner of smoked meats: pulled pork, smoked duck, and smoked pork tenderloin. The nachos are made with pork rinds. **Little Dooey** (100 Fellowship St., 662/323-6094, www.littledooey.com, 11:30am-9pm Mon.-Sat., 10:30am-2pm Sun.) is a time-honored Starkville barbecue favorite.

Harveys (406 MS-12 E., 662/323-1669, http://eatwithharveys.com, 11am-9:30pm Mon.-Thurs., 11am-10pm Fri., 10am-10pm Sat., 10am-9pm Sun., $9-27) is a Mississippi tradition, and this outpost is popular with students when Mom and Dad come to town. The menu is filled with fried appetizers (fried broccoli and mushrooms among them), plus salads, steaks, chops, and seafood.

Does one member of your party prefer Chicago-style pizza while another is all about New York-style pie? No worries, **Dave's Dark Horse Tavern** (410 Dr. Martin Luther King Jr. Dr. E., 662/324-3316, http://davesdarkhorse.com, 3:30pm-midnight Mon.-Wed., 3:30pm-1am Thurs.-Fri., noon-1am Sat., noon-midnight Sun., $7-32) serves both. Locals like the cracker crust pizza. The menu includes a few gluten-free and vegan items, too.

There's nothing wrong with a restaurant that has a different mac and cheese every week. People also like **The Camphouse** (409 University Dr., 662/769-5665, 11am-9pm Mon.-Thurs., 11am-10pm Fri.-Sat.) for its outdoor patio.

Restaurant Tyler (100 E. Main St., 662/324-1014, http://eatlocalstarkville.com, 11am-2pm Mon., 11am-9pm Tues.-Thurs., 11am-10pm Fri., 5pm-10pm Sat., 10am-2pm Sun., $8-38) serves elevated Southern classics with modern variations, such as jambalaya pasta and sweet potato gnocchi. The beautiful bar, called The Guest Room, boasts an excellent bourbon selection and knowledgeable bartenders. The Restaurant Tyler and Guest Room team gets more casual at **Bin 612** (612 University Dr., 662/324-6126, http://eatlocalstarkville.com, 2pm-midnight Sun.-Wed., 11am-1am Thurs.-Sat., $4-16) with a menu of burgers, panini, pizza, and wine.

It's worth getting up early to try the buttermilk biscuits made from scratch at ★ **The Biscuit Shop** (104 S. Washington St., 662/324-3118, www.thebiscuitlady.com, 6:30am-11:30am Thurs.-Sat., 7am-noon Sun., $1.50-2.50) before they sell out. They're known for their wacky flavors, like sausage-cheddar, s'mores, and peppermint-chocolate chip.

Accommodations

Hotel Chester (101 N. Jackson St., 662/323-5005 or 866/325-5005, www.historichotelchester.com, $77-260) is downtown's signature boutique hotel. In a restored 1925 building, Hotel Chester is a funny combination of styles and history, with modern (if small) rooms, a glass elevator, and a lobby and exterior that are old world. There are several restaurants on-site, including The Beer Garden, whose claims to fame are a menu courtesy of Gordon Ramsay and a serene patio, perfect on spring and fall nights. The included breakfast is made-to-order.

★ **The Courtyard by Marriott at the Mill at MSU** (100 Mercantile St., 662/338-316, www.marriott.com, $84-176) is an exceptionally well-located, well-appointed hotel adjacent to the convention center, which is located in a historic cotton mill; even if you don't have a meeting in the facility, it's worth taking a look at the art and architecture. It's easy to walk to many restaurants, drug stores, and other essentials nearby. The outdoor patio and pool are well-isolated from road noise and traffic.

There are several other serviceable chain hotels in Starkville, which book up early during football season (prices are higher on game days, too). **The Holiday Inn Express & Suites** (110 MS-12, 662/324-0076, www.ihg.com, $95-110) and the **Days Inn & Suites** (119 MS-12, 662/270-5995, www.wyndhamhotels.com, $65-158) both have Wi-Fi, a free breakfast bar, and an outdoor pool.

Information and Services

The **Greater Starkville Development Partnership** (200 E. Main St., 662/323-3322, http://starkville.org, 8am-5pm Mon.-Fri.) is the place to start for visitor information, maps, and more.

Boardtown Bikes (200 S. Montgomery St., Ste. C, 662/324-1200, www.boardtownbikes.com, 10am-6pm Mon.-Fri., 11am-6pm Sat.) sells road, mountain, and fitness bikes and can help with repairs and gear as you continue your ride on the Trace.

OCH Regional Medical Center (400 Hospital Rd., 662/323-4320, www.och.org) has a 24-hour emergency room.

The **SMART Shuttle Bus** (662/325-5204, www.smart.msstate.edu, free) is a free bus that connects the Mississippi State campus to downtown. There are seven different routes. Most run 7am-8pm Monday-Saturday, although a few are 7am-6pm Monday-Friday only.

Back to the Trace

To return to the Trace, take MS-182 northwest for nine miles to MS-82. Turn left, then take MS-82 west for 12 miles. Just before you pass underneath the Trace, exit to the right, then turn left to rejoin the Trace near **milepost 204.5** and continue south.

Jeff Busby Park (MP 193.1)

This park is named in honor of U.S. congressman Thomas Jefferson Busby, a Mississippian who, in 1934, introduced a bill authorizing a survey of the Old Natchez Trace. Just four years later, the road was incorporated into the National Park System. The park is nestled on Little Mountain, one of the higher elevation points in Mississippi (603 feet), which affords scenic views thanks to the Summit Overlook, which can be reached on foot or by car, with plenty of parking at the top. On a clear day from the overlook, you can see for about 20 miles. The park also contains one of the three free campgrounds on the parkway.

It's possible to drive to the scenic Summit Overlook, or you can see it by hiking Little Mountain Trail. Starting from the campground, you'll hike out to Summit Overlook, atop Little Mountain. It's an uphill walk on the way back for a total of 1.6 miles out and back.

For those who don't want to do the Little Mountain Trail, the park also features a 0.5-mile loop trail that heads into a shady hollow, which is particularly welcome during hot Mississippi summers. Allow yourself up to 20 minutes to complete the gently rolling loop. Neither of the trails is wheelchair-friendly.

The entrance to the park is on the left side of the parkway. This is your last stop for restrooms until the Kosciusko Welcome Center (milepost 160). The restrooms at the summit overlook include educational signage about the area, but are not wheelchair-accessible. The restrooms at the base of the hill are accessible.

Camping

The ★ **Jeff Busby Campground** (no reservations, free) has 18 first-come, first-served sites, with some primitive tent sites as well as RV sites. Most of the campsites are pull-throughs. There is also ample overflow parking.

Claim your spot by pitching your rent or parking your RV. There are picnic tables and a grill at each site. The campground has bathrooms but no showers or dumping stations.

French Camp Historic District (MP 180.7)

French Camp Historic District (1 Fine Pl., 662/547-6417, www.frenchcamp.org/historic) is one of the few tourist stops along the parkway. This area, named for Frenchman Louis LeFleur, who opened an inn (called a "stand") here in 1812, is today home to **French Camp Academy,** a

Christian boarding school, as well as a collection of businesses run by the academy and its students. French Camp has an unusual vibe: part national park, part Disneyland, and part Sunday school.

In the historic district, you can tour several restored buildings, including the Drane House, and visit the Children of God Pottery Studio, a working studio where you can buy pottery and also talk to the academy students who are working and learning here. The pottery studio is located in what was the village's old post office.

French Camp isn't to everyone's taste, and that will dictate how long you spend exploring. If you like what you see, you could spend the better part of a day exploring, eating, shopping, praying, and talking to students and teachers. Due to the religious nature of the institution, the businesses are closed on Sunday and no alcohol or tobacco is permitted.

Explore several gift shops, such as **Barlow Blue** (66 Lefleur Cir., 662/547-6220, http://barlowblue.com, 10am-5:30pm Mon-Fri., 10am-2pm Sat.), which is chock-full of souvenirs and clothing. Then head to the **Council House Café** (10:30am-8pm Mon.-Sat., $6-10) and walk over to the pottery studio and historical compound. Don't skip the bread! It is made by hand and served in the café and the B&B and is for sale in the gift shop.

The academy also runs the ★ **French Camp B&B** (662/547-6835, $115-160), with an option of three different cabins and cottages, including a historic log cabin. Wi-Fi is available in the main house. There's no alcohol or tobacco permitted. The included breakfast is served at the Council House Café. Pets are permitted for a $15 fee.

The academy's **Rainwater Observatory & Planetarium** (6810 MS-413, 662/547-7283, www.rainwaterobservatory.org, free) hosts monthly star-watching events for the public.

As you head south on the Trace, you'll pass two entrances to French Camp. The first is a U-shaped pullout on the east side of the Trace. You can park here and cross a footbridge to the French Camp Village. The second entrance is accessible by turning left (east) from the parkway on MS-413 and then immediately into the parking lot on your left.

Cole Creek (MP 175.6)

Stop here for an easy walk through a shaded cypress swamp. The turnout for Cole Creek is just past Bethel Mission on the east side of the parkway. The U-shaped parking area is visible from the road, but the hike and creek are not.

Cole Creek Trail

Distance: 0.4-mile loop
Duration: 10-15 minutes
Difficulty: Easy

This trail through a cypress swamp is flat with a few concrete steps on each side of the entrance. In some places you'll walk above the swamp on a wooden boardwalk, seeing cypress trees, tupelo, and other water-loving trees in their natural habitat. Cole Creek runs through the swamp. The walk shouldn't take more than 10-15 minutes.

Hurricane Creek (MP 164.3)

This stop offers a pretty little nature trail that makes for a perfect walk through the woods. The U-shaped pullout is on the right side of the parkway. The creek is not visible from the road, but the parking is. There are no other amenities.

Hurricane Creek Trail

Distance: 0.3-mile loop
Duration: 10 minutes
Difficulty: Easy

This loop trail is less than one-third of a mile, with a well-cleared path of dirt and pebbles. The terrain is stable and sure-footed, but you're walking into a creek bed, so there's a decline to get there and an incline to get back. You'll be shaded from the sun by a dense thicket of southern pines, American beech, and other trees. This walk will take you less than 10 minutes unless you linger to read the signage about the foliage.

Kosciusko Museum and Information Center (MP 160)

The **Kosciusko Museum and Information Center** (180-189 Natchez Trace Pkwy, 662/289-2981, 9am-4pm daily) is a useful resource offering maps and information about the Trace, and museum exhibits about the history of the adjacent town of Kosciusko. There are restrooms and ample parking and even a small campground for cyclists (although you need to be able to sleep through some traffic noise to appreciate a stay here). The exit for the center is on the west side of the parkway at milepost 160 and visible from the road.

Back in the days of the Old Trace, this was a campsite for travelers. It is named for a Revolutionary War hero, General Tadeusz Kościuszko.

Kosciusko

Sleepy Kosciusko (population 6,800) is known for a few things. It's named for Tadeusz Kościuszko, the Polish war hero who helped the United States during the American Revolution. (Note that the town name doesn't use the "z" in its spelling.) It is also the birthplace of several Americans of significance, including media mega-personality Oprah Winfrey

Top to bottom: Jeff Busby Park; French Camp Historic District; Kosciusko Museum and Information Center

Don't Be Shy

In many small towns, particularly in the Delta and along the Trace in Mississippi, life moves at a different pace. Shopkeepers may pop out to visit a friend down the block or pick up a kid from school. If there's a phone number taped to the door—suggesting that you call to be let in—by all means, go ahead and phone the number on the sign if you're interested in the shop or museum; it isn't an imposition. Things are just less formal 'round these parts.

and James Meredith, the civil rights activist who helped integrate the University of Mississippi. The town is also part of the Mississippi Blues Trail.

Many Trace travelers stop here because of its proximity to the parkway. Its B&Bs are easily accessible for cyclists, and restaurants are within walking and biking distance. There are gas stations and even a Walmart (on Veterans Memorial Dr.).

The downtown square is quaint, an actual four-sided square around the courthouse. There are some sweets shops and mom-and-pop restaurants in town, but nothing fancy.

Sights

In downtown Kosciusko, **Redbud Springs Park** (across from 120 S. Natchez St.) was created in 1976 for the United States' bicentennial. There's a statue of the city's namesake, General Tadeusz Kościuszko, and pretty foliage. The town was originally named Redbud Springs.

A Blues Trail marker at **Charlie Musselwhite Blues Trail** (Washington St. between Jackson and Madison) notes the birthplace of the famous harmonica player, who was born in 1944. Musselwhite's great uncle owned the shop that once stood on this spot. Musselwhite became known in the Memphis and Chicago blues scenes, winning Grammy and W. C. Handy awards.

Certainly media mogul Oprah Winfrey is Kosciusko's most famous daughter. But the **Oprah Winfrey First Home Site** (1 mile east of downtown at MS-12E and Oprah Winfrey Rd.) isn't much to see. A sign commemorates her birth in 1954, but the wood frame house in which she lived is long gone. Only the most diehard fans will appreciate this site, which is not particularly well cared for. If you really want to honor Oprah while in town, check out **The Oprah Winfrey Boys & Girls Club of Kosciusko/Attala County** (500 Knox Rd., 662/289-4252), which opened in 2001. Her philanthropy helps area kids get breakfasts and lunches, tutoring, medical care, and more.

The 1899 Gothic-style church now houses the **Mary Ricks Thornton Cultural Center** (Washington St. and Huntington St.). The center doesn't have resources (or regular hours) for tourists, but architecture fans should plan to stop by and admire the exterior, including the stained-glass windows.

Festivals and Events

The city of Kosciusko is proud of its connection to the Trace, and no time is this more obvious than in April when it hosts the **National Natchez Trace Festival.** Held in downtown Kosciusko since 1969, the day's festivities include food vendors, arts and crafts booths, a Miss Natchez Trace Pageant, and live music.

Since 1909 the annual **Central Mississippi Fair** has been a highlight of August. Held at the Attala County Coliseum (550 MS-12, 662/289-2981, admission $6) over four days, it features all the standard fair fun: carnival rides, livestock showings, and more food on a stick than you can eat.

Shopping

Stroll around the historic downtown Court Square and browse some of the small boutiques, including **Claude Julian's** (141 N. Madison St., 662/289-4821, 9am-5:30pm Mon.-Fri., 9am-5pm Sat., 1pm-5pm Sun.), which has contemporary men's and women's clothing; the family-owned **Patterson Jewelers** (122 N. Jackson St., 662/289-3731, http://pattersonjewelers.net, 9:30am-4:30pm Mon.-Fri., 9:30am-2pm Sat.), which has been in business since 1950; and **Coghlan Jewelers** (106 W. Washington St., 662/289-4811, 10am-5pm Mon.-Fri.).

Food

Located just off the Trace, **Old Trace Grill** (719 Veterans Memorial Dr., 662/289-2652, 10:30am-9pm Tues.-Sat., $7-10) serves fried chicken, barbecue, burgers, sandwiches, and ice cream. Lines are out the door in the summer. It has a drive-thru and takeout as well as eat-in dining.

The parking lot at **Rodeo Family Mexican Restaurant** (1050 Veterans Memorial Dr., 662/289-9802, 11am-9pm daily, $8-13) is almost always full, as locals like this affordable Mexican eatery. There are plenty of lunch specials in the $5-9 range if you are looking to fuel up before rejoining the parkway.

Kosciusko restaurants close early. If you're looking for something open later, try **Bel Piatto Italian Restaurant** (1050 Veterans Memorial Dr., 662/289-9999, 7am-10pm daily, $9-18). It's not just Italian; there are American and even Tex-Mex items on the menu, too.

Accommodations

Kosciusko's strength is its collection of bed-and-breakfasts, particularly those that cater to cyclists. The folks who own the **Maple Terrace Inn** (300 N. Huntington St., 662/289-4131, www.mapleterraceinn.com, $135) offer several places to stay in Kosciusko, with a total of 35 guest rooms. Maple Terrace is in a 1912 building just blocks from Court Square, with antique furniture and architectural detailing. There's a secure garage for locking up bicycles overnight. Some lore suggests the Maple Terrace Inn is haunted. If you believe that sort of thing, listen closely, particularly on nights when you're the only guest in the house. **Martha's Cottage** (401 N. Huntington St., $135-259) is more private, with two guest rooms, a porch swing, piano, and indoor bicycle storage. The innkeepers also own the **Presidents Inn** (100 E. Washington St., $135). Their **Hammond-Routt House** (109 S. Natchez St., $135) is located on the Old Trace itself. Finally, the **Niles-Bailey House** (305 N. Huntington St., $135) is a Queen Anne Victorian mansion with a wrap-around porch. Prices for all include breakfast, which is served either in the residence or at a restaurant on the square; Wi-Fi; and other modern amenities. These are unattended bed-and-breakfasts: Fill out your menu when you check in and someone comes to cook breakfast in the morning, but otherwise, there's no one on-site, although there is a phone number for emergencies.

Information and Services

If you need medical help, **Trace Medical Clinic** (530 Veterans Memorial Dr., 662/289-9155, www.tracemedicalclinic.com) offers basic services during the week. The nearest full-service hospital is in Jackson, nearly 100 miles south.

Red Dog Road (MP 140)

This road, built circa 1834, is historically important. Named for Choctaw chief Ofahoma, also called Red Dog, the road runs to Canton, Mississippi. Chief Ofahoma signed the Treaty of Dancing Rabbit Creek here on September 27, 1830, by which the Choctaws agreed to vacate their land and head west to Oklahoma.

The pullout is on the west side of the road, with a U-shaped parking area and informational signage.

Robinson Road (MP 135.5)

This is a historically significant road that's listed on the National Register of Historic Places. Robinson Road was built in 1821 through Choctaw country. It was this road that connected the towns of Jackson and Columbus, Mississippi. In 1822 this became the designated mail route north, taking some of the traffic off of the historic Trace.

The pullout is on the east side of the road, with a U-shaped parking area and informational signage.

Upper Choctaw Boundary (MP 128.4)

Signage here points to what was the Upper Choctaw Boundary, the border dividing the Choctaw nation from areas allocated for white settlers. The boundary was agreed to by the Choctaws and the American Commission under Andrew Jackson in the 1820 treaty of Doaks Stand. This was a reluctant agreement on the part of the Choctaw, as it forced them to give up about one-third of their land, some 5.5 million acres.

Near the parking lot, an easy 10-minute, flat loop trail will take you on a tour of southern pines in this area, with signage about different tree varieties along the way.

River Bend (MP 122.6)

A significantly larger stop than many on the parkway, River Bend provides access to the Pearl River. In 1698, the French explorer Pierre LeMoyne Sieur d'Iberville made his way into the mouth of this river and found pearls. Some 100 miles south, near Hattiesburg, Mississippi, the Pearl River has served as part of the border between Mississippi and Louisiana since 1812.

It's unlikely that you'll find any pearls here, but you can find a different kind of gem. There are beautiful views of lily-pad-filled waters, with wide grassy expanses for picnicking and playing, and grills and picnic tables on both sides of the parking lot.

The entrance is on the east side of the parkway. There are restrooms and covered picnic areas. The next restroom stop going south is at the **Bill Waller Mississippi Craft Center** (milepost 104.5).

Cypress Swamp (MP 122)

The Trace is full of astonishing natural beauty, but even with a lot of tough competition, this walk easily is one of the most scenic.

★ Cypress Swamp Loop Trail

Distance: 0.4-mile loop

Duration: 20 minutes

Difficulty: Easy

The **Cypress Swamp Loop Trail** takes you on a walk of just under half a mile, but don't judge it by its distance. It starts on a bridge that leads to a boardwalk, which spans a swamp of water tupelos and bald cypress. Because this trail is away from the parking lot and the road, it is unusually quiet and serene. If you're lucky, you may see some wildlife, such as herons or alligators.

The boardwalk leads to a dirt trail, shaded in the woods, that loops around and comes back to the parking area. This is a very easy trail, about a 20-minute walk, assuming a leisurely pace to take in the unusual views. There are a few steps on the bridge to get down to the swamp level, so it is not wheelchair accessible.

The entrance is on the east side of the parkway. The parking area is visible from the road, but the swamp is not.

To access the Natchez Trace National Scenic Trail from this stop, cross the parkway (to the west side) and look for the green hiking sign. From here it is 14.1 miles south to the West Florida Boundary or 8.9 miles north to the Yockanookany Trailhead.

Cypress Swamp

The Trace:
Southern
Mississippi

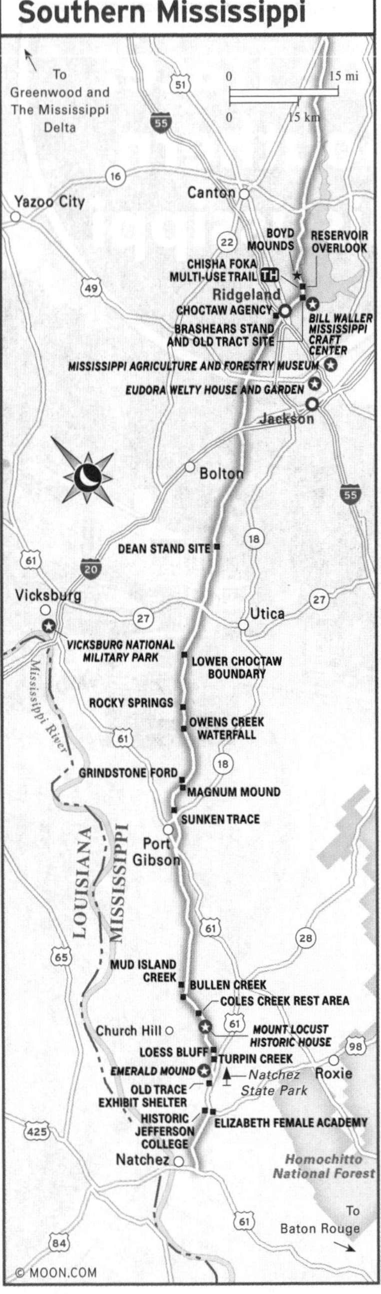

This drive includes sites of some of the Civil War's bloodiest battles. It cuts through Jackson, the state capital and home to many important civil rights era sites and blues music icons.

It also skirts several large Indian mounds, sacred sites of Native American tribes who once lived in this area but were pushed west.

But despite its tragic history, this part of Mississippi shines, too, through its friendly, welcoming residents; its reverence for history, particularly its architecture; its lush green landscapes and rolling hills along the banks of the mighty Mississippi; its love of music and art; and, of course, its delicious food. Pack your bags and come think, share, and explore.

Route Overview

Starting north of the Jackson metropolitan area and ending at the southern terminus of the Natchez Trace Parkway, this section of the drive covers **122 miles** of the National Park thoroughfare, plus side trips to some of Mississippi's most historic cities, including Port Gibson, Vicksburg, Jackson, and Natchez.

The amount of time you devote to this region depends on your personal interests. If Civil War battlefields and historic architecture appeal to you, you'll want to devote at least **four days** in the area, being sure to focus on Vicksburg and Natchez. If the American civil rights movement is a passion, allot the same number of days, but skew your time around and near Jackson. If it's the allure of the great outdoors that motivates you, plan to spend **1-2 days** exploring Native American mounds and villages.

Highlights

★ **Bill Waller Mississippi Craft Center:** Browse the works of local artists and see them practice their craft at this oasis along the Trace (page 293).

★ **2 Mississippi Museums:** This complex includes the powerful Mississippi Civil Rights Museum, a must-experience for anyone who wants to better understand the country's past (page 295).

★ **Mississippi Agriculture and Forestry Museum:** You can spend hours learning and exploring on these 39 acres (page 295).

★ **Vicksburg National Military Park:** Immerse yourself in Civil War history at this mammoth battlefield (page 303).

★ **Mount Locust Historic House:** Tour one of the few remaining historic structures on the parkway (page 309).

Best Restaurants

★ **Brent's Drugs:** Indulge in a shake or a malt at this old-fashioned soda fountain (page 300).

★ **Main Street Market Café:** Friendly service and Cajun cooking are a recipe for the perfect Vicksburg lunch (page 305).

★ **Old Country Store:** Mr. D sings while you feast on his famous fried chicken—some of the best in the South—at this all-you-can-eat spot (page 308).

★ **King's Tavern:** Wine and dine in the oldest restaurant in the state (page 314).

Driving Considerations

This section of the parkway is well maintained and there are ample pullouts to permit safe sightseeing. The speed limit is 50 mph, and there is likely to be bicycle traffic. You may encounter traffic on the Trace around Jackson, but likely very little south of the city until Natchez. Keep your eyes peeled for wild turkeys and deer on the road.

Southern Mississippi is considered to have a "subtropical" climate. That means highs in the 60s in the winter and above 100°F in the summer. Snow or ice on the Trace in this region is rare, although there is occasional flooding. Call 800/305-7417 for up-to-date road conditions.

Because of soft soil in the area, there are uneven road surfaces throughout Mississippi. Those in cars are unlikely to be significantly impacted by these potholes, but bicyclists and motorcyclists should use caution.

Fuel and Services

This section of parkway is less rural than others, and you likely will have a cell signal when on the Trace near **Ridgeland, Jackson, Clinton,** and **Natchez.** Service is spottier in the rural areas, particularly en route to **Vicksburg** (though you should be able to connect again once you arrive in Vicksburg itself).

Getting to the Starting Point

Car, Motorcycle, or Bicycle

If you've been following the Natchez Trace south, continue driving south from Cypress Swamp for about 15 miles to Boyd Mounds, the first stop of this leg.

It's about 20 miles from the **Jackson** airport to Boyd Mounds. Take MS-475 north to MS-25, then continue west to I-55. From here, it's about six miles until you hit the Trace. Turn right onto the parkway and then continue for about five miles until you reach Boyd Mounds. This drive will take around 40 minutes.

Nine rental car companies have counters in Terminal 1, including **Avis** (601/939-5882, www.avis.com), **Hertz** (601/939-5312, www.hertz.com), and **Budget** (137 Hangar Dr., 601/923-9504, www.budget.com). **Enterprise Rent-A-Car** (1010 S. State St., 601/948-0062, http://www.enterprise.com) is located near Baptist Medical Center.

Air

The **Jackson-Medgar Wiley Evers International Airport** (100 International Dr., www.iflyjackson.com) is served by American, Delta, United, and Southern Airways Express, with daily flights from select cities, including Atlanta, Charlotte, Chicago, Dallas, Memphis, Nashville, and Washington DC. The

Best Accommodations

★ **Hyatt Place Renaissance Colony Park:** A walkable location and suite layouts make this hotel most accommodating (page 294).

★ **Fairview Inn:** Step back in time at this 1908 hotel (page 302).

★ **Devereaux Shields House:** Hospitality is the watchword at this B&B (page 316).

★ **Monmouth Historic Inn and Gardens:** Escape at this old-world Southern resort (page 317).

airport has ATMs and free Wi-Fi, but no currency exchange.

The airport is about a 15-minute drive from downtown, and you'll want a rental car to explore the city.

Train and Bus

Amtrak operates out of Jackson's **Union Station** (300 W. Capitol St., 800/872-7245, www.amtrak.com), a stop on the 900-mile City of New Orleans route, which runs from New Orleans to Chicago. Union Station is centrally located in downtown Jackson.

Greyhound (601/353-6342, www.greyhound.com) serves Jackson out of Union Station. The Greyhound routes to Jackson are through Birmingham and Memphis.

MS-43 to Canton

Much of the town of Canton is on the National Register of Historic Places. Those who love all things old will be charmed by the courthouse square, which is a historical shopping district and home to the twice-annual Canton Flea Market, a draw for bargain hunters.

Leaving the Trace

To get to Canton, exit the parkway at MS-43, near **milepost 115.** (The Ross Barnett Reservoir will be to your east.) Take MS-43 north for 6.6 miles. Turn left onto Peace Street. Drive 1.7 miles and turn left onto MS-16 to reach downtown Canton. The drive should take 15 minutes.

Shopping

Thanks to its many sweet shops filled to the brim with vintage, antique, and specialty gift items, Canton is called the Antique and Gift Square of Mississippi.

Held in the town square twice a year, the popular **Canton Flea Market** (601/859-8055, http://cantonmsfleamarket.com, 7am-4pm second Thurs. of May and Oct.) hosts more than 1,000 vendors and artists, making it one of the largest of its kind in the South. The charming iron fence around the courthouse makes a great backdrop for artwork.

Canton Square Antiques (155 W. Peace St., 601/953-1141, 10am-5pm Mon.-Sat.) stocks vintage fine jewelry, furniture, and artwork. **La Di Da** (3334 N. Liberty St., 601/859-8106, http://shopladida.com, 10am-5pm Mon.-Tues. and Thurs.-Fri., 10am-2pm Wed., 10am-4pm Sat.) is a sweet gift boutique owned by two sisters. Come here for ceramics and other small home decor.

You can tell from the old cabinetry that **Unique Antiques** (171 W. Peace St.,

Fuel Up

On this section of the Trace, between major cities Jackson and Natchez, you're never particularly far from a gas station. You will easily find gas in the side trip destinations in this chapter, including Port Gibson and Vicksburg. Here's a quick list of places to exit the parkway in southern Mississippi so that you can refuel at the closest gas station. (Some stops may take you to small towns, others will be just a single service station.)

The National Park Service posts a list of supply stations at most of the Trace rest areas, although the list is not updated regularly.

- **Milepost 103.4:** Exit at Old Canton Road and head south. Drive 0.3 mile to the Chevron at the intersection with Rice Road.
- **Milepost 101:** Exit at I-55 North, then take exit 105B toward Ridgeland. Gas stations near this interchange include a Chevron on Old Agency Road. Exit 105C leads you to the only Costco in the state of Mississippi, which is an affordable place to fuel up.
- **Milepost 89:** Exit at Pinehaven Drive and turn south. Drive 0.4 mile to the Exxon or Quick Stop at the Northside Drive intersection in Clinton.
- **Milepost 79.0:** Exit at MS-467 and head southeast. Drive 2.5 miles to the Shell in Raymond.
- **Milepost 41.3:** Exit at MS-18 and drive west. There's a Citgo 1.3 miles from the parkway, or turn south onto US 61 to head into Port Gibson. There's a Shell on US 61 in the center of town.

601/667-3480, 10am-5pm Mon.-Sat.) is the real deal, located in the old Mosby Drugstore space. The space may be old, but the store is new, opened in 2016. They specialize in collectibles and antiques, including some primitive folk art styles.

The Emporium of Canton (3344 N. Liberty St., 601/667-3670, www.emporiumofcanton.com, 10am-5pm Mon.-Sat.) stocks the work of more than 40 Mississippi artisans and makers, including items like housewares, furniture, and jewelry.

Food

Canton Junction Sports Pub (399 Neponset St., 781/828-7878, www.junctionsportshub.com, 3pm-midnight Mon., 3pm-1am Wed., noon-midnight Thurs. and Sun., noon-1am Fri.-Sat, $7-16) has the standard fare like pizza, burgers, wings, and salads, plus a better-than-average craft beer list.

Have you ever had oysters on the half chip? That would be a fried oyster on a tortilla chip with pico de gallo and chipotle cream. You can try it at **Two Rivers** (1537 W. Peace St., 601/859-9999, www.tworiverscanton.com, 4:30pm-9pm Mon.-Wed., 5pm-9pm Thurs., 4:30pm-10pm Fri.-Sat., $10-37), which is the nicest restaurant in town.

Back to the Trace

Return to the parkway by taking Peace Street, the main thoroughfare, 1.7 miles east to MS-43. Turn right and drive 6.6 miles south on MS-43. Turn right to exit MS-43, then rejoin the parkway near **milepost 115** by turning left to continue heading south. The total drive should take 15 minutes.

A Day on the Trace: Southern Mississippi

Gas up and get going! You'll start your day in the state capital, where history and progress meet. Have a traditional pork breakfast at **Big Apple Inn,** then visit the hands-on **Mississippi Agriculture and Forestry Museum.** Before leaving town, stop by the **Medgar Evers Home Museum National Monument** to learn about the civil rights battle of one of Mississippi's bravest sons.

Jump on I-20 West near milepost 86 and you'll reach Vicksburg in about 30 minutes. Explore **Vicksburg National Military Park,** then take in the river views at this terminus to the Mississippi Delta during lunch at **10 South Rooftop Bar & Grill.**

Drive east to rejoin the parkway from I-20. As you approach the last 15 miles of the Trace, stop at **Mount Locust Historic House** and then **Emerald Mound,** one of the largest archaeological mounds in North America. For a complete list of every stop along the Trace, download the detailed National Park Service maps (www.nps.gov/natr).

Take a photo as you reach the **southern terminus** of the Natchez Trace Parkway, and then ease into **Natchez,** where dinner should be at **King's Tavern,** the oldest restaurant in Mississippi—and one that can make a fine cocktail to toast your milestone. Spend the night at **Devereaux Shields House,** a B&B set in a Queen Anne Victorian.

Boyd Mounds (MP 106.9)

When you first spy this area, it may appear to be one large mound, but it's really three separate mounds within the larger, 100-foot-long mound. Archaeologists date pottery found in these mounds from AD 700. Remains of more than 40 burials were also found here.

The road leading to the mound is on the left (east) side of the parkway. The mound isn't visible from the parkway. The site is open sunrise to sunset only.

Reservoir Overlook (MP 105.6)

This stop is both a pretty overlook and a place to play. Overlooking **Ross Barnett Reservoir** (which is accessible from the nearby town of Ridgeland), this is a popular place for locals to spend an afternoon with a blanket, some sunscreen, and a book.

Depending on the time of year, water lilies, wildflowers, and lush trees provide contrast to the wide watery openness of the reservoir. Sunrises and sunsets reflecting off the reservoir can be stunning. It's not unusual to catch a wedding or engagement photo shoot here.

The **Chisha Foka Multi-Use Trail,** which runs parallel to the Trace for about 10 miles, has its northern terminus in the overlook's parking lot.

The parkway hugs the reservoir for 15 miles. The driveway is on the left (east) side of the road; the reservoir and parking lot are visible from the road.

Chisha Foka Multi-Use Trail

Chisha Foka Multi-Use Trail

Yet another unexpected gem along the Natchez Trace Parkway is the **Chisha Foka Multi-Use Trail** (formerly the Natchez Trace Multi-Use Trail). Designed for cyclists, pedestrians, and others not in motorized vehicles, this paved recreational trail parallels the parkway, offering a safe way to enjoy the scenery without being in traffic. The trail starts at **Reservoir Overlook** (milepost 105.6) and runs along the parkway for almost 10 miles. The southernmost access point on the trail is at milepost 95.8. It runs by the **Chocktaw Agency** (milepost 100.7), which is the best place to park. (You can continue walking or cycling south, but there is no parking or access to the trail beyond this.) There are plans to eventually extend the trail to the Clinton Visitor Center at milepost 89.

The trail also traverses the city of Ridgeland, where you can access shopping and local parks. Download a full map at www.visitridgeland.com.

If you are cycling the Trace and are frustrated by traffic around Ridgeland, this is a non-motorized alterative. Remember to look both ways when crossing the trail, as bikers and those on inline skates may be traveling at a speedy clip.

Choctaw Agency

(MP 100.7)

This stop commemorates the Choctaw Agency. The agency was located here between 1807 and 1820, and functioned like an embassy in which the U.S. government and the Choctaw Nation would negotiate with each other. The U.S. government set up agencies within the borders of many Native American nations. Federal agents working out of this location would act as intermediaries between the two governments. The agents lived among the Choctaw and represented their interests while implementing U.S. policy.

All that's left of the agency today is a sign marking the site and explaining its significance. There's an access point for the **Chisha Foka Multi-Use Trail** in the parking lot; signs point the way. You can take the trail from here back to the Reservoir Overlook or continue onward. However, you'll have to turn around in about five miles, as there's no parking or other access to the trail beyond this stop.

Ridgeland

Ridgeland is essentially a suburb of Jackson, but thanks to its location on Ross Barnett Reservoir, proximity to the parkway, and commitment to outdoor recreation, it is a destination for those who travel the Trace.

Sights

Parkway Information Cabin

Staffed by park rangers, the **Parkway Information Cabin** (milepost 102.4 Natchez Trace Pkwy., 601/898-9417, 9am-4pm Fri.-Sat.) is a good stop to get questions answered from people who know the Trace. Various ranger-led programs (free) cover everything from wildlife to Indian mounds. Some programs are specifically designed for kids, but all are family-friendly.

The cabin has a small gift shop, information about nearby Ridgeland, and picnic tables.

★ Bill Waller Mississippi Craft Center (MP 104.5)

Run by the Craftsmen's Guild of Mississippi, the **Bill Waller Mississippi Craft Center** (950 Rice Rd., 601/856-7546, http://craftsmensguildofms.org, 9am-5pm Mon.-Sat., noon-5pm Sun., free) is a surprising cornucopia of art right off of the parkway. This large building houses classes, local events, artisan demos, and fine art exhibitions. Browse the large gallery store for quilts, wood-carvings, ceramics, baskets, sculpture, jewelry, and metalworking made by local and regional craftspeople.

The building also has some outdoor sculpture, a sizable deck, and places to sit both inside and outside. There's no café, but there are a few vending machines and restrooms.

You can access the building two different ways. Near milepost 104.5 there's a turnoff on the left side of the road. The signage reads "Brashears Stand," noting the inn that provided entertainment and shelter to travelers in the early 1800s. You can park here and walk down the shaded trail for a quick hike or cross a small, well-marked bridge to the back of the building. To get to the main entrance, continue another mile south on the parkway to Old Canton Road. Exit to the right to leave the Trace, then turn right onto Old Canton. Continue 0.2 mile to Rice Road. Turn left and drive one mile. The center will be on your left.

Shopping

Renaissance at Colony Park (1000 Highland Colony Pkwy., 601/519-0900, http://renaissanceatcolonypark.com) is Ridgeland's upscale, open-air shopping mall. Many of the stores are national chains, but there are boutiques, too, like women's clothing store **Libby Story** (601/717-3300, http://libbystory.com, noon-6pm Mon.-Sat., 1pm-6pm Sun.) and **Whimsy Cookie** (601/499-1955, 10am-6pm Mon.-Thurs., 10am-8pm Fri.-Sat., 1pm-6pm Sun.). Even if shopping is not your thing, the mall is a lovely place for a stroll. Each night on the hour between 6pm and 9pm there's a free fountain light show that is a draw for locals and visitors. The **Visit Ridgeland Tourist Information Center** (800/468-6078, 9am-5pm Mon.-Fri., 10am-4pm Sat.) is also located inside Renaissance at Colony Park.

Sports and Recreation

Ross Barnett Reservoir (115 Madison Landing Circle, 601/856-6574, www.therez.ms.gov, $5 Sat.-Sun. and holidays Apr.-Sept.) is the reason locals and visitors gravitate to Ridgeland. The 33,000-acre reservoir and surrounding area (another 17,000 acres) provide the water supply for Jackson residents, but recreation is the watchword here. There are 16 parks, multiple hiking and biking trails, two golf courses, five marinas, and 22 boat launches. The reservoir also has five campgrounds. There are a number of entrances to the reservoir. MS-43 crosses both the parkway and the reservoir itself, and is a well-trafficked place to enter.

For the largest selection of recumbent bikes in the South, head five miles south along the reservoir to **Ride South** (105 Avalon Ct., Brandon, 601/992-2490, www.ridesouth.com, 9am-5pm Mon.-Fri., 10am-4pm Sat., by appt. Sun.). **Bike Crossing** (115 W. Jackson St. Ste. 1D, 610/856-0049, http://thebikecrossing.com, 10am-6pm Mon.-Fri., 10am-5pm Sat.) is the closest bike shop to the parkway, in Ridgeland's charming Jackson Street historic district. Find all the gear you need, get your bike repaired, or join in Trace-centric cycling events. **Indian Cycle Fitness** (677 S. Pear Orchard Rd., 601/899-9755, www.indiancyclefitness.com, 10am-6pm Mon.-Fri., 10am-5pm Sat.) repairs bikes and sells both new and used bikes.

Food

It doesn't seem like it'd be enough to sustain a whole restaurant, but **Tom's Fried Pies** (827 US 49, 769/257-7351, www.tomsfriedpies.com, 10am-7pm Tues.-Sat., $3-6) has savory and sweet fried half-moon-shaped pies, with varieties ranging from Tex-Mex to spinach and mushroom. The fruit pies include berry flavors as well as peach, apple, apricot, and cherry.

Anjou (361 Township Ave., 601/707-0587, http://anjourestaurant.net, 11am-9pm Mon.-Thurs., 11am-10pm Fri.-Sat., 10:30am-9pm Sun., $13-36) is a traditional white-tablecloth French bistro serving dishes such as beef tartare and steak frites. Run by a father-daughter team, Anjou is located in The Township at Colony Park complex, which includes a hotel and shops.

With buzzy, high-energy ambience, beautiful decor, and an impressive seafood menu, **CAET** (1000 Highland Colony Pkwy., 601/321-9169, www.caetseafood.com, 11am-9pm Mon.-Thurs., 11am-10pm Fri.-Sat., $16-50) is a date-night favorite for locals.

If you are looking for organic or vegetarian options while on the road, **Crossroads Cafe** (398 US 51, 601/790-7141, 7:30am-6pm Mon.-Fri., 8am-6pm Sat., $3-14) is a good bet. In addition to made-to-order meals, it also has pre-made meals to go, perfect for a picnic out on the Trace. The breakfast smoothie business is brisk.

There are a number of good places to take in the views of the Rose Barnett Reservoir while dining out: **Shuckers** (116 Conestoga Rd., 615/853-0105, www.shuckersontherez.com, 11am-11:30pm Mon.-Thurs., 11am-2am Fri.-Sat., 10am-11pm Sun, $6-18) is an oyster bar with live music and big TVs, and **Cock of the Walk** (141 Madison Landing, 601/856-5500, www.cockofthewalkrestaurant.com, 11am-8:30pm Sun.-Thurs., 11am-9pm Fri.-Sat., $10-18) has a limited menu but serves large portions of fried catfish, chicken, and sides—and the servers will flip your cornbread in the air (and catch it) tableside.

The Prickly Hippie (500 US 51, Suite F, 601/910-6730, www.pricklyhippie.com, 8am-6pm Tues.-Sat., $12-30) is a charming bakery/plant shop with delicious baked goods and a friendly staff.

Accommodations

Ridgeland is a good place to stop and crash for the night, with lots of safe, convenient options, with all of the major chains represented. Many of these hotels offer suites with small kitchens and extra space for families or friends traveling together.

Thanks to sofa sleepers in the rooms, ★ **Hyatt Place Renaissance Colony Park** (1016 Highland Colony Pkwy., 601/898-8815, http://jacksonridgeland.place.hyatt.com, $80-173) is great for families. The lobby is a bustling hangout with a coffee shop and a wine café. The hotel is conveniently within walking distance to all Colony Park attractions, including the fountain, light show, shops, and restaurants. The **Hampton Inn** (600 Steed Rd.,

769/300-5556, www.hilton.com, $93-141) is a modern, clean hotel with Wi-Fi, a pool, and friendly service.

Ross Barnett Reservoir (115 Madison Landing Circle, 601/829-2751, www.therez.ms.gov, RVs $15-30, tents $14-17) has five campgrounds (Timberlake, Goshen Springs, Coal Bluff, Leake County, and Low Head Dam), some of which offer pools, Wi-Fi, and laundry. If you don't need amenities and just want to be one with the land, primitive up-river camping is allowed on Pearl River north of MS-43 and south of Lease County Water Park. A permit (free) is required and is good for up to 10 days. To get your permit, call Goshen Springs Campground (601/992-9703) or the Reservoir Control Tower (601/992-9703).

Jackson

The Natchez Trace Parkway runs near Jackson, Mississippi's energetic, complicated, and historic capital. Named after President Andrew Jackson, the city is known for its blues music, art museums, and complex civil rights history. It is the Magnolia State's biggest city.

Sights

★ 2 Mississippi Museums

A complex coined the **2 Mississippi Museums** (www.mdah.ms.gov/2MM) was developed as part of a celebration of Mississippi's bicentennial in 2017. In the short time it has been open, the Mississippi Civil Rights Museum (222 North St., 601/576-6800, mcrm.mdah.ms.gov, 9am-5pm Tue..-Sat., 1pm-5pm Sun., $10 adults, $8 seniors and military, $6 children ages 4-18, children 3 and under free) has become an international destination. The interactive museum fully documents the history of the state and its civil rights struggles. The subject matter, of course, can be upsetting, as the content doesn't shy away from the atrocities that took place, including lynchings, arrests, and church burnings. However, there are also elements that are uplifting and inspiring, particularly the central This Little Light of Mine gallery, which is filled with song and the opportunity for crowds to interact with a light sculpture. The museum is designed so that it is easy to accompany children and expose them to age-appropriate sections. Particularly graphic films, for example, are shown in enclosed areas with warning signs.

The connected **Museum of Mississippi History** covers everything that has happened in the state the last two hundred years, with lots of memorabilia and artifacts, and even a replica of the sunken Natchez Trace Parkway. There's a lot to explore in these two museums. If you are a person who likes to go in-depth, it may be worth breaking them into two sections (one before lunch and one after) to avoid overload.

★ Mississippi Agriculture and Forestry Museum

Oft referred to as the Mississippi Ag Museum, the mammoth **Mississippi Agriculture and Forestry Museum** (1150 Lakeland Dr., 601/432-4500, www.msag-museum.org, 9am-5pm Mon.-Sat., adults $5, seniors, students, and children $4, free for children under 3) is a hands-on experience. On 39 acres, the museum houses working printing presses, impressive model trains, arrowhead collections, a blacksmith shop, antique cars, and even a replica of an 1820s Mississippi town, complete with a general store that functions as the museum's gift shop. The staff is exceedingly knowledgeable and devoted to their mission of making Mississippi's agrarian roots interesting. Families of all ages could easily spend many hours here.

Mississippi Sports Hall of Fame

Learn about Mississippi's famous athletes, including Cool Papa Bell, Boo Ferriss, Dizzy Dean, Walter Payton, Archie Manning, Jerry Rice, Brett Favre,

Jackson

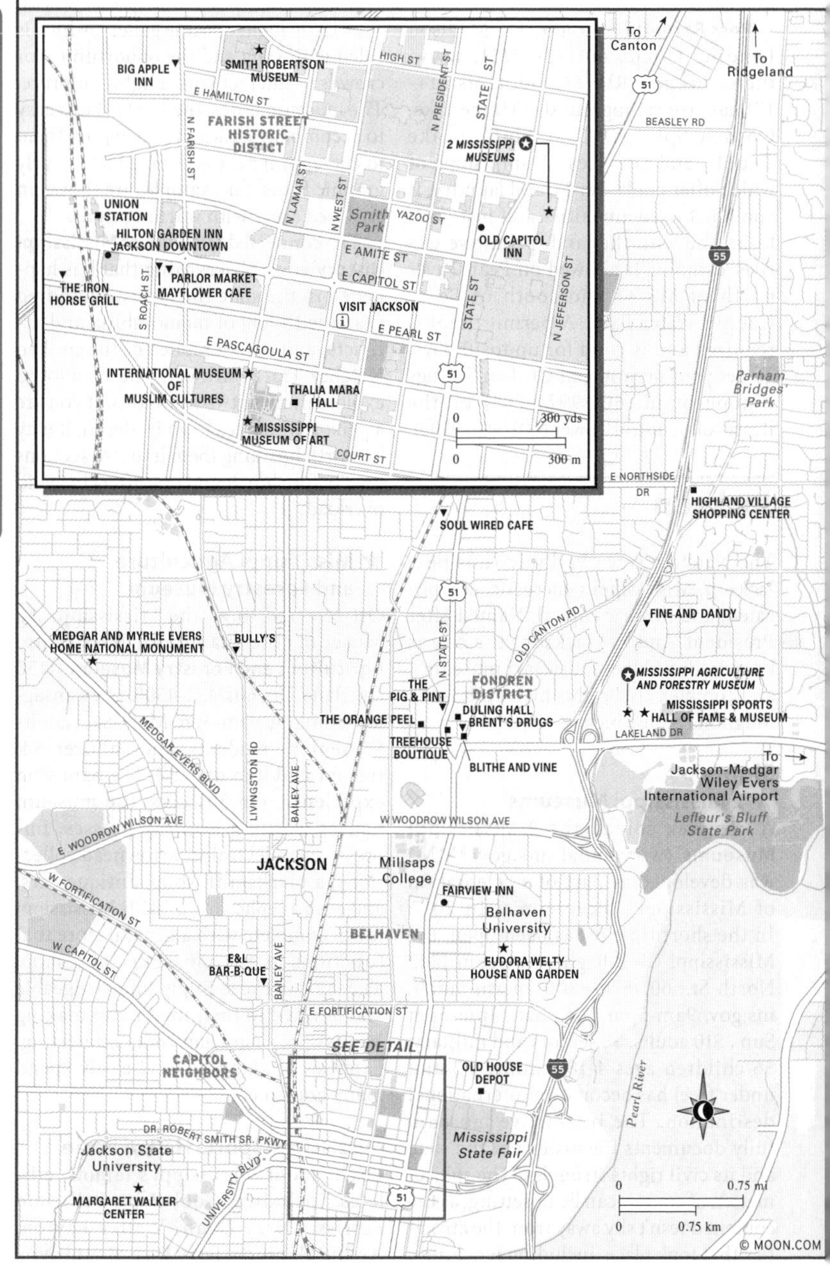
BIG APPLE INN
SMITH ROBERTSON MUSEUM
HIGH ST
E HAMILTON ST
FARISH STREET HISTORIC DISTICT
N FARISH ST
N PRESIDENT ST
STATE ST
2 MISSISSIPPI MUSEUMS
UNION STATION
N LAMAR ST
N WEST ST
Smith Park
YAZOO ST
HILTON GARDEN INN JACKSON DOWNTOWN
OLD CAPITOL INN
E AMITE ST
E CAPITOL ST
THE IRON HORSE GRILL
PARLOR MARKET
MAYFLOWER CAFE
S ROACH ST
VISIT JACKSON
E PEARL ST
STATE ST
N JEFFERSON ST
E PASCAGOULA ST
INTERNATIONAL MUSEUM OF MUSLIM CULTURES
THALIA MARA HALL
MISSISSIPPI MUSEUM OF ART
COURT ST
51
0
300 yds
300 m
To Canton
To Ridgeland
51
BEASLEY RD
55
Parham Bridges' Park
E NORTHSIDE DR
HIGHLAND VILLAGE SHOPPING CENTER
SOUL WIRED CAFE
51
OLD CANTON RD
FINE AND DANDY
MEDGAR AND MYRLIE EVERS HOME NATIONAL MONUMENT
BULLY'S
N STATE ST
FONDREN DISTRICT
MISSISSIPPI AGRICULTURE AND FORESTRY MUSEUM
MISSISSIPPI SPORTS HALL OF FAME & MUSEUM
THE PIG & PINT
THE ORANGE PEEL
DULING HALL
BRENT'S DRUGS
LAKELAND DR
TREEHOUSE BOUTIQUE
BLITHE AND VINE
MEDGAR EVERS BLVD
LIVINGSTON RD
BAILEY AVE
To Jackson-Medgar Wiley Evers International Airport
Lefleur's Bluff State Park
W WOODROW WILSON AVE
E WOODROW WILSON AVE
JACKSON
Millsaps College
FAIRVIEW INN
W FORTIFICATION ST
Belhaven University
BELHAVEN
W CAPITOL ST
E&L BAR-B-QUE
BAILEY AVE
EUDORA WELTY HOUSE AND GARDEN
E FORTIFICATION ST
SEE DETAIL
CAPITOL NEIGHBORS
OLD HOUSE DEPOT
55
Pearl River
DR. ROBERT SMITH SR. PKWY
Jackson State University
Mississippi State Fair
UNIVERSITY BLVD
MARGARET WALKER CENTER
51
0
0.75 mi
0.75 km
© MOON.COM

Bailey Howell, Davey Whitney, and Van Chancellor at the **Mississippi Sports Hall of Fame** (1152 Lakeland Dr., 601/982-8264, http://msfame.com, 10am-4pm Mon.-Sat., adults $5, seniors $3.50, students 6-17 $3.50, free for children 5 and under).

Eudora Welty House and Garden

A National Historic Landmark and listed on the National Register of Historic Places, the **Eudora Welty House and Garden** (1119 Pinehurst St., 601/353-7762, http://eudorawelty.org, tours 9am, 11am, 1pm, and 3pm Tues.-Fri., 9am and 11am second Sat. of the month, and by appt., adults $5, students $3, free for children under 6) offers an in-depth look into the life and work of one of Mississippi's favorite daughters. The prolific Pulitzer Prize-winning author was deeply connected to her native Mississippi. Everything about Welty's home (in which she grew up and lived until her death)—the exterior, interior, and furnishings—is as it was in 1986 when she donated it to the State of Mississippi. Look at her paintings, photographs, and thousands of books. Stroll in her garden and see what inspired her. The gift shop has many of Welty's books for sale (as well as some of her photographs); you'll likely be motivated to read them after your visit. Admission is free on the 13th of the month if it falls on a day when the museum is open.

Smith Robertson Museum

Housed in the building that was formerly Smith Robertson School, the first public school built in Jackson for African American children, **Smith Robertson Museum and Cultural Center** (528 Bloom St., 601/960-1457, www.jacksonms.gov, 9am-5pm Mon.-Fri., 10am-1pm Sat., adults $7, seniors $5, students $5, children 4-17 $4, free for children 3

Top to bottom: Mississippi Civil Rights Museum; Eudora Welty House; Medgar Evers Home Museum National Monument

Self-Guided Tours of Jackson

- Download a free brochure and take yourself on the self-guided **Belhaven Neighborhood Driving Tour** (www.finditfondren.com). It features 18 sites, all tied to different quotes or moments in the movie *The Help,* written by Jackson native Kathryn Stockett. Both the book and the movie include a number of damaging and unrealistic stereotypes about race relations, but fans may enjoy going by 805 Riverside Drive, headquarters of the Junior League of Jackson, and the homes of characters Hilly Hollbrook and Elizabeth Leefolt on Myrtle and Devine Streets.

- The self-guided **Historic Downtown Walking Tour** (www.visitjackson.com) provides precise walking directions for some of Jackson's prettiest sights. The downloadable brochure starts at the Old Capitol Museum (1839-1902) and includes the Old U.S. Post Office (circa 1875), Central Fire Station (circa 1904), City Hall, and others.

- Another downloadable, self-guided option, the **Civil Rights Movement Driving Tour** (www.visitjackson.com) includes a whopping 81 sites related to the civil rights movement in Jackson. The scope of the tour includes churches, public buildings, residences, and businesses in four different neighborhoods. The tour begins at the Smith Robertson Museum. Sites are marked by blue signs with a number in yellow that corresponds to the map. The stops on this tour are generally safe during daylight hours, but use common sense when visiting less populated areas.

and under) honors that legacy. The museum's exhibits focus on the experiences of African Americans in the Deep South. Exhibits cover slavery, including a powerful slave ship display that details passage from Africa; historically Black colleges and universities; Mississippi African American folk art; and the history of the building.

Medgar Evers Home Museum National Monument

Medgar Evers was the first field secretary for the NAACP in Jackson. He was assassinated in his own driveway in June 1963 during Jackson's difficult and violent fight for civil rights. The **Medgar Evers Home Museum National Monument** (2332 Margaret Walker Alexander Dr., 601/977-7839, tours by appt. only, free) was named a National Historic Landmark in 2017 and became a National Monument in 2019. Both inside and outside the home are panels detailing Evers's life, death, and work. Bullet holes are visible in the walls. Neighbor and local author Eudora Welty was moved by Evers's death, and during a sleepless night that followed his assassination, she wrote one of her most powerful stories, "Where Is the Voice Coming From?" from the point of view of Evers's killer.

The National Park Service is in the process of taking over the management and tours of the home from Tougaloo College. In the interim, you must call the school in advance to schedule a tour of the interior. This is a powerful and important experience and well worth the advance planning.

Margaret Walker Center

The **Margaret Walker Center** (1400 J. R. Lynch St., 601/979-3935, 8am-5pm Mon.-Sat., free) is a multi-story archive and museum about African American history and culture. Originally founded in 1968 by Margaret Walker as the Institute for the Study of the History, Life, and Culture of Black People, the center honors Walker's legacy and continues her work. The art exhibitions on display change, but they tend to be thought-provoking and powerful. The museum is inside Ayer Hall on the Jackson State University campus. Free on-campus visitor parking is easy to find.

Farish Street Historic District

Farish Street Historic District (between Fortification St. and Amite St.) was the center of commerce and social activity for African Americans in Jackson after World War II. At that time the area thrived, as Black-owned businesses attracted customers who were not welcome elsewhere in town. As the city became desegregated, the district fell into disrepair. There have been efforts to rehab and revitalize the area since the late 1970s, and it is a designated stop on the Mississippi Blues Trail, but it is still very much a work in progress. It's important to come here and read the signage to truly understand Jackson. But do so during daylight hours and pay attention to your surroundings. This area is not recommended at night.

International Museum of Muslim Cultures

The **International Museum of Muslim Cultures** (101 E. Capitol St., 601/960-0440, www.immuslimcultures.org, 10am-5pm Tues.-Sat., 1pm-5pm Sun., adults $18, seniors $14, students $9) is a fascinating and comprehensive look at Islamic culture via artifacts and other exhibitions. Many of the displays are hands-on and include music and other elements to keep kids' attention.

Mississippi Museum of Art

An impressive world-class art museum in the heart of downtown, the **Mississippi Museum of Art** (380 S. Lamar St., 601/960-1515, http://msmuseumart.org, 11am-7pm Tues.-Thurs., 10am-5pm Fri.-Sat., noon-5pm Sun., free; admission varies for special exhibits) has a permanent collection focused on Mississippi artists, in a building that will make you think you're in one of the world's art capitals. The brick and glass lobby is sleek and modern, yet welcoming, and flows into a 1.2-acre public garden with fountains and plants, where locals hang out for lunch. Extending the museum's collection to the outdoors, the sculptures in this outdoor patio area are vibrant.

The museum has a lovely café and a better-than-average gift shop.

Entertainment and Events

A 1906 smokehouse is now one of Jackson's best options for live blues. Head to **The Iron Horse Grille** (320 W. Pearl St., 601/398-0151, www.theironhorsegrill.com, 11am-9pm, $12-26) for live music, plus burgers, barbecue, and beers. This is a downtown hangout where you're sure to meet new friends. Tours of the **Mississippi Musicians Hall of Fame,** also on-site, are available.

Soul Wired Café (4147 Northview Dr., Ste. B, 601/790-0864, www.soulwiredcafe.com, 11am-6pm and 9pm-2am Sat., 11am-6pm Sun., $3-7) is a community-centric café with local art on the walls and live music and poetry readings on Thursdays and Saturdays. This is a good place for vegan and vegetarian options in a meat-centric city, thanks to the salad bar and extensive sandwich offerings.

More than 120 concerts are performed annually by the **Mississippi Symphony Orchestra** (601/960-1565, http://msorchestra.com). Most shows take place at **Thalia Mara Hall** (255 E. Pascagoula St.), but there are popular special performances, such as the Pepsi Pops concert at Old Trace Park on the Ross Barnett Reservoir in nearby Ridgeland.

Think of this as the Olympics of ballet. The **USA International Ballet Competition** (www.usaibc.com) takes place every four years (2022) for two weeks in June at Thalia Mara Hall, when the ballet world looks to Jackson. In addition to the competition itself, there are performances and also classes for students.

A former elementary school, **Duling Hall** (622 Duling Ave., 601/292-7121, http://dulinghall.com, ticket prices vary by concert) is now the city's best venue for indie music, with both indoor and outdoor space.

Held annually in October at the Mississippi State Fairgrounds, the 10-day **Mississippi State Fair** (1207 Mississippi St., 601/961-4000, www.mdac.ms.gov) is a big deal. Look for musical acts such as Boyz II Men and Travis Tritt, rides, contests (including a mother-daughter look-alike competition and a hula hoop contest), and lots of fair food. It's a nice bonus that the fairgrounds are in walking distance of downtown.

Shopping

In recent years the revitalized **Fondren District** (bounded by Northside Dr., I-55, Woodrow Wilson Ave., and the ICR railroad, www.finditinfondren.com) has become Jackson's hip arts district, home to many boutiques, galleries, and restaurants. If you're a browser and want one-of-a-kind items, this is where you should start.

Blithe and Vine (2943 Old Canton Rd. Ste. E., 601/427-3322, http://blitheandvine.com, 10am-5:30pm Mon.-Fri., 10am-5pm Sat.) features women's clothing, with an emphasis on upscale brands. Upscale brands like Trina Turk are also on the racks at **Treehouse Boutique** (3000 N. State St., 601/982-3433, 10am-5:30pm Mon.-Sat.). You'll know you're in the right place when you see the little white house with hot pink doors and shutters.

The Orange Peel (422 Mitchell Ave., 601/364-9977, noon-6pm Mon., 10am-6pm Tues.-Fri., 10am-5pm Sat.) is a vintage consignment shop selling clothing and jewelry.

Old House Depot (639 Monroe St., 601/592-6200, www.oldhousedepot.com, 9am-5pm Tues.-Sat. or by appt.) is the only Jackson store on the Mississippi Antique Trail. The focus here is on architectural salvage: building parts that have been rescued from a demolition site. Look for stained-glass panels, doors, doorknobs, and other hardware.

Highland Village Shopping Center (4500 I-55 N., 601/982-5861, http://highlandvillagejxn.com, 10am-9pm daily) is the area's upscale shopping center, with pretty stonework, elevated walkways, fountains, and seasonal landscaping. The center has nearly 50 stores, including , Lululemon, and Whole Foods.

Food

Since 1935 **Mayflower Café** (123 W. Capitol St., 601/355-4122, www.mayflowercafems.com, 11am-10pm Mon.-Fri., 4pm-10pm Sat., $12-35) has been a Jackson mainstay. It's the oldest restaurant in town, and was said to be Eudora Welty's favorite. Come here for seafood, steaks, and serious old-time ambience, plus an amazing neon sign.

Parlor Market (115 W. Capitol St., 601/360-0090, http://parlormarket.com, 11am-2pm and 4:30pm-10pm Mon.-Fri., 5pm-10pm Sat., $10-39) is one of Jackson's most compelling restaurants. A cozy yet modern decor complements what the chef calls "seasonal Southern." Think: duck carbonara, General Tso's pork cheeks, and duck breast in a sweet tea brine.

Located in a new building in historic Bellhaven, **Manship Woodfired Kitchen** (1200 N. State St., 601/398-4562, http://themanshipjackson.com, 11am-8:30pm Mon., 11am-10pm Tues.-Fri., 10am-10pm Sat., 10am-2:30pm Sun., $7-34) serves wood-fired pizzas and other Italian-inspired dishes from the dining room, patio, or large bar.

Opened in 1946, ★ **Brent's Drugs** (655 Dueling Ave., 601/ 366-3427, www.brentsdrugs.com, 7am-5pm Mon., 7am-8:30pm Tues.-Fri., 8am-8:30pm Sat., 10am-3pm Sun., $3-11) was once the traditional pharmacy/soda fountain that every neighborhood used to have. Today, the soda fountain/restaurant has taken over the whole space, but the old-time feel remains. Come here for burgers, salads, penny candy, shakes, and malts, and to pose in a location from the movie *The Help*.

Jackson's Legal Still

Cathead Distillery

Southerners are proud of **Cathead Distillery** (422 S. Farish St., 601/667-3038, http://catheadvodka.com, tours hourly 3pm-6pm Thurs.-Fri., noon-8pm Sat., or by appt.), which claims to be the state's first legal still (there are plenty of illegal moonshiners in these parts). The name comes from a phrase in the blues music community, "That cat can play," meaning someone was respected by their peers. Take a tour, hang out and have a drink, shop for a bottle to take home, or find a local restaurant to mix you a cocktail.

Pickle-brined chicken, meatloaf, wedge salads and other classics at the aptly-named **Fine and Dandy** (100 District Blvd. E., 601/202-5050, www.eatdandy.com, 11am-10pm Mon.-Thurs., 11am-11pm Fri.-Sat., 11am-9pm Sun., $8-30).

Barbecue

The Pig & Pint (3139 N. State St., 601/326-6070, http://pigandpint.com, 11am-9pm Mon.-Sat.,$7-27) offers barbecue and craft beer. What more could you want? Barbecued meats are served in fun dishes (nachos, tacos, disco fries, and even salads). The signature is a sweet Mississippi-style barbecue sauce.

E&L Bar-b-que (1111 Bailey Ave., 601/355-5035, 11am-9pm Tues.-Thurs., 11am-11pm Fri.-Sat. $5-21) is a local favorite with chicken wings, smoked turkey legs, hot links, and the Jackson specialty, the pig ear sandwich.

Named an "American classic" by the James Beard Foundation, **Bully's** (3118 Livingston Rd., 601/362-0484, 11am-6pm Mon.-Sat., $6-9) has a menu of traditional soul food dishes like ham hocks, smothered oxtails, chitterlings, smothered liver and onions, turkey necks, fried pork chops, fried okra, fried green tomatoes, and banana pudding.

For more than 70 years Jacksonians have been coming to the **Big Apple Inn** (509 N. Farish St., 601/354-9371, 10am-6pm Tues.-Thurs., 10am-8pm Fri.-Sat., $5-10) for pig ear sandwiches and hot smoked sausage sandwiches (known as "smokes"). This is strictly no-frills, and an acquired taste, but definitely a classic.

Accommodations

Jackson has many hotels to accommodate state legislators and others visiting on official state business, as well as fans of Jackson State University's Baby Tigers. If you're coming to town when the legislature is in session or a football game is scheduled, room availability might be low. If you find yourself stuck, try Ridgeland (to the north) or Clinton (to the south).

Once the historic King Edward Hotel, the **Hilton Garden Inn Jackson Downtown** (235 W. Capitol St., 601/353-5464, http://hiltongardeninn3.hilton.com, $104-179) has 186 rooms with old-world charm and modern amenities. The pretty lobby is appealing and the bar can be hopping at night. It also has a fitness room, lounge, and indoor pool.

Hilton Jackson Hotel & Convention Center (1001 E. County Line Rd., 601/957-2800, www.hiltonjackson.com, $82-302) is popular for convention-goers, with its location, a fitness center, outdoor pool, and the popular Fitzgeralds Lobby Bar.

Head to the ★ **Fairview Inn** (734 Fairview St., 601/948-3429, http://fairviewinn.com, $199-339) for a Southern experience. This former 1908 Colonial Revival mansion on the Register of Historic Places is Jackson's only small luxury hotel. Amenities include a library, bar, restaurant, spa, and lovely gardens in which to stroll. The rooms are large, some with parlors and fireplaces and giant soaking tubs. Service is attentive, but more like a B&B than a traditional hotel.

Locals love to hang at the rooftop bar of the **Old Capitol Inn** (226 N. State St., 601/359-9000, http://oldcapitolinn.com, $99-175), which is housed in a pretty brick building that was once a YWCA. In addition to the rooftop garden, the hotel has a ballroom and Jacuzzi suites. The fitness center is next door.

Information and Services

Visit Jackson (308 East Pearl St., Ste. 301, 800/354-7695, http://visitjackson.com) is a good place to stop in and find brochures and other basic information on the city.

Clinton Visitor Center (MP 89)

The **Clinton Visitor Center** (1300 Pinehaven Dr., 601/924-2221, www.clintonms.org, 9am-5pm Mon.-Sat., 1pm-5pm Sun.) is an impressive oasis on the parkway. Built in 2004, it has nice restrooms, a large parking area, a brick patio, a free "little library" book exchange space, plus a small museum with exhibitions on the Trace and a gift shop. There are a few snacks in the gift shop, and the knowledgeable staff will help you figure out where to go and what to see in historic Clinton (they'll even make reservations for you or let you use the Wi-Fi to make your own). Pets are not permitted inside the building, but there are plenty of places to walk the dog on the grounds.

I-20 to Vicksburg

Vicksburg, on the banks of the Mississippi and Yazoo Rivers, is best known for its bloody battle during the Civil War. It was during the 47-day Siege of Vicksburg that the Union troops gained control of the Mississippi River, an event that many cite as the turning point in the Union's ability to win the war. It is called "The Key to the South," thanks to President Abraham Lincoln who called the city the key to winning the Civil War.

Today, Vicksburg is a city of more than 22,000, an attraction for those interested in military history and river culture. The street along the Mississippi River, Levee Street, is often referred to as

"Catfish Row," in literature and lore, and is a great place to take in a Mississippi Delta sunset.

The **Vicksburg Convention and Visitors Bureau** (52 Old Hwy. 27, 800/221-3536, http://visitvicksburg, 8am-5pm Mon.-Sat., 10am-5pm Sun.) operates a visitors center with a wealth of information about the region. There are **Mississippi Welcome Center** (4210 Washington St., 601/638-4269, www.visitmississippi.org, 8am-5pm daily) locations all over the state, of course, but this one is especially helpful because of Vicksburg's historical significance.

Leaving the Trace

Near **milepost 86,** turn left to exit the Natchez Trace Parkway, following signs for I-20 West. Drive west on I-20 for 29 miles (about 20 minutes). Take exit 4B to Vicksburg. Follow Clay Street to get into central Vicksburg.

Sights

Check out 21 exhibits about life on the river at the **Jesse Brent Lower Mississippi River Museum & Riverfront Interpretive Site** (910 Washington St., 601/638-9900, www.lmrm.org, 9am-4pm Mon..-Sat., 1pm-4pm Sun., free). Highlights include exhibits about the steamboat and the river as a highway, a 1,515-gallon aquarium featuring local fish species, displays on the 1926 Great Flood, and a Mississippi Flood River Model.

A $2.4 million renovation of the old railroad depot into **The Old Depot Museum** (1010 Levee St., 601/638-6500, www.vicksburgbattlefieldmuseum.net, 9am-5pm Mon.-Sat. Apr.-Sept., 10am-4pm Mon.-Sat. Oct.-Mar., adults $5.50, seniors and military $5, students $3.25) has resulted in this museum focused on transportation. Check out railroad memorabilia and models of military ships and riverboats, and exhibits from the old Vicksburg Battlefield Museum. Near here you can see murals along Catfish Row.

Coca-Cola was first bottled (anywhere in the world, not just Mississippi) at the **Biedenharn Coca-Cola Museum** (1107 Washington St., 601/638-6514, www.biedenharncoca-colamuseum.com, 9am-5pm Mon.-Sat., 1:30pm-4:30pm Sun., adults and children over 12 $3.50, children 6-12 $2.50, free for children under 6) in 1894. The packed museum features vintage Coca-Cola ads and memorabilia.

A piece of outsider art and religious history, **Margaret's Grocery** (4535 N. Washington St., 601/668-9611, donations accepted) is located on the site of a former grocery store that the late Reverend H. D. Dennis decorated to show his affection for his wife, Margaret. From a bright pink pulpit, Preacher (which is what everyone called Dennis) welcomed all with a message of love and tolerance. Since Dennis passed away, locals have been working to preserve and restore this icon. As you are driving down US 61 you can see the remains of the old grocery from the road: bright pink buildings, love-conquers-all signage, and pink religious iconography. The grocery, the pulpit, and the different artistic embellishments are stunning examples of outside art. You are welcome to take photos without crossing any fences. Call in advance to arrange a tour.

★ Vicksburg National Military Park

Vicksburg National Military Park (3201 Clay St., 601/636-0583, www.nps.gov/vick, 8am-5pm daily, $20 per vehicle, $15 per motorcycle, $10 per pedestrian) should be the first stop for Civil War buffs in Vicksburg. This park includes 1,325 historical monuments and markers, 20 miles of reconstructed trenches, a 16-mile tour road, a 12.5-mile walking trail, two different antebellum homes, 144 cannons, a restored gunboat, and more. If you have the time and want to see everything in detail, allot 1.5-2 hours here. Vehicle and motorcycle admissions are good for seven days.

Pick up a map at the visitors center to

take the self-guided driving tour. Some of the 15 sites on the driving tour include Fort Hill, an anchor of the Confederates' northern lines; Vicksburg National Military Cemetery, where 17,000 soldiers are buried (13,000 of whom are unknown); and Battery Selfridge, a naval cannon battery manned by the U.S. Navy.

While it's not possible to actually "get in the trenches," as the saying goes, you can get pretty close at Vicksburg. There are 20 miles of reconstructed trenches depicting those used during the Civil War. Get out of your car and look at them up close and imagine what it was like for soldiers on this battlefield. Don't miss the Confederate Trenches Exhibit in the visitors center, which shows what a trench looked like during that time, with model soldiers and supplies.

If you time your visit right, you can also tour the two antebellum homes in the park. The **Shirley House,** built in the 1830s, is the park's only wartime structure that's still intact; it served as headquarters for the 45th Illinois Infantry. Confederate soldiers were ordered to burn the houses, but reportedly, the soldier assigned to set fire to this house was shot before he could do so. The Shirley House is open for interior tours on weekends from Memorial Day through Labor Day. **Pemberton's Headquarters** (also called the Willis-Cowan House) is open to visitors 9am-4pm Monday in June and July.

The **USS *Cairo* Gunboat and Museum** (3201 Clay St., 601/636-0583, www.nps.gov/vick) is part of the park complex. The large, ironclad gunboat, which was sunk in 1862, is a sight worth exploring. In 1964, the gunboat was pulled from the river in three pieces, after which it was restored and reassembled at Vicksburg. Check out the 13 mounted cannons, reconstructed wood beams, a few original

Top to bottom: Lower Mississippi River Museum & Riverfront Interpretive Site; USS *Cairo*; Vicksburg National Military Park

floorboards, and artifacts such as sailors' supplies. The Cairo is one of four surviving Civil War-era ironclads.

A free **cell phone tour** (601/262-2100) complements the self-guided tour. While you can see the park on your own, a licensed guide from Vicksburg Convention and Visitors Bureau (601/636-0583, $50 per car for two hours, $67 per van, $100 per bus, $25-50 for each additional hour) can help make the giant park manageable.

Shopping

Downtown Vicksburg is dotted with fun boutiques and galleries. Among the standouts are **Lorelei Books** (1103 Washington St., 601/634-8624, http://loreleibooks.com, 10am-5pm Mon.-Sat.), which has a deep collection of fiction and military history. **Attic Gallery** (1101 Washington St., 601/638-9221, 10am-5pm Mon.-Sat.) is the oldest independent art gallery in the state of Mississippi. The walls (and floors and shelves) are stuffed with the works of local artists, from paintings to jewelry. **H. C. Porter Gallery** (1216 Washington St., 601/661-9444, www.hcporter.com/intro.asp, 10am-5pm Mon.-Sat.) features the works of Porter, a local artist who documents blues legends and life in the Delta.

Sports and Recreation

Vicksburg is built on a hill, so you'll get a good workout if you decide to see it on two wheels. Grab a bike from **Mobile Bicycle Rentals** (908 Cherry St., 662/347-0789, http://battlefield-bicycle-llc.constantcontactsites.com, 7:30am-noon and 1pm-7pm Mon.-Sat.).

Food

Enjoy views of the city from 10 stories up at **10 South Rooftop Bar & Grill** (1301 Washington St., 601/501-4600, www.10southrooftop.com, 11am-2pm and 5pm-9pm Tues.-Thurs. and Sun., 11am-2pm and 5pm-10pm Fri., 11am-10pm Sat., $12-34). The restaurant has a casual vibe and Southern menu. For dessert, try the chocolate-covered bacon and moon pie bread pudding.

The Biscuit Company (610 Grove St., 601/429-0035, http://thebiscuitcompanyofvicksburg.com, 11am-4pm and 5pm-9:30pm Mon.-Thurs., 11am-4pm and 5pm-10:30pm Fri.-Sat., $8-29) is housed in the historic National Biscuit Company building. The lively bar hosts karaoke plus live music. The menu is full of Southern-inspired dishes.

Walnut Hills Restaurant (1214 Adams St., 601/638-4910, http://walnuthillsms.com, 11am-9pm Mon. and Wed.-Sat., 11am-2pm Sun., $11-30) serves po'boys, fried chicken, fried catfish, shrimp and grits, and boiled shrimp on round tables.

If you are looking for Vicksburg locals during lunch, you'll likely find them at ★ **Main Street Market Café** (902 Cherry St., 601/634-8088, http://mainstreetmarketcafe.com, 11am-2pm and 5:30pm-7:30pm Mon., 11am-2pm Tues.-Fri., $10-25). Lunches here are big on Southern and Cajun specialties, but the meals aren't heavy or overly fried. Monday night dinners are reservation-only. The menu changes, but you'll always find hospitality and prime rib.

The Mississippi Delta is known for its tamales, and Vicksburg has two great places to taste the Southern delicacy: **The Tamale Place** (2190 S. Frontage Rd., 601/634-8900, 10am-8pm Mon. and Wed.-Sat., $3.50-11) and **Solly's Hot Tamales** (1921 Washington St., 601/636-2020, 10:30am-7pm Tues.-Sat., $2.50-9).

Locally crafted beers can be found at **KeyCity Brewing** (1309 Washington St., 601/501-7712, www.keycitybeer.com, 11am-11pm Sun.-Mon., 4pm-midnight Tues.-Thurs., 11am-midnight Fri.-Sat., $5-8), located downtown inside the **Cottonwood Public House** (1311 Washington St., 601/501-7712, 11am-11pm Sun.-Mon., 4pm-midnight Tues.-Thurs., 11am-midnight Fri.-Sat., $10-15). Cottonwood servers pizza, fries, wings, a grilled kim-cheese (that's a grilled cheese sandwich with kimchi mayo) and other food, plus, of course, KeyCity beer.

Accommodations

After Civil War history, the thing Vicksburg is best known for is riverboat casinos. There are several from which to choose, if that's your thing. While the casinos have hotels, you may visit and gamble without staying overnight.

The Ameristar (4116 Washington St., 601/638-1000, www.ameristar.com/vicksburg, 24 hours daily, $89-179) riverboat casino and hotel has 149 large rooms with soaking tubs, free Wi-Fi, an outdoor pool, and a free shuttle between the hotel and casino (which are adjacent, but not connected). There are several on-site restaurants, including Bourbon's, a steakhouse with a river view.

Formerly Diamond Jacks, **WaterView Casino and Hotel** (3990 Washington St., 601/636-5700, www.waterviewcasino.com, $79-219) has Las Vegas-style table games as well as an event center and several restaurants. Both smoking and non-smoking rooms are available.

Anchuca reportedly means "happy home" in Choctaw. And, chances are, you'll be happy if you stay at **Anchuca Historic Mansion and Inn** (1010 1st East St., 601/661-0111, www.anchuca.com, $165-240). Some of the eight rooms in this Greek Revival mansion and neighboring carriage house have gas-burning fireplaces. There's an on-site restaurant worth visiting even if you are not a guest as well as a bar and an outdoor pool. Tours of the home are offered daily 9:30am-4pm and are free for guests, $10 for history buffs who aren't staying on site.

There are 33 different rooms in five different buildings at **Cedar Grove Mansion, Inn & Restaurant** (2200 Oak St., 601/636-1000, www.cedargroveinn.com, $87-215). People love the sherry and chocolate turn-down service.

One of the oldest homes in Vicksburg, circa 1826, **The McNutt House** (815 1st East St., 601/529-2695, http://themcnutthouse.com, $50-135) is walking distance to downtown Vicksburg. All six rooms have kitchens or kitchenettes, and the vibe is more like efficiency-style apartments than a fancy B&B.

Back to the Trace

Return to the Natchez Trace Parkway by taking I-20 east for 29 miles (about 30 minutes). Take exit 34 and follow signs for the Trace. Turn left at the stop sign to continue south on the Trace near **milepost 86.**

Author David Cohn said, "The Mississippi Delta begins in the lobby of the Peabody Hotel in Memphis and ends on Catfish Row in Vicksburg." There's some poetic license with the name Catfish Row, but it illustrates how Vicksburg operates with one foot in the Delta and one foot out. Instead of returning to the Trace, you can opt to drive down the parkway, detour to Vicksburg, and drive back up the Delta to catch many of the Blues Trail sights.

Mangum Mound and Grindstone Ford (MP 45.7)

This is one of the very few places on the parkway where the signage can be confusing or inconsistent. Official maps and signage at the site itself call this Mangum Mound. However, the official Trace sign just says "Indian Mound." Follow this sign to the turnoff on the right side of the road for several options.

Veer to the left when the road splits to get to Mangum Mound, a burial ground from the late prehistoric period, between AD 1350 and AD 1500. There is no informational signage here, so just look at the hill and pay respects to the 84 people who are buried inside.

If you head right when the road splits, you'll follow a half-mile loop to Grindstone Ford. From here you can park

Rodney, a Southern Ghost Town

In the 1800s, Rodney was so significant to this region that it was the state capital. At its peak in the 1860s, there were as many as 4,000 people living in Rodney, and it was the busiest river port between New Orleans and St. Louis. The town sustained multiple banks, newspapers, churches, stores, and even Mississippi's first opera house.

But the town suffered from epidemics of yellow fever, fires from Civil War battles, and a slow economy, a result of being bypassed by the railroads. To add insult to injury, a sandbar formed in the Mississippi River, shifting the river two miles west of town, permanently crippling the city's economy.

Rodney church

Visitors to Rodney today can see remains from two striking 19th-century churches—which are in the process of being preserved and worth seeking out for architecture buffs—plus a former store, cemetery, and several other buildings. But this isn't quite an Old West ghost town; there are more plants and wildlife than dusty tumbleweeds. Eight people still live in Rodney. Should you make the detour here, be respectful of those who live here.

Getting There

Rodney is 10.4 miles west of the parkway off of MS-552. But these are winding, rural roads, so it may take more than 30 minutes to get there. About 10 miles south of Port Gibson, take MS-552 west for two miles. At Fellowship Road, turn left and after 0.6 mile, turn left again on Firetower Road. Take that for a mile and then veer to the right onto Rodney Road and continue for 6.5 miles. Retrace your steps to rejoin the Parkway. There are no services or amenities on this route. This is an easy side trip before or after Windsor Ruins.

in the parking lot and take a relatively easy 0.4-mile walk through a section of the Old Trace. The path isn't difficult and should take about 10 minutes to walk. It is not paved and there are elevation changes.

There are no amenities at either end of this stop. Your vehicle must have a clearance of 11 feet 6 inches to access this site.

MS-18 to Port Gibson

When Union general Ulysses S. Grant led troops here in May 1863 as part of the Vicksburg campaign, a battle was waged and more than 200 soldiers from both sides perished. But unlike so many cities in the Civil War, Port Gibson wasn't scorched, as Grant felt the city "was too beautiful to burn."

Today the beautiful buildings are still in place. Explore the historic buildings, as well as plantations and military sites.

Leaving the Trace

To get to Port Gibson, exit the parkway (near **milepost 41**) to the right, following signs for Port Gibson. When you come to MS-18, turn right and drive west for about a mile. Turn left at the intersection with US 61 and drive south. US 61 bisects Port Gibson.

Sights

More than 40 houses that date back to 1800 are part of the **Port Gibson Historic District** (http://portgibsonms.org). The district runs along US 61, which becomes Church Street once you get to Port Gibson, in between Orange Street to the north and Greenwood Street to the south. Don't miss Engelson House, which has the oldest formal gardens in the state. City Hall has a display of historical photos from early Port Gibson.

Once an outpost during the Civil War, **Grand Gulf Military Park** (12006 Grand-Gulf Rd., 601/437-5911, adults $4, seniors $3, students $1) is now a lovely state park. Grand Gulf was once a port on the Mississippi River, but when the river shifted, it stopped being used and became uninhabited. Despite the vacant, ghost-town vibe of the empty buildings, and the remote location of the park, it is a surprisingly jam-packed site, with several lovely historic buildings, a submarine that was used by bootleggers during Prohibition, an observation tower with Mississippi River views, picnic tables, walking trails, Grand Gulf Cemetery, and a robust museum. You could spend an hour, a day, or a night as there's also a lovely campground (RV sites $25, tent sites $10-15). It's eight miles northwest of Port Gibson.

Accommodations

Isabella B&B (1009 Church St., 601/437-5097, $125-135 s/d, $25-25 for additional guests) is a B&B in a remodeled yellow Queen Anne home built in 1880. It features Wi-Fi, a full Southern breakfast, private bathrooms, and front porch with porch swing.

Back to the Trace

To return to the parkway, take US 61 south out of Port Gibson for about two miles. Exit the highway to the right, following signs for the Trace, then turn left to continue south (near **milepost 37**).

MS-552 to Lorman

Tiny Lorman is a delicious detour on exploring Port Gibson, Rodney, and the Windsor Ruins. It has a population of less than 2,000, but is a draw because of ★ **Old Country Store** (18801 US 61, 601/437-0661, 10am-4pm Sun.-Thurs., 10am-6pm Fri.-Sat., $13-23). It is here that you'll find some of the best fried chicken in the South (and that's saying something!). This is a combination store/flea market/restaurant. If you have a woman at your table, Mr. D will serenade you while you eat, singing songs about his grandmother. Food is served cafeteria-style and is all you can eat. Bring a business card to staple to the wall when you leave.

After you have eaten your weight in fried chicken, get back in the car and make the quick drive to **Windsor Ruins** (601/576-6952, open daily, dawn to dusk, free). It is about 12 miles from the Old Country Store and 4 miles from Lorman. As you drive up you'll see the ghostly remains of what was once the largest antebellum Greek Revival mansion ever built in Mississippi. In 1861 this stately home cost $175,000 to build. Enslaved people were forced to do much of the basic construction, and artists and craftsmen not just from Mississippi, but also from Europe, were hired to provide opulent finishes.

Windsor Ruins was used by both Confederate and Union troops during the Civil War. What's here now are 23 masonry Corinthian columns towering 45 feet above the Mississippi landscape. There's very little signage at the site, which is on the National Register of Historic Places, so you won't learn about the lives of those who lived, died, and were enslaved here. A visit to the ruins is one that is only visual in nature. The museum at nearby Grand Gulf Military Park has more information about

Windsor Ruins, including images and replicas of the home.

Getting There

Exit the parkway at milepost 30, which is MS-552, and drive one mile east. To continue to Windsor Ruins, stay on MS-552 for three more miles until you get to the fork in the road at Rodney Road. Continue straight for one mile and the ruins will be on your right. Retrace your steps to return to the parkway.

★ Mount Locust Historic House (MP 15.5)

Since it was built in 1780, **Mount Locust** (no phone, 8:30am-5pm daily, free) has been an important place on the Trace. The site has a rich and complicated history. John Blommart originally built it as his homestead, but he quickly lost it after being jailed for leading a failed rebellion against the Spanish. It was purchased by William and Polly Ferguson in 1784. After William died, Polly eventually began running the farm as a rest stop and inn for the Kaintuck boatmen who used the Trace to return north after boating their goods down the Mississippi, which was an unusual position of power for a woman at the time. By the mid-1820s, when development slowed the commercial traffic on the Trace, Polly turned Mount Locust into a vacation refuge for those from the town of Natchez.

Slavery was part of life at Mount Locust. The 1820 census lists 26 enslaved people at Mount Locust; a few decades later that number climbed to 51. Like many of the remote National Park sites, Mount Locust has detailed interpretive signage, and what is there and is in the handouts, gives detail on how cramped these quarters were for the enslaved and how little they received for their hard labor.

The National Park Service began restoring Mount Locust in 1954, and returned it to its 1820 state. Get a map from the ranger station and take a self-guided tour through the furnished home, former kitchen site, cemeteries, and more. The slave quarters are no longer standing and the slave cemetery did not have headstones, although there is a marker with names so that they may be honored. You can visit these sites, but you won't see physical structures. The pathway to the home is paved. Informative detailed signage is included throughout the site.

Mount Locust is visible from the parkway. The restrooms here are the last ones on the parkway, unless you exit at Natchez State Park. There are picnic areas as well. Mount Locust is a particularly good stop for kids and history buffs. Plan to stay 45 minutes to an hour.

Emerald Mound (MP 10.3)

Emerald Mound is, at 80 acres, the second largest ceremonial mound in the United States. Built between AD 1250 and 1600 by the Natchez people, this is the largest mound along the parkway.

Unlike at other mounds, you are encouraged to walk part way up the flat-top mound, which is about 70 feet high. There's a short but steep paved path to the base of the mound. This is wheelchair-accessible (if you are experienced with braking). You can walk around the site at this level. There used to be a wooden staircase to the very top; it's no longer here but there are still good views of the scenery, and area wildlife, including cardinals and other birds.

To get to Emerald Mound, turn right to exit at MS-553. When the highway curves to the right, stay straight and follow signs for Emerald Mound. This is a paved, but rough, road. The U-shaped parking lot is on the right after nearly one mile.

Natchez State Park (MP 10.3)

Natchez State Park (230 Wickliff Rd., 601/442-2658, day-use $4 per car) is a quick detour (5-10 minutes each way) off of the parkway. Here you'll find restrooms, showers, campsites ($15-28) and cabins (no pets permitted, $35-110), picnic areas, a boat launch, disc golf course, and a playground for kids. The park has more than 13 miles of hiking trails. Hunting and fishing are permitted with state licenses.

To get to Natchez State Park, turn left at MS-553. This is the same exit as Emerald Mound, but on the south side of the Trace. After about half a mile, the highway goes under US 61 and turns into State Park Road. Turn left on Wickliff Road and continue less than 0.4 mile to the park entrance.

Elizabeth Female Academy (MP 5.1)

Founded in 1818 by the Methodist church, this was the site of the first institution of higher learning for women in Mississippi. It is one of the few places on the parkway where you can see the ruins of the building itself, rather than just a marker. The site, which is on the National Register of Historic Landmarks, is open sunrise to sunset.

Check out the brick remains of the building, which was burned in a fire in 1870, long after it closed in 1845. The pathway to the ruins (0.3 mile) is wheelchair accessible and goes along the side road (Old US 84) to Washington, Mississippi. This is an out-and-back trail.

Exit the parkway on the right side and follow a long drive to the parking area, which is not visible from the road. There are no other amenities, but you're just five miles from the city of Natchez. This is your last stop on the parkway heading south.

Natchez

The Natchez Trace wouldn't exist without the city of Natchez. French settlers built a fort on the banks of the Mississippi River in 1716; archaeological excavations suggest that people have been living on this land since the 8th century AD. It's clearly the oldest city on the mighty Mississippi; it's been controlled by the French, the Spanish, and the British, and influences of all three still can be seen in the culture. You can delve into steamboat culture whether you arrive by riverboat cruise or not. As the southern terminus of the parkway, it's a great place to celebrate the end of your 444-mile trek and transition into Cajun culture before heading on to New Orleans.

Some people spend days in Natchez doing nothing but touring preserved and restored historical homes (and sleeping and eating in them, as some are B&Bs). Many do so during the Fall and Spring Pilgrimage, multi-week home and garden tour programs and dinners, combined with lectures, plays, and guides dressed in period costumes. Pilgrimage was the brainchild of local women in the 1930s who decided to open the city's preserved antebellum homes for tours to help reverse Natchez's economic decline. (More than one local says the reason that Natchez preserved these homes was not forethought, but that the town was too poor to knock them down.) Some feel that these tours glorify the city's past and ignore the human costs of Black enslavement, which is inexorably intwined with these homes. Today, discussions of slavery and race are often incorporated into tours, yet not all, and enslavement is often a side note, rather than the focus. Regardless of whether or not you intend to participate in Pilgrimage, you should be aware of its dates, as rooms book early, room rates are higher, and the area draws more crowds.

Leaving the Trace

The southern terminus of the parkway is just north of Liberty Road in Natchez, about 2.5 miles east of downtown. To get to downtown Natchez, exit to the right and take Liberty Road west, which will turn into John A. Quitman Boulevard, then Main Street. Consider turning into the small pullout on the left just before exiting to get a photo or two at the southern terminus and parkway signs.

Sights

A network of walkways and streets totaling 5.6 miles runs through downtown Natchez and along the boardwalk near the Mississippi River bluff. Color-coded signs help direct you on thematic walks, and there are informational signs along the way detailing local history, archaeology, and the environment. Pick up a map at the **Natchez Visitor Center** (640 S. Canal St., 800/647-6724 or 601/446-6345, http://visitnatchez.org, 8am-5pm Mon.-Sat., 9am-4pm Sun.), which should be your first stop when you get to town. With views of the Mississippi River, this is not your average visitors center. The National Park Service operates the building and maintains an office here. Exhibits about the city, a small movie theater showing a 20-minute film ($2) about Natchez can be found here, too.

The historic district of **Under-the-Hill** (between Canal St. and Broadway along the Mississippi River) was once the center of all activity in Natchez; in the 1700s it was like the Wild West, hosting outlaws of all types. Today it's home to a strip of restaurants, shops, and rental houses with great river views and a storied history. The neighborhood is part of the **Natchez National Historic Park,** which also includes **Fort Rosalie National Historical Park** and several other sites, and is managed by the National Park Service.

The **William Johnson House** (210 State St., 601/445-5345, www.nps.gov/natc, 9am-12pm & 1pm-5pm Mon.-Sat., noon-5pm Sun., free) is a brick building where freed-slave-turned-barber William Johnson and his family once lived. Downstairs is a museum that includes detailed excerpts from Johnson's diaries, giving a glimpse of what life was like for this former enslaved person who, once freed, had enslaved people performing tasks and labor at his home. The house is run by the National Park Service, and many of the interpretive materials are written in a way that makes them accessible to both children and adults. Upstairs the former Johnson family home is preserved. The stories told through Johnson's belongings and diaries aren't uplifting; Johnson is candid about his cruelty to his slaves. They tell a layered story of enslavement in early19th century Natchez.

The 128-acre **Grand Village of the Natchez Indians State Historic Site** (400 Jefferson Davis Blvd., 601/446-6502, www.nps.gov, 9am-5pm Mon.-Sat., 1:30pm-5pm Sun., free) offers a look at the political and religious capital of the Natchez chiefdom of the late 17th century and early 18th century. Start in the small museum with a seven-minute film to get an overview of the area. Check out the artifacts inside and then go outside and explore the three Natchez Indian mounds. These are thought to have been used as a ceremonial plaza and residential areas, rather than burial mounds. The Grand Village is one of the National Park Service sites in Natchez, and is undergoing a significant renovation and expansion. The gift shop has a particularly impressive selection of books, baskets, and jewelry.

During the 19th century, the **Forks of the Road** (232 St. Catherine St.) was one of the largest slave markets in the country easily the largest in the state of Mississippi, and enslaved people throughout the region were likely bought and sold here. Today this outdoor area consists of several solemn plaques that tell the brutal story of humans being treated like property, as well as the tasks which enslaved

people were forced to perform. This cruel marketplace was operational between 1808 and 1863, until Union troops occupied the city of Natchez. The signage also includes an ad about a runaway slave and a concrete display includes replicas of shackles used to keep humans in place. A future interpretive center is in the planning stages.

On the banks of the mighty Mississippi, the **Natchez National Cemetery** (41 Cemetery Rd., 601/445-4981, 8am-sunset daily) contains the headstones of many of Natchez's famous—and infamous—names, including two buffalo soldiers, members of the African American 24th U.S. Infantry regiments. The cemetery was established in 1866.

More than 500 photographs of Natchez throughout history are on display at the **Natchez in Historic Photographs at Stratton Chapel Gallery** (405 State St., 601/442-4741, 10am-4pm Mon.-Sat., $5 donation requested). Come see the ups and downs of this river town through the lens of photographers throughout time. The museum-quality exhibition is well organized, and is a must-see for anyone interested in Southern history.

Richard Wright, the author of *Uncle Tom's Children* and *Native Son,* grew up in Natchez. You can view the exterior of **Richard Wright's Childhood Home** (20 E. Woodlawn St.).

See exhibitions about African American life in Natchez during the Civil War and the civil rights era at the **Museum of African-American History and Culture** (301 Main St., 601/445-0728, 10am-4:30pm Mon.-Fri., 10am-2pm Sat., free, $7 donation encouraged).

Antebellum Architecture

Owned and operated by the Mississippi State Society Daughters of the American Revolution (MSSDAR), **Rosalie Mansion**

Top to bottom: Grand Village of the Natchez Indians State Historic Site; Mount Locust Historic House; Stanton Hall

and Bicentennial Gardens (100 Orleans St., 601/446-5676, http://rosaliemansion.com, 9am-5pm daily Mar.-Oct., 10am-4pm daily Nov.-Feb., $15) was built in 1823. Over its history families who lived here helped found the Natchez Children's Home and housed orphans. In addition to the mansion, there are several gardens on-site to tour: Janet Terreson Sims Memorial Rose Garden, Patricia Walton Shelby Bicentennial Garden, and Walter Reed Page Smith Garden. If you're interested in genealogical research, MSSDAR's library here is open to the public.

Stanton Hall (401 High St., 601/445-5151, tours every 30 min. 9am-4:30pm daily, $25 adults, $15 youth 12-17, children 11 and under free) is a massive Greek Revival mansion that takes up a whole city block. Built by cotton merchant Frederick Stanton in 1859, Stanton Hall was occupied by Union soldiers during the Civil War and also housed Stanton College for Young Ladies. Now owned by the Pilgrimage Garden Club, Stanton Hall also has the **Carriage House Restaurant** (601/445-5151, 11am-2pm Wed.-Sun.), which serves Southern cuisine, blue plate specials, and a Sunday buffet brunch.

Owned by the Pilgrimage Garden Club, **Longwood** (140 Lower Woodville Dr., 601/442-5193, tours every 30 min. 9am-4:30pm daily, $20) has a curious and sad story. What would have been the largest octagonal house in the world was begun in 1860 for Haller Nutt, a wealthy cotton planter. But Nutt's fortunes changed, and although he was a Union sympathizer, many of his fields were burned during the Civil War. The house was never completed and has been preserved as such, so you can see both the finished and unfinished sections, giving you an architectural tour unlike any other. Stroll around the gardens and see the family cemetery.

Entertainment and Events

Nightlife

Under-the-Hill Saloon (25 Silver St., 601/446-8023, 10am-3am daily or at bartender's discretion) has been around since the 1800s, features live music as well as karaoke, and serves beers. The courtyard is a nice place to hang out in temperate weather. In spring, you can see poppies blooming along the riverbank.

The family-run **Natchez Brewing Co.** (207 High St., 828/788-3315, www.natchezbrew.com, 11am-1:30pm and 4pm-9pm Mon.-Fri., noon-9pm Sat., noon-6pm Sun., $5-12) brews its own beers and has a nice patio on which you can enjoy them while listing to live music or hanging out with new friends.

Mississippi is known for its blues music and its biscuits, so of course you want to combine them at **Biscuits and Blues** (315 Main St., 601/446-9922, http://biscuitsandblues.com, 11am-2pm and 5pm-10pm Tues.-Thurs., 11am-11pm Fri.-Sat., 11am-9pm, $12-28). Call ahead to confirm it's open; this Southern fare restaurant is only open on days when live music performances are scheduled.

Smoots Grocery Blues Lounge (319 N. Broadway St., 601/653-0731, www.smootsgrocery.com, 4pm-midnight Thurs.-Fri., 3pm-midnight Sat., 3pm-8pm Sun., $3-12) was once a grocery store by day and a juke joint by night. Now it is a live music venue featuring a wide array (not just blues) of acts, largely consisting of local performers, rather than touring acts.

The **Magnolia Bluffs Casino** (7 Roth Hill Rd., 601/235-0045 or 888/505-5777, www.magnoliabluffscasinos.com) has 450 slot machines. It's also a venue for live music and has a buffet restaurant, a bistro, a steakhouse, several bars, and a full-service hotel.

Festivals and Events

The last weekend in February, the **Natchez Literary and Cinema Celebration** (www.colin.edu) brings authors and others to lead readings and discussions and to sign books, all around a different annual theme. Most events are free, but some higher-profile events may be ticketed.

Held annually in March at the Grand Village of the Natchez Indians, **Natchez Pow-Wow** (400 Jefferson Davis Blvd., www.natchezpowwow.com, adults $5, children $3) includes dancing, music, and booths selling food and Native American crafts.

The **Natchez Balloon Festival** (100 Orleans St., 601/442-2500, natchezballoonfestival.com) is one of Natchez's most beloved annual events, held at the grounds of Rosalie Mansion each October. Pilots launch their balloons twice daily (weather dependent) and sail over the Mississippi. Tethered balloon rides are offered to the public.

Shopping

The shopping in Natchez is heavily skewed toward antiques.

As You Like It Silver Shop (410 N. Commerce St., 601/442-0933, 11am-5pm Tues.-Fri., 10:30am-5pm Sat.) is located inside the carriage house on the Stanton Hall property. Hours can vary as it's a one-woman show, but it is a destination for those who collect silver. **Mrs. Holder's Antiques** (634 Franklin St., 601/442-0675, www.mrsholdersantiques.com, 11am-5pm Tues.-Sat. or by appt.) is a full-service antiques store, with furniture, housewares, and linens.

Turning Pages Bookstore (520 Franklin St., 601/442-2299, http://turningpagesbooks.com, 10am-5:30pm Mon.-Sat., 1pm-5pm Sun.) looks small but has a well-edited selection of books in a variety of genres. It has a particularly in-depth selection of garden and history books.

Across the street from Fort Rosalie National Historical Park, **Old South Trading Post** (600 S. Canal St., 601/446-5354, http://natchezshop.com, 9am-5pm Sun.-Fri., 9am-6pm Sat.) stocks some local jams and jellies, but this is also the place to find souvenirs, books, T-shirts, and other gifts to take home. The knowledgeable staff will offer you a cup of coffee and answer any questions about Natchez.

Both **Arts Natchez** (425 Main St., 601/442-0043, http://artsnatchez.com, 10am-5pm daily) and **Crafted Gallery** (209 Franklin St., 601/334-9759, http://craftedgallery.com, 10am-6pm Tues.-Sat.) feature works by local artists.

In the Under-the-Hill district, **Silver Street Gallery and Gifts** (27 Silver St., 601/870-1237, 10am-6pm Tues.-Sat., noon-5pm Sun.) is stocked with souvenirs, gifts, jewelry, and other lovely items, plus there's a great view of the Mississippi.

Food

Housed in the oldest building in Mississippi is ★ **King's Tavern** (613 Jefferson St., 601/446-5003, www.kingstavernnatchez.com, 5pm-10pm Thurs.-Fri., noon-10pm Sat.-Sun., $15-28), the oldest restaurant in Mississippi. While the building may have been constructed in 1789, the menu is anything but dated. Chef Regina Charboneau and her husband serve inspired flatbreads, sandwiches, and salads, many made with herbs and vegetables grown in their small plot. The cocktail bar serves small-batch spirits, including those from their adjacent **Charboneau Distillery** (617 Jefferson St., 601/861-4203, www.charboneaudistillery.com, tours hourly 5pm-7pm Fri., noon-6pm Sat., $10). Regina Charboneau is also known as the Queen of Biscuits; **Regina's Kitchen Wine Bar and Cooking School** (312 Main St., www.reginaskitchen.com, 601/392-1756, 5pm-10pm daily, $7-30) is more upscale than King's Tavern. You can have a drink at the wine bar, make a reservation for dinner, or sign up for a class and learn from the master.

A favorite among the innkeepers and locals in Natchez, **Cotton Alley Café** (208 Main St., 601/442-7452, http://cottonalleycafe.com, 11am-2pm and 5:30pm-9pm Mon.-Sat., $11-32) serves Southern- and Italian-inspired fare, including pastas, burgers, sandwiches, and seafood, plus delicious desserts, in a cozy downtown environment. The bar is a good place to eat if you're traveling alone. The kitchen will make vegetarian dishes on request.

As you'd expect from its name, **Fat Mama's Tamales** (303 S. Canal St., 601/442-4548, http://fatmamastamales.com, 11am-9pm Mon.-Thurs., 11am-10pm Fri.-Sat., noon-7pm Sun., $5-10) specializes in tamales sold by the half dozen and dozen. It also serves chili, taco salads, and taco soup. The frozen Knock-You-Naked margaritas are local favorites.

Restaurant 1818 (36 Melrose Ave., 601/442-5852, www.monmouthhistoricinn.com, 6pm-8:30pm daily, $12-38) is the city's most elegant restaurant, housed in two parlors of the Monmouth Inn. You'll experience first-class service while indulging in contemporary cuisine (think duck breast with green onion risotto, wilted spinach, blueberries, and crispy mushrooms). Hours are extended to seven days a week during Pilgrimage. Reservations are required.

It doesn't look like much, but **The Donut Shop** (501 John R. Junkin Dr., 601/442-2317, 6am-7pm Tues.-Sat., 6am-2pm Sun., $1-7) shouldn't be missed. The doughnuts, with creative varieties that change daily—like chocolate peanut butter chip—are the reason the parking lot is packed all day. Also available are salads, sandwiches, gyros, and dinner platters featuring items such as country-fried steak. Another blink-and-you'll-miss it Natchez staple, **The Malt Shop** (4 Homochitto St., 601/445-4843, 10am-9:30pm Mon.-Thurs., 10am-10pm Fri.-Sat., 11am-9pm Sun., $4-7) has been

Top to bottom: Under-the-Hill Saloon; The Donut Shop; Fat Mama's Tamales

offering burgers and shakes since the 1960s. Note there's no indoor seating.

Head to **The Camp** (21 Silver St., 601/897-0466, www.thecamprestaurant.com, 11am-9pm Sun.-Thurs., 11am-10pm Fri.-Sat., $12-18) in the Under-the-Hill district for local craft beer on tap and made-from-scratch sliders, burgers, sandwiches, fried catfish, ribs, and tacos. The backyard beer garden is serene, and the porch seating has a river view.

Started by then 16-year-old Hannah-Grace, **Rolling 'n' the Dough** (413 Franklin St., 601/653-0302, https://cookiedough-addict.com, noon-5pm Thurs.-Sat., $6-16) is essentially a scoop shop—but the scoops are cookie dough, not ice cream. Hannah-Grace's whole family now works in the dessert destination, which also sells baked goods and toffee.

Eat breakfast, grab a cup of joe, and talk to locals at **Natchez Coffee Company** (509 Franklin St., 601/304-1415, 7am-5:30pm Mon.-Sat., 7am-2pm Sun.), the city's bustling coffee shop.

Accommodations

Natchez is primarily a B&B and historic inn kind of town; staying in one is the best way to experience the city's culture and charm. If you are adamant about staying in a traditional hotel, there are a few options. For the B&Bs in this section, breakfast is included unless otherwise noted. Very few historic B&Bs are wheelchair-accessible and, if they are, have just one or two rooms that meet ADA requirements. If this is a necessity, call to discuss rather than booking online.

Hotel Vue (10 John R. Junkin Dr., 601/442-9976, www.hotelvuenatchez.com, $80-169) is one of the city's more contemporary spaces, with an outdoor pool, exercise room, and jaw-dropping views of the Mississippi River. **Pilot House** is the in-house restaurant and bar.

A free shuttle runs between the **Magnolia Bluff Casino-Hotel** (645 S. Canal St., 601/861-4600, www.magnoliabluffscasinos.com, $199-229) and the casino proper, as they are not in the same building. Breakfast is included in the room price. Magnolia Bluff also has Wi-Fi, a fitness center, and an outdoor pool.

It's hard to miss the **Natchez Grand Hotel and Suites** (111 N. Broadway St., 601/446-9994, www.natchezgrandhotel.com, $99-184), a large red brick building in downtown Natchez that was designed to look like the cotton baling factories of old. Rooms are either city view or river view. The hotel is adjacent to the Natchez Convention Center, and is walking distance to everything downtown. Cross the street to check out the stone marker that marks the start of the original Natchez Trace.

The three-room **1888 Wensel House** (206 Washington St., 888/775-8577, http://1888wenselhouse.com, $125) is a sweet Victorian home converted into a B&B within walking distance of the heart of downtown Natchez. Your stay includes fruit and wine in the parlor and Wi-Fi.

Built in 1836, **The Burn Bed & Breakfast** (712 N. Union St., 601/442-1344, http://theburnbnb.com, $168-180) is a three-story building with a lot of history. It was used as a hospital during the Civil War and is the setting of the 1994 novel *Pilgrimage: A Tale of Old Natchez*. In addition to plenty of modern amenities, such as private baths, Wi-Fi, and an outdoor pool, there's also bicycle storage for those who have cycled the Trace. Children under 12 are not allowed; neither are pets. A home and garden tour is included.

Owners Ron and Eleanor chose Natchez as their retirement destination and running a B&B as their second career, and their passion for both is clear at every turn at ★ **Devereaux Shields House** (709 N. Union St., 601/304-5378, www.dshieldsusa.com, $89-199). The main house is a restored 1893 Queen Anne Victorian; down the street are four more rooms in Aunt Clara's Cottage, which is pet-friendly. Both have gardens in back and private baths, plus amenities such as white noise machines, Wi-Fi, cable, and fluffy robes. Welcome receptions with wine and cheese occur every afternoon. The common areas are as luxurious as the private rooms, and the owners are enthusiastic about helping guests see the best of Natchez.

★ **Monmouth Historic Inn and Gardens** (1358 John A. Quitman Blvd., 601/442-5852, www.monmouthhistoricinn.com, $205-415) feels more like a resort than a B&B. There are 15 suites and 15 rooms between the historic main house and the smaller outbuildings, each with period furnishings and modern amenities. TVs and Wi-Fi are present, but hidden, so as not to detract from the old-world charm. The bathrooms are modern and luxurious. Some rooms have spa tubs or fireplaces. Fine-dining can be found at **Restaurant 1818,** while a full Southern breakfast is served in a garden building and evening hors d'oeuvres are in the bar. Tours of the home and grounds are offered at 10am and 2pm daily.

Housed in a restored 1836 clapboard home, **Garden Song B&B** (705 Washington St., 601/443-7664, www.gardensongbnb.com, $130-180) is a relaxing getaway, thanks to its gardens, extra touches like mini-fridges in each room, and owner Dan Gibson, who is known to play piano for his guests.

If river views are important to you, book a room at **Clifton House** (209 Clifton Ave., 601/445-6000, http://cliftonhousenatchez.com, $145-175) and be there during sunset.

Information and Services

Merit Health Natchez (54 Seargent Prentiss Dr., 601/443-2100, www.merithealthnatchez.com) is the hospital closest to the southern terminus of the parkway.

For motorcycle repair, try **Natchez Powersports** (730 US 61 N., 601/446-6211, www.natchezpowersports.com, 8:30am-6pm Tues.-Fri., 8:30am-2:30pm Sat.).

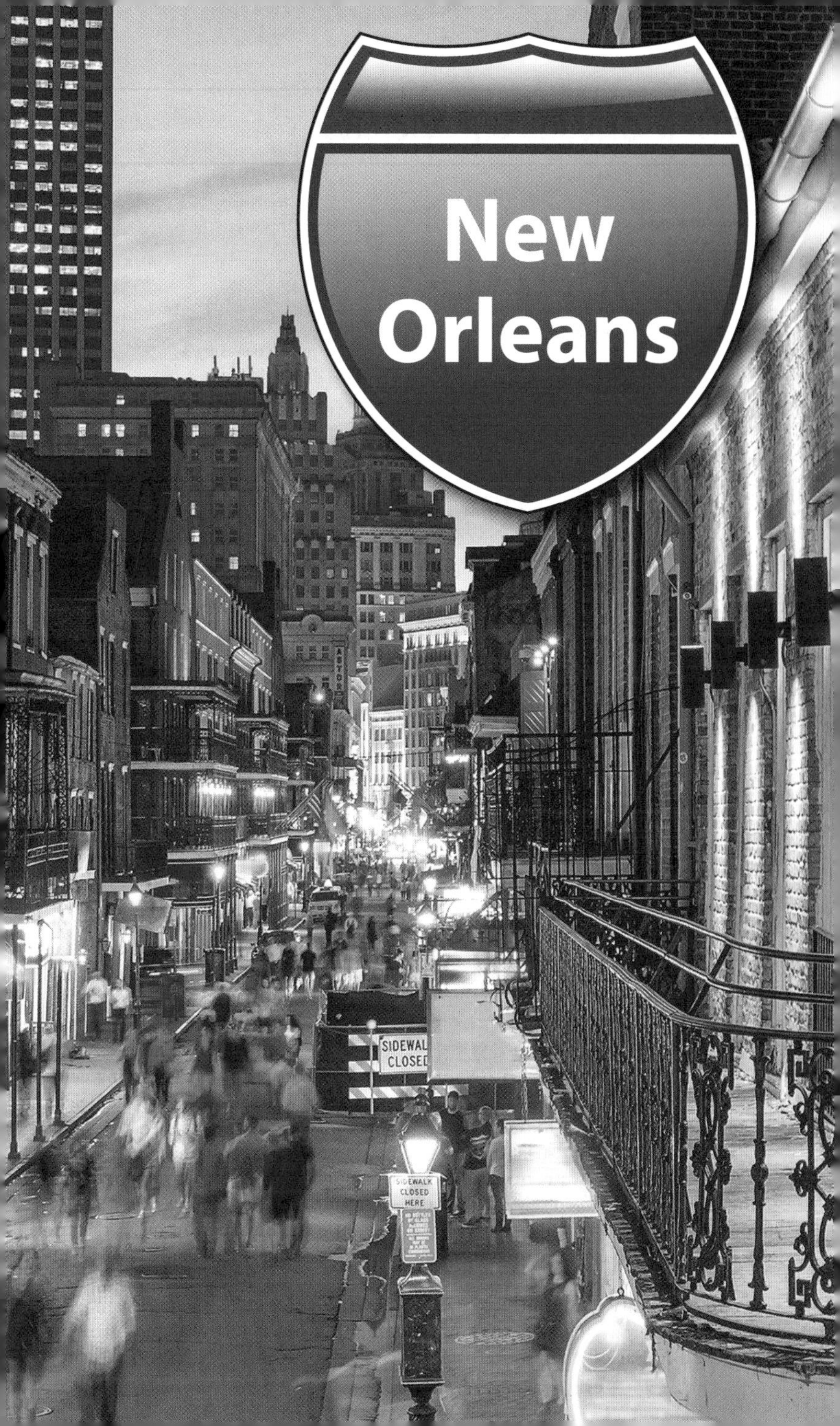
New
Orleans
ASTOR
SIDEWAL
CLOSED
SIDEWALK
CLOSED
HERE

New Orleans and Vicinity

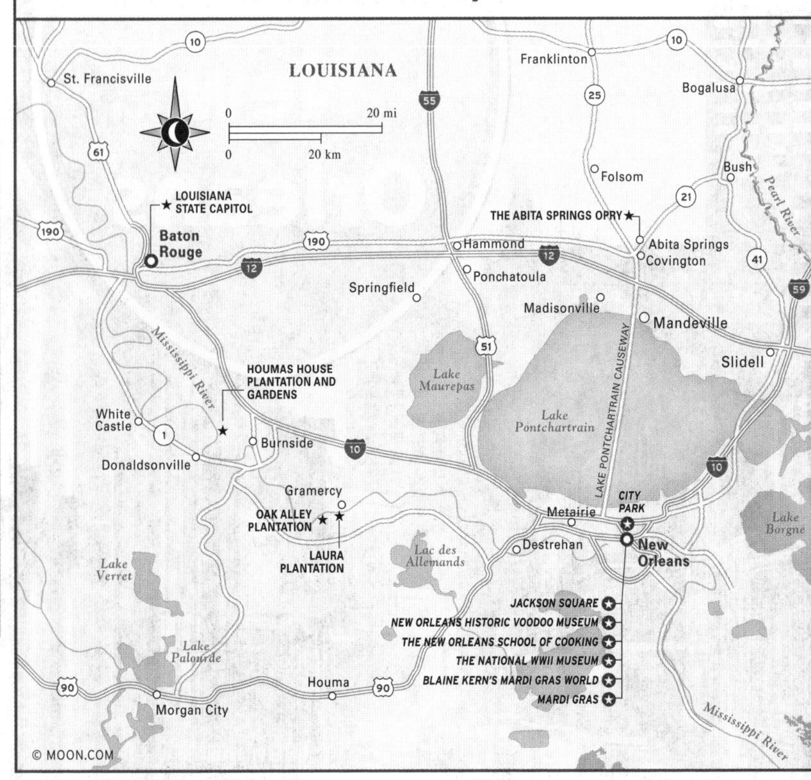

Although the city is famed for its raucous Mardi Gras, there's more to New Orleans. It's family-friendly, a mecca for art, and has countless historic sites.

Families come for kid-friendly places like the Audubon Aquarium of the Americas, Blaine Kern's Mardi Gras World, and the Audubon Zoo. Art lovers flock to the New Orleans Museum of Art, and outdoor enthusiasts appreciate oases like City Park. But it's history buffs who are particularly enamored with the Big Easy. Besides engrossing exhibits at The National WWII Museum, the Crescent City—and particularly the French Quarter—boasts an array of historic structures.

There's history beyond the Quarter, too, from the distinctive homes of the Garden District to the crumbling cemeteries in the Tremé and Mid-City neighborhoods. In a city defined by water, many natives enjoy simply wandering through Woldenberg Riverfront Park alongside the Mississippi River.

While the destruction of Hurricane Katrina is still evident in areas like Mid-City, the Ninth Ward, and New Orleans East, New Orleans has experienced a rebirth since 2005. This fast-growing city is brimming with refurbished

Highlights

★ **Jackson Square:** The heart and soul of the French Quarter, this scenic spot is the perfect place to start your Big Easy adventure (page 329).

★ **New Orleans Historic Voodoo Museum:** Dive into the city's colorful past, with tales of voodoo priestesses and zombies, ritual art, and a stroll through St. Louis Cemetery No. 1 (page 336).

★ **The New Orleans School of Cooking:** Want to make gumbo or shrimp Creole like a native? This is the place to hone your skills (page 341).

★ **The National WWII Museum:** You'll feel immersed in historic battles thanks to the interactive exhibits at this museum (page 344).

★ **Blaine Kern's Mardi Gras World:** Stroll amid kaleidoscopic parade floats in progress, observe artists at work, and get a behind-the-scenes look at Mardi Gras in the making (page 348).

★ **City Park:** This 1,300-acre swath of greenery boasts picturesque bridges, moss-covered oak trees, and the New Orleans Botanical Garden (page 350).

★ **Mardi Gras:** Nothing exemplifies the joyous spirit of New Orleans more than this annual celebration (page 365).

Best Restaurants

★ **Galatoire's Restaurant:** This quintessential old-school New Orleans spot serves superb Creole fare from time-tested recipes (page 381).

★ **Commander's Palace:** Book a table at this legendary restaurant in the Garden District (page 391).

★ **Jacques-Imo's Cafe:** This funky favorite is known for innovative Creole and Cajun food, huge portions, sassy service—and long waits (page 391).

★ **Angelo Brocato:** This quaint spot has doled out delicious homemade ice cream and Italian pastries for more than a century (page 392).

★ **Ralph's on the Park:** Part of the fun of brunch here is the creative and beautifully presented nouvelle Creole cuisine, but the other benefit is strolling adjacent City Park afterward (page 392).

★ **Elsie's Plate & Pie:** Indulge your cravings for comfort food at this Baton Rouge spot (page 406).

attractions, brand-new establishments, and re-energized residents.

Planning Your Time

While you can get a taste of New Orleans in a long weekend, staying **five days** (or more) allows you to fully experience the city.

Although New Orleans is a year-round destination, **summer** is the least crowded time to visit, except during major events like the **Essence Festival** and **Southern Decadence.** Temperatures are fairly high June-September, with an average high of about 91°F, when hurricane season is at its peak. While **fall** is more comfortable, **winter** and **spring** constitute the high season here. Annual events, such as **Mardi Gras,** the **French Quarter Festival,** and the **New Orleans Jazz & Heritage Festival,** lure the bulk of out-of-towners during these months.

The date for Mardi Gras shifts every season (it is always 47 days before Easter). Lodging rates are inflated in high season, as well as during major events and holiday weekends, and advance reservations may be necessary.

Getting There

Car

From Natchez

The drive south from Natchez, Mississippi, the southern terminus of the Natchez Trace Parkway, to New Orleans, is about three hours on US 61 if you don't make any stops. But these 174 miles are a lot more fun if you take your time and stop in Baton Rouge. From Natchez, take US 61 south for about 80 miles. Take the exit for I-110 South, then follow the interstate for about eight miles. Take exit 1G to reach downtown Baton Rouge. Continue to Baton Rouge by taking I-10 east for about 85 miles.

From Baton Rouge

From downtown Baton Rouge, follow I-10 east for roughly 85 miles. From I-10, take exit 234B to Poydras Street; at this point you'll be just a few blocks south of the French Quarter. Without any stops, the drive should take about two hours. Another scenic alternative is to take the Great River Road, which adds hours to the drive, but allows you to stop a Whitney Plantation.

Best Accommodations

★ **Royal Sonesta New Orleans:** Enjoy the revelry from this prime location on Bourbon Street (page 394).

★ **Hotel Monteleone:** This handsome hotel has long been a favored address among American writers (page 394).

★ **Hotel Peter and Paul:** A former church site is now one of New Orleans's most stylish places to sleep (396).

★ **International House New Orleans:** Creatively decorated, this hotel draws a hip crowd (page 398).

★ **Pontchartrain:** Imagine you live in New Orleans with a stay in this retro apartment-building-turned-hotel that boasts a lively bar scene (page 399).

★ **The Green House Inn:** This inn delights visitors with its funky, tropical decor, flower-named rooms, and clothing-optional pool (page 399).

From Jackson

If you want to skip to scenic route (and the southern terminus of the Natchez Trace Parkway), the drive from Jackson, Mississippi along I-55 is 187 miles of largely interstate driving. It takes just three hours and crosses Lake Pontchartrain. On this route you could easily add a 25-minute detour east on I-12 to see Abita Springs (page 401) and head south over the Lake Pontchartrain Causeway (toll required) and I-10 to reach New Orleans (45 miles, roughly one hour).

Air

Louis Armstrong New Orleans International Airport (900 Airline Dr., Kenner, 504/303-7500, www.flymsy.com), 15 miles west of downtown New Orleans via I-10, is a massive facility that accommodates the entire Gulf South with service on several airlines. It's easy to find direct flights from most major U.S. cities: Dallas, Houston, Atlanta, Orlando, Miami, Charlotte, Nashville, Newark, New York, Chicago, Minneapolis, Denver, Las Vegas, Reno, and San Francisco. British Airways flies direct from London four times per week. A $1 billion terminal, designed by Cesar Pelli, opened in 2019 and includes 30 gates, 2,000 parking spaces, lots of local boutiques and restaurants, and a new access road.

Commercial air service is also available to Baton Rouge and Lafayette. Situated roughly eight miles north of downtown Baton Rouge via I-110, **Baton Rouge Metropolitan Airport** (9430 Jackie Cochran Dr., 225/355-0333, www.flybtr.com) is served by American Airlines and Delta, with frequent direct flights to and from Atlanta, Dallas, Houston, and Memphis. **Lafayette Regional Airport** (200 Terminal Dr., 337/266-4400, www.lftairport.com) is three miles southeast of downtown Lafayette via US-90. It is served by American Eagle, the Delta Connection, and United Express, with direct flights to and from Atlanta, Dallas, Houston, and Memphis. If you choose to fly into one of these regional airports, you'll have to rent a car to reach New Orleans. Avis, Budget, Hertz, National, and Enterprise serve both locales.

Airport Transportation

Depending on traffic, the 15-mile trip from the airport to the French Quarter

Two Days in New Orleans

Day 1

Start your day in the French Quarter with some warm café au lait and sugar-covered beignets at the world-famous **Café Du Monde,** part of the historic **French Market,** a collection of eateries, gift stores, and praline shops.

After breakfast, stroll through picturesque **Jackson Square** and tour the stunning structures that surround this well-landscaped park and promenade. Besides the majestic **St. Louis Cathedral,** you'll see curious historical exhibits inside the **Cabildo** and the **Presbytère** and glimpse period Creole furnishings inside the **1850 House,** part of the lovely **Pontalba Apartments.**

Stroll past the quaint boutiques and verdant balconies of Chartres Street, then take a self-guided tour of the **Old Ursuline Convent.** Walk over to the **Old U.S. Mint,** a magnificent, red-brick edifice that now houses a state-of-the-art concert space and an engaging museum about the city's musical heritage.

At night, don your finest attire for a quintessential French Creole dinner at **Galatoire's Restaurant** on Bourbon Street. Afterward, walk to the world-famous **Preservation Hall** for a short jazz concert. End your evening at the candlelit **Lafitte's Blacksmith Shop Bar** for a late-night drink.

Day 2

Board the **St. Charles streetcar** and head to the **Garden District,** where you can visit **Lafayette Cemetery No. 1** and stroll amid historic homes. Take time to explore the antiques shops, art galleries, and boutiques along funky **Magazine Street.**

In the afternoon, head through the CBD to **The National WWII Museum,** where you can watch an immersive documentary and experience exhibits pertaining to the Allied victory in World War II. Afterward, take a quick tour of **Sazerac House,** and buy some rye to take home.

Head to **Thalia** for a community vibe and simple, delicious dinner. Then, kick it up a notch and catch some live rock, funk, jazz, and blues music at well-loved Uptown joint **Tipitina's.**

can take 25-35 minutes by car. A **taxi** from the airport to the Central Business District (CBD) usually costs $36 for one or two passengers and $15 per person for three or more passengers. Pickup occurs on the airport's lower level, just outside the baggage claim area. Credit cards are typically accepted.

Using a **ride-sharing service** like **Lyft** or **Uber** costs about $33, plus a $4 airport surcharge. There's a designated meeting place on the ground level for these services.

If you'd prefer to travel in style, consider **Airport Limousine** (504/305-2450 or 866/739-5466, www.airportlimousineneworleans.com), the airport's official limo service, which has handy kiosks in the baggage claim area. The number of passengers will determine the type of vehicle selected: sedans for up to three passengers, SUVs for up to five, and limos for six or more. For one-way trips to the French Quarter and CBD, rates start at $58 for one or two passengers; a nominal fuel charge is applied to all rides.

To save a little money, opt for the **Airport Shuttle** (504/522-3500 or 866/596-2699, www.airportshuttleneworleans.com, one-way adults $24, round-trip adults $44, free for children under 6), which offers shared-ride service to hotels in the French Quarter, the CBD, and Uptown. From the upper level of the airport outside Door 7, you can also hop aboard the **E2 Airport Bus** (504/248-3900 or 504/248-3900, www.

jeffersontransit.org, $2 pp). On weekdays, the bus takes about 35 minutes to reach the CBD; on weekends, it only travels to Mid-City and you'll have to rely on an RTA bus route to reach destinations in uptown or downtown New Orleans.

The **Tiger Airport Shuttle** (225/333-8167, www.tigerairportshuttle.com, rates vary) provides transportation to and from Baton Rouge.

Train

Amtrak (800/872-7245, www.amtrak.com) operates three rail routes across southern Louisiana, all of which include stops at the **New Orleans Union Passenger Terminal** (1001 Loyola Ave., 5am-10pm daily).

These rail routes serve New Orleans:

- **City of New Orleans** runs daily from Chicago to New Orleans, with major stops in Memphis, Jackson, and Hammond (19 hours).
- **Crescent** runs daily between New York City and New Orleans, with major stops in Philadelphia, Baltimore, Washington DC, Charlotte, Atlanta, Birmingham, and Slidell (30 hours).
- **Sunset Limited,** an east-west train, runs from Los Angeles to New Orleans three times weekly, with major stops in Tucson, El Paso, San Antonio, Houston, Lake Charles, and Lafayette (48 hours).

Bus

Greyhound (800/231-2222, www.greyhound.com) is the definitive bus provider for New Orleans, with frequent and flexible service throughout the country. Buses depart daily from the **New Orleans Greyhound Station** (1001 Loyola Ave., 504/525-6075, 5:30am-10:30pm daily) with multiple stops throughout Louisiana to many neighboring states. Travel times can be significantly longer than by train (although not always), but fares are generally much cheaper.

Starting from New Orleans

Because the Natchez Trace is well-marked from south to north, it's easy to begin your road trip here. Head northwest via US 61 to Baton Rouge (79 miles, roughly two hours), then onward to Natchez (another 92 miles, roughly two hours). I-10 may be a faster alternative route between New Orleans and Baton Rouge—but it may also be slower, depending on traffic conditions leaving the Big Easy.

Getting Around

Public Transportation

New Orleans is served by an extensive network of buses and streetcars, operated by the **New Orleans Regional Transit Authority** (RTA, 504/248-3900, www.norta.com). The standard fare is $1.25 per person (seniors $0.40, free for children under 2) plus $0.25 per transfer; express buses cost $1.50 per person. You must pay with exact change by depositing coins or inserting $1 bills into the fare box at the front of the bus or streetcar. Food, beverages, smoking, and stereos are not permitted on buses or streetcars.

The handy **Jazzy Pass,** a magnetized card presented upon boarding the bus or streetcar, allows unlimited rides during the active period; it's available in 1-day ($3), 3-day ($9), 5-day ($15), or 31-day ($55) increments. The 1-day pass can be purchased on the bus or streetcar, though only cash is accepted. Other passes are available from the RTA GoMobile app, online on the RTA's website, or from various hotels, banks, and retailers, such as Walgreens.

Bus

Bus service is available throughout the city, and all RTA buses can accommodate people with disabilities. The one-way fare is $1.25 (plus $0.25 per transfer), and passengers must pay with either exact change (coins or $1 bills) or the Jazzy Pass.

Tourists often utilize the **Magazine line** (11), which runs from Canal Street in the CBD through the Garden District and

Uptown, along a six-mile stretch of galleries, shops, and restaurants, before ending at Audubon Park. Another important route is the **Jackson-Esplanade line** (91), which runs from Rousseau Street in the Garden District, through the CBD, along the north edge of the French Quarter, up Esplanade Avenue, and past City Park, ending at the Greenwood Cemetery. For a complete map of all bus lines, plus individual maps and schedules, visit the RTA website (www.norta.com).

Streetcar

The RTA also operates New Orleans's iconic streetcars. The one-way fare is $1.25 per person (plus $0.25 per transfer), and passengers must pay with either exact change (coins or $1 bills) or the Jazzy Pass.

The famous **St. Charles streetcar** line, which operates 24 hours daily, runs along St. Charles and South Carrollton Avenues, from Canal Street to Claiborne Avenue; a one-way trip lasts about 45 minutes. Some passengers with disabilities may have trouble boarding, as they are not wheelchair-accessible. The St. Charles line has been in operation since 1835, when it began as the main railroad line connecting the city of New Orleans with the resort community of Carrollton, now part of the city; the olive-green cars date to the 1920s, when they were built by the Perley Thomas Company. Today, the line is a wonderful, scenic, and atmospheric way to travel between the CBD and Uptown. A one-way ride lasts about 40 minutes.

The **Canal Street streetcar** line extends from Canal Street to Mid-City before splitting into two branches. The Cemeteries branch (5am-3am daily) runs from the foot of Canal Street, not far from the ferry terminal for Algiers Point, all the way up to the historical cemeteries along City Park Avenue. The City Park/Museum branch (daily 7am-2am) takes North Carrollton Avenue to Esplanade Avenue, right beside City Park and the New Orleans Museum of Art. A one-way trip along either branch lasts about 30 minutes.

The **Riverfront streetcar** line (7am-10:30pm daily) uses newer streetcars and runs a short but scenic 1.8-mile route along the Mississippi River, from the French Quarter to the CBD. These modern red streetcars were built by New Orleans metal- and woodworkers; a one-way ride lasts about 15 minutes.

The **Rampart Streetcar** line (7am-10:30pm daily) runs from Union Passenger Terminal on Loyola Avenue through the Central Business District to Elysian Fields Avenue. It offers views of downtown skyscrapers and French Quarter architecture. This is a good way to get to Louis Armstrong Park.

Ferry

The **Algiers Point/Canal Street ferry** (504/248-3900, www.norta.com or www.friendsoftheferry.org, 6am-9:45pm Mon.-Thurs. and Sun., 6am-11:45pm Fri.-Sat., adults $2, seniors $1, free for children 2 and under) provides ferry service across the Mississippi River, from the foot of Canal Street in the CBD to Algiers Point. The five-minute service no longer transports vehicles; the boat departs every 30 minutes on either shore. The **Lower Algiers/Chalmette ferry** (6am-8:45pm daily, pedestrians or vehicle drivers $2, senior pedestrians, senior drivers or vehicle passengers $1, free for children 2 and under) offers hourly service between Lower Algiers and the East Bank community of Chalmette; the trip usually lasts 15-20 minutes.

Taxi and Pedicab

For safety reasons, taxis are *highly* recommended over public transportation at night, particularly when traveling solo. This is the sort of city where it's easy to lose track of time, particularly if you're bar-hopping, so it's always a smart idea to have the name and number of a couple of cab companies with you at all times.

Taxi rates within the city typically start at $3.50 per ride, plus $2 per mile thereafter; there's also a charge of $1 for each additional passenger. You will often find taxis waiting at major intersections near Bourbon Street and other nighttime hot spots in the Quarter. Be sure to use taxis operated by licensed and established cab companies, such as **New Orleans Carriage Cab** (504/207-7777, www.neworleanscarriagecab.com) and **United Cabs** (504/522-9771, www.unitedcabs.com). Taxi rates are often higher during peak times, such as Mardi Gras and Jazz Fest; expect to pay $5 per person at least.

Operated by knowledgeable guides and equipped with safety belts, headlights, and flashing taillights, ecofriendly pedicabs can accommodate up to three or four passengers. Currently, there are two pedicab companies in the city: **Bike Taxi Unlimited** (504/891-3441, http://neworleansbiketaxi.com), which serves the French Quarter, Marigny, the CBD, the Arts/Warehouse District, and Uptown; and **NOLA Pedicabs** (504/274-1300, www.nolapedicabs.com), which mainly serves the Quarter, the CBD, and the Arts District. Standard fares are $5 per passenger for the first six blocks, after which each passenger will be charged $1 per city block. During special events, such as Mardi Gras, expect to pay $50 per half hour and $100 hourly.

Ride-hailing companies, including **Lyft** (www.lyft.com) and **Uber** (www.uber.com), are popular in New Orleans. Download their apps to find a local to drive you to your destination.

Driving

Many streets are one-way and riddled with potholes, street parking is scarce, and garage and hotel parking is expensive. On the other hand, the main neighborhoods are easily walkable, taxis are easy to find, and public transportation is decent, particularly from the French Quarter to Uptown and Mid-City, so having a car isn't necessary. Given the city's compact size, many travelers rely on motorcycles and bikes, which are often much easier to park on the street.

Parking

Given New Orleans's high crime rate, parking requires caution: When parking on the street or in an unattended lot, keep as few of your belongings in your car as possible ("stow it; don't show it"). For a bit more security, you can pay $15-50 nightly to park your car at a hotel or commercial lot. Relying on hourly rates can be considerably more expensive, though many downtown businesses and stores offer free or discounted parking with minimum purchase and validated parking tickets. Even with secured parking areas, refrain from leaving valuables in plain sight.

Beyond the security concerns, finding street parking in the French Quarter, the CBD, and other tourist areas can be extremely difficult. Most blocks of the Quarter are restricted for residents with permits. Many hotel properties in the Quarter have no dedicated parking facilities. You'll find street parking meters throughout the city using the ParkMobile app or boxes midblock. If you're staying beyond the downtown area, it might be better to park in the Uptown or Mid-City neighborhoods and use public transportation to visit the French Quarter and CBD.

Avoid parking vehicles longer than 22 feet overnight in the CBD. For general questions about parking in New Orleans, consult the city's **Parking Division** (504/658-8200 or 504/658-8250).

Sightseeing Passes

Admission fees in New Orleans can add up quickly, but money-saving tricks do exist, particularly in the form of combination packages. If you're planning to visit the **Audubon Zoo, Audubon Butterfly Garden and Insectarium, Audubon Aquarium of the Americas,** and **Entergy Giant Screen Theatre,** go for the

Audubon Experience Package (www.auduboninstitute.org, adults $45, seniors $38, children 2-12 $35), which can save you up to $30 per person. The package (valid for 30 consecutive days) includes one visit to each facility. The **New Orleans Pass** (www.getyourguide.com; 1-day pass adults $74, children $55; 2-day pass adults $120, children $94; 3-day pass adults $160, children $129; 5-day pass adults $240, children $170) provides access to more than 25 tours, attractions, and other diversions throughout the Crescent City and beyond including, for example, Blaine Kern's Mardi Gras World.

Orientation

New Orleanians rarely refer to compass directions when discussing how to navigate the city. The city is bound on one side by the irregular Mississippi River, which forms the western, southern, or eastern border; main roads tend to run parallel or perpendicular to the river. Since the river's direction changes, this means that New Orleans's street grid also changes its axis in different places. As a result, most residents employ the terms "lakeside" (meaning north toward Lake Pontchartrain) and "riverside" (meaning south toward the Mississippi) when referring to streets perpendicular to the river. The terms "upriver" or "uptown" refer to westerly directions; the terms "downriver" or "downtown" are used for easterly directions. For example, Canal Street, which tourists generally consider a north-south thoroughfare, actually runs in a southeasterly direction toward the river. If you're still confused, be sure to have a city map with you at all times, as this is one place where it is indispensable—whether you're walking, driving, taking public transportation, or even using cabs. Residents refer to neighborhood names almost as much as specific streets.

The heart of New Orleans, the **French Quarter** beckons with its wealth of seafood restaurants, history museums, and varied street performers. Peruse the art galleries and antiques shops along Royal Street, stroll beside the Mississippi River, enjoy live music on Bourbon Street, or take a carriage ride through the fabled avenues. Iconic images like the St. Louis Cathedral, flickering gas lamps, and wrought-iron balconies make the Vieux Carré the city's most photographed neighborhood. While the Quarter gets all the headlines, it would be a mistake not to venture into other neighborhoods.

Northeast of the French Quarter, the residential **Faubourg Marigny** and **Bywater** neighborhoods lure their share of visitors. Sandwiched between Esplanade Avenue, the Mississippi River, and the Industrial Canal, this vast area is particularly popular among local music lovers, who flock nightly to the moody jazz clubs and low-key eateries on Frenchmen Street.

Southwest of the French Quarter lies the **Central Business District (CBD).** Here, you'll encounter some of the city's finest hotels, plus restaurants and diversions like the prominent Harrah's New Orleans casino. The adjacent **Arts District,** also known as the Warehouse District, contains numerous art galleries, the Contemporary Arts Center, The National WWII Museum, and Lee Circle.

The eclectic **Uptown** area is filled with as many rundown apartment buildings as well-landscaped estates. Shop for fashionable jewelry, clothing, and home furnishings along Magazine Street, ride the streetcars on oak-shaded St. Charles Avenue, and explore popular bars and eateries in the Riverbend neighborhood. Uptown is also home to the famous Audubon Zoo, part of verdant Audubon Park.

Technically part of the expansive Uptown area, the **Garden District** comprises several mansions and art museums. Most of the attractions, restaurants, inns, and stores worth noting lie along or within several blocks of St. Charles Avenue, between the Pontchartrain Expressway and Louisiana Avenue. Browse antiques shops and vintage clothing boutiques on funky Magazine Street, savor classic local cuisine at the award-winning Commander's Palace, and explore landmarks like Lafayette Cemetery No. 1.

Two areas flooded by Hurricane Katrina, the **Tremé** and **Mid-City** have slowly rebounded since that devastating storm. Northwest of Rampart Street, the Tremé has nurtured many local musicians over the years and now entices tourists with places like Louis Armstrong Park and St. Louis Cemetery No. 1, site of Marie Laveau's celebrated tomb. Farther north, Mid-City features several popular attractions, including City Park, the New Orleans Museum of Art, and the Fair Grounds Race Course, home to the annual New Orleans Jazz & Heritage Festival.

Sights

Yes, there are 'round-the-clock bicycles and cars, yet the French Quarter is a pedestrian-friendly neighborhood. Marked by traditional European architecture, lush Caribbean-style courtyards, high-end art galleries, Bohemian shops, traditional jazz clubs, and rowdy karaoke bars, this eclectic historical district appeals to tourists and residents alike. Walking amid the old-fashioned gas lamps constitutes a sight in itself—albeit a tantalizing, multisensory one. While strolling along the cracked, ankle-spraining sidewalks, enjoy the varied street musicians, the clip-clop of passing carriages, and an air often scented with the mingled perfume of sweet olive trees, chicory-laced coffee, boiled seafood, and, yes, mule manure.

Stay aware of your surroundings, particularly when walking at night. Crime rates in New Orleans are high.

French Quarter

★ Jackson Square

Jackson Square (Decatur St. and Chartres St. between St. Peter St. and St. Ann St., 504/658-3200, www.experienceneworleans.com, 8am-7pm daily summer, 8am-6pm daily winter, free) was named in honor of the seventh U.S. president, Andrew Jackson, who led the United States to victory during the Battle of New Orleans. A 14-foot-tall bronze statue of Jackson serves as the square's centerpiece and ranks among the city's favorite photo ops.

Filled with trees, benches, and grassy areas, Jackson Square is a wonderful place to sit and read a newspaper, eat a muffuletta from one of the nearby cafés, and absorb the oldest section of New Orleans. (No dogs or bikes are permitted.) More often than not, you'll spy mimes, musicians, and other entertainers along the promenades that fringe Jackson Square, sometimes even after the park has closed at night. Horse-drawn carriages usually line the gated park alongside Decatur Street, awaiting tourists for guided excursions through the Quarter.

This picturesque green space is surrounded by several historical buildings, including the gorgeous **St. Louis Cathedral,** as well as the **Cabildo** and the **Presbytère.** Along the northeastern and southwestern sides of the square lie the lower and upper **Pontalba Apartments,** the oldest apartment buildings in the country. Here, you'll find the historic **1850 House** and, on the lower levels, several eateries and shops.

1850 House and Pontalba Apartments

The Pontalba Apartments were commissioned by Baroness Micaela Almonester de Pontalba in 1849 (the lower building, on St. Ann St.) and 1851 (the upper building, on St. Peter St.). She had inherited the land from her father, Don Andres Almonester, the man who had financed the Cabildo, the Presbytère, and St. Louis Cathedral after the devastating fire of 1788.

The only Pontalba Apartment open to the public, the **1850 House** (523 St. Ann St., 504/524-9118, www.louisianastatemuseum.org, 10am-4:30pm Tues.-Sun., adults $5, seniors, military, and students $4, free for children 6 and under) was restored in 1955. Most of the interior furnishings were donated to the museum but are authentic to the exact period. Today, the 1850 House is a small but popular museum, which also has an excellent book and gift shop. The actual apartment occupies the two floors above the shop. Visitors can stand at edges of the doorways and peer into the rooms, gaining a sense of an 1850s row house owned by a family of somewhat considerable means. Plaques on the third floor detail the lives of the home's inhabitants from 1850 to 1861.

Sazerac House

Opened in 2019, **Sazerac House** (101 Magazine St., 504/910-0100, www.sazerachouse.com, 1pm-6pm Wed.-Sat., free) is an interactive museum about that thing for which New Orleans is known: the Sazerac cocktail. It offers an in-depth look at cocktail culture. Take a self-guided tour through the three floors of exhibits and learn how rye is distilled and how the drink is made. You can buy souvenirs to take home, including locally made bitters, plus rye and whiskey.

Presbytère

Built in 1797 as a home for the priests of the St. Louis Cathedral, and standing just on the downriver side of it, the two-story **Presbytère** (751 Chartres St., 504/568-6968 or 800/568-6968, www.louisianastatemuseum.org, 10am-4:30pm Tues.-Sun., adults $7, seniors, military, and students $6, free for children 6 and under) on Jackson Square bears a structural resemblance to the Cabildo. It was never used for its intended purpose, as its financier, Don Andres Almonester (a Spaniard of considerable means who also funded the Cabildo and St. Louis Cathedral), died before it was completed. The new U.S. government eventually completed it and used it to house the Louisiana state courts during the 19th century.

In 1911, it became part of the Louisiana State Museum, and today, it houses a colorful permanent exhibit on the history of Mardi Gras traditions both in the city and the state called Mardi Gras: It's Carnival Time in Indiana. Videos, audiotapes, and a wide array of artifacts detail how Louisianians have celebrated Carnival through the years and how this event has grown to become one of the most popular festivals in the world. You'll also encounter Living with Hurricanes: Katrina and Beyond, a heartbreaking yet inspiring exhibit that utilizes photographs, eyewitness accounts, artifacts, and multimedia displays to explore the history and science of hurricanes.

St. Louis Cathedral

The lakeside end of Jackson Square is dominated by the **St. Louis Cathedral** (615 Père Antoine Alley, 504/525-9585, www.stlouiscathedral.org, 8:30am-4pm daily, self-guided tour pamphlet for $1 donation), one of the most magnificent cathedrals in the United States. The current building was constructed in 1794 in the Spanish style, with two round spires rising from the facade, and then virtually rebuilt and remodeled in 1849. Simpler churches have stood on this site since the 1720s, not long after the arrival of the French explorer Jean Baptiste Le Moyne, Sieur de Bienville, who established New Orleans as a permanent settlement in 1718. During the 1849 remodel, huge steeples were added to the two symmetrical round towers, and the building has received additional restorations over the years. The cathedral was designated a minor basilica in 1964 by Pope Paul VI. Mass is held every day, and the gift shop (10am-3pm daily) offers an assortment of religious and spiritual items. Visitors are welcome to take a guided tour of the property; as an alternative, simply wander inside and explore the gorgeous architecture, including kaleidoscopic stained-glass windows, on your own. Keep in mind that this is a working church, so be respectful of those who have come for prayer and quiet reflection.

Cabildo

On the upriver side of the St. Louis Cathedral stands the **Cabildo** (701 Chartres St., 504/568-6968 or 800/568-6968, www.louisianastatemuseum.org, 10am-4:30pm Tues.-Sun., adults $10, seniors, students, and military $8), the building in which the formal transfer of Louisiana to the United States took place after the Louisiana Purchase. The Spanish first constructed the Cabildo as their seat of government in the 1770s, but it and its replacement were destroyed during both major city fires in the late 18th century. The current structure, made of brick and stucco and built in the Spanish style with Moorish influences, was erected in 1794, serving again as home to the Spanish administrative body, after which it became the Maison de Ville (Town Hall) during the brief time the French reclaimed New Orleans. It served as the Louisiana Supreme Court headquarters for much of the 19th and early 20th centuries, and it was actually the site where the landmark *Plessy v. Ferguson* decision (which legalized segregation) originated in 1892. Many prominent visitors have been officially received in the Cabildo, from the Marquis de Lafayette to Mark Twain. The building looks more French than Spanish today, because the original flat-tile roof was replaced with a Second Empire mansard roof in the late 1840s. Since 1908, the Cabildo has been part of the Louisiana State Museum.

Top to bottom: Jackson Square; Sazerac House; Pontalba Apartments

French Quarter

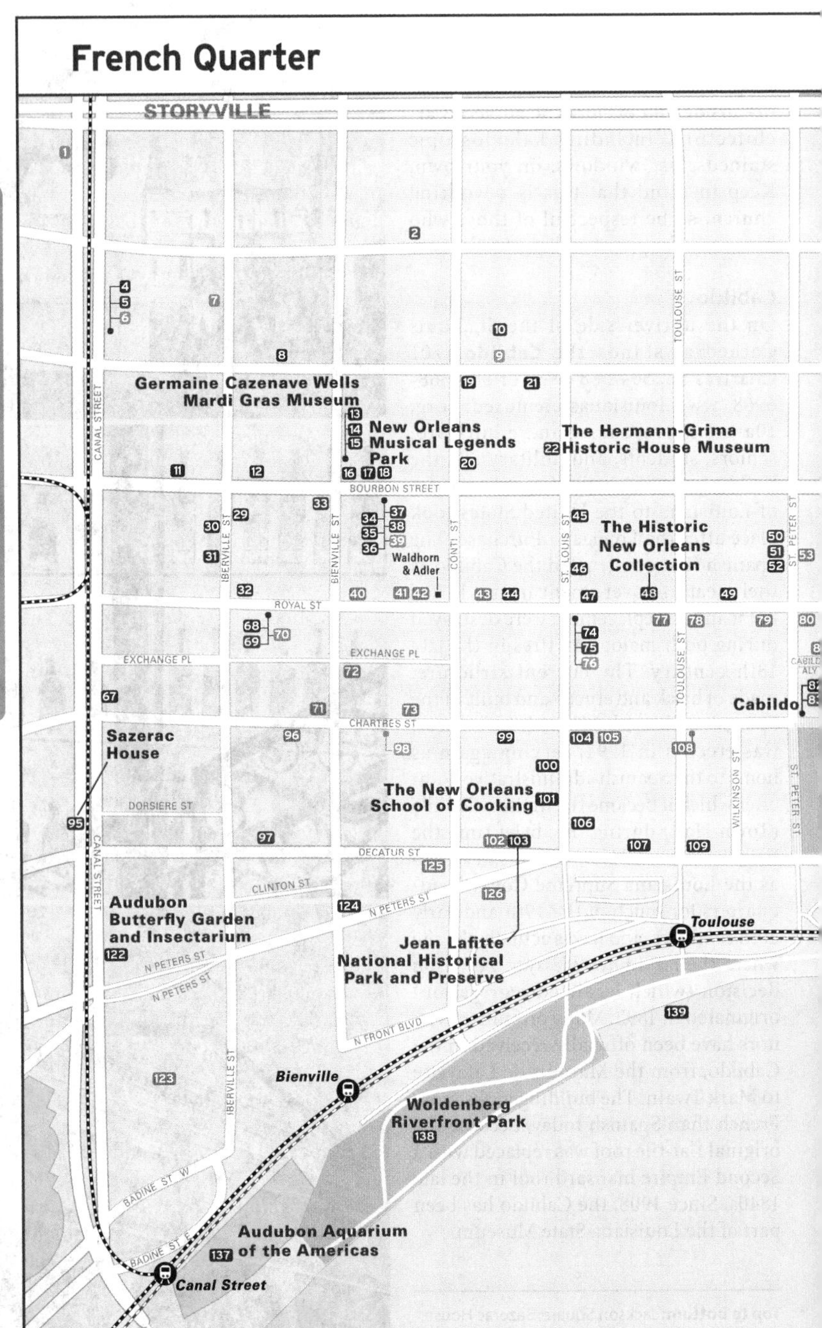

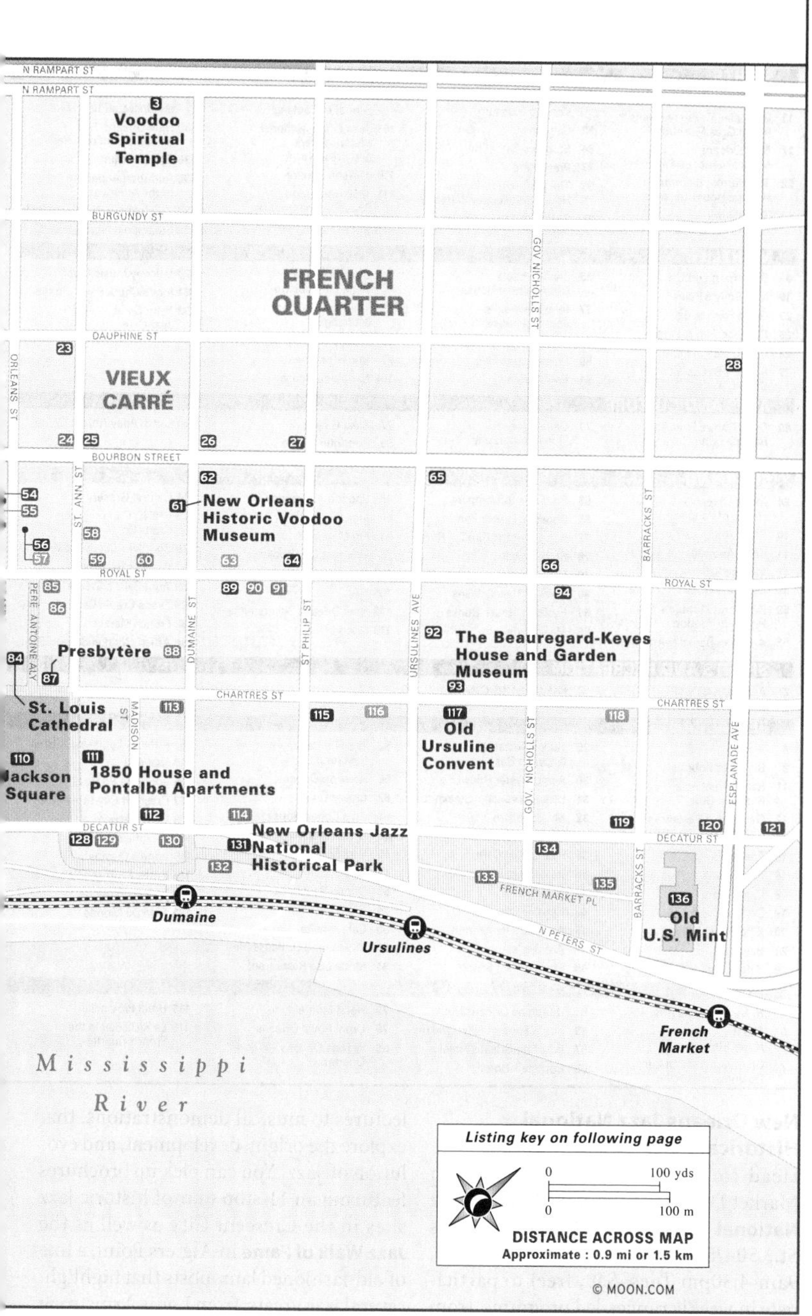

N RAMPART ST
N RAMPART ST
BURGUNDY ST
DAUPHINE ST
BOURBON STREET
ROYAL ST
CHARTRES ST
DECATUR ST
FRENCH MARKET PL
N PETERS ST
ORLEANS ST
ST. ANN ST
DUMAINE ST
ST PHILIP ST
URSULINES AVE
GOV NICHOLLS ST
GOV. NICHOLLS ST
BARRACKS ST
ESPLANADE AVE
PERE ANTOINE ALY
MADISON ST
FRENCH QUARTER
VIEUX CARRÉ
Voodoo Spiritual Temple
New Orleans Historic Voodoo Museum
Presbytère
St. Louis Cathedral
Jackson Square
1850 House and Pontalba Apartments
New Orleans Jazz National Historical Park
The Beauregard-Keyes House and Garden Museum
Old Ursuline Convent
Old U.S. Mint
Dumaine
Ursulines
French Market
Mississippi River
Listing key on following page
0
100 yds
0
100 m
DISTANCE ACROSS MAP
Approximate : 0.9 mi or 1.5 km
© MOON.COM

French Quarter Key

SIGHTS

3 Voodoo Spiritual Temple
13 Germaine Cazenave Wells Mardi Gras Museum
17 New Orleans Musical Legends Park
22 The Hermann-Grima Historic House Museum
48 The Historic New Orleans Collection
61 New Orleans Historic Voodoo Museum
82 Cabildo
84 St. Louis Cathedral
87 Presbytère
93 The Beauregard-Keyes House and Garden Museum
95 Sazerac House
101 The New Orleans School of Cooking
103 Jean Lafitte National Historical Park and Preserve
110 Jackson Square
111 1850 House and Pontalba Apartments
117 Old Ursuline Convent
122 Audubon Butterfly Garden and Insectarium
130 New Orleans Jazz National Historical Park
135 Old U.S. Mint
136 Audubon Aquarium of the Americas
137 Woldenberg Riverfront Park
138 Steamboat Natchez

NIGHTLIFE

5 Davenport Lounge
10 May Baily's Place
23 Good Friends Bar
25 Bourbon Pub & Parade
26 Cafe Lafitte in Exile
27 Lafitte's Blacksmith Shop Bar
33 Jean Lafitte's Old Absinthe House
37 Irvin Mayfield's Jazz Playhouse
38 Bar R'evolution
50 Preservation Hall
51 Pat O'Brien's
54 Orleans Grapevine Wine Bar & Bistro
69 The Carousel Bar & Lounge
75 Touché Bar
97 House of Blues
104 Napoleon House
120 Balcony Music Club
121 Igor's Check Point Charlie
133 Palm Court Jazz Cafe

ARTS AND CULTURE

60 Craig Tracy's Fine-Art Bodypainting Gallery
71 Gallery for Fine Photography
72 Michalopoulos Gallery
77 Kako Gallery
85 Rodrigue Studio New Orleans
131 Dutch Alley Artist's Co-op

SHOPPING

24 Marie Laveau's House of Voodoo
40 Royal Antiques
41 Keil's Antiques
42 Vintage 329
43 Moss Antiques
53 Reverend Zombie's House of Voodoo
55 Arcadian Books & Art Prints
58 Boutique du Vampyre
59 Bourbon French Parfums
73 Bottom of the Cup Tea Room
78 Roux Royale
79 M.S. Rau Antiques
80 Forever New Orleans
81 Faulkner House Books
86 Maskarade
88 Voodoo Authentica
90 Idea Factory
91 Fifi Mahony's
96 Crescent City Books
102 Cigar Factory New Orleans
105 UAL
108 New Orleans Silversmiths
113 Queork
114 Central Grocery
123 RHINO Contemporary Crafts Co.
125 Southern Candymakers
126 Peaches Records
128 Aunt Sally's Creole Praline's
129 Evans Creole Candy Factory
132 French Market
134 Artist's Market & Bead Shop

SPORTS AND RECREATION

2 American Bicycle Rental Company
83 Friends of the Cabildo

RESTAURANTS

4 Bistro
8 Big Killer Poboys
11 Ralph Brennan's Red Fish Grill
12 Galatoire's Restaurant
14 Arnoud's
15 French 75
16 Remoulade
18 Cafe Beignet
19 Déjà Vu Bar & Grill
20 Killer Poboys
21 Bayona
28 Port of Call
29 Felix's Restaurant & Oyster Bar
30 Acme Oyster House
31 Dickie Brennan's Steakhouse
32 Mr. B's Bistro
34 Desire Oyster Bar
35 PJ's Coffee Cafe
36 Restaurant R'evolution
44 Brennan's
45 Hermes Bar
46 Antoine's Restaurant
47 Antoine's Annex
49 Court of Two Sisters
52 The Old Coffeepot Restaurant
56 Roux on Orleans
62 Clover Grill
64 CC's Coffee House
65 Quartermaster
66 Verti Marte
67 Palace Café
68 Criollo Retaurant
74 Rib Room
89 Café Amelie
92 Croissant d'Or Patisserie
94 Mona Lisa Restaurant
99 K-Paul's Louisiana Kitchen
100 NOLA
106 Johnny's Po-Boys
107 Crescent City Brewhouse
109 Café Maspero
112 Tujague's
115 Irene's Cuisine
119 EnVie Espresso Bar & Cafe
124 Felipe's Taqueria
127 Café Du Monde

HOTELS

1 HI New Orleans Hostel
6 The Ritz-Carlton New Orleans
7 Courtyard New Orleans Downtown/Iberville
9 Dauphine Orleans Hotel
39 Royal Sonesta New Orleans
57 Bourbon Orleans Hotel
63 Cornstalk Hotel
70 Hotel Monteleone
76 Omni Royal Orleans
98 W New Orleans—French Quarter
116 Hôtel Provincial
118 Le Richelieu in the French Quarter

New Orleans Jazz National Historical Park

Head to the visitor center in French Market District at the **New Orleans Jazz National Historical Park** (916 N. Peters St., 504/589-4841, www.nps.gov/jazz, 9am-4:30pm Tues.-Sat., free) to participate in weekly ranger-led programs, from lectures to musical demonstrations, that explore the origin, development, and evolution of jazz. You can pick up brochures featuring an 11-stop tour of historic jazz sites in the Crescent City as well as the **Jazz Walk of Fame** in Algiers Point, a line of old-fashioned lampposts that highlight several jazz greats, from Louis Armstrong

An Architectural Driving Tour

For a fun cursory education of local architecture, take the following drive through this relatively compact city.

French Quarter

Jackson Square (700 block of Decatur St.) is a lovely park surrounded by the **Cabildo,** the **Presbytère,** and the **St. Louis Cathedral,** Spanish-style structures built in the 1790s. Along the southwestern and northeastern edges of the park lie the lower and upper **Pontalba Apartments,** commissioned in the mid-1850s and considered the oldest apartment buildings in America.

At the corner of Governor Nicholls and Royal stand the supposedly haunted **LaLaurie Mansion** (1140 Royal St.), an imposing gray structure built in the 1830s.

Head to Chartres Street to the expansive **Old Ursuline Convent** (1100 Chartres St.), constructed in 1745 and the oldest existing building in the Mississippi River Valley.

Garden District

On Constance Street is the regal **St. Mary's Assumption Church** (2030 Constance St.). Constructed between 1858 and 1866, St. Mary's is a massive, German Baroque Revival-style structure with an intricate facade and arched stained-glass windows.

End at St. Charles Avenue, home to the Victorian-inspired **House of Broel** (2220 St. Charles Ave.) and Italianate-style **Van Benthuysen-Elms Mansion** (3029 St. Charles Ave.), both erected in the mid- to late 19th century.

to Louis Prima. Self-guided audio tours are also available through the website or by phoning 504/613-4062.

Old U.S. Mint

Fashioned with a granite facade and made of stucco and Mississippi River mud brick, the **Old U.S. Mint** (400 Esplanade Ave., 504/568-6993 or 800/568-6868, www.louisianastatemuseum.org, 10am-4:30pm Tues.-Sun., free) was constructed in 1835 at the behest of U.S. president Andrew Jackson. This is the only building in the country to have functioned as both a U.S. and a Confederate mint. It also housed Confederate troops for a time during the Civil War. With the Union occupation, the mint was shut down until Reconstruction, at which time it resumed service.

In 1909, the mint was decommissioned, and in 1981, it was added to the state museum system. Today, it's home to the **Louisiana Historical Center,** an archive open to the public and containing priceless collections of colonial-era maps and manuscripts. The site is also home to **The New Orleans Jazz Museum** (adults $8, students, seniors and active military $6, free for children 6 and under), which features a variety of music-related artifacts, such as posters, sheet music, and memorabilia, from Sidney Bechet's soprano sax to Fats Domino's piano.

The Mint also houses historical musical recordings, showcases live performances, and presents on-site interviews of performing musicians. There's also a large tribute to Louis Armstrong, as well as three colorful murals depicting New Orleans's fabled Storyville red-light district, one of the city's cultivators of jazz. A small display is dedicated to the building's architect, William Strickland, who trained under famous Greek Revival architect Benjamin Latrobe and who also designed the Tennessee State Capitol.

Old Ursuline Convent

King Louis XV of France established the **Old Ursuline Convent** (1112 Chartres St., 504/529-3040, www.oldursulineconventmuseum.org, 10am-4pm Mon.-Fri., 9am-3pm Sat., adults $8, seniors $7, students $6) in 1745 to house the Ursuline nuns

Romeo Spikes and Haint Blue Paint

As the city's oldest neighborhood, the Vieux Carré (French Quarter) boasts the lion's share of photogenic architectural styles, including the upper-level galleries, wrought-iron railings, and hidden courtyards ironically influenced by the city's Spanish era. As you admire the architecture, you may notice protective spikes, broken glass pieces, and other deterrents atop gates and fences. Particularly ominous are the **Romeo spikes** at the top of ground-floor gallery polls; relics of 19th-century New Orleans, these cast-iron protrusions were installed to prevent male suitors from making nighttime visits to young women. Throughout the city, you'll also encounter curiosities like **haint blue** paint on the underside of porch ceilings, meant to repel evil spirits, or **shotgun houses,** one-level structures in which all rooms are positioned consecutively and interconnected by doors in lieu of a hallway.

who first came to New Orleans in the late 1720s, making them the first nuns to establish a permanent foothold in what is today the United States. This convent was their second home, completed in 1753 and now believed to be the oldest extant building in the Mississippi River Valley; they moved to Dauphine Street in 1824, and then to their present Uptown home, at 2635 State St., in 1912. In those early decades, the convent housed everyone from French orphans and wounded British soldiers to exiled Acadians and the city's destitute masses. During the early 1800s, the nuns conducted a school for the education of daughters of wealthy Louisiana plantation owners. Today, the Ursuline Academy still functions at its State Street locale as the country's oldest continuously operated school for women.

The entire Chartres Street complex—which includes the adjacent gardens, the attached **St. Mary's Church,** and several related outbuildings—is named for the first archbishop of New Orleans, Antoine Blanc. Today, the complex and the St. Louis Cathedral in Jackson Square form the Catholic Cultural Heritage Center of the Archdiocese of New Orleans. The **Old Ursuline Convent Museum,** which encompasses the exhibits on the first floor of the main convent building, is open for self-guided tours.

★ New Orleans Historic Voodoo Museum

Established in 1972, the small, somewhat cramped **New Orleans Historic Voodoo Museum** (724 Dumaine St., 504/680-0128, www.voodoomuseum.com, 10am-6pm daily, adults $7, seniors and students $5.50, children under 12 $3.50) offers a respectful overview of a practice still shrouded in mystery yet taken seriously by its practitioners. Displays include masks, ritual art, and artifacts from Africa and Haiti, where the city's distinctive brand of voodoo practice originated. The exhibits, though ominous, aren't gory in nature, so kids often find them appealing. The focus is on Marie Laveau, the anointed voodoo priestess who lived in New Orleans from the 1790s until her death in 1881. Though you can arrange private consultations and healing seminars with museum staff, the true highlight is the historian-led walking tour (call or book online more than 24 hours in advance to schedule, from $29), which includes a stroll through **St. Louis Cemetery No. 1** (supposed site of Marie Laveau's tomb), an encounter with a contemporary voodoo priestess, and plenty of engrossing stories about voodoo, zombies, jazz funerals, Mardi Gras Indians, and other curious aspects of the city's colorful history.

Marie Laveau: Voodoo Queen

Voodoo experienced its heyday in New Orleans in the 19th century, but while most voodoo paraphernalia available in the French Quarter today is bought by tourists, some people still take the practice seriously. Unfortunately, misconceptions about voodoo abound and are often encouraged by its depiction in popular culture. Voodoo is based on the worship of spirits, called Loa, and a belief system that emphasizes spirituality, compassion, and treating others well. Although there's nothing inherently negative about voodoo, its practice does allow its followers to perform rites intended to bring calamity upon their enemies. These traditions, such as burning black candles or piercing miniature effigies with pins, are the most familiar among outsiders.

The origins of voodoo as a religious practice are unclear. Voodoo rituals are based on a variety of African religious traditions, which were brought to the United States by enslaved West Africans. In 18th-century New Orleans, where enslaved people were kept by French and Spanish residents, voodoo began to incorporate some of the beliefs and rituals of Catholicism as well.

Marie Laveau (circa 1794-1881) is the historical figure most connected with southern Louisiana's rich voodoo tradition. A beautiful woman of French, African, and Native American extraction, she was New Orleans's high priestess of voodoo from roughly 1830 onward. She had numerous children, and at least one daughter continued to practice for many years after her mother's death, fueling rumors that the original Marie Laveau lived into the early 20th century. Her supposed grave in **St. Louis Cemetery No. 1,** on Basin Street, is still a site of pilgrimage for voodoo practitioners.

Laveau combined the understanding ear of a psychologist with the showmanship of a preacher to become one of the city's most vaunted spiritual figures. As a young woman, she practiced as a hair stylist in New Orleans, a position that afforded her the opportunity to work inside some of the city's most prominent homes. As she soaked up the gossip of the day, she also dispensed both practical and spiritual advice to her clients, no doubt sprinkling her words with healthy doses of voodoo mysticism and lore. Word of Laveau's talents as a voodoo priestess spread rapidly, and soon she was staging ceremonies in the small yard of her St. Ann Street home. Her most notorious ceremony, held annually in a swamp cabin along Bayou St. John on June 23 (St. John's Eve, the night before the Feast Day of St. John the Baptist), became the stuff of legend.

Laveau was the most famous priestess to captivate New Orleans's residents, but she wasn't the last. Throughout the centuries, a number of women and some men have carried on the tradition of the voodoo priestess. According to legend, believers can invoke her powers by marking her tomb with three X's (a gris-gris, or charm), scratching the ground three times with their feet, knocking three times on the grave, and leaving a small offering before making a wish. In addition, many people in New Orleans continue to celebrate St. John's Eve and believe that, on this night, the spirit of the Voodoo Queen makes herself known.

Voodoo Spiritual Temple

Operated by Priestess Miriam, the **Voodoo Spiritual Temple** (1428 N. Rampart St., 504/943-9795, www.voodoospiritualtemple.org, 10:30am-6pm Mon.-Sat., 11am-3pm Sun., free, donations accepted), a center of voodoo worship and healing, offers voodoo consultations, rituals, and workshops. An on-site gift shop sells handcrafted voodoo dolls, gris-gris and mojo bags, aroma oils, and books and CDs related to voodoo. The hours of the temple are flexible, so don't be surprised to find the front door locked at random times.

New Orleans Musical Legends Park

While strolling down Bourbon, note the small **New Orleans Musical Legends Park** (311 Bourbon St., 504/888-7608, www.

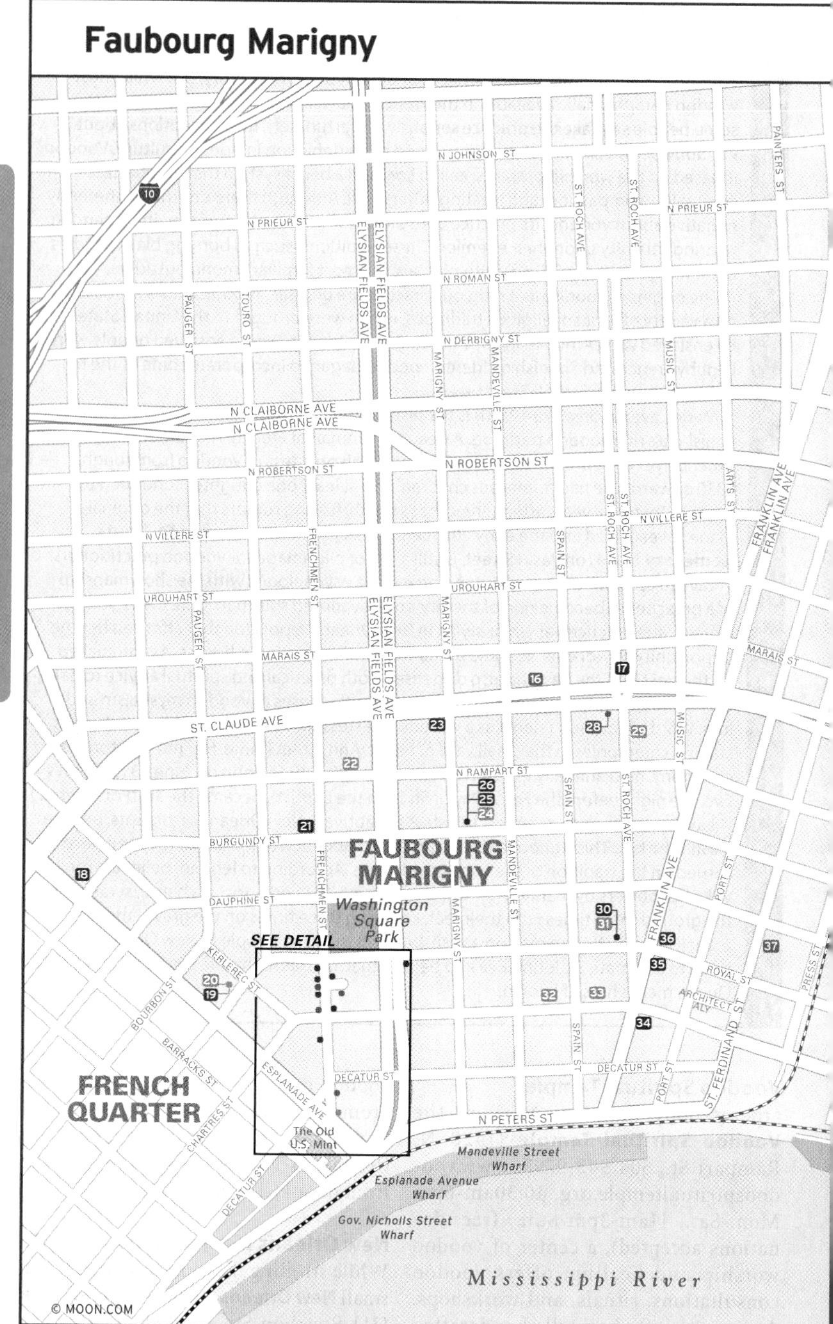
Faubourg Marigny
N JOHNSON ST
PAINTERS ST
ST. ROCH AVE
ST. ROCH AVE
N PRIEUR ST
N PRIEUR ST
10
ELYSIAN FIELDS AVE
ELYSIAN FIELDS AVE
N ROMAN ST
PAUGER ST
TOURO ST
N DERBIGNY ST
MUSIC ST
MARIGNY ST
MANDEVILLE ST
N CLAIBORNE AVE
N CLAIBORNE AVE
N ROBERTSON ST
N ROBERTSON ST
ARTS ST
FRANKLIN AVE
FRANKLIN AVE
ST. ROCH AVE
ST. ROCH AVE
N VILLERE ST
N VILLERE ST
SPAIN ST
FRENCHMEN ST
URQUHART ST
URQUHART ST
PAUGER ST
MARIGNY ST
ELYSIAN FIELDS AVE
ELYSIAN FIELDS AVE
MARAIS ST
MARAIS ST
ST. CLAUDE AVE
MUSIC ST
N RAMPART ST
SPAIN ST
ST. ROCH AVE
BURGUNDY ST
FAUBOURG MARIGNY
FRENCHMEN ST
MANDEVILLE ST
FRANKLIN AVE
PORT ST
DAUPHINE ST
Washington Square Park
MARIGNY ST
SEE DETAIL
KERLEREC ST
ROYAL ST
PRESS ST
BOURBON ST
ARCHITECT ALY
ST. FERDINAND ST
BARRACKS ST
SPAIN ST
DECATUR ST
PORT ST
ESPLANADE AVE
DECATUR ST
FRENCH QUARTER
CHARTRES ST
N PETERS ST
The Old U.S. Mint
Mandeville Street Wharf
DECATUR ST
Esplanade Avenue Wharf
Gov. Nicholls Street Wharf
Mississippi River
© MOON.COM
16
17
18
19
20
21
22
23
24
25
26
28
29
30
31
32
33
34
35
36
37

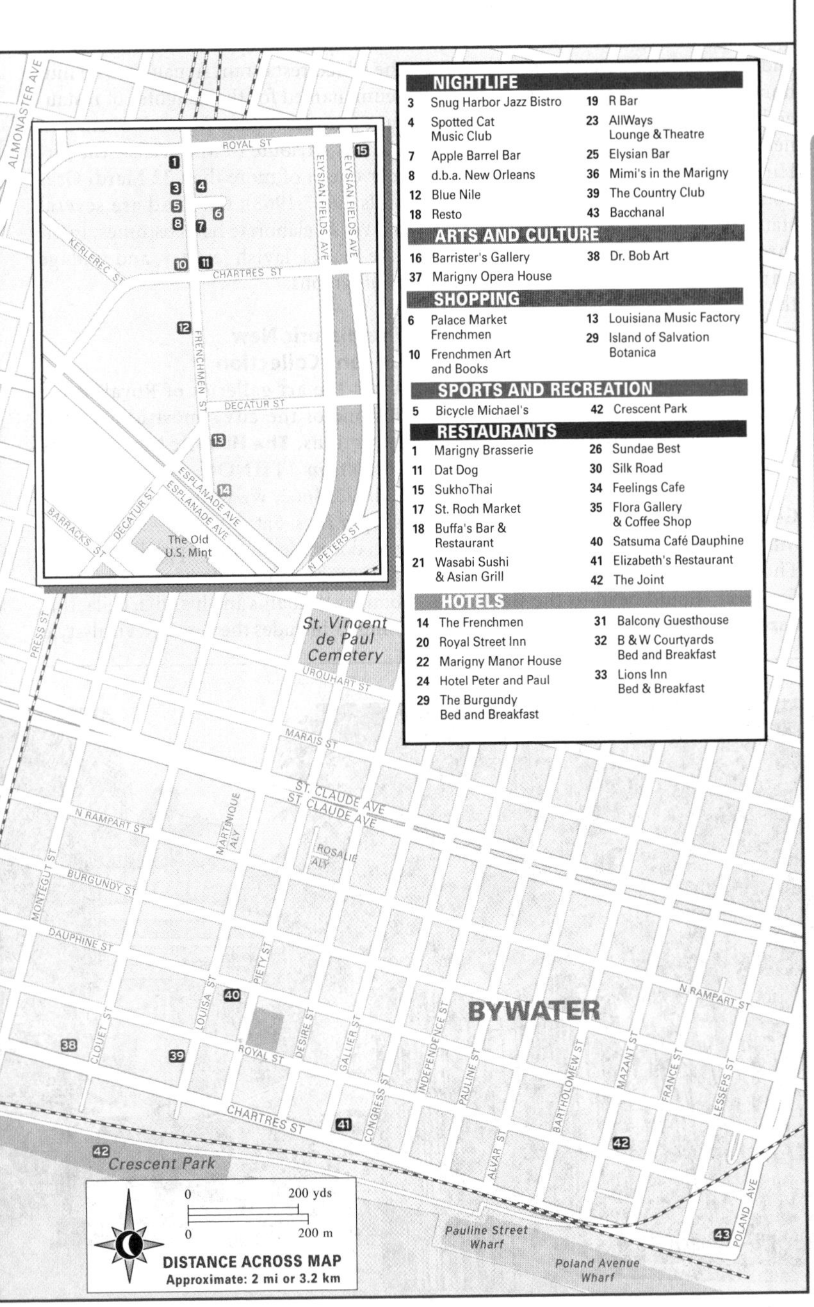

NIGHTLIFE
3 Snug Harbor Jazz Bistro
4 Spotted Cat Music Club
7 Apple Barrel Bar
8 d.b.a. New Orleans
12 Blue Nile
18 Resto
19 R Bar
23 AllWays Lounge & Theatre
25 Elysian Bar
36 Mimi's in the Marigny
39 The Country Club
43 Bacchanal
ARTS AND CULTURE
16 Barrister's Gallery
37 Marigny Opera House
38 Dr. Bob Art
SHOPPING
6 Palace Market Frenchmen
10 Frenchmen Art and Books
13 Louisiana Music Factory
29 Island of Salvation Botanica
SPORTS AND RECREATION
5 Bicycle Michael's
42 Crescent Park
RESTAURANTS
1 Marigny Brasserie
11 Dat Dog
15 SukhoThai
17 St. Roch Market
18 Buffa's Bar & Restaurant
21 Wasabi Sushi & Asian Grill
26 Sundae Best
30 Silk Road
34 Feelings Cafe
35 Flora Gallery & Coffee Shop
40 Satsuma Café Dauphine
41 Elizabeth's Restaurant
42 The Joint
HOTELS
14 The Frenchmen
20 Royal Street Inn
22 Marigny Manor House
24 Hotel Peter and Paul
29 The Burgundy Bed and Breakfast
31 Balcony Guesthouse
32 B & W Courtyards Bed and Breakfast
33 Lions Inn Bed & Breakfast
ROYAL ST
CHARTRES ST
DECATUR ST
KERLEREC ST
FRENCHMEN ST
ELYSIAN FIELDS AVE
ESPLANADE AVE
BARRACKS ST
N PETERS ST
The Old U.S. Mint
ALMONASTER AVE
PRESS ST
St. Vincent de Paul Cemetery
URQUHART ST
MARAIS ST
ST. CLAUDE AVE
N RAMPART ST
MARTINIQUE ALY
ROSALIE ALY
MONTEGUT ST
BURGUNDY ST
DAUPHINE ST
PIETY ST
LOUISA ST
CLOUET ST
DESIRE ST
GALLIER ST
CONGRESS ST
INDEPENDENCE ST
PAULINE ST
ALVAR ST
BARTHOLOMEW ST
MAZANT ST
FRANCE ST
LESSEPS ST
POLAND AVE
BYWATER
Crescent Park
Pauline Street Wharf
Poland Avenue Wharf
0 200 yds
0 200 m
DISTANCE ACROSS MAP
Approximate: 2 mi or 3.2 km

SIGHTS

neworleansmusicallegends.com, 8am-10pm Sun.-Thurs., 8am-midnight Fri.-Sat., free), which was established in 1999 and now contains several bronze statues honoring some of the city's most legendary performers, including jazz clarinetist Pete Fountain, trumpet greats Al Hirt and Louis Prima, and singers Allen Toussaint and Irma Thomas. Additional statues, busts, and plaques will be added through the years as notable jazz musicians are inducted. Besides the statues, the park includes a lovely fountain, several tables and chairs, and a few food stalls, selling surprisingly tasty fare, from gumbo to beignets. So, grab some food, find a seat, and listen to live jazz music (10am-close daily), courtesy of Steamboat Willie and other musicians.

Germaine Cazenave Wells Mardi Gras Museum

Those curious about the glamour of Carnival should head to the **Germaine Cazenave Wells Mardi Gras Museum** (813 Bienville St., 504/523-5433, www.arnaudsrestaurant.com, 6pm-close Mon.-Sat., 10am-2pm and 6pm-close Sun., free) at the fabled restaurant Arnaud's. The museum, named for the daughter of restaurant founder Count Arnaud, opened in 1983 as a tribute to Ms. Wells—the former queen of more than 22 Mardi Gras balls (1937-1968). On hand are several of Wells's elaborate ball costumes, intricate masks, lavish jewelry, and vintage photographs.

The Historic New Orleans Collection

Amid the art galleries of Royal Street lies one of the city's most underrated attractions, **The Historic New Orleans Collection** (THNOC, 533 Royal St., 504/523-4662, www.hnoc.org, 9:30am-4:30pm Tues.-Sat., 10:30am-4:30pm Sun., free, docent-led tours $5 pp). Established in 1966 by avid collectors General L. Kemper Williams and his wife, Leila, this complex includes the Greek Revival-style

New Orleans Musical Legends Park

Merieult House. Built in 1792, the house now contains the **Williams Gallery,** featuring rotating history exhibits, and the **Louisiana History Galleries,** 13 chambers that each explore a specific period of the state's history (from the French colonial years to the 20th century) by using authentic maps, books, furniture, and artwork.

From the courtyard, you'll notice a few other buildings, such as the Spanish colonial-style **Counting House** and the three-story **Maisonette,** which now contain administrative offices. One exception is the **Williams Residence,** an 1880s Italianate townhouse that the museum founders occupied until 1963. Docent-led tours (10am, 11am, 2pm, and 3pm Tues.-Sat., 11am, 2pm, and 3pm Sun.) last 45 minutes and enable you to view this room-by-room survey of how an upscale early-20th-century home would have been furnished, including several antiques, various watercolors, and vintage maps of New Orleans. You can also join a guided architectural tour of the buildings and courtyards that compose the Royal Street complex.

This impressive complex of interconnected buildings also includes three structures on Toulouse Street: a former banking house, a Creole cottage, and the two-story **Louis Adam House,** where Tennessee Williams once boarded. While here, you should also make time for the impressive museum shop in the Merieult House, where you'll find everything from local novels and history books to vintage maps and iconic jewelry. In addition, THNOC oversees the **Williams Research Center** (410 Chartres St., 504/523-4662, 9:30am-4:30pm Tues.-Sat., free), a Beaux Arts-style brick structure containing an extensive library of documents, manuscripts, photographs, drawings, prints, and paintings about the history of New Orleans.

★ The New Orleans School of Cooking

While most people visit New Orleans to taste its one-of-a-kind food, it's also possible to learn how to create such wonderful cuisine. Since 1980, **The New Orleans School of Cooking** (524 St. Louis St., 504/525-2665, www.neworleansschoolofcooking.com, 9am-6pm Mon.-Sat., 9am-5pm Sun.), situated in a renovated, 19th-century molasses warehouse, has invited local Cajun and Creole chefs to teach residents and visitors alike the basics of Louisiana-style cooking, sharing history and tall tales along the way. The popular **demonstration lunch classes** (10am-12:30pm and 2pm-4pm daily, $30-35) include generous samplings of the demonstrated menu items, plus recipes, coffee, iced tea, and Abita beer. Three-hour, hands-on **cooking classes** (10am-1pm and 4pm-7pm Sun., 10am-1pm and 6pm-9pm Mon., Wed., and Fri., 6pm-9pm Tues., 10am-1pm Thurs., 10am-1pm and 5pm-8pm Sat., $139 pp) are also available, provided you are 18 or older. Besides beverages and the prepared meal, you'll receive a souvenir apron and related recipes. Depending on the class, dishes may include gumbo, barbecue shrimp and grits, bananas foster crepes, and pralines. Non-chefs can peruse the on-site **Louisiana General Store,** which offers a plethora of Cajun and Creole products, from cookbooks and cookware to spices and gift baskets.

Jean Lafitte National Historical Park and Preserve

A couple of blocks upriver from Jackson Square is the main office of **Jean Lafitte National Historical Park and Preserve** (419 Decatur St.,504/589-3882, www.nps.gov/jela, 9am-4:30pm Tues.-Sat., free, donations accepted), established in 1978 to preserve natural and historical resources and properties throughout the Mississippi River Valley. The park actually has six distinct units: this one, the **French Quarter Visitor Center;** two others in metro New Orleans (**Chalmette Battlefield and National Cemetery,** just east of the city, as well as **Barataria Preserve** on the west bank); and three in Cajun Country (in Thibodaux, Lafayette, and Eunice) that deal in Cajun culture. Although the visitor center presents a film and several exhibits on various historical and cultural aspects of New Orleans, Louisiana, and the Mississippi River Delta, its best feature is its one-hour ranger-led history talks (9:30am-10:30am Tues.-Sat.).

Woldenberg Riverfront Park

Named for philanthropist Malcolm Woldenberg (1896-1982), lovely **Woldenberg Riverfront Park** (1 Canal St., Mississippi River between Canal St. and St. Peter St., 6am-10pm Sun.-Thurs., 6am-midnight Fri.-Sat., free) is a 16-acre green space and redbrick promenade that extends along the riverfront from the aquarium to Jackson Brewery. It's along this stretch that the site of New Orleans was established in 1718. Crape myrtle and magnolia trees shade the numerous park benches, affording romantic views of the Mississippi River. One of the original quays, **Toulouse Street Wharf,** is home to the palatial excursion riverboat, the **Steamboat *Natchez.*** Fringing the park is the **Moonwalk,** a wooden boardwalk that stretches along the riverfront, between St. Philip and St. Peter Streets. Musicians, tourists, and unhoused individuals are all drawn to this scenic spot, so you won't be alone when you visit. Note: this is an area where property crime takes place, so pay attention to your surroundings and do not leave belongings visible in parked cars.

Within the park are several significant sculptures. The stunning, 20-foot-tall ***Monument to the Immigrant*** marble statue, by noted New Orleans artist Franco Alessandrini, commemorates New Orleans's role as one of the nation's most prolific immigrant ports throughout the 19th century. The mesmerizing ***New Orleans Holocaust Memorial*** (www.holocaustmemorial.us), created by Israeli artist Yaacov Agam, features nine colorful panels that meld to form different images depending on where you're standing.

Audubon Aquarium of the Americas

Established in 1990 by the Audubon Nature Institute—the same folks who operate the Audubon Zoo—the **Audubon Aquarium of the Americas** (1 Canal St., 504/565-3033 or 800/774-7394, www.audubon institute.org, 10am-5pm Tues.-Sun., adults $30, seniors $25, children 2-12 $22, free for children under 2, $3 discount on tickets by purchasing online) is one of the most popular tourist destinations in downtown New Orleans. At the southern end of 16-acre Woldenberg Riverfront Park, alongside the Mississippi River, this contemporary glass-and-brick building houses several intriguing exhibits, most notably the 400,000-gallon Gulf of Mexico habitat, which features sharks, stingrays,

Bayou St. John

Bayou St. John may not draw in the tourists like the French Quarter, but it's an opportunity for a unique view of the city. Stretching from Lake Pontchartrain south along the edge of City Park on to Orleans Avenue, this waterway is what remains of the swamp that was drained to create the city of New Orleans. That doesn't sound appealing, but, in fact, the neighborhoods that back up to the canal, particularly along Moss Street between Esplanade Avenue and Lafitte Avenue, are some of the city's most charming and livable.

Explore the bayou on foot or by kayak or paddleboard. **NOLA Paddleboards** (504/717-8847, www.nolapaddleboards.com, by appt. only, $37) will meet you on the bayou for a pleasant, boat-free paddle in the heart of the city. Lessons and rentals are available. **Kayak-Ti-Yak** (512/964-9499 or 985/778-5034, http://kayakitiyat.com, $45-75) offers two-hour and four-hour guided tours by boat.

Also on the bayou is the **Pitot House** (1440 Moss St., 504/482-0312, 10am-3pm Wed.-Sat., www.pitothouse.org, $7-10), the only Creole colonial country house that is open to the public in the entire city. While in the neighborhood, stop at **Parkway Bakery & Tavern** (538 Hagan Ave., 504/482-3047, http://parkwaypoorboys.com, 11am-10pm Wed.-Mon., $7-17). Don't be intimidated by the lines: They move fast and the po'boys are well worth the wait.

and other saltwater creatures amid the barnacled pilings of an offshore oil rig replica. Kids particularly favor this family-friendly attraction, where they can touch cownose rays, climb above an Amazonian rainforest, and, via an underwater glass tunnel, stroll through the moray eels and tropical fish of a Caribbean coral reef.

Visitors to this exceptional, two-story aquarium will observe a wide array of aquatic and amphibious creatures. Adjacent to the aquarium is the **Entergy Giant Screen Theatre** (504/581-4629, 10am-5pm Tues.-Sun., admission included with aquarium ticket), which typically showcases vibrant 3-D nature documentaries.

Audubon Butterfly Garden and Insectarium

Part of the stately U.S. Custom House, a 30,000-square-foot intimidating gray structure that occupies an entire block, is home to the **Audubon Butterfly Garden and Insectarium** (423 Canal St., 504/524-2847 or 800/774-7394, www.auduboninstitute.org, 10am-4:30pm Tues.-Sun., adults $23, seniors $20, children 2-12 $18, free for children under 2, $3 discount on tickets by purchasing online), which contains the largest freestanding collection of insects in the United States—about 900,000 species in all. Visitors have the opportunity to touch all kinds of creatures, although many others (like the despised cockroaches) are presented through clever displays from a safe distance. Even the museum's Tiny Termite Café has an insect-themed appearance—and the glass-topped tables are actually terrariums, so you might find yourself eating directly over a live tarantula. The museum's bug-cooking demonstration "café," Bug Appétit, illustrates how people around the world routinely snack on insects as an excellent source of protein. Less harrowing for squeamish visitors is the massive butterfly room set within a Japanese-style garden.

Central Business and Arts Districts

St. Patrick's Church

Not far from Lafayette Square, **St. Patrick's Church** (724 Camp St., 504/525-4413, www.oldstpatricks.org, hours vary daily, free, donations accepted) was the first place of worship built in the city's American Sector. The sector was so named because it's where 19th-century Americans built their homes and businesses in order to distinguish their lifestyles from those of the Creoles residing in the French Quarter, New Orleans's original settlement. Blessed by Bishop Antoine Blanc in 1838 and completed by 1840, St. Patrick's Church is one of the few structures left in a district once filled with magnificent mansions and high-end mercantile stores. When the parish was first established in 1833, the area was known as the Faubourg St. Mary; the church itself developed from a need for the Americans, many of whom were Irish, to worship in a structure as noteworthy as the French Quarter's St. Louis Cathedral. This National Historic Landmark is celebrated not only for its historic significance but also for its lavishly ornate interior, high vaulted ceilings, majestic paintings, and fine stained-glass windows.

Lee Circle

Lee Circle (St. Charles Ave. and Howard Ave., 24 hours daily, free) is the hub for a small arts and museum district that has evolved on the streets just downriver from here since the mid-1990s. This is the one regal traffic circle in downtown New Orleans, and it imparts a slightly formal, urban air—a hint of Paris or London. Depending on which direction you're coming from, it serves as a gateway to the Garden District or the CBD. The circle was named for enslaver and Confederate General Robert E. Lee. A statue depicting Lee used to reside here. It has been taken down, though the name of the circle has not been changed.

★ The National WWII Museum

One of the nation's most exalted historians, the late Stephen Ambrose, founded **The National WWII Museum** (945 Magazine St., 504/528-1944, www.nationalww2museum.org, 9am-5pm daily, adults $28.50, seniors $24.50, military,

The National WWII Museum

students, and children 5-17 $18, free for children under 5) in the early 1990s. Ambrose, a professor at the University of New Orleans, lived in New Orleans until his death in 2002. He is best known for such riveting World War II histories as *Band of Brothers, The Wild Blue, D-Day, Citizen Soldiers,* and *The Victors.*

The museum opened to the public on June 6, 2000, the 56th anniversary of the amphibious World War II invasion. This is the only museum in the United States dedicated to this event, which involved more than a million Americans. The Andrew Higgins factory, which now houses the museum, built ships during World War II, including some of the vehicles that transported infantrymen to Normandy.

A museum visit can be an all-day (or multiday) affair; after all, it might take that long to absorb the enormous collection of exhibits documenting the Allied victory in World War II, not to mention exploring Final Mission: The USS *Tang* Submarine Experience (9:35am-4:35pm daily $7 pp), which allows visitors to relive the last epic battle of the most successful submarine in World War II, or watching the immersive 4-D, Tom Hanks-narrated documentary *Beyond All Boundaries* (10am-4pm Sun.-Thurs., 10am-5pm Fri.-Sat., $7 pp) in the 250-seat **Solomon Victory Theater.** If you have time, have a meal at the on-site restaurant, **The American Sector** (504/528-1940, 11am-6:30pm Mon.-Fri., 10am-6:30pm Sat.-Sun.), or an old-fashioned dinner theater experience in the **Stage Door Canteen** (hours vary depending on performance).

Museum of the Southern Jewish Experience

Opened in 2020, the **Museum of the Southern Jewish Experience** (818 Howard Ave., http://msje.org) covers the experience of Jewish people in 13 states through memorabilia and interactive educational displays. Exhibits cover the role of the Jewish community in the Civil War and the civil rights movement, as well as the migration of Jewish people away from the South when Ulysses S. Grant ordered them out of Mississippi, Tennessee, and Kentucky in 1862. This was just one example from a long list of anti-Semitic policies that made Jews feel unwelcome—or worse—in the area traditionally known as the Bible Belt. Today, Jews comprise just 2.1 percent of the American South.

Ogden Museum of Southern Art

Ogden Museum of Southern Art (925 Camp St., 504/539-9650, http://ogdenmuseum.org, 10am-5pm daily, adults $13.50, seniors, students, military $11, children 5-17 $6.75, free for children under 5), contains one of the country's largest collections of artwork related to the American South. This impressive complex comprises the contemporary, five-story Stephen Goldring Hall, the restored Howard Memorial Library, and the Clementine Hunter Education Wing,

Central Business District
Louisiana State University Health Sciences Center
To Handsome Willy's 1 Patio Bar & Lounge
TULANE AVE
LASALLE ST
S ROMAN ST
GRAVIER ST
S LIBERTY ST
GRAVIER ST
CLARA ST
MAGNOLIA ST
S ROBERTSON ST
FRERET ST
LASALLE ST
PERDIDO ST
New Orleans City Hall
POYDRAS ST
POYDRAS ST
2 3
Mercedes-Benz Superdome
DAVE DIXON DR
4 Smoothie King Center
S LIBERTY ST
LOYOLA AVE
LOYOLA AVE
GIROD ST
S RAMPART ST
HOWARD AVE
HOWARD AVE
CLIO ST
0 200 yds
0 200 m
DISTANCE ACROSS MAP
Approximate: 1.7 mi or 2.7 km
SIGHTS
2 Mercedes-Benz Superdome
32 St. Patrick's Church
42 Museum of the Southern Jewish Experience
43 Lee Circle
44 Ogden Museum of Southern Art
46 The National WWII Museum
52 Scrap House
54 Blaine Kern's Mardi Gras World
NIGHTLIFE
1 Handsome Willy's Patio Bar & Lounge
5 Pisco Bar
9 The Sazerac Bar
39 Mulate's
41 Republic New Orleans
50 Howlin' Wolf
51 The Metropolitan
ARTS AND CULTURE
33 New Orleans School of GlassWorks & Printmaking Studio
36 Søren Christensen Gallery
38 LeMieux Galleries
45 Contemporary Arts Center
SHOPPING
14 Rubensteins
15 Meyer the Hatter
SPORTS AND RECREATION
3 New Orleans Saints
4 New Orleans Pelicans
12 Waldorf Astoria Spa
20 Creole Queen
21 Spanish Plaza
22 Spanish Plaza
26 Lafayette Square
RESTAURANTS
7 Crystal Room
10 Teddy's Cafe
11 Domenica
17 Polo Club Lounge
18 The Grill Room
23 Bon Ton Cafe
24 Mother's Restaurant
27 Compére Lapin
29 Poydras & Peters
31 Herbsaint Bar and Restaurant
34 Tommy's Cuisine
35 Pêche Seafood Grill
37 Emeril's New Orleans
40 Root
47 The American Sector
48 Thalia
49 Cochon
HOTELS
6 Catahoula Hotel
8 Le Pavillon Hotel
13 Roosevelt New Orleans
16 International House New Orleans
19 Windsor Court Hotel
25 ACE Hotel
28 Old No. 77 Hotel & Chandlery
30 Loews New Orleans Hotel
53 Hampton Inn & Suites New Orleans Convention Center

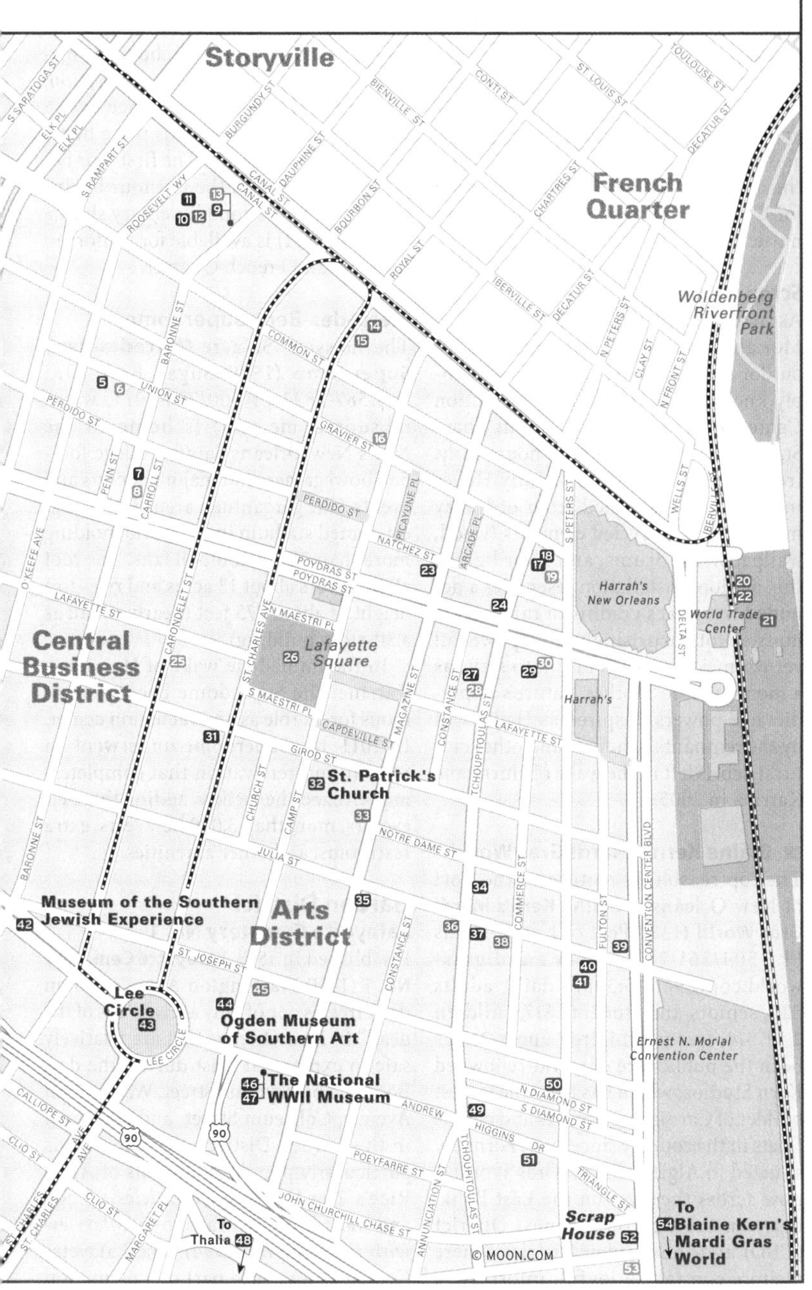
Storyville
French Quarter
Woldenberg Riverfront Park
Harrah's New Orleans
Harrah's
World Trade Center
Central Business District
Lafayette Square
St. Patrick's Church
Arts District
Museum of the Southern Jewish Experience
Lee Circle
Ogden Museum of Southern Art
The National WWII Museum
Ernest N. Morial Convention Center
Scrap House
To Blaine Kern's Mardi Gras World
To Thalia
© MOON.COM

named for the famous Louisiana folk artist who grew up on a cotton plantation in Cloutierville and produced about 4,000 works during her storied career. The artwork includes all mediums and spans the 18th to 21st centuries, representing artists from 15 Southern states as well as Washington DC. Thursday evenings the museum reopens from 6pm-8pm for Ogden After Hours, presenting live music.

Scrap House

As you drive past the enormous Ernest N. Morial Convention Center, keep an eye out for the colorful sculpture that's simply known as ***Scrap House*** (Convention Center Blvd. and John Churchill Chase St., www.sallyheller.com, 24 hours daily, free). Completed by artist Sally Heller in 2008 and fashioned from ordinary materials and recycled elements (wood, wallpaper, oil drums, and solar lights), this outdoor installation resembles a denuded tree that's cradling a ramshackle house. Not surprisingly, this powerful yet whimsical piece is meant to serve as a monument to Mother Nature's unpredictable powers, inspired as Heller was by the remnants of houses and other cultural debris left in the wake of Hurricane Katrina in 2005.

★ Blaine Kern's Mardi Gras World

The top reason to venture to the Port of New Orleans is **Blaine Kern's Mardi Gras World** (1380 Port of New Orleans Pl., 504/361-7821, www.mardigrasworld.com, 9am-5:30pm daily, adults $22, seniors and students $17, children 2-11 $14, free for children under 2). It's been the public face of world-renowned Kern Studios, which has been the largest builder of Carnival sculptures and parade floats in the country since 1947. Formerly situated in Algiers, Mardi Gras World is now across the river on the East Bank, between the Central Business District (CBD) and the Garden District, where visitors can take a joyful, informative guided tour of the facility. The one-hour tour includes a stroll amid kaleidoscopic floats, the observation of working artists and artisans, and a video about the history of the city's Mardi Gras celebration. Though Mardi Gras takes place over a short period each year, this place hums with activity every day. The first tour begins at 9:30am and the last tour begins at 4:30pm, and a complimentary shuttle (504/361-7821) is available for visitors in the CBD and French Quarter.

Mercedes-Benz Superdome

The massive, 52-acre **Mercedes-Benz Superdome** (1500 Sugar Bowl Dr., 504/587-3822 or 800/756-7074, www.mbsuperdome.com) is home to the NFL's New Orleans Saints, college football bowl games, and major concerts and events. The gargantuan arena is the largest domed stadium in the world, holding more than 76,000 football fans. The roof alone covers about 13 acres and rises to a height of about 273 feet (nearly as tall as a 30-story building).

In the immediate wake of Hurricane Katrina, the Superdome became infamous for its role as an evacuation center. In 2011, the Superdome underwent an $85 million renovation that completely modernized the facility, adding three elevators, more than 3,000 new seats, extra restrooms, and other amenities.

Garden District

Lafayette Cemetery No. 1

Established in 1833, **Lafayette Cemetery No. 1** (1400 Washington Ave., 7am-3pm daily free) is one of only a few "cities of the dead" in New Orleans that are relatively safe to explore, at least during the day. Bordered by Prytania Street, Washington Avenue, Coliseum Street, and 6th Street in the Garden District, the cemetery is particularly popular with fans of Anne Rice's *The Vampire Chronicles* trilogy and was featured in the movie *Interview with the Vampire* (1994). The Lafayette Cemetery was once part of a plantation

Mister Mardi Gras

For many years, families have flocked to **Blaine Kern's Mardi Gras World** (www.mardigrasworld.com). This vibrant attraction offers visitors a behind-the-scenes glimpse at the magic of Mardi Gras, one of the city's oldest traditions. Here, you'll see a variety of colorful floats and get the chance to watch the artists and artisans of **Kern Studios** (www.kernstudios.com) hard at work.

Blaine Kern's Mardi Gras World

As the names indicate, the heart and soul behind Blaine Kern's Mardi Gras World (also known simply as Mardi Gras World) and Kern Studios is Blaine Kern Sr. himself—the man known as Mister Mardi Gras. Born in 1927, Blaine grew up on the west bank of the Mississippi River. His early interest in the arts was inspired by his proximity to New Orleans as well as the vocation of his father, Roy, a sign painter who survived the Depression by painting names on the bows of freighters.

When Blaine's mother was hospitalized, he offset the family's medical bills by painting a mural in the hospital—a mural that captured the attention of a surgeon who was also the captain of a Mardi Gras krewe. Blaine began designing floats soon afterward and was eventually hired to fashion a complete parade. In 1947, he established Blaine Kern Artists (which eventually evolved into Kern Studios) in Algiers and, over time, became the Big Easy's leading parade creator, working with Rex, Zulu, Bacchus, and all the legendary krewes.

Following his travels to Italy, where he was impressed by the extravagant animation and prop concepts that distinguished the European style of float building, Blaine began to embrace the monumental scale and lavish ornamentation that mark contemporary Mardi Gras parades. Today, Kern Studios produces floats and props for more than 40 New Orleans parades, including Endymion and Orpheus, as well as pageants throughout the world. Kern props and sculptures also enhance themed environments in Walt Disney World, Universal Studios, and Japan's Toho Park.

owned by the Livaudais family. As a cemetery, it has always been nonsegregated and nondenominational; you'll see the tombs of American merchants, African families, and German, Irish, Italian, English, Scottish, and Dutch immigrants, not to mention several Civil War soldiers.

The office is at 1427 6th Street. Taking a properly vetted, guided tour is preferable, particularly for history buffs. Tours are offered by various companies, most notably **Save Our Cemeteries** (SOC, 501 Basin St., #3C, 504/525-3377, www.saveourcemeteries.org, adults $15, free for children under 12), a nonprofit organization that preserves the city's burial grounds. The one-hour walks occur daily at 10:30am, which means that it's still possible to experience the cemetery on Sunday, when it's normally closed to the public. Please be respectful; this is an active cemetery that still welcomes mourners.

Southern Food & Beverage Museum

In a city that is celebrated around the world for its cuisine, it's not surprising that the **Southern Food & Beverage Museum** (SoFaB, 1504 Oretha Castle Haley Blvd., 504/569-0405, http://natfab.org, 11am-5:30pm Wed.-Mon., adults $10.50, seniors and students $5.25, free for children under 12) is a huge draw. It features the **Museum of the American Cocktail** as well, included in the price of admissions. Dedicated to the discovery and appreciation of the food, drinks, and related culture of the American South, the museum's temporary and permanent exhibits explore an assortment of tasty topics, including Southern barbecue and liquor, Gulf Coast seafood, and praline vendors.

Uptown

Audubon Zoo

Below Magazine Street lies 58-acre **Audubon Zoo** (6500 Magazine St., 504/861-2537 or 800/774-7394, www.auduboninstitute.org, 10am-4pm Tues.-Fri., 10am-5pm Sat.-Sun., adults $23, seniors $20, children 2-12 $18, free for children under 2), a significant part of the larger Audubon Park. Established in 1914, it contains historical buildings, notable sculptures, and nearly 2,000 animals from around the world.

The award-winning **Louisiana Swamp** exhibit is the next best thing to taking a swamp tour and even better in one respect: You're guaranteed to see marsh wildlife up close and personal. The swamp exhibit is a recreation of a Depression-era Cajun swamp settlement, complete with old bayou shacks and a trapper's cottage. The albino alligators never cease to amaze, and the ever-frisky river otters are endlessly amusing.

St. Charles Streetcar

No one should leave New Orleans without taking a ride on one of the city's famous, oft-photographed streetcars. While there are six separate lines—the St. Charles, the Loyola-UPT, the Canal-Cemeteries, the Canal-City Park/Museum, the Rampart, and the Riverfront—the most famous by far and most beloved by residents and tourists alike is the **St. Charles line** (Canal St. and Carondelet St. to S. Carrollton Ave. and S. Claiborne Ave., 504/248-3900, www.norta.com, hours vary daily, $1.25 one-way), which dates back to 1835 and has been featured in numerous films over the years. Because of the line's presence on the National Register of Historic Places, the olive-green Perley Thomas streetcars currently in use must be preserved as they looked in 1923, which makes for a retro riding experience. A one-way ride on the St. Charles line, which runs 24 hours daily, lasts about 45 minutes and is well worth the time.

Tremé and Mid-City

★ City Park

Near the Lakeview and Mid-City neighborhoods, **City Park** (1 Palm Dr., 504/482-4888, http://neworleanscitypark.com, hours vary seasonally, free) is bordered by Robert E. Lee Boulevard, Marconi Drive, City Park Avenue, and Wisner Boulevard.

Considerably larger than New York City's Central Park, this 1,300-acre spread sits on what was once a swampy oak forest. It still contains the nation's largest collection of mature live oaks, some believed to date to the 1400s or earlier. Stop by the **Timken Center,** housed in a 1913 Spanish Mission-style building, for sandwiches, ice cream, and refreshments before exploring the park.

City Park encompasses several worthwhile attractions. The **New Orleans Botanical Garden** (10am-5pm daily, adults $8, children ages 3-12 $4, free for children 2 and under) is filled with thematic gardens, making it a wonderful place for a relaxing stroll. Another tranquil locale is the **Sydney and Walda Besthoff Sculpture Garden,** a free outdoor extension of the New Orleans Museum of Art.

Children are particularly fond of the **Carousel Gardens Amusement Park** (504/483-9402, hours vary seasonally, $5 admission, $4 per ride, $18 unlimited rides, free for kids 36 inches and under), which features numerous rides and a mini train that tours the park. The historic carousel was established here in 1906 and eventually listed on the National Register of Historic Places; it's now the last antique wooden carousel in Louisiana.

Since the 1950s **Storyland** (10am-5pm daily, $5 pp, free for kids 36 inches and under) has captivated New Orleanians and their kids. Remodeled in 2019, the property features 25 larger-than-life sculptures, each based on a different fairy tale, from Captain Hook's pirate ship to the Three Little Pigs. Paid admission to Storyland, the New Orleans Botanical Garden, or the Carousel Gardens Amusement Park allows you access to all three.

Across the street from City Park is the somber **Hurricane Katrina Memorial** (5056 Canal St.), a memorial to those who lost their lives in 2005. It features a hurricane-shaped walkway and is the

City Park

final resting place of the unknown victims of the storm.

New Orleans Museum of Art

The vast holdings of the fabulous **New Orleans Museum of Art** (NOMA, 1 Collins Diboll Circle, City Park, 504/658-4100, http://noma.org, 10am-6pm Tues.-Fri., 10am-5pm Sat., 11am-5pm Sun., adults $15, seniors and military $10, college students $8, free for ages 19 and under) total about 40,000 objects that span a variety of cultures and eras—from pre-Columbian, Native American, and Mayan artwork to French Impressionist paintings. The city's oldest fine arts institution is justly known for its excellent rotating exhibits, including everything from creative bookmarks to the 19th-century mass production of British decorative arts. The museum is also an architectural marvel, an imposing Beaux Arts-style building that dates to 1911. A cleverly appended modern addition was completed in 1971 and renovated in the 1990s.

The **Sydney and Walda Besthoff Sculpture Garden** (10am-6pm daily Apr.-Sept., 10am-5pm daily Oct.-Mar., free) is a jaw-dropping outdoor attraction. Peppered with magnolias, pines, and Spanish moss-draped live oaks, this peaceful, 11-acre spread encompasses lagoons, pedestrian bridges, and more than 86 impressive sculptures. Noted works include sculptures by Pierre-Auguste Renoir, Ida Kohlmeyer, and Claes Oldenburg. A free cell-phone tour is available.

St. Louis Cemetery No. 1

Arguably the oldest and most famous of New Orleans's "cities of the dead," **St. Louis Cemetery No. 1** (425 Basin St., 504/482-5065, http://nolacatholiccemeteries.org, 9:15am-4pm daily, free) was established in 1789, following the Great

Top to bottom: Backstreet Cultural Museum; Le Musée de f.p.c.; Longue Vue House & Gardens

Fire of 1788, and set outside what was then the city border. Since New Orleans sits below sea level and has a high water table, bodies were buried aboveground, as earlier attempts to bury the dead underground had resulted in caskets floating to the surface during floods.

Bordered by Basin, Conti, Tremé, and St. Louis Streets, the cemetery currently contains more than 700 tombs and has interred thousands of people. Most of these aboveground structures are owned by families and designed to hold multiple sets of remains. Though constructed of brick, the elaborate tombs are often covered in concrete or stucco; some of the oldest ones are little more than crumbled ruins and piles of brick dust. One curious element is the segregated Protestant section near the rear of the predominantly Catholic cemetery. Famous residents here include Homer Plessy (of *Plessy v. Ferguson* fame) and the much-loved voodoo priestess **Marie Laveau,** whose supposed tomb is a frequent stop on daily tours.

The Archdiocese of New Orleans requires all tourists (those unrelated to the deceased) to enter the premises with a licensed tour guide. While several organizations offer guided tours, one of the most well-respected is **Save Our Cemeteries** (504/525-3377, www.saveourcemeteries.org, tours daily, times vary, adults $25, free for children under 12), which leads hour-long excursions through the cemetery. Tours depart from the lobby of the nearby Basin Street Station. View the full list of licensed guides on the website (http://nolacatholiccemeteries.org).

Backstreet Cultural Museum

If you were a fan of HBO's acclaimed show *Treme* or simply curious about the Big Easy's vibrant African American culture, you're in for a treat. Not far from Louis Armstrong Park—the original site of Congo Square—lies the fascinating **Backstreet Cultural Museum** (1116 Henriette Delille St., 504/606-4809, www.backstreetmuseum.org, 10am-4pm Mon.-Fri., 10am-3pm Sat., $10). The museum contains the world's most comprehensive collection of costumes, films, and photographs from jazz funerals and pleasure clubs, plus Carnival-related groups like the Mardi Gras Indians, Baby Dolls, and Skull and Bone Gang. Beyond the permanent exhibits, the museum presents public performances of traditional music and dance.

Le Musée de f.p.c.

While there were freed people of the color all over the U.S. before the Civil War, New Orleans was the city with the largest population of people of African descent who were not enslaved. The lives and history of some of these free people of color is told at **Le Musee de f.p.c.** (2336 Esplanade Ave., 504/323-5074, www.lemuseedefpc.com, $15, tours by appointment only, tour availability 1-4pm Tues.-Fri., 11am and noon Sat., 1pm and 2pm Sun.). The museum is packed into a Greek Revival house with artifacts on every surface, all from a private collection. Tours are led by knowledgeable scholars, offering perspective on the experiences of freed people of color, which included those of African and Creole decent, and how those experiences were different both from the enslaved and from free white people that many other museums don't. Time periods covered include pre-Civil War through Reconstruction and into the Civil Rights Movement.

Greater New Orleans

Longue Vue House & Gardens

One of the city's most impressive attractions is often overlooked by visitors simply because it's slightly off the beaten path. Near the border between New Orleans and Old Metairie, the **Longue Vue House & Gardens** (7 Bamboo Rd., 504/488-5488, www.longuevue.com, 10am-5pm Mon.-Sat., 1pm-5pm Sun., adults $12, seniors $10, students 11-17 $8, children 3-10 $5, free for active military and children under 3) is a lush, exotic, eight-acre estate that once belonged to local community pillars Edgar and Edith Stern and their children. Designed and constructed between 1939 and 1942 by architects William and Geoffrey Platt and landscape architect Ellen Biddle Shipman, the tranquil property was intended to be one organic whole, uniting the house and gardens seamlessly. Today, this serene place represents one of the last Country Place Era homes built in America. It comprises a period-furnished Classical Revival-style manor house, several outbuildings, 14 spectacularly landscaped garden areas, and 22 ponds and fountains.

Guided and Walking Tours

Photogenic New Orleans boasts a slew of guided tour companies. One of the most authentic is **Historic New Orleans Tours** (various locations, 504/947-2120, www.tourneworleans.com, hours vary, adults $25, seniors, students, and active military $18, children 6-12 $7, free for children under 6). Walking tours focus on French Quarter history, voodoo culture, the city's jazz scene, the Garden District, and legendary hauntings. On the two-hour Garden District Tour, guides explain the history of the city's American Sector, point out notable buildings (including the former homes of Anne Rice and Peyton Manning), and discuss their colorful heritage; you'll also get the chance to explore the aboveground tombs within Lafayette Cemetery No. 1. The company also offers swamp tours, plus van excursions through the city's varied neighborhoods.

For an intimate tour of the French Quarter, take one of the two-hour, narrated strolls led by the nonprofit **Friends of the Cabildo** (701 Chartres St., 504/523-3939, www.friendsofthecabildo.org, 9am-4:30pm Mon.-Fri., adults $22, seniors, students, and active military $17). Conducted by licensed guides, these well-respected tours highlight the history, folklore, and architecture of one of the country's oldest neighborhoods, known alternatively as the Vieux Carré. Tours depart from the **1850 House Museum Store** (523 St. Ann St., 504/524-9118, 10am-4:30pm Tues.-Sun., $5 adults, $4 students, seniors, and active military, children 12 and under free) and are offered daily at 10:30am and 1:30pm. All proceeds benefit the Friends of the Cabildo, a volunteer group that supports the Louisiana State Museum.

Riverboat Tours

Launched by the **New Orleans Steamboat Company** (504/586-8777 or 800/233-2628, www.neworleanssteamboatcompany.com) in 1975, the **Steamboat *Natchez*** (Toulouse St. Wharf, 504/586-8777 or 800/233-2628, www.steamboatnatchez.com) is an authentic, steam-powered sternwheeler modeled after the *Virginia* and the *Hudson*, two sternwheelers of old. The *Natchez* offers two-hour **harbor cruises** (11:30am and 2:30pm Mon.-Sat., adults $36, seniors $32.50 children 6-12 $15.50, free for children under 6), departing from the foot of Toulouse Street. While on board, you can visit the steam engine room, listen to live narration about the history of the port, enjoy a concert of the onboard, 32-note steam calliope, and opt for a Creole lunch (adults $48, seniors $43.50, children 6-12 $24, children 2-5 $10.50, price includes cruise). Alternatively, you can board a **dinner jazz cruise** (7pm daily, adults $85, seniors $76.50, children 6-12 $40, children under 6 $19.25), which features decent buffet-style dining, live jazz by the Dukes of Dixieland, and gorgeous views of the city. Although sightseeing on the deck is a highlight of any *Natchez* excursion, climate-controlled indoor seating is always available (and particularly welcome on hot or rainy days).

For a memorable excursion along the Mississippi River, board the majestic **Creole Queen** (1 Poydras St., 504/529-4567 or 800/445-4109, www.creolequeen.

com), an authentic paddlewheeler that, with its Victorian-style furniture and wrought-iron deck railings, harkens back to those of the mid-1800s. Operated by New Orleans Paddlewheels, Inc., the *Creole Queen* offers two daily historical river cruises (9:30am and 1:30pm, adults $36, children 6-12 $15, free for children under 6). You can also opt for the nightly three-hour **dinner jazz cruise** (6:30pm daily, adults $52-84, children 6-12 $26-40, free-$15 for children 3-5), which includes a scenic river cruise, a Creole buffet, and live jazz music.

For all cruises, it's a good idea to arrive 30 minutes before boarding time.

Entertainment and Events

Nightlife

New Orleans is synonymous with nightlife. The city boasts a cornucopia of funky watering holes, festive gay bars, stylish hotel lounges, and legendary tourist magnets like Pat O'Brien's, famous for its knock-me-under-the-table hurricanes.

The Big Easy's reputation as a party town is well deserved, and the pulse of that party is often found on Bourbon Street in the French Quarter. Unabashed strip clubs, karaoke bars, daiquiri shops, pulsating dance spaces, and a few well-respected jazz venues line the colorful strip. But it can also be a loud, sometimes obnoxious, often smelly thoroughfare that can become frighteningly crowded at Mardi Gras and Halloween. A drunken scene most nights, Bourbon is not for everyone, but it's worth a look.

It's the boisterous music scene that truly distinguishes New Orleans. This is one of the world's premier destinations for jazz, blues, rock, soul, zydeco, and Cajun music. The city's live music venues are equally varied, ranging from friendly neighborhood bars to capacious music halls.

Many bars are cash-only, and restrooms are typically reserved for paying customers. Given the prevalence of 24-hour bars and restaurants, New Orleans is a wonderful place for night owls.

Safety

The city's revelry can be disarming. This is a town with drive-through daiquiri shops, where you can walk down Bourbon with enormous "go-cups" of beer, and where residents tend to be a friendly bunch. Unfortunately, though, this is still a relatively dangerous city, where tourists have been known to wander off the beaten path and encounter aggressive muggers. This is particularly true in the French Quarter, where criminals expect to find tourists unaware, but happens throughout the whole city, too. The best advice is to travel in groups, have fun in moderation, be aware of your surroundings at all times, and make sure that someone is sober enough to find a safe path back to your hotel.

Bars and Lounges

French Quarter

Even if you're not staying at the legendary Hotel Monteleone, you can still enjoy a libation in the colorful **Carousel Bar & Lounge** (Hotel Monteleone, 214 Royal St., 504/523-3341, http://hotelmonteleone.com, 11am-close daily) on the first floor. The prime attraction—the kitschy, 1940s-style, 25-seat bar—is festooned with bright lights and garish decorations, but the real treat is that, as its name implies, the bar slowly revolves around the center of the room. Stop by to savor the old-world ambience, watch passersby on Royal Street, and listen to live music in the adjacent lounge.

Contained within a building that dates back to the early 1800s, **Jean Lafitte's Old Absinthe House** (240 Bourbon St., 504/523-3181, www.ruebourbon.com/old-absinthe-house, 9am-4am daily) is popular among lawyers and other professionals. Furnished with antique

Greater New Orleans

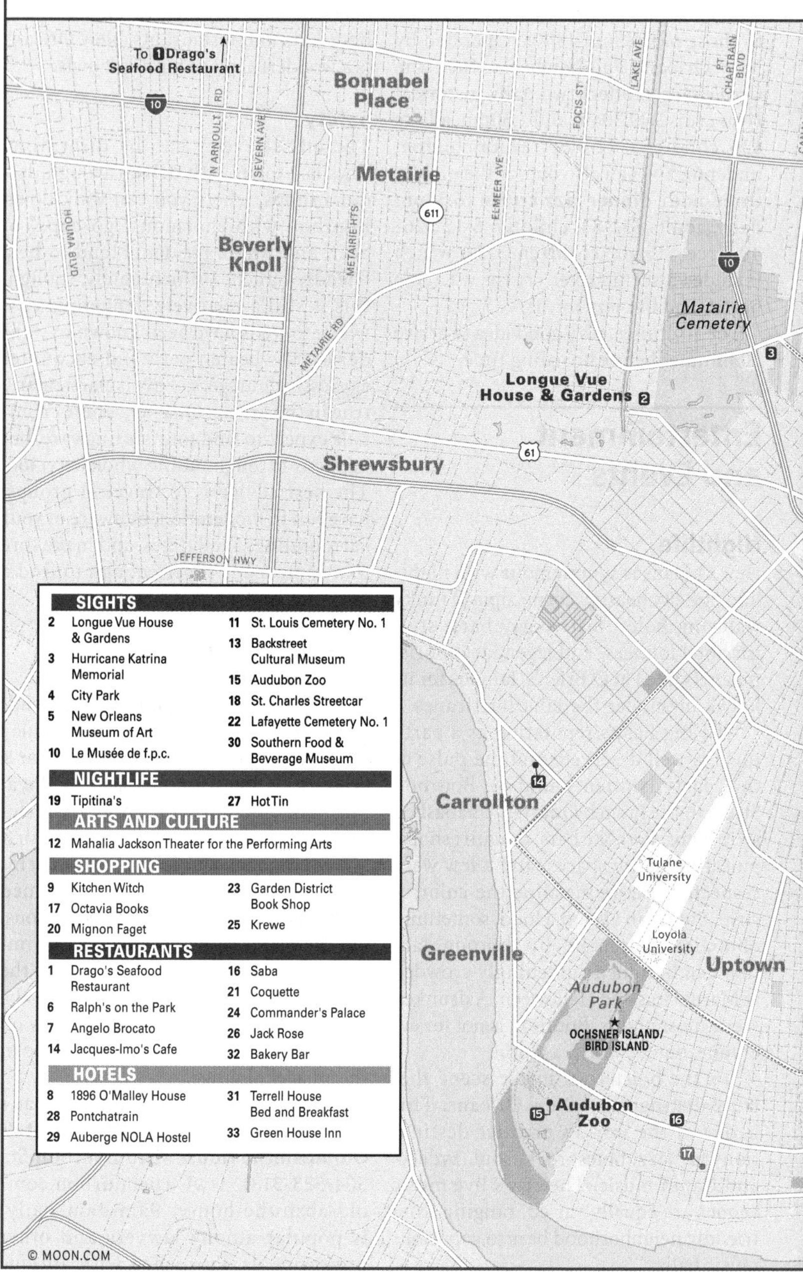

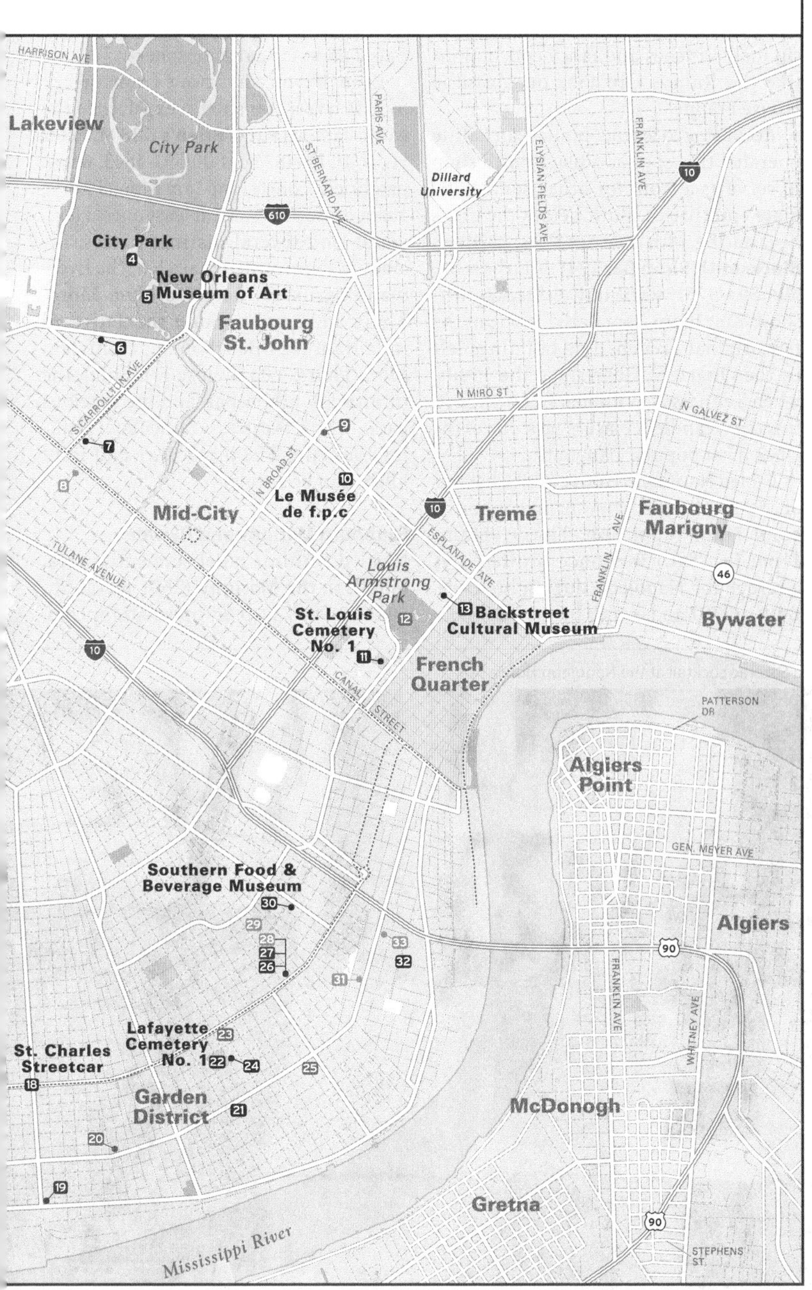

Lakeview
City Park
Dillard University
City Park
New Orleans Museum of Art
Faubourg St. John
Mid-City
Le Musée de f.p.c
Tremé
Faubourg Marigny
Louis Armstrong Park
St. Louis Cemetery No. 1
Backstreet Cultural Museum
Bywater
French Quarter
Algiers Point
Algiers
Southern Food & Beverage Museum
Lafayette Cemetery No. 1
St. Charles Streetcar
Garden District
McDonogh
Gretna
Mississippi River
HARRISON AVE
PARIS AVE
ST BERNARD AVE
ELYSIAN FIELDS AVE
FRANKLIN AVE
S CARROLLTON AVE
N BROAD ST
N MIRO ST
N GALVEZ ST
TULANE AVENUE
ESPLANADE AVE
CANAL STREET
PATTERSON DR
GEN. MEYER AVE
WHITNEY AVE
STEPHENS ST

chandeliers, a copper-topped bar, and the paraphernalia of famous football legends, this cozy tavern is an ideal spot to sip malt scotches and fancy concoctions like the Ramos Gin Fizz or Absinthe House Frappe.

According to legend, pirate Jean Lafitte operated this spot as a blacksmith shop to serve as a front for other, less legitimate enterprises. Built before the city's devastating 18th-century fires, **Lafitte's Blacksmith Shop Bar** (941 Bourbon St., 504/593-9761, www.lafittesblacksmithshop.com, 10am-3am daily) is one of the few original French-style buildings left in the Quarter. A bar since the 1940s, when Tennessee Williams frequented it, this cozy, candlelit place is now one of the city's most popular hangouts.

Fabled **Napoleon House** (500 Chartres St., 504/524-9752, www.napoleonhouse.com, 11am-10pm Sun.-Thurs., 11am-11pm Fri.-Sat.) was once proffered as a refuge for Napoleon during his exile. Built in 1797 and owned by the Impastato family since 1914, this world-famous landmark is a terrific place to park your feet, particularly if you favor classical music and a casual atmosphere.

Even if you shy away from pricey tourist traps, you should experience the world-famous **Pat O'Brien's** (718 St. Peter St., 504/525-4823 or 800/597-4823, www.patobriens.com, 11am-2am Mon.-Thurs., 10am-close Fri.-Sun.) at least once. Here, you'll find several distinct spaces, including the crowded main bar, the lively piano bar (show begins at 6pm Mon.-Thurs. and 2pm Fri.-Sun.), the courtyard restaurant (624 Bourbon St., 11am-2am Mon.-Thurs., 10am-close Fri.-Sun.), the intimate Bourbon Bar, and the spacious patio, which features a rather cool flaming fountain. The hurricanes and mint juleps can be strong.

Faubourg Marigny and Bywater

Nestled within a quiet residential area, **Mimi's in the Marigny** (2601 Royal St., 504/872-9868, http://mimismarigny.com,

a Sazerac cocktail at the Napoleon House

11am-close daily, no cover) has long been a popular hot spot, particularly among locals. Downstairs, you'll find a neighborhood bar with couches, stools, and a pool table, while the upstairs space is often a live music venue, with a decent amount of room for dancing. At times, you can expect concerts and DJ-helmed dance parties, not to mention dance lessons. Try the tasty tapas on offer, from almond-stuffed dates to beef empanadas; the kitchen is typically open 1pm-close daily.

Central Business and Arts Districts

The Sazerac Bar (The Roosevelt New Orleans, 130 Roosevelt Way, 504/648-1200, www.therooseveltneworleans.com, 11am-2am daily), at the CBD's grand Roosevelt New Orleans, is perhaps the most famous hotel lounge in the city. Named for the noted cocktail—a concoction of rye whiskey, Pernod, sugar, lemon oil, and the local Peychaud's bitters—the bar was once a favored haunt of Governor Huey P. Long, the infamous "Kingfish" of Louisiana.

Named for the Peruvian liquor made from grapes, **Pisco Bar** (Catahoula Hotel, 914 Union St., 504/603-2442, http://catahoulahotel.com, 5pm-10pm daily) serves the classic Peruvian pisco sour, of course, plus more unusual beverages, such as the cinnamon-topped Chinguerito. The bar is packed early in the evening, as it is a popular post-work stop for locals before venturing out for the night. The bartenders are knowledgeable and friendly, making this a great place to try something new.

LGBTQ Nightlife

French Quarter

One of the most popular gay dance clubs sits at the often-rowdy corner of Bourbon and St. Ann. The **Bourbon Pub & Parade** (801 Bourbon St., 504/529-2107, www.bourbonpub.com, 11am-3am Sun.-Thurs., 10am-5am Fri.-Sat., cover varies) has a typically packed video bar on the ground level, a slick dance floor upstairs, and a long wraparound balcony on the second floor—a favorite perch from which to gaze at the throngs of revelers on Bourbon Street. Music lovers can expect to see plenty of retro music videos downstairs, while everything from drag and burlesque shows to hot guy contests to karaoke nights is happening upstairs.

Cafe Lafitte in Exile (901 Bourbon St., 504/522-8397, www.lafittes.com, 24 hours daily, no cover) has been serving the local gay community for roughly as long as any bar in town. It draws a 30- to 50-something crowd. You can watch music videos in the downstairs bar and observe curious passersby from the upstairs balcony, which can be particularly eye-opening during uninhibited, skin-baring events like Mardi Gras and Southern Decadence.

The mellow, longstanding **Good Friends Bar** (740 Dauphine St., 504/566-7191, www.goodfriendsbar.com, 24 hours daily, no cover) isn't too loud or flashy.

It's just a casual, pet-friendly neighborhood watering hole, where you'll find a pool table, affordable beer and cocktails, a slightly fancier upstairs area, and attentive bartenders. Saints fans come here, as do low-key locals, and no matter your sexual orientation, you're welcome to join in the karaoke fun every Tuesday night (8pm-11pm).

Faubourg Marigny and Bywater

Definitely not for the faint-hearted, the rowdy **AllWays Lounge & Theatre** (2240 St. Claude Ave., 504/321-5606, www.theallwayslounge.net, 6pm-close daily, cover varies) welcomes everybody, though it has a predominantly gay and lesbian following. Nudity, wacky sexual acts, and strange musical performances are common in the lounge. The theater features ever-changing productions, including bizarre concerts and counterculture musicals like *The Rocky Horror Picture Show*. Shows generally start at 10pm.

Although **The Country Club** (634 Louisa St., 504/945-0742, www.thecountryclubneworleans.com, 10am-1am daily, no cover), set in a magnificent Bywater mansion, isn't technically a gay bar, it definitely embraces an anything goes vibe, with its clothing-optional pool, sauna, Jacuzzi, and on-site massage and spa services. You can sip cocktails in the indoor or outdoor bars, enjoy creative cuisine in the restaurant (Sun.-Thurs. 10am-9pm, Fri.-Sat. 10am-10pm), or watch movies, music videos, and sporting events on the 25-foot screen. If the crowd is really hoppin', the joint might not close until 2am or later. Expect to pay $15 to access the area that houses the pool.

Jazz

French Quarter

Since 1961, **Preservation Hall** (726 St. Peter St., 504/522-2841, www.preservationhall.com, box office 11am-4pm daily, shows 5pm-11pm daily, cover $20) has been one of the city's top places to hear true New Orleans jazz. The band and the venue were formed expressly to keep the legacy of the city's distinctive style of jazz music alive for generations to come, and top musicians continue to perform in the surprisingly intimate concert hall. Housed within a weathered, 1750s-era house, it's a charming, laid-back place, with vintage wooden benches, folding chairs, and a good bit of standing room. After the all-too-brief concert (usually less than an hour), feel free to stroll along the carriageway, to the landscaped courtyard for a breath of fresh air. Get here early, as the line forms quickly for these nightly concerts (5pm, 6pm, 8pm, 9pm, and 10pm daily). If you'd rather skip the line altogether, opt for the limited "Big Shot" seating ($40-50).

No matter the evening, it's difficult to cross the corner of Decatur Street and Esplanade Avenue without catching some of the fantastic tunes coming from the open doors of the funky **Balcony Music Club** (1331 Decatur St., 504/301-5912, 5pm-2am Mon.-Thurs., 3pm-4am Fri., noon-4am Sat., noon-2am Sun., cover varies), known colloquially as the BMC. Though you're most likely to hear brass, jazz, or funk, anything is possible. If you're still in the mood for fun after this place closes, just hop across Esplanade to **Igor's Check Point Charlie** (501 Esplanade Ave., 504/281-4847, 24 hours daily), a lively 24-hour bar, grill, music club, game room, and self-service laundry.

On the ground floor of the elegant Royal Sonesta hotel, in the heart of Bourbon Street's revelry, the stylish **Irvin Mayfield's Jazz Playhouse** (Royal Sonesta New Orleans, 300 Bourbon St., 504/553-2299 or 504/586-0300, 4pm-midnight Sat.-Thurs., 4pm-1am Fri., showtimes vary, no cover) welcomes jazz aficionados and curious tourists every night of the week. Although the musicians rotate nightly, you're always guaranteed to hear some stellar performers. On Friday night, stick around until midnight to experience a classy burlesque show. You can purchase a limited number of reserved seats online for $20 (one-drink minimum), and the remainder of seating is for walk-ins.

One of the Big Easy's most famous and delightful live jazz venues is the **Palm Court Jazz Cafe** (1204 Decatur St., 504/525-0200, www.palmcourtjazzcafe.com, 7pm-11pm Wed.-Sun., no cover), in a handsome, 19th-century building near the historic French Market. Besides Southern-style ceiling fans and an elegant mahogany bar, the restaurant features exposed-brick walls lined with photos of jazz greats, plus a kitchen producing tasty Creole fare. Because seating is arranged at tables over dinner, reservations are a must.

Faubourg Marigny and Bywater

At the aptly named **Snug Harbor Jazz Bistro** (626 Frenchmen St., 504/949-0696, www.snugjazz.com, 5pm-10:45pm Sun.-Thurs., 5pm-11:45pm Fri.-Sat., $15-35 pp), a cozy, classy, contemporary spot, you can sip cocktails in the downstairs bar or relish tasty regional cuisine in the adjacent dining room, before heading upstairs to catch some of the city's top jazz acts. Occupying a renovated, 19th-century storefront on Frenchmen, Snug Harbor has been showcasing top musicians, from Ellis Marsalis to Charmaine Neville, as well as nurturing young talent for more than three decades.

Practically across the street from Snug Harbor lies the **Spotted Cat Music Club** (623 Frenchmen St., www.spottedcatmusicclub.com, 2pm-2am Sat.-Sun. daily, no cover, one-drink minimum), a less famous, cash-only jazz club that qualifies as one of the coolest little music finds in the city. This happily cramped, dark, and sweaty dance hall offers a long happy hour, a nice selection of designer martinis, and terrific live bands. Although you'll occasionally hear rock, blues, bluegrass, salsa, and other dance-worthy musical styles, modern and traditional jazz are definitely the mainstays here.

Blues and Rock

French Quarter

Part of the famous chain, the predictably popular tourist haunt **House of Blues** (225 Decatur St., 504/310-4999, www.houseofblues.com/neworleans, 11:30am-close daily, cover varies) has been enticing legions of music fans since its 1994 opening. Home to a large folk art collection, the funky, colorful concert venue features two music halls, which can accommodate about 370 and 840 guests, respectively. Various performers play here, from major rock bands to local jazz and blues musicians. Particularly popular is Sunday's Gospel Brunch, which combines world-class performances with a Southern-style buffet.

Faubourg Marigny and Bywater

In the heart of the Marigny's lively music scene, the intimate, somewhat dingy **Apple Barrel Bar** (609 Frenchmen St., 504/949-9399, 3pm-4am Mon.-Thurs., 1pm-4am Fri.-Sun., no cover, one-drink minimum) lures an ever-revolving crowd of blues and jazz lovers nightly. Hip yet happily low-key, this is an ideal spot for sipping cocktails before heading out to the noisier music clubs along Frenchmen—though, be advised, it can still get pretty loud in here, depending on who's playing.

A Faubourg Marigny mainstay, the spacious **Blue Nile** (532 Frenchmen St., 504/766-6193, http://bluenilelive.com, 8:30pm-1am Tues., 8pm-2am Wed., 7pm-4am Thurs.-Sat., 7pm-1am Sun., cover varies) presents a broad mix of cool music, from blues and jazz to reggae and garage rock. Frequent acts include the Honey Island Swamp Band and local fave Kermit Ruffins and the BBQ Swingers. Typically, there are two shows each night, with the first starting around 7 or 8pm and the second kicking off at 10 or 11pm. With its plush lounge seating and tile floors, it's a funky yet elegant place to socialize early in the evening.

Located in a building from the late 19th

century, the dimly lit **d.b.a. New Orleans** (618 Frenchmen St., 504/942-3731, www.dbaneworleans.com, 5pm-close Mon.-Thurs., 4pm-close Fri.-Sun., cover varies) is a good place to meet locals, hear live rock and blues bands, and, on occasion, catch performances from the likes of Jimmy Buffett and Stevie Wonder.

Central Business and Arts Districts

For the most part, you'll catch top blues and funk acts at the **Howlin' Wolf** (907 S. Peters St., 504/529-5844, www.thehowlinwolf.com, 11pm-11pm Mon.-Thurs., 11am-2am Fri.-Sun., cover varies), a cavernous nightclub in the Arts District, not far from the city's convention center. This is one of the Big Easy's largest and most prominent live music venues, which has been known to host rock, alternative, pop, and R&B bands, too.

Uptown

For catching rock (both hard-edged and down-home), jazz, zydeco, Cajun, and blues, there may be no club in the city more acclaimed or more festive than **Tipitina's** (501 Napoleon Ave., 504/895-8477, www.tipitinas.com, box office 10am-4:30pm Mon.-Fri., hours and cover vary depending on show), a longstanding venue in the heart of Uptown. Purists may tell you that Tip's has lost its edge and no longer presents the best—or at least most distinctive—local acts, but anybody looking for an introduction to the city's eclectic music scene should head here. Entertainment varies greatly, but no matter what's playing, you can probably dance to it.

Cajun and Zydeco

Central Business and Arts Districts

Mulate's (201 Julia St., 504/522-1492, www.mulates.com, 11am-10pm Sun.-Thurs., 11am-11pm Fri.-Sat., no cover) features live bands, plenty of dancing space, and a menu filled with Louisiana favorites. In the Arts District, this down-home Cajun restaurant and dance hall occupies a large building. The music is far superior to the food. Expect live entertainment nightly (7pm-10pm).

Wine Bars

French Quarter

The intimate **Orleans Grapevine Wine Bar & Bistro** (720 Orleans St., 504/523-1930, www.orleansgrapevine.com, 4pm-midnight daily) is one of the rare reasonably priced yet sophisticated bars in the French Quarter. Set inside a restored 1809 building, it's a classy yet casual bistro in the oft-overlooked block between the peaceful rear garden of the St. Louis Cathedral and the craziness of Bourbon Street. Besides featuring an extensive list of 450 bottled wines and 75 varietals by the glass, the Grapevine turns out an elegant and tasty menu, including revolving delicacies like baked brie and stuffed flounder. Expect meal service Sunday-Thursday 5pm-10:30pm and Friday-Saturday 5pm-11pm.

Faubourg Marigny and Bywater

Spotted in HBO's acclaimed show *Treme,* **Bacchanal** (600 Poland Ave., 504/948-9111, www.bacchanalwine.com, 11am-midnight daily) is a stylish wine bar and retail shop, a New York-style deli, an international bistro, and, when weather allows it in the exposed courtyard, a live music venue. Come for the wine list and the views, stay for the experience. This local favorite offers an ever-changing, culinary experience that you must embrace firsthand to understand.

The Arts

A longtime haven for artists, writers, and musicians, New Orleans has a rich, multicultural tradition in the arts.

The city is home to numerous outstanding galleries, with particularly strong concentrations along Royal and Chartres Streets in the French Quarter, around Julia Street in the Arts District, and along funky Magazine Street in Uptown.

Galleries

French Quarter

The eye-catching **Craig Tracy's Fine-Art Bodypainting Gallery** (827 Royal St., 504/592-9886, http://craigtracy.com, 10am-6pm daily) presents the innovative creations of Craig Tracy, an internationally known artist who paints landscapes, storms, animal prints, and other patterns on naked human bodies, then photographs his living creations. Gorgeous and mesmerizing, his artwork typically requires intense concentration to discern the human form. At the gallery, you can often speak to the artist himself and watch videos that document his fascinating process.

As you stroll through the historic French Market, visit the **Dutch Alley Artist's Co-op** (912 N. Peters St., 504/412-9220, www.dutchalleyartistsco-op.com, 10am-6pm daily), founded in 2003 by artist Ric Rolston. Operated by the two dozen artists whose work is on display, the gallery features a wide array of creations, from John Fitzgerald's prints to Kimberly Parker's seafood collages to Linda Sampson's beaded accessories and mourning jewelry.

Although New Orleans boasts several art galleries that focus exclusively on photography, you'll find the largest assortment at the **Gallery for Fine Photography** (241 Chartres St., 504/568-1313, www.agallery.com, 10:30am-5pm Thurs.-Mon.). Established in 1973, this prestigious emporium features the work of such titans as Ansel Adams, Walker Evans, and Diane Arbus, plus the visionary creations of newer artists. Be prepared for hefty price tags.

If you favor offbeat contemporary art from local artists and artisans, then the **Kako Gallery** (536 Royal St., 504/644-2451, www.kakogallery.com, 11am-7pm Mon.-Thurs., 11am-9pm Fri.-Sun.) might be right up your alley. You'll find unique sculptures, paintings, and jewelry from artists like Don Picou, who frequently paints muted scenes of bayous and swamps, and Stan Fontaine and Diane Millsap, two visionaries whose kaleidoscopic paintings feature the city's most famous landmarks and neighborhoods, from the St. Louis Cathedral to Pirate's Alley.

Owned by one of the most respected artists in Louisiana, the eponymous **Michalopoulos Gallery** (617 Bienville St., 504/558-0505, www.michalopoulos.com, 10am-6pm Mon.-Thurs., 10am-8pm Fri.-Sat.) carries dozens of James Michalopoulos's vibrant architectural renderings, with their trademark skewed angles and impressionistic brushwork. Many of his works feature Creole houses or classic French Quarter townhouses. His studio is in the nearby Marigny (527 Elysian Fields Ave.).

Although the famous Cajun "Blue Dog" artist George Rodrigue passed away in 2013, you can still visit his **Rodrigue Studio New Orleans** (730 Royal St., 504/581-4244, http://georgerodrigue.com, 11am-6pm Mon. and Thurs.-Sat., noon-5pm Sun.) on Royal Street, in a warmly lighted space not far from the St. Louis Cathedral. Here, you can buy everything from inexpensive gifts to original oil paintings, depicting the "Blue Dog" amid swamps, cemeteries, and other picturesque places. The inspiration for these works was twofold: a Cajun legend about the *loup-garou* (werewolf) and the owner's terrier, Tiffany, who had died several years before.

Faubourg Marigny and Bywater

The curious **Barrister's Gallery** (2331 St. Claude Ave., 504/710-4506, www.barristersgallery.com, 11am-5pm Tues.-Sat.) is located at the edge of the funky neighborhood of Faubourg Marigny and features a variety of Asian, African, Haitian, and Oceanic folk and outsider art. Its primary focus is on monthly contemporary exhibits that have an eclectic, unorthodox bent.

"Be Nice or Leave" is the motto that **Dr. Bob Art** (3027 Chartres St., 504/701-7297, www.drbobart.net, 10am-5pm daily,

10am-4:20pm summer hours) paints on everything. The fun Bywater studio features lots of art made from found objects and signs painted in bright colors. You know the drill: Be nice.

Central Business and Arts Districts

LeMieux Galleries (332 Julia St., 504/522-5988, www.lemieuxgalleries.com, 10am-5:30pm Mon.-Sat. and by appt.) presents a wide assortment of visionary, contemporary artwork, including Bobby Wozniak's infrared photographs, Theresa Honeywell's knitted pieces, and John Donovan's small yet impactful sculptures, which invariably make political statements about America's military history.

At the 25,000-square-foot **New Orleans School of GlassWorks & Printmaking Studio** (727 Magazine St., http://neworleansglassworks.com, 10am-5pm Mon.-Sat., free), you can observe highly skilled glassblowing, torchworking, printmaking, metalworking, and stained-glass artisans in action. Besides browsing their wares, you can also learn how to create your own glasswork, jewelry, and paper arts by taking one of the studio's exceptional classes.

Performing Arts

Within walking distance of Lee Circle, the **Contemporary Arts Center** (CAC, 900 Camp St., 504/528-3800 or 504/528-3805, http://cacno.org, event and ticket prices vary) is a multipurpose venue that houses an innovative art gallery (11am-5pm Wed.-Mon.) as well as performing arts spaces. In addition to staging lectures, performances, and concerts, the CAC often serves as a main location for the New Orleans Film Festival and other annual events. Stop by the on-site café (9am-3pm Mon.-Fri., 11am-3pm Sat.) for refreshments.

Within Louis Armstrong Park, the **Mahalia Jackson Theater for Performing Arts** (1419 Basin St., 504/287-0350, www.mahaliajacksontheater.com, hours and ticket prices vary) is a popular venue for live concerts, operas, musicals, comedy shows, dance performances, and festival events, particularly since its complete restoration following Hurricane Katrina. Named for New Orleans-born gospel singer Mahalia Jackson, the theater hosts regular performances by the **New Orleans Opera Association** (504/529-2278 or 504/529-3000, www.neworleansopera.org), the **Louisiana Philharmonic Orchestra** (504/523-6530, www.lpomusic.com), and the **New Orleans Ballet Association** (504/522-0996, www.nobadance.com), which books some of the world's most important ballet companies. Parking is inside the gated park, accessible via the Orleans Avenue entrance. This can be an unsafe part of town, especially at night, so avoid coming to the theater alone, and be aware of your environs at all times.

The imposing structure that now houses the **Marigny Opera House** (725 St. Ferdinand St., 504/948-9998, www.marignyoperahouse.org, hours and ticket prices vary) once served as the Holy Trinity Catholic Church, which was founded in 1847 for German Catholics, built in 1853 by architect Theodore Giraud, and known for its excellent music. Perhaps it's fitting then that the Marigny Opera House considers itself a nondenominational, neighborhood "church of the arts." Home to the Marigny Opera Ballet, a professional contemporary ballet company founded in 2014, the Opera House hosts various musical concerts, spotlighting everything from classical to jazz, as well as other cultural events.

Festivals and Events

The Big Easy offers a cornucopia of festivals worth planning a trip around, especially in fall, winter, and spring. Well-known events like Mardi Gras and the New Orleans Jazz & Heritage Festival are just the tip of the iceberg. Most events revolve around food and music. During popular events—particularly Mardi Gras and Jazz Fest—the city can fill up quickly, so book your trip well ahead of time.

★ Mardi Gras

Few festivals exemplify the joyous spirit of New Orleans more than **Mardi Gras** (various locations, www.mardigrasday.com, hours vary, free), a French term meaning "Fat Tuesday." If you're a fan of colorful, exciting festivals, there's no better time to visit New Orleans than during Mardi Gras season, which usually falls in February or early March and lasts 2-3 weeks prior to Lent (from Epiphany to Ash Wednesday). Festivities include everything from colorful street masks and costumes to gala balls and events. But Mardi Gras's most famous events are the free public parades sponsored by krewes and featuring colorful floats, marching bands, motorcycle squads, dancers, entertainers, and, sometimes, a royal court (the king, queen, maids, and dukes of a krewe). Participants often toss beaded necklaces, stuffed animals, commemorative doubloons, and other trinkets to spectators lining the route. For most krewes, each year brings a new theme, usually with a historical, mythical, or topical bent. Some of the most worthwhile parades include the krewes of Endymion, Bacchus, Orpheus, Zulu, and Rex. Dog lovers might appreciate the Mystic Krewe of Barkus in the French Quarter, while sci-fi and fantasy fans look forward to the Intergalactic Krewe of Chewbacchus.

Planning Checklist

Know when to go. Carnival season technically begins on January 6 (known as Twelfth Night, or the Feast of the Epiphany), but Mardi Gras Day shifts every season (Mar. 1 in 2022, Feb. 21 in 2023, and Feb. 13 in 2024). Mardi Gras parades usually start about two weeks prior to Fat Tuesday, but most revelers venture to New Orleans for the weekend preceding the climactic day—from the Friday before Fat Tuesday through midnight on Mardi Gras.

Book a bed. Make reservations at least six months in advance. Note that many hotels require a minimum stay of three nights during Mardi Gras weekend, and costly special-event rates may apply. Although you'll find cheaper hotels near the airport, staying there will require long commutes to reach the main festivities. You'll save time by staying in a more convenient neighborhood, such as the French Quarter. For a good night's sleep, stay in the CBD or Faubourg Marigny, both of which lie within walking distance of the Quarter. As an alternative, you can stay in some of the quieter inns throughout the Garden District, Uptown, and Mid-City, most of which are accessible via the streetcar lines.

Beware of scams. During Mardi Gras, many residents rent out rooms and cottages. While you may find a good deal this way, make arrangements as early as possible and be aware of unscrupulous landlords.

Pick your neighborhood. If you seek debauchery, the French Quarter will not let you down. However, celebrations elsewhere in the city—notably in Uptown along the St. Charles Avenue parade route or in Metairie along Veterans Memorial Boulevard—are much more family-oriented and tend to be dominated by locals, or at least Louisianians.

Plan your transportation. During Mardi Gras, the French Quarter is closed to non-essential vehicular traffic. Hailing a cab can be difficult, so many visitors prefer getting around town via bus, streetcar, or foot. Some even opt to rent a bicycle (or bring their own).

Prepare for mayhem. The French Quarter might be the rowdiest neighborhood, but the less wholesome aspects of Mardi Gras, such as public nudity, drunkenness, crowds, and opportunistic crime, can occur anywhere. Travel in groups, arrange regular meeting spots

Mardi Gras Lingo

- **ball:** a masquerade or lively extravaganza that usually occurs at the end of a parade
- **boeuf gras** (BUFF grah): the fatted bull or ox, the ancient symbol of the final meat eaten before the Lenten season of fasting
- **captain:** the leader of each krewe
- **doubloon:** large coins made from aluminum, plastic, or other materials and stamped with the insignia and theme of a krewe
- **favor:** a souvenir, given by krewe members to friends attending the ball and usually bearing the krewe's name, insignia, and year of issue
- **flambeaux** (FLAM-bohz): naphtha-fueled torches, once carried by white-robed Black men as the only source of nighttime parade illumination, still used in many nighttime parades today.
- **king cake:** an iced or sugared coffee cake, often shaped like a ring, served during the Mardi Gras season and containing a small plastic baby, the finder of which, according to tradition, must purchase the next king cake or throw the next party
- **krewe:** private Carnival organization
- **Lundi Gras** (LUN-dee grah): the day before Mardi Gras, also known as Fat Monday
- **Mardi Gras Indians:** groups of local Black men who, led by separate Big Chiefs, chant, dance, and compete with one another in ceremonial processions along ever-changing routes through residential neighborhoods on Mardi Gras Day, all while wearing handmade beaded and feathered costumes as a tribute to American Indians, who often assisted escaping enslaved people.
- **throw:** an inexpensive trinket, such as an aluminum doubloon or plastic medallion necklace, tossed by krewe members

with friends, avoid quiet streets at night, conceal money and valuables, and exercise caution at all times. Float riders in the major parades, like Endymion and Bacchus, tend to hurl trinkets with unnecessary force, so look out.

Stake out seats. If you want to be close to the floats, it's often necessary to arrive several hours early. For major parades, such as Endymion, many people set up blankets, chairs, and ladders the day before. (It's illegal to leave such marked areas unattended.) It's best to choose a spot near a public restroom. Consider bringing snacks, beverages, and portable chairs. Make restaurant reservations or dine at off-peak times.

Wear a costume. On Mardi Gras Day, you'll see costumed revelers dressed as everything from pop culture icons to political statements. Do as the locals do and wear a costume (or at least purchase a mask, available in shops throughout the Quarter). Prepare for the possibility of cold, rainy weather, which is common in February and March.

Eat king cake. King cake, essentially a large, colorful cinnamon roll, is the season's most famous treat. Grab a slice at a local coffeehouse or pick up an

Laissez les Bon Temps Rouler!

Only a few official **Mardi Gras parades** run through the French Quarter, including the raunchy Krewe du Vieux, the wine-themed Krewe of Cork, and the dog-filled Krewe of Barkus. Most of the other parades in and around the city (including Uptown, Mid-City, Metairie, and communities on the west bank and north shore) are family-friendly. Some have special throws, such as the hand-decorated shoes offered by the Krewe of Muses, which usually rolls on the Thursday before Mardi Gras weekend. Parade routes are listed in the *New Orleans Times-Picayune* and online (www.nola.com, www.mardigras.com, www.mardigrasday.com, www.mardigrasneworleans.com). Here are the major parades.

Endymion

The Krewe of Endymion (www.endymion.org) is the city's largest parade, a "super-krewe" that features enormous floats, magnificent court costumes, and celebrity grand marshals.

When: 4:15pm on the Saturday prior to Mardi Gras.

Where: Starts near City Park and travels down Canal Street and St. Charles Avenue, culminating with its ball in the New Orleans Ernest N. Morial Convention Center.

Bacchus

The Krewe of Bacchus (www.kreweofbacchus.org) is a "super-krewe" that features incredible floats and celebrity kings, from Danny Kaye to Will Ferrell. Signature floats include the Bacchasaurus, Bacchagator, and Baby Kong.

When: 5:15pm on the Sunday prior to Mardi Gras.

Where: From Napoleon Avenue and Tchoupitoulas Street, it rolls through Uptown on Napoleon Avenue, along St. Charles Avenue, and down Canal Street, ending at the Ernest N. Morial Convention Center.

Orpheus

Co-founded by Harry Connick Jr., the Krewe of Orpheus (www.kreweoforpheus.com) has featured a slew of celebrity monarchs, from Stevie Wonder to Anne Rice.

When: 6pm on Lundi Gras.

Where: From the corner of Napoleon Avenue and Tchoupitoulas Street, it rolls through Uptown on Napoleon Avenue, then along St. Charles Avenue, down Canal and Tchoupitoulas Streets, to the Orpheuscapade, a black-tie event at the convention center.

Zulu

The Zulu Social Aid & Pleasure Club (www.kreweofzulu.com) presents one of the season's most anticipated parades, during which spectators vie for painted coconuts, the krewe's signature throw. Zulu also hosts the Lundi Gras Festival, a free music event on the day before Fat Tuesday.

When: 8am on Mardi Gras.

Where: From the corner of Jackson and South Claiborne Avenues in Uptown, it travels along Jackson Avenue, continues north on St. Charles Avenue, follows Canal and Basin Streets, and ends at Orleans Avenue and Broad Street.

Rex

Since 1872, the king of the Krewe of Rex (www.rexorganization.com) has reigned as the king of Mardi Gras. The parade features majestic floats, masked riders, and a royal court. Mardi Gras officially ends with the Rex Ball at the Sheraton New Orleans Hotel on Canal Street.

When: 10am on Mardi Gras.

Where: The parade travels down Napoleon Avenue from the intersection with South Claiborne Avenue in Uptown, then along St. Charles Avenue and down Canal Street toward the Mississippi River.

entire cake at Rouses Market, Gambino's Bakery, Haydel's Bakery, Maurice French Pastries, or the seasonal Manny Randazzo King Cakes.

New Orleans Jazz & Heritage Festival

Established in 1970, this musical extravaganza, which takes place at Mid-City's Fair Grounds Race Course, has grown to be nearly as popular as Mardi Gras. Held on two long weekends in late April and early May, the **New Orleans Jazz & Heritage Festival** (Fair Grounds Race Course & Slots, 1751 Gentilly Blvd., 504/410-4100, www.nojazzfest.com, hours vary, adults $70-85, children 2-10 $5, free for children under 2), also known as Jazz Fest, features music workshops, artisanal and culinary demonstrations, Native American powwow performances, arts-and-crafts vendors, an unbelievable array of food stalls, and numerous stages that buzz with jazz, blues, zydeco, rock, gospel, and folk musicians. Among the top acts who have performed at Jazz Fest are Fats Domino, Etta James, and various members of the Marsalis and Neville clans.

French Quarter Festival

Begun in 1984 to support local musicians, the four-day **French Quarter Festival** (various locations, 504/522-5730 or 800/673-5725, http://frenchquarterfest.org, hours vary, free), which typically occurs in early or mid-April, has since evolved into Louisiana's largest free music event. The roughly 20 outdoor stages—from the Old U.S. Mint to Jackson Square to Woldenberg Riverfront Park—host local and regional jazz, gospel, funk, zydeco, classical, bluegrass, folk, and blues acts, so you likely won't see mega-stars here.

Top to bottom: Mardi Gras marching band; Nitmeaux Krewe member at the Mardi Gras Parade; Mardi Gras Indian at the New Orleans Jazz & Heritage Festival

Other Festivals

Spring

If you're a "mudbug" lover, do yourself a favor and head to Chalmette in late March for the **Louisiana Crawfish Festival** (Frederick J. Sigur Civic Center, 8245 W. Judge Perez Dr., Chalmette, http://louisianacrawfishfestival.com, hours and costs vary). Since 1975, this popular, family-friendly event has celebrated crawfish season with live music, arts and crafts, amusement games and rides, and, of course, regional cuisine.

Typically held in late March, the **New Orleans Spring Fiesta** (various locations, 504/581-1367, www.springfiestanola.com, $25-30 pp for home tours, $15-20 pp for walking tours) grants you the unique opportunity to step inside nearly two dozen private homes, gardens, and courtyards in the French Quarter, Garden District, and Uptown neighborhoods—an unparalleled experience that is completely worth the cost.

Devotees of the city's most famous literary luminary rush to the Big Easy in late March or early April to attend the **Tennessee Williams/New Orleans Literary Festival** (various locations, 504/581-1144 or 800/990-3378, www.tennesseewilliams.net, hours and costs vary). For three decades, this event has celebrated the playwright who gave us such iconographic works as *A Streetcar Named Desire* and *The Glass Menagerie.* The five-day gathering is replete with writing classes helmed by experts, celebrity interviews, panel discussions, stagings of Williams's plays, fiction and poetry readings, and the endlessly entertaining Stanley and Stella Shouting Contest. For more on the author, see the Tennessee Williams Rectory Museum in Clarksdale.

Summer

In late June and/or early July, visitors typically descend upon New Orleans for the annual **Essence Festival** (various locations, www.essence.com/festival, hours and costs vary), a four-day celebration of African American music and culture. Besides DJ parties at the Sugar Mill, the main events of this much-anticipated festival consist of concerts and comedy shows at the Mercedes-Benz Superdome and empowerment presentations at the Ernest N. Morial Convention Center.

Every Labor Day weekend, the French Quarter and the Faubourg Marigny are flooded with eager participants and onlookers of **Southern Decadence** (various locations, www.southerndecadence.com, hours and costs vary), an annual Mardi Gras-like festival that's been celebrating the city's gay lifestyle, music, and culture since 1972. Held at various gay-friendly venues, from Rawhide 2010 to Bourbon Pub & Parade, the six-day event includes dance and pool parties, beefcake contests, singles' mixers, drag shows, and a leather-gear block party.

Fall

For one day in October or November, residents and out-of-towners converge at the intersection of Oak Street and South Carrollton Avenue in Uptown's Riverbend area for the **Oak Street Po-Boy Festival** (Oak St. and S. Carrollton Ave., www.poboyfest.com, free). Besides listening to a slew of live music, attendees can peruse arts and crafts, learn about the history of the po'boy, and, of course, sample a variety of local cuisine from more than 40 restaurants.

Winter

Introduced to New Orleans during the 19th century by its many Sicilian immigrants, **St. Joseph's Day** (various locations, www.mardigrasneworleans.com/supersunday.html, hours vary, free) is still celebrated with great ardor in the city's Italian American community. The observance of this feast on March 19 traces back to the Middle Ages, when people built altars to St. Joseph, who they believed had answered their prayers and

Halloween in the Crescent City

New Orleans is a wildly popular place for All Hallows' Eve. People venture here to visit the many voodoo shops and cemeteries, take a haunted walking tour of the French Quarter, and mingle with hordes of costumed revelers along Bourbon and Frenchmen Streets. Locals and visitors alike flock to seasonal attractions like **The Mortuary Haunted House** (www.themortuary.net), set inside a former mortuary that's supposedly haunted.

Many horror aficionados also appreciate the city's longtime vampire connection. The principal setting for Anne Rice's famous novel *Interview with the Vampire,* New Orleans is home to two annual vampire balls: the **New Orleans Vampire Ball,** sponsored by Anne Rice's Vampire Lestat Fan Club (www.arvlfc.com), and the **Endless Night Vampire Ball** (www.endlessnight.com). Vampire tours, which are available through **Haunted History Tours** (www.hauntedhistorytours.com) and **Bloody Mary's New Orleans Tours** (www.bloodymarystours.com), are also popular.

Take a walking ghost tour through **Historic New Orleans Tours** (www.tourneworleans.com) or **Spirit Tours New Orleans** (www.spirittoursneworleans.com).

In a town known for gay-friendly bashes, it's no surprise that there's also a gay-friendly Halloween celebration. Simply known as **Halloween in New Orleans** (www.gayhalloween.com), this weekend-long bash has evolved from a small gathering in 1984 into one of the biggest gay-and-lesbian parties in the country. If you're looking for well-dressed drag queens, this is definitely the time to visit the Big Easy.

New Orleans also hosts family-friendly events like Audubon Zoo's **Boo at the Zoo** (http://audubonnatureinstitute.org/batz), which usually occurs during the last two weekends of October and features trick-or-treat fun, a ghost train, and a haunted house. On Halloween itself, Molly's at the Market presents **Jim Monaghan's Halloween Parade** (www.mollysatthemarket.net), a spirited procession through the French Quarter. Since 2007, the **Krewe of Boo!** (www.kreweofboo.com) has been the city's official Halloween parade, typically entailing a downtown procession of colorful, mildly scary floats created by Kern Studios.

New Orleans is predominantly Catholic, which means that **All Saints' Day** (Nov. 1) and **All Souls' Day** (Nov. 2) are important holidays—a time when many residents make a point of visiting their loved ones at cemeteries. Simultaneously, lots of locals celebrate the Mexican holiday of **Día de los Muertos** by dressing in black, painting skulls on their faces, and congregating in front of the St. Louis Cathedral—truly a sight to behold.

delivered them from famine. Modern participants continue to celebrate by constructing elaborate and riotously colorful altars in their homes and churches. Besides a public parade in the French Quarter, smaller celebrations take place in private homes; signs welcome friends and strangers alike to view family altars and enjoy cakes and breads. The Italian holiday has also become significant for the city's Mardi Gras Indians, an African American troupe of Carnival revelers who usually host a vibrant parade on **Super Sunday,** the Sunday preceding or following St. Joseph's Day.

Shopping

In New Orleans, shopping opportunities embrace the most popular aspects of the city's heritage—its cuisine, music, art, literature, and historical preservation.

The most interesting shops and boutiques lie in the French Quarter, Arts District, and Uptown neighborhoods. The French Quarter is rife with praline shops, and visitors rarely leave without strolling through the varied food stalls of the historic French Market. Art and antiques hounds can browse the emporiums along Royal and Chartres Streets, while the Garden District stretch of Magazine Street is considered a less pricey yet still ample source of art, antiques, jewelry, and vintage clothing.

New Orleans is an easygoing town, with a flexible sense of time. When it comes to shops, that means that posted hours aren't always strictly enforced. Hours can also change from season to season; in the summer, when the weather is unbearable and tourism slows, shops tend to close earlier.

Shopping Districts

Known for upscale antiques and first-rate art galleries, **Royal Street** is the most exclusive address for shopping in the French Quarter, though parallel **Chartres Street** has similarly high-end emporiums. In the **Lower Quarter,** from Jackson Square to Esplanade Avenue, you'll find funkier, more youthful boutiques, such as mod clothiers and edgy galleries. **Decatur Street,** meanwhile, is a good place to find cheesy T-shirts, Tabasco sauce, crawfish-embroidered items, souvenir "go-cups."

Magazine Street, which follows the curve of the Mississippi River for about six miles from the CBD to Audubon Park, offers an astonishing variety of shops and boutiques. Sassy secondhand clothiers, colorful oyster bars, jamming music clubs, convivial java joints, and historic homes line the way, but it's the lower stretch of Magazine—from about Canal Street to Jackson Avenue—that possesses the city's most fascinating antiques district. Uptown also boasts the **Riverbend** area, which features several curious shops around the intersection of St. Charles and Carrollton Avenues.

French Quarter

Antiques and Vintage

Since 1899, when it was established by Hermina Keil, **Keil's Antiques** (325 Royal St., 504/522-4552, www.keilsantiques.com, 9am-5pm Mon.-Sat.) has been specializing in 18th- and 19th-century antiques from France and England. The inventory includes everything from marble mantels to magnificent crystal chandeliers to garnet chokers. The Keil family operates two other well-respected stores in the Quarter, **Moss Antiques** (411 Royal St., 504/522-3981, www.mossantiques.com, 9am-5pm Mon.-Sat.) and **Royal Antiques** (309 Royal St., 504/524-7033, http://royalantiques.com, 9am-5pm Mon.-Sat.), but Keil's has the most enticing window displays, particularly at Christmastime.

A family-owned, French Quarter landmark since Max Rau opened its doors in 1912, **M.S. Rau Antiques** (630 Royal St., 888/711-8084, www.rauantiques.com, 9am-5:15pm Mon.-Sat.) is one of the oldest antiques shops in New Orleans. Today, the 30,000-square-foot showroom houses a stupendous collection of 19th-century paintings and sculptures, exquisite clocks and music boxes, and striking bedroom and dining sets.

At **Vintage 329** (329 Royal St., 504/525-2262, www.vintage329.com, 10am-5:30pm daily), you might find signed Hemingway novels, an autographed Aerosmith guitar, or an oversized golf ball bearing the signatures of Rodney Dangerfield, Bill Murray, Chevy Chase, Ted Knight, and Michael O'Keefe—the principal cast members of *Caddyshack*. In addition to signed first editions, music memorabilia, and vintage movie posters, you'll spy old maps, swords, and sports-related items, including football helmets signed by entire NFL teams.

Arts and Crafts

The **Artist's Market & Bead Shop** (85 French Market Pl., 504/561-0046, www.artistsmarketnola.com, 9am-5pm Mon.-Fri.) is filled with paintings, photographs, pottery, textiles, woodwork, and hand-blown glass from more than 75 local and regional artists and artisans, plus curious gifts and decorative items, such as snow globes and red velvet Carnival masks. Beading enthusiasts will find a large selection of glass and sterling silver beads, semiprecious stones, and beading tools. Newbies can even take a jewelry-making class. The shop has two entrances; the second one is at 1228 Decatur Street.

A half block from Jackson Square, charming **Maskarade** (630 St. Ann St., 504/568-1018, www.themaskstore.com, 10am-5pm daily) presents a wide assortment of masks, crafted by artists from New Orleans and elsewhere around the country. You'll spy feathery Carnival masks, golden Venetian-style masks, and black leather masks, as well as masks that resemble creatures like ladybugs, leopards, and dragons. If, despite such a selection, you don't spot what you like, an artist can customize a mask for you—just in time for Mardi Gras, Halloween, or any other occasion.

The mission of **RHINO Contemporary Crafts Co.** (2028 Magazine St., 504/523-7945, www.rhinocrafts.com, 10am-6pm Sun.-Fri., noon-5pm Sat.) is to promote and sell the handcrafted ceramics, jewelry, furniture, accessories, and decorative arts of local talents. RHINO stands for Right Here in New Orleans, which is where all the goods were created.

Books and Music

On the relatively quiet block behind the St. Louis Cathedral, **Arcadian Books & Art Prints** (714 Orleans St., 504/523-4138, 9:30am-5:30am Mon.-Sat.) is the quintessential well-used bookstore, filled with cramped, musty pathways and stacks upon stacks of new and secondhand volumes, some stretching close to the high ceiling. Owned and operated by one of the friendliest, most helpful, and most knowledgeable proprietors in the French Quarter, this shop particularly appeals to locals and visitors in search of French books as well as titles related to New Orleans and Louisiana. Vintage postcards and art prints are also available.

Crescent City Books (124 Baronne St., 504/524-4997, www.crescentcitybooks.

the French Market

com, 10am-7pm Mon.-Sat., noon-6pm Sun.) contains two floors of out-of-print and antiquarian titles, plus antique maps and prints. Open since 1992, it's always been an exceptional source for local history and literature, scholarly books, and hard-to-find titles on philosophy, ancient history, and literary criticism—a real book lover's bookstore.

Hidden in the alley between the Cabildo and the St. Louis Cathedral, the small **Faulkner House Books** (624 Pirate's Alley, 504/524-2940, http://faulknerhousebooks.com, 10am-6pm daily) occupies the same space that novelist William Faulkner inhabited in 1925, when he first arrived in New Orleans as a young poet. It was here, in fact, that he wrote *Soldiers' Pay.* Operated by a knowledgeable staff, frequented by writers and collectors alike, this charming place sells new and used books, including rare first editions, titles about Southern Americana, and literature by Faulkner, Tennessee Williams, and Walker Percy.

Peaches Records (4318 Magazine St., 504/282-3322, www.peachesrecordsandtapes.com, 10am-7pm daily) features a slew of local tunes, from traditional jazz standards by Louis Armstrong and Jelly Roll Morton to modern funk by the Meters and the Neville Brothers—plus blues, rap, and zydeco. Ernie K-Doe, Rockin' Dopsie, and the Dukes of Dixieland are just some of the local performers represented. Beyond music, there's a small selection of local books.

Gifts and Souvenirs

If you need a late-night cigarette fix, you can always stop by Mary Jane's Emporium in the 1200 block of Decatur, but for something more distinctive, venture to the **Cigar Factory New Orleans** (415 Decatur St., 504/568-1003, www.cigarfactoryneworleans.com, 10am-10pm Sun.-Thurs., 10am-11pm Fri.-Sat.), where you can actually watch cigars being rolled. Besides various tables for enjoying a smoking break, cigar lovers will appreciate the wide selection, walk-in humidor, and knowledgeable staff. There are two smaller Cigar Factory branches on Bourbon Street and Decatur Street.

On the first floor of one of the most photographed buildings in the entire French Quarter, gift shop **Forever New Orleans** (700 Royal St., 504/586-3536, http://shopforeverneworleans.com, 9am-10pm daily) gets quite a lot of foot traffic. It doesn't hurt that it's halfway between Jackson Square and Bourbon Street. You'll be lured inside by the plethora of fleur-de-lis souvenirs, from jewelry sets to stationery to glassware. The inventory seems to change often, so it's easy to find a new trinket that you never noticed before. Forever New Orleans is particularly popular with tourists, so much so that there are now four other locations in the French Quarter.

Owned by a local named Ken Ford, the **Idea Factory** (924 Royal St., 800/524-4332 or 504/524-5195, http://ideafactoryneworleans.com, 10am-6pm daily) is a local favorite. This cozy place contains a treasure-trove of handcrafted wooden objects, including clocks, mechanical toys, and chessboards. This fascinating place sells marvelous gifts, from gorgeous clipboards and odd-looking back massagers to curious puzzle boxes and ingenious cooking utensils.

Unlike most tourist-focused shops, **Roux Royale** (600 Royal St., 504/565-5272 or 855/344-7700, http://shoprouxroyale.com, 9am-10pm daily) has a definitive purpose: to celebrate the unique cuisine of New Orleans. From colorful aprons and fleur-de-lis glassware to fabulous local cookbooks and Tabasco products, you'll find almost everything you need to bring the taste of the Big Easy home with you—even boxed pralines. If you can't find the right cookbook here, try **Kitchen Witch** (1452 N. Broad St., 504/528-8382, www.kwcookbooks.com), a bookstore that specializes in rare secondhand cookbooks, including those that pertain to Cajun, Creole, and Louisiana cuisine.

Gourmet Treats

For specialty food items, there's no place quite like the **Central Grocery** (923 Decatur St., 504/523-1620, http://centralgrocery.com, 9am-5pm daily) on bustling Decatur. Famous for its oversized muffulettas—and the orderly, strictly enforced line that's required to purchase them—this often-crowded grocery stocks all manner of gourmet goodies and seasonings, from olive salad to Italian cookies to Zatarain's crawfish boil.

Not surprisingly, the French Market boasts more than one praline vendor. A few doors down from **Aunt Sally's Creole Pralines** (810 Decatur St., 800/642-7257, http://auntsallys.com, 8am-8pm daily), you'll encounter one of the city's oldest such stores. For more than a century, **Evans Creole Candy Factory** (848 Decatur St., 504/522-7111, 9am-6pm Sun.-Thurs., 9am-7pm Fri.-Sat.) has been crafting delicious pralines. Still today, you can watch the candy-makers working on a fresh batch of pralines through the big windows of this shop, which is also an excellent source for hand-dipped chocolates, dark-chocolate turtles, and chocolate-covered maraschino cherries.

Southern Candymakers (334 Decatur St., 504/523-5544 or 800/344-9773, www.southerncandymakers.com, 9am-7pm daily) stands out among the French Quarter's longstanding praline shops. A couple blocks from Canal Street, this is a full retail shop with pralines, toffees, nut clusters, chocolate alligators, marzipan, peanut brittle, and fudge. If you find yourself closer to Esplanade, stop by the Quarter's other location in the French Market (1010 Decatur St., 504/525-6170, 9am-6pm daily).

Health and Beauty

For more than 160 years, the aromatic **Bourbon French Parfums** (805 Royal St., 504/522-4480, www.neworleansperfume.com, 10am-5pm daily) has been creating custom-blended fragrances. Schedule a one-hour private sitting with a specialist who will analyze your body chemistry, assess your personality, and record your preferred scents. Once your "secret" formula is created, you can order an entire set of toiletries, including perfume, lotion, and foaming bath gel. If you lack the time or patience, you can just as easily choose from the perfumes, musk oils, and voodoo potions available on-site.

Jewelry and Accessories

Whether you have a Halloween parade, Mardi Gras party, or special occasion in your future, outrageous **Fifi Mahony's** (934 Royal St., 504/525-4343, www.fifimahonys.com, noon-6pm Sun.-Fri., 11am-7pm Sat.) is your one-stop salon and makeup counter if you're hoping to make a bold statement. Pop in and browse the wigs that come in every color of the rainbow, Tony and Tina cosmetics, and offbeat handbags.

A French Quarter fixture since 1938, **New Orleans Silversmiths** (600 Chartres

St., 504/522-8333 or 800/219-8333, www.neworleanssilversmiths.com, 10am-5pm Mon.-Sat., 11am-4pm Sun.) specializes in modern gold jewelry, estate jewelry, and antique silver holloware. You'll also find decanters, candlesticks and candelabra, and handcrafted, sterling silver animal figurines. For a taste of New Orleans, the shop even offers café au lait sets as well as fleur-de-lis jewelry and cuff links.

Queork (838 Chartres St., 504/481-2585, www.queork.com, 10am-6pm daily) features all sorts of high-end accessories made from cork fabric: shoes, handbags, dog collars, glasses cases, wallets, hats, and more. The cork wears like leather—it develops a patina over time—but it is stylish and vegan. Queork has two other stores—in New Mexico and Florida—but is headquartered in New Orleans, and many of the products are made locally.

Occult and Voodoo

Besides offering more than 100 varieties of fine tea, the cozy **Bottom of the Cup Tea Room** (327 Chartres St., 800/729-7148, www.bottomofthecup.com, 10am-6pm daily) has been giving authentic psychic readings since 1929. In fact, the name of the store is derived from its early days, when the resident psychic would read the tea leaves left at the bottom of a customer's cup. This is also a good spot for tarot cards and metaphysical gifts like crystals, amulets, and wands.

In a city obsessed with vampire lore and Anne Rice's legacy, it's hard to believe that **Boutique du Vampyre** (709 1/2 St. Ann St., 504/561-8267, www.feelthebite.com, 10am-9pm daily) is one of its only vampire shops. In this cozy spot between Bourbon and Royal Streets, you'll find plenty of vampire accoutrements, from sexy capes and old-fashioned hats to customizable fangs and temporary bite tattoos. The proprietors, Marita and Steve, stock candles, books, soap, tarot cards, wine-related paraphernalia, and Gothic jewelry.

Amid the inebriated tourists on Bourbon Street lies **Marie Laveau's House of Voodoo** (739 Bourbon St., 504/581-3751, http://voodooneworleans.com, 10am-11:30pm Sun.-Thurs., 10am-1:30am Fri.-Sat.), a small, often crowded space filled with incense, voodoo literature, symbolic pendants and figurines, locally crafted voodoo dolls, and souvenir posters and T-shirts. Opposite the register, you'll spy a cluttered, hands-off voodoo altar, while in the rear room, you can experience private tarot-card readings (noon-close daily). The folks behind Marie Laveau's also operate **Reverend Zombie's House of Voodoo** (723 St. Peter St., 504/486-6366, 10am-11:30pm Sun.-Thurs., 10am-1:30am Fri.-Sat.), which offers many of the same items and services, plus a wide array of cigars. Photos aren't allowed in either store.

Owned and operated by voodoo practitioners since 1996, **Voodoo Authentica** (612 Dumaine St., 504/522-2111, www.voodooshop.com, 11am-7pm daily) carries the typical French Quarter voodoo shop items: incense, potions, gris-gris bags, ritual kits, handmade voodoo dolls, Haitian crafts, helpful books and DVDs, and unusual jewelry, such as necklaces made of alligator claws and teeth. Besides offering spiritual consultations, this unique cultural center presents **Voodoofest,** a free annual festival that occurs on Halloween and celebrates the voodoo religion's influence on New Orleans traditions through educational presentations, book signings, and an ancestral healing ritual.

Shopping Centers and Malls

Not far from Jackson Square lies the **French Market** (Decatur St. and N. Peters St. btwn. St. Peter St. and Barracks St., 504/636-6400, www.frenchmarket.org, 10am-6pm daily, hours vary by business), a picturesque, multi-block collection of shops, eateries, and stalls that partially date to 1813. Besides **Café Du Monde** (800 Decatur St., 504/525-4544, www.

Voodoo vs. Hoodoo

Given the Big Easy's historical ties to the voodoo religion, it surely comes as no surprise that the city is still home to several voodoo practitioners. So, whether you're seriously interested in the faith or just curious about this often misunderstood aspect of New Orleans's culture, you'll find several voodoo-related shops in town, most of which provide everything from gris-gris bags to potion oils to handmade African crafts, not to mention rituals and readings. In the French Quarter, such emporiums include **Voodoo Authentica, Reverend Zombie's House of Voodoo,** and **Marie Laveau's House of Voodoo.**

You might be aware that some southern Louisianians also practice hoodoo. So, what, you might wonder, is the difference between voodoo and hoodoo? Well, depending on who you ask, that can be a rather complicated question.

The voodoo of New Orleans is similar to that of Haiti, Cuba, and other Caribbean islands, where the ancient West African religion of Vodoun has been heavily influenced by Catholicism. Hoodoo, by contrast, is not a religion, but a folk magic that blends the practices of various cultures, from African and Native American traditions to European grimoires. Often referring to magic spells, potions, and charms that include conjuration, witchcraft, rootwork, and Biblical recitation, hoodoo supposedly enables people to access supernatural forces in order to improve aspects of their daily lives, including love, luck, health, wealth, and employment. Naturally, some people also use hoodoo for more nefarious reasons, such as revenge on those who have "crossed" them. No matter what your intentions, though, as with other magico-religious traditions, hoodoo often involves the utilization of herbs, roots, minerals, animal bones, candles, bodily fluids, and an individual's possessions.

In truth, many modern-day voodoo followers integrate hoodoo folk magic into the practice of their religion. For more information about both traditions, consult Jim Haskins's *Voodoo & Hoodoo: Their Tradition and Craft as Revealed by Actual Practitioners* (New York: Original Publications, 1978), Stephanie Rose Bird's *Sticks, Stones, Roots & Bones: Hoodoo, Mojo & Conjuring with Herbs* (St. Paul: Llewellyn Publications, 2004), and Denise Alvarado's *The Voodoo Hoodoo Spellbook* (San Francisco: Red Wheel/Weiser, LLC, 2011).

cafedumonde.com, 24 hours daily) and other eateries, the market houses retail shops that sell everything from toys, souvenirs, and candies to African oils, Latin American hammocks, and local artwork. One of the highlights is the open-air pavilion at the eastern end. It features a small **farmers market** offering bottled hot sauce, Cajun spices, homemade pralines, fresh seafood and produce, sandwiches, and sno-balls, plus a collection of locally made arts and crafts. There's also a daily **flea market,** which presents a wide array of jewelry, dresses, cookbooks, and African masks. Though it's rather crowded on the weekends, nothing here costs much.

Faubourg Marigny and Bywater

Books and Music

Located at the corner of Chartres and Frenchmen Streets in the heart of the Marigny's famous music scene, the cramped, no-frills **Frenchmen Art and Books** (600 Frenchmen St., noon-midnight daily) is often still open when the bands are starting to play. Somehow fitting with its authentic environs, this eclectic secondhand store is rife with curious choices, including New Orleans cookbooks, local short-story collections, and vintage gay adult publications.

The **Louisiana Music Factory** (421 Frenchmen St., 504/586-1094, www.

Farmers Markets

Farmers markets have been a part of life in New Orleans since the French and Spanish governments ruled the city in the 18th century, and they remain just as vibrant to this day. In fact, the farmers market in the historic **French Market** is perhaps the most famous place in the city to procure gourmet edibles. Here, you'll find pralines and baked goods, fresh seafood and produce, Cajun spices and cooking kits, plus an array of freshly prepared foods, from gumbo and boudin to smoothies and sno-balls.

If you love browsing market-fresh food, also consider the **Crescent City Farmers Market** (504/861-4485 or 504/861-4488, www.crescentcityfarmersmarket.org), held four times a week at different locations around town and featuring a phenomenal roster of vendors and chefs. Throughout the year, you'll spy pastries, Creole cream cheese, tamales, alligator sausage, Cornish hens, and freshly cut flowers. Depending on the month, you might also see fresh shrimp, soft-shell crabs, kumquats, and figs. It's held in Uptown on Tuesday (200 Broadway St., 9am-1pm), in Mid-City on Thursday (3700 Orleans Ave., 3pm-7pm), and in the Arts District on Saturday (750 Carondelet St. at Julia St., 8am-noon). Vendors accept only cash and market tokens, a special currency that comes in $1 and $5 increments and can be purchased in the Welcome Tent via credit card.

louisianamusicfactory.com, 10am-7pm daily) isn't far from the famous music clubs of Frenchmen Street. This noted music shop offers a great selection of local and regional blues, jazz, funk, R&B, gospel, Cajun and zydeco, reggae, swamp pop, rock, and hip-hop. This is a particularly great place if you're looking for Mardi Gras music, performers of which range from brass bands to Mardi Gras Indians to the Neville Brothers. You'll find both used and new CDs, plus vinyl records, books, DVDs, videos, and T-shirts.

Gifts and Souvenirs

Run by longtime voodoo practitioner Sallie Ann Glassman, the spiritual supply shop **Island of Salvation Botanica** (2372 St. Claude Ave., Ste. 100, 504/948-9961, http://islandofsalvationbotanica.com, 10am-5pm Mon.-Sat., 11am-6pm Sun.) is a good place to find herbs, oils, specialty candles, Haitian artwork, decorated spirit boxes, and dashboard statues. You can even purchase custom-made gris-gris bags, made with various herbs, stones, and other materials—including a clipping of your own hair or nails. Housed within a ramshackle building along the edge of the Faubourg Marigny (admittedly, not the best part of town), the Island of Salvation Botanica also provides readings and healings.

Central Business and Arts Districts

Clothing and Shoes

If you need a men's jacket for your dinner at Galatoire's, consider **Rubensteins** (102 St. Charles Ave., 504/581-6666, http://rubensteinsneworleans.com, 10am-5:45pm Mon.-Thurs., 10am-6pm Fri.-Sat.), a classic, family-owned outfitter carrying such exclusive lines as Hugo Boss, Ralph Lauren, and Brioni. Situated in the CBD since 1924, this well-respected emporium is one of the finest men's specialty stores in the country, featuring suits, sweaters, jeans, and fine footwear.

Fashionistas and bargain-hunters love to go through the racks at **UAL** (3306 Magazine St., 504/354-2777, http://store.shopual.com, 10am-8pm daily). The name stands for United Apparel Liquidators, and while the shop looks small, it is chock-full of discount designer goods. There's also a location in the French Quarter (518 Chartres

St., 504/301-4427, 10am-8pm daily), in Metairie (en route to Baton Rouge), and Nashville, all of which have different inventory.

Jewelry and Accessories

Your future's so bright in NOLA, you gotta wear shades. Why not buy them at local sunglass designer **Krewe** (1818 Magazine St., 504/342-2462, www.krewe.com, 10am-7pm Mon.-Sat., noon-6pm Sun.)? Each style is named after something NOLA-specific, and the boutique makes glasses shopping feel like jewelry shopping. It also stocks jewelry and other accessories.

Established by Sam H. Meyer in 1894 as Meyer's Hat Box, the family-run **Meyer the Hatter** (120 St. Charles Ave., 504/525-1048 or 800/882-4287, http://meyerthehatter.com, 10am-5:45pm Mon.-Sat.) boasts the South's largest collection of headwear, from stylish Stetsons and satin top hats to jazz band caps and black-and-gold Saints visors.

Markets

It's very fun—and very NOLA—to shop for art late at night. The **Palace Market Frenchmen** (7pm-midnight Sun.-Wed., 7pm-1am Thurs.-Sat.) is a hub of activity after the sun goes down, with local artists showing off jewelry, paintings, textiles, and more. Twinkling lights transform the empty lot into an outdoor gallery space. Remember to be aware of your surroundings as you walk back to the hotel with your purchases after midnight.

Garden District

Books and Music

Nestled inside a funky neighborhood building with plenty of other shops (and a designated parking garage), **Garden District Book Store** (2727 Prytania St., 504/895-2266, www.gardendistrictbookshop.com, 10am-6pm Mon.-Sat., 10am-5pm Sun.) features books about New Orleans and Louisiana, as well as current fiction, non-fiction, and kids' books.

Jewelry and Accessories

A modern-day general store, **Whites Mercantile** (3811 Magazine St., 504/354-8629, http://whitesmercantile.com, 10am-6pm Mon.-Sat., 10am-5pm Sun.) stocks jewelry, books, clothing, gifts, and other pretty things that country singer Holly Williams finds when she is out on tour. She also has a shop in Nashville.

Uptown

Books and Music

Within easy driving distance of Audubon Park and Tulane University, and only a couple blocks south of Magazine Street, **Octavia Books** (513 Octavia St., 504/899-7323, www.octaviabooks.com, 10am-6pm Mon.-Sat., 10am-5pm Sun.) is particularly popular among local residents and college students. Besides offering biographies, memoirs, and fiction, the store features plenty of local travel guides and cookbooks, as well as books about New Orleans's unique history, art, and celebrations.

Jewelry and Accessories

Mignon Faget (3801 Magazine St., 509/891-2005 or 800/524-1402, www.mignonfaget.com, 10am-6pm Mon.-Sat., noon-5pm Sun.) has an enthusiastic following among New Orleans's devotees of fine jewelry. Faget has won countless awards for her creations, many of which incorporate icons and images familiar to Louisianians, such as oyster earrings, red-bean charm necklaces, and fleur-de-lis cuff links.

Sports and Recreation

Parks and Plazas

South of Poydras Street lies the attractive **Lafayette Square** (St. Charles Ave. and Camp St., www.lafayette-square.org, 24 hours daily, free), which was laid out in the late 18th century as the American Quarter's version of the Place d'Armes (now Jackson Square). Bound by St.

Charles Avenue, Camp Street, and North and South Maestri Places, it is named in honor of the Marquis de Lafayette, who visited the city in 1825. With its ample park-bench seating, the shaded, landscaped park—one of the CBD's few patches of greenery—continues to be a pleasant place to relax, read, or listen to live music. In fact, you can catch free concerts by some of the city's top bands and musicians every Wednesday in spring at **YLC Wednesday at the Square** (504/585-1500, http://wednesdayatthesquare.com, 5pm-8pm Wed. mid-Mar.-late May). Local bars and restaurants sell food and drinks to benefit the Young Leadership Council. You can also purchase the work of local artisans in the Artist Village.

Between the Audubon Aquarium of the Americas and The Outlet Collection at Riverwalk, the pleasant **Spanish Plaza** (1 Poydras St., 24 hours daily, free) is an ideal spot to gaze at the bustling Mississippi. The square was rededicated by Spain in 1976 to commemorate its influence on the Crescent City's history and to serve as an ongoing promise of fraternity. As a symbolic reminder, the seals of Spanish provinces encircle the central fountain. Spanish Plaza is a common gathering place for residents and tourists alike, as well as the site of free public concerts throughout the year.

Since **Crescent Park** (Mississippi riverfront btwn. Elysian Fields Ave. and Mazant St., 504/636-6400, www.crescentparknola.org, 6am-7:30pm daily, free), an edgy Bywater sanctuary, opened in February 2014, the 1.4-mile-long, 20-acre strip has lured countless recreationists. Besides scenic views of the downtown New Orleans skyline, the Mississippi River, and Algiers Point, you'll find picnic areas, a fenced dog run, and a network of paths suitable for walking, jogging, and biking. A parking lot is situated near Piety and Chartres Streets, where you'll also spot the Piety Street Bridge, a rusted steel arch that safely delivers pedestrians over the active riverfront railroad tracks. Certain activities, such as cooking, swimming, and littering, are not allowed, as are skateboards, motorcycles, and bottles.

The 23,000-acre **Barataria Preserve** (6588 Barataria Blvd., Marrero, 504/689-3690, www.nps.gov/jela, 9am-5pm daily, free), a unit of Jean Lafitte National Historical Park and Preserve, is a popular **bird-watching** spot among locals and visitors. On the west bank of the Mississippi River, this enormous preserve comprises bayous, swamps, marshes, forests, and roughly nine miles of hiking trails (where pets, even leashed ones, aren't allowed). Don't miss the **Bayou Coquille Trail,** a half-mile, pavement-and-boardwalk path that's known for myriad sightings of snakes, alligators, nutrias, and some of the more than 300 bird species that dwell here. At the **visitor center** (9:30am-4:30pm Wed.-Sun.), you'll spot exhibits that highlight how the Mississippi River created Louisiana's wetlands, the national significance of this region, and the relationship between the land and its people. In the bookstore, you'll find music, field guides, and children's books. Free guided wetlands walks are available Wednesday-Sunday at 10am. The park, which is closed only on Mardi Gras Day, is also favored among kayakers, boaters, and anglers.

Spectator Sports

The NFL Super Bowl has been held in the iconic 73,000-seat **Mercedes-Benz Superdome** (1500 Sugar Bowl Dr., 504/587-3822, www.superdome.com) several times since 1978. It's home to the **New Orleans Saints** (504/731-1700, www.neworleanssaints.com). The Saints' unusual name derives from both the popular jazz anthem "When the Saints Go Marching In" and the fact that this predominantly Catholic city was awarded the NFL franchise on November 1, 1966 (All Saints' Day).

Adjacent to the Mercedes-Benz Superdome, the 18,000-seat **Smoothie**

Who Dat!

While in town, particularly during the NFL football season, you'll notice "Who Dat" flags and banners hanging from many porches and balconies, and you might hear someone shout "Who Dat!" at no one in particular. If you're wondering about the origins of such a funny-sounding call of solidarity, just know that you've arrived in the heart of the **Who Dat Nation** (www.whodatnation.com), a popular term used to describe the entire community of fiercely loyal Saints' fans.

Once a common dialogue exchange between performers and spectators at minstrel shows and vaudeville acts in southern Louisiana, the "Who Dat" chant was eventually adopted by the **New Orleans Saints** in the 1980s. Part of a longer chant—"Who dat say dey gonna beat dem Saints?"—that is often heard at Saints' games, "Who Dat" has now become a rallying cry of team support for New Orleanians everywhere.

King Center (1501 Dave Dixon Dr., 504/587-3822, www.smoothieking-center.com) is the official home of the **New Orleans Pelicans** basketball team (504/525-4667, www.nba.com/pelicans).

Mid-City's **Fair Grounds Race Course & Slots** (1751 Gentilly Blvd., 504/944-5515 or 504/948-1111, www.fair-groundsracecourse.com, 9am-midnight daily, clubhouse $10 pp, grandstand $0-5 pp) offers live horse races from Thanksgiving through March. Events at the track include the Louisiana Derby and the Fair Grounds Oaks. It's also the longtime home of the annual **New Orleans Jazz & Heritage Festival** (www.nojazzfest.com).

Food

The city's reputation for culinary excellence is well deserved. This is the place that shaped famous chefs Paul Prudhomme, Emeril Lagasse, and Alon Shaya—all of whom have embraced the Big Easy's Cajun and Creole roots, not to mention its abundance of fresh seafood.

While New Orleans certainly has its share of upscale restaurants celebrated for their impeccable service, creative fusion cuisine, and reliance on fresh, seasonal ingredients, it also boasts a wide array of old-time neighborhood haunts. Historic joints, such as Café Maspero in the French Quarter, are often known for classic local staples like roast beef po'boys, gumbo, and crawfish étouffée.

Restaurants can fill up quickly around Christmas and Mardi Gras, and during special events, such as Jazz Fest. At such times, reservations are highly recommended; for places where reservations aren't accepted, it's best to go on weekdays, when it's generally less crowded. You'll often avoid crowds and save money by visiting at lunchtime.

French Quarter

Cajun and Creole

One of the true granddaddies of old-fashioned French-Creole cooking, **Antoine's Restaurant** (713 St. Louis St., 504/581-4422, www.antoines.com, 11:30am-2pm and 5:30pm-9pm Mon.-Sat., 10:30am-2pm Sun., $18-48) opened in 1840 and has served everyone from President Coolidge to Judy Garland. Several well-known dishes, from oysters Rockefeller to eggs Sardou, were invented at this elegant restaurant, and the solicitous waitstaff will happily explain the endless menu of culinary options. Deciding what to eat is only half the challenge: You'll also have to choose from one of 14 dining rooms, including the Mardi Gras-themed Rex Room. Before dinner, have a cocktail in the on-site **Hermes Bar,** and during the day, enjoy a treat at **Antoine's Annex** (513 Royal St.), a small coffeehouse offering gelato and pastries.

The active corner of Bourbon and

The City Is Your Oyster

While in town, oyster-lovers should sample some versions of the shellfish for which New Orleans is known:

- **Oysters Bienville:** Oysters that have been baked in their shells, along with shrimp, mushrooms, green onions, herbs, and seasonings in a white wine sauce. Since the dish was invented at **Arnaud's** (page 381), you should sample it there first.
- **Oysters Rockefeller:** Baked oysters on the half-shell, topped with bread crumbs, butter, and a green sauce made of puréed herbs (such as parsley). **Antoine's Restaurant** (page 380), where it was invented, serves some of the city's finest (and keeps the recipe a closely guarded secret).
- **Oyster Pernod:** This dish consists of raw oysters served with a dipping sauce made with Pernod, an anise-flavored French aperitif. Try one of the best versions at **Adolfo's** (page 389).

Bienville might seem an unlikely place for a fine-dining establishment, but **Arnaud's** (813 Bienville St., 504/523-5433, www.arnaudsrestaurant.com, 6pm-10pm Mon.-Sat., 10am-2pm and 6pm-10pm Sun., $27-37) is a terrific spot to sample traditional Creole cuisine and enjoy friendly, attentive service. Established by Arnaud Cazenave, a French wine salesman, in 1918, Arnaud's serves favorites like baked oysters, seafood gumbo, and speckled trout amandine. Dine in the elegant main dining room or the smaller jazz bistro. Before dinner, have a cocktail in **French 75,** the on-site bar, and check out the stunning costumes at the **Germaine Cazenave Wells Mardi Gras Museum** (free). For a more casual meal, head next door to Arnaud's other eatery, **Remoulade** (309 Bourbon St., 504/523-0377, www.remoulade.com, 11:30am-11pm daily).

It's hard to bypass **Brennan's** (417 Royal St., 504/525-9711, www.brennansneworleans.com, 9am-2pm and 6pm-10pm Mon.-Fri., 8am-2pm and 6pm-10pm Sat.-Sun., $21-38), the legendary pink eatery that initiated the Brennan clan's rise as the Crescent City's first family of the restaurant business. Opened in 1946 by Owen Edward Brennan, the restaurant encompasses several dining areas, plus a lush courtyard. While the atmosphere can be loud, and visiting celebrities tend to get better service than regular folks, the food is definitely worth sampling. Two of the dishes invented onsite include eggs Hussarde (which combines poached eggs with Canadian bacon, hollandaise, and Marchand de Vin sauce) and bananas Foster.

The French Quarter boasts several historic restaurants, including the **Court of Two Sisters** (613 Royal St., 504/522-7261, www.courtoftwosisters.com, 9am-3pm and 5:30pm-10pm daily, $25-37), established in 1880 by two Creole sisters, Emma and Bertha Camors. It's now run by the Fein brothers. Though the old-fashioned interior can be an elegant yet casual spot for a romantic dinner, the real appeal is the lush, spacious courtyard, particularly during the daily jazz brunch buffet, which features a live jazz trio and made-to-order omelets, turtle soup, and shrimp rémoulade.

Among those few remaining New Orleans restaurants where men must wear a jacket in the evening (and all day Sunday)—and no patron may stroll in wearing shorts—is ★ **Galatoire's Restaurant** (209 Bourbon St., 504/525-2021, www.galatoires.com, 11:30am-10pm Tues.-Sat., noon-10pm Sun.,

$24-42), which opened in 1905 and has been run by the Galatoire family ever since. Galatoire's lures many loyal patrons, and true regulars have been coming here for generations, often taking their seat at the same table. The enormous French-Creole menu includes everything from lavish high-end dishes, such as filet béarnaise, to affordable chicken and seafood entrées. Though the lower dining room doesn't accept reservations, you can reserve a seat in the upstairs area.

Celebrity Chef Paul Prudhomme was largely responsible for popularizing Cajun cooking outside Louisiana, and his restaurant, **K-Paul's Louisiana Kitchen** (416 Chartres St., 504/596-2530, www.kpauls.com, 5:30pm-10pm daily, $29-37), is an excellent, albeit pricey, place to learn why. Situated within an 1834 building with a cozy courtyard, K-Paul's has an open kitchen on both the 1st and 2nd floors, allowing diners the chance to watch their dishes being prepared.

Opposite the imposing Hotel Monteleone, **Mr. B's Bistro** (201 Royal St., 504/523-2078, www.mrbsbistro.com, 11:30am-9pm Mon.-Sat., 10:30am-9pm Sun., $28-38) is a popular place for business lunches. Given its fashionable bar, attentive service, and classy decor, it's easy to understand why. Though the ever-changing menu depends on seasonal ingredients, you can expect classic dishes like gumbo ya-ya, barbecue shrimp, and pasta jambalaya. Save some money by opting for weekday cocktail specials and two-course luncheons. Mr. B's also offers a wonderful jazz brunch on Sunday, and there's usually live piano music 7pm-10pm.

The **Palace Café** (605 Canal St., 504/523-1661, www.palacecafe.com, 8am-11am, 11am-2:30pm, 5pm-close Mon.-Fri., 10:30am-2:30pm and 5pm-close Sat.-Sun., $22-36) ranks among the most cosmopolitan of the Brennan family restaurants in New Orleans. It can seem touristy, but don't let that dissuade you—the kitchen prepares some of the city's best and most exciting local fare, and the staff is highly personable and efficient. Signature dishes include andouille-crusted fish, an oyster pan roast, and a crabmeat cheesecake baked in a pecan crust. Every dish is tasty and presented with great flourish. Housed within the historic Werlein's building, this classy restaurant also serves an enjoyable Sunday jazz brunch.

Nestled inside the posh Royal Sonesta New Orleans, **Restaurant R'evolution** (777 Bienville St., 504/553-2277, www.revolutionnola.com, 5:30pm-10pm Mon.-Thurs., 11:30am-2:30pm and 5:30pm-10pm Fri., 5:30-10pm Sat., 10:30am-2pm and 5:30pm-10pm Sun., $24-58) is the brainchild of award-winning chefs John Folse and Rick Tramonto. The menu consists of varied, reimagined versions of classic Cajun and Creole cuisine. The Sunday jazz brunch (10:30am-2pm) brings together local favorites like crab beignets, eggs Sardou, and strawberry pain perdu. Grab a drink in the on-site **Bar R'evolution** (5pm-10pm Mon.-Fri., noon-7pm Sat., 10:30am-7pm Sun.).

Tujague's (823 Decatur St., 504/525-8676, www.tujaguesrestaurant.com, 5pm-9pm Mon.-Thurs., 11am-2:30pm and 5pm-10pm Fri., 10am-2:30pm and 5pm-10pm Sat., 10am-2:30pm and 5pm-9pm Sun., $29-42) is an atmospheric corner tavern that's been around since 1856, making it the second-oldest continuously operated restaurant in New Orleans. It sits opposite the French Market and serves much of the local Louisiana produce and seafood sold there. The six-course Creole menu varies little from what diners might have eaten more than a century ago, including beef brisket in Creole sauce and shrimp rémoulade. In addition to the usual cocktails and wines, Tujague's serves its own microbrewed beer. Drinking here has quite a legacy—the cypress-wood bar is original, shipped from France the

Round-the-Clock Eats

For night owls, the Big Easy really delivers. In addition to bars, pubs, and live music venues that stay open until the wee hours, you'll find a slew of 24-hour eateries, ideal for late-night or early-morning cravings.

Perhaps the most well known of these round-the-clock joints is **Café Du Monde,** which, except for a brief time around Christmas (6pm on Dec. 24 to 6am on Dec. 26, $2-5), is open 24 hours daily. Stop in for late-night coffee and beignets.

If you have a yen for more than dessert in the French Quarter, head to the **Clover Grill** (900 Bourbon St., 504/598-1010, www.clovergrill.com, $4-7), a cozy diner where seating is often hard to snag and sassy waiters serve up hamburgers, sandwiches, and omelets.

A couple blocks down Bourbon, the **Quartermaster** (1100 Bourbon St., 504/529-1416, www.quartermasterdeli.net, $6-10) offers only a few seats alongside the front window, but plenty of culinary options at the deli counter in the rear of this often crowded, albeit dingy, store. After a night of tireless bar-hopping, the Quartermaster, also known as The Nellie Deli, is a popular place to stock up on junk food in addition to jambalaya, stuffed potatoes, and roast beef po'boys. Be aware; the employees here are rife with attitude.

Just a block east on nearby Royal, in the shadow of the supposedly haunted LaLaurie Mansion, stands another longtime, 24-hour market and deli. Popular with the late-night crowd, particularly post-shift bartenders and servers, **Verti Marte** (1201 Royal St., 504/525-4767, $4-6) prepares a slew of options, from omelets to barbecue and seafood entrées to scrumptious desserts.

Patrons 21 years old and over might prefer the **Déjà Vu Bar & Grill** (400 Dauphine St., 504/523-1931, www.dejavunola.com, $8-18), where you'll find a wide selection of beers, cocktails, and snacks—from burgers and po'boys to seafood platters and breakfast specialties. The Quartermaster, Verti Marte, and Déjà Vu offer free delivery for all phone-in food orders.

If you find yourself near Frenchmen Street in the wee hours, you can always head to **Buffa's Bar & Restaurant** (1001 Esplanade Ave., 504/949-0038, www.buffasbar.com, $7-14), a 24-hour bar and music club that lies on the border between the French Quarter and the Faubourg Marigny. It also happens to serve some terrific American, Cajun, and Creole grub, such as shrimp Creole omelets, redfish po'boys, and bratwurst jambalaya, any time of the day.

year that the restaurant opened, and it's played host to everyone from President Truman to Harrison Ford.

American

Red-meat lovers swear by the hefty cuts served at **Dickie Brennan's Steakhouse** (716 Iberville St., 504/522-2467, www.dickiebrennanssteakhouse.com, 3pm-close Sun.-Thurs., 3pm-close Fri.-Sat., $26-49), which is known for its oyster-topped filet served with creamed spinach and roasted potatoes. Though a clubby, upscale space, the restaurant has a relaxed mood, and presentable casual attire is customary.

Johnny's Po-Boys (511 St. Louis St., 504/524-8129, www.johnnyspoboy.com, 8am-4:30pm daily, $7-11, cash only) opened in 1950 as an unprepossessing, family-owned eatery with tables sheathed in red-checkered cloths and surrounded by bentwood chairs. Though it's only open until the afternoon, Johnny's fills up daily for breakfast and lunch. Not surprisingly, it's best known for its namesake sandwiches, but you can also order omelets, seafood platters, and ice cream treats.

Dark and divey **Port of Call** (838 Esplanade Ave., 504/523-0120, www.portofcallnola.com, 11am-midnight

Sun.-Thurs., 11am-1am Fri.-Sat., $10-23) is so popular for its hefty burgers—made with freshly ground beef and piled high with mushrooms or melted cheddar—that there's often a line outside the door. Besides burgers, the simple menu also features traditional comfort foods. The nautical decor and strong cocktails make Port of Call a worthy stop.

Inside Erin Rose Bar, **Killer Poboys** (811 Conti St., 504/252-6745, http://killerpoboys.com, 10am-midnight Wed.-Mon., $8-13) twists the po'boy on its ear. The menu includes many traditional sandwiches, like beef debris. But what people love here are the unusual takes, such as cheddar omelets and peanut butter po'boys. This location is 21 and older. **Big Killer Poboys** (219 Dauphine St., 504/462-2731) is open to all.

Coffee and Desserts

Beginning as a humble coffee stand to serve the customers and employees of the produce stalls in the French Market in 1862, **Café Du Monde** (800 Decatur St., 504/525-4544 or 800/772-2927, www.cafedumonde.com, 24 hours daily, $2-5) has grown into one of the most legendary food operations in the country. Part of its mystique and popularity is due to its round-the-clock hours (except for Christmas) and its small menu, conveniently plastered on the napkin dispensers. The mainstays are beignets and dark-roasted coffee laced with chicory and traditionally served *au lait*. The mostly open-air café has dozens of small marble tables beneath the green-and-white awning, the sides of which can be unfurled on chilly days, though you can also sit inside the small, fully enclosed dining area. Servers clad in white shirts with black bow ties and white-paper hats whisk about gracefully, delivering plates of beignets at almost breakneck speed. While no visit to New Orleans is complete without experiencing this original location, you may notice other branches throughout the city, including those in the Riverwalk (500 Port of New Orleans, Ste. 27, 8am-9pm Mon.-Sat., 8am-7pm Sun.) and Lakeside malls (3301 Veterans Blvd., Ste. 104, 7am-9pm Mon.-Fri., 8am-9pm Sat., 11am-6pm Sun.).

The Quarter has a branch of one of the city's most famous coffeehouse chains, **CC's Coffee House** (941 Royal St., 504/581-6996, www.ccscoffee.com, 6am-9pm Mon.-Fri., 7am-9pm Sat.-Sun., $2-5), at the corner of Royal and Dumaine Streets, just opposite the neighborhood's only elementary school. It's a cozy spot, meaning that seating is limited, but it's also warmly lit and charmingly furnished, with several cushy armchairs. Numerous other CC's coffeehouses can be found throughout Louisiana.

A source of delightful pastries, from napoleons to dark chocolate mousse, the **Croissant d'Or Patisserie** (617 Ursulines Ave., 504/524-4663, 6:30am-3pm Wed.-Mon., $2-6) is a classic French bakery that also serves delicious sandwiches, fresh salads, and yummy breakfasts. In the Lower Quarter, not far from the Old Ursuline Convent, this spacious café—with plenty of tables, local artwork, and a simply furnished courtyard—makes a nice break from exploring the neighborhood's rich architecture. Be prepared for long lines, particularly in the morning.

A wonderful place to while away an afternoon, hang out with friends, and watch curious passersby, **En Vie Espresso Bar & Cafe** (1241 Decatur St., 504/524-3689, www.cafeenvie.com, 7am-midnight Sun.-Thurs., 7am-1am Fri.-Sat., $6-12) brews a strong coffee and serves plenty of interesting teas and pastries. This local favorite prepares decent salads and sandwiches, not to mention excellent breakfasts. There's another location at 308 Decatur Street (504/598-5374).

Cafe Beignet (311 Bourbon St., 504/525-2611, http://cafebeignet.com, 8am-midnight daily, $4-10) may not be as famous as Café Du Monde, but many locals think their beignets are just as good, if not better. The location, nestled next to

Musical Legends Park, makes for a lovely alfresco dining experience. Expect a line, but it will be worth the wait.

Eclectic

A highly regarded restaurant on a quiet stretch of Dauphine, **Bayona** (430 Dauphine St., 504/525-4455, www.bayona.com, 5:30pm-9:30pm Mon.-Tues., 11:30am-1:30pm and 5:30pm-9:30pm Wed.-Sat., $28-34) fuses traditions, recipes, and ingredients from a handful of cultures, namely American, French, Italian, Mediterranean, Asian, and North African. Award-winning chef Susan Spicer dreams up such imaginative combos as peppered lamb loin with goat cheese-zinfandel sauce. Desserts are no mere afterthought, and there's a commendable wine list. The setting—an 18th-century Creole cottage filled with trompe l'oeil murals of the Mediterranean countryside, plus a lush courtyard—is the quintessence of romance, though the interior acoustics can make it rather loud on certain nights.

Opposite the oft-photographed Cornstalk Hotel, you'll encounter the enticing **Café Amelie** (912 Royal St., 504/412-8965, www.cafeamelie.com, 11am-3pm and 5pm-9pm Sun. and Tues.-Thurs., 11am-3pm and 5pm-10pm Fri.-Sat., $16-29), a cute, warmly furnished spot that sits beyond a lush, intimate courtyard, which is favored for anniversaries and other romantic occasions. Locals and tourists alike often pause before the simple, ever-changing menu that's posted daily by the wrought-iron gates. The menu, while eclectic, embraces Louisiana-style cuisine, including such classics as citrus-drizzled crab cakes and jumbo shrimp and grits with corn maque choux.

Occupying the first two floors of a white-brick building on Decatur, the **Crescent City Brewhouse** (527 Decatur

Top to bottom: Court of Two Sisters; Café Du Monde; Saba

St., 504/522-0571, www.crescentcitybrewhouse.com, 11am-10pm Sun.-Thurs., 11am-11pm Fri.-Sat., $15-18) is considered by some locals a tourist magnet. As brewpubs go, it serves surprisingly decent and varied food. Offerings include baked brie, shucked oysters, and seafood cheesecake. This inviting space lures passersby with its exposed brick walls, shiny brewing equipment, and live music. If possible, opt for balcony or courtyard dining.

Italian

In the quieter Lower Quarter, at the corner of Chartres and St. Philip Streets, stands a nondescript building that looks more like a warehouse than a fine-dining establishment. Nevertheless, the well-favored **Irene's Cuisine** (529 Bienville St. St., 504/529-8811, www.irenesnola.com, 5:30pm-10pm Mon.-Sat., $17-30) is popular among gourmands, particularly for romantic dinners and special occasions. The service is attentive, and the Italian and French cuisine is often quite tasty, with highlights like bruschetta, soft-shell crab pasta, and crème brûlée.

If you appreciate well-prepared Italian cuisine and would rather avoid the crazier end of the French Quarter, head to the more residential part of Royal Street, where you'll find a local favorite, the **Mona Lisa Restaurant** (1212 Royal St., 504/522-6746, www.monalisaneworleans.com, 5pm-10pm Wed.-Mon., $13-16). As ideal for romantic dinners as it is for family outings, this cozy eatery has at least three things going for it: friendly service; affordable yet delicious food; and warm, homey decor, including ceiling fans, red-and-white checkered tablecloths, and walls that are covered with assorted *Mona Lisa* renditions, from copies of the classic da Vinci painting to a Picasso-style version.

Mexican

A favorite late-night haunt for inexpensive and tasty tacos, burritos, and tamales is **Felipe's Taqueria** (301 N. Peters St., 504/267-4406, www.felipestaqueria.com, 11am-midnight daily, $4-8). The space is attractive and inviting, with high ceilings, solid wood tables, and a separate bar area, where the television is always tuned to sporting events. The menu is fairly simple, and all dishes are made right in front of you, which explains why everything tastes so fresh. Order the Felipe's Special, an appetizer consisting of corn chips, salsa, guacamole, and queso dip. There are also locations in Uptown (6215 S. Miro St.) and Mid-City (411-1 N. Carrolton Ave.).

Seafood

Since 1910, the **Acme Oyster House** (724 Iberville St., 504/522-5973, www.acmeoyster.com, 10:30am-10pm Sun.-Thurs., 10:30am-11pm Fri.-Sat., $9-22) has been a reliable option for fresh bivalves. Decked out with red-checkered tablecloths and packed with tourists, this casual place is crazy at times, but for some, it's worth braving the frenzy for tasty soft-shell crab po'boys, shrimp platters, and a first-rate oyster Rockefeller bisque. While it might not be oyster nirvana, Acme's rich history and convenient location make it a decent choice. There are additional Acme Oyster Houses in Harrah's casino (8 Canal St.), Metairie (3000 Veterans Blvd.), Covington (1202 N. Hwy. 190), and Baton Rouge (3535 Perkins Rd.).

For more than four decades, **Café Maspero** (601 Decatur St., 504/229-4341, www.cafemaspero.com, 8am-10pm Sun.-Thurs., 8am-11pm Fri.-Sat., $7-14) has been one of the Quarter's most popular eateries. Ideal for budget-conscious travelers, it features several local staples, including jambalaya and muffulettas. Despite the reasonable prices, portions are usually gigantic, and while there are occasional lulls, this spacious, admittedly dingy joint is typically hopping with full tables, bustling servers, and long lines of tourists and locals. The oft-open French doors invite refreshing breezes from the Mississippi River.

Just off crazy Bourbon Street, **Felix's Restaurant & Oyster Bar** (739 Iberville St., 504/522-4440, www.felixs.com, 11am-10pm Sun.-Thurs., 11am-11pm Fri.-Sat., $11-20) has been serving local seafood fanatics since the early 1900s. Though known for its oysters on the half shell, this casual joint prepares all of New Orleans's seafood favorites well, including the shrimp rémoulade, blackened alligator, and oysters Bienville.

Ralph Brennan's Red Fish Grill (115 Bourbon St., 504/598-1200, www.redfishgrill.com, 11am-10pm Sun.-Thurs., 11am-11pm Fri.-Sat., $23-34) on exuberant Bourbon Street is worth seeking out. Opened in 1996, the restaurant, just a block from Canal, helped to revive a block that once felt a bit dark and ominous at night. The cavernous main dining room reverberates with piped-in rock music, and huge redfish mobiles dangle overhead. The noisy, festive ambience makes it fun for singles, friends, and anybody hoping to experience Bourbon's nightlife. To one side lies a spacious oyster bar with huge oyster half-shell sculptures; you can order from the main menu in here, too.

Faubourg Marigny and Bywater

Cajun and Creole

Situated within a modest white-frame house by the levee, along the southern edge of the Bywater, easygoing **Elizabeth's Restaurant** (601 Gallier St., 504/944-9272, www.elizabethsrestaurantnola.com, 8am-8pm Mon.-Fri., 8am-3pm Sat.-Sun., $18-26) serves exceptional breakfast and lunch, though it does require a lengthy journey from the Quarter. Elizabeth's is operated by chef Bryon Peck, who maintains the beloved eatery's commitment to imaginative meals and friendly service. One popular choice is the salmon and brie grilled cheese on rye, topped with fried eggs and hash or grits, but be sure to order a side of praline-flavored bacon.

American

The enormous, garishly colored **Dat Dog** (601 Frenchmen St., 504/309-3362, http://datdognola.com, 11am-midnight Sun.-Wed., 11am-1am Thurs., 11am-3am Fri.-Sat., $7-10), an outpost of a local chain, offers a variety of tasty hot dogs and sausages, from Polish kielbasas to Louisiana-style sausages made from crawfish or alligator meat. Various condiments, fries, shakes, and cocktails round out the menu, but it's the dogs that draw the crowds, particularly those with a case of the late-night munchies. A friendly, casual joint, Dat Dog has indoor and outdoor seating. You'll find two other Dat Dog restaurants in the Uptown area.

New Orleans might not be known for its barbecue, but that doesn't stop local meat lovers from heading to **The Joint** (701 Mazant St., 504/949-3232, www.alwayssmokin.com, 11:30am-10pm Mon.-Sat., $8-12), a super-casual dive on the eastern end of the Bywater celebrated throughout the city for its "carnivore cuisine." Featured on Guy Fieri's popular Food Network show *Diners, Drive-Ins, and Dives,* this down-home, often crowded place offers delicious pork spareribs, beef brisket plates, and Cajun sausage. Even the sides are stellar, so save room for the macaroni and cheese, baked beans, and cole slaw. If you're really hungry, you won't go wrong with the desserts either, particularly the peanut butter pie.

Plenty of locals swear by the spacious, art-filled **Satsuma Café Dauphine** (3218 Dauphine St., 504/304-5962, www.satsumacafe.com, 7am-4pm daily, $6-10). In addition to standard coffeehouse fare, such as espresso drinks and lemon-blueberry muffins, the café has a wide array of delectable breakfast and lunch options that are often healthy and gluten-free. The freshly squeezed juices are worth sampling, particularly the Popeye, which consists of spinach, lemon, kale, and apple. Some of the soups, sandwiches, and muffins are vegan. There are two other Satsuma Café locations (7901 Maple St. and 1320 Magazine St.).

Asian

For some of the best Thai food in the city, drop by **SukhoThai** (2200 Royal St., 504/948-9309, www.sukhothai-nola.com, 11:30am-2:30pm and 5:30pm-10pm Tues.-Fri., 11:30am-10pm Sat.-Sun., $20-30), a relatively quiet eatery. Here, the friendly service and local artwork help to create a hip yet informal vibe, and the menu is quite extensive, offering tasty soups, vegetarian dishes, and seafood specialties, including the glass noodle shrimp bake. In case you get hungry while antiques shopping, there's also a location in the Uptown area.

Near the edge of the Faubourg Marigny, just a few blocks up Frenchmen Street from the main cluster of bars and restaurants, sits the dark, cozy **Wasabi Sushi & Asian Grill** (900 Frenchmen St., 504/943-9433, www.wasabinola.com, 11:30am-2:30pm and 5pm-10pm Mon.-Thurs., 11:30am-2:30pm and 5pm-11pm Fri.-Sat., 5pm-10pm Sun., $16-23), at once a mellow neighborhood bar and a stellar Japanese restaurant. Besides excellent sushi and sashimi, Wasabi serves crab asparagus soup, squid salad, and wasabi honey shrimp, plus daily specials.

Coffee and Desserts

Occupying a busy corner about four blocks east of Washington Square Park, the **Flora Gallery & Coffee Shop** (2600 Royal St., 504/947-8358, 7am-midnight daily) is a funky little place with sidewalk seating, worn-in furnishings, big portions of coffee elixirs, and home-style cooking. While it's not a bad place to read a book, peruse groovy art, or chat with eccentric locals, it's admittedly not for everyone—particularly at night, when it is wise to be aware of your surroundings around the border between the Marigny and Bywater.

To satisfy your sweet tooth, venture to the homey **New Orleans Cake Cafe & Bakery** (2440 Chartres St., 504/943-0010, www.nolacakes.com, 7am-3pm Wed.-Mon.), which prepares to-die-for treats, such as red velvet cake with cream cheese frosting, plus specialty cupcakes flavored with champagne, mimosa, and chocolate mousse. The service is friendly and easygoing, and the crowd is a comfortable mix of students, retirees, artists, and hipsters. Be prepared for long lines, particularly during the weekend brunch.

Eclectic

Located in the same block as Frenchmen Street's most famous music clubs, the **Marigny Brasserie** (640 Frenchmen St., 504/945-4472, www.marignybrasserie.com, 3pm-11pm Mon.-Thurs., noon-1am Fri.-Sat., noon-11pm Sun., $14-32) is a slick, modern space whose kitchen puts a unique spin on Louisiana, Southern, Italian, French, and Mexican ingredients and recipes. The BBQ shrimp with rosemary grits reflects the kitchen's simple approach to contemporary food. Besides tasty salads, tacos, and sandwiches, classic New Orleans dishes are available, including fried green tomatoes and shrimp rémoulade. The stylish bar is a pleasant place to sip creative cocktails and listen to live music before heading to one of the nearby clubs.

Perched on the edge of the St. Roch neighborhood, sandwiched between the Faubourg Tremé and the Faubourg Marigny, stands the cavernous, high-ceilinged **St. Roch Market** (2381 St. Claude Ave., 504/609-3813, www.strochmarket.com, 7am-10pm Sun.-Thurs., 7am-11pm Fri.-Sat.), a refurbished gathering place for foodies and families alike. With its white, minimalist decor, plentiful indoor and outdoor seating, and assorted stalls, offering everything from cold-pressed juices and savory crepes to raw oysters and Korean-Creole dishes like the "Japchalaya," it's a welcome addition to the local food scene.

It's also a decent place to pick up coffee, pastries, specialty meats, fresh produce, and wine.

Indian

Set inside a strikingly restored historic building, **Silk Road** (2483 Royal St., 504/944-6666, www.silkroadnola.com, noon-10pm Wed.-Mon.) is a full-service restaurant offering both highly praised Indian fare as well as classic New Orleans dishes. On any given day, you might sample BBQ shrimp and grits for breakfast, Louisiana crawfish eggrolls and masala shrimp wraps for lunch, and samosas, chicken and andouille gumbo, and lamb vindaloo for dinner. If you really love it here, you can even spend the night, as the family-owned **Balcony Guesthouse** (504/810-8667, www.balconyguesthouse.com) is located upstairs.

Italian

Large portions of traditional Italian and Creole fare are heaped onto the plates at **Adolfo's** (611 Frenchmen St., 504/948-3800, 5:30pm-10:30pm daily), a longtime neighborhood standby that's particularly strong on seafood dishes, such as oysters Pernod and the "ocean sauce," which features shrimp, crawfish, and crab. Granted, it's a small hole-in-the-wall, where the service can be slow, reservations are typically not accepted, and no credit cards are allowed, but it's a good choice for dining before heading to one of Frenchmen's nearby music clubs. Downstairs, the **Apple Barrel Bar** (609 Frenchmen St.) is a dark and cozy spot to nurse a cocktail before or after dinner.

Central Business and Arts Districts

Cajun and Creole

Housed within a building erected in the 1840s and featuring brick walls, wrought-iron chandeliers, and red-checkered tablecloths, the nostalgic, amiable **Bon Ton Cafe** (401 Magazine St., 504/524-3386, www.thebontoncafe.com, 11am-2pm and 5pm-9pm Mon.-Fri., $19-36) has been serving well-favored Cajun cuisine since 1953 (although other restaurants have been in this location since 1900). Dishes like the turtle soup, seafood gumbo, and bread pudding with whiskey sauce are legendary among the regulars. Given the challenging street-parking situation, arriving by foot, cab, or streetcar is recommended. Dinner reservations are strongly recommended; the wait is long without one.

Noted chef Donald Link, of Herbsaint Bar and Restaurant, runs **Cochon** (930 Tchoupitoulas St., 504/588-2123, http://cochonrestaurant.com, 11am-10pm Sun.-Thurs., 11am-11pm Fri.-Sat., $9-32) in a rustic, renovated warehouse space. It serves a stellar blend of Cajun and contemporary American victuals, specializing in small, tapas-style portions. Highlighted entrées include rabbit and dumplings, smoked ham hocks with bitter greens, and smoked beef brisket with horseradish potato salad. Save room for the hummingbird cake, made with pecans, pineapples, bananas, and a cream cheese frosting.

The celeb photos lining the walls of **Mother's Restaurant** (401 Poydras St., 504/523-9656, www.mothersrestaurant.net, 7am-10pm daily, $12-18) attest to its longstanding popularity. Opened in 1938, this glorified cafeteria with brash lighting, Formica tables, and chatty servers draws a mix of downtown office workers, hungry tourists, and local politicos. The most famous dishes are the roast beef and baked ham po'boys, but you'll also find delicious jambalaya, seafood gumbo, and crawfish étouffée. It opens earlier than most CBD restaurants—a handy fact if you happen to be returning to your hotel with hunger pangs after a night of barhopping.

American

Named in honor of the CBD's former moniker, **The American Sector** (The

National WWII Museum, 945 Magazine St., 504/528-1940, ww2eats.com, 11am-6:30pm Mon.-Fri., 10am-6:30pm Sat.-Sun., $13-20) is a better-than-average museum eatery. With decor that resembles an old-fashioned airport, this delightful eatery features creative versions of American staples, such as mini-cheeseburgers with bacon-onion marmalade, heirloom tomato soup with grilled ham and cheese, and bananas Foster shakes. The portions are generous. Try a vintage cocktail, such as the Last Waltz, which blends vodka, strawberries, mint, ginger, and champagne. Parking is validated during happy hour (4:30pm-6pm).

Eclectic

If you can reserve a table at **Emeril's New Orleans** (800 Tchoupitoulas St., 504/528-9393, www.emerils.com, 11:30am-2pm and 5pm-10pm Mon.-Fri., 5pm-10pm Sat.-Sun., $29-50), go for it—Emeril didn't become famous for no reason. He's an excellent cook with a great kitchen staff, and the food here is more complex and imaginative than at NOLA, his French Quarter restaurant. The bigger and louder of Emeril Lagasse's acclaimed restaurants, Emeril's takes its hits from critics who complain about haughty service and high prices, but this is the domain of one of the world's most famous chefs, and it's always packed. The space is airy, high-ceilinged, and dramatic, the quintessence of Arts District chic.

Like many places in New Orleans, it is easy to walk by **Thalia** (1245 Constance St., 504/655-1338, www.thalianola.com, 5pm-10pm Tues.-Sat., $10-21) and not realize what lies behind its doors. Head inside to find some of the city's least complicated food and a homey atmosphere. The restaurant has a zero-waste ethic, which is a nice counterbalance to many of the city's (admittedly pleasurable) excesses. Thalia's owners are also the team behind the acclaimed **Coquette** (2800 Magazine St.).

French

A boisterous power-lunch bistro that's also a hit with the dinner crowd, trendy **Herbsaint Bar and Restaurant** (701 St. Charles Ave., 504/524-4114, www.herbsaint.com, 11:30am-10pm Mon.-Fri., 5:30pm-10pm Sat., $27-36) sits along a nondescript stretch of St. Charles, its setting brightened by tall windows, soft-yellow walls, and a youthful, good-looking staff. The wine selection is terrific, though you can also try a variety of cool cocktails.

Italian

Tommy's Cuisine (746 Tchoupitoulas St., 504/581-1103, www.tommysneworleans.com, 5:30pm-10pm Mon.-Thurs., 5:30pm-10:30pm Fri.-Sat., 10am-2:30pm Sun., $22-36) is a reliable pick for creative, Creole-inspired Italian fare. Housed within a charming space in the Arts District, the warmly lit dining room—with its paneled walls, mirrors, and old-fashioned sconces—creates an appealing scene.

Seafood

The **Pêche Seafood Grill** (800 Magazine St., 504/522-1744, www.pecherestaurant.com, 11am-10pm Sun.-Thurs., 11am-11pm Fri.-Sat., $16-27) is focused on regional seafood and owned by local culinary star Donald Link, the man behind other CBD favorites (Cochon, Cochon Butcher, and Herbsaint Bar and Restaurant). Save for the elegant bar area, Pêche exudes a chic rustic vibe, and the menu includes entrées as well as small plates and raw bar items. Reservations are recommended, particularly on the weekend.

Desserts

What's not to love at **Bakery Bar** (1179 Annunciation St., 504/513-8664, http://bakery.bar, 11am-midnight Tues.-Fri.,

Sweet Treats

Beignets aren't the only dessert worth sampling in New Orleans. Here are some of the city's quintessential treats and where to try them:

- **Bananas Foster:** A rich dessert consisting of bananas, butter, brown sugar, cinnamon, and rum, invented by Paul Blangé at **Brennan's** (page 381) in 1951. It's often prepared as a flambé in a tableside performance, then promptly served over vanilla ice cream.
- **Bread pudding:** A traditional dessert made from soaked French bread and often served with rum or whiskey sauce. For the classic version, head to the CBD's **Bon Ton Cafe** (page 389).
- **Calas** (KAH-luhs): Creole rice fritters usually covered with cane syrup or powdered sugar. Similar to beignets, they're a popular breakfast dish at **The Old Coffeepot Restaurant** in the French Quarter, though you'll see them as "callas cakes" on the menu.

10am-midnight Sat.-Sun., $6-13)? This spot is, as the name suggests, both a bakery and a bar. Sip on a Suffering Bastard and snack on a deep-friend chocolate chip cookie—then carry on with your revelry.

Garden District

Cajun and Creole

If you must put one place at the top of your restaurants list, make it ★ **Commander's Palace** (1403 Washington Ave., 504/899-8221, www.commanderspalace.com; 11:30am-1:30pm Mon.-Fri., 11am-1pm Sat., 10am-1:30pm Sun.; dinner service starting between 6pm and 6:30, hours vary seasonally, $39-45), which was established in 1880 and became part of the famed Brennan family empire in 1974. Nestled within a blue-and-white Victorian mansion in the Garden District, this local landmark is a terrific place to try turtle soup, griddle-seared Gulf fish, and bread pudding soufflé. Lunch isn't too expensive, particularly if you opt for the wonderful two-course Creole luncheon (about $40). The weekend jazz brunches are the stuff of legend, and advance reservations are a must for any meal.

Uptown

Cajun and Creole

On bustling Oak Street, funky ★ **Jacques-Imo's Cafe** (8324 Oak St., 504/861-0886, http://jacques-imos.com, 5pm-10pm Mon.-Thurs., 5pm-10:30pm Fri.-Sat., $20-34) presents a mix of eclectic contemporary dishes and New Orleans standbys. Reservations are available for large groups, and the place fills up quickly, so expect a wait on most nights. You can always pass the time at the charming bar. To reach the loud, rambling dining room, you have to walk through the oft-crowded bar and bustling kitchen, where you can take a peek at the dishes being prepared.

Mediterranean

Alon Shaya is one of the masters of Mediterranean cooking, and **Saba** (5757 Magazine St., 504/324-7770, http://eatwithsaba.com, 11am-10pm Wed.-Thurs., 11am-11pm Fri., 10am-11pm Sat., 10am-10pm Sun., $10-60) shows off his skills. Come here for perfect pita bread, lamb, hummus, and more. The atmosphere is refined. Note there is another restaurant in town, Shaya, which bears the chef's name, but he is no longer associated with it.

Tremé and Mid-City

Coffee and Desserts

After a day of exploring City Park, head southwest on Carrollton, toward Canal Street, and take a snack-break detour at ★ **Angelo Brocato** (214 N. Carrollton Ave., 504/486-1465, www.angelobrocatoicecream.com, 10am-10pm Tues.-Thurs., 10am-10:30pm Fri.-Sat., 10am-9pm Sun., $3-6), an old-world bakery and ice cream parlor that's famous not only for its superb Italian pastries, such as the classic cannoli, but for tantalizing house-made ice cream, Italian ice, and gelato in all kinds of tempting flavors, such as spumoni, chestnut, and amaretto. The most popular treat is the lemon ice, a simple yet expertly blended concoction of water, granulated sugar, and fresh lemons.

Eclectic

Within steps of leafy City Park, the aptly named ★ **Ralph's on the Park** (900 City Park Ave., 504/488-1000, www.ralphsonthepark.com, 5:30pm-9pm Mon., 11:30am-2pm and 5:30pm-9pm Tues.-Thurs., 11:30am-2pm and 5:30pm-9:30pm Fri.-Sat., 10:30am-2pm and 5:30pm-9pm Sun., $24-32) is one of only two Brennan family-helmed dining operations in Mid-City, and it's absolutely worth the trip. It's far from the crowds of the Quarter and CBD, making for a relaxed, convivial dining experience. It's also set inside a lovely historical building.

Greater New Orleans

Seafood

Try to make a reservation a few days in advance for **Drago's Seafood Restaurant** (3232 N. Arnoult Rd., Metairie, 504/888-9254, www.dragosrestaurant.com, 11am-9pm daily, $17-51), a riotously popular restaurant with limited seating and parking. As the name indicates, the emphasis is on seafood, much of it prepared with a Louisiana slant. The lobster dishes are particularly noteworthy; try the lobster Marco, a whole lobster stuffed with fresh sautéed shrimp and mushrooms in a light cream sauce over angel hair pasta. You can sit at the bar, which affords a clear view of the grill-cooked charbroiling oysters, or dine in one of the noisy but festive dining rooms. There's also a Drago's inside the CBD's Hilton New Orleans Riverside (2 Poydras St., 504/584-3911), but it doesn't have the same atmosphere.

Accommodations

At once classic and Bohemian, New Orleans contains a wide array of unique lodging options. Historic hotels dot the French Quarter, like the literary Hotel Monteleone and the elegant Royal Sonesta New Orleans, not to mention smaller, more affordable guesthouses. Beyond high-end chain establishments, such as the pet-friendly Loews New Orleans Hotel, the Central Business District (CBD) houses boutique-style options like the International House New Orleans. The Garden District and Uptown areas feature elegant inns, such as the traditional Terrell House Bed and Breakfast. The Tremé and Mid-City areas encompass laid-back hostels and guesthouses, such as the 1896 O'Malley House.

You'll find plenty chain hotels here, particularly in the CBD and near Louis Armstrong New Orleans International Airport. Besides standard amenities, these often spacious hotels typically offer swimming pools, business centers, meeting rooms, and off-street parking.

Where you choose to stay will greatly depend on whether you have a car. Staying in the main neighborhoods of the French Quarter, the CBD, the Garden District, and Mid-City will ensure convenient access to public transportation, namely the streetcar lines. Accommodations are completely smoke-free. Most of the privately owned inns have minimum stay requirements, particularly during the peak winter and spring seasons. During events like New Year's Eve, the Sugar Bowl, Mardi Gras, French Quarter Fest, and Jazz Fest expect higher rates as well as the need to book further in advance. Even in the slower summer season, certain annual events—such as the Essence Festival and Southern Decadence—might necessitate a reservation.

Choosing a Hotel

There's no shortage of motels, hotels, inns, and cottages available in the Big Easy, and many websites and organizations can help narrow down the options. If you're looking for a bed-and-breakfast, consult the **Professional Innkeepers Association of New Orleans** (PIANO, www.bbnola.com) or the **Louisiana Bed & Breakfast Association** (LBBA, www.louisianabandb.com). You might also benefit from local reservation services like **New Orleans Bed & Breakfasts** (www.neworleansbandbs.com) and the **Inn the Quarter Reservation Service** (800/570-3085, www.innthequarter.com). For more specific accommodations, check out **Historic Hotels of America** (800/678-8946, www.historichotels.org) and **Bluegreen Resorts** (800/755-1848, www.bluegreenrentals.com).

French Quarter

Essentially a complex of historic buildings that includes a former 1830s military hospital, the **Hôtel Provincial** (1024 Chartres St., 504/581-4995 or 800/535-7922, www.hotelprovincial.com, from $119) has been owned by the Dupepe family since 1961. The cheery guest rooms are decorated with Southern antiques and reproduction French period furnishings; some feature balconies, views of the river, or access to sunny, private courtyards. Amenities include a free continental breakfast, two swimming pools, an on-site bar, and secured valet parking ($31 daily). The staff is efficient and friendly, reason enough to stay at this upscale, family-run inn.

One of the Quarter's most popular mid-priced hotels, **Le Richelieu in the French Quarter** (1234 Chartres St., 504/529-2492 or 800/535-9653, www.lerichelieuhotel.com, from $95) books up quickly. Contained within two historic buildings, the 69 guest rooms are clean and simple, but with reproduction antiques, varying color schemes, and, in some cases, pleasant views. There are also 17 suites with spacious sitting areas. This European-style property lies along a quiet stretch in the Lower Quarter, not far from the French Market and the Marigny. An on-site café serves breakfast all day, and there's also a lounge, an unheated swimming pool, and 24-hour concierge services. The hotel offers satellite TV, laundry and babysitting services, and secured self-parking ($30 daily).

The lovely, pet-friendly **Courtyard New Orleans Downtown/Iberville** (910 Iberville St., 504/523-2400 or 877/703-7072, www.marriott.com, $150-190) features clean, spacious suites with separate sleeping and sitting areas, wet bars and refrigerators, and Bath & Body Works toiletries. It's ideal for families, business travelers, and small groups. Laundry service, pricey valet parking ($38 daily), and simple continental breakfasts are available. As a bonus, guests can access the pampering services offered by its elegant neighbor, **The Ritz-Carlton New Orleans**, whose spa (504/524-1331) features a fitness center, a resistance pool, a retail store, and an assortment of spa treatments.

Opened in 1969, the elegantly simple **Dauphine Orleans Hotel** (415 Dauphine St., 504/586-1800 or 800/521-7111, www.dauphineorleans.com, from $106) provides tranquility only a block from boisterous Bourbon. Inside the magnificent main building, you'll find 111 comfortable, contemporary guest rooms. The Dauphine Orleans also manages the 14-unit Hermann House, which features whirlpool tubs, and the 9-unit Carriage House, with period antiques and courtyard views. Other in-room amenities include bathrobes, free bottled water, and spa services. At the main property, guests can take a dip in the saltwater pool, enjoy the fitness room, and imbibe in **May Baily's Place,** the hotel bar. Concierge services, secured valet parking ($36 daily), and free continental breakfasts and afternoon teas are available.

Many folks choose the ★ **Royal Sonesta New Orleans** (300 Bourbon St., 504/586-0300 or 800/766-3782, www.sonesta.com/royalneworleans, from $230) for its prime location on Bourbon Street, particularly if they're able to snag a balcony room. From this perspective, you can oversee and participate in the late-night revelry, as many partygoers expect you to toss down a Mardi Gras-bead necklace or two. An even better enticement is the on-site jazz club, not to mention the hotel's hospitable staff, stylish decor, and pet-friendly policy. The 483 well-appointed guest rooms and suites feature standard amenities plus king-size pillows. Guests also appreciate the fitness center, outdoor swimming pool, spa services, and on-site eateries **PJ's Coffee Café,** the **Desire Oyster Bar,** and **Restaurant R'evolution.**

The enormous **Bourbon Orleans Hotel** (717 Orleans St., 504/523-2222 or 866/513-9744, www.bourbonorleans.com, $150-509) occupies most of a block at Bourbon and Orleans Streets. It also lies within a heartbeat of Bourbon's all-night craziness, so if you plan to sleep, book a room facing one of the side streets. This historic, European-style hotel is one of the Quarter's finest properties. The rooms and suites are large and elegant, with tall windows, luxurious beds, and, in some cases, balconies. Amenities include concierge and in-room spa services, a heated outdoor pool, and valet parking. The on-site contemporary Creole restaurant, **Roux on Orleans,** serves breakfast daily and dinner Tuesday-Saturday.

With its distinctive, cornstalk-inspired, cast-iron fence, the gorgeous, Victorian-style **Cornstalk Hotel** (915 Royal St., 504/523-1515, www.thecornstalkhotel.com, $125-320) offers 14 sumptuous guest rooms, all of which feature high ceilings and antique furnishings. Besides the amicable staff, another advantage is the location, which offers an ideal spot for people-watching and easy access to art galleries, carriage tours, seafood restaurants, and late-night bars.

Topped by a large red neon sign, the marvelous ★ **Hotel Monteleone** (214 Royal St., 504/523-3341, www.hotelmonteleone.com, $240-400) hosted Tennessee Williams many times, as well as Ernest Hemingway, Truman Capote, and Anne Rice. The enormous hotel offers 600 luxurious rooms and 55 suites, equipped with marble-and-granite bathrooms. The sumptuous suites feature Jacuzzi tubs and, in some cases, wet bars and sofa beds. On-site amenities include the rotating **Carousel Bar & Lounge,** the **Criollo Restaurant,** a spa, a modern fitness center, and a rooftop pool that's heated year-round.

With a prime spot in the Quarter and a hospitable staff, the lavish, rambling **Omni Royal Orleans** (621 St. Louis St., 504/529-5333 or 888/444-6664, www.omnihotels.com, from $169) contains 346 smartly furnished rooms with 19th-century decor and marble bathrooms. Premier rooms and certain suites feature balconies, and just about all options afford an impressive view of the Quarter. On the roof, you'll find a state-of-the-art fitness center, a heated pool, and a year-round observation deck. Other on-site amenities include a beauty salon, a full-service barber shop, a 24-hour business center, concierge and babysitting services, the cozy **Touché Bar,** and the hallowed **Rib Room** restaurant. Pricey valet parking ($49.58 daily) is available.

This is the perfect choice for the ultimate pampering vacation: **The Ritz-Carlton New Orleans** (921 Canal St., 504/524-1331 or 800/542-8680, www.ritzcarlton.com, from $289) has a state-of-the-art day spa and fitness center; the **Davenport Lounge,** which presents live

Illegal Guesthouses

Some of the most charming rooms in the city are found in unlicensed, illegal B&Bs, Airbnbs, guesthouses, or vacation rentals. Many of these "underground" establishments advertise heavily online, particularly during major annual events, such as Mardi Gras and French Quarter Fest. There are so many other options for places to stay, think twice before booking a room at such a property.

The city of New Orleans requires all short-term rentals to be licensed, and restricts rentals to certain neighborhoods, and yet it seems to make little effort to enforce this rule. Consequently, upstanding innkeepers who have gotten the approval (and paid the various fees) to open an inn are at a competitive disadvantage compared to those who run properties illegally.

By staying at an illegal B&B, you have little or no recourse for remedying any disputes that arise, and you have no legal protection should you be injured. Illegal short-term rentals often fail to comply with fire and safety regulations, as nobody inspects them. They also rarely carry the proper commercial insurance that is required of licensed inns.

Finally, choosing to patronize only licensed, legal establishments actually helps the city of New Orleans. Illegal vacation rentals don't contribute taxes to the city.

The easiest way to ensure that the B&B in which you're interested is licensed, legal, and adhering to proper standards is to choose one of the more than 50 properties that are members of **PIANO, the Professional Innkeepers Association of New Orleans** (www.bbnola.com), an organization that's been going strong since 2000. Note that New Orleans regulations require a renter to be at least 21-years-old.

jazz and afternoon tea service; and **Bistro,** serving fresh, local cuisine. The well-trained staff tends to guests' every need, from valet parking to babysitting services to a free overnight shoeshine. Richly furnished rooms feature 400-thread-count sheets, goose-down pillows, and Italian marble baths. For extra-special attention, stay at the hotel's club-level **Maison Orleans** (904 Iberville St.).

The **W New Orleans—French Quarter** (316 Chartres St., 504/581-1200, www.wfrenchquarter.com, from $206) combines the alluring pizzazz and old-world charm of the French Quarter with the modern elegance and high-tech sophistication associated with this pet-friendly chain. The 98 rooms, which include two deluxe suites and four carriage houses, are decorated in cool earth tones with pillow-top mattresses, 350-thread-count linens, Wi-Fi, and Bliss bath products. Sip cocktails in the W Living Room or take a dip in the courtyard pool. The helpful staff will make your stay memorable.

Faubourg Marigny and Bywater

Situated above the **Silk Road Restaurant** (504/944-6666, www.silkroadnola.com)—a popular hangout for artists, musicians, and other Bohemian types—the airy **Balcony Guesthouse** (2483 Royal St., 504/810-8667, www.balconyguesthouse.com) offers four guest rooms and one suite, all of which have hardwood floors, simple furnishings, microwaves, and mini-fridges. Two of the rooms also feature French doors and direct balcony access. The guesthouse lies only four blocks from Washington Square Park and the music clubs along Frenchmen Street. Be prepared for tight bathrooms and the possibility of noisy revelers on the sidewalk below.

Nestled within the residential Faubourg Marigny, the whimsical, red-white-and-blue cottage of **The Burgundy Bed and Breakfast** (2513 Burgundy St., 504/261-9477, www.theburgundy.com) epitomizes the 19th-century, Eastlake-style shotgun doubles prevalent throughout New Orleans. Boasting original hardwood floors, 12-foot ceilings, and louvered shutters, this lovingly restored inn houses four cozy guest rooms, each of which has distinctive decor. Guests can utilize the communal kitchen, relax in the parlor, and enjoy the clothing-optional spa and sunbathing area. Smoking is allowed on the back porch or in the courtyard.

The Frenchmen (417 Frenchmen St., 504/945-5453, www.frenchmenhotel.com) is an ideal lodging option for those hoping to explore the Marigny and the Quarter, as it's literally steps from the border between these two distinctive neighborhoods. This hospitable, though somewhat aging, hotel offers cozy guest rooms and spacious suites, some of which contain canopy beds, decorative fireplaces, and private balconies. Additional amenities include a free continental breakfast, affordable on-site parking, and a romantic brick courtyard with lush plants, wrought-iron tables, and a small pool and Jacuzzi. You're also close to the popular clubs of Frenchmen Street, so music can be heard into the wee hours.

Near the northern edge of this funky neighborhood, the **Marigny Manor House** (2125 N. Rampart St., 504/943-7826, www.marignymanorhouse.com) sits along a quiet stretch that offers a wonderful sampling of vintage 19th-century residential architecture typical of New Orleans. Built in 1848, this lovingly restored Greek Revival-style house presents four color-themed, high-ceiling rooms, neatly furnished with designer fabrics, antique furnishings, and, in some cases, crystal chandeliers, four-poster beds, and Oriental rugs over hardwood floors. One room has a balcony overlooking the brick fern-and-flower-bedecked courtyard. Amenities include delicious Southern breakfasts. The offbeat bars and restaurants of Frenchmen Street are only a short walk away.

If you're adventurous and don't mind noisy places, then you'll likely love the **Royal Street Inn** (1431 Royal St., 504/948-7499, www.royalstreetinn.com), a funky guesthouse situated above a popular neighborhood bar. You'll find five unique, unpretentious suites, from the cozy Marigny to the spacious Royal. All feature queen-size beds and couches; three suites offer balcony access. This so-called bed-and-beverage even divvies out drink tickets to its overnight guests in an attempt to entice you downstairs, where the boisterous **R Bar** has a pool table, a decent jukebox, and endless opportunities to mingle with eccentric locals and wide-eyed fellow travelers.

An architectural stunner, ★ **Hotel Peter and Paul** (2317 Burgundy St., 504/356-5200, http://hotelpeterandpaul.com, $150-360) took a former church and turned it into a hotel unlike any other. Stay in one of the unique rooms, and you'll be treated to a New Orleans experience. Give yourself time to stroll the property to absorb all the thoughtful touches. On-site you'll also find the jaw-dropping **Elysian Bar** and an ice cream shop, **Sundae Best.** Space in the former church is still open for community meetings and yoga classes, which helps the hotel stay connected to the neighborhood.

Central Business and Arts Districts

Constructed in 1907, the world-renowned **Le Pavillon Hotel** (833 Poydras St., 504/581-3111, www.lepavillon.com, from $121) offers some of the most elegant rooms and suites in the CBD. Besides tall ceilings, mahogany armoires, and handmade drapes, you can expect terry-cloth robes, designer bath products, and minibars. There are also seven exquisite suites; each has a unique theme, from art deco to presidential. Relax in the stunning lobby or take a dip in the heated rooftop pool, which affords incredible views. Also onsite is the well-regarded **Crystal Room**.

Just blocks from the French Quarter, **Old No. 77 Hotel & Chandlery** (535

Tchoupitoulas St., 504/527-5271, http://old77hotel.com, from $120) is fun, funky, and affordable. It has an art gallery, the Where Y'Art annex, just off the lobby, and artwork by students of the New Orleans Center for the Creative Arts, the city's tuition-free arts high school, adorns the hotel's 167 rooms. As is not uncommon given New Orleans's quirky building designs, some rooms don't have windows—though the high ceilings prevent them from being claustrophobic—but staff will advise you about this before you book one of these rooms. Caribbean and Creole food is served at **Compére Lapin,** the hotel's restaurant helmed by celebrity chef Nina Compton. The hotel is pet-friendly, too.

HI New Orleans Hostel (1028 Canal St., 504/603-3850, www.hiusa.org, $31-189) is a hostel with both traditional shared dormitory-style rooms and private rooms. Dine in the café, meet other hostel travelers, and hang out on the lively patio. Bike storage and free breakfast are included.

The **Hampton Inn & Suites New Orleans Convention Center** (1201 Convention Center Blvd., 504/566-9990 or 800/446-6677, www.neworleanshamptoninns.com, $115-246) differs a bit from the usual modern chain properties—it's set inside a five-story, redbrick, early-20th-century building where burlap sacks were once manufactured. Though completely renovated, the 288-unit hotel still contains original hardwood floors, exposed brick walls, tall windows, and high ceilings. Airy, spacious guest rooms, studios, and suites—some with kitchens—are available. An outdoor pool, business and fitness centers, a lobby bar, concierge services, and a free hot breakfast round out the amenities.

Stay at the **ACE Hotel (**600 Carondelet St., 504/941-9191, http://acehotel.com/neworleans, $150-250) to see and be seen. The art deco building is a modern oasis

Top to bottom: Old No. 77 Hotel & Chandlery; Catahoula Hotel's bar; Pontchartrain

with a rooftop pool and bar that attracts beautiful people for drinks and merry-making. The 234 guest rooms are sleek and modern. Local touches include work by New Orleans artists and suites with turntables and Martin guitars. Dark hallways, a live music venue, and a Stumptown Coffee outlet cement its ultra-hip reputation. Full-service restaurant Josephine Estelle rounds out the offerings.

Part of the Loews hotel chain, the towering downtown **Loews New Orleans Hotel** (300 Poydras St., 504/595-3300 or 866/550-4743 or 888/647-9197, www.loewshotels.com, from $144) contains 285 spacious rooms and suites, featuring 300-thread-count linens, all-natural bath products, luxurious robes, Keurig coffeemakers, and, in many cases, spectacular views. Other draws include the on-site **Poydras & Peters** restaurant and bar and the indoor swimming pool. Guests may also appreciate the babysitting and laundry services, complimentary shoeshine, valet parking ($45 daily), and live weekend entertainment in the lobby lounge. Pets ($25 daily, $100 nonrefundable fee) are both welcome and pampered here.

The stunning ★ **International House New Orleans** (221 Camp St., 504/553-9550 or 800/633-5770, www.ihhotel.com, $125-335) occupies a 1906 Beaux-Arts building that once served as a bank and is now one of the coolest addresses in town. The 117 rooms, suites, and penthouses are decorated in stylish, muted tones with stereo systems, down comforters, and Aveda bath products. There's no pool, but you can work out in the fitness center and relax in the top-notch spa afterward. Given the fashionable clientele it courts, it's no surprise that the hotel's **Loa** bar is a favorite spot for the well-heeled to rub elbows. Several times each year, the ornate lobby is reborn to celebrate a particular festival or holiday that's dear to New Orleanians, from All Saints' Day in early November to the voodoo-based St. John's Eve in late June.

The **Catahoula Hotel** (914 Union St., 504/603-2442, http://catahoulahotel.com, $140-350) feels straight out of a Wes Anderson movie, with 35 minimalist rooms on a small side street, around a signature NOLA courtyard. Amenities include luxury bath products, Wi-Fi, and more. Showers don't have doors, better for couples than just friends, but the Bunk Room is ideal for a group of four who just want a place to crash. The on-site Pisco Bar, rooftop deck, and coffee shop are perfect places to sit and stay for awhile. The pet-friendly hotel is named after the state dog of Louisiana.

Operated by the Waldorf Astoria hotel chain, the magnificent **Roosevelt New Orleans** (130 Roosevelt Way, 504/648-1200 or 800/925-3673, www.therooseveltneworleans.com, from $229) has exuded old-world charm since 1893. Fringing the French Quarter, this landmark features 369 stunning guest rooms and 135 sumptuous suites with 300-thread-count sheets, down-filled comforters, and Ferragamo bath products. **The Sazerac Bar** is a highlight of this property, as is **Teddy's Café,** a coffee lounge and sweets shop. The well-regarded **Domenica** restaurant, a rooftop pool, and the **Waldorf Astoria Spa** round out the amenities. Pets up to 25 pounds are allowed with a $175 fee.

The art-filled **Windsor Court Hotel** (300 Gravier St., 504/523-6000 or 888/897-6345, www.windsorcourthotel.com, $280-515) has been ranked among the top hotels in the world. The large rooms, most of them full suites, contain elegant furnishings and Italian-marble baths, giving them the air of a posh English country home. Amenities include valet parking, 24-hour concierge services, in-room spa sessions, and afternoon teas. Guests can take advantage of the 24-hour business center, the pool and health club, a stylish boutique, the upscale **Polo Club Lounge,** and **The Grill Room**. Pets are welcome (two up to 40 pounds each) for a $150 fee.

RV Resources

New Orleans is a challenging destination for RV travelers. Besides the pothole-riddled streets, tight corners, and numerous blind spots, there aren't many RV parks in the Greater New Orleans area. These campgrounds offer cable television, Internet access, 50-amp electrical service, full hookups, and a swimming pool. Weekly and monthly rates are often available.

- **French Quarter RV Resort** (500 N. Claiborne Ave., 504/586-3000, www.fqrv.com, $105-250): Though in a sketchy part of town, between I-10 and Louis Armstrong Park, this gated, pet-friendly resort is the most convenient choice for those interested in exploring the nearby French Quarter. Besides the 52 paved sites, amenities include showers, a hot tub, a recreation room, fitness and laundry facilities, and 24-hour on-site management and security.

- **Jude Travel Park of New Orleans** (7400 Chef Menteur Hwy., 504/241-0632 or 800/523-2196, http://judetravelpark.com, $38): Situated in New Orleans East, this gated, pet-friendly park is relatively far from the city's major attractions. Take advantage of the laundry area, hot tub, heated showers, and shuttle service.

- **Mardi Gras RV Park & Campground** (6050 Chef Menteur Hwy., 504/286-8157 or 877/376-7850, www.mardigrasrvparkandmotel.com, $20-25): In New Orleans East, this gated, pet-friendly campground lies within easy driving distance of the French Quarter. Offering 100 grassy and paved lots (including tent and pull-through sites), the park also provides a convenience store, meeting and exercise rooms, laundry and dining areas, gas and dump stations, barbecue facilities, phone access, and 24-hour surveillance and patrol.

- **Pontchartrain Landing** (6001 France Rd., 504/286-8157 or 877/376-7850, www.pontchartrainlanding.com, $57-153): This waterfront campground offers easy access to Lake Pontchartrain. This well-lit, gated community offers 125 sites (some pull-through), 24-hour camera surveillance, 24-hour laundry access, a convenience store, a bar and seafood restaurant, a playground, a boat launch ramp, a dumping station, showers, propane gas, shuttle service to the French Quarter, furnished villas and campers, and proximity to a full-service marina.

Garden District

Laundry services, maps, charging stations, and other amenities make **Auberge NOLA Hostel** (1628 Carondelet St., 504/524-5980, http://aubergehostels.com, $26-67) an incredibly good-value option with a great location. And this is not the hostel of your youth. There are both dorm rooms—that sleep up to six people—and private rooms.

★ **Pontchartrain** (2031 St. Charles Ave., 800/708-6652, http://thepontchartrainhotel.com, $138-465) feels like it's straight out of a movie, located in a gem of a renovated building that retains all of its old-world charm. The rooms used to be apartments and are spacious, with lots of closet space, and each room has a unique theme and decor—one of the rooms even has a piano. Multiple bars are also in the building, including the rooftop **Hot Tin,** which is a neighborhood gathering space (it can be hard to get into the elevator when it's hopping). The 1st-floor **Jack Rose** is a destination restaurant; order the Mile High Pie for dessert.

The unusual ★ **Green House Inn** (1212 Magazine St., 504/525-1333, www.thegreenhouseinn.com, $149-289), set in the Lower Garden District, offers a pleasant change of pace from many of New Orleans's richly urbane B&Bs.

Constructed in 1840, the Greek Revival-style townhouse has a tropical, whimsical vibe, from the palm tree-shaped, clothing-optional pool to the verdant landscaping. The flower-named rooms are well outfitted with the kind of amenities you'd expect at a much pricier hotel: king-size beds, deluxe sheets and towels, all-natural bath products, and guest robes. Additionally, the pet-friendly inn offers gated off-street parking and an oversized hot tub near the pool.

Set amid the historic homes of Uptown's Lower Garden District, the hospitable **Terrell House Bed and Breakfast** (1441 Magazine St., 504/237-2076, www.terrellhouse.com, $370-550) is a magnificent, Italianate-style mansion. Built in the mid-19th century, it offers luxurious accommodations, plus delicious Southern-style breakfasts. Only a block from restful Coliseum Square, this beloved B&B ensures convenient access to the shops and eateries along Magazine Street, plus the St. Charles streetcar line. Two-night minimums may apply.

Tremé and Mid-City

$150-200

Not far from the busy intersection of Canal Street and North Carrollton Avenue, the **1896 O'Malley House** (120 S. Pierce St., 504/488-5896 or 866/226-1896, www.1896omalleyhouse.com, $155-200) is one of the more hidden, less-touristy inns in the city. This gracious, Colonial Revival-style mansion features original cypress-wood mantels, pocket doors, and other artful details. The eight sumptuous suites are filled with exceptional antiques, handsome Oriental rugs, plush four-poster beds, and elegant tables. Most rooms have whirlpool tubs. Run by exceedingly hospitable hosts, the house lies within walking distance of several restaurants and just steps from the Canal streetcar line, which links City Park to the French Quarter. A bounteous continental breakfast is included.

Information and Services

Visitor Information

New Orleans Welcome Center (529 St. Ann St., 504/568-5661, www.crt.state.la.us, 8:30am-5pm daily) is the place to grab Louisiana highway maps, as well as literature about New Orleans attractions and free coffee.

Emergency Services

Dial 911 for police, fire, or ambulance in an emergency. For non-emergency, but still urgent service, call the **New Orleans Police Department** (715 S. Broad St., 504/821-2222) or the **New Orleans Fire Department** (317 Decatur St., 504/658-4700).

If your emergency is medical in nature, you have a lot of options. **New Orleans Emergency Medical Services** (2929 Earhart Blvd.) is open 24 hours. **Tulane Medical Center** (1415 Tulane Ave., 504/988-5263) is a world-class facility. Other choices, depending on where you are in town, include: **Children's Hospital New Orleans** (200 Henry Clay Ave., 504/899-9511), **New Orleans East Hospital** (5620 Read Blvd., 504/592-6600), and **University Medical Center New Orleans** (2000 Canal St., 504/702-3000).

Bicycle Rental and Repair

A bike is a great way to get around the Crescent City. **Arts District Bike Rental** (1121 Margaret Pl., 504/521-6390, 8am-9pm Mon.-Thurs., 8am-10pm Fri., 9am-10pm Sat., 10am-9pm Sun., 24-hour rentals $20) is one block from The National WWII Museum. Stop here for rentals that include a lock, lights, and helmet. Some bikes also have cup holders and baskets. **New Orleans Bike & Board Shop** (8136 Oak St., 504/866-4439, www.neworleansbikeshop.net, 10am-6pm Tues.-Fri., 10am-3pm Sat.) offers bike sales and rentals, plus parts and repairs,

 Detour to Abita Springs

Once a Choctaw village named after the nearby springs, today Abita Springs is a sweet town of just 2,300 people. But it's known to beer-drinkers worldwide: **Abita Brewing Co.** was founded here in 1986, making beer from the namesake medicinal springs. If you love your ale, a visit here is worth a detour.

Obviously, you have to visit the **Abita Tap Room** (166 Barbee Rd., 985/893-3143, http://abita.com, 11am-7pm Sun.-Thurs., 10am-8pm Fri.-Sat.). Sit inside the taproom or outside in the beer garden and have a pint; they also do growler fills. The only food is chips and pretzels, but food trucks can usually be found on Saturday. Guided tours (2pm and 4pm Wed.-Thurs.; 1pm, 2pm, 3pm, and 4pm Fri.; 11am, noon, 1pm, 2pm, 3pm, and 4pm Sat.; noon, 1pm, 2pm, and 3pm Sun.), but you can also take a self-guided tour (11am-4pm Mon.-Tues., 11am-1pm Wed.-Thurs., 11am-noon Sun.).

When you're hungry, head to **Abita Brew Pub** (72011 Holly St., 985/892-5837, www.abitabrewpub.com, 11am-9pm Tues.-Thurs., 11am-10pm Fri.-Sat., 11am-9pm Sun., $9-17), a restaurant housed in Abita Brewery's original brewery and bottling facility. You can buy growlers and six-packs to take home, too.

Right next to the pub is **Abita Springs Trailhead & Park** (22049 Main St., dawn-dusk daily, free, donations accepted), which has a lovely pagoda, walking trails, and the **Abita Springs Trailhead Museum** (22049 Main St., 985/871-5327, 10am-4pm Fri.-Sat., 11am-4pm Sun.), a small art and history museum.

Getting There

To get to Abita Springs from New Orleans, take I-10 West to the Lake Pontchartrain Causeway. (Make sure someone has a camera ready for the beautiful views as you cross the lake.) The causeway continues for about 24 miles. Once you're on the north side of the lake, merge onto I-12 East, then exit at LA-59 toward Abita Springs, about five miles north. You could take I-10 around the east side of the lake, but skipping the bridge is far less scenic and doesn't necessarily save you time. Abita Springs is a 45-mile, one-hour drive from New Orleans.

and also carries skateboards. **Mike the Bike Guy** (4411 Magazine St., 504/899-1344, www.mikethebikeguy.com, 10am-6pm Mon.-Fri., 10am-5pm Sat., $30-40 daily) has rentals that include a helmet, lock, and light.

To tour the Big Easy at your own pace, head to the helpful **American Bicycle Rental Company** (318 N. Rampart St., 504/324-8257, www.bikerentalneworleans.com, 9am-5pm daily, $10 hourly, $36 daily), which rents cruisers by the hour or by periods of 4, 8, or 24 hours. Each rental includes a lock, helmet, basket, and cycling map, plus lights for nighttime riding. You can also book an excursion with the on-site **Free Wheelin' Bike Tours** (504/522-4368, www.neworleansbiketour.com, $50).

Amid the live music clubs of Frenchmen Street stands laid-back, full-service **Bicycle Michael's** (622 Frenchmen St., 504/945-9505, www.bicyclemichaels.com, 10am-5pm Sun.-Tues., 10am-7pm Thurs.-Sat., $40-125 daily, $175-560 weekly), which offers rentals, sales, and repair services, perfect if you intend to bike the Trace from south to north and need a tune-up before you start. Choose among city hybrids, mountain bikes, off-road bikes, and tandems. Depending on how long you keep the rental (from a half day to a full week), you can explore the Faubourg Marigny, the nearby French Quarter, City Park, the Lake Pontchartrain shoreline, and other key areas in this relatively compact city. Although locks, biking advice, and local tips are free, there are nominal costs for helmets ($5 daily), baskets ($5), and maps

($6-8). In the Marigny, **Bokah Bikes** (4233 St. Claude Ave., 504/942-0732, 10am-6pm Tues.-Sat.) sells new and vintage cycles.

Motorcycle Rental and Repair

Redbeard Cycles (8022 Orpheus Ct., 504/483-3232, 9am-5pm Mon.-Fri., 9am-noon Sat.) is a local motorcycle repair shop. **FX Motorsports** (3248 Chippewa St., 504/267-4517, 9am-5pm Mon.-Fri.) offers weekday-only sales and repairs for mopeds, scooters, and motorbikes. **New Orleans Harley-Davidson** (6015 Airline Dr., Metairie, 504/667-5171, 10am-7pm Mon.-Fri., 9am-5pm Sat.) is a full-service dealership with a parts and service department.

Baton Rouge

Baton Rouge often gets overshadowed by its more popular neighbor to the east, New Orleans. But as Louisiana's capital city and home to Louisiana State University, with a metro population of 825,000 people, it is a worthy destination it its own right.

When French-Canadian explorer Pierre Le Moyne d'Iberville came along the banks of the Mississippi River in 1699, he saw a red cypress pole marking the boundary between the hunting territory of the Houma and the Bayougoula peoples. He dubbed the town Red Stick or, in French, Baton Rouge, and the name stuck. You'll see sculptures with allusions to red sticks around town.

Getting There

From the southern terminus of the Natchez Trace Parkway in Natchez, it's a 90-mile drive south along US 61. After 80 miles, take the exit for I-110 South. Continue on I-110 for eight miles, then take exit 1E for Capitol Access Road/Capitol Park to get into downtown Baton Rouge. The drive takes under two hours and takes you through lush swamps as well as affords vistas.

If you're starting in New Orleans, Baton Rouge is an 81-mile, 1.5-hour drive northwest. Take I-10 west out of the city for 80 miles. At the junction with I-110, keep right to merge onto I-110 North. After a mile, take exit 10 to the left to get to downtown Baton Rouge.

Sights

Downtown has a particularly rich public art collection. Make time to stroll on foot to enjoy the many interesting sculptures, particularly by the library and near the riverfront. You'll find several of Louisiana's most engaging attractions here.

Mid City (not to be confused with New Orleans's Mid-City) is the neighborhood east of downtown Baton Rouge, and historically was the first urban expansion in the area. It is nestled east of I-10, south of I-110, and west of Choctaw Street. Downtown Baton Rouge is the dense area between I-10 and the Mississippi River.

Louisiana State Capitol

The **Louisiana State Capitol** (State Capitol Dr. and N. 3rd St., 225/342-7317, www.crt.state.la.us, 8am-4:30pm daily, free) was completed in March 1932. A nifty 34-story art deco wonder, complete with stylized concrete pelicans, it took 14 months to build with a resulting price tag of about $5 million. It is, at 450 feet, the tallest U.S. capitol building and unlike any other you've seen. One of the highlights of a visit here is touring the 27 acres of spectacularly landscaped gardens. In addition, you can look around the grand entrance and Memorial Hall; peek inside the chambers (when the state legislature is not in session); ride the elevator to the 27th-floor observation deck, which affords spectacular views of the city; and see exactly where flamboyant governor Huey P. Long was assassinated.

Taking the Great River Road

The most direct drive from Baton Rouge to New Orleans is along I-10. But if you really want to get a feel for the region, skip the interstate and take the **Great River Road** to Baton Rouge from New Orleans. This road runs for about 70 miles on both sides of the Mississippi and is nicknamed Plantation Alley. Along this route you'll witness a juxtaposition of grand plantation homes and trees dripping with Spanish moss against small working-class towns and petrochemical plants.

Very few of the existing plantations are complete and honest about the horrors of enslavement that took place in this area, as well as the labor of enslaved people which resulted in the building of these impressive homes. The exception is **Whitney Plantation Museum** (5099 Highway 18, Wallace, www.whitneyplantation.org, $25, $11 children ages 6-18, free children under 6, 9:30am-4-30pm Fri.-Mon.). This former sugar, rice, and indigo plantation focuses exclusively on the lives of the enslaved, with memorials to honor those who died here. Structures include original slave cabins, the owner's 1790 house, and a freedman's church. Tours are self-guided and mostly outdoors, although there are some museum-style exhibits in the visitor's center.

The Great River Road route from Baton Rouge to New Orleans takes about three hours to drive without stops—but if you're not going to stop and spend a little time looking around, there's little reason to drive this way.

Louisiana's Old State Capitol

Louisiana's Old State Capitol (100 North Blvd., 225/342-0500 or 800/488-2968, http://louisianaoldstatecapitol.org, 10am-4pm Tues.-Fri., 9am-3pm Sat., free) is different from the Louisiana State Capitol. Built in 1847, this national landmark has been carefully restored and now houses the city's political history museum. Come here for artifacts and memorabilia about the state and for temporary exhibitions, such as one about the first ladies of Louisiana. Don't miss the lovely garden of established live oak trees around the building.

Old Louisiana Governor's Mansion

First resident (and 40th governor of the state) Huey Long wanted this building to look like the White House. And that it does. The **Old Louisiana Governor's Mansion** (502 North Blvd., 225/387-2464, http://preserve-louisiana.org, tours 10am-3pm Tues.-Fri., adults $10, seniors $9, students $8, free for children under 5) is a stucco Georgian edifice, built in 1930.

Louisiana State University

Don't miss the opportunity to check out the beautiful magnolia-lined campus of **Louisiana State University** (225/578-5000, www.lsu.edu), including its stadium and the LSU Lakes (2883 E. Lakeshore Dr.), where you can stand-up paddleboard with **Muddy Water Paddle Co.** (4355 Perkins Rd., 225/800-6848, http://muddywaterpaddleco.com, 10am-2pm Fri.-Sat. and by appt., rentals $25/hour, lessons $45/hour).

The school, established in 1860, has more than 45,200 students (graduates and undergraduates). The campus has some 250 buildings and covers about 2,000 acres just south of downtown Baton Rouge. One of the campus highlights, across from Tiger Stadium, is **Tiger Walk,** a 15,000-square-foot sanctuary and home to Mike the Tiger (www.lsu.edu/miketh-etiger), the school's live tiger mascot. A lovely semicircular sanctuary allows visitors to view Mike and learn about worldwide tiger conservation.

LSU Rural Life Museum

Only a short drive southeast of downtown, the **LSU Rural Life Museum** (4560 Essen Ln., 225/765-2437, http://rural-life.lsu.edu, 8am-5pm daily, adults $10,

seniors $9, children 6-11 $8, free for children under 6) is a living-history museum situated on the 450-acre **Burden Research Plantation.** Dedicated to preserving and interpreting the lifestyles and cultures of preindustrial Louisiana, the museum comprises numerous buildings and exhibits, which show different aspects of early Louisiana living. The plantation quarters constitute a complex of authentically furnished 19th-century structures, including a kitchen, a schoolhouse, and slave cabins (note: beginning in the 1970s, the LSU Rural Life Museum was one of the first museums in the state to accurately depict the horrors of slavery). Inside a large barn, you can examine tools and vehicles spanning more than 300 years. You'll also spy several historical houses that reveal Louisiana's rich tradition of folk architecture, from a country church to an Acadian house to a shotgun home. You can also tour ($3) the extensive Windrush Gardens, a 25-acre plot of semiformal gardens abundant with winding paths, ponds, and flora typically found in 19th-century plantation gardens.

Bluebonnet Swamp Nature Center

The **Bluebonnet Swamp Nature Center** (10503 N. Oak Hills Pkwy., 225/757-8905, http://brec.org, adults $3, seniors and students $2.50, youth ages 3-17 $2, free for children 2 and under) is 103 acres and features gravel paths and boardwalks, as well as picnic areas and an education center.

USS *Kidd* Veterans Museum

The **USS *Kidd* Veterans Museum** (305 S. River Rd., 225/342-1942, www.usskidd.com, 9am-3:30pm Mon.-Fri., 10am-4pm Sat.-Sun., adults $12.53, seniors $10.45, children 5-12, $8.36) is the only ship of its kind that's still in its wartime camouflage paint. This World War II-era

Top to bottom: LSU Mike the Tiger; LSU Rural Life Museum; Bluebonnet Swamp Nature Center

Fletcher-class destroyer was awarded 12 battle stars for serving during World War II and the Korean War; it was struck by a Japanese kamikaze plane during the World War II Battle of Okinawa, an attack that killed 38 members of the *Kidd*'s crew. It has been carefully restored and can now be toured, along with the nearby Veterans Memorial Museum, which features a nuclear-powered submarine, a World War II-era fighter plane and a Vietnam-era bomber, and the South's largest model ship collection.

Spanish Town

Established in 1805, **Spanish Town** (bounded by State Capitol Dr., 5th St., North Ave., and 9th St., http://spanishtownbr.org) is Baton Rouge's oldest neighborhood. Just west of downtown, the neighborhood is characterized by bright, colorful homes and an offbeat character. It is listed on the National Register of Historic Places. It's best to visit Spanish Town during daylight hours.

Entertainment and Events

Nightlife

Between bars, music clubs, and casinos, Baton Rouge provides a decent share of nightlife options. The low-key **Phil Brady's Bar & Grill** (4848 Government St., 225/927-3786, 11am-2am Mon.-Fri., 5pm-2am Sat.) is a fun place to drink with pals, play a round of pool, or enjoy some live music, particularly the well-attended Thursday night blues jams.

The city's favorite gay and lesbian dance club is **Splash Nightclub** (2183 Highland Rd., 225/242-9491, www.splashbr.com, 9pm-2am Wed.-Sat.), situated in a slightly dodgy neighborhood near LSU's campus. Featuring multiple rooms and several bars, Splash presents a variety of music, from country to techno, plus one of Baton Rouge's best drag shows.

If you're in more of a gambling mood, head to the **Belle of Baton Rouge Casino** (103 France St., 225/242-2600 or 800/266-2692, www.belleofbatonrouge.com, 24 hours daily), which is housed inside a three-deck riverboat that's docked permanently on the Mississippi River. There are restaurants and bars in the casino, including Shucks on the Levee.

Inside the renovated Electric Depot, **Red Stick Social** (1503 Government St., 225/223-6637, http://redsticksocial.com, 3pm-10pm Mon-Tues., 3pm-midnight Wed.-Thurs., 11am-2am Fri.-Sat., 11am-10pm Sun.) is a happening, multistory venue with outdoor space, live music, bowling, and billiards.

The Arts

For a bit of culture, head to the **Theatre Baton Rouge** (7155 Florida Blvd., 225/924-6496, www.theatrebr.org), which has been presenting live theater since the late 1940s. Each season's lineup typically includes several well-known plays and musicals, such as *A Streetcar Named Desire* and *Hairspray*. Another cultural option is the **Varsity Theatre** (3353 Highland Rd., 225/383-7018, www.varsitytheatre.com), a legendary concert venue that features salsa, alternative rock, and everything in between.

Festivals and Events

From balloon festivals to Fourth of July fireworks displays, Baton Rouge presents a slew of crowd-pleasing events throughout the year. One of the most popular is the **Baton Rouge Blues Festival** (www.batonrougebluesfestival.org), a free, one-day event that usually takes place in mid-April in the city's Town Square. Founded in 1980, it's one of America's oldest blues festivals, featuring a lineup of well-respected blues guitarists, pianists, and bands.

In late October, literary fans will appreciate the **Louisiana Book Festival** (www.louisianabookfestival.org), a free, one-day event that typically occurs at various locations in downtown Baton Rouge, such as the Louisiana State Capitol and the State Library of Louisiana. Activities include readings, workshops, and a book discussion group.

Food

Where there are politicians, there are almost always good restaurants, and Baton Rouge confirms this rule with its wide variety of well-favored eateries. It's also a college town, which means you can find lots of decent, relatively affordable joints around LSU's campus.

Perhaps the most stylish restaurant in Baton Rouge is **Juban's** (3739 Perkins Rd., 225/346-8422, www.jubans.com, 5:30pm-9pm Mon., 11am-2pm and 5:30pm-9pm Tues.-Thurs., 11am-2pm and 5:30-10pm Fri., 5:30-10pm Sat., 10:30am-3pm Sun., $14-40). Juban's has been serving innovative Louisiana-influenced fare since the early 1980s, when owner-chef John Mariani's temple of fine cuisine was named one of America's "Best New Restaurants" in *Esquire*. The restaurant is known for such signature dishes as Louisiana crawfish pasta with shiitake mushrooms and white truffle Madeira cream, seafood-stuffed soft-shell crab topped with Creolaise sauce, and a pork rib chop with honey-bourbon glaze.

For local flavors that won't blow your budget, head to **Jasmines on the Bayou** (6010 Jones Creek Rd., 225/753-3668, www.jasminesonthebayou.com, 11am-2pm Mon., 11am-8pm Tues.-Thurs., 11am-9pm Fri.-Sat., $11-17). Essentially a Cajun seafood restaurant, Jasmines offers such tasty regional fare as corn and crab bisque, grilled shrimp rémoulade, and pasta jambalaya. Start with an order of rocket shrimp, which are lightly battered and tossed in a spicy chili aioli sauce.

An old-school, fast-food restaurant, **Frostop** (402 Government St., 225/344-1179, www.frostoprestaurant.com, 10am-8pm Mon.-Sat., 11am-6pm Sun., $2-12) serves burgers, fries, soft-serve ice cream, and root beer in a frosted mug.

A charming and welcoming eatery, ★ **Elsie's Plate & Pie** (3145 Government St., 225/636-5157, www.elsiespies.com, 11am-9pm Mon., 11am-10pm Tues.-Thurs., 11am-11pm Fri.-Sat., 10am-9pm Sun., $4-18) serves sweet and savory pies in Mid City, as well as other comfort foods. Grab a slice, a whole pie, or a hand pie.

White Star Market (4624 Government St., 225/224-8092, www.whitestarmarket.com, 8am-3pm Mon., 8am-9pm Tues.-Thurs., 8am-10pm Fri.-Sat., 8am-8pm Sun., hours vary by vendor) is a favorite Mid City hangout, with several food and drink vendors serving items from pizzas to tacos, communal tables, and trivia nights and other evening activities.

The Overpass Merchant (2904 Perkins Rd., 225/508-4737, www.theoverpassmerchant.com, 11am-midnight Mon.-Wed., 11am-2am Thurs.-Sat., 11am-8pm Sun., $6-13) is, aptly, nestled right under the I-10 overpass. But despite its location, it's a cozy place, with a patio and a large menu of bar food.

LSU AgCenter Dairy Store (40 S. Stadium Dr., 225/578-4392, 8:30am-5pm Mon.-Fri. $1-10) sells ice cream scoops, as well as some cheeses and meats, all from the animals in the university's agriculture department. If there is a guard at the LSU gate, just tell him or her that you are going to get ice cream. Like many college campuses, most parking is by permit, but there are labeled spots for the Dairy Store.

New Orleans-based **French Truck Coffee** (2978 Government St., 225/406-7776, http://frenchtruckcoffee.com, 6:30am-6pm Mon.-Fri., 8am-6pm Sat.-Sun.) is a regional favorite for small-batch coffee. Stop here—look for the bright yellow truck—before heading out on an adventure.

Accommodations

Most of the city's lodging options comprise major chain hotels and motels, primarily set just off I-12 and I-10, on the southeast side of town. The **Hilton Baton Rouge Capitol Center** (201 Lafayette St.,

225/344-5866 or 888/225-9664, www.hiltoncapitolcenter.com, $149-250) is located in historical buildings that once housed the Heidelberg and Capitol House Hotels. In addition to 290 rooms, it offers a full-service spa and fitness center, a pool overlooking the Mississippi River, and steakhouse **The Kingfish Grill.**

Other downtown options include the **Hotel Indigo** (200 Convention St., 225/343-1515 or 877/666-3243, www.ihg.com, $115-385), which has modern decor and a fun bar scene. Valet parking is $20 per day, and pets are allowed for a $50 fee. The historic **Watermark** (150 Third St., 225/408-3200, www.watermarkbr.com, $145-345) is a luxury hotel built in an old bank. Check out the old bank's murals, or ask to see the private dining room in the old safe in the basement. There are several restaurants on-site, including **Milford's on Third,** a quick deli, and **The Gregory,** a high-end restaurant with an extensive wine list. Valet parking is $25 per night.

The **Renaissance Baton Rouge** (7000 Bluebonnet Blvd., 225/215-7000, www.marriott.com, $175-239) is a very contemporary, clean, and sleek hotel with eclectic lobby decor and a decidedly big-city feel. Some rooms have a view of Jimmy Swaggart's mammoth bible college.

If you're coming to town to visit the LSU campus, try the **Cook Hotel and Conference Center at LSU** (3848 W. Lakeshore Dr., 225/383-2665, http://thecookhotel.com, $139-179).

The **Stockade Bed & Breakfast** (8860 Highland Rd., 225/769-7358, http://thestockade.com, $150-215) has four regular guest rooms, plus one two-bedroom suite. Leave time to walk the on-site nature trails.

Information and Services

For more information about the state's charming capital city, consult **Visit Baton Rouge** (359 3rd St., 225/383-1825 or 800/527-6843, www.visitbatonrouge.com, 8am-5pm Mon.-Fri.).

Baton Rouge General Hospital (www.brgeneral.org) has two locations, one in Mid City (3600 Florida Blvd., 225/387-7000) and one in Bluebonnet (8585 Picardy Ave., 225/763-4000).

Essentials

Getting There

Getting to Nashville

Thanks to a friendly, accessible airport, easy access to several interstates, reliable bus services, and a plethora of rental cars, getting to Music City shouldn't be a hassle (although no guarantees about the rush-hour traffic once you arrive).

Many visitors to Nashville drive their own cars. In fact, the city is said to be within a day's drive of one-half of the U.S. population. The highways are good, distances are manageable, and many, if not most, destinations in the city and surrounding area are not accessible by public transportation.

Air

The **Nashville International Airport** (BNA, http://flynashville.com) brings back some of the pleasure to air travel. Despite shuttling 18 million passengers annually, it is easy to navigate, affordable to park at, and only overwhelmingly crowded during big events like CMA Music Festival. BNA offers email updates that tell travelers when to expect congestion, so they can plan accordingly. BNA is about nine miles east of downtown, a 20-minute drive in average traffic.

The terminal is filled with local art and live music and comfortable waiting areas for those picking up in-bound passengers. There's even a health clinic for routine medical care. Exchange currency at **SunTrust Bank** near A/B concourse or at the **Business Service Center** (Wright Travel, 615/275-2660) near C/D concourse.

Airport Transportation

Many of the major hotels offer shuttles from the airport; a kiosk on the lower level of the terminal can help you find the right one.

BNA was the first airport in the United States to include "transportation network companies," such as Lyft and Uber, in their plans. A designated ride sharing area is on the ground floor where hotel shuttles wait, past the taxi stand.

Taxis are also a feasible option for ground transport from BNA. Rates start at $7 plus $2.10 per mile. To downtown or Opryland, the flat rate is $25.

Bus

Greyhound (709 5th Ave. S., 615/255-3556, www.greyhound.com) fully serves Music City, with daily routes that crisscross the state in nearly every direction. In 2012 the city opened a LEED-certified depot. The environmentally friendly building has parking for picking up passengers, a restaurant, a vending area, and ample space for buses coming and going. Service goes to major cities in most directions, including Atlanta, Chattanooga, Memphis, and Louisville.

Budget-friendly **Megabus** (http://us.megabus.com) leaves from the same station. Megabus boasts free Wi-Fi on board.

Getting to Memphis

Air

Memphis International Airport (MEM, 901/922-8000, www.flybymemphis.com) is 13 miles south of downtown Memphis.

Air Transportation

TennCo Express (901/527-2992, www.tenncoexpress.com) provides a shuttle service from the airport to many downtown hotels. Tickets are $20 one-way and $30 round-trip. Look for the shuttle parked in the third lane near column number 14 outside the airport terminal. Shuttles depart every half hour 7:30am-9:30pm. For a hotel pickup, call at least a day in advance. The airport website (www.flymemphis.com/hotel-shuttles) lists which hotels offer shuttles.

Uber and Lyft pickup areas are located outside each of the three (A, B and C).

Train

Amtrak (800/872-7245, www.amtrak.com) runs the **City of New Orleans** train daily between Chicago and New Orleans, stopping in Memphis on the way. The southbound train arrives daily at Memphis's **Central Station** (545 S. Main St., 5:45am-11pm daily) at 6:27am, leaving about half an hour later. The northbound train arrives at 10pm every day. It is an 11-hour ride overnight between Memphis and Chicago, and about 8 hours between Memphis and New Orleans.

Bus

Greyhound (3033 Airways Blvd., 800/231-2222, www.greyhound.com) runs daily bus service to a **Memphis station** (3033 Airways Blvd., 901/395-8770, 24 hours daily) from around the country. Direct service is available to Memphis from a number of surrounding cities, including Jackson and Nashville, Tennessee; Tupelo and Jackson, Mississippi; Little Rock and Jonesboro, Arkansas; and St. Louis, Missouri. Budget-friendly **Megabus** (http://us.megabus.com) also serves Memphis from six cities—Atlanta, Birmingham, Chicago, Dallas, Little Rock, and St. Louis—from the same station. Megabus boasts free Wi-Fi on board.

Getting to New Orleans

New Orleans's airport is well served by most major airlines and has direct flights to many of the nation's largest cities. The city also has direct Amtrak train service and Greyhound bus service from many big cities, but these modes of transport are often quite time-consuming and, especially in the case of trains, not always less expensive than flying.

Air

Louis Armstrong New Orleans International Airport (MSY, 900 Airline Dr., Kenner, 504/303-7500, www.flymsy.com), 15 miles west of downtown New Orleans via I-10, is a massive facility with service on several airlines. It's easy to find direct flights from most major U.S. cities. British Airways flies direct from London four times per week. A new $807 million terminal at Louis Armstrong opened in 2019 with 30 new gates, 2,000 more parking spaces, and a new access road.

Commercial air service is also available to Baton Rouge, Lafayette, and Lake Charles. Situated roughly eight miles north of downtown Baton Rouge via I-110, **Baton Rouge Metropolitan Airport** (9430 Jackie Cochran Dr., 225/355-0333, www.flybtr.com) is served by American Airlines, Delta, and United, with frequent direct flights to and from Atlanta, Charlotte, Dallas, and Houston. **Lafayette Regional Airport** (200 Terminal Dr., 337/266-4400, www.lftairport.com) is three miles southeast of downtown Lafayette via US-90. It is served by Delta, American Airlines, and United, with direct flights to and from Atlanta, Dallas, and Houston. **Lake Charles Regional Airport** (500 Airport Blvd., 337/477-6051, www.flylakecharles.com) is nine miles south of downtown Lake Charles via LA-385. You can take direct flights to and from Houston, courtesy of United, and Dallas, courtesy of American Airlines. If you choose to fly into one of these three regional airports, you'll have to rent a car to reach New Orleans. Avis, Budget, Hertz, National, and Enterprise serve all three locales.

Airport Transportation

Depending on traffic, the 15-mile trip from the airport to the French Quarter can take 25-35 minutes by car. A **taxi** from the airport to the Central Business District (CBD) usually costs $33 for one or two passengers and $14 per person for three or more passengers. Pickup occurs on the airport's lower level, just outside the baggage claim area. Extra baggage might require an additional charge; credit cards are typically accepted.

Using a ride-sharing service like Lyft or Uber costs about $33, plus a $4 airport surcharge. There's a designated meeting place on the ground level for these services.

If you'd prefer to travel in style, consider **Airport Limousine** (504/305-2450 or 866/739-5466, www.airportlimousineneworleans.com), the airport's official limo service, which has handy kiosks in the baggage claim area. The number of passengers will determine the type of vehicle selected: sedans for up to three passengers, SUVs for up to five, and limos for six or more. For one-way trips to the French Quarter and CBD, rates start at $58 for one or two passengers; a nominal fuel charge is generally applied to all rides.

To save a little money, opt for the **Airport Shuttle** (504/522-3500 or 866/596-2699, www.airportshuttleneworleans.com, adults one-way $24, adults round-trip $44, free for children under 6), which offers shared-ride service to hotels in the French Quarter, the CBD, and Uptown. From the upper level of the airport outside Door 7, you can also hop aboard the **E2 Airport Bus** (504/248-3900, www.jeffersontransit.org, $2 pp). On weekdays, the bus takes about 35 minutes to reach the CBD; on weekends, it only travels to Mid-City and you'll have to rely on an RTA bus route to reach destinations in uptown or downtown New Orleans.

If you're headed north of New Orleans, there are two helpful services at the airport. **Northshore Airport Transportation** (985/445-4544, www.northshoreairporttransportation.com) offers shuttle service to and from Slidell, Covington, Hammond, and other north shore communities. Advance reservations are required. The **Tiger Airport Shuttle** (225/333-8167, www.tigerairportshuttle.com) provides transportation to and from Baton Rouge.

Train

Amtrak (800/872-7245, www.amtrak.com) operates three rail routes across southern Louisiana, all of which include stops at the **New Orleans Union Passenger Terminal** (1001 Loyola Ave., 5am-10pm daily). There are rental car agencies at Amtrak stations in most big cities.

These rail routes serve New Orleans:

- **City of New Orleans** runs daily from Chicago to New Orleans, with major stops in Memphis, Jackson, and Hammond (19 hours).
- **Crescent** runs daily between New York City and New Orleans, with major stops in Philadelphia, Baltimore, Washington, D.C., Charlotte, Atlanta, Birmingham, and Slidell (30 hours).
- **Sunset Limited,** an east-west train, runs from Los Angeles to New Orleans three times weekly, with major stops in Tucson, El Paso, San Antonio, Houston, Lake Charles, and Lafayette (48 hours).

Bus

Greyhound (800/231-2222, www.greyhound.com) is the definitive bus provider for New Orleans, with frequent and flexible service throughout the country. Buses depart daily from the **New Orleans Greyhound Station** (1001 Loyola Ave., 504/525-6075, 5:30am-10:30pm daily) with multiple stops throughout Louisiana to many neighboring states. Travel times can be significantly longer than by train, but fares are generally much cheaper.

Road Rules

Car and RV Rental

If you don't bring your own car, a dozen major rental agencies have fleets of cars, trucks, and SUVs at Nashville's airport. Agencies include **National** (615/340-6546 or 888/826-6890, www.nationalcar.com), **Avis** (615/361-1212 or 800/331-1212, www.avis.com), and **Hertz** (615/361-3131 or 800/654-3131, www.hertz.com).

U.S. car rental companies charge a significant fee if you want to drop off your rental at a different location than where you picked it up. Depending on the time of year and the return location, this fee can be $200 or more. However, if you want to drive the length of the Natchez Trace Parkway one way, this may be the best method.

Driving along the Natchez Trace Parkway in an RV is one of the most popular ways to see its 400-plus miles. But there are some limitations. According to the National Park Service, RVs must be less than 40,000 pounds and fewer than 55 feet long (including a tow vehicle, if you have one). Almost all parkway stops are RV-accessible. If not, they are well-marked with "no circular drive" signage at the entrance. These include: Devil's Backbone (milepost 394), Old Trace Drive (mileposts 375.8 and 401.4), Twentymile Bottom Overlook (milepost 278.4), Grindstone Ford/Mangum Mound (milepost 45.7), and the southern trailhead of the Potkopinu section (milepost 17).

One of the largest RV rental companies is **Cruise America** (www.cruiseamerica.com), which has locations in Nashville (B&C Rentals, 201 Donelson Pike, 800/671-8042 or 615/885-4281), Memphis (Interstate Rental Store, 12043 US 64, Lakeland, 800/671-8042 or 901/867-0639), and Birmingham (Pee Wee Turners Motors Inc., 512 South Quintard Ave., Anniston, 256/237-6619; Adair Tire, 2253 Decatur Hwy., Gardendale, 205/631-0042). Because Cruise America does not have a New Orleans location, you may have to adjust your route if you want to do a one-way drive with a rented RV. Otherwise, inquire with regional RV rental companies in Nashville or New Orleans. Renters should be 25 years or older. Rental rates vary depending on the size of the vehicle and other factors. They also charge for mileage, and you can buy kits that include sheets, towels, dishes, and other basic necessities. Cruise America rents RVs of standard (five-person) and large (seven-person) sizes.

Driver's Licenses

Alabama, Mississippi, Louisiana, and Tennessee recognize other U.S. driver's licenses and learner's permits. The legal driving age in all four states is 16. Most driving regulations are similar to those in other states.

Traffic Regulations

Speed limits in this region vary. Along the Trace, the speed limit is never more than 50 miles per hour, and it's as low as 40 mph in some sections. The charm of the Trace is its scenic, slow pace.

It is required by law that all drivers and passengers in a moving vehicle wear their **seatbelts.** In all four states covered in this guide, infants less than one year old must be restrained in a rear-facing car seat; children 1-3 years must be restrained in a front-facing car seat. A child of 4-8 years who is less than four feet, nine inches tall must have a booster seat. When in doubt, check the applicable state's Department of Transportation website for specific regulations.

Drunk driving is dangerous and against the law. It is illegal to drive with a blood alcohol concentration of 0.08 percent or higher in Alabama, Mississippi, Louisiana, and Tennessee.

If a police car or other authorized vehicle is on the right shoulder, and you can safely do so, you should pull into the left lane.

Slow Down

The Natchez Trace Parkway is meant to be enjoyed at a slower pace. The speed limit is no more than 50 mph (and in some places, 40 mph). You should adhere to it not only to avoid a pricey speeding ticket, but also because at a faster pace you'll miss the many breathtaking sights and wildlife. In addition, the Natchez Trace is a designated bicycling route, so drivers need to be alert and watch out for two-wheeled tourists. Lanes are just 11 feet wide and, in most places, there is no road shoulder. Bicyclists are permitted to ride in the road, and signage directs cars to drive in the opposite lane (when possible to do so safely) to pass. Driving the route prescribed in this guide (north to south) means that the Trace's milepost markers will appear in descending order. Markers will be on the left side of the parkway as you drive south and generally have the number printed on both sides of the post.

The parkway is open to RVs of 55 feet in length or less, although some sections of the Old Trace—the original (sunken) road that intersects the parkway in many places—are not. The same is true of trailers and other large vehicles. The parkway is off-limits to commercial vehicles, with exceptions for those that have secured a permit (800/305-7417) in advance.

Texting while driving is illegal in all four states included in this guide, with Louisiana imposing the heftiest fines ($100) on offenders. Having Bluetooth or other technology that allows you to use your phone hands-free is your best option.

Fuel Availability

There are no gas stations along the Natchez Trace Parkway, so you'll need to plan accordingly to fuel up at locations off of the Trace. Each chapter of this guide has details on where to exit the Trace to reach a gas station. Options may be limited in rural areas, particularly if your car requires premium gasoline.

Roadside Assistance

Despite the rural nature of the Trace and the Mississippi Blues Trail, you're never too far from help. However, there are no gas stations or service stations on the Trace itself. Fuel up in advance to avoid issues on the parkway.

Breaking down on the road doesn't have to be a vacation killer. A few preventive measures (including a full tank of gas, flares, and a spare tire) can help. Even when you're on what feels like the most remote section of the Natchez Trace, you're never that far from cell service and park rangers, who patrol the parkway with some regularity.

Need help while on the interstate in Tennessee? Text *847 while on state highways and a HELP Program emergency responder will reply. HELP trucks patrol the area to help motorists in trouble. For non-emergency incidents in Nashville, dial 615/862-8600 to report a traffic incident or request roadside assistance. In Memphis, the local non-emergency number is 901/545-2677.

For AAA Roadside Assistance in Tennessee, Alabama, Mississippi, or Louisiana, call 800/222-4357.

The **HONK app** (www.honkforhelp.com) can be useful for roadside assistance, provided you are somewhere with strong enough cell service to run the app.

Because so many people bicycle the Trace, there are bike repair shops in most nearby cities.

Road Conditions

The weather from Nashville to New Orleans is generally mild. It's rare that significant snowfall accumulates on any portion of the Natchez Trace or surrounding roadways. However, because snow, sleet, and hail aren't common in these parts, few municipalities have equipment for significant snow removal. If it comes down, prepare for roads to be slick, with little salt or sand; local drivers will be unfamiliar with how to best drive on those roads and the parkway itself isn't treated for snow or ice.

Park rangers have good information on road conditions and frequently communicate with rangers elsewhere on the Trace. Start by calling the **Natchez Trace Parkway Headquarters and Visitor Center** (milepost 266, 662/680-4027) in Tupelo or check under "Current Conditions" on the Trace website (www.nps.gov/natr/planyourvisit/conditions.htm). Depending on where you are along the Trace, the rangers at the **Parkway Information Cabin** (milepost 102.4) in Ridgeland or the **Mount Locust Historic House** (milepost 15.5) near Natchez may also be helpful. They can call ahead to ranger stations along your route to get you the current weather conditions of your destination.

Other than snow or hail in **winter,** heavy rain and wind can make driving difficult in this area. These can happen any time of the year, but **spring** is when tornadoes are most likely to whip through the area. Tornadoes aren't a common occurrence, but heed weather warnings that suggest you take shelter in a windstorm. Pay attention to flood warnings, particularly around Jackson and Ridgeland and in the Mississippi Delta.

Early **summer** is thunderstorm season in the South. Pull over in a strong rainstorm if you are having any visibility issues. Southern rainstorms can be intense, but they're over quickly. If you are considering taking any of the unpaved sections described in this guide, check for significant rainfall to avoid getting stuck in the mud. Summer can be hot and humid in the South. Bring water; don't leave pets in parked cars. Heatstroke is a real risk.

In **fall,** you may be slowed down by leaf-peepers, but you aren't likely to run into weather complications. The end of summer through fall is hurricane season in New Orleans (Hurricane Katrina took place August 23-31, 2005), however, so listen to weather reports and heed any warnings to head inland.

As always, adjust driving speeds in inclement weather. When driving in rural areas, it's wise to keep an emergency kit in the trunk of your car.

The Trace by Motorcycle

The absence of commercial traffic, stop signs, and stoplights and the abundance of scenic views make the Trace a popular route for motorcycle travel. Motorcyclists must abide by speed limits and other road regulations. Many of the inns, B&Bs, and restaurants nearby cater to motorcyclists.

Tennessee, Alabama, Mississippi, and Louisiana all require both drivers and passengers on a motorcycle to wear a helmet. In addition, you'll want to have eye protection, a protective jacket, long pants, boots, gloves, and a tool kit for basic repairs. Consider wearing bright colors to ensure that you're easily visible to other vehicles on the road. Check the applicable state's Department of Transportation website for specific regulations as they pertain to motorcyclists.

The Trace by Bicycle

There are no designated bicycle lanes on the Natchez Trace; instead the National Park Service has designated the Trace in its entirety as a bicycle route. Bicyclists share the road with recreational vehicles. This means that when it's safe, drivers should move into the left lane to give cyclists more room.

If you'd like to cycle a portion of the Trace, it's possible to leave your car parked for an extended period in one of several parking lots, provided you complete a vehicle contact form (www.nps.gov/natr/planyourvisit/extended-vehicle-parking.htm). A few of the lots recommended by the park service are at Garrison Creek (milepost 427.6), Gordon

Motorcycle Repair Shops

Franklin, Tennessee

- **Moonshine Harley-Davidson** (7128 S. Springs Dr., Franklin, 615/266-0333, http://hdcoolsprings.com)

Memphis, Tennessee

- **Bumpus Harley Davidson** (2160 Whitten Rd., 901/401-9279, http://bumpushd-memphis.com)

Jackson, Mississippi

- **Cycle Service Plus** (2607 US 80 E., Pearl, 601/939-5077, www.cycleserviceplus.net)

New Orleans, Louisiana

- **Redbeard Cycles** (8022 Orpheus Ct., 504/483-3232)
- **New Orleans Harley-Davidson** (6015 Airline Dr., Metairie, 504/667-5171)

House and Ferry Site (milepost 407.7), Natchez Trace Parkway Headquarters and Visitor Center (milepost 266), and the Parkway Information Cabin (milepost 102.4). See the NPS website for more recommended lots.

Because so many people bike the Trace, most hotels and bed-and-breakfasts offer secure places for guests to lock bicycles. Park bikes, cars, and motorcycles in well-lit parking lots. Use locking bike racks if traveling with bicycles on your car.

There are five bike-only campgrounds on the parkway:

- junction with TN-50 (milepost 408)
- Colbert's Ferry Site (milepost 327)
- Witch Dance (milepost 234)
- Natchez Trace Parkway Headquarters and Visitor Center (milepost 266)
- town of Kosciusko (milepost 159)

To get your bicycle to the start of this epic adventure, you'll want to ship it ahead. **Bike Flights** (541/705-2453, www.bikeflights.com) is a concierge service that will help you pack and ship your bike—and get it back home when you're done. They offer several shipping speeds and methods. Prices vary based on shipment origin but start at around $60 each way.

Bike Tours and Shuttles

If you don't want to do it alone, there are tour companies and shuttles to help you out:

Lizard Head Cycling Guides (970/728-5891, http://lizardheadcyclingguides.com, $2,890 pp) has both spring and fall guided trips, on which you can bring your bike or rent one. The cost of the seven-day trek includes meals, lodging, shuttles, and mechanical support. These trips begin in Natchez and head north to Nashville.

Cycle of Life Adventures (303/945-9886, http://cycleoflifeadventures.com, $2,895 pp) offers Trace trips four times a year. If you need a little extra boost, you can rent an e-bike (an electric bike) instead of a traditional bike.

VBT (800/245-3868, www.vbt.com, from $1,945 pp) offers a six-day tour of the Mississippi section of the Trace, including lodging, meals, tours of

Vicksburg National Military Park, and more.

Natchez Trace Cycle Tours (615/300-8224, http://natcheztrace.bike/natchez-trace-tours, $1,099 pp) offers four-, five,- or seven-day trips, based on your schedule, not set dates.

Black Bear Adventures (888/339-8687, http://blackbearadventures.com, $3,600 pp) takes 10 days to tour the Trace on bicycle, with options in both spring and fall.

Downtown Karla Brown (907/540-0001, www.downtownkarlabrown.com, $600), based in Natchez, offers a shuttle service. Leave your car in Natchez, let Karla drive you and your bikes to the northern terminus, then bike south. Karla also offers a three-day, 100-mile bike tour of the Trace ($949-1,599 pp).

For more information on cycling on the Trace, see the **National Park Service** website (www.nps.gov/natr/planyourvisit/bicyclinghome.htm) and **Natchez Trace Travel** (www.natcheztracetravel.com/biking-the-trace.html).

The Trace on Horseback

Horseback riding is a popular way to see portions of the Natchez Trace, along horse trails that run adjacent to the parkway in Tennessee and Mississippi. They include:

- Natchez Trace National Scenic Trail, Leiper's Fork Segment (milepost 408-428)
- Natchez Trace National Scenic Trail, Tupelo Segment (milepost 260)
- Witch Dance Horse Trail, Tombigbee National Forest (milepost 233)
- Natchez Trace National Scenic Trail, Ridgeland Segment (milepost 115)
- Natchez Trace National Scenic Trail, Rocky Springs Segment (milepost 59)

Horses aren't allowed in the campgrounds or picnic areas along the Trace, but there are hitching posts on the trails. Plenty of private campgrounds near the parkway allow horses, and many have horse stalls and private trails.

Note that if you are bringing a horse trailer, the Park Service has regulations:

- Bring proof of an official negative test for equine infectious anemia (EIA) dated within the last year.
- Horse trailers combined with their tow vehicle must be no longer than 55 feet.
- Load and unload horse trailers only at designated horse staging areas (marked on parkway maps).
- Only one rider per horse is allowed.

Sports and Recreation

Cruising the Delta

Due to its proximity to the Mississippi River, the Delta is a popular destination for riverboat cruises. Greenville, Cleveland, Clarksdale, Vicksburg, Natchez, and New Orleans all have active ports. Most cruisers eat and sleep on the luxury boats and then head out to explore and shop during the day. Most cruise companies have options for one-day and round-trip cruises, both on the Lower Mississippi (Memphis to New Orleans) and headed farther north to St. Louis and beyond. Three of the leading companies include:

- **Viking River Cruises** (www.vikingrivercruises.com)
- **American Cruise Lines** (www.americancruiselines.com)
- **USA River Cruises** (http://usarivercruises.com)

Fishing

If you plan to fish on the great waterways covered in this book, you'll need to get a license.

In **Tennessee** (www.tn.gov/twra/license-sales/fishing-licenses.html) licenses are based on species. Three-day licenses for nonresidents are $40.50, or

Bike Repair Shops

Nashville, Tennessee

- **Cumberland Transit** (2807 West End Ave., 615/321-4069, http://cumberlandtransit.com)
- **Shelby Avenue Bicycle Co.** (1629 Shelby Ave., 615/925-3274, http://shelbybicycle.com)
- **Trace Bikes** (8080B TN-100, 615/646-2485, http://tracebikes.com)
- **Halcyon Bike Shop** (2802 12th Ave. S., 615/730-9344, http://halcyonbike.com)

Memphis, Tennessee

- **Peddler Bike Shop** (3548 Walker Ave., 901/327-4833, http://peddlerbikeshop.com; three other locations in greater Memphis)
- **Bikes Plus** (7007 Stage Rd., 901/385-8788, www.bikesplus.net)

Florence, Alabama

- **Spinning Spoke Cycle Hub** (221N S. Seminary St., 256/349-5302, www.spinningspoke.com)

Tupelo, Mississippi

- **Trails and Treads** (549B Coley Rd., 662/690-6620)
- **Bicycle Pacelines** (2120 W. Jackson St., 662/844-8660, www.bicyclepacelines.net)

Starkville, Mississippi

- **Boardtown Bikes** (200 S. Montgomery St., Ste. C, 662/324-1200, www.boardtownbikes.com)

Ridgeland, Mississippi

- **Bike Crossing** (115 W. Jackson St., 601/856-0049, http://thebikecrossing.com)

Jackson, Mississippi

- **The Bike Rack** (2282 Lakeland Dr., Flowood, 601/936-2100)
- **Indian Cycle Fitness and Outdoor** (677 S. Pear Orchard Dr., 601/956-8383, www.indiancyclefitness.com)

Natchez, Mississippi

- **Trippe's Western Auto** (180 Sgt. S. Prentiss Dr., 601/445-4186)

Baton Rouge, Louisiana

- **The Bicycle Shop South** (3315 Highland Rd., 225/344-5624)

New Orleans, Louisiana

- **New Orleans Bike & Board Shop** (8136 Oak St., 504/866-4439)

$20.50 if you're not fishing for trout. One-day licenses for residents are $6.50.

Alabama has different fishing licenses for flatwater and saltwater fish (www.outdooralabama.com/license-information). Three-day licenses for nonresidents are $29.95. Annual permits for residents are $13.85. Residents of Florida, Georgia, Louisiana, Mississippi, and Tennessee may have reciprocal agreements.

Three-day **Mississippi** fishing licenses (601/432-2400, http://mdwfp.com/license/fishing) are $15 for nonresidents and $3 for residents.

A Brief History of the Natchez Trace

The Natchez Trace Parkway runs between Nashville and Natchez, Mississippi, winding 444 miles through Tennessee, Alabama, and Mississippi.

According to researchers, some **10,000 years ago,** herds of bison likely made their way along what's now the Natchez Trace from the mighty Mississippi, which was their water source, to salt licks in Tennessee. Humans followed in their four-legged footsteps, using the same route.

In 2019 the Natchez Trace Parkway was the eighth most-visited National Park site in the country, with 6.3 million people—more visitors than to the Grand Canyon!—driving, cycling, and walking its winding way. This achievement was possible thanks to people who saw the Trace's historical and recreational value; originally, each section of the Trace was maintained (or, in many cases, neglected) by local municipalities, and getting them to work together was a challenge.

Prehistoric and Early Native American Life

Several thousand years ago, Native Americans also walked this way, perhaps in search of the migrating bison—perhaps, too, in search of resources like salt and water, following the topography of the land through the Mississippi Hills and along waterways. They found this land and made it their home, creating communities based on agriculture and trading, and building thriving villages.

Throughout the route there are places to stop and see **Indian burial mounds** and sites of these **former villages,** including the **Chickasaw Village Site, Pharr Mounds,** and **Grand Village of the Natchez Indians State Historic Site.** Tribes that lived in this region include (from north to south) **Cherokee, Shawnee, Chickasaw, Choctaw,** and **Natchez.** During this period the Trace began to take on clear marks of a major route as trails were blazed. Sections of the Trace were referred to as The Path to Choctaw Nation and Chickasaw Trail.

European Colonizers

European explorers probably first reached the Mississippi Valley in the **1500s,** when Spaniard Hernando de Soto and his army traveled west from what is now Florida. He spent the winter of 1540 in Chickasaw villages, and brought diseases such as small pox, to the Natchez people, who were the last American Indians to live in this region. According to the National Park Service, "Nearly all the villages and ceremonial centers that de Soto's men had seen were abandoned by the late 1600s."

Over the next centuries colonizers founded cities up and down the Trace, displacing Native Americans from their ancestral lands, either through disease or by force. At different points in this period this land was controlled by the French, the Spanish, and the British. While the Indigenous people didn't disappear, their traditional way of life on the land did. It was during this period that white settlers brutally battled with Native Americans over land and resources along the Trace. Natchez was founded in 1716 and Nashville in 1806 and Jackson, Mississippi in 1821.

By the **end of the 1700s,** not only was Natchez a booming city, but Nashville was also a thriving region and there needed to be a way to get goods to and from these cities. So-called "Kaintucks," who may or may not have been from Kentucky, traveled on boats down the Mississippi to sell their wares in Natchez and New Orleans. Then they'd head home on foot, along the then-sunken Trace. It would take as many as 30 days to make the return trip. By the late 1700s the Natchez Trace was becoming a more popular road, as the first documented cargo reached Natchez via the Mississippi River. But the route home was rough: It was an unregulated expanse heavy with crime, particularly horse thievery. Travelers also had to contend with wild animals and insects (mosquitos were no joke then or now).

Road Improvements

President Thomas Jefferson wanted to connect the disparate sections of the United State frontier, and he saw the Natchez Trace as a way to do that. As early as **1801** the postmaster general of the United States suggested making the Trace easier to navigate to improve mail service. By **1803** about 264 miles had been widened and smoothed. These improvements led to increased use, and more "stands"—akin to a humble inn—opened to accommodate weary travelers; these stands were generally one-room shelters offering some food and company. To learn more about them, you can visit sites along the route today including **Colbert's Stand and Ferry Site** and **French Camp Historic District.**

In 1806 Congress appropriated $6,000 to improve the Trace, and by 1809 the route was considered traversable by wagon. However, that initial $6,000 didn't include funding for maintenance, so improvements were short-lived. Jefferson began calling it the "Columbian Highway," but those who traveled it called it "The Devil's Backbone" due to its remoteness, wilderness, and continued lawlessness.

In 1809 Meriwether Lewis died on the Trace.

Government Use and Abuse

When General Andrew Jackson needed to move his troops from Nashville to New Orleans during the War of **1812,** the Trace was a natural choice for a route, and this portion was dubbed "Jackson's Military Road."

In 1830 President Andrew Jackson signed the Indiana Removal Act, a cruel piece of legislation that forced Native Americans from their ancestral land in Georgia, Alabama, Florida, North Carolina, and Tennessee. By 1837, the U.S. government forced their departure. The routes they took west to Oklahoma (www.nps.gov/trte/planyourvisit/maps.htm) were referred to as the **Trail of Tears.** One such land route, the Deas-Whiteley Route, intersects with the Natchez Trace Parkway in Alabama. Another route, the Bell Route, went through Memphis, while others used the Mississippi River as a means of transport. Visit the Wichahpi Commemorative Stone Wall to learn about one particularly poignant story of this brutality and heartbreak.

There are many examples of war-time use of the Trace, including battlegrounds and gravesites. The trace was used as a direct and efficient way for troops to get from town to town.

Before and after the **Civil War,** iron ore mining near the northern sections of the Trace kept local economies humming, which made the Trace a business thoroughfare for a few decades. But, as time ticked by, the Trace began to be passed over in favor of other modes of transportation. Steamboats could travel upstream, unlike the Kaintucks' self-propelled boats, and the U.S. Postal Service opted for steamboats rather than the Trace to get mail back and forth.

New roadways bypassed the Trace. Railroads made other routes faster, too. The Trace fell into disrepair. It was possible that this historic route could be lost to time, overgrown by vines, and forgotten.

National Park Service and Preservation

In the **early 1900s, women in the Mississippi chapter of the** Daughters of the American Revolution (DAR) began to advocate for restoration and preservation of the Trace. In 1892, Elizabeth Jones was the first DAR member from the state of Mississippi when she began advocating for a group to preserve what she called "the once famous military road." She was followed later by Lucille Mayfield, another DAR member who became the first president of the Natchez Trace Military Highway Association (later renamed the Natchez Trace Association). Mayfield and others had commemorative markers erected at important sites, often traversing the woods in the long dresses of the time to do the work themselves. They lobbied in Washington DC to have the road paved and made part of the National Park Service.

In **1934** Congress approved a survey of the "Old Indian Trail" with the idea of making the national Natchez Trace Parkway. Marketing materials from 1934 called it "the Road to Yesterday; the Pathway to Tomorrow."

Completion and Modern Day

Federal construction on the parkway began in **1938, but the** Old Trace wasn't added to the National Register of Historic Places until **1976. This was essential for fund raising to** finish construction of the roadway.

The **Double Arch Bridge,** near the northern terminus, was finished in **1994,** and it was featured as part of the celebration of the Tennessee Bicentennial in **1996.**

The final sections of the parkway, between Ridgeland and Natchez, were completed in **2005.**

Travel Tips

Visas and Officialdom

Passports and Visas

Visiting from another country, you must have a valid passport and a visa to enter the United States. The U.S. government's Visa Waiver Program allows tourists from many countries to visit without a visa for up to 90 days. To check if your country is on the list go to http://travel.state.gov. To qualify, you must apply online with the **Electronic System for Travel Authorization** (www.cbp.gov) and hold a return plane or cruise ticket to your country of origin dated less than 90 days from your date of entry. Even with a waiver, you still need to bring your passport and present it at the port of entry.

Take note that in recent years the United States has begun to require visa-waiver participants to have upgraded passports with digital photographs and machine-readable information. They have also introduced requirements that even visa-waiver citizens register in advance before arriving in the United States. For more information about the Visa Waiver Program, contact the **Customs and Border Protection Agency** (www.travel.state.gov).

All foreign travelers are required to participate in **U.S. Visit,** a program operated by the Department of Homeland Security. Under the program, your fingerprints and photograph are taken—digitally and without ink—as you are being screened by an immigration officer. The visa requirements and screening process are subject to change. If you're traveling from overseas, check current visa requirements before setting out.

Embassies and Consulates

Many consulates have offices in Chicago and Houston, which are significantly far from the Natchez Trace Parkway. The exception is the **Consulate-General of Japan** (1801 West End Ave. #900, Nashville, 615/340-4300) in midtown Nashville. Your best bet is to check with the appropriate agencies before your departure.

Customs

Upon entering the United States, international travelers must declare any dollar amount over $10,000 as well as the value of any articles that will remain in the country, including gifts. A duty will be assessed for all imported goods, though visitors are usually granted a $100 exemption. Illegal drugs, Cuban cigars, obscene items, toxic substances, and prescription drugs (without an accompanying prescription) are generally prohibited. In order to protect American agriculture, customs officials will also confiscate certain produce, plants, seeds, nuts, meat, and other potentially dangerous biological products. For more information, consult **U.S. Customs and Border Protection** (U.S. 877/227-5511, outside the U.S. 202/325-8000, www.cbp.gov).

Visitor Information

Many cities have their own tourist organizations. In some rural areas, counties have teamed up to develop visitor information for the region. Other organizations, such as the National Park Service, Army Corps of Engineers, and state parks, publish visitor information for certain attractions. Specific listings for visitor information are found throughout this book.

Tennessee

The **Tennessee Department of Tourism Development** (615/741-2159, www.tnvacation.com) is a source of visitor information about Tennessee. It publishes an annual guide that contains hotel and attraction listings. The website also offers specialty itineraries for wine lovers, whiskey drinkers, musicians, and Civil War buffs. Tennessee State Park information is included as well.

Several regional tourism organizations provide useful information and publications: Middle Tennessee has the **Middle Tennessee Tourism Council** (www.middletennesseetourism.com), which covers the counties around Nashville; the **Upper Cumberland Tourism Association** (www.uppercumberland.org), which promotes the region surrounding the Cumberland River and the northern plateau; and the **South Central Tennessee Tourism Association** (www.sctta.net).

Visit Music City (615/259-4747, www.visitmusiccity.com) operates two visitors centers in Nashville. The website offers concert listings, hotel booking services, and useful visitor information with lots of good discounts and trip-planning advice.

Visit Franklin (615/591-8514, http://visitfranklin.com) has maps and information on the Battle of Franklin Civil War sights.

Alabama

For information on the tiny corner of the Yellowhammer State through which the Trace cuts, there are several tourism organizations with good information and Southern hospitality. Start with the **Shoals Chamber of Commerce** (20 Hightower Pl., 256/764-4661, www.shoalschamber.com) and **Visit Florence** (200 Jim Spain Dr., 256/740-4141, www.visitflorenceal.com), which serves the city of Florence in the Quad Cities area. **Colbert County Tourism** (719 US 72 W., 256/383-0783, www.colbertcountytourism.org) covers Muscle Shoals, Tuscumbia, Florence, and Sheffield and operates a **visitors center** (8am-5pm Mon.-Fri.). The **Florence-Lauderdale Tourism Convention & Visitors Bureau** (256/740-4141) has information on specific tours.

Mississippi

If you take the Natchez Trace Parkway

or the Mississippi Blues Trail, you'll be covering much of the Magnolia State. **Visit Mississippi** (501 N. West St., Ste. 500, 601/359-3297, www.visitmississippi.org) fields general inquiries and provides travel guides.

Visit Vicksburg (52 Old Hwy. 27, Vicksburg, 800/221-3536, http://visitvicksburg.com) offers a free guide for visitors and is particularly well-versed in information for veterans and others interested in military history. **Corinth Area Convention and Visitors Bureau** (www.corinth.net) allows you to go deep into Civil War sights. **Visit Jackson** (http://visitjackson.com) has free travel guides to "the City with Soul." Immerse yourself in the history of the 300-year-old city on the Mississippi with information from **Visit Natchez** (http://visitnatchez.org). From tamales to juke joints to civil rights sights, **Visit the Delta** (www.visitthedelta.com) is rich in information on touring the Mississippi Delta.

The **Greater Starkville Development Partnership** (662/323-3322 or 800/649-8687, www.starkville.org/visit) has a prime downtown location in Starkville and lots of information on the college town. **Visit Oxford Visitor's Center** (1013 Jackson Ave. E., Oxford, 662/232-2477, http://visitoxfordms.com, 8am-5pm Mon.-Fri., 11am-3pm Sat., 1pm-4pm Sun.) is well-located in the town of Oxford and chock-full of maps, information, and Southern charm.

Louisiana

For general information about traveling in southeastern Louisiana, your best resource is the state-run **Louisiana Office of Tourism** (800/677-4082, www.louisianatravel.com), which offers a tour guidebook, interactive maps, travel tips, and oodles of information about the state's accommodations, restaurants, attractions, events, live entertainment, and outdoor activities, plus live operators willing to assist with your tourism needs.

Visitors to the Big Easy should consult the **New Orleans Convention & Visitors Bureau** (2020 St. Charles Ave., 800/672-6124, www.neworleanscvb.com, 8:30am-5pm Mon.-Fri.) or the **New Orleans Tourism Marketing Corporation** (2020 St. Charles Ave., 504/524-4784, www.neworleans.com), both of which provide a slew of information about the city's myriad lodging, dining, and activity options. The **New Orleans Welcome Center** (529 St. Ann St., 504/568-5661, www.crt.state.la.us, 8:30am-5pm daily) also provides maps and brochures and arranges tours.

For information about the Greater New Orleans area, consult the **Jefferson Convention & Visitors Bureau** (1221 Elmwood Park Blvd., Ste. 411, 504/731-7083 or 877/572-7474, www.visitjeffersonparish.com).

Visit Baton Rouge (359 3rd St., Baton Rouge, 225/383-1825 or 800/527-6843, www.visitbatonrouge.com) is the official travel resource for visitors to Louisiana's capital city.

Access for Travelers with Disabilities

Several national organizations offer information and advice about traveling with disabilities. The **Society for Accessible Travel and Hospitality** (www.sath.org) publishes links to major airlines' accessibility policies and publishes travel tips for people with various disabilities, including blindness, deafness, mobility disorders, diabetes, kidney disease, and arthritis. The society publishes *Open World,* an online magazine about accessible travel.

Accessible Vans of America (877/275-4915, www.accessiblevans.com) is a national chain specializing in van rentals that are wheelchair-accessible or otherwise designed for drivers and travelers with disabilities. Accessible Vans of America has locations in Memphis, Tennessee (888/432-9387) and New Orleans, Louisiana (888/433-6862), and it will deliver to other locations.

Rental car company Avis offers **Avis**

Access, a program for travelers with disabilities. Call the dedicated 24-hour toll-free number (888/879-4273) for help renting a car with features such as transfer boards, hand controls, spinner knobs, and swivel seats.

Some of New Orleans's older hotels, cobblestone streets, and other charms can make accessible travel a challenge. Within new hotels, some large restaurants, and most major attractions, you can expect to find wheelchair-accessible restrooms, entrance ramps, and other helpful fixtures; RTA buses are wheelchair-accessible. But New Orleans has many hole-in-the-wall cafés, tiny B&Bs, historical houses with narrow staircases or uneven thresholds, and other buildings that are not easily accessible to people using wheelchairs. Unfortunately, the city's historic streetcars are also not wheelchair-accessible. If you're traveling with a guide animal, be sure to contact every hotel or restaurant in question to confirm access and accommodation. Some of these issues also apply in older cities in this region, such as Vicksburg and Natchez.

Traveling with Children

A leisurely, 444-mile drive down a historic parkway with limited Internet connectivity isn't the first choice of vacation for many small children. Stopping at Mississippi Blues Trail sights may not be compelling for kids, and certainly juke joints and nightclubs and New Orleans's Bourbon Street aren't kid-centric stops. Nevertheless, there are some outstanding attractions for kids in each city and town, plenty of child-centric eateries, and lots of wide-open spaces for them to run and play, making for a Southern road trip the family will remember for decades.

- **Nashville:** Check the calendar for events for the Taylor Swift Education Center at the **Country Music Hall of Fame and Museum** and the **Nashville Zoo at Grassmere.** Explore cars from a different time and place at the **Lane Motor Museum.** The **Adventure Science Center** and its **Sudekum Planetarium** offer education disguised as entertainment and is a great option for rainy days. **Nashville Children's Theatre** has been offering stage productions for little ones since 1931. If you are staying at the **Gaylord Opryland Resort,** choose the package that gives access to its mammoth **SoundWaves** water park. For more tips, check out **Nashville Parent** (http://nashvilleparent.com).
- **Memphis:** On a nice day there's nothing like walking over the mighty Mississippi at **Big River Crossing,** and later catching it lit up at night. The **Memphis Zoo, Children's Museum of Memphis and its restored Grand Carousel,** and **Cotton Museum** have exhibits geared to the under-age set. And don't miss the **Peabody ducks** at **The Peabody Memphis. Memphis Parent** (http://memphisparent.com) is chock-full of information.
- **New Orleans:** The **Audubon Aquarium of the Americas, Audubon Butterfly Garden and Insectarium, Blaine Kern's Mardi Gras World, Audubon Zoo,** and **Storyland** are some great attractions for kids. Many excursions offered throughout the city, such as swamp tours, riverboat rides, and haunted strolls, are also a big hit with kids, especially teenagers. For more ideas, consult **New Orleans Kids** (www.neworleanskids.com), which offers a slew of tips regarding family-friendly hotels, restaurants, attractions, and activities.

Senior Travelers

Both the Natchez Trace Parkway and the Mississippi Blues Trail are popular trips for seniors. Want some help getting started? **Road Scholar** (800/454-5768, www.roadscholar.org), formerly called Elderhostel, organizes educational tours in Memphis, Nashville, Baton Rouge, and New Orleans for people over 55.

For discounts and help with trip planning, try the **AARP** (800/454-5768, www.aarp.org), which offers a full-service travel agency, trip insurance, a motor club, and the AARP Passport program, which provides seniors with discounts for hotels, car rentals, and other things.

Travelers over 55 should always check for a senior discount. Most attractions and some hotels and restaurants have special pricing for senior citizens. In general, the concept of Southern hospitality is put into action daily: People are exceptionally helpful, so senior travelers should have little trouble finding assistance here.

LGBTQ Travelers

Lesbian, gay, bisexual, transgender, and queer travelers are presented with a mixed bag when visiting the South. In 2013, Tennessee lawmakers introduced a bill, often referred to as the "Don't Say Gay" bill, that would have banned teachers from even saying the word *gay* in the classroom. (It failed to make it through the legislative process.) Mississippi state law does not address discrimination on basis of sexual orientation—although some cities in the Magnolia State, including Oxford and Jackson, have such laws. Similar laws exist in Alabama; some officials there have been outspoken about their opposition to same-sex marriage. In 2016, the British Foreign Office issued a warning to British LGBTQ travelers to be aware of a Mississippi law that permits businesses to refuse service to someone based on sexual orientation.

On the other hand, there has been no better time to be gay in the South. More and more social, civic, and political organizations are engaging the gay community, and there are vibrant gay scenes in several of the region's larger cities.

For gay travelers, this means that the experience on the road can vary tremendously. You can find gay nightlife and gay-friendly lodging in many cities, but you may experience chilly treatment in the countryside. Memphis is progressive and welcoming, but rural areas along the Mississippi Blues Trail may be more conservative.

New Orleans is a bastion of gay-friendliness, with gay newspapers, numerous gay and lesbian organizations and gay-owned businesses, and several gay-dominated bars and nightclubs, many of which are in the midst of the nightlife district in the French Quarter. The Quarter, the Faubourg Marigny, and Uptown tend to have the highest lesbian and gay populations.

Three annual events—Mardi Gras in the late winter, the Southern Decadence celebration over Labor Day weekend, and Halloween in the fall—draw the greatest numbers of gay and lesbian visitors to New Orleans, but the city is always popular with gay and lesbian travelers. Many inns and B&Bs, especially in the Faubourg Marigny, are gay-owned.

Resources for LGBTQ Travelers

Several guidebooks and websites give helpful listings of gay-friendly hotels, restaurants, and bars. The **Damron LGBT Travel Guides** (www.damron.com) offer Tennessee listings; the **International Gay and Lesbian Travel Association** (IGLTA, www.iglta.org) is a trade organization with listings of gay-friendly hotels, tour operators, and much more. San Francisco-based **Now, Voyager** (www.nowvoyager.com) is a gay-owned and gay-operated travel agency that specializes in gay tours, vacation packages, and cruises.

Out and About (http://outandaboutnashville.com) is a free monthly newsmagazine for the gay, lesbian, bisexual, and transgender community in Nashville. **OUT Memphis** (892 S. Cooper St., Memphis, 901/278-6422, www.outmemphis.org) is a clearinghouse of information for the gay and lesbian community. They offer a directory of gay-friendly businesses, host social events, and promote tolerance and equality.

Mid-South Pride (www.midsouthpride.org) organizes Memphis Pride in June.

For more information about gay and lesbian activities in New Orleans, consult the free bimonthly ***Ambush Mag*** (www.ambushmag.com). The same publication also has a website just for gay goings-on during Mardi Gras (www.gaymardigras.com). Another helpful website is www.gayneworleans.com.

Resources for Travelers of Color

Many parts of the South have a notorious reputation and a violent history in treatment of non-white people; therefore, it is understandable there may be a concern for some in traveling in these areas. However, today most of the areas covered in this book rely on tourism, and in general, it is unlikely that travelers of color will experience unsafe conditions while road tripping through the region. Care has been taken in the research of this book to include businesses, including those owned by people of color, that welcome people from all backgrounds.

In addition, many of the stops in this book feature locations with majority populations of people of color. Memphis, Jackson, and New Orleans are three of the U.S. cities with the largest African American populations. Nashville has the largest Kurdish population in the United States.

The following organizations may offer more resources:

- **National Association for the Advancement of Colored People:** The NAACP offers rare travel advisories (the last one was in Missouri in 2017) and keeps on top of incidents of racial violence and unrest; www.naacp.org.
- **We Go, Too:** This membership organization works with Black travel bloggers and other experts to provide tourism tips that go beyond local hot spots; http://wegotooworld.com/.
- **Black & Abroad:** While it is primarily focused on international travel, this website, focused on Black travelers, includes updated travel advisories; https://www.weareblackandabroad.com/.
- **Travel Noire:** Offers travel guides to various cities, with an emphasis on Black-owned businesses; https://travelnoire.com/.

Traveling without Reservations

Part of the serendipity of a road trip is traveling without reservations and staying where the spirit moves you. Unless you are traveling during a special event (like CMA Music Festival in Nashville, Pilgrimage in Natchez, Juke Joint in Clarkdale, or Mardi Gras in New Orleans), traveling without booking reservations ahead of time is generally possible.

However, many of the inns and bed-and-breakfasts listed in this guide have just a handful of rooms, so they may be sold out by the time you arrive. In cities such as Florence, Tupelo, and Jackson, you'll be able to find a decent hotel without trouble. If you have special requests or needs, you're best off booking in advance.

Communications and Media

Area Codes

Tennessee has seven different area codes. Of those, Memphis and vicinity use 901; Nashville and the counties immediately north of the city are in 615 and 629.

In the Shoals area of Alabama area codes are 256 and 938.

Mississippi has four area codes. Southern Mississippi is covered by 769 and 601, and northern Mississippi uses 662.

In Louisiana, Baton Rouge uses 225 and New Orleans uses 504.

Cell Phones

Cell phone signals are powerful and reliable in cities and along the interstates. On rural sections of the Natchez Trace and less populated sections of the Mississippi Blues Trail, you should not count on your cell phone having service.

Money

Bank debit cards and major credit cards are accepted throughout the southeastern region, particularly in major cities. However, it's not unusual for gas stations, markets, roadside stands, and other shops in rural areas to be cash-only. Don't rely solely on credit cards on this road trip, particularly along the Natchez Trace Parkway and the Mississippi Blues Trail.

Banks and ATMs

In Tennessee, the most prevalent banks are **SunTrust** (800/786-8787, www.suntrust.com), **First Horizon** (800/382-5465, www.firsttennessee.com), and **Regions** (800/734-4667, www.regions.com). Alabama is also **Regions** territory, and you may find plenty of **BBVA Bank** (844/228-2872, www.bbvausa.com) locations. In Mississippi **Regions** and **BancCorpSouth** (888/797-7711, www.banccorpsouth.com) are reliable choices. In Louisiana, try **Chase** (800/935-9935, www.chase.com), **Iberia Bank** (800/682-3231, www.iberiabank.com) and **Bank of Louisiana** (800/288-9811, www.bankoflouisiana.com).

Automated teller machines (ATMs) are prevalent throughout the region, and most banks provide access to ATMs inside and/or outside their branches. Be prepared to pay $2-3 per transaction if the machine isn't operated by your bank.

Currency Exchange

For up-to-date exchange rates, consult www.xe.com. In Nashville, the **Wright Travel Business Center** has a currency exchange location on the departures level of Nashville International Airport (http://flynashville.com), between Southwest and Delta Airlines.

In New Orleans, foreign currency can be exchanged at **Whitney Bank** (900 Airline Dr., Kenner, 504/838-6491 or 800/844-4450, www.whitneybank.com, 9am-5pm Mon.-Thurs., 9am-5:30pm Sat.) in the ticket lobby of the Louis Armstrong New Orleans International Airport; cash advances and travelers checks are also available.

Sales Tax

Tennessee

In Tennessee, sales tax is charged on all goods, including food and groceries. Sales tax is split between the state and local governments. Tennessee's sales tax is 5 percent on food and groceries and 7 percent on all other goods. Cities and towns add an additional "local use tax" of 1.5-2.75 percent, making the tax as high as 9.25 percent in Nashville and Memphis.

Alabama

Alabama's sales tax is 4 percent, but in some cities the combined rate reaches 11 percent. The combined rate in Florence is 8.5 percent.

Mississippi

Mississippi's statewide sales tax is 7 percent.

Louisiana

The combined state and city sales tax in New Orleans is 10 percent, making it one of the highest in the nation. Baton Rouge doesn't have a city sales tax, so you'll just pay the state sales tax of 5 percent.

Hotel Tax

Tennessee

There is no statewide tax on hotel rooms, but 45 different cities have established their own hotel tax, ranging 5-7 percent.

Alabama

A statewide hotel tax of 4 percent applies everywhere except the Alabama Mountain Lakes Region in North Alabama, which includes the part of Alabama through which the Natchez Trace runs.

Mississippi

There's a 2 percent tax on hotel rooms (but not food or entertainment) in Jackson County.

Louisiana

There is no statewide tax on hotel rooms, but Jefferson and Orleans parishes have a 4 percent room tax.

Tipping

Tipping is standard in this region. You should tip servers at least 20 percent in a sit-down restaurant. It's acceptable to tip 15 percent in a cafeteria-style or counter-service restaurant.

Tip bellhops or bag handlers $1 per bag—more if they went out of their way to help you. Same goes for valets and anyone who helps you with your bicycle.

Health and Safety

Medical Services

Dial 911 for police, fire, or ambulance in an emergency. Most medical and dental facilities will require insurance or a partial payment before admitting patients for treatment or dispensing medication.

Tennessee

Health care is a big industry in Nashville, so there are a lot of hospitals. Should you need emergency medical care, the majority of the hospitals are clustered in midtown, near Vanderbilt. **The Monroe Carell Jr. Children's Hospital** (2200 Children's Way, 615/936-1000, www.childrenshospital.vanderbilt.org) at Vanderbilt is among the best in the country. **TriStar Skyline Medical Center** (3441 Dickerson Pike, 615/769-2000, http://tristarskyline.com) is the closest hospital to Music Valley and parts of east Nashville.

Nashville's local number for "urgency without emergency" is 615/862-8600.

Midtown Memphis is referred to as Medical Center for the number of hospitals and medical facilities there. Among them are **Regional One Health** (877 Jefferson Ave., 901/545-7100, www.regionalonehealth.org) and the **Methodist University Hospital** (1265 Union Ave., 901/516-7000, www.methodisthealth.org).

In east Memphis, **Baptist Memorial Hospital** (6019 Walnut Grove Rd., 901/226-5000, www.baptistonline.org/memphis) is the cornerstone of the huge Baptist Memorial Health Care System.

Alabama

If you need medical attention in Muscle Shoals, head to **Shoals Hospital** (201 W. Avalon Ave., Muscle Shoals, 256/386-1600, www.shoalshospital.com), which has a full emergency room.

In nearby Sheffield, **Helen Keller Hospital** (1300 S. Montgomery Ave., 256/386-4196, www.helenkeller.com) is a full-service hospital with an emergency room.

Mississippi

In Oxford, **Baptist Memorial Hospital-North Mississippi** (1100 Belk Blvd., 662/636-1000, www.baptistonline.org) is a full service hospital.

Starkville's **OCH Regional Medical Center** (400 Hospital Rd., 662/323-4320, www.och.org) has a 24/7 emergency room and other services.

In Natchez, **Merit Health Natchez** (54 Sergeant Prentiss Dr., 601/443-2100, www.merithealthnatchez.com) is the hospital closest to the southern terminus of the parkway.

Louisiana

Baton Rouge locals call it Mid City or The General. The official name is **Baton**

Rouge General Medical Center (3600 Florida Blvd., 225/387-7000), and it's the place to go in a medical emergency. It is open 24 hours.

There are several well-regarded hospitals and clinics in New Orleans and its environs, including the **Tulane Medical Center** (1415 Tulane Ave., 504/988-5263, www.tulanehealthcare.com), the closest general hospital to the French Quarter and the CBD; the **Interim LSU Public Hospital** (2021 Perdido St., 504/903-3000, www.lsuhospitals.org), the active part of a major medical center still in progress; and the **Ochsner Baptist Medical Center** (2700 Napoleon Ave., 504/899-9311, www.ochsner.org), an Uptown hospital with a 24-hour emergency room.

If you're in need of emergency dental care, consider the **Louisiana Dental Center** (4232 St. Claude Ave., New Orleans, 504/947-2958, www.ladentalcenter.com, 8am-4pm Mon.-Thurs., 8am-3pm Fri., 8am-1pm Sat.), which offers several locations in southeastern Louisiana, from Metairie to Gonzales.

In the event of a hurricane or other natural disaster, contact the **New Orleans Office of Homeland Security and Emergency Preparedness** (504/658-8700) for instructions and evacuation assistance.

Wilderness Safety

West Nile Virus

West Nile virus was first recorded in humans in the United States in the early 2000s, and by 2007 nearly every state, including Tennessee, Alabama, Mississippi, and Louisiana, had reported confirmed cases of the disease. West Nile is spread by mosquitoes.

Summer is mosquito season in the southeast. You can prevent mosquito bites by wearing an insect repellent containing 30-50 percent DEET. An alternative to DEET, picaridin, is available in 7 and 15 percent concentrations and would need to be applied more frequently. Wearing long-sleeved pants and shirts and not being outdoors during dusk and dawn are also ways to avoid exposure to mosquitoes.

Fever, chills, weakness, drowsiness, and fatigue are some of the symptoms of West Nile virus.

Lyme Disease

Lyme disease is a bacterial infection spread by deer ticks. The first indication you might have Lyme disease is the appearance of a red rash where you have been bitten by a tick. Following that, symptoms are flu-like. During late-stage Lyme disease, neurological effects are reported.

Ticks are external parasites that attach themselves to warm-blooded creatures like dogs, deer, and humans. Ticks suck blood from their host.

Tick bites are unpleasant enough, even if there is no infection of Lyme disease. After coming in from the woods, especially if you were walking off-trail, carefully inspect your body for ticks. If one has attached itself to you, remove it by carefully "unscrewing" it from your body with tweezers.

You can avoid ticks by wearing long sleeves and pants, tucking in your shirt, and wearing a hat. You can minimize your exposure to ticks by staying on trails and walking paths where you don't brush up against trees and branches.

White-Nose Syndrome

In 2006 in upstate New York, a caver noticed a substance on the noses of hibernating bats, as well as a few dead bats. The next year, more of both were found. Now bats dying of a fungus called white-nose syndrome have been found across the country.

Researchers are still trying to find out what causes the deadly (to bats, not people) fungus. Until then, certain caves may be closed to prevent the disease from spreading. Check individual cave listings before heading out.

Poison Ivy

If there is one plant that you should learn to identify, it is poison ivy. This woody vine grows in woods all around the southeast. Touching it can leave you with a painful and terribly uncomfortable reaction.

Poison ivy is green, and the leaves grow in clusters of three. There are no thorns. Its berries are a gray-white color, and if the vine is climbing, you will notice root "hairs" on the vine. The following mnemonic might help: "Leaves of three, let it be; berries white, danger in sight."

An estimated 15-35 percent of people are not allergic to poison ivy. But after repeated exposure this protection is worn down. People who are allergic will experience more and more severe reactions with each episode of exposure.

Poison ivy is easily spread over your body by your hands or from person to person through skin-to-skin contact. Never touch your eyes or face if you think you may have touched poison ivy, and always wash yourself with hot soapy water if you think you may have come into contact with the vine.

Treat poison ivy rashes with over-the-counter itch creams. In severe cases, you may need to go to the doctor.

Heatstroke

Hot, sunny days are common in the southeast, and it's crucial to prepare for them. Apply sunscreen frequently and liberally. Prolonged sun exposure, high temperatures, and little water consumption can cause dehydration, which can lead to heat exhaustion—a harmful condition whereby your internal cooling system begins to shut down. Symptoms may include clammy skin, weakness, vomiting, and abnormal body temperature. In such instances, you must lie down in the shade, remove restrictive clothing, and drink some water.

If you do not treat heat exhaustion promptly, your condition can worsen quickly, leading to heatstroke (or sunstroke), a dangerous condition whereby your internal body temperature starts to rise to a potentially fatal level. Symptoms can include dizziness, vomiting, diarrhea, abnormal breathing and blood pressure, cessation of sweating, headache, and confusion. If any of these occur, head to a hospital as soon as possible.

Wildlife

Venomous Snakes

The vast majority of snakes in Tennessee are nonvenomous. Only four species of venomous snakes exist there. Copperheads (northern and southern) live throughout the state, along with the timber rattlesnake.

In both Alabama and Mississippi, there are six species of venomous snakes, five of them related to pit vipers. Rattlesnakes, cottonmouths, and copperheads are among the seven species of venomous snakes in Louisiana.

Crime

Wherever you are, to minimize any threat to your safety and your belongings, follow these commonsense precautions:

- Never leave valuables in plain view on a car seat; secure them in the trunk where they can't be seen.
- In case of an accident on the highway, do not abandon your vehicle.
- Don't display money, valuables, or jewelry conspicuously.
- Keep your money, credit cards, identification, and other important items hidden on your person; purses and backpacks are much easier to steal.
- Leave all but the most necessary items at home or at your hotel.
- Store laptop computers, cameras, jewelry, or any other expensive or irreplaceable items in the hotel safe.
- Secure your bike whenever it's left unattended.

- Lock your hotel and car doors at all times.
- Pay attention to your surroundings and walk along well-lit, well-traveled streets.
- Avoid dark and mostly residential areas.
- Don't go into cemeteries after dark.
- Travel in groups of at least two whenever possible.
- Take cabs to parts of town with which you're unfamiliar.
- If you're traveling via RV, do not boondock alone in an isolated place; try to stay in an RV park, a campground, or, at the very least, a well-lit parking lot.

Tennessee

Areas that cater to tourists in Nashville are popular with pickpockets. Call **Nashville Crime Stoppers** (615/742-7463, www.nashvillecrimestoppers.com) if you see suspicious activity.

Memphis's crime rates are a topic of discussion, and certain neighborhoods can shift from generally safe to not-as-safe fairly quickly. Single travelers, especially women, should take special care to stay in well-lit and highly populated areas, especially at night. It's a good idea to avoid walking alone down Beale Street at night, although security cameras have made the area safer in the last few years. Downtown and Midtown are considered the safest neighborhoods. Though Graceland is a heavily touristed area during the day, it's not a good idea to wander the area at night, when it's quieter and more isolated.

Mississippi

Jackson has a varied reputation when it comes to crime. Parts of the capital are picture-perfect for a stroll; others see their share of crime. Farish Street and downtown in particular have a different vibe at night than they do during the day. If you're traveling alone, consider staying in Ridgeland, which is close enough to visit Jackson during the day but safer at night and closer to the Trace.

Louisiana

New Orleans has a reputation for crime—partially deserved, partially exaggerated. While crime is prevalent in neighborhoods like the Tremé and Bywater, a lot of crime is also centered in or near tourist areas, and muggings or carjackings, while infrequent, do occur.

The most frequent targets of crime in New Orleans are inebriated tourists, and these, unfortunately, are easy to find in the French Quarter late at night. If you're planning a night of revelry, keep the name and address of your hotel written down someplace safe—but never write your hotel room number down somewhere that a thief or pickpocket could get it. Also be sure to carry the name and number of at least one or two cab companies, and keep your cell phone handy.

If you require assistance while in downtown New Orleans, contact **SafeWalk** (504/415-1730, 6am-10pm daily), a free service provided in the CBD and Arts District. With at least 20 minutes' advance notice, Public Safety Rangers will escort residents and visitors to their cars or other areas within the designated zone. If you do find yourself in trouble, whether in the CBD or another area of New Orleans, don't hesitate to find a phone and dial **911.**

If you witness a crime of any kind while in New Orleans, contact the **Greater New Orleans Crimestoppers** (504/822-1111 or 877/903-7867, www.crimestoppersgno.org) to offer an anonymous tip. Likewise, you can consult the **Orleans Parish Sheriff's Office** (504/822-8000, www.opcso.org).

Suggested Reading

General

Egerton, John. *Speak Now Against the Day: The Generation Before the Civil Rights Movement in the South.* Chapel Hill: University of North Carolina Press, 1995. Nashville native Egerton tells the relatively unacknowledged story of Southerners, white and Black, who stood up against segregation and racial hatred during the years before the civil rights movement.

Grant, Richard. *The Deepest South of All: True Stories from Natchez.* Mississippi. NY: Simon & Schuster, 2020. Grant, a white Brit who moved to Mississippi, looks at the history of racial conflict, from garden clubs to slavery, in Natchez.

Grant, Richard. *Dispatches from Pluto: Lost and Found in the Mississippi Delta.* NY: Simon & Schuster, 2015. A compelling read about an Englishman who moves to the Mississippi Delta.

Lost Delta Found: Rediscovering the Fisk University-Library of Congress Coahoma County Study, 1941-1942. Nashville: Vanderbilt University Press, 2020. This reissue includes a comprehensive study of one part of the Delta at one moment in time.

Sides, Hampton. *Hellhound on His Trail: The Stalking of Martin Luther King, Jr. and the International Hunt for His Assassin.* New York: Doubleday, 2010. A well-written, captivating account of MLK's murder and the efforts to nab his killer. Sides provides perspective on Memphis's troubled history.

Fiction

Taylor, Peter. *Summons to Memphis.* New York: Knopf Publishing Group, 1986. Celebrated and award-winning Tennessee writer Taylor won the Pulitzer Prize for fiction for this novel in 1986. Phillip Carver returns home to Tennessee at the request of his three older sisters to talk his father out of remarrying. In so doing, he is forced to confront a troubling family history. This is a classic of American literature, set in a South that is fading away.

Wright, Richard. *Black Boy.* New York: Chelsea House, 2006. The 1945 memoir of African American writer Wright recounts several years of residency in Memphis. His portrayal of segregation and racism in Memphis and Mississippi is still powerful today.

Food

Lundy, Ronni, ed. *Cornbread Nation 7.* Chapel Hill: University of North Carolina Press, 2006. The seventh in a series of collections on Southern food and cooking. Published in collaboration with the Southern Foodways Alliance, which is dedicated to preserving and celebrating Southern food traditions, the *Cornbread Nation* collection is an ode to food traditions large and small. Topics include pawpaws, corn, and pork.

Puckett, Susan. *Eat Drink Delta: A Hungry Traveler's Journey through the Soul of the South. Athens:* University of Georgia Press, 2013. From barbecue in Memphis, Tennessee, to okra in Cleveland, Mississippi, this guide surveys the South's regional specialties and must-visit restaurants, city by city.

Music

Berry, Jason, Jonathan Foose, and Tad Jones. *Up from the Cradle of Jazz: New Orleans Music Since World War II.* Lafayette, LA: University of Louisiana at Lafayette Press, 2009. A terrific survey tracing the history of music in the Big Easy, from the 1940s to the post-Katrina era.

Escott, Colin. *Hank Williams The Biography*. New York: Back Bay Books, 2004. No country star had a bigger impact on Nashville's evolution to Music City than Hank Williams. This detailed history shares his failings, downfall, and remarkable legacy.

Gioia, Ted. *Delta Blues: The Life and Times of the Mississippi Masters Who Revolutionized American Music*. New York: W. W. Norton & Company, 2009. A music critic, historian, and musician himself, Gioia walks through blues history with the help of archival research, interviews, and narrative accounts.

Guralnick, Peter. *Last Train to Memphis: The Rise of Elvis Presley*. Boston: Little, Brown and Company, 1994. Quite possibly the definitive biography of the King. In volume one, Guralnick recreates Presley's first 24 years, including his childhood in Mississippi and Tennessee, his remarkable rise to fame, and the pivotal events of 1958, when he was drafted into the army and buried his beloved mother.

Handy, W. C. *Father of the Blues*. New York: The Macmillan Company, 1941. This memoir by Memphis's most famous bluesman depicts the city during the first quarter of the 20th century. It is an entertaining and endearing read.

Havighurst, Craig. *Air Castle of the South: WSM and the Making of Music City*. Champaign, IL: University of Illinois Press, 2007. Havighurst is known as the preeminent Nashville music historian and this tome delves deep into an important piece in Nashville's musical hierarchy.

Kingsbury, Paul, ed. *Will the Circle Be Unbroken: Country Music in America*. London: DK Adult, 2006. An illustrated collection of articles by 43 writers, including several performing artists, this book is a useful reference on the genre's development from 1920 until the present.

Kossner, Michael. *How Nashville Became Music City: 50 Years of Music Row*. Milwaukee, WI: Hal Leonard, 2006. This profile of country music focuses on the people you've never heard of: the executives, songwriters, and behind-the-scenes technicians who really make the music happen. An interesting read for fans who don't mind seeing how the sausage is made; a good introduction for people aspiring to be a part of it.

Lomax, Alan. *Mister Jelly Roll: The Fortunes of Jelly Roll Morton, New Orleans Creole and "Inventor of Jazz."* Los Angeles: University of California Press, 2001. Originally published in 1950, this fascinating examination of a New Orleans jazz luminary also explores the development of the city's music scene.

Murphy, Michael. *Hear Dat New Orleans: A Guide to the Rich Musical Heritage & Lively Current Scene*. New York: Countryman Press, 2016. Take an in-depth look at music venues in New Orleans in this guide also featuring photos from photographer Marc Pagani.

Palmer, Robert. *Deep Blues: A Musical and Cultural History of the Mississippi Delta*. New York: Penguin Books, 1982. An oldie but a goodie, this tome chronicles blues from its early beginnings through its heyday, touching on key figures such as Muddy Waters, B. B. King, and Robert Johnson.

Stolle, Roger, and Lou Bopp. *Hidden History of Mississippi Blues*. Mount Pleasant: The History Press, 2011. The background of Mississippi bluesmen and their legacies are detailed in this book by Clarksdale's Stolle.

Stolle, Roger, and Lou Bopp. *Mississippi Juke Joint Confidential: House Parties, Hustlers and the Blues Life*. Mount Pleasant: The History Press, 2019. Everything you need to know about the iconic juke joint is examined in this book.

Travel Guides

Cheseborough, Steve. *Blues Traveling: The Holy Sites of Delta Blues*. Jackson: University Press of Mississippi, 2018. Blues fans can check out maps, photos, and descriptions of musical history sights and sounds through Mississippi.

Jackson, Tim W., Taryn Chase Jackson and F. Lynne Bachleda. *Guide to the Natchez Trace Parkway*. Birmingham, AL: Menasha Ridge Press, 2018. A survey of the Trace's merits and history, plus a Top 20 list of sights to stop at during your trip along the Trace.

Littman, Margaret. *Moon Memphis*. Berkeley: Avalon Travel, 2020. A stand-alone guide to the Bluff City and Mississippi Delta, with excursions to Little Rock and Hot Springs, Arkansas.

Littman, Margaret. *Moon Nashville*. Berkeley: Avalon Travel, 2020. A stand-alone guide to Music City.

Littman, Margaret. *Moon Tennessee*. Berkeley: Avalon Travel, 2019. A comprehensive guide to the Volunteer State.

McGunnigle, Nora. *Moon New Orleans*. Berkeley: Avalon Travel, 2020. A stand-alone guide to the Big Easy.

Steed, Bud. *The Haunted Natchez Trace*. Charleston, SC: Haunted America/The History Press, 2012. Paranormal tales along the Trace are detailed in this book, written in a conversational tone.

Summerlin, Cathy and Vernon. *Traveling the Trace: A Complete Tour Guide to the Historic Natchez Trace from Nashville to Natchez*. Nashville: Rutledge Hill Press, a Thomas Nelson Company, 1995. This guide features a narrative retelling of sights and points of interest in communities within 30 miles of the Natchez Trace Parkway, slanted toward visitors traveling by bicycle.

Timme, S. Lee, and Caleb C. K. Timme. *Wildflowers of the Natchez Trace*. Jackson: University Press of Mississippi, 2000. More of a field guide, this volume is full of photos to help you identify what you see.

Wanner, Glen and Ann Richards. *Bicycling the Natchez Trace: A Guide to the Natchez Trace Parkway and Nearby Scenic Routes*. Nashville: Pennywell Press, 2005. Written by two musicians in the Nashville Symphony who are also avid outdoorspeople, this guide focuses on traversing the Trace on two wheels.

Internet and Digital Resources

General

Civil Rights Trail
http://civilrightstrail.com
More than 100 sights in 15 states are plotted on this trail.

Civil War Trail
www.civilwartrails.org
Explore an interactive map of Civil War sights.

Elvis Presley Driving Tour
www.scenictrace.com/elvis-presley-driving-tour
Visit all the places that made the King who he was.

Mississippi Delta National Heritage Area
www.msdeltaheritage.com/delta-divide
Learn about the rich diversity and history of the region.

Mississippi Mound Trail
http://trails.mdah.ms.gov/mmt/index.html
Learn about the Native Americans who lived in this region at archaeologic sites along 350 miles of the Mississippi River.

Music

Americana Music Triangle
http://americanamusictriangle.com
The roads between Nashville, Memphis, and New Orleans are paved with gold records. Explore this website full of photos and suggested itineraries.

Mississippi Blues Trail
http://msbluestrail.org
There are more 200 landmarks along this trail. Use this website to plot a trip or just immerse yourself in armchair travel, or download the app and check them out as you go.

Mississippi Country Music Trail
www.mscountrymusictrail.org
Find markers that show where Mississippi country musicians were born, lived, and played.

The Roots of American Music Trail
http://musictrail.una.edu
Documents where to explore music of the 20th and 21st century, including hits from the 1960s, 1970s, and 1980s, in Northern Alabama.

Natchez Trace Parkway

Natchez Trace Parkway Guided Cell Phone Tour
http://natr.oncell.com
Listen to recordings about sights along the Trace.

Natchez Trace Travel
www.natcheztracetravel.com
Each sight along the Natchez Trace Parkway is detailed on this website, with extensive photos and maps. Itineraries are available for cyclists. There are reservation links to bed-and-breakfasts and other lodging options.

National Park Planner
http://npplan.com
An unofficial website comprised of one photographer's impressions of each stop along the Natchez Trace Parkway, as well as other national parks.

Scenic Trace
www.scenictrace.com
A comprehensive website by the Natchez Trace Compact suggests places to do and things to do along the way. Check out the interactive maps.

INDEX

C

G

H

IJ

K

L

M

N

O

P

QR

S

WXYZ

LIST OF MAPS

PHOTO CREDITS

All interior photos © Margaret Littman except: page 7 © (top) Helgidinson | Dreamstime.com; page 8 © Rolf52 | Dreamstime.com; page 10 © Roberto Galan | Dreamstime.com; page 11 © (top) James Kirkikis | Dreamstime.com; (bottom) Bhofack2 | Dreamstime.com; page 13 © (top) Jdpphoto12 | Dreamstime.com; (bottom) C5Media | Dreamstime.com; page 14 © (top) Calvin L. Leake | Dreamstime.com; (middle) Jai Mo | Dreamstime.com; (bottom) Gerry Matthews / Shutterstock; page 15 © Jordan Hill | Dreamstime.com; page 17 © (top) Karen Foley | Dreamstime.com; (bottom) F11photo | Dreamstime.com; page 23 © (top) Marekuliasz | Dreamstime.com; (bottom) Chris Granger; page 25 © (top) Tupelo CVB; (bottom) Bob LaCour | Dreamstime.com; page 26 © Tupelo CVB; page 30 © F11photo | Dreamstime.com; page 43 © (top) Brenda Kean | Dreamstime.com; (bottom) Abigail Volkmann, courtesy of Clearbrook Hospitality; page 45 © courtesy of the Nashville Public Library; page 55 © (top) Jiawangkun | Dreamstime.com; (middle) Brenda Kean | Dreamstime.com; (bottom) Sean Pavone | Dreamstime.com; page 62 © (middle) Alexis Kirkman | Dreamstime.com; (bottom) Kerry Woo for Lane Motor Museum; page 64 © Paul Brady Photography / Shutterstock; page 67 © Erik Lattwein | Dreamstime.com; page 69 © (top) Erik Lattwein | Dreamstime.com; (middle) Icon Entertainment Group; (bottom) Christopher Lyzcen | Dreamstime.com; page 78 © Calvin L. Leake | Dreamstime.com; page 82 © courtesy of The Bookshop; page 86 © Erik Lattwein | Dreamstime.com; page 102 © Deebrowning | Dreamstime.com; page 112 © Kenn Stilger | Dreamstime.com; page 117 © (top) Debbie Smartt; (bottom) Amber Beckham Photography; page 120 © Erik Lattwein | Dreamstime.com; page 125 © President James K. Polk Home and Museum; page 129 © (bottom) Marek Uliasz | Dreamstime.com; page 150 © (bottom) Chris Granger; page 152 © Chris Granger; page 155 © (middle) Visit The Shoals, AL; page 157 © Visit The Shoals, AL; page 162 © Visit The Shoals, AL; page 164 © Mkojot | Dreamstime.com; page 167 Elvis statue "Becoming" sculpted by Michiel Van der Sommen; page 177 © National Park Service; page 188 © Sean Pavone | Dreamstime.com; page 199 © Ginosphotos | Dreamstime.com; page 201 © (top) Daniel Schreurs | Dreamstime.com; (middle) Andrea Zucker/The Blues Foundation; (bottom) The Peabody Memphis; page 207 © (bottom) Calvin L. Leake | Dreamstime.com; page 208 © Arenaphotouk | Dreamstime.com; page 221 © Calvin L. Leake | Dreamstime.com; page 224 © Melissa McMasters; page 230 © (top) Margaret Littman; (middle) Dan Ball; page 235 © (top) The Peabody Memphis; page 254 © Anne Donnarumma | Dreamstime.com; page 262 © Visit Oxford Mississippi; page 267 © (top) James Kirkikis | Dreamstime.com; (bottom) Visit Oxford Mississippi; page 270 © Anton Foltin | Dreamstime.com; page 274 © (top) Msucarliann | Dreamstime.com; page 282 © Jerry Whaley | Dreamstime.com; page 284 © Brenda Kean| Dreamstime.com; page 297 © (middle) C5Media | Dreamstime.com; page 304 © (top) Visit Vicksburg; (middle) Gary Millett; (bottom) Gary Millett; page 312 © (top) Visit Natchez; page 318 © F11photo | Dreamstime.com; page 331 © (top) James Kirkikis | Dreamstime.com; (bottom) Richard Espenant | Dreamstime.com; page 340 © Tony Bosse | Dreamstime.com; page 344 © Wenling01 | Dreamstime.com; page 351 © Rebeccaannphotography | Dreamstime.com; page 352 © (bottom) Dan Oberly | Dreamstime.com; page 358 © Zimmytws | Dreamstime.com; page 368 © (top) Eugene Ballard | Dreamstime.com; (middle) Roberto Galan | Dreamstime.com; (bottom) Allenalo | Dreamstime.com; page 372 © Tony Bosse | Dreamstime.com; page 385 © (middle) Redwood8 | Dreamstime.com; page 397 © (middle) Catahoula Hotel 2016/Elsa Hahne; page 408 © Chris Granger

ACKNOWLEDGMENTS

Every book I've ever written requires a long list of "thank yous." This list feels like it should go on for 444 miles. It was a return trip filled with tornadoes, floods, and a global pandemic.

First and foremost are the rangers and employees of the National Park Service who care for this land and the people who use it. To the men and women who had the foresight to protect the tales these roads tell, I hope my encouraging others to visit and appreciate them are "thank you" enough.

Since my first guidebook (*The Dog Lover's Companion to Chicago*) was published by Avalon Travel, I've been aware that I work with the most supportive publishers around. This is even more evident on this book, which at times overwhelms me with its 10,000 years of history, and miles (and miles) of must-sees. All of the crew was top-notch, including Kat Bennett, Kimberly Ehart, Rue Flaherty, Nikki Ioakimedes, and Kevin McLain.

Ally Willis kept on top of my random emails about an amazing boutique or trail we *had* to add at the last minute, checking facts and seeking photo permissions.

Georgia Carter Turner was the first person, more than a decade ago, to encourage me to drive the Natchez Trace. She's no longer with The Shoals Tourism, but her colleagues, including Randa Hovater, fill her shoes.

Others who came through with essential assistance include: Heather Middleton of Nashville Convention & Visitors Corp.; Lisa Konupka of Tunica Convention & Visitors Bureau; Meredith Conger of Visit Baton Rouge; Jennie Bradford Curlee of Visit Tupelo; Danielle Morgan of Visit Greenwood; Lisa Winters of Washington County; Julia Hollings in New Orleans; Ashley Gaitan of Visit Vicksburg; Kelly Mott of Visit Ridgeland; and Kelli Carr of Cleveland Tourism. Cole Ellis not only fed me food and drink, but also kept me full of stories of the Delta. No one loves Memphis more than Milton Howery. Kinney Ferris introduced me to the amazing Jack Mayfield as we uncovered Oxford's many charms. A day with Emily Steen at the Corinth Convention and Visitors Bureau is as entertaining as a stand-up comedy marathon. A day with Stratton Hall of Visit Natchez is filled with more desserts than you can eat. A day with Bubba O'Keefe of Visit Clarksdale is filled with more stories than your local library.

Having an excuse to reconnect with my old friend Cynthia Joyce in Oxford—and for emergency hummus in Jackson or to find a dog-friendly bar in Memphis—is one of my favorite things about this project.

I hope reading this book inspires everyone to explore this piece of American magic.

MOON
the OPEN ROAD
50 BEST ROAD TRIPS in the USA
From Weekend Getaways to Cross-Country Adventures
JESSICA DUNHAM

MOON
NASHVILLE TO NEW ORLEANS
Road Trip
NATCHEZ TRACE PARKWAY • MEMPHIS • TUPELO • MISSISSIPPI BLUES TRAIL
MARGARET LITTMAN

MOON
NEW ENGLAND
Road Trip
BOSTON, ACADIA NATIONAL PARK, WHITE MOUNTAINS, BERKSHIRES, NEWPORT, AND CAPE COD
JEN ROSE SMITH

MOON
NORTHERN CALIFORNIA
Road Trips
DRIVES ALONG THE COAST, REDWOODS, AND MOUNTAINS WITH THE BEST STOPS ALONG THE WAY
STUART THORNTON & KAYLA ANDERSON

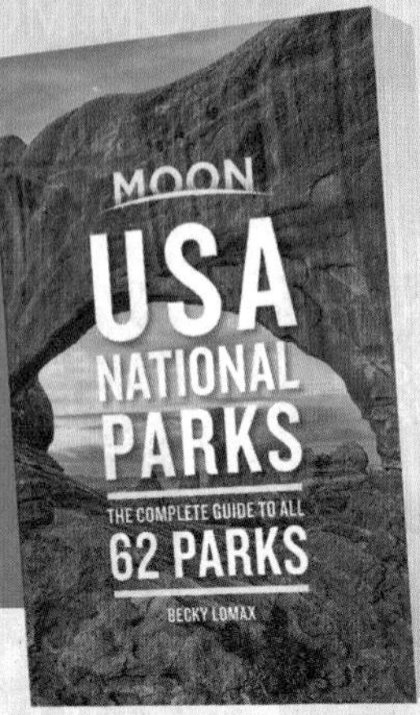
MOON
USA
NATIONAL
PARKS
THE COMPLETE GUIDE TO ALL
62 PARKS
BECKY LOMAX

MOON
ACADIA
NATIONAL PARK
HILARY NANGLE

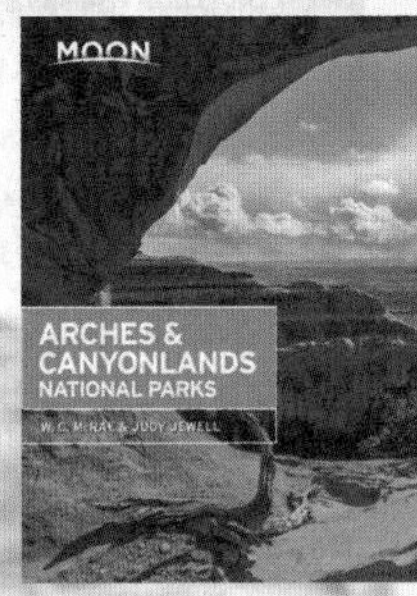
MOON
ARCHES &
CANYONLANDS
NATIONAL PARKS

MOON
BANFF
NATIONAL
PARK
HIKE·CAMP
SEE WILDLIFE
ANDREW HEMPSTEAD

MOON
DEATH VALLEY
NATIONAL PARK
JENNA BLOUGH

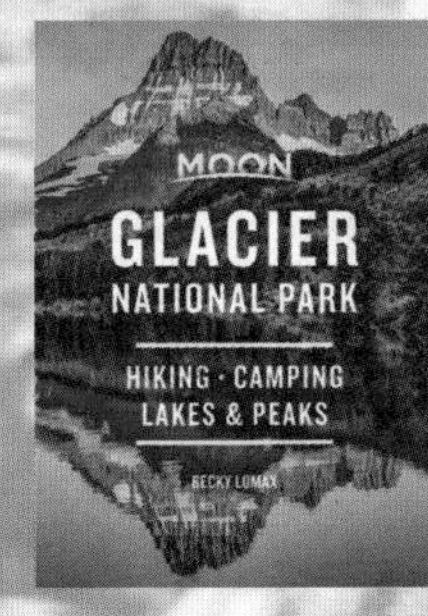
MOON
GLACIER
NATIONAL PARK
HIKING · CAMPING
LAKES & PEAKS
BECKY LOMAX

MOON
GRAND
CANYON
HIKE·CAMP
RAFT THE
COLORADO RIVER
TIM HULL

MOON
MOUNT RUSHMORE
& THE BLACK HILLS
Including the Badlands
LAURA K. BIDWELL

MOON
ROCKY
MOUNTAIN
NATIONAL PARK
HIKE·CAMP
SEE WILDLIFE
ERIN ENGLISH

MOON
SEQUOIA &
KINGS CANYON
HIKING·CAMPING
WATERFALLS & BIG TREES
LEIGH BERNACCHI

MAP SYMBOLS

Expressway	City/Town	Information Center	Park
Primary Road	State Capital	Parking Area	Golf Course
Secondary Road	National Capital	Church	Unique Feature
Unpaved Road	Highlight	Winery/Vineyard	Waterfall
Trail	Point of Interest	Trailhead	Camping
Ferry	Accommodation	Train Station	Mountain
Railroad	Restaurant/Bar	Airport	Ski Area
Pedestrian Walkway	Other Location	Airfield	Glacier
Stairs			

CONVERSION TABLES

°C = (°F - 32) / 1.8
°F = (°C x 1.8) + 32
1 inch = 2.54 centimeters (cm)
1 foot = 0.304 meters (m)
1 yard = 0.914 meters
1 mile = 1.6093 kilometers (km)
1 km = 0.6214 miles
1 fathom = 1.8288 m
1 chain = 20.1168 m
1 furlong = 201.168 m
1 acre = 0.4047 hectares
1 sq km = 100 hectares
1 sq mile = 2.59 square km
1 ounce = 28.35 grams
1 pound = 0.4536 kilograms
1 short ton = 0.90718 metric ton
1 short ton = 2,000 pounds
1 long ton = 1.016 metric tons
1 long ton = 2,240 pounds
1 metric ton = 1,000 kilograms
1 quart = 0.94635 liters
1 US gallon = 3.7854 liters
1 Imperial gallon = 4.5459 liters
1 nautical mile = 1.852 km

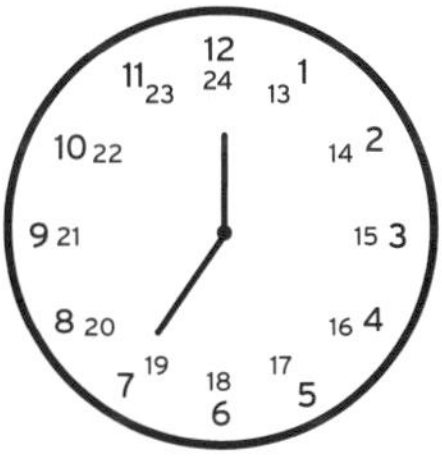

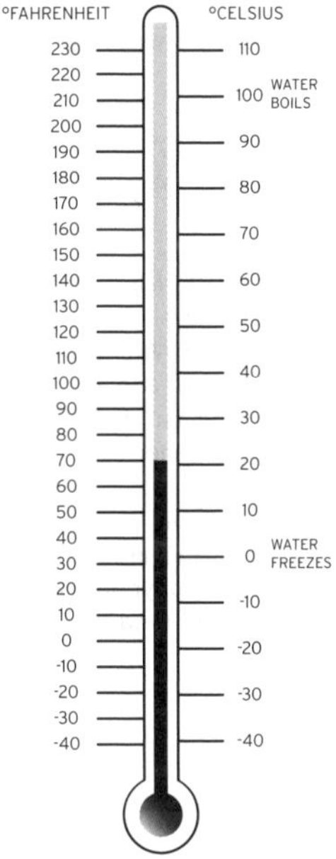

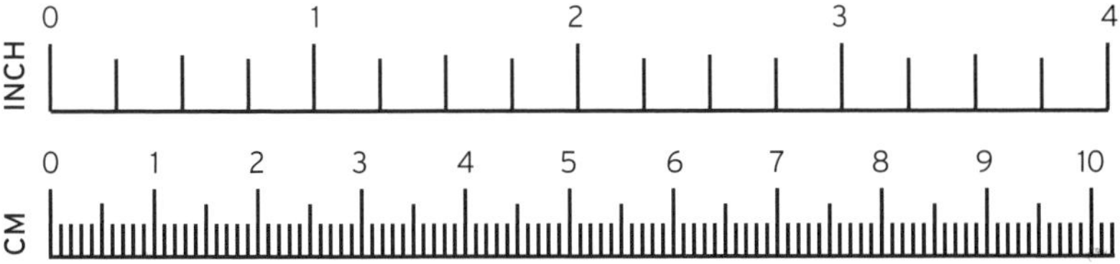

°FAHRENHEIT °CELSIUS

WATER BOILS

WATER FREEZES

INCH

CM

MOON NASHVILLE TO NEW ORLEANS ROAD TRIP

Avalon Travel
Hachette Book Group
1700 Fourth Street
Berkeley, CA 94710, USA
www.moon.com

Editor: Kimberly Ehart
Acquiring Editor: Nikki Ioakimedes
Copy Editor: Kristi Mitsuda
Graphics and Production Coordinator: Rue Flaherty
Cover Design: Erin Seaward-Hiatt
Interior Design: Darren Alessi
Moon Logo: Tim McGrath
Map Editor: Kat Bennett
Cartographers: Karin Dahl, Brian Shotwell, Kat Bennett
Indexer: Greg Jewett

ISBN-13: 978-1-64049-924-9

Printing History
1st Edition — 2018
2nd Edition — March 2021
5 4 3 2 1

Front cover photo: Legendary Crossroads in Clarksdale Mississippi © James Kirkikis / Alamy Stock Photo

Printed in China by RR Donnelley